2004
Report

Economic and Social Progress
in Latin America

Good Jobs Wanted
Labor Markets in Latin America

Published by the Inter-American Development Bank
Distributed by The Johns Hopkins University Press
Washington, D.C.

ACKNOWLEDGMENTS

The Research Department, under the direction of Guillermo Calvo, was responsible for this Report. Carmen Pagés was the academic director of the project in collaboration with project assistant director Mauricio Olivera. Daron Acemoglu (Massachusetts Institute of Technology) and Eduardo Engel (Yale University), members of the Editorial Committee, provided guidance since the early stages of the project. Eduardo Lora provided essential help and advice throughout the process. The Overview and Chapter 1 were written by Carmen Pagés; Chapter 2 was coauthored by Matías Busso and Alejandro Micco; Chapter 3 was written by Eduardo Lora, based on research results by Suzanne Duryea and Emmanuel Skoufias and drawing on a background paper prepared by Ximena Clark, Timothy Hatton, and Jeffrey Williamson; Chapter 4 was written by Ugo Panizza, with contributions by Arturo Galindo, Alejandro Izquierdo, and Kevin Cowan; Chapter 5 was authored by Eduardo Lora; Chapter 6 was written by Andrés Rodríguez; Chapter 7 was written by Eduardo Lora and Carmen Pagés; and Chapter 8 was produced by Gustavo Márquez. Alejandro Micco provided contributions to Chapters 5 and 7. Additional contributions by Roberto Iunes and Alberto Chong are also acknowledged. Reyes Aterido, Gabriela Cordourier, Virgilio Galdo, María Eugenia Genoni, Carlos Andrés Gómez, Ana María Loboguerrero, Álvaro Mezza, Guillermo Ordóñez, Alejandro Riaño, and Cristóbal Ruiz-Tagle provided valuable research assistance.

María Ariano, Elisabeth Boggs-Davidson, César Bouillon, José Ernesto López-Córdova, Jacqueline Mazza, Josefina Monteagudo, André Medici, Andrew Morrison, Claudia Piras, Ferdinando Regala, Consuelo Ricart, José Seligman, and Jaime Vargas provided useful comments on early drafts of the chapters. The study was enriched by the comments of Manuel Agosín, René Caceres, Ciro de Falco, Eduardo Fernández-Arias, Richard Fletcher, Christof Kuechemann, Elio Londero, Paulo Paiva, Ricardo Santiago, and Graciela Schamis, as well as participants at workshops and seminars conducted at the Bank during the process of preparation of the Report. Mariela Semidey provided administrative support throughout the entire process.

The principal source of information for the Report was the household surveys generously provided by the governments of Argentina, Bolivia, Brazil, Chile, Colombia, Costa Rica, the Dominican Republic, Ecuador, El Salvador, Guatemala, Honduras, Mexico, Nicaragua, Panama, Paraguay, Peru, Uruguay, and Venezuela. The Improvement of Surveys and Measurement of Living Standards Program contributed to gathering and distributing the surveys. Chapter 2 benefited from firm-level survey data from Brazil, Chile, Colombia, and Mexico. The Economic Commission for Latin America and the Caribbean, International Labour Organization, International Monetary Fund, United Nations Industrial Development Organization, and World Bank provided international databases. Reyes Aterido, Gabriela Cordourier, María Eugenia Genoni, Carlos Andrés Gómez, Álvaro Mezza, and Cristóbal Ruiz-Tagle, under the direction of Suzanne Duryea, processed the information contained in the Data Appendix (on the CD-ROM accompanying the Report).

The IDB's Office of the External Relations Advisor was responsible for the editorial production of the Report. Larry Hanlon (English); Donaldson Garschagen, Maria José Cyhlar Monteiro, and Carlos Ramires (Portuguese); and Álvaro Correa, Stella Covre, Roberto Donadi, Eleana Gómez, and Carlos Trípodi (Spanish) translated the text. Sandra Gain (English), Eloisa Marques (Portuguese), and Claudia Pasquetti (Spanish) edited the Report. Rita Funaro provided editorial suggestions. Cathy Conkling-Shaker provided valuable editorial assistance and, along with Viviane Azevedo, Julia Gomila, Katia Rossini, and John Smith, proofread the volume. Leilany Garron and Valkiria Peizer created the cover and graphic design and typeset the volume along with Alejandra Luzardo and Dolores Subiza.

**Good Jobs Wanted:
Labor Markets in Latin America**

Distributed by
The Johns Hopkins University Press
2715 North Charles Street
Baltimore, MD 21218

To order this book, contact
IDB Bookstore
Tel: 1-877-PUBS IDB / 202-623-1753
Fax: 202-623-1709
E-mail: idb-books@iadb.org
www.iadb.org/pub

ISBN: 1-931003-50-5
ISSN: 0095-2850

Preface

Ordinary citizens are more concerned about employment-related problems than other social or economic issues. According to opinion polls, the majority of Latin Americans live with the constant threat of unemployment, low and unstable wages, and lack of employment benefits.

Deficiencies that have traditionally characterized labor markets in the region have increased in recent years, undermining efforts to reduce poverty and improve social and economic conditions. Unemployment rates have increased in a number of countries since the mid-1990s and are now at their highest level in at least two decades. The percentage of workers covered by labor regulations and social protection measures is less than it was in the early 1990s. Wages have risen slowly, and almost without exception wage gaps between more skilled and less skilled workers have widened.

Nonetheless, in some aspects labor markets have moved in a favorable direction. Employment opportunities for women have increased and improved, and employment discrimination based on gender has declined. And in a number of countries, employment creation and working conditions have improved at an encouraging pace in the export and service sectors. But these developments have not been sufficient to alter the prevailing climate of dissatisfaction in the region. This year's edition of *Economic and Social Progress in Latin America* analyzes these problems from a new perspective, calling into question assumptions and policies that have not proved successful.

In the discourse on labor markets, there are two main positions. On the one hand, those who worry more about the social implications of the labor problem often advocate for greater government involvement to enforce stronger and more effective labor regulations, protect wages, and implement more active job creation policies. On the other hand, those who want to dismantle the tools for state intervention seek to make the labor market more flexible. Both approaches are extreme. One fails to see that the effectiveness of labor policies largely depends on whether they are compatible with the incentives of workers and companies, and with the government's ability to enforce them. The other glosses over the fact that the labor market is far from the ideal textbook market; it is not characterized by perfect competition or complete information on the goods being traded.

Labor markets are full of surprises that conventional analysis cannot anticipate. In Latin America, for example, typically when the relationship between labor supply and demand changes, the main adjustment mechanism is not unemployment or even informal labor, but wages. And informal labor is not the last refuge for those who have no other opportunities. Rather, for many workers, it is an option that they prefer because of its flexibility and pay. In some countries, the minimum wage is more effective among those who are regarded as informal workers than in other segments of the labor market.

Naturally, what happens in the labor market often reflects policy decisions made elsewhere in the economy. Given the depth of the structural reforms adopted by the countries of the region since the late 1980s, it is hardly surprising that labor has been affected. However, this Report indicates that this is also an area of unexpected developments, where traditional approaches have gone wrong. For example, contrary to what its advocates expected, liberalization has not favored less skilled workers. And contrary to its opponents' expectations, liberalization has not resulted in unemployment. Instead, it has caused much less reallocation and loss of employment than either side expected.

The 2004 Report aspires to be as novel in its approach as it is cautious in its recommendations. It recognizes the limited knowledge in the area of labor, and the conflicting objectives facing policy decisions in this area. The express goal is to contribute to an understanding of the problems and to stimulate governments, labor organizations, and civil society to analyze the options for solving labor problems without resorting to dogmatic approaches. The Bank hopes that with this study it is making a valuable contribution to the well being of Latin Americans.

Enrique V. Iglesias
President
Inter-American Development Bank

Contents

Overview

Labor markets in Latin America are ailing. Unemployment is at its highest in many years and although wages have improved in some countries, they have done so at a very slow pace. Many workers receive pay that is too low to escape poverty, and wage inequality, which is among the highest in the world, is not getting any better. Instead, unskilled workers have seen their wages decline relative to the wages of skilled workers. Moreover, while the probability of losing a job is high, only a dwindling minority of workers is insured against this risk. Not surprisingly, public opinion surveys, such as the Latinobarometer, have identified unemployment, low wages, and job instability as the most pressing problems in the region, ahead of corruption, crime, and other difficult social problems.

Employment-related concerns are not new in the region. For years, population dynamics and increasing labor force participation rates have resulted in a rapidly growing supply of labor. Employing this ever-increasing reserve of workers at a decent wage and with the benefits prescribed by labor laws has been a perennial challenge for policymakers. What seems to be new is that unemployment, a problem that was only supposed to occur in richer countries where workers can afford to search for jobs, is now reaching levels above those of developed countries. Moreover, many indicators of the quality of jobs seem to have deteriorated during the 1990s. Employment in small firms increased and the share of workers with the protection mandated by labor laws declined from levels that were already low.

Many explanations have been proposed for this state of affairs. Some analysts argue that trade reforms and the privatization of state-owned firms have displaced workers from noncompetitive manufacturing sectors and public jobs, while new jobs have been created in low-productivity sectors.[1] Others claim that trade reforms and the process of globalization of trade are behind the increasing demand for skilled workers and the declining relative wages of the unskilled.[2] Some observers blame the process of trade integration—globalization—for the decline in the proportion of workers with social protection as firms seek to reduce labor costs to stay competitive.[3] Some point to the increasing adoption of new technologies—in part fuelled by trade and other structural reforms—as part of the explanation since, on the one hand, new technologies are less labor intensive and, on the other hand, they use more skilled labor than older technolo-

[1] ILO (1996). Saavedra (2003) makes the case that many changes observed in Latin American markets are likely to be associated with sector reallocations of output and employment induced by structural reforms.

[2] See, for example, Robbins and Gindling (1999).

[3] Stallings and Peres (2000); Goldberg and Pavcnik (2003).

gies.[4] Other suggested explanations for increasing unemployment are increasing female labor force participation and the rapidly increasing labor supply. Excessively rigid labor regulations and increasing wage rigidities are also often mentioned as the cause of labor market problems.

How can Latin America and the Caribbean improve the availability and quality of jobs? The treatments to be prescribed depend on the diagnosis of the problems. While it is often claimed that it is necessary to focus on solutions, this Report contends that the solutions must be based on a clear understanding of the way labor markets work, the tasks they perform, and the effects that policies and institutions within and outside the labor market have on them. Labor markets, that is, the daily exchange of productive skills between workers and firms as well as the institutions that govern them, perform the key task of allocating resources and incomes across firms and workers. While well-designed institutions and policies can enhance the performance of labor markets, poorly conceived policies and institutions may slow down economic activity and reduce social welfare. Therefore, this Report explores the anatomy and dynamics of labor markets in the region as well as the effects that demographic and labor force participation trends, migration, macroeconomic shocks, structural reforms, education, technology adoption, and policies and institutions have on the labor market. In doing so, some popular assumptions regarding labor market behavior are reexamined and new data sets are uncovered and analyzed.

Several Important Findings Emerge

Increasing labor supply is neither the cause nor the consequence of worsening labor market conditions.

In a typical workday, more than 210 million Latin Americans offer their skills to the labor market, and about five million additional workers join the labor supply every year. At 2.5 percent, the rate of growth of the labor force is among the highest in the world. Demographic trends and higher female participation rates are the main two factors behind these trends, while emigration—the highest in the world—is responsible for only a slight decrease in the rate of growth of the labor force.

In spite of its rapid pace, growth in the supply of labor is not the cause of the increase in unemployment or unregulated employment. Nor are the changes in the characteristics of the labor force that are taking place in the process. The labor force is becoming older, more gender balanced, more urban, and more educated, but there is no basis to argue that any of these changing patterns is an important explanation for the ills of the labor market.

Female labor force participation rates are growing fast from levels that are still low by international standards. However, there is no evidence that across countries increasing female participation is causing increasing unemployment rates. Instead, it has been the most important source of growth of income per capita in the region. There is no evidence that in general women are being forced into the labor market by the dire economic situation of their families, although that may be the case in a few countries. Over the medium term, relative wages, although still unfavorable to women, have been moving in their favor, which suggests that the reason for their higher labor force participation has been the improvement in their relative labor opportunities. In some countries and periods, short-term participation rates increase when macroeconomic conditions deteriorate, adding pressure to the labor market and probably contributing to an increase in temporary unemployment.

Structural reforms did not alter the labor market in the expected ways.

The 1990s witnessed major changes in economic policies aimed to facilitate the operation of markets and to improve efficiency and economic growth. Inflation and fiscal deficits were reduced, govern-

[4] See de Ferranti and others (2003) for a link between trade, technology, and increasing returns to education.

ments lifted restrictions on trade and capital markets, tax systems were reformed, and many state-owned firms were privatized.

Reformers predicted that these reforms would stimulate the demand for labor and lead to wage gains, although, in the short run, there could be a temporary increase in unemployment because jobs in noncompetitive sectors would be lost. The reformers also predicted that wage inequality between skilled and unskilled workers would be reduced as the demand for unskilled workers—the most abundant factor in the region—would increase relative to the demand for skilled workers. Instead, critics claimed that reforms brought sizable losses in employment, particularly in small and medium-size firms and good public sector jobs, as well as losses in the quality of jobs because many employers stopped offering benefits as the pressure to remain competitive increased.

The reality is that, contrary to the critics' predictions, employment losses were small and when they occurred they had no discernable effects on the unemployment rate. There were no massive losses in employment because, surprisingly, contrary to the reformers' predictions, there were limited shifts in resources to potentially more efficient sectors, which may explain why productivity and earnings increased at such a slow pace.

There were more surprises. For example, the wage gap between skilled and unskilled workers widened. However, the relative demand for skilled labor increased in all sectors, and not only in those that were affected by trade reforms, suggesting that other factors were at work. Contrary to the expectations of some reformers, in some countries, wages in the manufacturing sector fell as workers lost part of the rents they used to share with employers as a result of trade protection. But contrary to the critics of globalization, new jobs in the export sector have usually offered comparable and sometimes better wage and employment conditions than other jobs. Unfortunately, as trade barriers came down, some countries—particularly those with restrictive labor laws—have reported a reduction in jobs that provide the benefits mandated by law.

Although it eliminated many jobs in some specific sectors, the privatization of state-owned firms had little effect on unemployment. In Argentina, the most extreme case, close to 150,000 workers were made redundant as a result of privatizations between 1987 and 1997. Although large in number, these redundancies accounted for only 13 percent of the increase in unemployment in the period. In Bolivia, privatizations explained just 3 percent of the rise in unemployment in 1995-2000. Furthermore, the private firms created in the privatized sectors directly or indirectly rehired many of the laid-off workers.

In sum, the picture of the effects of the reforms is full of surprises and lessons for reformers and critics alike.

The problem is not technology, but the lack of it.

It is often stated that modern technology reduces the demand for workers, particularly those with low levels of education, but history and the evidence for Latin America indicate that this is not the case. There is no evidence that employment rates have declined in countries that adopted new or better technologies. Nor is it true that industries that experienced fast technology growth had slow employment growth. Indeed, higher productivity growth, the best indicator available for technological improvements, has been associated with faster employment growth at the industry level.

It is not technology, but the lack of it that has been behind some of the unsatisfactory labor outcomes. On average, labor shares were constant in the region during the 1990s, indicating that the slow growth of wages has been due to meager growth of labor productivity, a direct consequence of the slow pace of technological change. During 1985-2000, the average productivity of physical capital, labor, and skills combined declined 0.1 percent a year in the Latin American and Caribbean countries. This implies that technological progress did not contribute to improving labor productivity and wages in the region. Thus, the problem has been not so much that labor markets have allocated incomes in a way that has hurt workers, but the fact that economies have failed to generate incomes that can be allocated to workers.

Demand drives the increasing skill premium, but it is unclear what drives this demand.

To some extent, increasing returns to tertiary education are driven by the region's success in increasing the supply of workers with secondary education relative to workers with primary and tertiary education. However, changes in supply alone cannot explain why returns to tertiary education are increasing relative to those for secondary education, or why returns to secondary education have not plummeted relative to returns to primary education. Therefore, changes in the relative returns to education are also driven by increasing demand for skills.

Although some of the rise in the demand for skills is due to the shift in employment toward services, overall this effect tends to be small. Instead, most of the effect comes from an increase in the demand for skills that occurred within both the manufacturing and service sectors. However, the evidence on what explains this rising demand for education within all sectors remains inconclusive. The popular claim that skill-biased technological change is the cause of recent increases in the returns to education has proved difficult to substantiate.

For instance, there is no evidence that countries with faster technological growth—as measured by total factor productivity—have increasing demand for skills, nor is there evidence that the skill premium is explained by the evolution of the ratio of human to physical capital as some recent theories have suggested. Moreover, the evidence at the plant level is not supportive of the thesis that plants (or firms) that adopt production automation technologies demand more skilled workers. If anything, the reverse is true. Plants with more skilled workers tend to adopt more automation technologies, suggesting that the low levels of education in the region may slow down technological growth. And even if the evidence supported the hypothesis that automation technologies explained the increasing demand for skills, this could not account for the increasing demand for skills in the service sector where automation technologies are less common. The alternative hypothesis that the use of information technologies leads to increasing demand for skills in both services and manufacturing awaits confirmation for Latin America.

The popular hypothesis that trade reforms of the magnitude experienced in Latin America have fostered increasing imports of skill-intensive technology is also difficult to substantiate. Tariffs on capital goods were already low before the trade reforms, and while the share of imported capital in the capital stock is increasing, there is no clear relationship between this trend and trade reforms. And although there is some evidence that higher import penetration is associated with increasing demand for skills, other measures of trade liberalization, such as tariffs, do not show a relationship with the demand for skills.

More research is necessary to understand whether and how technology affects the returns to education. Meanwhile, a more important issue concerns why the region has not been able to benefit more from technology to increase the incomes and standards of living of all workers.

Many workers are poor, but focusing on informal work may be misleading.

Many workers are having a hard time in the labor market. Many are unemployed and many are employed in jobs that pay very little or offer little protection against the risk of unemployment, sickness, work accidents, or old age. Over the years, labor market analysts in developing countries have focused on following the evolution of informal labor as a measure to track the quality of employment and well being of workers. However, focusing on informal work may be misleading and risk turning a blind eye to other serious maladies.

An emphasis on informal work may be misleading because it is both unclear who informal workers are and whether they are suffering more than formal sector workers. Some analysts define informal work as noncompliance with official norms (for instance, the share of unregistered businesses); others identify informal work with certain types of employment assumed to be low-paying, low-advancement jobs (such as self-employment, unpaid family work, or employment in firms with five or fewer employees). There is some overlap among these categories, but many workers fall in only one category.

The evidence challenges the popular notion that workers are in the informal sector against their will and would prefer to move to the formal sector if given the opportunity. Recent studies for Brazil and Mexico document that a large majority of self-employed workers prefer this status to a formal sector job because they earn higher wages and enjoy more independence. And although many jobs in the smallest firms fall into the low-advancement, low-productivity category, there are also thriving new small enterprises. Consistent with this idea, there is no indication that the differences in wages between small and large firms are larger in Latin America than in the Unites States. This observation also challenges the notion that labor markets in Latin America are abnormally segmented. In reality, there is substantial mobility between sectors traditionally considered formal and informal in the labor market.

Given these complications, the Report tracks the quality of jobs by using direct measurements of the wages and benefits received by workers. This has the following advantages: first, it clearly defines the phenomenon of study; and second, it avoids attaching a value judgment to sectors of the labor market based on predetermined criteria of the welfare of those employed in a given sector. These measures indicate that on average one in every two workers earns wages that are too low to lift an average family out of poverty, and that more than half of all workers are not protected by labor laws or social security programs. However, the evidence also suggests that, to a large extent, low earnings and lack of social protection reflect low worker productivity rates in the region. Higher rates of productivity growth would increase the earnings of the poorest workers and improve coverage of labor laws and social security programs.

Focusing on wages and benefits shifts the emphasis of labor policies toward increasing labor productivity and reassessing the structure of social protection so it can cover more workers. It also brings attention to those workers who, despite being employed in sectors considered formal, still earn very low wages or are not covered by labor laws. And it is a way out of the contradiction in the widely shared view that laments the growth of the informal sector, but also laments the destruction of many small and micro enterprises when the informal sector shrinks.

Earnings inequality reflects inequality in education, but education alone is not enough to solve the problem of low wages.

The level of earnings inequality in Latin America is among the highest in the world, but this inequality is not so much created in the labor market as reflected by it. A large share of earnings inequality is associated with large differences in endowments, such as education and experience that workers bring to the labor market. Only a small fraction of earnings inequality is explained by the fact that similar workers obtain different pay depending on the characteristics of their jobs. Differences in the wages of workers employed in small and large firms, as well as interindustry wage differentials, are within the range observed in the United States, a country with substantially lower earnings inequality than Latin America, but higher than that in most other developed countries. Moreover, the share of national income that goes to workers falls within the range observed for more developed countries and has been stable for the past decade.

Thus, addressing the problem of earnings inequality is more a matter of leveling the playing field in terms of endowments rather than altering prices in the labor market. The observed increasing returns to education may raise the incentives for families to keep their children in school longer, or for adult workers to go back to school. However, increasing returns also contribute to further increasing the earnings differences between those who have high levels of education and those who do not. More resources should be devoted to reducing early age dropout rates and improving adult education.

Although more education for all could help to reduce inequality substantially, it would not necessarily diminish poverty in a substantial way. Inequality would be reduced if all workers attained similar years of education, but poverty might still affect many of them if education does not allow workers to escape poverty. Of course, education does increase earnings, and returns to education in most Latin American countries are high by international standards. However, if workers without education earn very little, increasing wages by a fixed percentage would still leave workers with low wages in absolute terms. Since the basic level of productivity of all workers largely depends on the quality of the institutional and economic environment in which firms operate, efforts to raise the average level of education may turn out to be a slow (and even inefficient) way to eliminate poverty, unless efforts are also made to improve the conditions for firms to invest, innovate, and achieve higher levels of productivity.

Labor markets in the region appear to be losing their traditional mechanisms of adjustment to macroeconomic shocks.

The region's labor markets operate in a volatile environment. Over the past 30 years, only Africa and the Middle East have been more volatile than Latin America. This pervasive aggregate volatility requires large adjustments in the labor market. Thus, even if the share of national income that goes to workers did not vary much, a reduction in national income would manifest itself in a decline in employment or wages.

Is it better to adjust to shocks through lower wages or higher unemployment? Although it is difficult to make value judgments regarding how to adjust to a crisis, the reality is that wage adjustments help to spread the cost of a recession while unemployment concentrates it among a few. In Latin America, despite large volatility in output, volatility in employment has not been higher than in more stable regions. This is because, with a few exceptions, shocks have been traditionally absorbed through very high wage volatility. This has helped to spread the costs of crisis more evenly among the employed, which is an important feature in countries where only a minority of workers has access to unemployment insurance or severance pay.

However, the traditional adjustment mechanisms appear to be changing, and this change can explain why unemployment rates have reacted so virulently to the decline in economic activity in the past few years. In Latin America, high wage flexibility seems to be the result of two bad outcomes: high inflation and low enforcement of labor regulations. As inflation levels have dropped to single digits, less adjustment via wages has implied a larger reaction of employment and unemployment to macroeconomic shocks. Higher investments in improving the enforcement of labor laws might produce a similar effect.

As economies grow, joblessness will subside. However, to the extent that unexpected and unavoidable shocks will continue to occur, unemployment will continue to react strongly unless policies and institutions facilitate wage adjustments. This is not to say that Latin America should go back to the days of high inflation or weaken enforcement of labor laws. Instead, the mix of recurring shocks and low inflation should be accompanied by institutions that facilitate wage adjustment—helping to contain the consequences of macroeconomic shocks on unemployment—and ameliorate the welfare costs associated with job loss.

At the micro level, there is a large but not atypical amount of reallocation of workers and jobs.

While changes in unemployment during the 1990s seem to be mostly explained by the interaction of macroeconomic volatility and declining wage adjustment, unemployment is only the tip of the iceberg of the vast majority of activity that occurs in the labor market. In any given year, a large number of firms expand their workforces while others trim their payrolls. This activity occurs in recessions and booms, and within all sectors of the economy regardless of how narrowly they are defined. To give an idea of the magnitudes, every year in the countries studied about one in every four jobs is either created or destroyed. This implies that at any given moment a large number of workers lose their jobs, while at the same time many workers are hired.

Focusing only on unemployment rates assumes that all workers who both lose and find jobs are winners. However, this may not be the case. There is a large probability of job loss for all workers, particularly the unskilled. Many workers, especially the poorest, cannot afford periods of job search and therefore are forced to accept the first job that comes their way, even if waiting would have meant finding a job in which they were more productive and would earn higher wages. Workers who are involuntarily displaced from their jobs tend to find jobs that pay lower wages than the ones they had before. The fact that workers who shift sectors, have higher skills, or have higher tenure tend to suffer higher wage losses suggests that some specific skills are lost in the process and that some inefficient churning may be taking place. Imperfect or insufficiently developed capital markets may explain why employers are forced to lay off workers who, given their particular skills, are difficult to replace.

Should layoffs be forbidden or indemnities for dismissal be increased? Although it is true that stringent job security measures reduce reallocation, they may have adverse consequences for productivity and earnings growth. In all economies, productivity growth is associated with productivity gains within existing firms and productivity increases because workers move from less productive firms to more productive ones. The latter component explains between 20 and 50 percent of total productivity growth. By inhibiting the process of allocating workers from less productive uses to more productive ones, economic growth could be stalled. Indeed, it is possible that the stringent job security provisions found in the region hold up productivity growth. The solution to this dilemma is not simple. Policies designed to contain the welfare cost of this perennial motion should be crafted with extreme care; otherwise, the cure might be worse than the disease.

Labor regulations are not cost-free, but deregulation is not the answer.

Across countries, labor regulations govern the rules of the game in labor markets, which are complex and cannot function properly without regulations. Yet, this is not to say that the more regulations the better. The fact is that regulations come in many forms and although some might bring clear welfare gains, others might not. Although the dogma is often that workers' welfare can be improved by legislating benefits and labor warranties, workers' welfare also depends on how well labor markets work. Benefits associated with regulated jobs are of little use to unemployed workers or workers excluded from the system of social protection.

Although it has been argued that labor regulations have little costs in terms of employment, unemployment, and other labor market variables, the empirical evidence gathered in this Report suggests that this is not the case. The implication is not that all regulations should be eliminated, because in most cases they serve an important role. Instead, it is important to recognize that when regulations are not cost-free, their effects should be continuously monitored and balanced against their benefits. In the medical sciences, some illnesses have treatments that can greatly disrupt the life of a patient. Such treatments, if unchecked or provided without care, can even kill. As in that discipline, the dilemmas posed by social policies can be resolved by constantly evaluating the health of the labor market and changing treatments when the risks become too large.

Unions are neither the sand in the wheels of the labor market nor the solution to low wages.

Labor unions have made possible substantial gains in working conditions for significant groups of workers. However, similar to other institutional arrangements in the labor market, union action can bring substantial benefits but also important costs for society. On the benefit side, unions increase their members' earnings between 5 and 10 percent. Although this is a sizable number, these gains are small when compared with the gains associated with experience or education. Thus, typically, every year of secondary education increases earnings by 11 percent relative to the earnings of workers with primary education; therefore, a five-year degree increases earnings more than 50 percent. These numbers suggest that few workers would be able to lift their wages above poverty relying solely on union activity.

However, unions also bring important benefits to their members in terms of reduced turnover and higher employment. Unions may also open important channels of communication between workers and management and contribute to productivity. Collective bargaining can help to reconcile the interests of workers and companies in the aggregate and prevent the adverse consequences that may result from uncoordinated bargaining activities. For society as a whole, unions appear to reduce overall earnings inequality. Moreover, research suggests that countries with highly coordinated collective bargaining experience lower unemployment and higher employment rates than countries with highly decentralized wage setting.

At the same time, unions can also bring important costs. At the firm level, unions may reduce investment, a key variable for earnings growth. Thus, unions may tend to maximize current wage gains at the expense of future wage increases. At the macro level, unions may reduce the ability of economies to adjust and adopt reforms.

Whether benefits outweigh costs is difficult to foresee because the balance is sensitive to the legal framework governing unions, the level of internal and external competition, the nature of labor relations, and their degree of coordination and centralization. An element of concern is that, according to the opinions of workers and employers, labor relations in Latin America seem to be mired in conflict and distrust. This in turn may deter firms and workers from performing the long-term investments in training and new technologies that are essential for sustained growth.

What Should Labor Policies Do?

Given these lessons, what can governments do to minimize workers' difficulties and help them to lead better and more productive lives? What can labor policies do to improve the performance of the labor market?

Governments can help by adopting policies to reduce macroeconomic volatility and create stable, growth-friendly macroeconomic conditions. In those countries where real wage rigidities are increasing the response of unemployment to declining growth, mechanisms such as profit sharing or reducing the transaction costs of wage contracts could increase wage flexibility. But the quest for a better macroeconomic environment and a better response to macroeconomic shocks should not blind policymakers to the everyday demands that a well-functioning labor market places on labor policy. There is a need to readdress the labor policy agenda from temporary solutions to economic crisis to structural policies; and from the philosophy of "protecting workers from the power of employers" to an agenda driven by the objectives of expanding workers' opportunities and improving the performance of labor markets. This does not diminish the importance of workers' rights, as established in conventions on core labor standards and in national labor codes. On the contrary, they should be taken more seriously. The status quo of low enforcement and low compliance undermines the rule of law and leaves many workers ill-equipped to weather the consequences of the continuous process of labor reallocation.

However, in order for regulations to be enforceable, the philosophy of granting warranties in the legal codes, and sometimes even in constitutions, without assessing their consequences in the labor market should also be reassessed. The evidence collected in this Report suggests that there might be important trade-offs between different objectives in the labor market. For instance, full employment may not be compatible with full insurance against unemployment. But the Report also suggests that there are important complementarities. For instance, better labor market performance is compatible with lower earnings inequality. Complementarities can be maximized and trade-offs can be minimized by paying due attention to the consequences of policies. Doing otherwise has led to the current dilemmas, in which workers are highly protected on paper, but noncompliance is the norm and, because there is little focus on policies that expand workers' opportunities, earnings grow painfully slowly. The new agenda requires a strengthened labor authority and a complex network of public and private institutions to fill the following four specific functions.

Increase the efficiency of the job-worker matching process.

A large amount of reallocation creates gaps and lags between firms that seek workers and workers that seek jobs. Policymakers, in partnership with the private sector, could increase the efficiency of the matching process by creating vacancy registries and providing job search assistance. Evaluations in OECD countries suggest that such systems are highly cost-effective mechanisms for putting workers in jobs. Although these policies do not help to create new job vacancies, they reduce frictional unemployment by more quickly filling the available openings. These policies also reduce the income losses associated with unemployment and the demand for social services or unemployment insurance, if applicable. But the main advantage probably lies in the potential to increase the quality and therefore the productivity of job-worker matches. This is because better job-worker matches would likely result in greater investment in training by firms and learning by workers, which are essential for achieving growth in earnings.

Labor intermediation services in the region are less extensive than their counterparts in OECD countries. Nonetheless, there are a number of public national employment services and a growing private sector market in labor intermediation and placement. The reform of these systems requires fostering an appropriate regulatory environment for nonprofit providers, improving information systems, and expanding the range and coverage of the services provided.

Insure workers against the risk of job churning.

Macroeconomic volatility and vigorous job churning have created strong demand for mechanisms of protection against income loss. This demand has been met by regulating employment stability mechanisms that are more stringent than those encountered in more developed countries. However, such mechanisms constitute a primitive method of insurance and can be costly. In addition, more than half of all workers do not participate in such systems and therefore are not covered against the risk of loss of employment.

Although the current system is flawed, the main question is whether alternative forms of insurance would be better suited for the particular characteristics of the region. Most countries in Latin America have reached a level of development that is comparable to the level the developed countries had reached when they implemented unemployment insurance mechanisms.[5] However, the creation or expansion of such systems is challenged by the lack of adequate registries of firms and workers, the high degree of informality in the labor market, the small size of the state, and the lack of fiscal room to pursue countercyclical social expenditures. Under these conditions, the type of unemployment insurance systems in place in developed countries may be infeasible in the region. Moreover, although unemployment insurance does not impede the reallocation of resources, the experience of developed countries suggests that it could have adverse side effects on the labor market.

It is clear that the road to better insurance mechanisms is plagued with obstacles. An important criterion should be to promote the sound functioning of the labor market. After all, the best unemployment insurance is the possibility of quickly finding a good job. But when this is not enough, each country needs to find a solution to

[5] Average per capita GDP in 20 developed nations when they first enacted unemployment insurance law was US$3,539 (Maddison 1995), and the average per capita GDP for 22 countries in the region was of $3,964 in 2000. Most developed countries enacted their first unemployment insurance laws between 1900 and 1944.

these dilemmas that adequately reflects the characteristics of its economy and the preferences of its citizens. In the process, policymakers and legislators should continuously monitor the potential risks that insurance systems bring to the performance of labor markets.

Enhance opportunities for workers.

There is a widespread perception that globalization and trade integration are making training policies more important. At the same time, however, increasing use of temporary contracts and other measures to achieve flexibility are reducing firms' and workers' incentives to invest in skills. Therefore, any policy that seeks to expand the supply of training must foster a regulatory and institutional environment in which incentives for training exist. In this new paradigm, training reforms go beyond the objective of overhauling public training institutions or making training more responsive to the needs of the market. The reforms involve changes in taxes, regulations, and collective bargaining. The objective is to move away from the direct provision of training and improve the incentives for firms, workers, and training providers to fund, seek, and provide high-quality training.

Another promising area for policy is adult education. Although it has been a low priority in most countries, research suggests that bringing adults back to school can be an effective policy for increasing productivity (particularly compared with the results of public job training for unskilled workers). Latin American governments should devise ways to bring adults back to school. Possible measures include issuing tax credits to employers that provide time or resources for employees to attend school or giving tax relief to adult workers while they complete their formal schooling.

Monitor labor policies, enforce regulations, and promote harmonious labor relations.

Countries should invest in developing institutions that collect, analyze, and process information, and those that implement policies and enforce regulations. Assessing the benefits and evaluating the costs of labor policies requires skills that most labor administration authorities (normally the ministry of labor) do not have. Although researchers at universities and specialized firms can perform such monitoring, labor authorities ought to be the ones that contract the analysis, weigh the benefits and costs, and decide on and design the treatments to follow. This requires rebuilding the capacity of the labor administration authority and staffing it to perform such new roles.

The tasks of the authorities are challenged by massive noncompliance. To some extent, noncompliance is the response to poorly designed regulations, but it also reflects the government's lack of effectiveness in enforcing labor laws. Countries with more effective governments tend to exhibit more compliance with social security regulations.[6] New approaches are needed to improve regulations and expand the coverage of inspections and other mechanisms to increase compliance.

Labor authorities should also pay close attention to the quality of labor relations. Labor policies require cooperation between unions and employers to be successful. More transparent wage and collective bargaining rules would go a long way toward improving these relations.

The good news is that many countries are already working hard in these new directions. They have to. Discontent with the current state of affairs is too high to be left unattended. The hope is that the set of policies and institutions that will emerge from the crisis will go beyond quick fixes and help establish a new labor market agenda.

[6] For instance, regressing the percentage of workers that are affiliated with (and make contributions to) social security programs on income per capita and the index of the quality of the government (collected by Kaufman, Kraay, and Zoido-Lobatón [1999]) indicates that while compliance increases with income per capita, the quality of the government also contributes to expanding the coverage of labor regulations.

Chapter 1

The Performance of Latin American Labor Markets

Every day many workers go to work and many firms hire workers. Some firms close, others reduce their size, and new firms emerge; workers switch jobs and enter and exit employment. The decisions and actions of thousands of workers and firms, as well as their interactions with institutions and policies, constitute the labor market. As in many other markets, the labor market has to continuously allocate resources to their most productive uses. The magnitude of this activity is astounding. On average, as many as one in four jobs are created or destroyed in a given year, and a large percentage of workers transit between jobs and between employment, unemployment, and inactivity. This perennial churning is typical of many markets. However, labor markets are special because they deal with the most complex "commodities" of all: people's effort and skills.

The daily business of exchanging labor services for wages provides the main source of income to workers and households. In Latin America and the Caribbean, between one-half and two-thirds of total income is allocated in the labor market and more than 70 percent of Latin American households depend entirely on labor income to live.[1] Moreover, the labor market also creates many economic risks that affect the livelihoods of workers and their families. Workers might involuntarily lose their jobs, but, because fewer than half the workers are protected against this risk, a large share of the labor force is not insured against the distress and suffering that results from the loss of labor income.

What happens in the labor market dramatically affects individuals and households. Therefore, failures in the labor market and in the institutions that support it amount to much more than output losses or lower economic growth; they become difficult social problems as well. Across countries, low wages, low and unequal opportunities for advancement, high unemployment, and low job creation tend to be associated with poverty, inequality, youth alienation, and crime.

Thus, it would seem that this market is too important to fail. Yet, according to the people of Latin America, something is wrong with labor markets in the region. In the Latinobarometer, a public opinion survey that covers 17 countries in Latin America, problems directly related to the labor market have ranked first in the list of population concerns year after year since the survey was started in 1996. Moreover, the importance assigned to these problems has been increasing. On average, in 2001, more than 20 percent of the survey responses pointed to unemployment as the most pressing

[1] This is the average labor share for 10 countries in the region (Bernanke and Gurkaynak 2001). The proportion of households that depend entirely on labor income is from the most recent available household surveys (1999 or 2000). The number reported is the simple average for 11 countries.

Figure 1.1 The Most Pressing Problem in the Region
(Percentage of respondents)

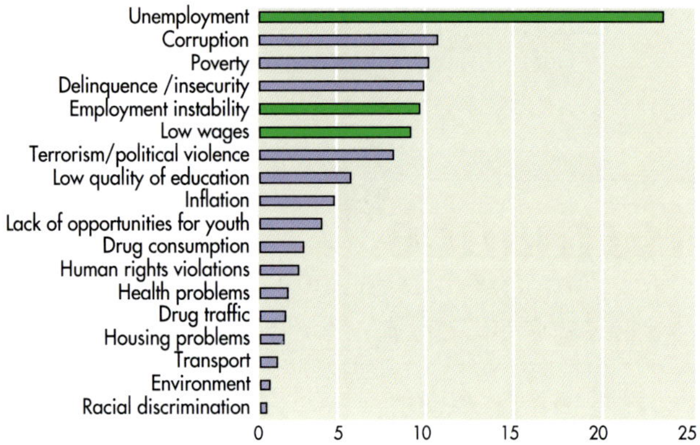

Note: Average of responses for 17 countries in Latin America.
Source: Latinobarometer (2001).

Figure 1.2 The Most Important Problem, by Country
(Percentage of respondents)

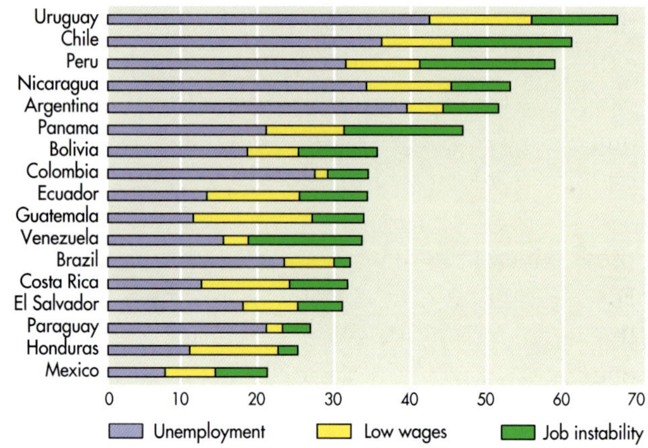

Source: Latinobarometer (2001).

problem in the region, while more than 40 percent of the responses identified low wages, job instability, or unemployment as the most important problem, ahead of corruption, crime, and other difficult social problems (Figure 1.1). In Argentina, Chile, Nicaragua, Peru, and Uruguay, this percentage climbed to 50 percent (Figure 1.2). It is clear that whatever is going on in the labor market tops the list of concerns of Latin American citizens.

This chapter analyzes the performance of Latin American labor markets during recent years to understand whether they are fit to perform the important tasks they need to do. It compares critical parameters of the regional markets with those of countries outside the region to identify areas in need of improvement. And it develops summary measures of performance, ranking labor markets in the region along the dimensions of labor market efficiency, income equity, and insurance against risks.

The following main conclusions emerge about labor markets in the region:

- Labor markets show increasing difficulty in allocating workers to jobs, although there are substantial disparities within the region.
- Wages have grown slowly and one in two workers earns wages that may be too low to afford consumption above poverty levels. However, these factors are not so much due to excessive bargaining power of employers relative to workers, but to low and stagnant labor productivity.
- Although the region suffers from very high levels of earnings inequality, the labor market reflects rather than creates inequality. Nonetheless, labor market-generated inequality increased during the 1990s.
- Labor relations are mired in conflict and distrust, which may deter labor productivity growth in the region.
- More than half of the workers do not receive the protection mandated by labor laws. Thus, many workers are vulnerable to the risks of income loss due to unemployment, illness, or old age. Moreover, coverage has declined during the 1990s. Although labor policies should strive for better allocation of resources and better and more widespread risk insurance, there may be important trade-offs between these dimensions. Keeping the allocation engine running while providing sufficient insurance to workers constitutes one of the major challenges for labor policies in the region.

Dimensions of Labor Market Performance

It is commonplace to summarize the performance of labor markets with the unemployment rate. However, many other dimensions of performance should be assessed as well. This chapter evaluates the performance of Latin American labor markets based on how they perform the key tasks of allocating resources, earnings, and risks across workers and firms. It also examines the quality of labor relations, that is, the quality of the special relationship that bonds employers with workers and unions, to determine whether it is conducive to rewarding work experiences and productivity growth or mired in conflict and distrust. For each country, the indicators are computed along three dimensions—efficiency, social insurance, and equity—to examine whether there are any relevant trade-offs among them.

Box 1.1 describes the difficulties involved in gathering labor market data. In general, data were only available for the 1990s, so the analysis does not provide a long-term assessment of the evolution of the labor market. Given these limitations, the focus is on describing cross-country differences by comparing the average values of all variables in the 1990s across countries. The evolution of most variables is documented both for the region as a whole as well as for the individual countries for which data are available.

Allocation of Resources

A key function of labor markets is to continuously match workers to their most productive use. As shown in chapter 2, a labor market that performs the allocation task well not only ensures that workers are well allocated to jobs, it is also an important source of economic growth. The labor market allocates the available resources efficiently if no workers willing to work are left without jobs, no job vacancies are left unfilled, and workers and jobs are well matched. Clearly, a labor market that regularly functions with a high level of unemployment is not allocating resources well. However, while a persistently high level of unemployment signals problems in the labor market, low unem-

Box 1.1 Labor Market Data

The paucity and lack of comparability of data on labor market variables in Latin America remain a large obstacle for the analysis of labor markets in the region. The Labour Statistics Database of the International Labour Organization (ILO) includes data for a noteworthy number of countries and years and for numerous indicators; however, the data are not yet fully cross-country or time-series comparable. For instance, the geographic area and the age range used to compute the indicators are not fully consistent across countries and the definitions used to compute the indicators are not always equivalent. Furthermore, the sources and sample coverage fluctuate over time. The ILO faces large obstacles because it must rely on countries' capability to provide the data. Nevertheless, the quality of data is improving substantially and the ILO is working toward releasing comparable data.

To overcome some of these difficulties, this study has processed a large number of household surveys, making a special effort to address time-series and cross-country comparability. However, while the Inter-American Development Bank's (IDB's) data offer a good picture of the cross section of countries, for many countries, the time-series dimension is not large enough to provide a good description of changes over time.

The IDB's collection of harmonized household surveys is not exhaustive; in particular, coverage of the Caribbean is poor and the IDB is working toward expanding information on these countries. This would be facilitated by the collection of comparable information from Caribbean countries as well as the timely release of surveys.

Facing all these constraints, this chapter and the volume in general use a mix of data sources, depending on the dimensions analyzed. In general, the cross-country comparisons and analysis of labor market dynamics are performed using IDB data, and the time-series analysis relies on IDB data and data from published sources, such as the ILO or the Economic Commission for Latin America and the Caribbean. In addition, individual firm, plant, and worker panel data are available only for a small number of countries. Thus, the analysis of labor market dynamics is limited to a few countries (see chapter 2).

Box 1.2 Labor Market Indicators

Labor force participation rate. The number of persons in the labor force as a percentage of the working-age population. The labor force is the sum of the number of persons employed and unemployed. The working-age population is the population within a certain age range. Although this range varies across countries, in all the IDB computed variables, the age considered is 15 to 64 years.

Employment rate. The proportion of people in the working-age population that is employed. The employed comprise all persons who during a specified reference period, either one week or one day, worked for at least one hour for profit or family gain, in cash or in kind in (a) paid employment, (b) self-employment, or (c) as contributing family workers (also termed unpaid family workers).

Unemployment rate. The proportion of unemployed in the labor force. The unemployed comprise all persons in a specified age range who during the reference period were: (a) without work, that is, not employed, (b) currently available for work, that is, available for paid employment or self-employment during the reference period, and (c) seeking work, that is, had taken specific steps in a specified reference period to seek paid employment or self-employment.

Underemployment rate. The proportion of workers whose working hours total less than full time as a proportion of total employment. In this study, up to 30 hours a week is established as the number of hours that is less than full time.

Voluntary underemployment. The proportion of workers whose working hours are less than 30 a week and who do not desire to work more hours.

Involuntary underemployment. The proportion of workers whose working hours are less than 30 a week and who desire to work more hours.

Coverage rate. The proportion of either wage employed or total employed workers participating in a program of social security benefits and who are entitled to benefits. (The social security system covers the risk of old age, unemployment illness, disability, and death.) It is assumed that workers who are not participating in a social security system are not covered by all the other benefits prescribed by labor laws.

ployment rates are not necessarily a signal of labor market health. Unemployment rates might be low because workers have given up searching for jobs, a phenomenon known as the discouraged worker effect, or because workers cannot afford to search for the best job and therefore take any job available. In the latter case, workers have jobs, but the quality of the job-worker match might be poor. (See Box 1.2 for definitions of unemployment and other labor market variables.)

A related problem in evaluating how workers are matched with jobs is that while resource allocation is a dynamic concept, most labor market statistics measure static concepts. Thus, while the problem at hand is to assess whether unemployed workers have trouble finding jobs that match their abilities, whether displaced workers are forced to accept large wage cuts, or whether workers who have unemployment insurance find better jobs, labor market statistics measure how many workers are unemployed or employed by occupation or sector. Thus, it is possible to analyze whether workers *are* allocated to jobs, but there is little that can be said about whether they are *well* allocated to jobs.

Chapter 2 analyzes labor market dynamics for a few countries in which longitudinal data on workers and firms are available. This chapter takes advantage of information from household and labor force surveys to obtain a rough but broader picture of how labor markets allocate resources in Latin America. It analyzes the unemployment rate, the duration of unemployment, and the unemployment gaps between different types of workers across countries and time. While the unemployment rate measures the number of people who wish to work and are actively searching for jobs, the duration of unemployment measures the extent to which the pool of unemployment is stagnant. Unemployment gaps measure whether unemployment is concentrated in a particular type of worker. In addition, since it could be argued that unemployment rates hide the true degree of "joblessness," the chapter examines other measures, such as the level and evolution of the share of self-employed or underemployed workers, to complete the picture of how Latin American labor markets allocate workers to jobs. Unfortunately, little can be said about how job vacancies are filled because data on vacancies are not available in most countries.

Rising Unemployment

Unemployment has become a significant problem in Latin America. The region ended the 1990s with much higher unemployment rates than at the beginning (Figure 1.3). By contrast, unemployment rates have experienced a sustained decline in the Caribbean since 1993 (Figure 1.4). It should be noted, however, that in Latin America, much of the rise in unemployment occurred after 1994 and again after 1998, coinciding with periods of low economic growth. Indeed, figure 1.3 suggests that throughout the 1980s and the 1990s, periods of low economic growth tended to be accompanied by increased unemployment. Nonetheless, by 2000, the median unemployment rate was above 10 percent, and as high as the rates seen in the region during the height of the debt crisis (1983-85), despite the fact that economic activity did not contract nearly as much in the late 1990s as in the 1980s. It appears that unemployment rates are reacting much more virulently to changes in economic activity than they did in earlier periods. It is also clear that joblessness is not only an issue in rich countries; by 2001, average unemployment rates were substantially higher in Latin America than in Continental Europe and Eastern Europe, two regions often singled out for their high unemployment rates (Figure 1.5).

Despite the increase in Latin America's regional unemployment rate, each country has had its own trajectory, and some ended up with lower unemployment rates. Comparing the average rate during the 1990s and the 1980s, some countries—particularly Mexico and the Central American countries—experienced lower unemployment rates during the 1990s than the 1980s. In others, average unemployment rates increased, although in most cases the difference was small (Figure 1.6). Looking instead at the annual change in unemployment rates during the 1990s, in Mexico, Bolivia, and Panama, unemployment rates declined. By contrast, the Southern Cone countries experienced a large average annual increase in unemployment.[2] This was also true in Colombia and Venezuela.

But beyond differences in trajectories, there are large and persistent differences in average

Figure 1.3 Urban Unemployment Rate and GDP Growth in Latin America

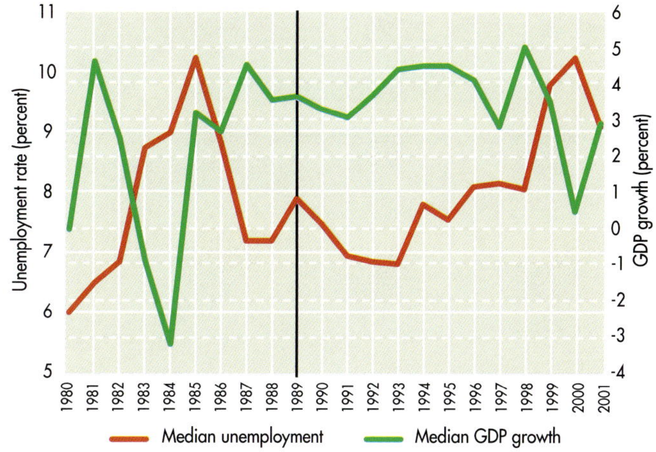

Note: The figure includes data from Argentina, Bolivia, Brazil, Chile, Colombia, Costa Rica, Ecuador, Guatemala, Honduras, Mexico, Nicaragua, Panama, Peru, Paraguay, Uruguay, and Venezuela.
Source: Unemployment rate from ECLAC; GDP in constant prices (national currency) from IMF.

Figure 1.4 Urban Unemployment Rate in the Caribbean
(Percent)

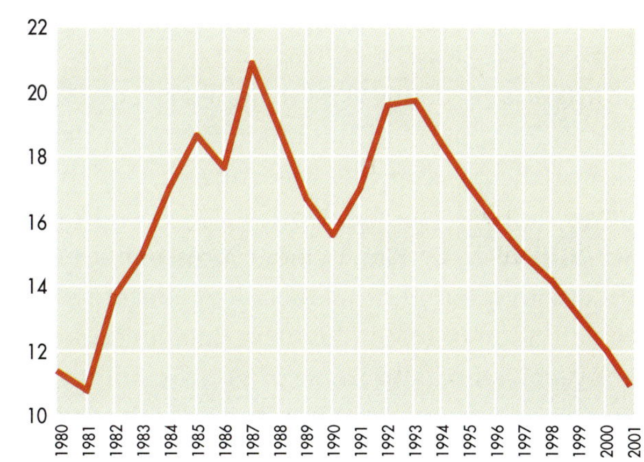

Note: Includes data for Barbados, Jamaica, and Trinidad and Tobago.
Source: ILO.

[2] The countries in the Southern Cone are Argentina, Brazil, Chile, and Uruguay.

Figure 1.5 Average Unemployment Rate by Region, 2001
(Percent)

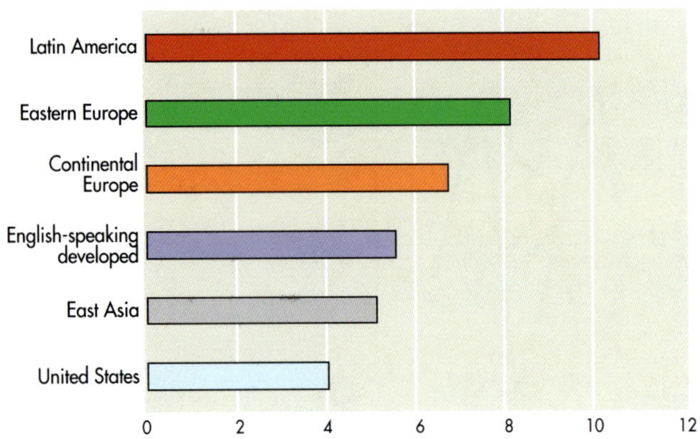

Source: ILO (LABORSTA and *Employment Outlook*) and OECD statistics.

Figure 1.6 Urban Unemployment Rate: 1980-89 vs. 1990-2001

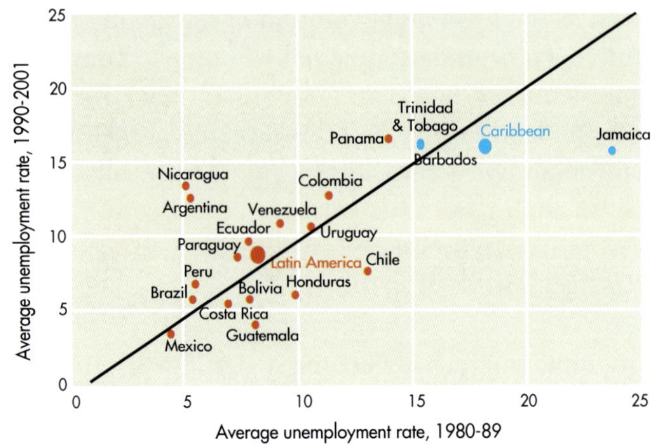

Note: Unemployment rates in the Caribbean are not comparable to the rates in Latin American countries due to methodological differences.
Source: ECLAC and ILO.

unemployment rates across countries. Although some countries can be characterized as high-unemployment countries, others have persistently low unemployment rates. On average, for the 19 countries in Figure 1.6, urban unemployment rates during the 1990s were more than 10 percent in eight countries and below 6 percent in six countries. With the exception of the unemployment rates in the Caribbean countries and Panama, which cannot be directly compared with the rates in other countries in Latin America because they are computed with a different methodology, differences in the definition of unemployment do not account for such persistent differences in unemployment. Thus, with few exceptions, countries that endured high unemployment rates during the 1980s also experienced high unemployment during the 1990s, suggesting that structural factors account for differences in unemployment levels across countries.

In most countries, rising unemployment rates were not associated with declining employment opportunities (at least in terms of the number of jobs). In practically all the countries in Figure 1.7, a larger share of the population was drawn to the labor market during the 1990s. Thus, the share of the overall population that was employed declined significantly only in Brazil, Argentina, and Colombia.

The rise in employment and labor force participation rates came from women. While on average male labor force participation rates remained constant, female labor force participation increased at a rate of 0.7 points a year during the 1990s (Table 1.1). Moreover, in at least four countries, female labor force participation rates went up by at least nine points during the decade. These rates largely outpaced the rise in female labor force participation in other regions of the world during the 1990s, suggesting that while female labor force participa-

Figure 1.7 Annual Change in Unemployment and Employment Rates, 1990-2001
(Percent)

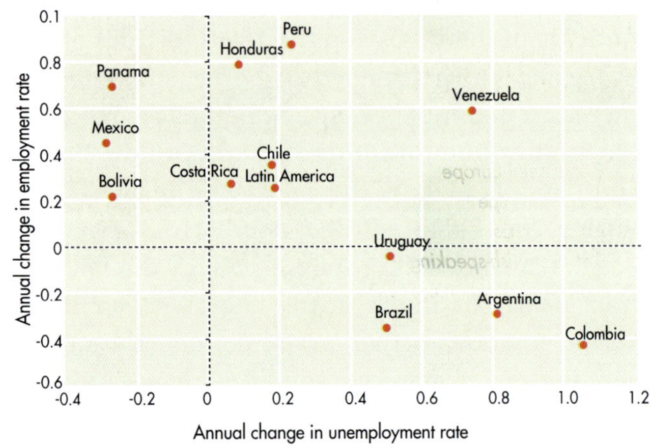

Note: National data except for Argentina, Mexico, and Uruguay, which are urban data.
Source: IDB household surveys.

Table 1.1 Labor Force Participation by Gender, 1990-2001
(Percent)

Country	Number of observations	Male: Mean	Male: Annual change	Female: Mean	Female: Annual change
Latin America	77	83.3	0.04	47.6	0.73*
Argentina	10	81.7	–0.23*	50.0	0.72*
Bolivia	6	75.6	–0.29*	50.9	0.32
Brazil	7	86.4	–0.48*	53.2	0.43*
Chile	5	79.4	0.02	38.8	0.90*
Colombia	6	85.0	–0.38*	48.8	0.84*
Costa Rica	6	85.5	0.00	38.3	0.62*
Dominican Republic (1998)		83.4		49.1	
Ecuador (1998)		89.8		58.4	
El Salvador (1999)		79.9		47.2	
Guatemala (1998)		89.5		47.0	
Honduras	5	88.4	0.42*	42.4	1.28*
Mexico	12	79.2	0.07	39.1	0.51*
Nicaragua (2001)		82.4		45.1	
Panama	6	79.4	0.49	40.3	0.66*
Paraguay (1999)		86.1		50.3	
Peru	4	81.2	0.89*	55.5	1.20*
Uruguay	5	84.9	–0.15	58.7	0.72*
Venezuela	5	82.4	0.47*	43.5	1.79*
East Asia	38	80.1	–0.14*	51.7	0.07
Continental Europe	112	80.0	–0.08*	61.0	0.46*
Eastern Europe	30	74.3	–0.25*	59.5	–0.40*
United States	11	85.6	–0.18*	70.4	0.33*
Other English-speaking developed countries	59	82.8	–0.05	62.7	0.57*

* Significant at 15 percent.

Note: Male (female) labor force participation is expressed as a percentage of male (female) working-age (15–64 years) population. For East Asia, the age group varies by country. The data are incomplete; the mean and trend were computed when data included three or more years, spread over three periods: early (1990–93), mid (1994–97), and late (1998–2001). The countries included in the regions are as follows: East Asia: Indonesia, Korea, Malaysia, Philippines, and Thailand; Eastern Europe: Czech Republic, Hungary, and Poland; Continental Europe: Denmark, France, Germany, Greece, Italy, Netherlands, Norway, Portugal, Spain, and Sweden; other English-speaking developed countries: Australia, Canada, England, Ireland, and New Zealand. Country trends were obtained by regressing available data on a time trend. Regional trends were obtained by regressing available data on a time trend and a set of country fixed effects.

Source: Latin America and the Caribbean: IDB calculations based on household surveys; national data except for Argentina, Bolivia, Mexico, and Uruguay, for which urban data are used. East Asia: ILO LABORSTA Labour Statistics Database. OECD: OECD online databases for labor force data.

tion rates remain low in the region—particularly in Chile, Costa Rica, and Mexico—when compared with East Asia or developed countries, there is a process of convergence to international levels. This process would imply that large increases in female labor force participation would continue in the future. In comparison, male labor force participation rates are within the range observed in other parts of the world.

Duration of Unemployment

During the 1990s, there were no significant changes in the regional incidence of long-term unemployment, defined as the share of unemployed workers that spent one year or more searching for a job. Some countries experienced an increase in duration and in others, the percentage of long-term unemployed workers declined. However, the incidence of long-term unemployment is low in the region, at least compared with long-term rates in Eastern European countries and other developed countries (Table 1.2). Nonetheless, in half the countries for which data are available, the incidence of long-term unemployment was higher than in the United States during the 1990s. This is quite surprising because only a relatively small and declining share of workers had access to unemployment insurance or severance pay; therefore, for many workers, it was difficult to sustain long periods of job search. Moreover, by the end of the 1990s, more than 50 percent of unemployment was long term in Uruguay and more than 40 percent in Colombia.

At the other end of the employment distribution, Table 1.2 shows that as much as 36 percent of the unemployed had been in that state for a month or less in Latin America, compared with 8 percent in Eastern Europe, 11 percent in Continental Europe, and 17 percent in other English-speaking developed countries (excluding the United States). This suggests that on average, Latin American labor markets reallocated unemployed workers to jobs faster than richer regions of the world, although at a slower pace than the United States. In some individual countries, about 50 percent or more of the unemployed had been in that state for a month or less. These figures can be interpreted as a sign that the labor market reallocated workers with amazing efficiency or, alternatively, as an indication that workers were seriously constrained in their ability to search for good jobs.

Large Unemployment Gaps

During the 1990s, women and youth in Latin America experienced abnormally high rates of unemployment relative to the rates of males and prime-age workers. However, such unemployment gaps did not change much during the decade (Table 1.3). The ratio between male and female unemployment rates was much larger in Latin America than in other regions of the world, with the exception of Continental Europe. Moreover, in some countries, such as Brazil, Chile, Colombia, and Uruguay, the gender unemployment gap was larger than in Continental Europe. The unemployment rates for young workers were also high relative to the unemployment rates of adult workers compared with other regions, except for the United States. In some countries, the youth unemployment rate was more than three times the adult rate.

Such large differentials indicate the presence of substantial and troublesome labor market problems; however, the source of the problems is unclear because various phenomena may give rise to large unemployment gaps. Thus, on the one hand, large unemployment gaps may be the result of existing barriers, regulations, or discrimination practices that make it difficult for women and young people to enter the labor market. On the other hand, such large gaps may signal that, on average, women and youth can take more time to search for jobs relative to male and prime-age workers who, in many cases, are the main earners and therefore are pressed to find any job. In the first case, the problem is concentrated on women and youth in the labor market; in the second, the problem relates to adults. The inability to search interpretation is more credible in countries such as Mexico, where male and adult unemployment rates are extremely low. The barrier to insertion interpretation is more likely in countries where unemployment rates for adult and male workers are not low. In this second group of countries, youth unemployment rates—which are much higher than adult rates—are reaching high levels in absolute terms. This worrisome development constrains the economic opportunities of this group of workers and may have important and undesired consequences in terms of youth alienation and juvenile violence and crime.

Urban-rural unemployment gaps were also large, although the relative difference fell during the 1990s. On average, unemployment rates in cities were more than four times greater than the rates in rural areas (Table 1.3). Among the exceptions, in Peru, the ratio was 20 and in Bolivia it was 13. These outcomes suggest that there are still large differences between the labor market structures in rural and urban areas. Workers in rural areas may have a much lower ability to engage in job search than workers in urban settings.

Table 1.2 Duration of Unemployment, 1990-2001
(Percentage of unemployment)

Country	Number of observations	Short-term (up to one month) Mean	Short-term (up to one month) Annual change	Long-term (one year or longer) Mean	Long-term (one year or longer) Annual change
Latin America	50	36.14	–0.17	11.18	0.47
Argentina	10	27.05	–0.03	9.22	0.83*
Bolivia (1997)		15.22		22.60	
Chile (1996)		49.16		2.74	
Colombia	6	20.06	–2.56*	33.72	0.76
Costa Rica	6	37.26	–0.80	10.57	0.66*
Dominican Republic (1996)		44.55		3.30	
Ecuador (1998)		57.35		5.20	
Guatemala (1998)		52.24		0.08	
Honduras	5	46.01	2.25	4.01	–1.24*
Mexico	12	49.66	0.51*	0.78	0.08*
Nicaragua (2001)		65.37		1.16	
Panama	6	13.20	0.62*	24.63	–1.35*
Paraguay (1999)		9.25		21.61	
Peru (2000)		52.00		1.10	
Uruguay	5	19.92	–2.67*	23.48	4.52
Venezuela (1999)		19.91		14.75	
Continental Europe[a]	104	11.36	0.48*	42.04	0.20
Eastern Europe	29	8.28	–0.60*	41.52	1.93*
United States	12	39.65	0.33	7.35	–0.19
Other English-speaking developed countries[b]	48	17.32	0.70*	32.51	–0.46*

* Significant at 15 percent.

[a] There are 115 observations for long-term unemployment.

[b] There are 57 observations for long-term unemployment.

Note: The data are incomplete; the mean and trend were computed when data included three or more years, spread over three periods: early (1990–93), mid (1994–97), and late (1998–2001). For countries included in the regions, see note in Table 1.1. Short-term unemployment does not include Ireland or Portugal. Country trends were obtained by regressing available data on a time trend. Regional trends were obtained by regressing available data on a time trend and a set of country fixed effects.

Source: Latin America and the Caribbean: IDB calculations based on household surveys; national data except for Argentina, Bolivia, Mexico, and Uruguay, for which urban data are used. OECD: OECD online databases.

Many analysts have documented that across firms, economic sectors, and countries, there is an increasing demand for skilled workers. Is there any evidence that unemployment is becoming increasingly concentrated in unskilled workers? Are increasing unemployment rates a consequence of shifting demand for skills? Although this is a reasonable hypothesis, there is little evidence that this is the case. While unemployment rates tend to be higher for workers with secondary education than for workers with primary or college education (Table 1.4), there is no indication that unemployment rates are becoming more concentrated in the unskilled. Instead, if anything, the opposite seems to be true: on average, workers with tertiary education were increasingly more likely to be unemployed than their less skilled counterparts (Table 1.4).

Could it be that unskilled workers left the labor force discouraged by their inability to find jobs? Murphy and Topel (1997) report that in the United States, unemployment has become less informative for gauging the changing opportunities of the unskilled. This is because these workers are increasingly withdrawing from the labor force in the face of adverse economic opportunities. Over-

Table 1.3 Unemployment Gaps by Gender, Age, and Area, 1990-2001

(Ratio of unemployment rates)

		Female/male		Young/ prime-age male[a]		Urban/rural	
Country	**Number of observations**	**Mean**	**Annual change**	**Mean**	**Annual change**	**Mean**	**Annual change**
Latin America[b]	77	1.30	0.00	2.65	–0.05	4.31	–0.72*
Argentina	10	1.24	–0.02	2.55	–0.10*		
Bolivia[c]	6	1.16	0.02	2.23	0.09	13.27	
Brazil	7	1.57	0.02*	2.56	0.04*	3.54	–0.16*
Chile	5	1.45	–0.01	2.82	–0.03	1.40	–0.04
Colombia	6	1.94	–0.07*	2.74	–0.08	2.06	–0.08*
Costa Rica	6	1.56	0.03	3.31	–0.05	1.08	–0.01
Dominican Republic (1998)		2.75		3.64		1.47	
Ecuador (1998)		1.03		1.88		4.47	
El Salvador (1999)		0.62		1.93		1.20	
Guatemala (1998)		0.52		1.97		2.59	
Honduras	5	0.95	–0.01	1.80	0.13	3.30	–0.07
Mexico	12	1.23	–0.01	3.20	–0.01		
Nicaragua (2001)		1.10		1.39		2.55	
Panama	6	1.39	0.01	2.75	0.06*	2.00	–0.06
Paraguay (1999)		1.36		2.83		3.32	
Peru	4	1.11	–0.01	3.45	–0.44	20.67	–4.45
Uruguay	5	1.63	–0.01*	4.62	–0.24*		
Venezuela[d]	5	0.85	0.02	1.99	–0.08*	1.72	
East Asia	35	1.04	–0.03*				
Continental Europe[e]	185	1.43	–0.005*	2.42	0.01		
Eastern Europe[f]	31	1.19	0.00	2.46	0.00		
United States[g]	11	1.00	0.01*	2.825	0.10*		
Other English-speaking developed countries[h]	60	0.90	0.00	2.16	0.05*		

* Significant at 15 percent.

[a] The total working-age group is 15–64 years old, the young group is 15–24 years, and the prime-age group is 25–49 years.

[b] Based on 39 observations for the urban/rural gap.

[c] Data for the urban/rural gap are for 1999.

[d] Data for the urban/rural gap are for 1995.

[e] Based on 118 observations for the young/prime-age male gap.

[f] Based on 29 observations for the young/prime-age male gap.

[g] Based on 12 observations for the young/prime-age male gap.

[h] Based on 55 observations for young/prime-age male gap.

Note: Unemployment is the share of the labor force (age 15–64 years) that is unemployed. For East Asia, the age group varies by country. The data are incomplete; the mean and trend were computed when data included three or more years, spread over three periods: early (1990–93), mid (1994–97), and late (1998–2001). For countries included in the regions, see note in Table 1.1. Norway is included only for the young/prime-age male gap. Country trends were obtained by regressing available data on a time trend. Regional trends were obtained by regressing available data on a time trend and a set of country fixed effects.

Source: Latin America and the Caribbean: IDB calculations based on household surveys; national data except for Argentina, Bolivia, Mexico, and Uruguay, for which urban data are used. East Asia: ILO LABORSTA Labour Statistics Database. OECD: OECD online databases.

all, however, there is little evidence that unskilled workers are abandoning the labor force in Latin America since the employment rates of skilled relative to unskilled workers did not change in the region (Table 1.4). The lack of an overall trend hides differences in performance across countries. In Bolivia, Colombia, and Costa Rica, employment opportunities shifted toward the most skilled workers; in Chile and Peru, employment rates for workers who have completed secondary school increased at a faster pace than for workers with some college education.

Table 1.4 Unemployment and Employment Gaps by Education Level, 1990-2001

		Unemployment rate				Employment rate			
		Secondary/primary		Some tertiary/ secondary		Secondary/primary		Some tertiary/ secondary	
Country	Number of observations	Mean	Annual change	Mean	Annual change	Mean	Annual change	Mean	Annual change
Latin America[a]	77	1.68	–0.01	0.67	0.01*	1.07	0.000	1.07	0.00
Argentina	10	0.81	0.01	0.71	–0.01*	1.17	0.005	1.08	0.00
Bolivia	6	2.43	0.15*	0.77	0.01	0.86	–0.006*	1.04	0.01*
Brazil	7	1.28	0.00	0.55	0.00	1.15	0.002	1.12	0.00
Chile[b]	5	1.22	–0.03	0.67	0.01	1.23	0.007*	1.01	–0.01*
Colombia	6	1.82	–0.05*	0.60	0.00	1.05	–0.007	1.12	0.01*
Costa Rica	6	0.95	0.00	0.59	0.00	1.06	–0.001	1.12	0.01*
Dominican Republic (1998)		1.27		0.68		1.11		1.15	
Ecuador (1998)		2.88		0.55		0.91		1.13	
El Salvador (1999)		1.79		0.68		1.14		0.89	
Guatemala (1998)		2.53		0.39		1.08		1.02	
Honduras	5	1.22	0.00	0.71	0.04*	1.11	–0.003	0.97	–0.01
Mexico	12	1.39	0.02*	0.88	0.04*	1.07	–0.004*	1.15	0.00
Nicaragua (2001)		1.36		1.00		1.06		1.02	
Panama	6	2.16	–0.12*	0.60	0.00	1.04	0.008*	1.16	0.00
Paraguay (1999)		1.78		0.40		1.06		1.15	
Peru	4	3.33	–0.17	0.90	0.03*	0.90	–0.002	1.06	–0.01*
Uruguay	5	0.92	–0.03*	0.68	0.01	1.16	–0.003	1.07	0.01
Venezuela	5	1.12	0.01	0.73	–0.01	1.03	0.004*	1.06	0.00
United States		0.56		0.80					

* Significant at 15 percent.

[a] There are 78 observations for the employment rate.

[b] There are 6 observations for the employment rate.

Note: Unemployment and employment rates are expressed as a percentage of working-age (15–64 years) population in the labor force. The data are incomplete; the mean and trend were computed when data included three or more years, spread over three periods: early (1990–93), mid (1994–97), and late (1998–2001). Schooling level definitions vary somewhat across countries. Country trends were obtained by regressing available data on a time trend. Regional trends were obtained by regressing available data on a time trend and a set of country fixed effects.

Source: IDB calculations based on household surveys; national data except or Argentina, Bolivia, Mexico, and Uruguay, for which urban data are used. Data for the United States are from the U.S. Bureau of Labor Statistics.

Other Indicators of Labor Market Slack

It has been argued that unemployment rates do not measure the true degree of joblessness because many workers, particularly the unskilled, cannot afford to remain unemployed, as suggested by the low unemployment rates of workers with primary education relative to workers who have finished secondary education (Table 1.4). To overcome this problem, many analysts have constructed measures to capture the share of workers employed in precarious, low-quality jobs or, as they are often called, informal jobs. The International Labour Organization, for instance, classifies as informal workers those who are self-employed, employed without wages in a family business, employed as domestic service workers, or employed in a firm with five or fewer employees.[3]

According to these categories, the unemployment rate might not properly reflect a deterioration in labor market conditions in Bolivia, Mexico, or Panama. Figure 1.8 plots yearly changes in unemployment against the changes in the share of workers who were self-employed, did not receive wages for their work, or were employed in firms with five

[3] See *Employment Outlook*, which is published by the regional office of the International Labour Organization in Lima, Peru.

or fewer employees in the 1990s. The share of workers in each category increased in all cases in Mexico and Bolivia, despite the fact that, on average, there was a negative trend in unemployment rates.

In the other countries, unpaid and self-employed workers did not show a clear trend despite generalized increases in unemployment rates. For instance, the share of unpaid workers, which for the region averaged 6.8 percent of employment during the 1990s, declined in seven out of 11 countries and increased in the other four (Figure 1.8b). Regarding the share of self-employment, the average rate of change was positive, although not statistically different from 0 (Figure 1.8a). This was the case because performance differed across countries, although unemployment increased in many. The share of self-employment, which for the whole region averaged 27 percent of employment, increased in six out of 11 countries and fell in five. In some countries, large increases in unemployment were accompanied by a rise in the share of self-employed workers. In other cases, unemployment increased substantially, while the share of self-employed workers fell. By contrast, the share of workers employed in very small firms (five or fewer employees) increased in all countries for which data are available for the 1990s, with the exception of Chile (Figure 1.8c).

Judging from the evolution of these categories of employment, labor market conditions deteriorated in some countries in which unemployment rates did not increase during the 1990s. However, a fundamental problem with these measures is that it is unclear which phenomena they are measuring. For instance, while the trend toward a larger share of workers employed in very small firms could be interpreted as a deterioration in the capacity of the labor market to allocate workers to good jobs, this same trend could also be caused by an increasing share of thriving, newly created firms. This is because in general new firms are small. Similarly, a rise in the share of self-employment does not necessarily imply deterioration in the labor market; it may reflect increasing opportunities for small-scale activities and independent workers. (See Box 1.3 for further discussion regarding the problems associated with measures of the informal sector.)

Figure 1.8 Unemployment and the Share of Workers in Total Employment, 1990-2001

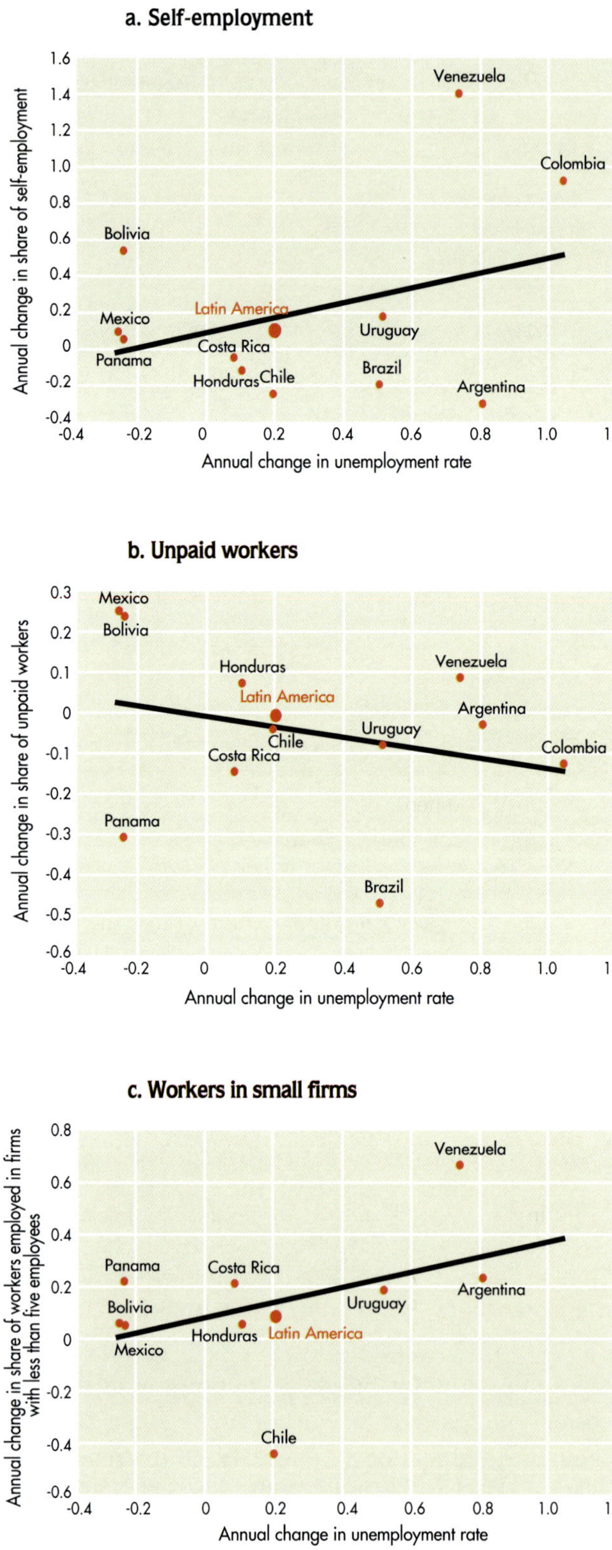

Note: Annual rates are computed by estimating a linear trend for each country. National data except for Argentina, Mexico, and Uruguay, which are urban data.
Source: IDB calculations based on household and labor force surveys.

A final measure of the degree to which labor markets allocate all the available resources is given by the number of workers that declare that they would like to work more hours than they do. This measure captures the percentage of the labor force that is involuntarily underemployed. According to the data summarized in Table 1.5, on average during the 1990s, about 8.4 percent fell into that category. In five countries, more than one in 10 workers were restricted in the number of hours they worked. Moreover, this variable exhibited a positive (and statistically significant) rate of growth during the 1990s in the small sample of countries for which time-series data are available.

Summary Indicator of Resource Allocation

The performance of Latin American labor markets in their task of allocating workers to jobs is ranked based on average unemployment, long-term unemployment, and unemployment gaps. The unemployment gap is the simple average of the gender, age, and skill unemployment gaps, and the skill unemployment gaps are measured across differences between workers with primary and secondary education and between workers with completed secondary and any college education. Measures of the informal sector are not included in

Box 1.3 What Is the Informal Sector?

In studies of labor markets in developing countries, it is traditional to include a discussion of the informal sector. However, given that this variable has come to measure different outcomes in different studies, the term has lost some of its usefulness. Thus, for example, in some studies, the term informal describes jobs that provide low incomes, few benefits, and little possibility of advancement to the workers that perform them. A second strand of studies refers to the informal sector as a measure of noncompliance with the state (evading labor laws or taxes).

In the spirit of the first type of studies, the International Labour Organization defines the informal sector as the sum of nonprofessional self-employed workers, domestic workers, unpaid workers, and workers employed in firms with at most five (or sometimes, depending on the country, 10 employees). An obvious problem with this definition, however, is that it is not necessarily clear that all jobs classified in that group fall into the low productivity, low advancement category. This is especially relevant in the small firms sector, which may be populated by low productivity, low-paying firms, but also by thriving newborn enterprises. But it is also relevant in the self-employment sector. Thus, while it is true that most street vendors and other traditional manifestations of self-made, low-productivity work will be classified as own-account workers, it is also possible that many self-employed workers may be in that sector by choice.

Indeed, there is a remarkable split in the literature between the developed and developing countries on this particular topic: studies analyzing self-employment in developed countries usually emphasize the flexibility and independence afforded to workers in this segment (Blanchflower 2000). They also stress the importance of self-employment as part of a new trend toward more decentralization of production as economies of scale are becoming less important in service-dominated economies (Belussi 1998). By contrast, most literature on labor markets in developing countries associates an increase in the share of self-employment with a decline in workers' welfare.

While chapter 4 shows that the share of self-employed workers tends to move countercyclically, that is, it increases in bad times, it is unclear whether this occurs because workers take refuge in self-employment or because this sector contracts less than the wage employment sector in recessions. Similarly, it is unclear whether all self-employed workers in developing countries would rather work in the wage employment sector. For instance, a recent study reports that roughly four out of five self-employed Brazilians prefer this status to a formal job. Similarly, Maloney (1999) reports that in Mexico, two-thirds of those that moved from the formal sector to self-employment did so voluntarily, mentioning a desire for more independence or higher pay as an explanation.

Given the above-mentioned shortcomings, this study uses the term "informal labor" sparingly and measures instead the manifestations that the literature sometimes associates with the informal sector, such as low productivity or lack of compliance (referring to the percentage of workers with low wages or the percentage of workers without social security). This has several advantages: first, it clearly defines the phenomenon of study; and second, it avoids attaching a value judgment to sectors of the labor market based on prejudging the welfare of those employed in a given sector.

Table 1.5 Underemployment in Latin America, 1990-2001
(Percentage of employment)

Country	Number of observations	Involuntary underemployment: Mean	Involuntary underemployment: Annual change	Voluntary underemployment: Mean	Voluntary underemployment: Annual change
Latin America[a]	57	8.42	0.48*	8.77	–0.07
Argentina	10	13.98	1.16*	8.30	–0.23*
Bolivia (1999)		10.22		12.34	
Colombia	6	4.56	0.36*	7.86	–0.56*
Costa Rica	6	8.08	0.26	7.59	–0.19*
Ecuador (1998)		21.78		5.90	
El Salvador (1999)		3.80		0.47	
Guatemala (1998)		13.95		10.90	
Honduras	5	2.75	0.08*	14.16	0.39*
Mexico	12			0.36	0.04*
Nicaragua (2001)		13.39		5.77	
Panama	6	6.56	–0.02	6.72	0.37*
Paraguay (1999)		5.93		7.59	
Peru[b]	4	3.30		25.38	–0.18
Uruguay	5	7.61	0.45*	13.17	–0.13
Venezuela	3	2.03	0.48*	5.09	–0.50

* Significant at 15 percent.
[a] There are 41 observations for involuntary underemployment.
[b] Data for involuntary underemployment are for 2000.
Note: The data are incomplete; the mean and trend were computed when data included three or more years, spread over three periods: early (1990–93), mid (1994–97), and late (1998–2001). Country trends were obtained by regressing available data on a time trend. Regional trends were obtained by regressing available data on a time trend and a set of country fixed effects.
Source: IDB calculations based on household surveys; national data except for Argentina, Bolivia, Mexico, and Uruguay, for which urban data are used.

the summary ranking because it is unclear that a high rate of self-employment or a high share of workers in small firms signals poor labor market performance (see Box 1.3). Moreover, Figure 1.9 shows that the shares of self-employed and unpaid workers are highly negatively correlated with the levels of productivity per worker, suggesting that in the long run these variables capture the level of development of a country rather than the performance of its labor market. However, if a country's unemployment rate does not capture the true degree of joblessness, it will tend to be reflected in large skill, gender, or age unemployment gaps because poorer workers and main earners will tend to be more constrained in their job search than other workers.

Figure 1.10 reports the resulting summary measure of the efficiency in resource allocation across countries. Higher values indicate better performance in this area, while lower values point to difficulties in allocating workers to jobs. According to this measure, Latin America on average displays a lower capacity to allocate workers than the United States, the reference country. Within the region, some countries display a combination of lower unemployment, lower unemployment duration, and lower unemployment gaps than the reference country, suggesting that in these countries, labor

Figure 1.9 Informal Work and GDP per Worker

a. Self-employment

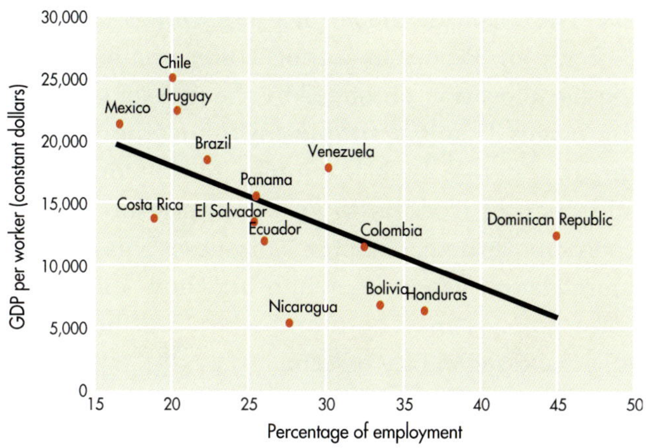

b. Unpaid workers

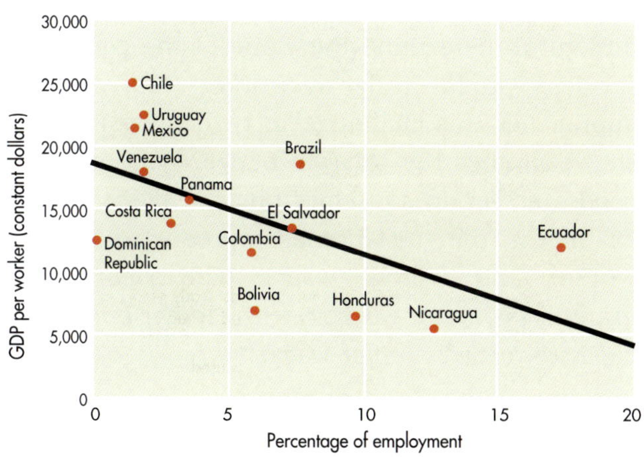

c. Employment in small firms

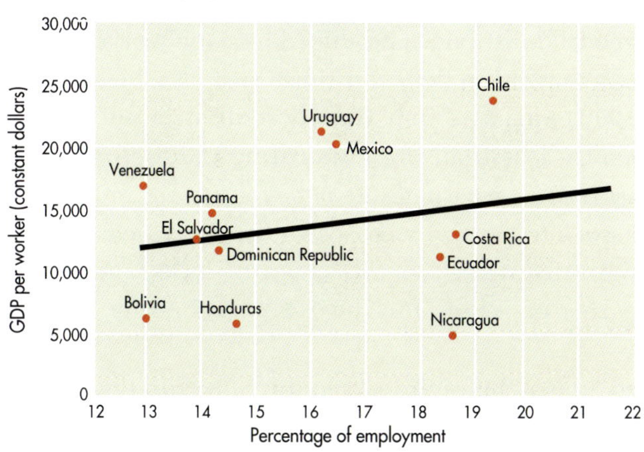

Note: Annual rates are computed by estimating a linear trend for each country. National data except for Argentina, Mexico, and Uruguay, which are urban data.
Source: IDB calculations based on household and labor force surveys for labor data, and World Bank data for GDP.

Figure 1.10 Summary Measure of Efficiency in Allocation of Resources, 1990-2001
(Index, 0-1)

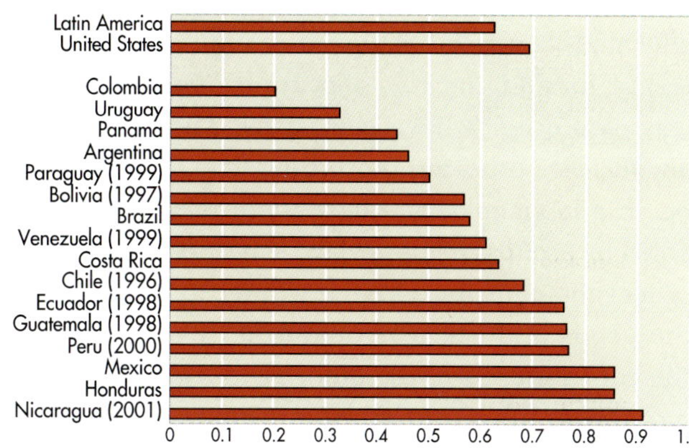

Source: IDB calculations based on individual country household and labor force survey data.

markets are quite efficient in allocating workers to jobs. Nonetheless, it could also be argued that higher values of the index reflect that workers cannot afford to search for jobs. However, if that is the case, these difficulties arise for all workers, not only for the poorest or more pressed to find jobs. The worst job allocation performance is found in Colombia, Uruguay, Panama, and Argentina. In these countries, many workers seek jobs for long periods of time and unemployment is highly concentrated among some groups of workers.

Allocation of Earnings

It is often assumed that many workers are poor because employers abuse their power by keeping wages low. If minimum wages or other regulations could force employers to pay more, the argument goes, many workers would be able to escape from poverty and live decent lives, and the appalling levels of income inequality observed in the region would be reduced. This section examines how well or how poorly labor markets in Latin America have allocated earnings to workers by examining the pricing behavior of the labor market as well as the sources of the high levels of earnings inequality and poverty in the region.

Two Criteria

A difficulty in evaluating how well labor markets allocate incomes is that there is more than one criterion for judging the allocation of earnings. At least two criteria have been used. The first one is an *efficiency* criterion. According to economic theory, in a labor market where there is enough competition among firms to hire workers, wages will reflect the contribution of a worker to the value of the goods and services produced by a firm, once the contributions of the other factors of production have been taken into account. This contribution is known as the marginal product of labor. Therefore, the efficiency criterion assesses how much workers' earnings reflect their productivity.

In an efficient allocation, equally productive workers would receive identical wages, regardless of the firm, sector or activity, or gender of the worker. With this premise, gender wage differentials or differentials in wages between workers employed in large and small firms or across different industries have often been used to assess the earnings allocation efficiency of labor markets. In practice, however, not all wage differentials between seemingly similarly productive workers are a sign of inefficient allocation of incomes. Two workers may look similar in terms of observed factors, such as age and education, but differ across dimensions like type of degree or motivation, which are rewarded in the labor market. Wage differences can also reflect compensation for differences in working conditions. For instance, workers employed in more dangerous industries may be compensated with higher wages. Similarly, employers in larger firms may set higher effort and productivity standards and therefore pay higher wages. Nonetheless, abnormally high differentials are likely to signal lack of competition and lack of mobility in the labor market, which prevent workers from getting the value of their marginal product.

The second criterion that has been used to assess how well labor markets allocate incomes is *equity*. Large wage differentials across similar workers will lead to wage inequality. However, even in an efficient labor market in the sense defined above, that is, when all similarly productive workers get similar wages, inequality may be large if some workers are much more productive than others. The resulting disparities in earnings might be difficult for society to accept. Unfortunately, altering the allocation produced by the market via altering wages is not a simple task. Income policies might generate high unemployment, worsen the allocation of workers to jobs, and possibly reduce economic growth. Chapter 7 discusses this issue in more detail, assessing when and how minimum wage policies may help and when and how they may have secondary effects.

Efficiency

Assessing whether workers' wages reflect the value of the goods and services they produce is not simple because wages are poorly measured and it is difficult to determine the value of the goods and services produced by a worker. The analysis approaches this challenge in two ways. The first step examines the relation between the value of goods and services produced by the average worker—that is, the gross domestic product (GDP) per worker—and average wages. The second step examines whether workers with similar productive capacity receive similar wages.

Wage Increases

The empirical evidence suggests that, at least for the region as a whole, wage growth is intimately related to the growth of the average value of the goods and services produced by each worker. A linear regression between these two variables for the 1990s suggests that the coefficient is not significantly less than one, indicating that across countries increases in GDP per worker are one-to-one associated with increases in wages, at least in the manufacturing sector (Figure 1.11).[4] Although series of wages for the whole economy are not

[4] Wages for the overall economy are not available for most countries. Therefore, manufacturing wage data compiled by ILO (2002a) were used. The coefficient of the linear regression is 0.86, with a standard error of 0.12; therefore, the null hypothesis that the coefficient is equal to 1 is not rejected.

Figure 1.11 Wages and Labor Productivity in Latin America

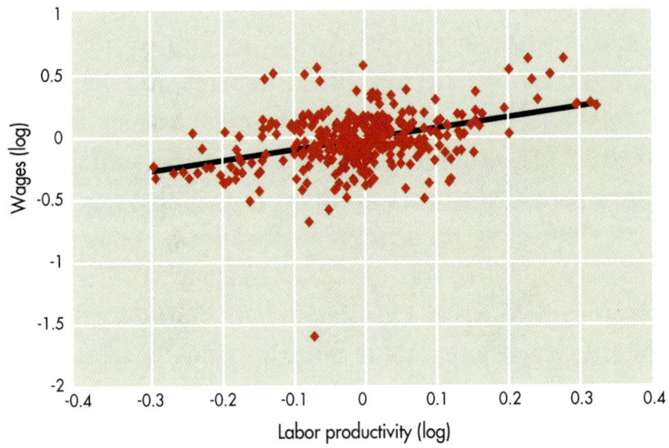

Note: Each point in the scatter corresponds to one Latin American country and one year.
Source: IDB calculations based on ILO data.

Figure 1.12 Annual Change in the Labor Share, 1990s
(Percent)

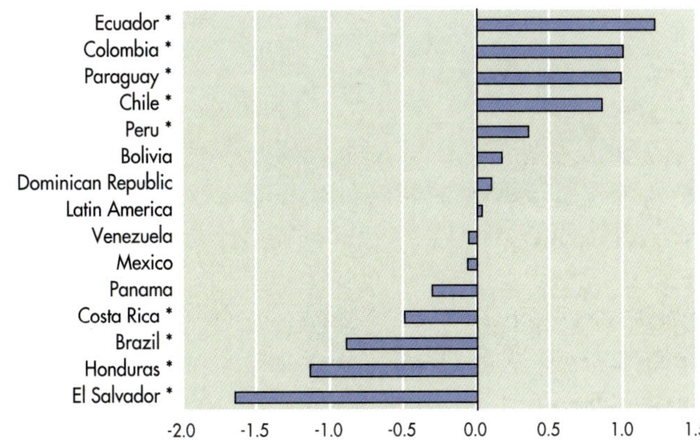

* Significant at 15 percent.
Note: The annual rate of change is computed from regressing labor shares on a time trend.
Source: UN National Accounts statistics.

available, an indication of the evolution of wages and productivity at the aggregate level can be obtained from the evolution of the labor share, that is, the share of value added that goes to pay workers' wages and benefits. Although on average the labor share fell during the 1980s, it remained constant during the 1990s. Therefore, at the aggregate level and in terms of the average for the region, wages increased at the same pace as productivity (Figure 1.12).[5]

A fundamental problem, however, is that despite substantial structural reforms, product per worker—also referred to as labor productivity—has grown slowly in the region. Figure 1.13 plots the annual growth rate of this variable across countries in 1990-95 and 1995-2000. Performance has been uneven, but in general most countries achieved productivity growth rates that are below those attained in the United States and other developed countries.

For the region as a whole, labor productivity growth was practically zero. This underscores the limited scope for wage increases in the region. In only a few countries, productivity grew enough to grant substantial increases in workers' wages. The scarce available data on wages suggest that, on average, real manufacturing wages grew by about 1 percent a year during the 1990s (ILO 2002a). However, in some countries, real wages experienced a large decline (Figure 1.14).

Figure 1.13 Annual Growth in Labor Productivity
(Percent)

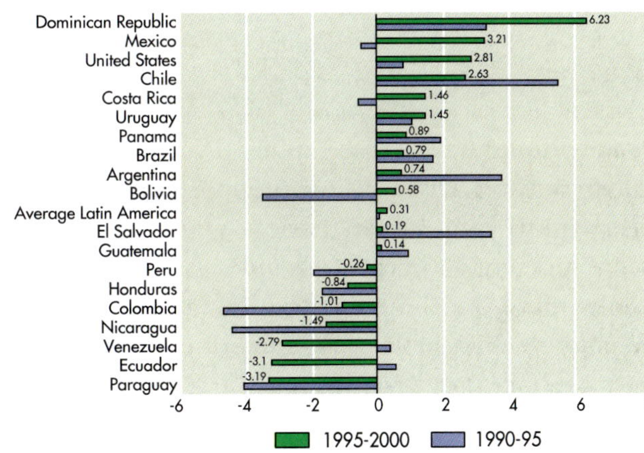

Source: Heston, Summers, and Bettina (2002) database.

In a few countries, labor shares increased in the 1990s, suggesting that wages increased above labor productivity growth (Figure 1.12); in others, wage increases fell short of productivity growth. It is quite remarkable that labor shares tended to fall in Mexico and Central America, where unemployment rates declined or stayed constant, while they increased in Ecuador, Colombia, and Paraguay, where unemployment rates increased. As is shown

[5] These results are obtained by regressing labor shares from the UN National Accounts Statistics on a set of fixed effects and a time trend.

Figure 1.14 Change in Real Wages in Manufacturing, 1990s
(Percent)

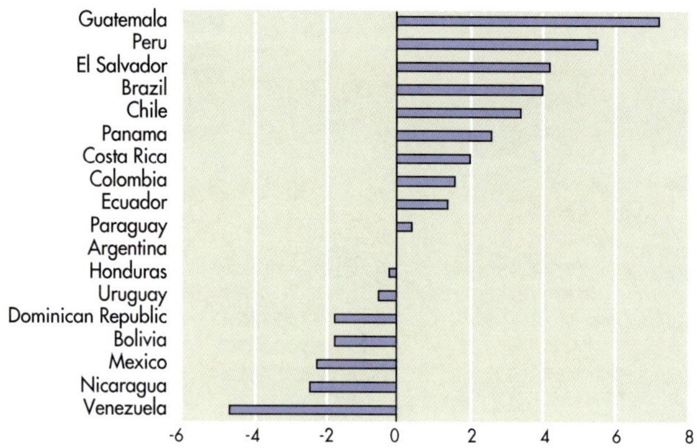

Source: ILO (2002a).

in chapter 4, rising wage rigidity is a strong candidate for explaining the sharp increases in unemployment during the second part of the 1990s.

Wage Differentials

Wage differentials across gender, firm size, and sector of activity have not been abnormally large in the region. Thus, although these wage differentials were not small, they were not unlike the ones observed in the United States, the only nonregional country for which comparable reference indicators could be constructed.

On average in Latin America, a worker employed in a firm with more than five employees earned about 29 percent more than a worker employed in a smaller firm, while the comparable wage gap in the United States in 1996 was about 27 percent (Table 1.6).[6, 7] It is unclear whether such wage gaps are the result of unobservable differences between workers employed in small and large firms or instead reflect barriers to entry or rents in large firms.[8] However, the fact that these differentials are similar in Latin America and the United States suggests that there does not seem to be an abnormal degree of labor market segmentation between large and small firms in Latin America relative to the United States.

Industry wage differentials in Latin America were also within the range of differentials in the United States (Table 1.7). In both parts of the world, construction and retail, restaurants, and hotels paid less than manufacturing, while the business services and finance sector tended to pay more, even when controlling for differences in the age and education of workers. By contrast, transport and communications paid more than manufacturing in some countries and less in others.

Although industry differentials tended to increase during the 1990s, at least for the limited sample of countries for which data on the evolution of the wage gaps are available, there was no discernible trend in size differentials. These increased in some countries and became smaller in others despite the fact that, on average, the percentage of workers in small firms increased in all countries, with the exception of Chile. Therefore, it is not in general true that the increase in the proportion of workers employed in small firms was accompanied by wages in this sector falling relative to wages in the large firm sector.

Finally, average gender wage gaps were also in line with the U.S. gender gap (Table 1.6). Hence, on average during the 1990s, Latin American men earned 26.5 percent more than women of comparable age and education, while in the United States, male workers earned 26.7 percent more. Moreover, gender differentials decreased during the 1990s in many countries. Nonetheless, there are still large gender differentials in some countries, including Brazil, Honduras, and Guatemala. Cox Edwards, Duryea, and Ureta (2002) provide an explanation for why wage differentials may be high in countries like Brazil. These authors noticed that there is a positive relationship between female labor force participation and wage gaps. They explain this fact by hypothesizing that in

[6] Wage gaps are computed for prime-age male workers to minimize the selection problems that arise when working with a sample that includes women. These selection problems are due to the fact that only a minority of women participates in the labor market and therefore the sample of working women is not likely to be a random selection of women in a given country.

[7] The average size differential for Latin America excluding Paraguay, an extreme case, is even closer to the differential for the United States.

[8] See for instance Oi (1999) for a recent survey of this literature.

Table 1.6 Wage Differentials by Gender and Firm Size, 1990-2001

(Percent)

		Male/female		Firm size large/small	
Country	**Number of observations**	**Mean**	**Annual change**	**Mean**	**Annual change**
Latin America[a]	81	26.54	–0.23	29.27	0.06
Argentina	10	16.66	0.17	26.87	1.60*
Bolivia[b]	6	29.83	0.34	33.94	–0.38
Brazil[c]	12	46.78	–1.17*	26.35	–1.36*
Chile	5	30.00	–1.08*	25.13	0.02
Colombia	7	14.03	–1.14*		
Costa Rica	6	20.91	0.03	27.57	–1.14*
Dominican Republic (1998)[d]		28.46		17.26	
Ecuador (1998)		30.12		51.43	
El Salvador (1999)		24.72		37.40	
Guatemala (1998)		33.38		15.17	
Honduras	5	40.40	3.30*	2.58	–8.34*
Mexico	10	11.89	–0.46*	29.15	2.73*
Nicaragua (2001)		27.12		28.44	
Panama	6	28.71	0.45	43.50	0.01
Peru[e]	4	20.48	–0.19	35.88	
Uruguay	5	26.74	–0.22	39.60	0.69*
Venezuela	5	20.88	0.14	28.08	0.71
United States (1996)		26.65		26.74	

* Significant at 15 percent.
[a] There are 64 observations for the firm size gap.
[b] There are 5 observations for the firm size gap.
[c] There are 7 observations for the firm size gap.
[d] Data for the firm size gap are for 1996.
[e] Data for the firm size gap are for 2000.

Note: Values are Mincerian rates expressed as a percent. For the male/female wage differentials, data are for urban wage employees age 25–49 years, working more than 30 hours a week. For the firm size wage differentials, data are for urban male wage employees age 25–49 years, working more than 30 hours a week. The rates are derived from the following regression models:

Gender wage differentials: Log wagehr = A + B*gender + C*X + E

where the dependent variable is logarithm of hourly wage; independent variables are a dummy for gender, X = dummies for six educational levels, and potential experience and its square.

Firm size wage differentials: Log wagehr = A + B*SIZE + C*X + E

where the dependent variable is logarithm of hourly wage; independent variables are a dummy for firm size, X = dummies for six educational levels, and potential experience and its square. Note the omitted category for the dummy is firms with fewer than five employees, with the exception of the United States, for which it is firms with fewer than 10 employees. Country trends were obtained by regressing available data on a time trend. Regional trends were obtained by regressing available data on a set of country fixed effects.

Source: IDB calculations based on household surveys. National data except for Argentina, Bolivia, Mexico, and Uruguay, for which urban data are used.

countries with very low female labor force participation rates, women who do participate are highly motivated or able. Therefore, the wage gaps between these exceptional women and their male counterparts tend to be lower than in countries where more women participate and the sample of employed women is less selected. This could explain why female wage gaps are large in Brazil, where the labor force participation of women is high, and low in Mexico, where participation is very low. However, the argument does not explain why the gap is high in countries like Honduras or Guatemala, where female labor force participation rates are at or below average levels.

Indicator of Income Allocation Efficiency

There are some wage differentials between workers of seemingly equal productivity, but these differences are of the same order of magnitude as

Table 1.7 Industry Wage Differentials by Sector, 1990-2001

(Percent)

Country	Number of observations	Construction: Mean	Construction: Annual change	Retail trade, restaurants and hotels: Mean	Retail trade, restaurants and hotels: Annual change	Transport, storage, and communications: Mean	Transport, storage, and communications: Annual change	Finance, insurance, real estate, and business: Mean	Finance, insurance, real estate, and business: Annual change
Latin America	80	–0.68	0.00	–11.13	–0.47*	–2.19	–0.59*	13.16	–0.68
Argentina	10	–9.49	–1.70*	–18.11	–1.38*	–13.62	–0.89*	2.67	–0.52
Bolivia	5	14.22	1.29	1.11	3.06	–11.76	–3.40*	40.29	5.34
Brazil	12	–29.69	0.32	–30.88	0.77*	–8.72	0.15	15.75	0.77*
Chile	5	–0.23	–0.04	–13.25	0.10	–7.31	–1.67*	18.89	–0.30
Colombia	7	2.09	0.28	–12.07	–0.77*	–3.70	0.19	1.24	0.15
Costa Rica	6	–8.73	0.33	–8.98	–0.23	–4.72	–0.96	8.88	–3.40*
Dominican Republic (1998)		25.97		–7.84		–2.06		14.21	
Ecuador (1998)		–19.62		–8.97		–34.69		5.85	
El Salvador (1999)		–3.62		–10.77		–3.69		–2.48	
Guatemala (1998)		–5.91		–5.94		1.60		14.12	
Honduras	5	–3.65	0.29	–22.14	–4.11*	11.14	2.83*	–25.50	–8.53*
Mexico	10	–3.98	–1.49*	–15.45	–0.36	–6.18	–1.18*	30.63	1.19
Nicaragua (2001)		26.45		–3.71		11.52		39.75	
Panama	6	8.26	–0.05	–6.99	–0.99*	47.65	–2.07*	6.56	–2.70*
Peru	4	–0.63	1.30	–10.16	–2.82*	–9.03	–1.82*	18.98	0.36
Uruguay	5	–8.62	1.14*	–14.72	0.58	–5.37	1.51*	32.18	–3.59*
Venezuela	5	5.56	2.13	–10.54	–0.42	1.78	–1.04	1.75	–1.60
United States (1996)		–2.44		–21.80		–3.89		14.52	

* Significant at 15 percent.

Note: Values are Mincerian rates expressed as a percent. Data are for urban male wage employees age 25–49 years, working more than 30 hours a week. The rates are derived from the following regression model:

Log wagehr = A + B*sector + C*X + E.

The dependent variable is logarithm of hourly wage; independent variables are dummies for sector of activity, six educational levels, and potential experience and its square. Note the omitted category for the dummy is the manufacturing sector. Country trends were obtained by regressing available data on a time trend. Regional trends were obtained by regressing available data on a time trend and a set of country fixed effects. The data are incomplete; the mean and trend were computed when data included three or more years, spread over three periods: early (1990–93), mid (1994–97), and late (1998–2001).

Source: IDB calculations based on household surveys, and national data for Argentina, Bolivia, Mexico, Uruguay, and Venezuela.

those measured in the United States. This is an important finding because it suggests that focusing on the evolution of the share of workers in small firms as an indicator of labor market performance, as is traditional in the literature on labor markets in developing countries, may be misguided.

It is true that workers in smaller firms tend to earn less and enjoy fewer benefits, such as health insurance or old age pensions. However, this is true across many countries, not only developing ones, and there is no indication that this is more of a problem in Latin America than in developed countries. Nonetheless, some countries exhibited larger than average wage gaps. Therefore, in these countries, lack of competition or mobility across firms and sectors may reduce wages below marginal productivity. To identify such countries, a summary measure is constructed by standardizing all wage differentials between 0 and 1 and averaging across them. Higher values of this measure imply lower wage differentials. The resulting measure is plotted in Figure 1.15. On average, wage differentials were larger in Brazil, Ecuador, Nicaragua, and Panama, and lower in Guatemala, Costa Rica, El Salvador, and Venezuela.

Figure 1.15 Summary Measure of Efficiency in Allocation of Incomes
(Index, 0-1)

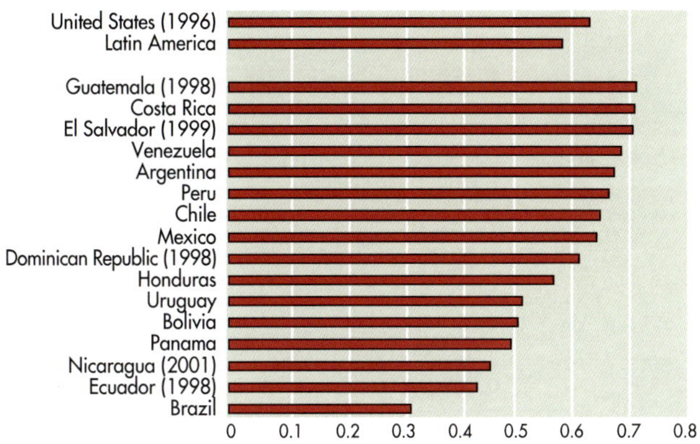

Source: IDB calculations.

Figure 1.16 Relative Earnings: Median Worker/Poorest 10 Percent of Workers, 1990s

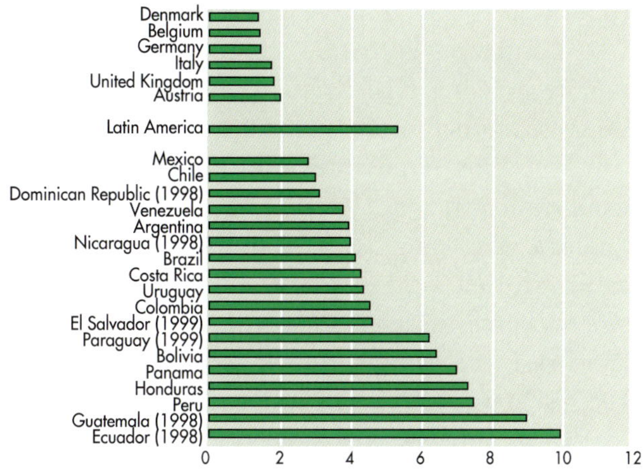

Source: Latin America: IDB calculations based on household and labor force surveys; other countries: OECD data.

Equity

It is well known that the countries of the region suffer from the greatest income inequality in the world (IDB 1999). This is also true for labor earnings. A comparison with developed countries, for example, indicates that on average in Latin America, the median worker earns five times as much as the poorest 10 percent of workers in society, while in most developed countries, this difference is less than two (Figure 1.16).[9]

Not all inequality is created in the labor market. Thus, when assessing the role of labor markets in generating earnings inequality, it is important to distinguish how much inequality is created in the labor market and how much is reflected by it. For example, inequalities may arise because workers with different levels of education earn very different wages or because similar workers obtain different wages depending on the type of job.

IDB (1999) examines the causes of wage inequality in Latin America and finds that differences in the characteristics of the individuals—such as education, gender, and experience—explained an average of 35 percent of the labor income concentration in the region, and approximately half the concentration in Argentina, Costa Rica, El Salvador, Panama, and Honduras. Among the individual characteristics, educational differences had the most significant effects on inequality, explaining an average of one-fourth of the labor income concentration. Differences in experience accounted for 10 percent of income concentration, while gender differences accounted for approximately 4 percent.

By comparison, IDB (1999) finds that job type, geographic area, and economic sector explained a small share of labor income concentration. This is compatible with the information presented in Tables 1.6 and 1.7, indicating that, on average during the 1990s, wage differentials between workers employed in firms of different size or in different economic sectors were comparable to those in the United States, a country with a lower concentration of income than Latin America, although higher than in other developed countries. Thus, earnings inequality is to a large extent a reflection of differences in the endowments that workers bring to the workplace.

Unequal Distribution of Education

Labor income inequality attributed to differences in education arises from patterns of distribution of education as well as from the way the labor market compensates education. Slow progress in education, high educational inequality, and rising skill

[9] Earnings inequality is also much higher in Latin America when measured by the Gini coefficient.

premia contribute to make differences in education a key source of earnings inequality in Latin America.

Compared with other regions, particularly the rapidly growing East Asian countries, educational progress has been slow. In 1960, mean years of education for the population age 25 years and older were similar in South Korea, Singapore, and Taiwan and in Latin America. In 2000, mean years of education in these Asian countries were between 35 and 75 percent higher than in Latin America.[10] In East Asia, the rate of growth of education during 1980-2000 was 1.4 years per decade; in Latin America, it was only 0.75 years per decade (Figure 1.17). However, there were important differences within the region. The fastest improvements in education per decade took place in Mexico (1.36), Panama (1.00), Chile (0.97), and Argentina (0.94). At the other extreme, educational attainment grew at a dismal rate in Venezuela (0.3), Guatemala (0.35), and Colombia (0.54).

Not only has educational progress been slow, but it has also been poorly distributed, not so much as a result of lack of initial access, but as a consequence of higher dropout rates among children from poor households. For instance, among the current school age generation in 18 countries in Latin America, children from the poorest 30 percent of households are less likely to attend school than children from the richest 20 percent (Figure 1.18). The gaps are most pronounced in the early years, at ages 6 and 7, and after age 12. Although many children attend some years of primary school, few continue to secondary and higher education, and those who do tend to come from richer households. This gives rise to a stratified system that, rather than being a vehicle for social mobility, perpetuates existing inequities.

However, educational inequality matters for income inequality only if workers with higher education obtain higher earnings. Table 1.8 shows that on average, a worker with completed secondary schooling earned 10 percent more than a worker with only primary education per year of secondary education. Depending on the length of secondary education, a worker with secondary education earned around 40-50 percent more than a worker

Figure 1.17 Change in Schooling Attainment, 1980-2000
(Years of schooling per decade)

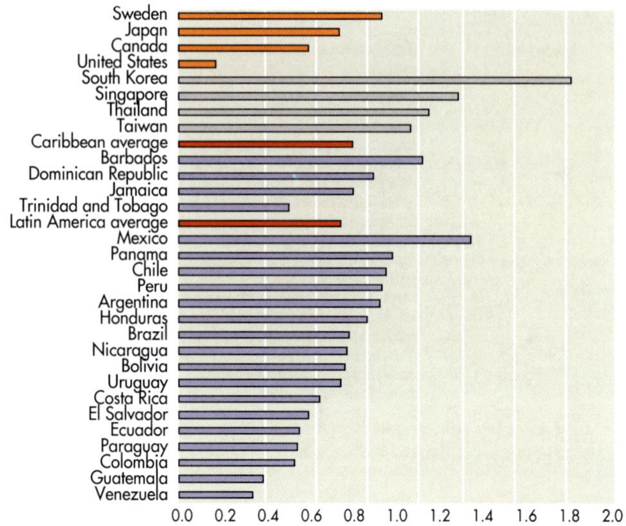

Source: Barro and Lee (2000).

Figure 1.18 School Attendance Rates by Per Capita Household Income, Latin America, 1999

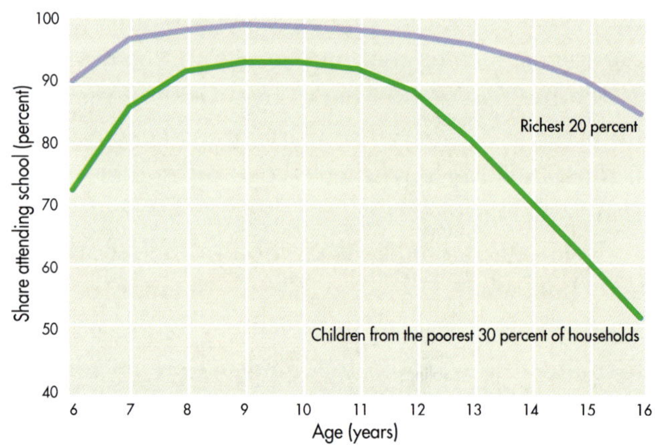

Source: Duryea and Pagés (forthcoming) based on individual data from household surveys for 18 countries.

with only primary. This differential was even larger for workers with tertiary education. On average, a worker with completed college studies earned about 17 percent more than a worker with secondary education. This implies that a four-year college degree increased earnings by another 85 percent.

---

10 Values are based on data assembled by and described in Barro and Lee (2000).

Table 1.8 Wage Differentials by Education Level, 1990-2001
(Percentage change per additional year of schooling)

Country	Number of observations	Secondary/primary schooling: Mean	Secondary/primary schooling: Annual change	Tertiary/secondary schooling: Mean	Tertiary/secondary schooling: Annual change
Latin America[a]	81	9.85	-0.19*	17.26	0.40*
Argentina	10	9.15	-0.01	15.86	0.39*
Bolivia[b]	6	5.57	-0.05	14.15	1.99*
Brazil[c]	12	15.99	-0.36*	23.29	0.40*
Chile	5	14.15	0.15	21.27	0.40*
Colombia	7	8.47	-0.03	20.38	0.18
Costa Rica	6	9.68	-0.14	16.40	0.06
Ecuador (1998)		12.46		6.99	
El Salvador (1999)		8.56		21.56	
Guatemala (1998)		10.74		14.59	
Honduras	5	5.46	-2.11*	13.14	-0.88*
Mexico	10	8.47	0.09	16.66	0.32*
Nicaragua (2001)		10.31		18.46	
Panama	6	9.77	-0.30*	16.36	0.10*
Paraguay (1999)		8.12		0.00	
Peru[d]	4	8.12	-0.23	15.60	0.72
Uruguay	5	8.29	0.11	12.20	0.46*
Venezuela	5	8.37	-0.05	15.99	0.50
United States (1996)		9.18		13.48	

* Significant at 15 percent.
[a] There are 64 observations for the tertiary/secondary differential.
[b] There are 5 observations for the tertiary/secondary differential.
[c] There are 7 observations for the tertiary/secondary differential.
[d] Data for the tertiary/secondary differential are for 2000.

Note: Values are expressed as a percent. Data are returns to completed degrees for urban male wage employees 25–49 years old, working more than 30 hours a week. The wage differentials are derived from the following regression model, which was run separately for each country and year:

Log wage = A + B*educ + C*X + E.

The dependent variable is logarithm of hourly wage; independent variables are dummies for seven levels of education, and X = potential experience and its square. The rates are obtained by dividing the coefficient on completed schooling level by the years necessary to attain a degree. The data are incomplete; the mean and trend of the wage differentials were computed when data included three or more years, spread over three periods: early (1990–93), mid (1994–97), and late (1998–2001). Schooling level definitions vary somewhat across countries.

Source: IDB calculations based on household surveys; national data, except for Argentina, Bolivia, Mexico, Uruguay, and Venezuela, for which urban data are used.

Such numbers suggest that initial differences in the level of education that workers bring to the workplace are translated into substantial differences in earnings. On average, tertiary education in Latin America pays more than in the United States. This suggests that the extraordinary levels of inequality in the region are in part generated by the high value placed on education. In addition, they reflect the high levels of educational inequality in the region.

A few countries stand out in terms of the price of education. Returns to secondary schooling are extraordinarily high in Brazil, where each year of secondary schooling brings almost twice the additional return measured for the United States, and also in Chile. The returns to a college degree are also very large in Brazil, Chile, Colombia, and El Salvador. In these countries, labor markets greatly contribute to accentuating the original differences in endowments.

During the 1990s, the wages of workers with college degrees increased in relation to the wages of workers with lower levels of education.[11] Table 1.8 shows that, on average, returns to tertiary schooling increased in the region. Instead, returns to secondary schooling declined relative to returns to primary education.[12]

The majority of countries experienced this effect. Wages for workers with tertiary education increased relative to wages for workers with secondary education in most countries. Similarly, in most countries, returns to secondary education declined relative to the returns of workers with lower levels of education. The results for individual countries are somewhat sensitive to the method used to compute the differentials (see Box 1.4); however, the conclusion that the returns to college education have increased for the region during the 1990s is not altered by the specific method used in the computation of the returns. Although such trends may increase the incentives to pursue a college education, the decline in returns to secondary schooling may accentuate the tendency for poor children to drop out at the end of primary school. This may be particularly true for those children who do not have the necessary resources to attend college.

Low Wages

An important dimension of inequality relates to whether some workers are left behind others because their level of education is low, their skills are obsolete, or they are paid wages below their productivity. In the same way that poverty measures attempt to capture all those individuals that fall below a certain agreed threshold, it is feasible to investigate how many workers in Latin America obtain wages that put them at risk of poverty. A worker is considered to earn low wages if she/he makes less than a dollar an hour in the primary job.[13] The one-dollar threshold has been adjusted in each country to reflect differences in the cost of living according to purchasing power parity (PPP). This definition of low wages is simple and it meaningfully relates to the moderate poverty measure. Thus, considering that the average worker in the region works an average of 44 hours a week and shares his or her income with two dependents, earnings of less than PPP$1 an hour result in a per capita household income of less than PPP$2 a day, a standard measure of moderate poverty. Not all workers earning less than this threshold are poor, since they may work more than 44 hours or live in a household with less than the average number of dependents. However, workers earning wages below this threshold are at a higher risk of poverty.

There is a strong relationship between this measure of low wages and standard measures of poverty based on per capita income, such as the moderate poverty indicator. For instance, the correlation between the percentage of workers with low wages and the percentage of individuals in moderate poverty is 0.87 despite the fact that the latter measure is computed by aggregating all incomes from all sources within a household and dividing by household size (Figure 1.19). Thus, low wages are an important determinant of poverty in the region.

By the end of the decade, the percentage of "working poor" was more than 50 percent in Honduras, Bolivia, Nicaragua, and El Salvador, and more than 20 percent in all countries except Venezuela, Mexico, and Chile (Figure 1.20). Therefore, a large percentage of workers fell into the poverty category unless they worked long hours or formed households with better-paid workers or a lower than average number of dependents.

Across the region, the incidence of low-paying jobs falls disproportionately on certain groups of workers. Thus, with a few exceptions, the proportion of people in low-paying jobs is higher among

[11] In most countries, household surveys do not provide a way to identify when a person has completed a college degree. Therefore, it is assumed that in each country a college degree is attained in the fourth or fifth year of college, depending on whether there are more people in the sample with four or five years of college education.

[12] These conclusions do not depend on whether the analysis is performed comparing the returns of completed or incomplete levels of schooling.

[13] All results are computed based on income from the primary job. However, except when otherwise noted, the results do not differ much if a more comprehensive measure of income is used including all jobs.

Box 1.4 Returns to Education: Measurement Issues

The measurement of returns to education is quite sensitive to the method used to compute them. The returns to schooling reported in Table 1.8 are computed using regression analysis, which compares wages across workers with different educational degrees, but with the same potential experience (computed as age-years of schooling–6). To limit selection bias problems that are common in this type of methodology (Mincer regression), the analysis is restricted to workers with high labor force attachment rates (men, 25-49 years old). However, if instead of using regression analysis, wage differentials are computed using the unadjusted average wages of workers with primary, secondary, and tertiary schooling for the same group of workers considered in Table 1.8, it turns out that returns to tertiary schooling show a decline in Brazil, Panama, and Honduras. However, the conclusion that, overall, returns to college education increased during the 1990s does not change.

Similarly, de Ferranti and others (2003) find that, during the 1990s, returns to tertiary education increased relative to returns to secondary education in all the countries they considered (Argentina, Bolivia, Brazil, Chile, Colombia, and Mexico), except Chile. The difference between their methodology and the methodology applied here has to do with the way education is measured. Here, returns are compared between workers that have completed primary, secondary, or college education. Instead, de Ferranti and others use a methodology that also includes people who have not completed degrees. In their study, workers are assigned to two educational levels, the group corresponding to the highest educational level they have completed and the group corresponding to the next educational level they have not completed.

Figure 1.19 Moderate Poverty and the Percentage of Low-paid Workers, Late 1990s

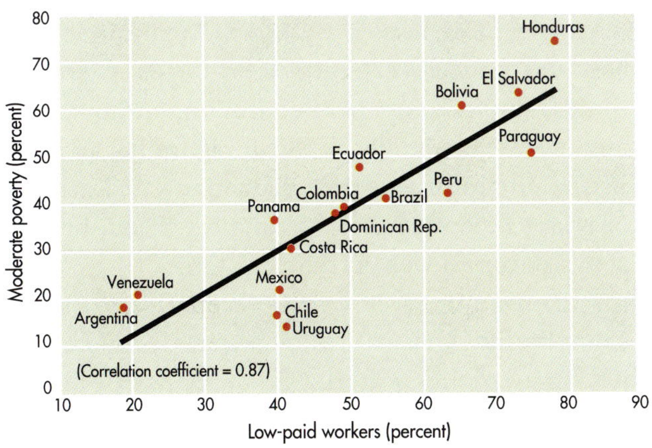

Source: IDB calculations.

Figure 1.20 Proportion of Workers with Secondary Education Completed and Earning Less Than PPP$1 an Hour
(Percent)

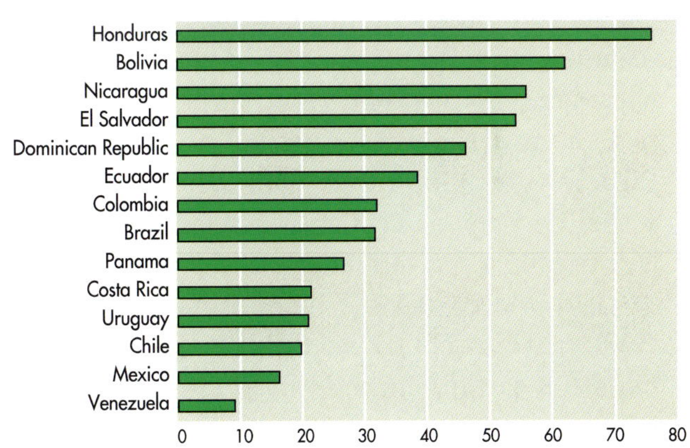

Note: All data are national except for Uruguay, Bolivia, and Mexico, which are urban.
Source: Household surveys.

women than among men, among workers with lower levels of schooling, and among workers in rural areas (Figure 1.21). Across countries, the incidence of poor jobs is also higher among young workers (age 15-19) and among workers employed in small firms (less than five employees) relative to workers employed in large firms or self-employed (Duryea and Pagés forthcoming).[14]

However, despite the effect of individual characteristics, such as gender, education, or age in explaining an individual's probability of earning low wages, there are important cross-country differences that can only be explained by country-spe-

[14] The exceptions are Honduras and Paraguay, where the incidence of low-paying jobs among the self-employed is higher than among salaried workers.

Figure 1.21 Poor Workers by Category, Latin America
(Percent)

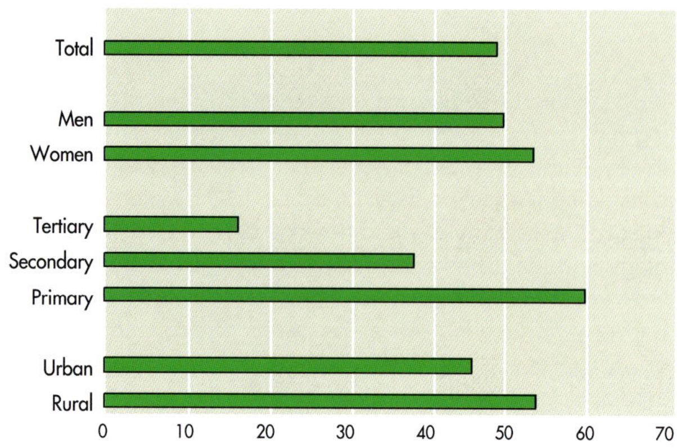

Source: Duryea, Jaramillo, and Pagés (2003).

Figure 1.22 Real GDP per Worker and Low Wages

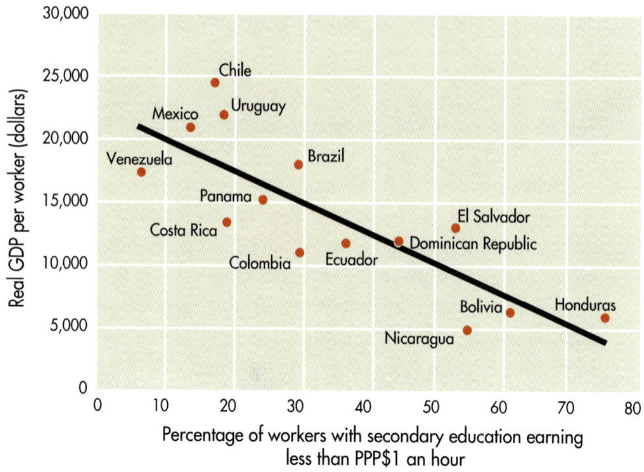

Note: Coefficient trend: -25242.27 , t-statistic -4.96.
Source: Data on percentage of workers with low wages from Duryea, Jaramillo, and Pagés (2003). Real GDP per worker from Heston, Summers, and Bettina (2002) Version 6.1.

cific effects. This is particularly striking in a comparison of the incidence of low-paying jobs among workers with completed secondary schooling. Figure 1.22 shows that in only five countries less than one in four workers with these characteristics earns low wages. In many other countries—for instance, the Dominican Republic, El Salvador, Nicaragua, Bolivia, and Honduras—more than 40 percent of these workers still fall in this category. Clearly, education alone does not warrant good wages, despite the fact that education does increase earnings by a substantial amount.

To understand the limited impact of education, it is useful to consider that returns to schooling are measured in percentage rates, so the final impact on absolute wages depends on the base to which the percentage applies. Because a Latin American worker without education or skills earns very little, a relatively large increase in wages (in percentage terms) due to education may still leave the worker with very low wages.

What determines the overall level of wages? Figure 1.22 suggests that there is a high correlation between the percentage of workers with secondary education who earn low wages and GDP per worker. Therefore, for any level of education, a worker's hourly wage reflects the productivity the worker is able to obtain with other factors of production, such as physical capital, utilities and telecommunications, or public goods like institutions or infrastructure. Thus, workers can productively apply their skills only when the economic and institutional environment in which they live and work is sufficiently fertile. In other words, although wage inequality is to a large extent explained by educational differences, absolute wage levels cannot be raised exclusively through improvements in education. Without simultaneous investments in the institutional and economic environment, the productivity and earnings of a large share of the population will not be lifted above poverty levels in the near term.

During the 1990s, some countries made considerable advances in reducing the proportion of jobs that pay low wages. The incidence of low pay declined mostly in the Southern Cone countries, while it increased in Mexico and Central America.

Summary Indicator of Equity

Although Latin America suffers from high levels of earnings inequality, there is only limited evidence that the source of inequality lies in the way markets price labor services. Thus, although on average returns to education are high, sector, firm size, and gender wage differentials are comparable with those in the United States, the reference country. However, the price of education and the returns to working in a given sector or firm vary substantially

Figure 1.23 Summary Measure of Equity in Allocation of Incomes
(Index 0-1)

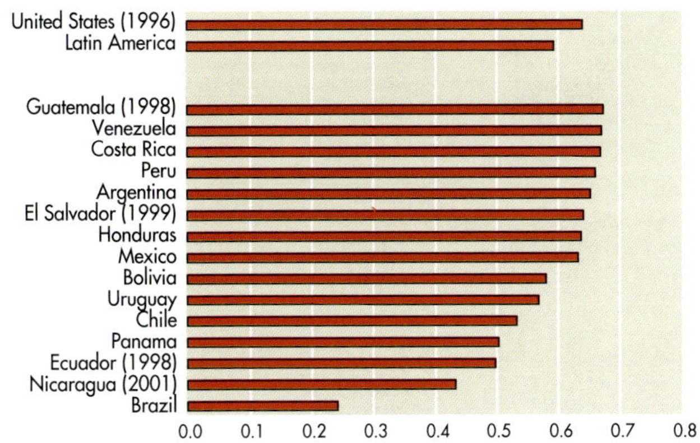

Source: IDB calculations based on household surveys.

across countries. This section constructs a summary index of equity in the allocation of incomes based on the simple average of the following components standardized between 0 and 1: gender wage gaps, returns to sector of activity, returns to size, returns to secondary education, and returns to college education. The percentage of low-paid workers is important but is not included because, from a policy standpoint, it is not necessarily determined by the behavior of the labor market. Instead, it is determined by the same array of factors that determine labor productivity, of which some are within the labor market, but many, such as the provision of infrastructure or communications, are outside it.

The index takes higher values the higher is equity, that is, the lower are the wage differentials associated with education, gender, and job characteristics. Latin America ranks close to the reference country (the United States) in terms of this indicator of equity (Figure 1.23). This implies that the source of the extreme inequality in earnings does not lie so much in the pricing behavior of the labor markets as in the extreme inequality of education and perhaps other endowments (such as family contacts) that are unobservable in household surveys but have a price in the labor market. Nonetheless, in Brazil, Nicaragua, Ecuador, and Panama, price differences greatly contribute to inequality in earnings (Figure 1.23). These countries also ranked lowest in the summary index of efficiency of allocation of incomes.

Allocation of Risks

The normal activity of labor markets creates risks for workers. As firms create and destroy jobs, some workers are displaced. Some might find jobs immediately and obtain similar pay. For others, however, losing their jobs can result in a temporal loss of income while unemployed, compounded by the potential loss of income associated with finding a job that pays less than the former one. The longer a worker spent and the more specific were the skills in the former job, the greater might be the loss of income associated with job loss.

In addition to job loss, old age, sickness, and work accidents constitute other important sources of risk of loss of labor income. Across the world, many workers obtain insurance against these risks through their jobs, participating in national public social security programs. However, not all workers have access to these benefits, and many are left uninsured.

Therefore, the level of protection of workers against the risk of income loss constitutes another important dimension for evaluating the performance of a labor market. It is evident, however, that the allocation of risks is not independent of the resource allocation dimension. The faster a worker finds a good job, the lower will be the income loss associated with joblessness and the lower will be the insurance premium necessary to hedge that risk. Similarly, the shorter are the periods of involuntary joblessness throughout the lifetime of a person, the longer the person would be able to contribute to an old age pension program and the higher would be the retirement payments in the future. The implications also go from insurance to allocation of resources. High levels of unemployment insurance might motivate unemployed workers to search less intensely for jobs, which in turn results in higher unemployment rates.

Chapter 2 explores the process of reallocation of jobs and workers at greater length and documents the size of these risks. Chapter 7 explores the effects that laws and regulations that seek to protect workers have on the labor market. This section characterizes the mechanisms that different countries have developed to protect workers against the loss of income as well as the degree of enforcement of these mechanisms.

Severance Pay

Most countries in the region do not have unemployment insurance mechanisms that cover workers against the risk of job loss. Instead, the mechanism of choice in Latin America to insure against these risks has been mandatory severance pay and indemnities for dismissal. These transfers that firms have to pay workers in case of a firm-initiated dismissal constitute an insurance mechanism that channels funds to unemployed workers. Indeed, labor laws in Latin America prescribe sizable transfers, much larger than the ones mandated in the Caribbean or other developed countries (Figure 1.24). Moreover, and contrary to common perception, these transfers increased during the 1990s in many countries (Figure 1.24). Deregulation, when it occurred, came more from the increased possibility of offering temporal labor contracts than from reducing the dismissal costs associated with indefinite contracts.

Figure 1.24 The Cost of Job Security, 1988 and 1999

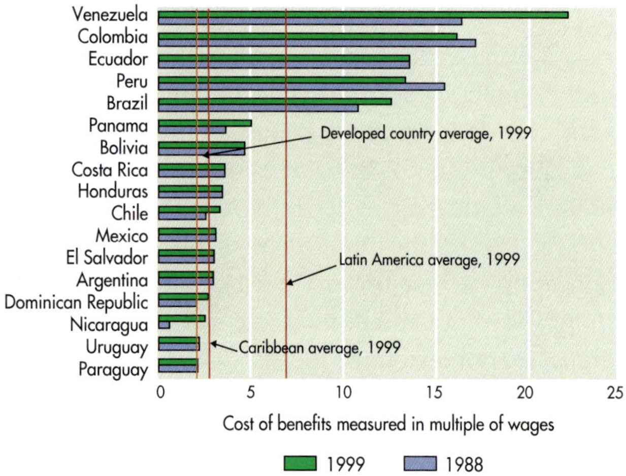

Source: Heckman and Pagés (forthcoming).

Figure 1.25 Social Security Index
(Index, 0-3)

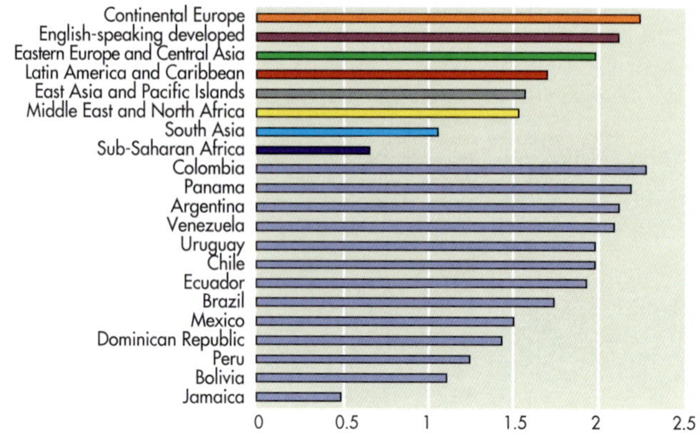

Source: Djankov and others (2003).

Social Security Programs

By contrast, the protection awarded by social security programs is lower in Latin America than in developed countries. Figure 1.25 displays a measure of the benefits awarded by old age pensions, health, maternity, and (when available) unemployment insurance programs.[15] The index takes a greater value for programs with greater benefits and for those with greater benefits relative to contributions. According to this measure, social security regulations are less protective of workers in Latin America than in developed countries and countries in Eastern Europe and Central Asia. However, the index for Latin America is higher than for other developing regions, including East Asia. Within the region, Jamaica, Bolivia, and Peru have the lowest social security benefits, whereas Colombia, Panama, and Argentina have the highest level of protection, with levels that are similar to the ones observed in developed countries.

[15] This index was developed by Djankov and others (2003) and is the normalized sum of the following components: the difference between retirement age and life expectancy; months of contributions required for normal retirement to qualify for health and unemployment insurance programs, if available; contributions to pensions, disability, health, and unemployment insurance programs; the replacement rate for pensions; the replacement rate for health insurance benefits; months of contributions to qualify for health insurance benefits; and the waiting period for health insurance benefits.

Table 1.9 Social Insurance, 1990s

Country	Number of observations	Country has unemployment insurance	Share of employed workers with social security (percent)		Share of wage workers with social security (percent)	
			Mean	Annual change	Mean	Annual change
Latin America[a]	48		42.76	-0.35*	60.05	-0.17
Argentina	10	YES	48.45	-0.29*	66.56	-0.83*
Bolivia (1999)		NO	26.36		38.56	
Brazil	7	YES	48.18	-0.05	64.04	0.28
Chile	6	YES	64.47	0.05	77.45	0.04
Colombia (1999)		NO	46.13		66.77	
Costa Rica	5	NO	65.92	-0.88*	74.61	-0.88*
Dominican Republic (1998)		NO	29.08		49.40	
Ecuador (1995)		NO	30.94		43.02	
El Salvador (1998)		NO	33.49		50.04	
Guatemala		NO				
Honduras		NO				
Jamaica		NO				
Mexico	12	YES [b]	52.53	-0.57*	67.96	-0.43*
Nicaragua		NO				
Panama (2001)		NO	55.66		74.50	
Paraguay (1995)		NO	16.70		30.66	
Peru (2000)[c]	4	NO	17.99		51.90	-0.47*
Trinidad and Tobago		NO				
Uruguay	4	YES	74.12		93.12	1.27*
Venezuela (1998)		NO	31.37		52.22	
English-speaking developed countries		YES				
Continental Europe		YES				
Eastern Europe		YES				
United States[d]		YES	82.00			

* Significant at 15 percent.

[a] There are 40 observations for the share of wage workers with social security.

[b] Only for workers age 60 years old or older.

[c] Data are from the metropolitan area of Lima, for the share of wage workers with social security in 2000.

[d] Data for the United States reflect the percentage of the labor force with medical insurance (Medical Expenditure Panel Survey, MEPS, 1996).

Note: Unemployment insurance includes payments in lieu of advance notice, severance pay, and funds accumulated in individual savings accounts. For all regions except Latin America and the Caribbean, it is assumed that 100 percent of employed workers are covered by social security. The data are incomplete; the mean and trend were computed when data included three or more years, spread over three periods: early (1990–93), mid (1994–97), and late (1998–2001). Country trends were obtained by regressing available data on a time trend. Regional trends were obtained by regressing available data on a time trend and a set of country fixed effects.

Source: Data on whether the country has unemployment insurance are from Government of the United States (1998). Shares of workers with social security are from IDB calculations based on household surveys; national data except for Argentina, Bolivia, Mexico, Panama, and Uruguay, for which urban data are used; and ILO (2002b) for Panama, Peru, and Uruguay.

Low Coverage

While the levels of protection prescribed by law are not that different, and in some instances are even higher than the protection mandated in developed countries, a large and growing majority of workers is not covered by labor laws, and therefore most workers work under the constant threat of unexpected illness, job loss, or poverty in old age.[16]

Table 1.9 shows that, on average, only 40 percent of workers were protected by labor laws and had access to social security benefits. The coverage weighted by the number of workers in each country was 44 percent. However, the dispersion in cov-

[16] This Report assumes that workers who are registered in publicly managed social security programs enjoy all the other benefits prescribed by labor laws, such as mandatory severance pay and compensation for overtime work.

Figure 1.26 Workers with Wages Less Than 75 Percent of the Minimum Wage, Late 1990s
(Percent)

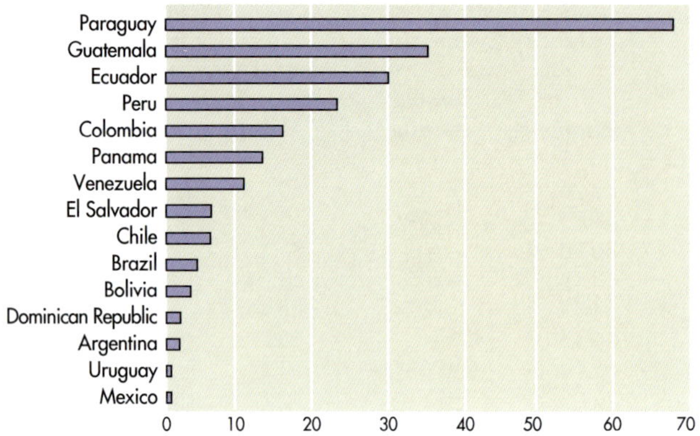

Note: National data except for Argentina, Mexico, and Uruguay which are urban data. Restricted to primary job and workers working more than 35 hours a week.
Source: IDB calculations based on household surveys.

Figure 1.27 Summary Measure of Insurance
(Index, 0-1)

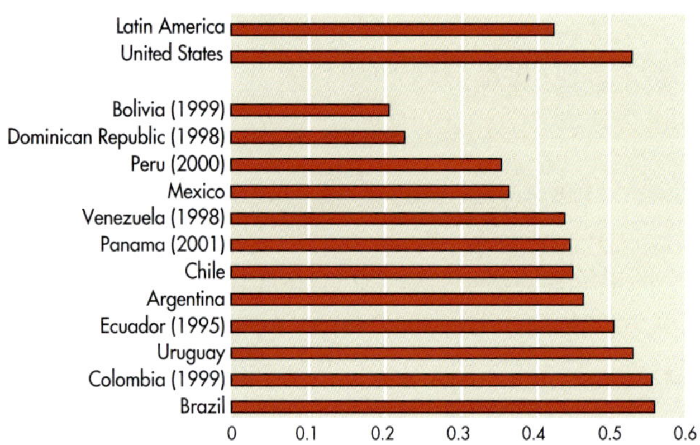

Source: IDB calculations based on household survey data and data on severance pay, indemnities for dismissal, and advance notice from Heckman and Pagés (forthcoming).

erage levels within the region was high. Uruguay, Costa Rica, and Chile had the largest percentage of covered workers, while Paraguay, Peru, Brazil, and Ecuador were on the other end, with less than one in three workers covered against sickness, old age poverty, and unemployment risk.

Although in part low coverage levels are associated with the large share of workers who are self-employed, coverage rates were also low for wage employees. Moreover, the share of workers that had access to social security or the benefits prescribed by labor laws declined during the 1990s, both among all workers and among wage employees. This suggests that the increasing rates of self-employment that some countries, for instance, Mexico, experienced are not the only cause behind this decline. And the cause does not lie in the increasing share of workers employed in small firms. At least this is not the case in Mexico and Argentina, which were studied in detail on this issue. In both countries, the percentage of workers with social security declined across firms of all sizes.

It is clear that enforcement of labor laws and mandatory contributions to social security programs in the region are poor. This lack of enforcement is also reflected in the low compliance with minimum wage laws. Figure 1.26 displays the percentage of workers across countries that earn less than 75 percent of the minimum wage. More than 60 percent of wage employees in Paraguay, and more than 25 percent in Guatemala, Ecuador, and Peru earn wages that are below statutory minimums.

In sum, benefits are not enforceable for all. This implies that for too many workers, the risk of losing the source of income is a real and often catastrophic possibility. It is not surprising that poor labor market performance is a main source of concern for a growing majority of people.

Summary Indicator of Insurance

The performance of individual countries in the area of social insurance is summarized by averaging over the following indicators: the amount of severance pay, the index of social security, the percentage of workers enrolled in social security programs, and whether workers have unemployment insurance. The first three indicators are standardized between 0 and 1. Having unemployment insurance is standardized with a value of 0.25 if available; 0.125 if available but only covering certain unemployed workers, as in Brazil (low-income workers) or Mexico (workers age 55 or older), and 0 if not available. Figure 1.27 presents the summary measure for 12 countries in Latin America, the United States, and the average for Latin America. Higher values of the index indicate higher insurance levels.

Figure 1.28 **Unionization Rates, 1980s and 1990s**

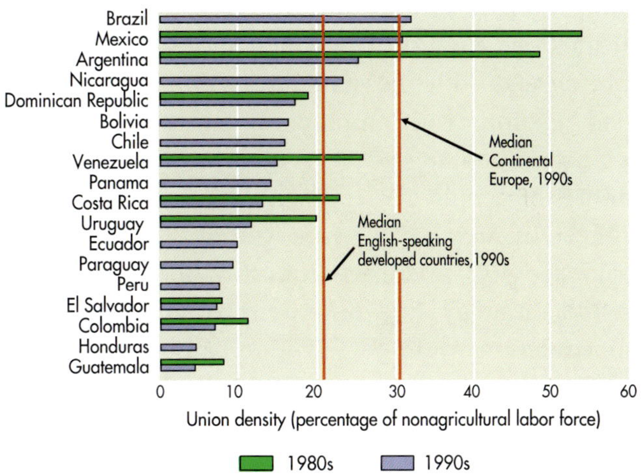

Source: ILO (1997); ILO database.

Figure 1.29 **Workers Involved in Strikes, 1990-95**

(Percentage of total employment)

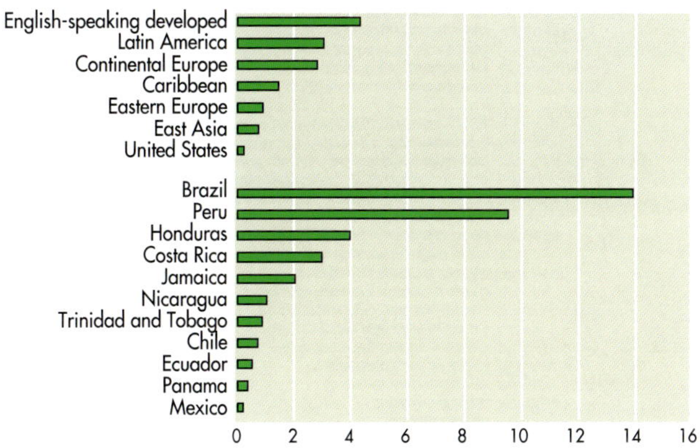

Source: ILO (1997).

According to this summary measure, only Brazil and Colombia have insurance levels that are comparable to those in the United States. The other countries are below the levels of insurance attained by the North Americans, which are low by developed country standards. Thus, although certain components, such as severance pay, are high, these programs do not cover many workers, and the overall levels of insurance turn out to be very low, particularly in Mexico, Peru, the Dominican Republic, and Bolivia. Social insurance coverage is probably even lower in countries such as Nicaragua, Honduras, and Guatemala, which are excluded for lack of complete data on all the dimensions.

Quality of Labor Relations

Labor relations define the employment relationship between employers and employees or their unions. There is large turnover in the labor market, but most employment relationships are more than short-run affairs. The attitudes of employers toward workers and workers toward employers, the quality of management, the channels of communication, and the methods of giving voice to workers and resolving conflicts determine the quality of labor relations. These, in turn, influence workers' effort, motivation, and willingness to learn and become more productive, as well as firms' long-term investments in training and technology adoption. This process of learning and innovation is a key component of productivity growth and essential to improving the standard of living of workers in the region.

According to IDB (2001), labor relations in Latin America are characterized by declining union density and weak labor unions. Figure 1.28 shows that union density has declined in the 1990s relative to the 1980s in all countries for which information is available. On average, only 14 percent of the nonagricultural labor force is unionized, which is below the average for developed countries.

Labor relations in the region seem to be mired in conflict. The percentage of workers involved in strikes as a percentage of total employment is high compared with the percentage in the United States, East Asia, Continental Europe, and Eastern Europe (Figure 1.29). But there are also important differences across countries. Although a large share of workers took part in strikes in Brazil and Peru, strike activity in Panama and Mexico was as low as in the United States.

According to employers, labor relations could improve. According to World Economic Forum (2001), Latin America ranks low in the degree of cooperation in labor relations. This information is based on the opinions of a sample of employers in each country. The ranking goes from 1 to 7, where one is confrontational and seven is cooperative

Figure 1.30 Degree of Cooperation in Labor Relations

(1=confrontational, 7=cooperative)

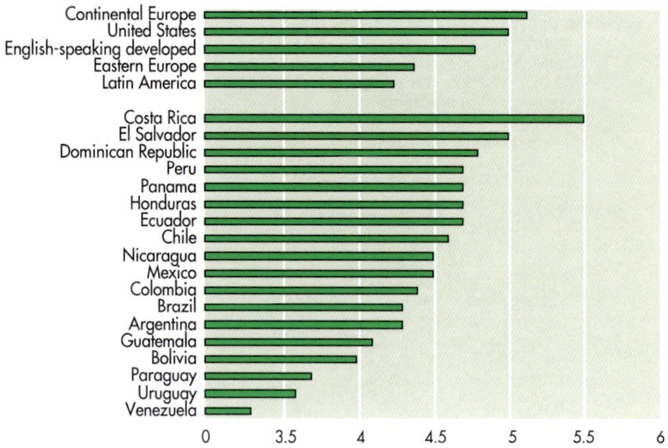

Source: World Economic Forum (2001).

Figure 1.31 Percentage of Respondents Who Agree That "Employers Have Good Relations with Employees"

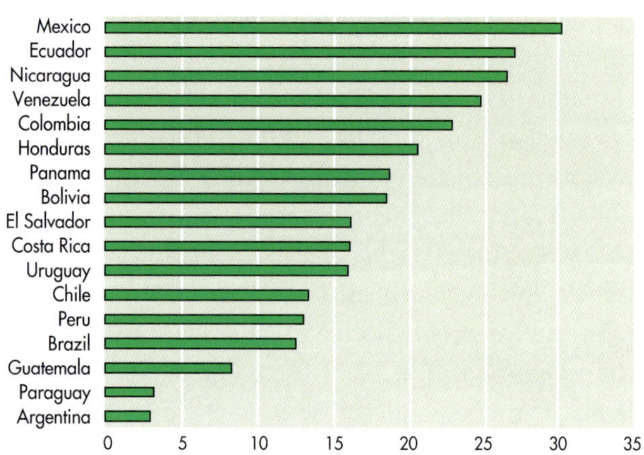

Source: Latinobarometer (1997).

(Figure 1.30). The average value for Latin America (4.3) is lower than the average for Continental Europe (5.15), the United States (5.0), other English-speaking developed countries (4.7), and Eastern Europe (4.4). However, as is the case with strike activity, heterogeneity is wider within the region than across regions. In Central American countries, employers tend to report more cooperative labor relations than employers in the Southern Cone. Employers rank Venezuela and Uruguay as having the most conflictive labor relations in the region. Labor relations are ranked most cooperative in Costa Rica.

It is important to assess how workers rate labor relations as well. In 1997, the Latinobarometer included a question asking whether the respondent agreed with the statement "Employers have good relations with employees." Across countries, not many people agreed (Figure 1.31). The percentage of people agreeing with this statement was highest in Mexico (a country that recorded low strike activity), and extraordinarily low in Argentina and Paraguay. It is quite telling that once again, labor relations were perceived to be better in most Central American countries than in the Southern Cone.

Summary Indicator of the Quality of Labor Relations

Figure 1.32 summarizes labor relations across Latin American countries by aggregating the perspectives of workers and employers. The summary index is built by scaling all answers between 0 and 1 and taking the simple average of the two indicators. Unfortunately, there is no reference country for this indicator because information regarding the views of workers is available only for Latin America. Therefore, it is not possible to assess whether labor relations are abnormally poor relative to other regions. Within the region, the summary index suggests that labor relations are better in Mexico and Central American countries than in the Southern Cone, especially Paraguay, Argentina, and Uruguay. The higher incidence of unemployment in the latter countries may have hindered long-term relations between workers and employers in the Southern Cone.

Efficiency, Equity, and Insurance

This chapter has developed several measures for evaluating the performance of labor markets. A question that arises is whether these measures can be aggregated into one unique measure of performance. Although it might be tempting to do so, it would not be useful to aggregate them because they reflect different criteria of evaluation, which could conflict with each other. Thus, for instance, many observers praise the good performance of the United States for its low unemployment rates and seemingly high ability to adapt to changes in the economic environment relative to labor markets in Europe. Others instead emphasize the high rates of inequality and low levels of insurance against economic risks that are prevalent in the United States relative to European countries.

The citizens of a country are the ones who, through their political institutions, decide where they want their labor markets to be placed along the dimensions of efficiency, equity, and insurance. People in some countries may have a lower tolerance for risk or inequality than in others, and this will be reflected in the set of labor policies. However, the public and policymakers should consider that there might be important complementarities but also trade-offs between these components. While complementarities help, trade-offs may get in the way of achieving the most preferred situation. For example, many observers blame the high levels of social protection in Europe for its persistently high levels of unemployment. Transferring income to unemployed people may reduce the urgency to search for a job and increase the duration of unemployment. Mandatory social security programs require contributions that could increase the price of labor and reduce employment.

Where does each country stand in terms of efficiency, social insurance, and equity? Since the chapter has discussed various aspects of efficiency, they are aggregated to form a synthetic indicator of labor market efficiency by averaging the following three indices: efficiency of resource allocation, efficiency of income allocation, and quality of labor market relations. The aggregate measure not only reflects how well the market allocates resources and incomes, but also the degree to which workers and employers cooperate toward a shared objective of income and productivity growth. Figure 1.33 presents the results. According to this measure, labor markets function best in Mexico, Costa Rica, Nicaragua, and Honduras, while they show the highest opportunities for improvement in Uruguay, Brazil, Argentina, and Bolivia.

To what extent are there important trade-offs across efficiency, insurance, and equity within the countries of the region? Figure 1.34 plots the measure of labor market efficiency against the measure of equity. Interestingly, there is not a negative relationship between these variables. In general, when the labor market functions better, wage differentials between workers with similar characteristics tend to be lower and the measure of equity improves. This does not imply that if a country were to follow aggressive policies to change market

Figure 1.32 Quality of Labor Relations
(Index, 0-1)

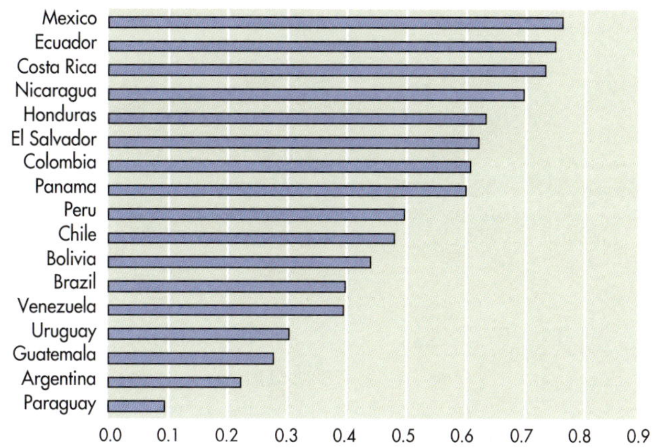

Source: IDB calculations.

Figure 1.33 Summary Measure of Overall Efficiency in Labor Market Performance
(Index, 0-1)

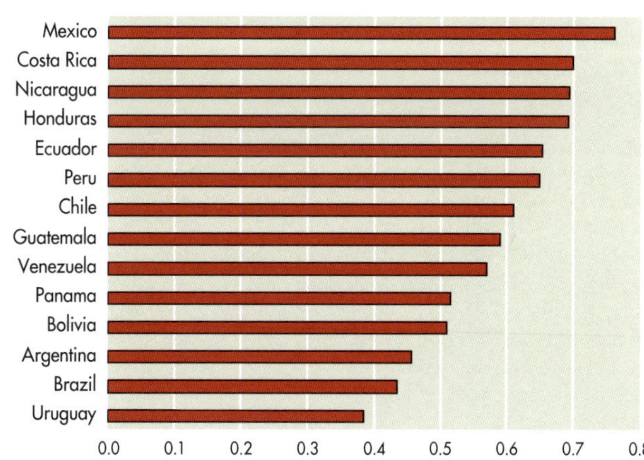

Source: IDB calculations based on household survey data; Latinobarometer (1997); World Economic Forum (2001).

Figure 1.34 **Efficiency and Equity in Labor Markets**
(Index, 0-1)

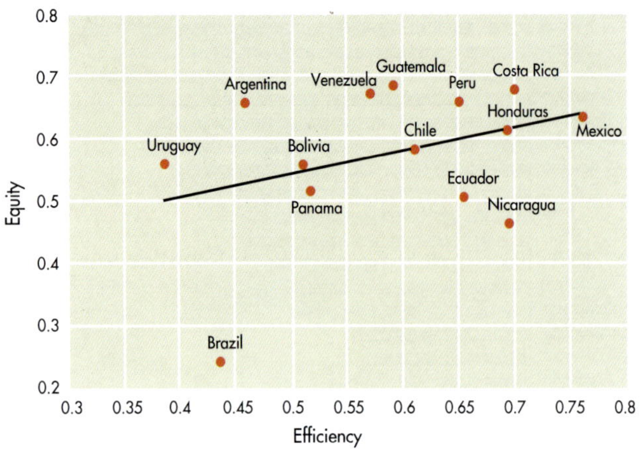

Source: IDB calculations based on household survey data.

Figure 1.36 **Insurance and Equity in Labor Markets**
(Index, 0-1)

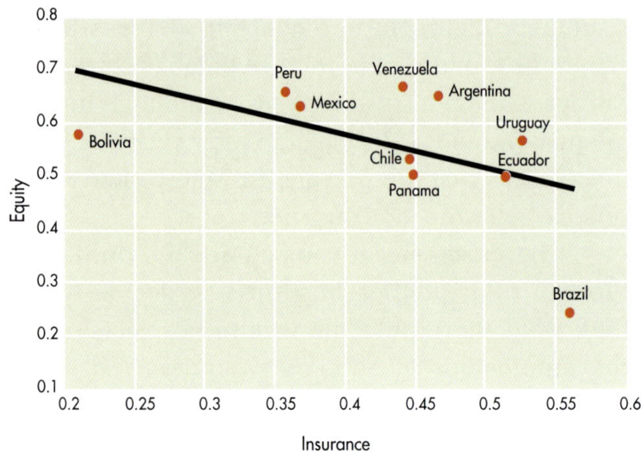

Source: IDB calculations based on household survey data; data from Djankov and others (2003); Heckman and Pagés (forthcoming).

Figure 1.35 **Efficiency and Insurance in Labor Markets**
(Index, 0-1)

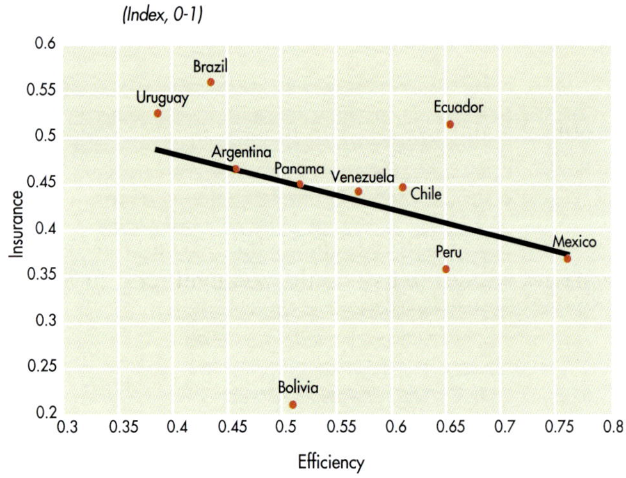

Source: IDB calculations based on household survey data; data from Djankov and others (2003); Heckman and Pagés (forthcoming).

prices, for instance, in favor of unskilled workers, unemployment and other labor market problems would not arise.

Instead, Figure 1.35 suggests that there might be a negative relationship between protection against risk and labor market efficiency. Those countries where workers were more protected against the risk of losing labor income are also the countries with the worst labor market functioning. Figure 1.35 would seem to indicate that the pattern in the United States and Europe also applies to Latin America. Nonetheless, the relationship is only suggestive. Chapter 7 explores the nature of these trade-offs for a range of labor market policies. The findings suggest that the nature and size of these trade-offs depend on the type of policies as well as the way they are implemented. The guiding principle, however, should be that insurance and labor market policies in general can bring unintended effects whose costs should be carefully balanced against the benefits of the policies.

Finally, Figure 1.36 examines whether there is a trade-off between insurance and equity. Again, the data suggest that this could be the case. If increased levels of insurance force more workers to work in sectors not covered by regulations, wage differentials between sectors traditionally covered—such as manufacturing or large firms—and sectors not covered—such as retail trade, construction, or employment in small firms—could increase, increasing labor market inequality. Again, these relationships are only suggestive, but the conclusion stated above remains the same. The public and policymakers should pay attention to the possible trade-offs and evaluate the benefits and costs of labor market policies with extreme care.

Conclusions

This chapter has examined the performance of Latin American labor markets based on how well they accomplish the tasks of allocating resources, income, and risks. It has also evaluated the nature of labor relations in the region. A few conclusions emerge from this analysis.

First, judging from unemployment rates, the duration of unemployment, and unemployment gaps between different types of workers, labor markets in Latin America are not allocating resources well. During the 1990s, and particularly at the end of the decade, unemployment was very high relative to historical values and relative to other regions of the world, which are often characterized as high-unemployment regions. Moreover, because less than 50 percent of the workers are insured against the risk of job loss, unemployment is likely to be more painful and more distressing in Latin America than in other more developed regions, where social insurance mechanisms are widespread. In Latin America, such mechanisms exist, but compliance is minimal; therefore, the design and enforcement of social insurance should be reevaluated. Moreover, the observation that there may be trade-offs between insurance and efficiency and between insurance and equity in the labor market implies that the benefits of any insurance mechanism have to be carefully weighed against the possible costs. Only when the benefits outweigh the costs can insurance improve the overall performance of the labor market.

Second, the patterns of unemployment suggest that, if anything, unemployment rates underestimate the problem of allocation of resources in the region. Thus, the short duration of unemployment and its concentration among women and youth suggest that primary earners cannot afford to remain unemployed and search for jobs as long as other workers can. However, an alternative hypothesis is that the large concentration of unemployment among women and youth may be an indication that these workers have problems finding jobs and entering the labor market.

Third, although unemployment rates increased, employment rates also increased as a consequence of higher participation rates among women. In addition, some forms of employment traditionally considered low quality increased as well. This was the case for the proportion of workers employed in small firms. Instead, the share of self-employment or the share of family (unpaid) workers did not show any discernible overall trend. It is unclear whether an increasing share of workers in small firms is a negative development in and of itself, but the fact that the share of jobs that provide the benefits mandated by law is dwindling suggests that the quality of employment may have deteriorated during the 1990s.

Fourth, although Latin American economies are characterized by high levels of earnings inequality, the source of this problem lies in the high levels of inequality in the educational attainment of the labor force. Increasing returns to education may increase the incentives for families to keep their children in school, but also may increase the differences between those who can afford education and those who cannot. If inequality is to be reduced, it is necessary to attack the source of the problem, that is, the inequality of endowments, especially education. To do so, more resources should be devoted to reduce the school dropout rates among children at an early age. In addition, a system of incentives should be developed to foster investments in education by those who are currently in the labor market. These incentives may take the form of subsidized adult education or tax breaks for individuals or firms that invest in human capital formation.

Fifth, on average, one in two workers in the region earns low wages. Moreover, wage increases during the 1990s were quite meager. This pattern is not so much a reflection of the low levels of education that prevail in the region or the excessive bargaining power of employers vis-à-vis workers. Instead, it is a direct reflection of low and stagnant levels of labor productivity. Since there is a one-to-one relation between productivity and wage growth, policies to foster the productivity of the labor force should be given priority. More and better investments in formal education and on-the-job training could lift productivity. However, without complementary investments in improving the economic and institutional environment, additional investments in human capital will not have large returns.

Sixth, the low quality of labor relations is also likely to be a contributing factor in low and stagnant labor productivity. In Latin America, a low degree of cooperation between workers and employers, distrust, and conflict seem to pervade the workplace. These conditions are clearly not conducive to the investments in technology and skills that guarantee rewarding work experiences and sustainable productivity growth.

What accounts for this disappointing performance? Some factors have already been hinted at in this chapter. Low and stagnant productivity per worker explains low wage levels and painfully slow increases in wages, but what accounts for rising unemployment rates? Is this a persistent phenomenon or is it only transitory? And if it is only transitory, why is it so high? And what explains the rising returns to education? Is globalization to be blamed for this phenomenon? Is it technological change? Why is the share of formal jobs declining? The rest of the Report is devoted to further understanding how labor markets work and what drives their performance in Latin America and the Caribbean.

Chapter 2 explores labor market dynamics using available worker and firm-level panel data. Chapter 3 focuses on the relationship between the changing nature of the supply of labor and labor market outcomes. Chapter 4 analyzes the effects of macroeconomic shocks on labor market performance. Chapter 5 studies whether the ambitious structural reforms launched in the 1990s have been responsible for poor labor market outcomes. Chapter 6 shows how technology affects employment and wages. Chapter 7 examines the role of labor market regulations and institutions in the performance of labor markets. Finally, chapter 8 presents a range of available policy options to face up to these challenges.

Chapter

2

Job and Worker Dynamics: The Hidden Side of the Labor Market

Although most studies focus on net changes in employment, unemployment, or inactivity, it turns out that relatively small net changes in these variables hide a phenomenal amount of reallocation activity in the labor market. In a given year, in all the countries examined here, a large number of firms are expanding their staff, while simultaneously many others are reducing employment. This occurs independently of whether the economy is going through a period of expansion or recession. It also occurs across sectors of activity and across firms of different ages and sizes. Thus, market economies are extremely fluid, require a constant reallocation of employment across uses, and have large worker flows. At any point in time, a large percentage of workers are transiting between jobs and between employment, unemployment, and inactivity. High levels of informal employment do not drive these large turnover rates; large levels of turnover in Latin America are also found among registered firms and skilled workers.

The evidence suggests that most reallocation is associated with firm-specific rather than aggregate shocks. This is true even in Latin America's highly volatile macro environment. The heterogeneity of firm-specific factors explains the large degree of job turnover in the market. It also explains why important productivity gains can be made by shifting resources from less productive to more productive activities. Thus, the analysis explains that this perennial churning is a cause and a consequence of productivity growth. A significant share of productivity growth is associated with the reallocation of workers from less productive to more productive firms and from underperforming firms exiting the market to new firms.

Although some workers benefit from mobility, involuntary turnover can impose large welfare costs on workers. Perennial churning forces workers to go through involuntary periods of unemployment and to find new jobs. However, in Latin America, most workers are ill prepared for this. Current forms of social insurance based on mandatory severance payments reach only a minority of workers. Therefore, most workers cannot properly search for jobs because they cannot afford to remain without income. These workers are forced to accept the first job that comes their way, without insuring a proper match between their abilities and the requirements of the job. Indeed, involuntarily unemployed workers accept jobs that pay less than their former jobs. The fact that these losses tend to be greater for workers that change sectors or have more tenure also suggests that some specific skills are lost in the process of displacement. At least some job destruction may be inefficient from a social point of view.

New evidence of the strikingly high level of job and worker reallocation as well as large heterogeneity in productivity give rise to a new vision of the labor market, which has important implications for economic policies. First, market economies are extremely fluid and require a constant reallocation of resources (employment) to their new, most efficient use. If the entry-exit process of new firms is at the core of this reallocation of resources, bureaucratic burdens that increase start-up costs may undermine aggregate growth. Second, the fact that worker turnover is even greater than job reallocation underscores the importance for workers to have flexible skills and for countries to institute widespread social insurance to reduce the cost of job instability. Third, social insurance not only serves an important role in consumption smoothing, but also can bring productivity gains by promoting better job searches. Fourth, the dominant role of idiosyncratic factors in firms' performance hampers the efficiency of targeted industrial policies to promote employment, first because the group of targeted firms would most likely be composed of efficient as well as inefficient firms, and second because the heterogeneity of shocks makes it more difficult to identify the final effect of these policies on employment and firm performance. And fifth, credit market development may be a way to avoid the destruction of efficient matches between workers and firms due to liquidity problems.

The evidence presented in this chapter offers little support for the dualistic view of the labor market. This view considers the informal sector as a marginal sector where workers are unlikely to progress or move to formal jobs. Contrary to this view, there is evidence of great mobility between formal and informal employment, regardless of the definition of formality considered.

The Flow of Jobs and Workers

It is useful to begin the analysis of labor market dynamics with an assessment of employment changes in individual firms based on data sets that follow individual firms or plants over time. Unfortunately, only a few countries in the region have this type of data. Therefore, the coverage of countries is not as wide as in other chapters. Despite the limited coverage, the results from a small, heterogeneous sample of countries are surprisingly consistent.

Total job turnover is defined as the sum of job creation (new jobs created in a given year) and job destruction (old jobs destroyed in a given year). (See Box 2.1 for more detailed definitions of the variables described in this chapter.) Figure 2.1 shows the annual average job creation and destruction rates for a sample of 12 countries.[1] Gross rates of job creation and destruction range between 8 and 20 percent, adding up to total job turnover rates that range between 16 and 35 percent.

To put these numbers in perspective, consider that a rate of 35 percent implies that about one in every three jobs is created or destroyed in a given year. In comparison, changes in net employment, that is, the difference between job creation and destruction, are about one full order of magnitude smaller than total job turnover. For instance, in Brazil, a rate of job creation of 1.1 percent a year hides an impressive amount of activity in the labor market: every year, 16.1 percent of all jobs are created while 15 percent are lost.

This constant churning of job positions characterizes both developed and emerging market countries (see Figure 2.1). The two Latin American economies for which data on turnover for the whole economy are available—Brazil and Mexico—show turnover rates that are within the ranges observed in developed countries. Since data from Mexico and Brazil come from social security registries, it is not the case that high rates of turnover for these two countries are driven by high rates of informal employment.[2] Instead, the data suggest that there are high rates of turnover within formal sector firms. In addition, a large fraction of job reallocation comes through firms that start up or shut down each year. New firms entering the market explain 40 percent of total job creation; firms that shut down explain 30 percent of job destruction.

[1] Brazil, Canada, Denmark, Estonia, Finland, France, Germany, Italy, Mexico, New Zealand, Sweden, and the United States.

[2] The high levels of job creation in Mexico may reflect an increase in the number of jobs that pay social security benefits.

Box 2.1 Definitions of Gross Flows

Job creation. The sum of employment changes for firms that increase the workforce between years *t*–1 and *t*, divided by average total employment in *t*–1 and *t*.

Job destruction. The negative of the sum of employment changes for firms that decrease the workforce between years *t*–1 and *t*, divided by the average total employment in *t*–1 and *t*. By construction, job destruction is positive.

Net employment rate. The sum of employment changes for all firms between years *t*–1 and *t*, divided by the average total employment in *t*–1 and *t*. This statistic is equal to job creation minus job destruction.

Job turnover or job reallocation. The sum of the absolute value of firms' employment changes, divided by the average total employment in years *t*–1 and *t*. This statistic is equal to job creation plus job destruction.

Excess reallocation. Job turnover minus the absolute value of the net employment rate.

Job creation by entering firms (entry). The sum of employment for firms that enter the market in year *t*, divided by the average total employment in *t*–1 and *t*. Job creation by entering firms is part of the previously defined job creation.

Job destruction by exiting firms (exit). The negative of the sum of employment (in year *t*–1) for firms that exit the market between *t*–1 and *t*, divided by the average total employment in *t*–1 and *t*. By construction, this statistic is positive.

Accession rate. The sum of all workers hired between years *t*–1 and *t*, divided by the average total number of employees in *t*–1 and *t*.

Separation rate. The sum of all workers that leave a firm between years *t*–1 and *t*, divided by the average total number of employees in *t*–1 and *t*. This statistic includes fired workers as well as employees who quit.

Worker turnover or worker reallocation. The sum all workers who are hired or who leave a firm between years *t*–1 and *t*, divided by the average number of workers in *t*–1 and *t*. This statistic is equal to the sum of the accession and separation rates.

Source: Davis and Haltiwanger (1999).

Figure 2.1 Average Annual Gross Job Flows

Source: OECD (1996); Davis and Haltiwanger (1999); Kaplan, Robertson, and Martínez (2003); Menezes Filho and others (2002).

High levels of job turnover can be observed in all areas of the economy. For the nine countries for which data are available for manufacturing, job turnover rates range between 15 and 30 percent (Figure 2.2). As for the whole economy (Figure 2.1), levels of job reallocation in the manufacturing sector in the countries in Latin America for which data are available (Chile, Colombia, and Mexico) are comparable to those in developed countries (Figure 2.2). This is a surprising result, considering the differences in labor market regulatory regimes across countries (see chapter 7).

Job flows are related to worker flows. As firms close positions, workers are forced to relocate to new jobs. However, workers also move across jobs and between employment, unemployment, and inactivity as a result of their own personal decisions. Thus, worker turnover is larger than job turnover. Figure 2.3 presents job and worker reallocation in five developed countries (Canada, Fin-

Figure 2.2 Average Annual Gross Job Flows in Manufacturing
(Percentage of employment)

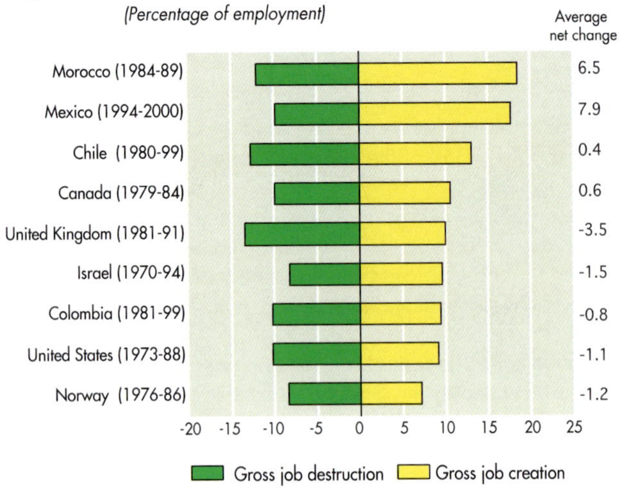

Source: IDB calculations; Davis, Haltiwanger and Schuh (1996); Barnes and Haskel (2002); Gronau and Regev (1997); Kaplan, Robertson, and Martínez (2003); Medina, Meléndez, and Seim (2003).

Figure 2.3 Average Annual Gross Worker Flows
(Percentage of employment)

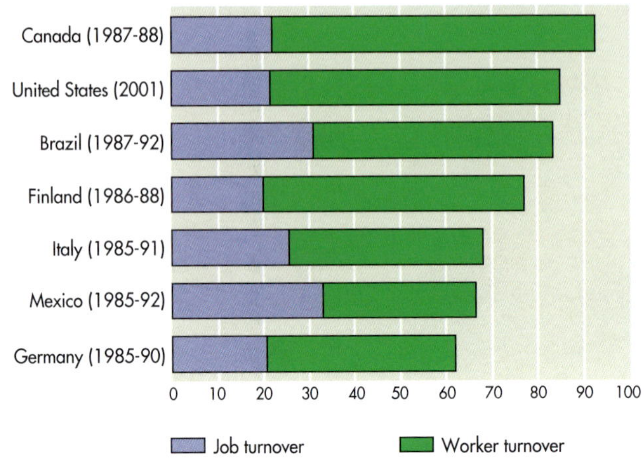

Source: Bertola, Boeri, and Cazes (1999); Davis, Haltiwanger, and Schuh (1996); Barnes and Haskel (2002); Kaplan, Robertson, and Martínez (2003); Menezes Filho and others (2002).

land, Germany, Italy, and the United States) and two developing countries (Brazil and Mexico). It shows that worker flows are larger than gross job flows by a factor of three. For each job created or destroyed in a year, approximately three workers either change from one job to another or change their employment status.[3] Again, Mexico and Brazil have patterns of job and worker reallocation that are within the ranges of those observed for the developed countries included in the sample.

This extreme level of job reallocation implies a large degree of heterogeneity in firms' behavior. Even within the same industry, firms face a broad range of shocks to the demand for their products, the cost of their inputs, and their production technology. The result is an equally broad range of productivity and employment patterns.

Three types of factors can drive changes in employment within firms: firm-specific shocks, sector shocks, and economywide aggregate shocks. Firm-specific factors are associated with changes in the demand for firms' products, changes in the cost of inputs, or changes in the technology used by individual firms. Sector shocks are driven by changes in price, technology, or the cost of inputs at the sector level. Economywide aggregate shocks tend to be associated with changes in the macroeconomic conditions of a country.

What is the relative importance of aggregate, sector, and firm-specific shocks in explaining job reallocation? Figure 2.4 shows that the lion's share of reallocation is associated with firm-specific rather than aggregate shocks. This is surprising given the volatility of Latin American economies.[4,5] These results imply that firm-specific factors play a dominant role in individual firms' performance even within narrowly defined sectors. This large heterogeneity in firms' performance explains why there is a large degree of turnover in the market. (Box 2.2 describes the importance of idiosyncratic shocks.)

Reallocation over Time

Some studies based on household survey data find that worker mobility increased in several countries in the region during the 1990s (Saavedra 2003). Figure 2.5 shows that excess turnover rates (see Box

[3] Employment status could be employed, unemployed, or inactive (out of the labor force).

[4] See Davis, Haltiwanger, and Schuh (1996) for a description of the methodology for this decomposition.

[5] Of course, the relative importance of sector shocks depends on the definition of the sectors. In this case, sectors were defined using the four-digit SITC classification.

Figure 2.4 Job Reallocation by Type of Shock

(Percentage of employment)

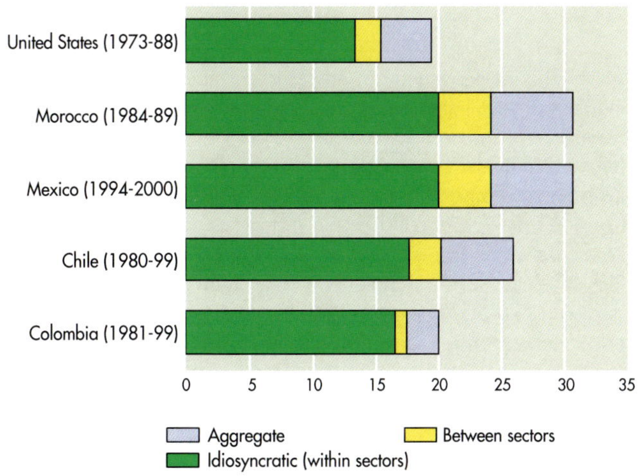

Source: IDB calculations; Barnes and Haskel (2002); Bergoeing, Hernando, and Repetto (2003); Davis, Haltiwanger, and Schuh (1996); Kaplan, Robertson, and Martínez (2003); Medina, Meléndez, and Seim (2003); Menezes Filho and others (2002); Roberts and Tybout (1996).

Figure 2.5 Excess Job Reallocation over Time, 1980-2000

(Percent)

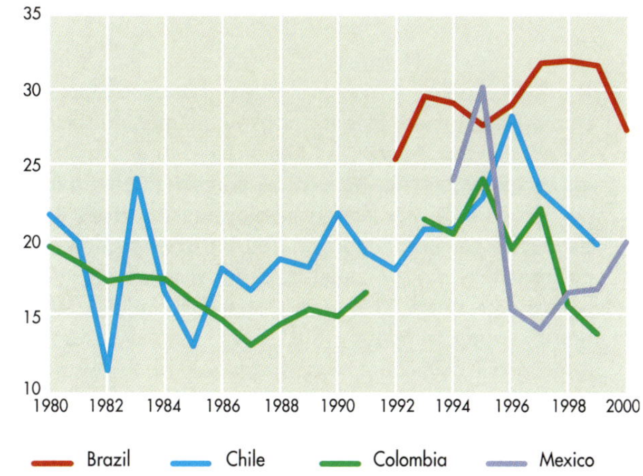

Source: Bergoeing, Hernando, and Repetto (2003); Kaplan, Robertson, and Martínez (2003); Medina, Meléndez, and Seim (2003); Menezes Filho and others (2002).

2.1) in manufacturing (that is, turnover net of the effect of aggregate shocks) increased in Colombia after 1992.[6] The figure also shows a trend toward higher excess reallocation in Chile and Brazil during the 1990s. By contrast, turnover declined in Mexico in the 1990s. In principle, increasing turnover rates could be associated with higher reallocation across sectors of activity brought about by the far-reaching trade reforms implemented during the 1990s in most countries in the region. However, as shown in chapter 5, there is no statistical association between trade reforms and increased reallocation across sectors. Therefore, if structural reforms brought increased reallocation, this effect came from increased reallocation within narrowly defined sectors, that is, increasing heterogeneity across individual firms' performance.

Reallocation as a Source of Productivity Gains

The evidence provided so far indicates that high rates of job reallocation are caused by firm-specific factors. It also indicates that firm entry and exit account for an important share of job turnover. These patterns suggest that firms may go through a process of learning in which trial and error plays an important role. This is confirmed by the observation that in both Colombia and Chile, younger firms have higher levels of reallocation (Figure 2.6). Moreover, younger firms tend to be less productive than firms that have been in operation for a longer time (Figure 2.7).

The fact that younger firms experience higher turnover rates suggests that new firms are uncertain about their costs of production and the demand for their final goods. The owners or managers of young firms continuously adjust their production and workforce based on their changing perceptions of market conditions and production costs. Some of them realize they cannot stay in business and close after a short time in operation.

As firms age, the learning process slows down and changes in employment become smaller and less frequent. In Chile, the probability that a new entrant exits after one year in business is 11 percent. After this initial difficult year, the probability of exiting the market goes down with the firm's age. After a decade in operation, the probability of exit

[6] Figure 2.5 plots excess reallocation (see Box 2.1 for a description).

Box 2.2. The Importance of Idiosyncratic Shocks

The figure below presents the distribution of the annual employment growth rate for firms in the manufacturing and bakery products sectors in Chile in 1995. In the manufacturing sector, employment grew at 1 percent, but more than 21 percent of firms contracted employment by more than 15 percent, 6 percent shut down, and 9 percent started up. This heterogeneity mainly comes from differences within narrowly defined subsectors. In particular, the Figure focuses on the bakery products industry (SITC 3117), and shows a level of heterogeneity similar to what is observed for the whole manufacturing sector.

This heterogeneity in employment has its counterpart in labor productivity. The figure shows the level (log deviation from the mean) and the rate of growth of firms' labor productivity in the bakery products industry in Chile. Firms in the 75th percentile had labor productivity three times larger than firms in the 25th percentile; the difference is more than 10 times between the 90th and 10th percentiles. Although industry-level labor productivity remained almost constant during 1994-95, more than 25 percent of establishments observed a drop in labor productivity larger than 15 percent.

a. Employment Growth Distribution in Manufacturing in Chile, 1995

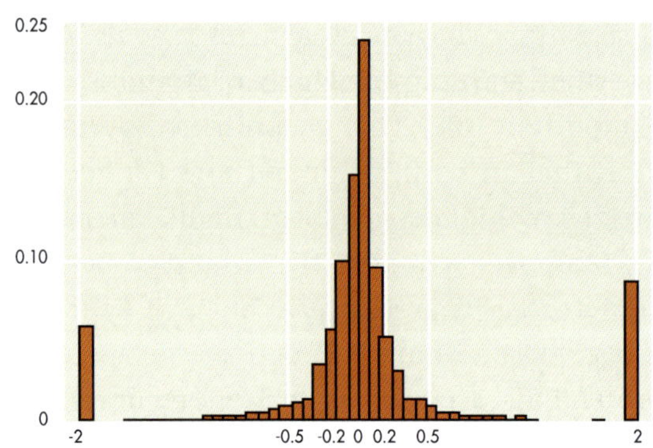

b. Employment Growth Distribution in Bakery Products in Chile, 1995

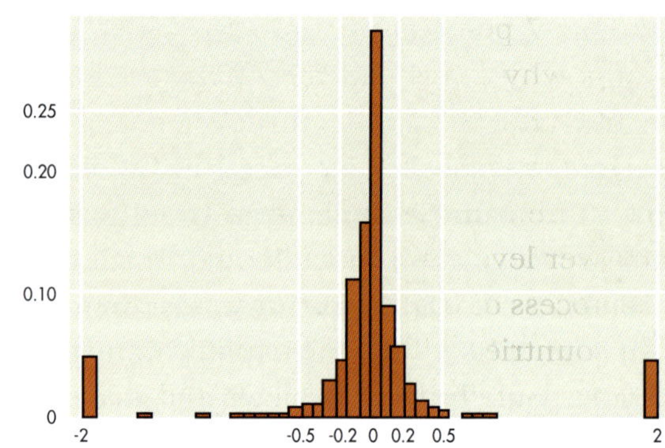

c. Labor Productivity Distribution in Bakery Products in Chile, 1995 (log deviation from the mean)

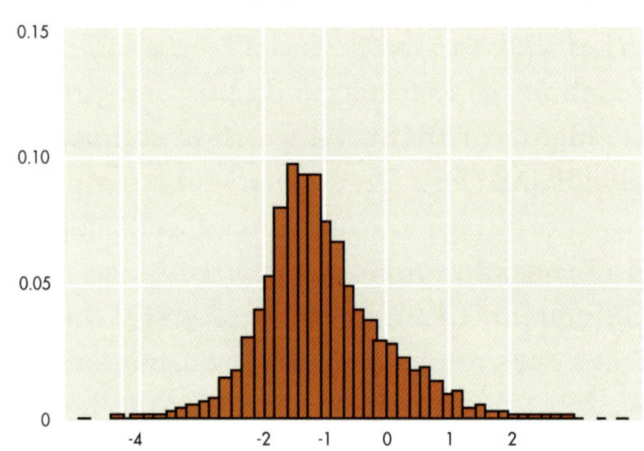

d. Rate of Growth of Labor Productivity in Bakery Products in Chile, 1995

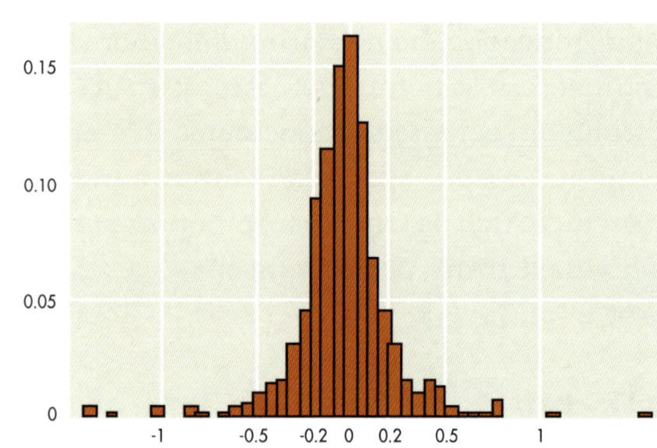

Note: The rate of growth in figure d is calculated without entry and exit of firms.
Source: IDB calculations.

Figure 2.6 Job Reallocation by Age of Firm
(Percentage of employment)

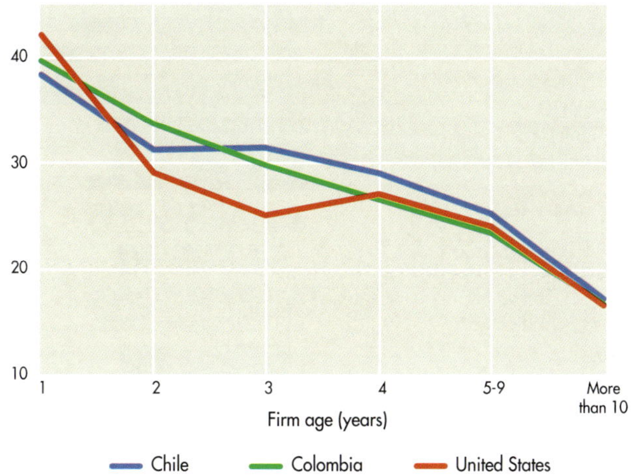

Source: IDB calculations; Davis, Haltiwanger, and Schuh (1996); Bergoeing, Hernando, and Repetto (2003); Medina, Meléndez, and Seim (2003).

Figure 2.7 Labor Productivity by Age of Firm in Chile and Colombia
(Percent)

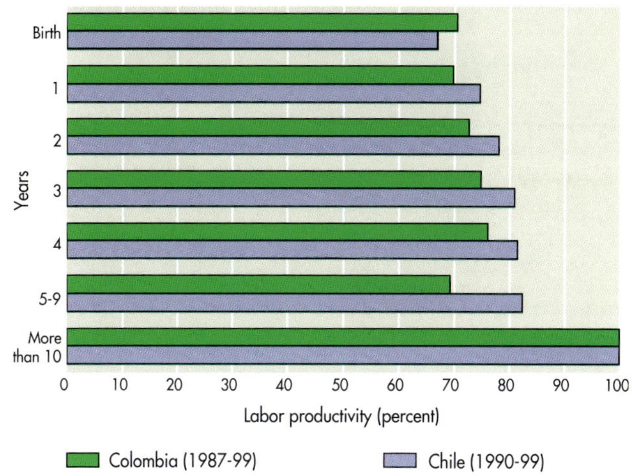

Note: Labor productivity is relative to firms age 10 years or older.
Source: IDB calculations; Bergoeing, Hernando, and Repetto (2003); Medina, Meléndez, and Seim (2003).

is reduced to 5-7 percent. This process of learning also explains why firms become more productive as they age. Over time, firms develop ways of producing more efficiently, leading to a learning curve in which mature firms tend to have higher productivity but lower levels of productivity growth.

This process of trial and error is important for growth. In countries with low entry and exit costs, entrepreneurs launch many projects and maintain the ones that end up being successful. In countries with high entry and exit costs, entrepreneurs have limited incentives to experiment and many good projects may never be tried.[7] Little is known about the costs of experimenting. However, Figure 2.8 suggests that the cost of starting a new firm is quite hefty in Latin America. This is reflected in the fact that the size of new entrants relative to incumbents is 60 and 45 percent in Chile and Colombia, respectively. In relative terms, entrants in these countries are greater than start-up firms in Canada, the United Kingdom, and the United States, but comparable to those in France and Italy (Figure 2.9).

An economy's productivity may grow because existing firms become more productive as they age and invest in new ways to produce (learning), less productive firms exit the market (selection), or less productive firms shrink while more productive firms expand (reshuffling). To find the share of productivity growth that is due to each of these factors, aggregate labor productivity growth can be decomposed into three components: (1) productivity growth in existing establishments, (2) productivity growth from shifts in market shares among existing firms with different productivity levels, and (3) productivity growth from reallocation of workers from exiting firms to more productive entering establishments. This accounting procedure does not take into account that strategic interactions among firms may induce important interactions among the three components of aggregate productivity growth. For example, entry of new firms may stimulate productivity-enhancing investment by incumbents to preserve their market shares.

Figure 2.10 presents the decomposition of labor productivity growth in manufacturing at five-year intervals.[8] The sample includes eight developed countries and two economies in Latin America.

[7] The costs of not experimenting are even higher considering that successful entrepreneurs could generate positive externalities by revealing a country's comparative advantage (Hausmann and Rodrik 2002).

[8] The productivity decompositions depend on the period in which productivity growth is calculated. The larger is the period, the larger is the importance of entry and exit in aggregate productivity growth. When the period is increased, a larger percentage of firms either enters or exits, and a larger percentage of the learning-by-doing process is accounted for by the entry-exit component.

Figure 2.8 Start-up Costs Ranked by Region
(Index)

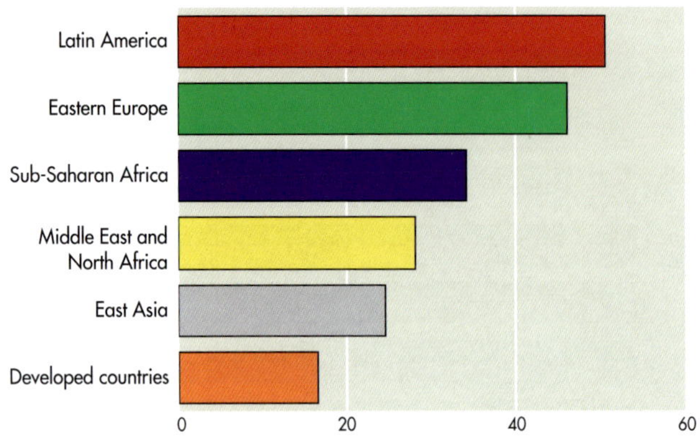

Note: For each region, the index is for the median country. Lower rank indicates lower cost of starting a new firm.
Source: World Economic Forum (2003).

Figure 2.10 Labor Productivity Growth Decomposition
(Percent)

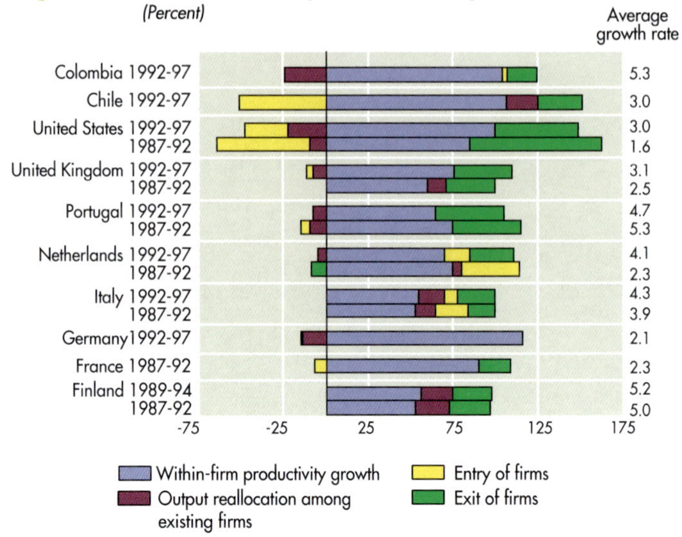

Source: Scarpetta, and others (2002); Bergoeing, Hernando, and Repetto (2003); Medina, Meléndez, and Seim (2003).

Figure 2.9 Relative Size of Entering Firms with Respect to Incumbents
(Percent)

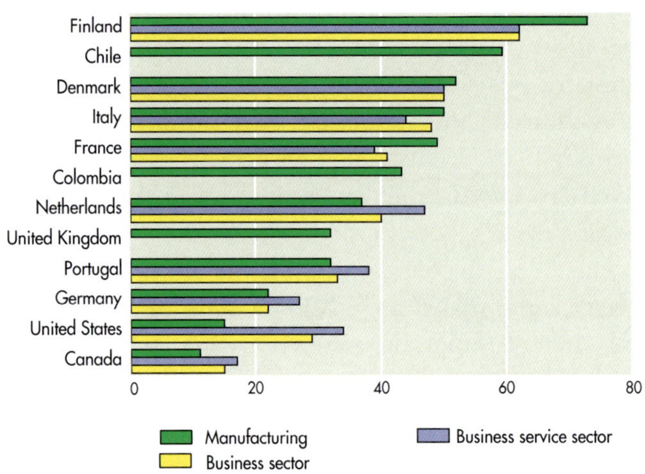

Source: IDB calculations; Scarpetta and others (2002); Medina, Meléndez, and Seim (2003).

Results suggest that firms' learning accounts for most of the growth in aggregate productivity (50-85 percent). The reshuffling component is typically small. The entry-exit component is positive in all but one case and accounts for 20-40 percent of total productivity growth. Focusing on Latin America, the exit component is lower than for the United States, but comparable to that for Italy, France, Finland, and the Netherlands.

In general, the selection process contributes to productivity growth because exiting firms have lower productivity than incumbent ones. Entering firms reduce aggregate productivity because, just after entering the market, they have on average lower productivity levels than incumbent firms. This is particularly the case in Chile, despite the fact that Figure 2.9 indicates that the typical entering firm is large. In general, the low average productivity of new firms is explained by the fact that these entrepreneurs have not yet experienced learning and the process of selection has not yet taken place.

Summing up, Figure 2.10 suggests that the reallocation process, which includes between-firm and entry-exit components, accounts for around 15 to 50 percent of aggregate productivity growth in the sample. In developed countries, these results have been interpreted as an indication of the importance of having low entry and exit costs. Reallocation has also been found to be important for explaining total productivity growth (Barnes and Haskel 2002; Scarpetta and others 2002). Thus, the high costs of adjusting employment could reduce productivity growth.

Factor Specificity

A factor of production is specific to a firm when its contribution to output within the firm is larger than its contribution outside the firm. For workers, this specificity may arise from specialized training, experience gained on the job that is only relevant in the current workplace, or the time required to search for a new job. In turn, capital may be specific to a firm because it has been adapted to a particular process and location, or because it is worth less in the hands of other workers and/or entrepreneurs.

If employers and workers share the returns of this specificity, both parties have incentives to maintain the employment relationship. Hence, specificity may provide a buffer against firm-specific, sector, or aggregate shocks, and therefore reduce employment volatility. In fact, employers will be more reluctant to lay off workers that are difficult to replace. Variations in the specificity of labor may therefore explain differences in employment volatility across different types of workers.

Specificity is likely positively associated with the level of human capital. Therefore, higher levels of turnover would be expected for less-skilled jobs (Mincer and Jovanovic 1981; Bulow and Summers 1986). Surprisingly, white and blue-collar jobs do not demonstrate this relationship in Chile, Colombia, and Uruguay according to the measure of job reallocation in Figure 2.11a. Contrary to the hypothesis that job turnover decreases with specificity, the figure shows that in Chile and Colombia, blue collar jobs appear to be more stable than white collar jobs in manufacturing. (The opposite is true in Uruguay, although the difference in turnover between white and blue collar jobs is small and not statistically significant.[9])

A possible explanation is that the implicit assumption that blue collar workers are less skilled than white collar workers is incorrect. Another way to approach the problem is to proxy specificity with the average level of wages of a firm. It is expected that firms that pay higher wages employ more skilled workers. Under this measure, reallocation clearly declines with the skill level. Figure 2.11b measures job reallocation across wage quintiles. It shows that the higher the level of human capital, the lower the level of job reallocation. For example, job turnover for Mexican firms with very low wages is almost twice as large as job flows for firms with very high wages. This negative relationship is monotonic and does not change, even controlling for other firm characteristics such as sector, age, and firm size. These results suggest that most of the burden of employ-

Figure 2.11 Job Reallocation

(Percent)

a. White and blue collar jobs

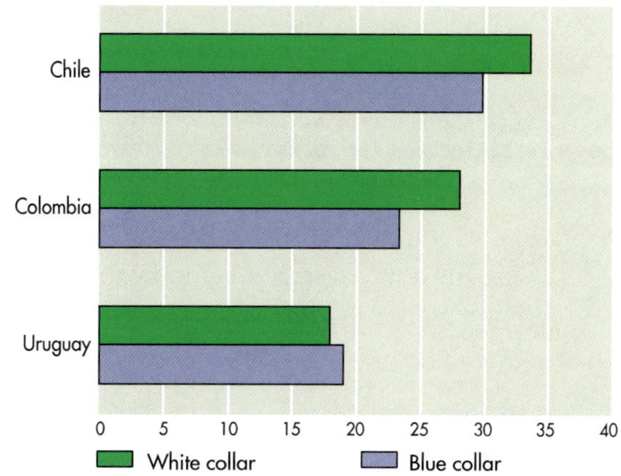

b. Wage quintile

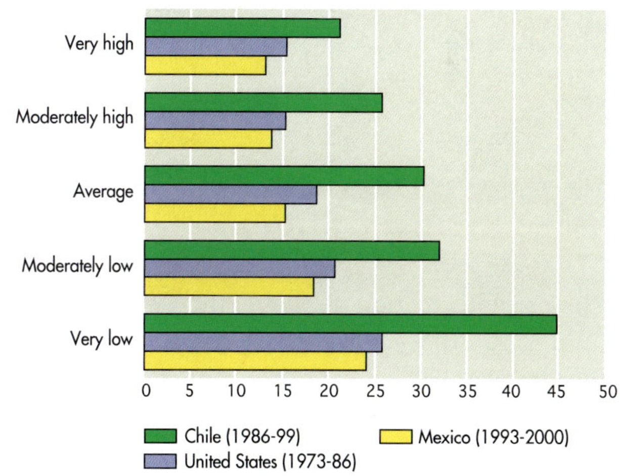

Note: The data on job reallocation in Mexico and Uruguay are only for continuous firms.
Source: IDB calculations; Bergoeing, Hernando, and Repetto (2003); Medina, Meléndez, and Seim (2003); Casacuberta, Fachola, and Gandelman (2003); Davis, Haltiwanger, and Schuh (1996).

[9] The data on job reallocation in Uruguay are only for continuous firms in manufacturing.

ment reallocation falls on workers with low levels of human capital and low wages.

Firm Size

In general, small firms have higher probabilities of exiting the market and pay lower wages than larger firms. It is therefore expected that turnover would be higher in smaller firms than in larger ones. The available data confirm that there is a strong association between firm size and turnover rate (see Figure 2.12). For each of the five countries in Figure 2.12, there is a negative monotonic relationship between firm size and job reallocation. In the case of Brazil, for instance, establishments with fewer than 50 workers have on average a level of job reallocation twice as large as that of firms with 250 or more employees.

Figure 2.12 Firm Size and Job Reallocation in the Manufacturing Sector

(Percentage of employment)

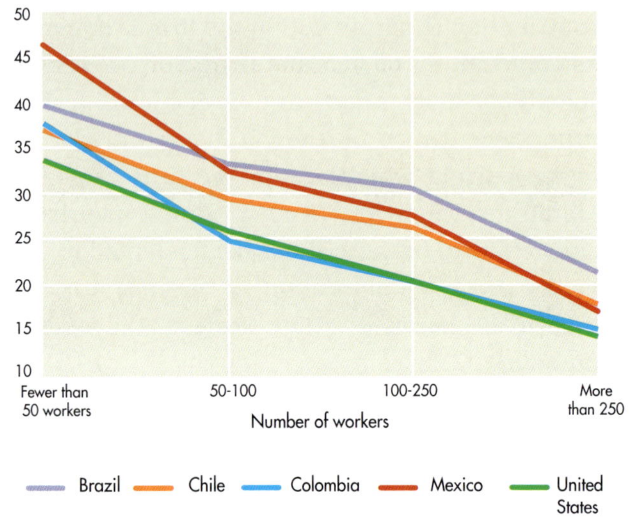

Source: IDB calculations; Bergoeing, Hernando, and Repetto (2003); Davis, Haltiwanger, and Schuh (1996); Kaplan, Robertson, and Martínez (2003); Medina, Meléndez, and Seim (2003); and Menezes Filho and others (2002).

Excessive Destruction and Liquidity Shocks

The previous section discussed the importance of a fluid labor market for the process of learning, reshuffling, and selection to take place. It highlighted that in the presence of uncertainty regarding the varieties of goods to be produced or the type of technology that should be used, the optimal production structure can be found only through a process of trial and error. A fluid labor market is also at the core of the Schumpeterian process of creative destruction. According to this view, aggregate productivity increases thanks to the continuous incorporation of new technologies that displace obsolete ones. Firms that incorporate new, efficient production processes gain market share and force inefficient producers to shut down.

These mechanisms assume that job reallocation is socially efficient, and that obstacles to reallocation reduce welfare. This may not always be the case. The following sections of the chapter discuss cases in which job creation and destruction are socially inefficient. Evidence for this perspective comes, in part, from studies of the private costs of job separations; the findings suggest that displaced workers take substantial wage cuts in their new jobs.[10]

Why would firms inefficiently destroy jobs? A possible explanation is that when negative shocks hit firms, imperfect capital markets constrain the ability of the firms to keep valuable workers, leading to the destruction of profitable firms and jobs. This factor is likely to be important in many Latin American countries that have underdeveloped financial markets. To date, no study has analyzed whether capital market underdevelopment leads to inefficient destruction of jobs. However, some indirect evidence suggests that small firms, in particular, may be severely credit constrained and destroy too many jobs. Thus, the results in Appendix Table 2.1 show that small firms have high levels of reallocation even after controlling for firm age, sector of activity, and level of wages.[11] This excess of turnover could be explained by the fact that small

[10] See Hall (1995) and Jacobson, LaLonde, and Sullivan (1993) for the United States and the references in the next sections for the region.

[11] In all specifications, dummies for larger firms are negative, indicating that larger firms have on average a lower level of job reallocation even after controlling for age and wage levels.

firms face lower adjustment costs and therefore their employment levels react more to shocks. Caballero, Engel, and Micco (2003) do not find support for this hypothesis. An alternative hypothesis is that small firms are more severely credit constrained, and therefore more vulnerable to inefficient destruction when faced with a liquidity shock.

Worker Flows and Worker Welfare

In market economies, the constant reallocation of labor is a key engine of productivity and wage growth. However, the process of labor reallocation may also bring large costs to displaced workers if it takes some time to find a new job or if workers have to accept jobs that pay lower wages than their previous jobs. Opinion surveys suggest that mobility may impose substantial costs on workers. According to the Latinobarometer, a public opinion survey conducted annually in Latin American countries, 85 percent of Latin Americans were either unemployed or worried about losing their jobs in 1996 (Figure 2.13a). In 2001, this feeling of malaise had increased in 11 of the 17 countries in which the survey was done. This concern is shared even in countries like Mexico, Costa Rica, and Guatemala, where unemployment rates are below 6 percent. In comparison, workers are more anxious about their jobs in Latin America than in Europe, despite the fact that the available data suggest that rotation rates are similar in the two regions. Thus, according to the Eurobarometer, only 32 percent of the workers in Europe felt insecure about their jobs in 1996 (Figure 2.13b).[12] What factors explain these differences?

The following sections assess whether reallocation is costly for workers. It turns out that, although job mobility can bring substantial welfare gains for many workers, for others the process of reallocation is not smooth. The absence of widespread social insurance may explain why Latin American citizens are especially concerned about keeping their jobs.

Figure 2.13 Public Opinion Survey Results

a. Unemployed or worried about losing current job, 1996-97 and 2000-01

(Percent)

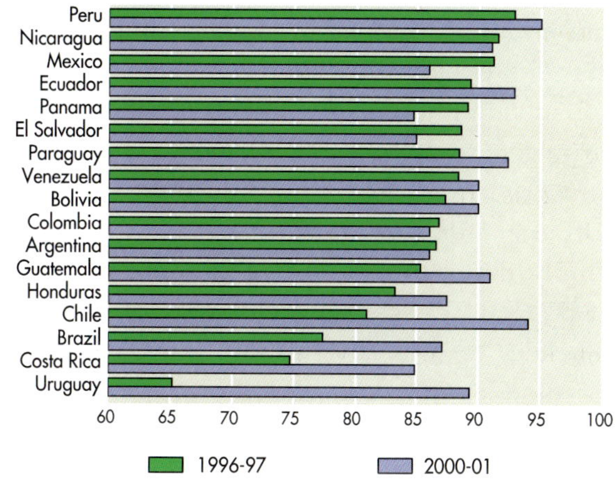

b. Current job is not very secure or not secure, 1996-97

(Percent)

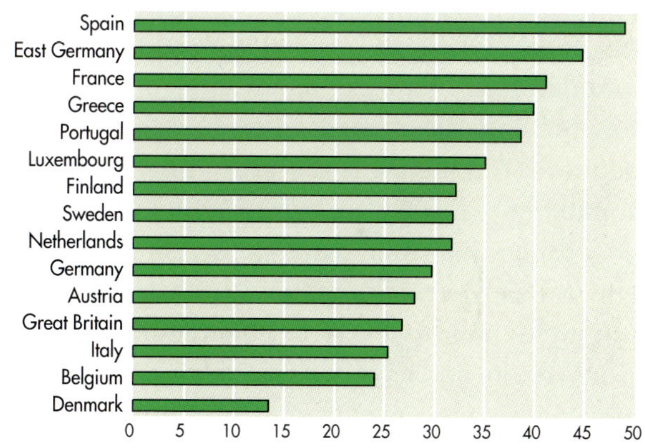

Source: Latinobarometer (various years); Eurobarometer (1996, 1997).

[12] This was estimated from Gallie (1997) for Austria, Belgium, Denmark, East Germany, Finland, France, Greece, Ireland, Italy, Luxembourg, the Netherlands, Northern Ireland, Portugal, Spain and Sweden, the United Kingdom, and West Germany based on data from the Eurobarometer (1996).

The Welfare Cost of Displacement

From a worker's standpoint, the continuous creation and destruction of jobs introduce opportunities and uncertainty. On the one hand, large gross job creation flows allow workers to move from less attractive to more attractive jobs. This reallocation process is generally associated with welfare gains. On the other hand, large job destruction flows imply that workers always face the threat of job loss. How this constant churning of labor affects workers' welfare depends on three factors: the risk of unemployment, the short-term income loss associated with unemployment, and the possible long-run losses associated with accepting jobs that pay less than previous jobs.

The earnings foregone and the length of the unemployment spell determine the short-run income losses associated with unemployment. Obviously, the existence of some form of social insurance (such as unemployment insurance or mandatory severance payments) alleviates the income loss associated with unemployment. In addition, the higher is the probability of finding a suitable job, the lower is the welfare loss associated with an unemployment spell.[13] In Latin America, the per-period income loss associated with unemployment is likely to be large because many workers do not have access to mandatory severance payments. On average, only 44 percent of the workers are covered by this form of social insurance (see chapter 1). Moreover, because severance pay depends on the number of years a worker has been in a firm, there are many workers who, despite having access to benefits, receive small amounts. These are, for instance, workers who have just entered the labor market (in general, young people), intermittently enter and exit the labor market (for example, women), or had a previous spell of unemployment. Chapter 7 analyzes the level and availability of social insurance. The next two sections focus on the probabilities of losing and finding a job and the post-unemployment conditions that determine the long-run cost of unemployment.

The Probability of Losing or Finding a Job

On average during the 1990s, workers in Latin America experienced a higher inflow to unemployment than workers in OECD countries. Some of this difference could be explained by increasing unemployment rates due to low growth in gross domestic product in the region. Box 2.3 shows the correlation between growth in gross domestic product and worker flows from employment to unemployment and from unemployment to employment in Argentina and Mexico in the 1990s. Figure 2.14 shows the number of workers that spent one month or less in unemployment as a share of total employment in Latin America and OECD countries. This measure offers a proxy for the probability that an employed worker enters unemployment. The probability of moving from employment to unemployment is particularly large in Argentina and Nicaragua, two countries that experienced high unemployment rates during the 1990s.

These measures are only approximations of the probability of finding a job. This is because newly unemployed workers could also come from inactivity (instead of only from employment, as assumed above). To better assess the probabilities of transitions across labor market states, that is, employment (E), unemployment (U), and being out of the labor force (N), requires information on the labor market state of a worker in a given period and in the following period. Thus, it is necessary to have panel data following individuals over time, but the data are available for only a few countries.

To get a more detailed view of the dynamics of the labor market from the workers' side, Figure 2.15 presents panel data on workers in Argentina in 1993-2001, a period of high and increasing unemployment. Comparing the labor status of an individual between two points in time, there are nine potential transitions or worker flows. For instance, an employed worker in time t might be unemployed in $t+1$ (E-U in Figure 2.15) or an unem-

[13] Gruber (1997a) finds that workers who receive higher unemployment insurance payments face a smaller reduction in consumption (a typical measure of welfare).

Box 2.3. How Does Aggregate Volatility Affect Worker Flows?

If worker flows respond to movements in gross domestic product (GDP), then greater volatility would lead to greater volatility in worker flows, greater uncertainty, and, thus, greater welfare loss. The effect of volatility is calculated based on simple correlations between worker flows and GDP growth. The Figure below illustrates the change in GDP and some transition probabilities (from employment to unemployment and from unemployment to employment) in Argentina and Mexico in the 1990s. As expected, in both countries, higher GDP growth is correlated with a lower risk of becoming unemployed and with a higher chance of finding a new job.

Worker Flows and GDP Growth

(Percent)

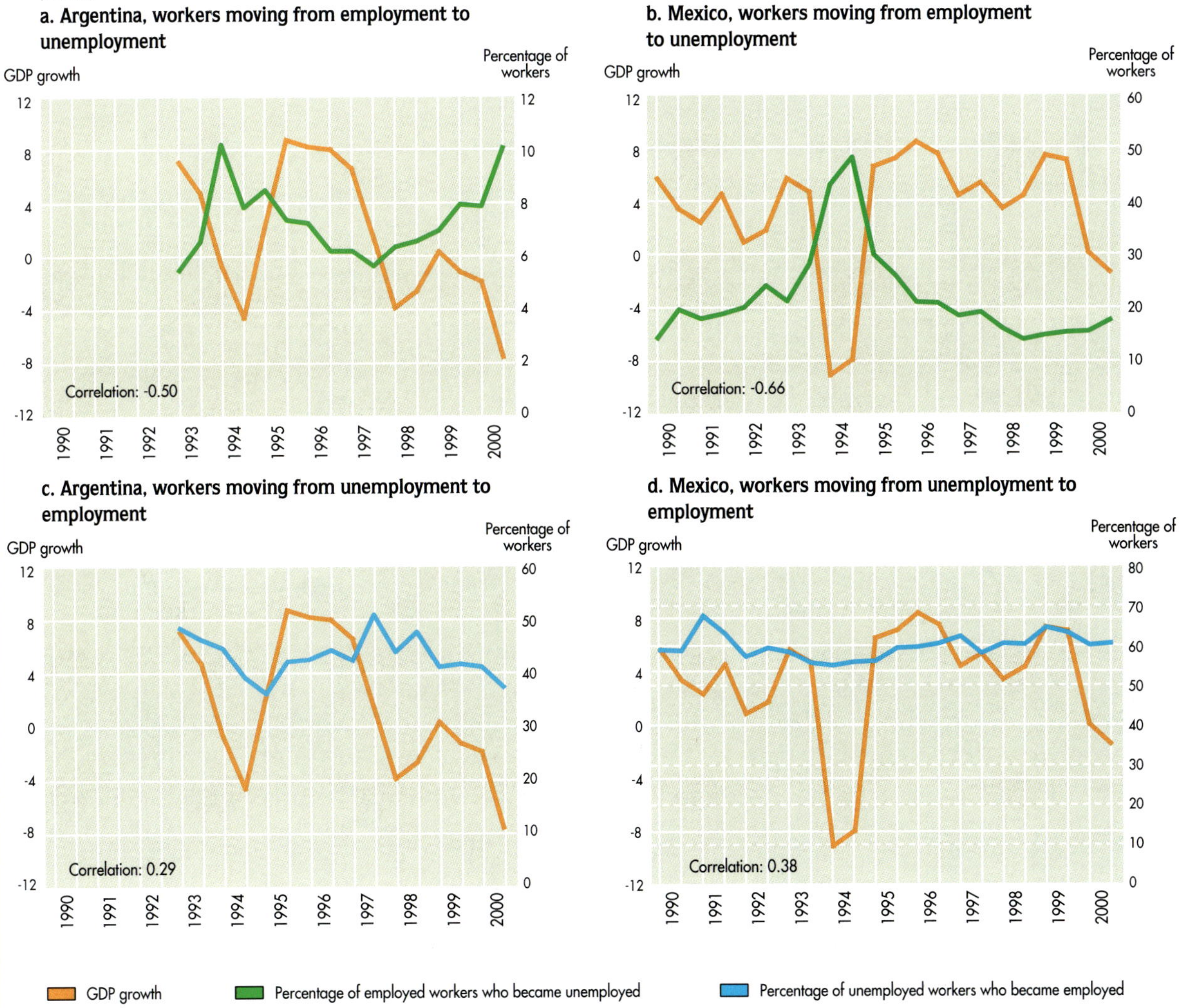

Note: Data for Argentina cover only the Gran Buenos Aires area.
Source: IDB calculations based on INDEC and INEGI rotating panel data from household surveys.

Figure 2.14 Workers Unemployed for One Month or Less
(Percentage of total employment)

a. Latin America **b. OECD countries**

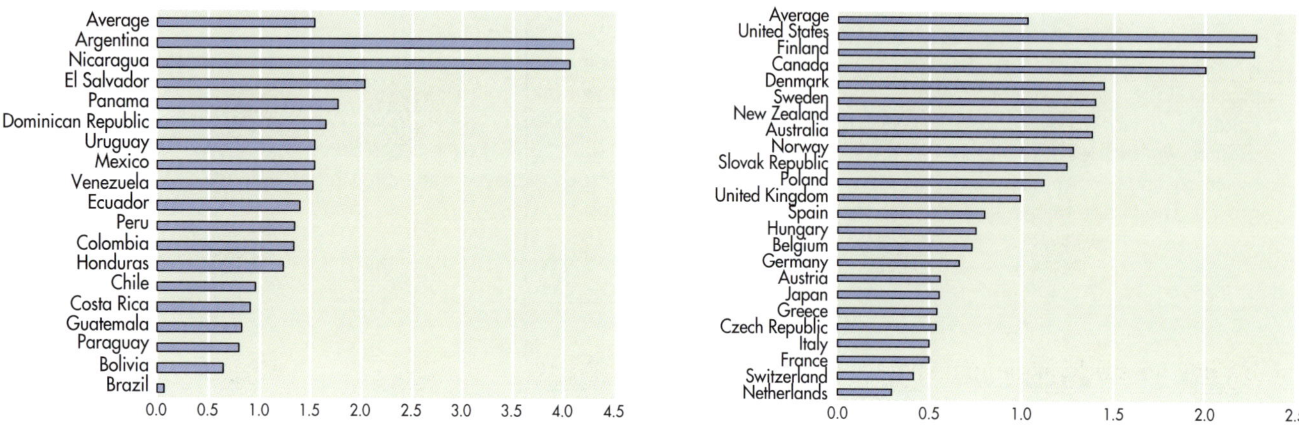

Source: IDB household surveys. Source: OECD.

Figure 2.15 Six-month Transitions across Labor Market States, Argentina, 1993-2001

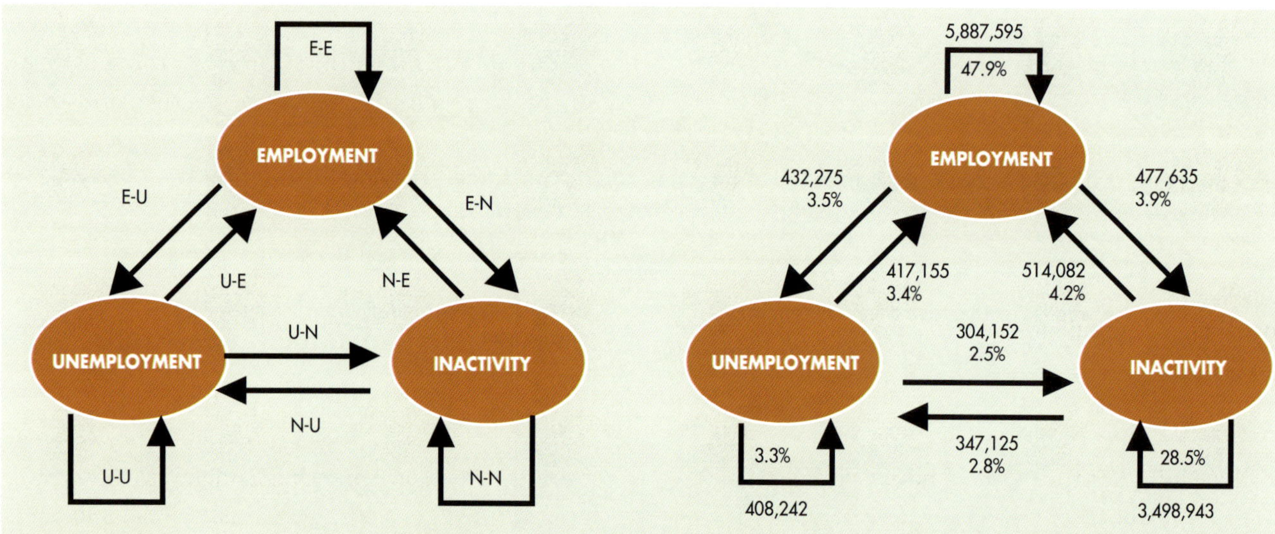

Note: E denotes employment; U, unemployment; and N, inactivity. E-U denotes movement from employment to unemployment. Values for Argentina were estimated using: (i) flows as a percentage of population (calculated as the average for 1993-2001 to avoid cyclical patterns), and (ii) the working-age population for 2002 (as reported by INDEC).

ployed worker in t might be employed in $t+1$ (U-E in Figure 2.15).

Dividing the expected worker flows by the population in Argentina in 2003 gives an idea of the magnitudes involved.[14] In a six-month period, about 3.5 percent of the population between ages 15 and 64 transits from employment to unemployment, while 3.4 percent makes the reverse (U-E) transition. These are large flows; for example, approximately 400,000 workers move from employment to unemployment and vice versa. The percentage of people entering and leaving the labor market is also significant: 4.2 percent of the popu-

[14] The number of people transiting from one state to another is computed using the period average flows multiplied by the projected population in 2003. All the data for Argentina correspond to the Gran Buenos Aires area.

lation moves from inactivity to employment (N-E) and 2.8 percent from inactivity to unemployment (N-U), while 3.9 percent moves from employment to inactivity (E-N) and 2.5 percent from unemployment to inactivity (U-N). Consequently, behind small movements in observed employment, unemployment, and participation rates, there are large flows of people.

Note that this information can be used to calculate, for instance, the gross probability of transition from employment to unemployment by dividing the number of people that made the transition by the stock of people that were employed. In more general terms, the transition between state i (in time t) and state j (in $t+1$) is calculated by dividing the flow between i and j by the stock of workers that were in state i in time t. So E-U, for example, represents from now on the probability that an individual is unemployed at time t, conditional on being employed at time $t-1$.

Comparing these probabilities across countries in Latin America and across regions yields the following results (see Appendix Table 2.2). First, as also suggested by the measures shown in Figure 2.14, the probability of entering unemployment during the 1990s was higher for the average of the three countries in the region for which data are available (Argentina, Mexico, and Peru) than for the United States or Eastern European countries (Figure 2.16). The probability of entering unemployment is two times larger in Latin America than in the United States. This finding contradicts the widespread perception that unemployment is not an issue in developing countries. Approximately 5 percent of the employed workers exited employment and entered unemployment as an intermediate step between jobs or between activity and inactivity. Within the region, the risk of unemployment was higher in Argentina and Peru, and much lower in Mexico.

During the 1990s, flows from employment to inactivity were also larger in the three Latin American countries than in the United States or Eastern Europe. Within the region, these transitions were higher in Mexico and Peru than in Argentina. These figures suggest that labor force attachment increases with the level of development and, as workers become more attached to the labor force, there are more transitions through unemployment and less to inactivity. This explains part of the differences in unemployment levels between Mexico, Peru, and Argentina.

The probability of exiting unemployment and finding a job was higher in the United States than in the other regions, followed by the average for the three Latin American countries. This confirms the results presented in chapter 1, showing that during the 1990s, the duration of unemployment in Latin America was higher than in the United States and lower than in Eastern and Western Europe. These results may reflect the fact that social insurance in Europe is more widespread and more generous than in Latin America and the United States. Europeans may just be spending more time finding a good job compared with unemployed workers in Latin America. In fact, Ehrenberg and Oaxaca (1976) show that increasing unemployment insurance benefits can induce further productive job searching, which in turn has a positive impact on post-unemployment wages. However, the literature also indicates that too generous unemployment insurance can be inefficient because it reduces job search effort. There is consequently an optimal level of unemployment insurance (Shavell and Weiss 1979; Hopenhayn and Nicolini 1997; Acemoglu and Shimer 1999a).

Within the region, the probability of exiting unemployment and finding a job is higher in Mexico than in Peru or Argentina. Indeed, in Argentina, the probability of finding a job is as low as in Western Europe. The probability of leaving unemployment to inactivity is also higher in the three countries in Latin America than in any other region. It is particularly high in Peru and Mexico and lower in Argentina. These figures suggest again the lower level of labor force attachment in Peru and Mexico relative to Argentina or the developed countries. These results are also consistent with the much higher rates of transition from inactivity to employment in Mexico and Peru than in Argentina.

Transitions across labor market states differ substantially across demographic groups. Data for Argentina and Mexico show that female, young, and unskilled workers are the most vulnerable

Figure 2.16 Six-month Transitions between Labor Market States

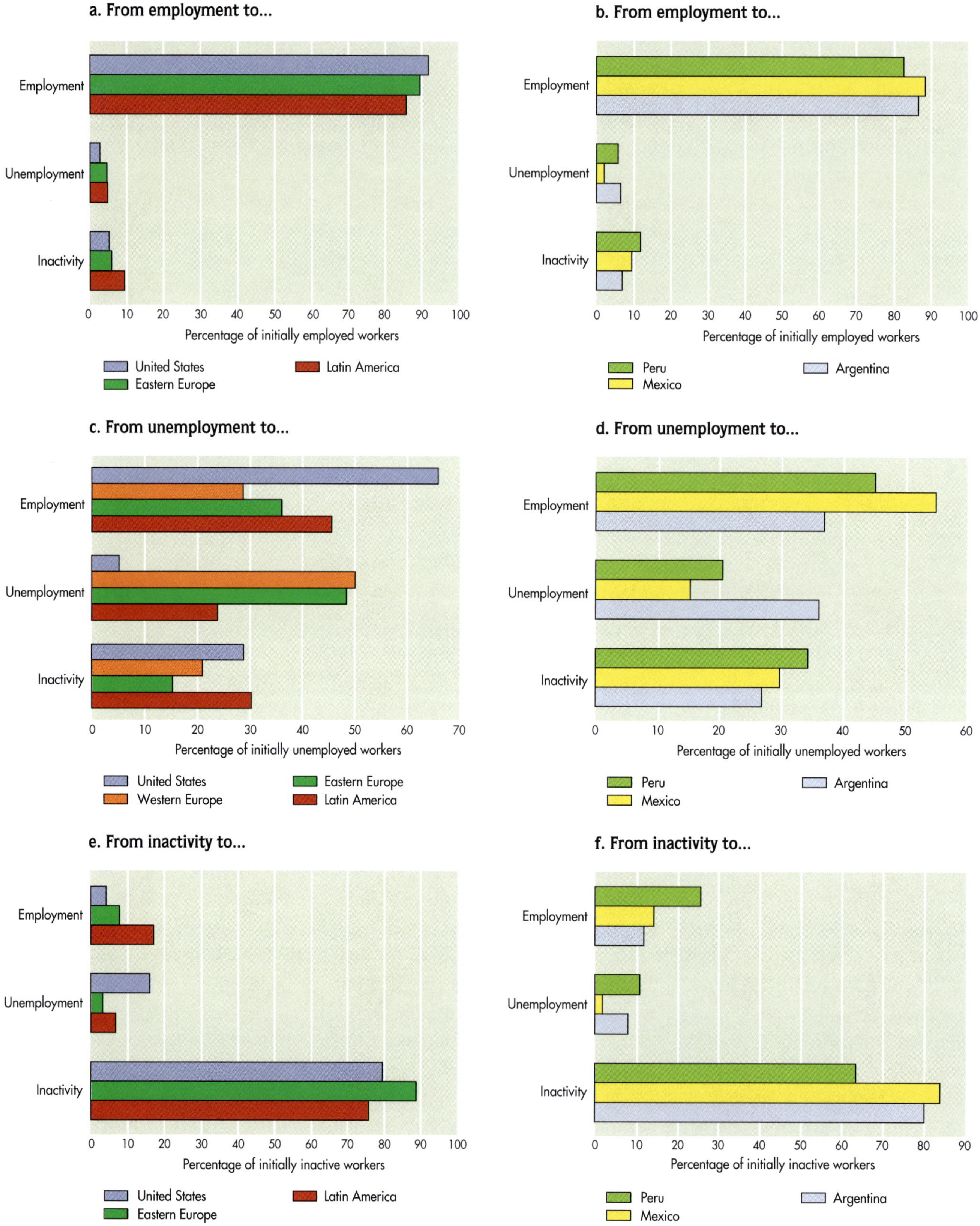

Source: IDB household surveys for Argentina, Peru, and Mexico; OECD data for regions and the United States.

Table 2.1 Labor Market Transitions by Group in Argentina and Mexico, 1990s

(Percent)

Country and group	From employment to: Employment	Unemployment	Inactivity	From unemployment to: Employment	Unemployment	Inactivity	From inactivity to: Employment	Unemployment	Inactivity
Argentina, 1993–2001									
Total	86.6	6.4	7.0	36.9	36.1	26.9	11.8	8.0	80.2
Male (prime age)	91.8	5.9	2.2	53.7	37.9	8.4	37.9	17.8	44.3
Female (prime age)	84.9	4.5	10.5	28.2	31.0	40.8	12.1	7.6	80.3
Prime age	89.2	5.4	5.4	40.8	34.4	24.8	14.2	8.5	77.3
Young	79.1	10.6	10.3	34.9	37.6	27.5	11.8	9.8	78.3
Skilled (prime age)	92.7	3.6	3.7	38.5	37.6	23.9	14.4	8.5	77.1
Unskilled (prime age)	86.1	7.1	6.8	41.9	32.7	25.4	13.9	8.3	77.8
Mexico, 1990–2001									
Total	88.4	2.0	9.6	54.9	15.3	29.8	14.3	1.8	83.9
Male (prime age)	96.8	1.8	1.3	75.9	16.2	7.9	40.7	6.1	53.2
Female (prime age)	83.3	1.1	15.6	38.6	14.1	47.3	13.4	1.2	85.4
Prime age	91.9	1.6	6.5	60.3	15.2	24.5	15.0	1.4	83.6
Young	82.4	3.6	14.0	50.5	15.8	33.7	14.6	2.7	82.7
Skilled (prime age)	94.0	1.4	4.6	56.9	18.1	24.9	16.9	2.4	80.7
Unskilled (prime age)	90.6	1.7	7.7	62.9	13.3	23.8	14.0	1.1	84.9

Note: Data are for six-month transitions. Data for Argentina are for the Gran Buenos Aires area.
Source: IDB estimates based on EPH-INDEC for Argentina, and Encuesta Nacional de Empleo Urbano (ENEU)-INEGI for Mexico.

groups to the risks of unemployment and exit from the labor market (Table 2.1).[15] Thus, the probability of losing a job is higher among women, youth, and unskilled workers than among prime-age, male, and skilled workers. Workers without social insurance are at high risk. They are not entitled to benefits in case of job loss, and their risk of unemployment is higher than for covered workers (see Figure 2.17 c and d and Appendix Tables 2.3, 2.4, and 2.5).

Youth and female workers have a lower probability of exiting unemployment than prime-age and male workers (Table 2.1). Instead, unskilled unemployed workers tend to exit unemployment toward a job faster than their skilled counterparts. These patterns could be explained by more job opportunities for prime-age, male, or unskilled workers, but most likely respond to a higher eagerness to accept jobs by primary earners and poorer workers relative to secondary earners (women and youth) and richer workers (skilled). Finally, women, youth, and unskilled workers tend to have higher transitions from and to inactivity than prime-age and male workers, perhaps as a result of lower levels of attachment to the labor market.

This research yields important results for the countries for which data are available. First, the probability of moving from employment to unemployment is as high (or higher) in the three considered countries in Latin America than it is in other regions. This implies that Latin American workers face a high risk of losing their jobs and going through a spell of unemployment. Second, women, youth, and unskilled workers tend to have a higher risk of unemployment than other workers. Third, workers in the uncovered sector bear a higher risk of unemployment than workers with the benefits mandated by labor laws. Fourth, transitions from unemployment to employment are also high by international standards, although lower than in the United States. Fifth, unskilled workers and prime-age workers tend

[15] This is based on rotating panel data on households. INDEC gathered Argentina's panel, which covers 1993-2001. INEGI generated Mexico's panel, which covers 1990-2001.

Figure 2.17 Six-month Transitions in Employment Status by Type of Job, Mexico and Argentina
(Percentage of workers in initial job status)

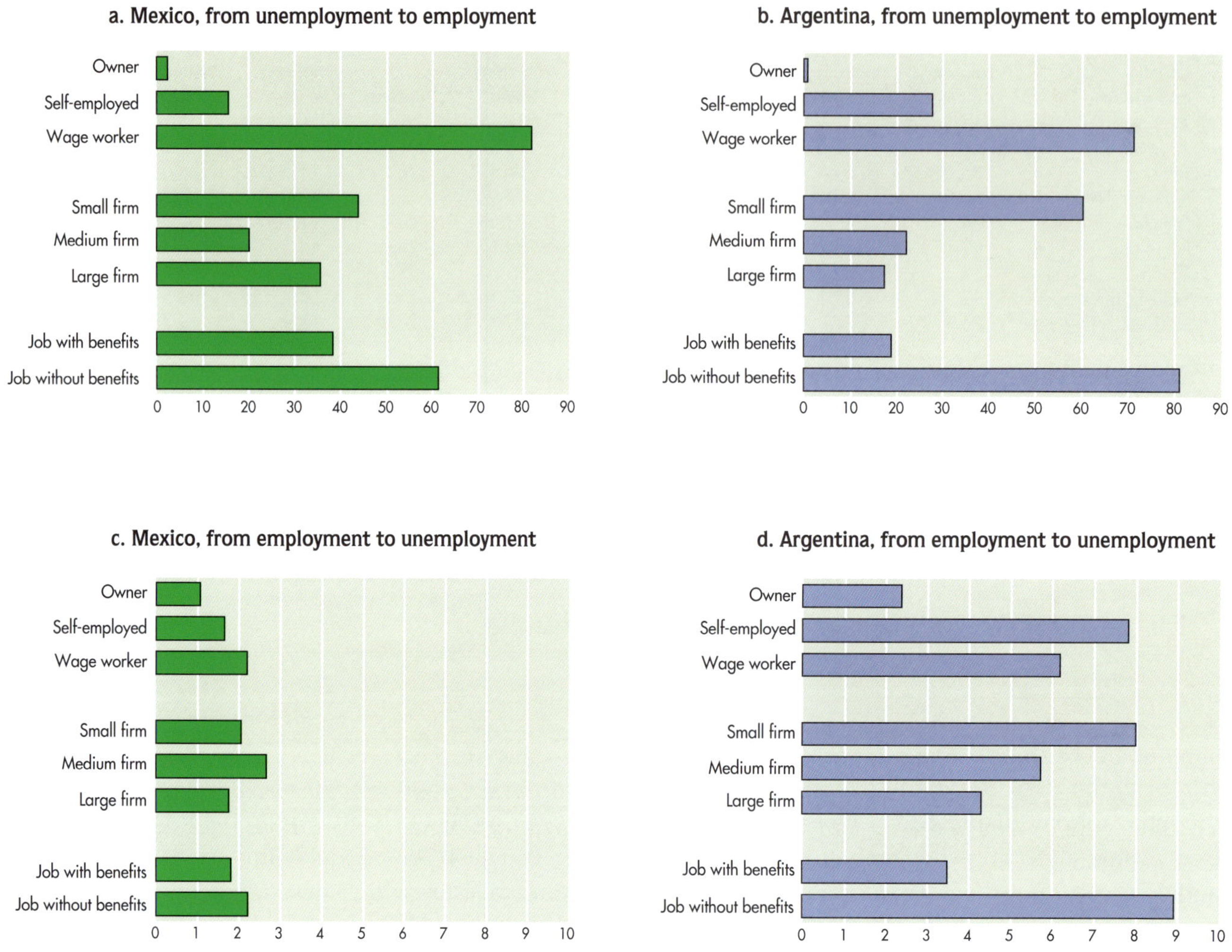

Source: IDB estimates based on data from EPH-INDEC for Argentina, and Encuesta Nacional de Empleo Urbano (ENEU)-INEGI for Mexico.

to exit unemployment faster than women and youth. These high transitions may reflect the lack of widespread social insurance, in particular for unskilled workers, and the existence of informal within-household insurance for women and young workers.

These findings suggest that some common perceptions about the incidence and importance of unemployment in Latin America are unwarranted. The first common perception is that workers without the benefits mandated by labor laws are less affected by unemployment than formal workers. As has been shown in the data for Mexico and Argentina, workers without benefits have a high risk of unemployment, in some cases higher than formal workers. The second common perception is that for poorer and more vulnerable workers, such as the unskilled, unemployment is not the issue; the issue is the low quality of jobs. The reality is that Latin American workers are much more vulnerable to the risk of unemployment than workers in developed countries, regardless of the aggregate rate of unemployment. This is because unskilled workers in Latin America not only have a higher probability of entering unemployment, but also are much less likely to receive some form of insurance while searching for new jobs compared with unskilled workers in developed countries.

Post-Unemployment Conditions

The welfare consequences of an unemployment spell depend crucially not only on the probability of finding a *new* job, but on the probability of finding a *similar* job, that is, a job with similar characteristics, pay, and benefits. Imagine that two workers face the same probability of unemployment with the same level of social insurance if unemployed. At time t, the firms at which they work go bankrupt and exit the market, leaving both workers (involuntarily) unemployed. After some period of time, one of the workers finds a similar job, earning the same wage. The other worker cannot find a similar job and, being the main household breadwinner, accepts a job offer with a lower wage. Clearly, the welfare outcomes of these two workers are very different. Thus, it is important to study not only the probability of becoming unemployed, but also the conditions under which a worker that becomes unemployed finds another job. This is particularly relevant in Latin America, where unequal levels of social insurance imply that many workers may not have the means to search for jobs that provide good matches for their abilities. To determine whether this is the case, it is useful to address the following two questions: Which jobs do the unemployed find? And do they indeed accept lower wages?

To address these questions, the analysis exploits the panel dimensions of the labor force surveys of Argentina and Mexico. In both countries, most unemployed workers find jobs in the uncovered (or informal) sector. In Argentina, 81 percent of the unemployed that find jobs do so in jobs that do not offer social security (see Figure 2.17 and Appendix Table 2.3). In Mexico, the corresponding figure is 61.5 percent (Appendix Table 2.4). A substantial proportion of the unemployed that become employed do so by creating their own jobs and becoming self-employed (28 percent in Argentina, 15.7 percent in Mexico). In comparison, in OECD countries, transitions from unemployment to self-employment are 7 percent (OECD 2000).[16] Moreover, of those that find jobs as employees, a large proportion of the unemployed enter employment via small firms (60 percent in Argentina and 44 percent in Mexico).

These patterns differ across workers (see Appendix Tables 2.3 and 2.4). Unskilled workers are more likely than skilled workers to create their own jobs. They are also more likely than their skilled counterparts to find jobs in small firms and in firms that do not provide the benefits mandated by law. Instead, women and youth are much less likely than men and prime-age workers to exit unemployment creating their own jobs. Moreover, youth and female workers tend to have a higher probability of exiting unemployment through a job in a medium or large firm, and a job that pays social security benefits, compared with men and prime-age workers. This is also true if the analysis adjusts for the percentage of employment in each category by population group (see Appendix Tables 2.3 and 2.4). These results suggest that taking the time to search pays off. Thus, while young and female workers are less likely to exit unemployment in six months, they are more likely to find jobs with benefits than other types of workers.

The evidence suggests that unemployment is associated with wage loss after reemployment. Assessment of the magnitude of this wage loss is based on the average wage change of an individual that is employed in time t and $t+2$, but in $t+1$ is unemployed, involuntarily unemployed, or inactive. However, the assessment requires a basis of comparison because workers who have been employed from t through $t+2$ may also suffer wage losses due to poor economic outcomes. Therefore, a so-called "control group" is constructed. For instance, the control group for an individual who is employed in t, becomes unemployed in $t+1$, and finds a job in $t+2$ is comprised of individuals that ex ante have the same probability of transiting

[16] It should be noted, however, that these estimations do not take into account that some of these flows might be voluntary. That is, some workers might decide to enter a small firm, enter a firm with no social security, or become self-employed.

through those states (although ex post they do not) and share similar demographic characteristics (such as age, education, and gender).

During the 1990s, the average monthly wage loss of an individual who became involuntarily unemployed in $t+1$ and found another job in $t+2$ was very large in Argentina and Mexico. Relative to the control group, displaced workers lost 15 percent of their monthly wages in Mexico and 8 percent in Argentina (see Figure 2.18).[17] Average monthly and hourly wage losses relative to the control group were greater for workers who had an involuntary spell of unemployment (because their firm went bankrupt or they were laid off) compared with workers who voluntarily left the labor force in $t+1$.[18]

In both Mexico and Argentina, on average, displaced men tended to experience higher wage losses than displaced women, both in absolute terms and relative to the counterfactuals (see Figure 2.19). Similarly, displaced workers whose previous jobs did not entitle them to social security and severance pay benefits had higher wage losses than covered workers. Finally, in Mexico, prime-age workers experienced higher wage losses than younger and older workers; in Argentina, the association between age and the cost of unemployment is less clear.

Wage losses associated with the event of re-employment may be related to a number of factors. First, displacement may induce the loss of some firm-specific skills that are useless in other jobs. The available data give some support to this hypothesis. The evidence that wage losses are higher for skilled workers than for unskilled workers suggests the loss of specific skills. This is because skilled workers tend to acquire more specific skills than unskilled workers.

Second, post-displacement wage losses could also be associated with the stigma of unemploy-

[17] The wage loss is computed by subtracting the wage change of the displaced workers from the wage change of the control group.

[18] Involuntary unemployed workers are those who do not have a job, are searching for one, and were laid off or the firm in which they used to work closed. See Appendix Table 2.5.

Figure 2.18 Average Wage Loss of a Displaced Employed Worker in Mexico and Argentina

(Percent)

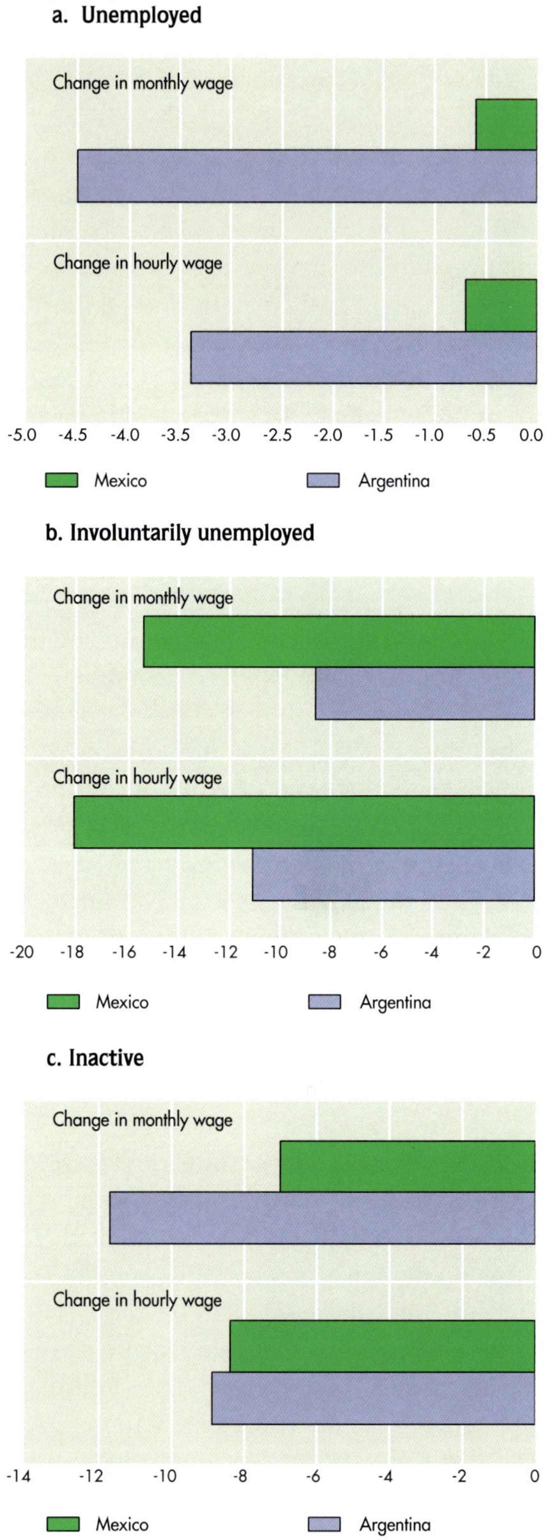

Note: The figure shows the difference between treatment and control groups.
Source: IDB estimates based on EPH-INDEC (1993-2001) for Argentina, and Encuesta Nacional de Empleo Urbano (ENEU)-INEGI (1990-2001) for Mexico.

Figure 2.19 **Average Wage Loss for Displaced Workers by Worker and Job Characteristics in Argentina and Mexico**
(Percent)

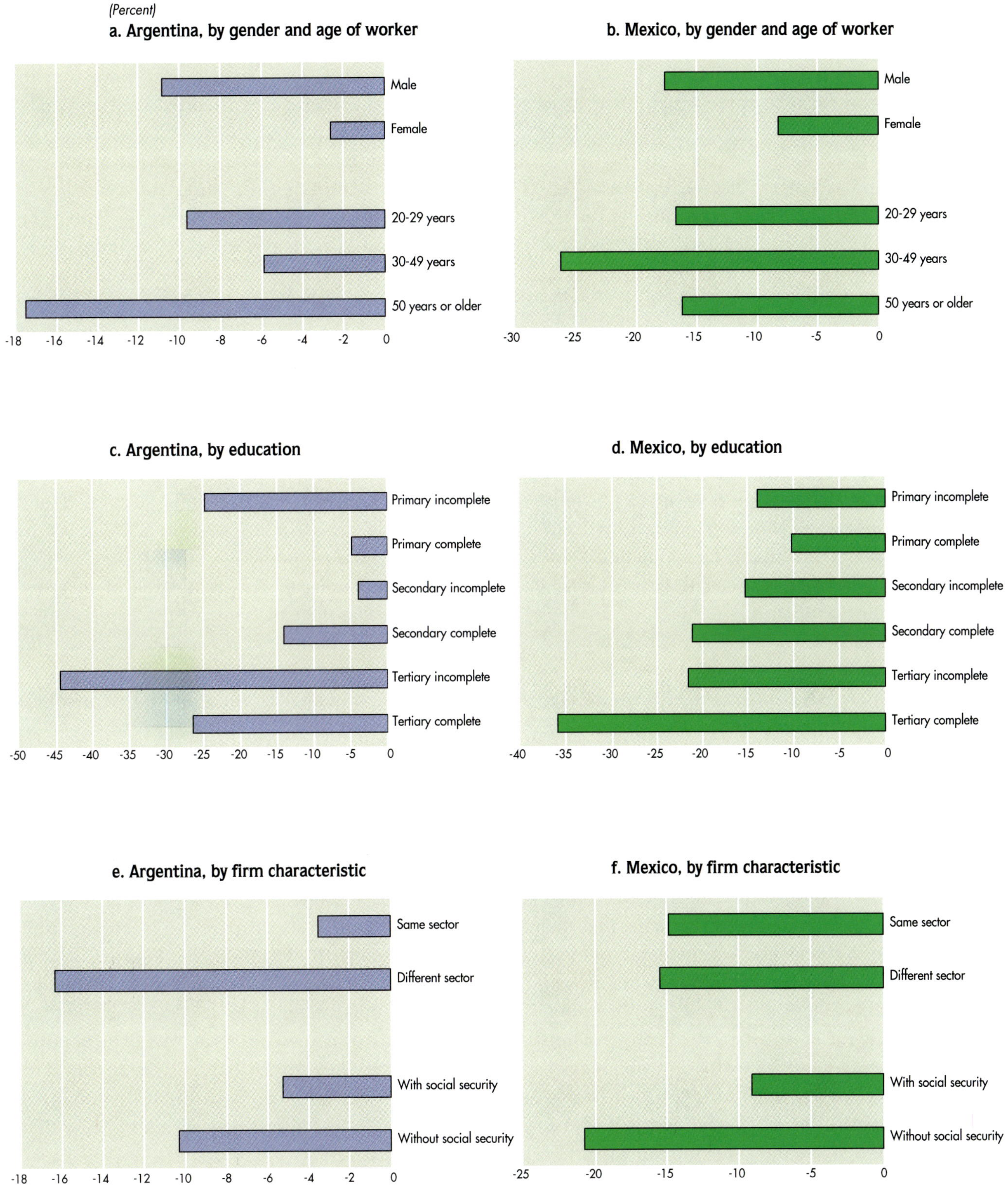

Note: Changes in wages are relative to individuals in a control group. See text discussion.
Source: IDB estimates based on EPH-INDEC (1993-2001) for Argentina, and Encuesta Nacional de Empleo Urbano (ENEU)-INEGI (1990-2001) for Mexico.

ment. If firms are more likely to dismiss lower-performing workers than other workers, laid-off workers may have a "mark" that indicates their lower than expected performance. This could explain why workers take some wage losses after displacement, but not why some types of workers bear higher displacement costs than others.

Recent studies suggest that an important component of post-displacement wage loss is indeed associated with the loss of specific skills. To discriminate between the specific skills and the "stigma" hypotheses, the studies concentrate on workers who have been displaced from firms that have reduced their labor forces by more than 60 percent. The idea here is that when firms have to undergo such large adjustments, they have to lay off their good workers along with their poorer-performing employees. Therefore, the stigma effect should be lower for workers displaced in mass layoffs. Another important advantage of these studies is that they use data that follow individuals for a long time. This allows the authors to measure whether wage losses are permanent or temporary.[19]

In the case of Mexico, Kaplan, Robertson, and Martínez (2003) find that workers displaced in bad periods and in regions of low economic activity endure higher long-term losses compared with workers displaced in better periods and in thriving regions. To estimate these results, the authors use the social security administration data set, which records individual employment histories for affiliated workers from 1993 to 2000. Menezes Filho and others (2002) use a similar data set for 1992 to 1998 and a similar methodology to estimate the displacement cost in Brazil. He finds evidence of long-term wage losses associated with displacement. He also finds that these losses tend to be larger among workers employed in small firms, highly skilled workers, and workers with greater tenure. This evidence suggests that an important reason why displaced workers suffer wage declines is because they are not able to use their specific skills in other jobs.

It is important to mention that mobility is not always bad for workers. For many workers, changing jobs is a way to achieve higher wage gains. In Mexico, people who transit to inactivity and move back to employment do not suffer wage losses. Moreover, some people improve their situation by moving to another job even when they have involuntarily lost their jobs. In addition, note that in every case, the wage gains and losses of those individuals who left employment were higher than the average wage gains and losses for those who did not change (the control group). Similarly, for the case of Brazil, Menezes Filho (2003) finds that many workers who switch jobs receive an increase in pay, and that on average the raise is larger than for workers who remain in the same job.

Job-to-Job Transitions

This chapter has documented the large degree of rotation in registered jobs and how within those jobs, small firms are more volatile. This evidence suggests that there is a large degree of volatility in all sectors of the economy.

This section explores the degree of mobility across jobs. The dualistic view of the labor market maintains that there are two sectors—formal and informal—and that these sectors operate in segmented labor markets, that is, there is limited mobility between the two.

The evidence suggests that there is high mobility across the formal and informal sectors. Some authors define an informal worker as one who does not receive the benefits mandated by labor laws. Using this definition, the average probability of an informal worker transiting to a job with these benefits is 16 percent in Mexico and about 12 percent in Argentina (see Figure 2.20 and Appendix Table 2.6). The probability of the reverse shift is of similar magnitude, 15.6 percent in Mexico and about 10 percent in Argentina. These numbers are large: they imply that in a given period of six months, about 32 percent of the workers in Mexico and 22 percent of the workers in Argentina

[19] Long panel data allow comparing wages some periods before displacement with wages some periods after reemployment. This is important because wages in distressed firms could have started declining some periods prior to the event of displacement. If that is the case, the estimates here underestimate the cost of displacement.

move from a formal to an informal job or from an informal to a formal job. Thus, it is difficult to justify the segmented view of the labor market with this evidence.

Not all workers have the same probability of moving from jobs without benefits to jobs with benefits. The probability is higher for young workers and for the skilled. The lower opportunities are found among women and unskilled workers. These findings suggest that while young workers may enter the market with worse jobs, there is considerable upward mobility for this group. There is also considerable upward mobility for skilled workers. Instead, women and unskilled workers are less likely to move to jobs that provide social security. This could be because these workers are rationed away from those jobs, or because they are less willing to pay for those benefits.[20]

Using instead the International Labour Organization's definition of informal workers, which is based on category of employment, there is also ample evidence of mobility. In a given six-month period, about 23 percent of workers transit from self-employment to wage employment in Mexico and Argentina (see Figure 2.21). The reverse transition is smaller. About 5.3 percent of the wage employees in Mexico and 6.1 percent in Argentina transit from wage employment to self-employment.

About 16-17 percent of the workers employed in firms with fewer than five employees move to larger firms in a given six-month period in Mexico and Argentina (Figure 2.21). The reverse transition is also large. Thus, 6.6 percent of workers employed in large firms and about 25 percent of workers employed in medium firms transit to small firms in a given six-month period.

So regardless of the definition of informal workers considered, the evidence does not support the segmentation approach. At least for Mexico and Argentina, transitions to and from informal work are large, suggesting that even if all transitions from the formal sector to the informal sector were forced by involuntary displacement, opportunities to return to the formal sector abound.

Maloney (1998) studies the evidence on wage changes for movements from the formal sector to

Figure 2.20 Six-month Job Transitions, Mexico and Argentina

(Percentage of workers in the initial state)

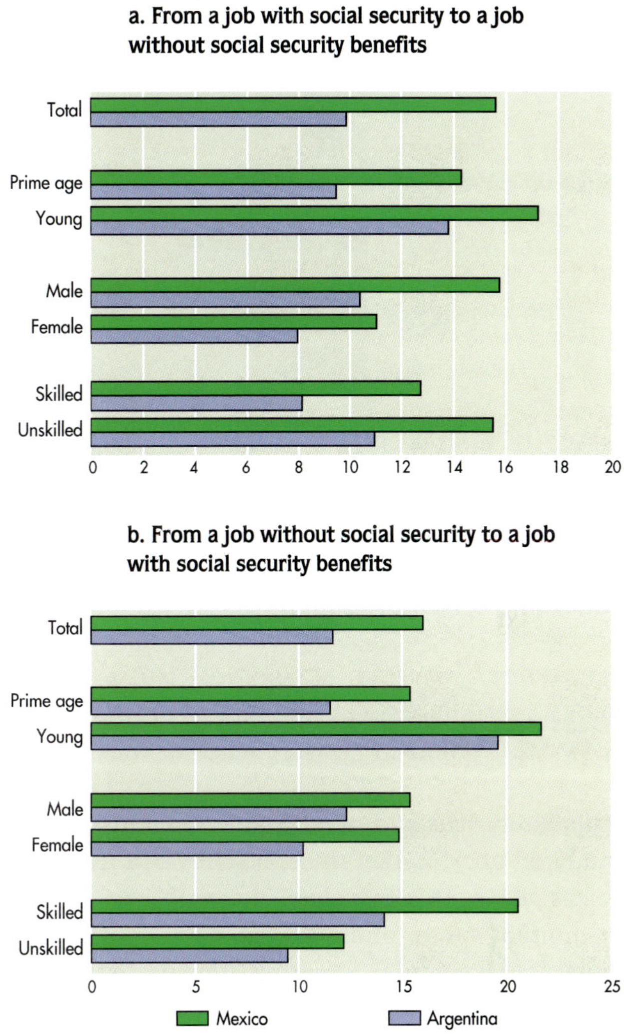

Source: IDB estimates based on EPH-INDEC (1993-2001) for Argentina, and Encuesta Nacional de Empleo Urbano (ENEU)-INEGI (1990-2001) for Mexico.

the informal sector and vice versa, using the same panel data for Mexico as those used in this study. From Maloney's results, it is not clear that the formal sector should always be preferred to the alternatives. Movements from formal salaried employment always lead to increases in wages; movements to formal salaried employment from self-employment or contract employment are associated with a wage decline.

[20] See chapter 7 for a discussion of the incidence of mandatory benefits.

Figure 2.21 Six-month Job Transitions: Small Firms and Self-employment in Mexico and Argentina

Source: IDB estimates based on EPH-INDEC (1993-2001) for Argentina, and Encuesta Nacional de Empleo Urbano (ENEU)-INEGI (1990-2001) for Mexico.

Conclusions

This study has presented a new approach to the study of labor market dynamics in Latin America. It has shown that the relatively small net changes in employment, unemployment, and inactivity hide a large amount of activity in the labor market. This change in view is important not only because it exposes the process by which productivity growth takes place, but also because it reveals the high risk that workers bear throughout the process. For the countries and sectors studied, there are no significant differences between the rates of turnover in developed and emerging economies; however, there are important differences in how well equipped workers are to navigate through this process. In Latin America, current forms of social insurance based on mandatory severance payments only reach a minority of workers. Many workers cannot search for good jobs because they cannot sustain themselves without income. Inefficient job-worker matching could be one explanation for the low productivity levels and low productivity growth rates in Latin America.

This analysis has important consequences for policy. First, it suggests the importance of reducing bureaucratic barriers to the entry and exit of firms and to the reallocation of workers and jobs. Second, it underscores the importance of developing better social insurance systems that extend coverage to the large majority of the workforce (see chapters 7 and 8 for further discussion on this issue). Third, it emphasizes the importance of building flexible and adaptable skills as an insurance mechanism for workers. Fourth, it highlights the challenges inherent in industrial policies targeted at sectors: even within a narrowly defined sector, there will be efficient as well as inefficient firms. Finally, the analysis points to the importance of credit market development as an instrument to prevent the inefficient destruction of specific skills.

Appendix Table 2.1 Reallocation of Employment by Firm Size in Chile and Mexico, 1990s

Variable	Chile, 1990–99	Mexico, 1993–2000[a]	Mexico, 1999–2000[a]
49–99 workers	–0.096	–0.014	–0.030
	(0.007)***	(0.003)***	(0.005)***
100–249 workers	–0.105	–0.026	–0.032
	(0.008)***	(0.003)***	(0.005)***
More than 249 workers	–0.157	–0.043	–0.044
	(0.010)***	(0.003)***	(0.005)***
Second wage quintile	–0.072	–0.028	–0.025
	(0.008)***	(0.003)***	(0.006)***
Third wage quintile	–0.063	–0.044	–0.041
	(0.008)***	(0.003)***	(0.006)***
Fourth wage quintile	–0.058	–0.052	–0.043
	(0.008)***	(0.003)***	(0.006)***
Fifth wage quintile	–0.032	–0.055	–0.040
	(0.008)***	(0.003)***	(0.006)***
Average	0.441	0.159	0.133
Number of observations	48,344	39,822	10,432
Age fixed effect	Yes	No	Yes
Year fixed effect	Yes	Yes	Yes

*** Significant at 1 percent.

[a] Does not include entry or exit of firms.

Note: Results are from OLS regressions using data on manufacturing firms. Standard errors are in parentheses.

Source: IDB calculations.

Appendix Table 2.2 Labor Market Transitions by Region

(Percent)

Region or country	From employment to: Employment	Unemployment	Inactivity	From unemployment to: Employment	Unemployment	Inactivity	From inactivity to: Employment	Unemployment	Inactivity
Latin America									
Argentina, 1993–2001	86.6	6.4	7.0	36.9	36.1	26.9	11.8	8.0	80.2
Mexico, 1990–2001	88.4	2.0	9.6	54.9	15.3	29.8	14.3	1.8	83.9
Peru, 1997–2000	82.6	5.7	11.7	45.1	20.5	34.4	25.7	10.8	63.5
Unweighted average	85.9	4.7	9.4	45.6	24.0	30.4	17.3	6.9	75.9
Eastern Europe									
Bulgaria, 1994–95	84.9	5.9	9.2	32.3	43.3	24.4	9.2	4.4	86.4
Czech Republic, 1994–99	96.1	1.3	2.6	42.9	46.4	10.7	3.9	1.2	94.8
East Germany, 1990–91	83.6	9.3	7.1	35.0	37.3	27.7	16.0	4.1	79.9
Poland, 1992–94	89.1	4.0	7.0	35.8	48.4	15.9	8.5	4.4	87.2
Slovakia, 1994–95	93.2	2.3	4.5	23.7	68.5	7.8	1.8	1.7	96.5
Estonia, 1997–97	91.3	4.7	4.0	37.2	56.4	6.4	7.4	3.8	88.8
Russia, 1992–96	89.6	4.4	6.0	45.8	39.2	15.1	8.2	2.4	89.5
Unweighted average	89.7	4.6	5.8	36.1	48.5	15.4	7.8	3.1	89.0
United States, 1992–93	91.9	2.8	5.3	65.9	5.3	28.8	4.3	16.1	79.6
Western Europe									
Austria, 1995–97				33.6	43.3	23.1			
Belgium, 1990–97				23.6	50.8	25.6			
Denmark, 1990–97				35.3	36.8	27.9			
Finland, 1995–97				26.9	45.9	27.2			
France, 1990–97				32.2	51.6	16.2			
Germany, 1992–97				25.4	49.6	25.0			
Greece, 1990–97				27.1	61.4	11.5			
Ireland, 1990–97				19.1	58.2	22.7			
Italy, 1992–97				22.4	47.4	30.2			
Portugal, 1990–97				35.8	41.8	22.4			
Spain, 1990–97				29.2	63.6	7.2			
Sweden, 1996–97				29.4	52.0	18.6			
United Kingdom, 1990–97				33.3	49.3	17.4			
Unweighted average				28.7	50.1	21.2			

Source: For Argentina, Mexico, the United States, and regional averages, IDB calculations; for Peru, Herrera and Shady (2003); for countries in Eastern Europe, Boeri and Terrel (2001); for countries in Western Europe, OECD (2000).

Appendix Table 2.3 Labor Market Transitions in Argentina, 1993–2001

(Percent)

Transition	All	Prime age	Young	Prime age: Male	Prime age: Female	Prime age: Skilled	Prime age: Unskilled
From unemployment[a]							
To unemployment	36.2	34.4	37.6	37.9	31.1	37.6	32.7
To inactivity	26.9	24.8	27.5	8.4	40.8	23.9	25.4
To employment	36.9	40.8	34.9	53.7	28.1	38.5	41.9
From unemployment to employment[b]							
Owner	0.8	1.0	0.5	0.8	1.5	1.2	0.9
Self-employed	27.9	32.2	13.6	36.3	24.5	27.0	35.5
Wage worker	71.3	66.8	85.8	62.9	74.0	71.8	63.7
Small firm	60.4	61.5	51.0	61.7	61.2	47.5	68.5
Medium firm	22.2	19.7	28.4	20.8	17.6	23.5	18.0
Large firm	17.4	18.8	20.6	17.5	21.2	28.9	13.5
Job with benefits	18.8	19.3	23.4	19.3	19.3	31.1	13.3
Job without benefits	81.2	80.7	76.6	80.7	80.7	68.9	86.7
From unemployment to employment, adjusted by share of employment in each category[a]							
Owner	14.6	15.2	43.7	9.0	53.6	14.7	16.6
Self-employed	151.2	167.3	179.0	190.7	124.9	226.8	143.6
Wage worker	94.0	90.1	94.1	87.1	95.3	90.0	91.0
Small firm	143.6	153.9	135.2	152.0	157.6	180.4	137.0
Medium firm	137.0	135.6	125.5	132.3	142.5	191.4	111.1
Large firm	41.7	41.3	52.0	40.1	43.4	47.2	40.0
Job with benefits	41.0	39.6	49.1	39.8	39.4	53.2	32.2
Job without benefits	150.2	157.2	146.4	156.5	158.3	166.2	147.8
From unemployment to unemployment	36.2	34.4	37.6	37.9	31.1	37.6	32.7
From inactivity to unemployment	8.0	8.5	9.9	17.8	7.6	8.5	8.3
From employment to unemployment	6.4	5.4	10.6	5.9	4.5	3.6	7.1
From employment to unemployment[c]							
Owner	2.4	1.7	8.2	1.6	1.9	1.2	2.4
Self-employed	7.8	7.4	12.6	8.7	5.3	4.9	9.1
Wage worker	6.2	5.0	10.4	5.4	4.4	3.5	6.6
Small firm	8.0	7.0	13.0	7.7	5.9	4.9	8.3
Medium firm	5.7	5.1	8.6	5.7	3.9	3.5	6.7
Large firm	4.3	3.4	9.0	3.8	2.8	2.6	4.7
Job with benefits	3.5	3.2	6.0	3.5	2.6	2.6	3.8
Job without benefits	8.9	7.7	14.1	8.9	6.3	5.1	9.4

[a] Values are the percentage of workers who were unemployed.

[b] Values are the percentage of workers who moved from unemployment to employment.

[c] Values are the percentage of each type of worker that became unemployed.

Source: IDB calculations based on EPH (1993–2001)-INDEC.

Appendix Table 2.4 Labor Market Transitions in Mexico, 1990–2001

(Percent)

Transition	All	Prime age	Young	Prime age: Male	Prime age: Female	Prime age: Skilled	Prime age: Unskilled
From unemployment[a]							
To unemployment	15.4	15.3	15.9	16.3	14.2	18.3	13.3
To inactivity	30.0	24.6	34.0	7.9	47.5	25.1	23.9
To employment	54.6	60.1	50.1	75.8	38.3	56.6	62.8
From unemployment to employment[b]							
Owner	2.4	3.6	0.7	4.6	0.9	4.0	3.3
Self-employed	15.7	22.0	6.8	24.0	17.2	19.7	23.4
Wage worker	81.9	74.3	92.5	71.4	81.9	76.2	73.4
Small firm	44.0	46.6	38.7	49.0	40.9	36.2	53.3
Medium firm	20.2	18.0	23.0	18.0	17.7	18.7	17.4
Large firm	35.8	35.4	38.3	33.0	41.4	45.1	29.3
Job with benefits	38.5	37.2	41.8	35.8	40.1	42.7	33.5
Job without benefits	61.5	62.8	58.2	64.2	59.9	57.3	66.5
From unemployment to employment, adjusted by share of employment in each category[a]							
Owner	48.8	74.4	85.2	75.0	31.5	59.6	105.0
Self-employed	73.4	99.2	65.5	106.7	78.8	105.9	91.8
Wage worker	111.1	102.0	104.2	100.0	108.8	102.2	102.7
Small firm	97.8	107.0	92.1	117.5	87.8	106.6	101.8
Medium firm	76.3	68.3	71.3	66.9	70.0	65.8	71.7
Large firm	125.7	117.5	148.9	105.2	147.0	119.9	125.4
Job with benefits	82.1	74.6	96.5	70.0	83.8	72.0	81.4
Job without benefits	115.8	125.2	102.7	131.3	114.8	140.7	113.0
From unemployment to unemployment	15.4	15.3	15.9	16.3	14.2	18.3	13.3
From inactivity to unemployment	1.9	1.4	2.8	6.2	1.2	2.4	1.1
From employment to unemployment	2.0	1.6	3.6	1.8	1.1	1.4	1.7
From employment to unemployment[c]							
Owner	1.1	1.1	1.9	1.1	0.8	0.8	1.4
Self-employed	1.7	1.6	3.5	1.9	1.0	1.8	1.5
Wage worker	2.2	1.7	3.6	1.9	1.2	1.4	1.8
Small firm	2.1	1.7	3.6	2.0	1.2	1.7	1.8
Medium firm	2.7	2.1	3.7	2.4	1.6	2.1	2.1
Large firm	1.8	1.3	3.4	1.5	0.9	1.2	1.4
Job with benefits	1.8	1.3	3.3	1.8	0.9	1.2	1.5
Job without benefits	2.2	1.8	3.8	2.2	1.3	1.7	1.9

[a] Values are the percentage of workers who were unemployed.
[b] Values are the percentage of workers who moved from unemployment to employment.
[c] Values are the percentage of each type of worker that became unemployed.
Source: IDB calculations based on ENEU (1990–2001)-INEGI.

Appendix Table 2.5 Labor Market Transitions by Group Including Voluntary and Involuntary Unemployment in Argentina and Mexico, 1990s

(Percent)

Country and transition	Unskilled	Prime-age skilled	Female	Prime-age male	Young	Prime age	All
Argentina, 1993–2001							
From employed to							
Employed	86.2	92.8	85.0	91.9	79.8	89.2	86.8
Voluntarily unemployed	1.0	0.7	1.0	0.8	2.4	0.9	1.1
Involuntarily unemployed	6.0	2.8	3.4	5.1	7.4	4.5	5.1
Inactive	6.8	3.7	10.5	2.2	10.4	5.4	7.0
Mexico, 1990–2001							
From employed to							
Employed	90.6	94.0	83.3	96.8	82.4	91.9	88.4
Voluntarily unemployed	0.8	0.6	0.6	0.7	2.1	0.7	1.1
Involuntarily unemployed	0.9	0.8	0.5	1.1	1.4	0.9	1.0
Inactive	7.8	4.6	15.6	1.3	14.0	6.5	9.6

Note: Involuntarily unemployed workers are those who do not have a job, are searching for one, and were laid off or the firm in which they used to work closed.
Source: IDB estimates based on EPH-INDEC (1993–2001) for Argentina, and Encuesta Nacional de Empleo Urbano (ENEU)-INEGI (1990–2001) for Mexico.

Appendix Table 2.6 Labor Market Transitions by Job Type in Argentina and Mexico

(Percent)

Transition	All	Prime age	Young	Prime age		Prime age	
				Male	Female	Skilled	Unskilled
Argentina, 1993–2001							
From employment[a]							
To unemployment	6.4	5.4	10.6	5.9	4.5	3.6	7.1
To inactivity	7.0	5.4	10.3	2.2	10.5	3.7	6.8
To employment	86.6	89.2	79.1	91.9	85.0	92.7	86.1
To employed[b]							
Owner – owner	58.3	55.2	25.0	57.0	48.5	61.4	43.5
Owner – self-employed	27.6	29.5	25.0	28.7	32.6	25.4	38.1
Owner – wage worker	14.0	15.3	50.0	14.3	18.9	13.2	18.4
Self-employed – owner	7.2	7.5	2.3	8.8	4.9	10.9	5.2
Self-employed – self-employed	70.1	69.7	48.3	70.0	69.0	69.8	69.6
Self-employed – wage worker	22.7	22.9	49.3	21.2	26.1	19.3	25.2
Wage worker – owner	0.8	0.9	0.4	1.0	0.6	1.0	0.6
Wage worker – self-employed	6.1	6.5	4.5	6.6	6.3	4.4	8.5
Wage worker – wage worker	93.1	92.6	95.1	92.4	93.1	94.6	90.9
Small firm – small firm	83.7	82.3	73.4	82.3	87.2	81.3	86.3
Small firm – medium firm	10.9	12.0	18.7	12.0	7.9	12.3	9.3
Small firm – large firm	5.3	5.7	7.9	5.7	4.9	6.4	4.4
Medium firm – small firm	16.8	18.9	19.5	18.9	11.4	12.7	19.6
Medium firm – medium firm	60.8	58.5	59.4	58.5	65.7	62.1	60.7
Medium firm – large firm	22.3	22.5	21.1	22.5	22.9	25.2	19.7
Large firm – small firm	7.4	7.4	9.4	7.4	6.5	5.5	9.2
Large firm – medium firm	18.8	17.9	24.2	17.9	19.1	17.2	19.9
Large firm – large firm	73.8	74.7	66.4	74.7	74.4	77.3	70.9
With social security – with social security	90.1	90.5	86.2	89.6	92.0	91.9	89.0
With social security – without social security	9.9	9.5	13.8	10.4	8.0	8.1	11.0
Without social security – with social security	11.7	11.5	19.6	12.3	10.2	14.1	9.4
Without social security – without social security	88.3	88.5	80.4	87.7	89.8	85.9	90.6
Mexico, 1990–2001							
From employment[a]							
To unemployment	2.0	1.6	3.6	1.8	1.1	1.4	1.7
To inactivity	9.6	6.5	14.0	1.3	15.6	4.6	7.7
To employment	88.4	91.9	82.4	96.9	83.3	94.0	90.6
To employed[b]							
Owner – owner	54.3	54.2	35.8	54.6	52.4	62.0	45.5
Owner – self-employed	26.4	26.3	27.3	25.8	30.5	19.9	34.0
Owner – wage worker	19.3	19.5	36.9	19.6	17.1	18.1	20.5
Self-employed – owner	8.8	9.4	5.0	11.4	4.6	14.1	7.8
Self-employed – self-employed	67.8	67.4	51.2	63.7	77.4	63.4	69.3
Self-employed – wage worker	23.3	23.2	43.7	24.9	18.0	22.5	22.9
Wage worker – owner	1.5	1.8	0.5	2.4	0.5	1.9	1.6
Wage worker – self-employed	5.3	5.5	3.4	6.5	3.4	2.9	7.7
Wage worker – wage worker	93.2	92.7	96.1	91.1	96.0	95.2	90.7
Small firm – small firm	82.5	82.7	73.8	82.7	87.2	81.3	85.2
Small firm – medium firm	10.2	10.0	16.4	10.0	7.3	9.0	9.3
Small firm – large firm	7.3	7.3	9.8	7.3	5.5	9.7	5.5
Medium firm – small firm	24.5	25.5	24.3	25.5	18.0	18.4	26.2
Medium firm – medium firm	50.9	49.2	51.9	49.2	56.1	51.0	51.2
Medium firm – large firm	24.6	25.3	23.8	25.3	25.8	30.5	22.6
Large firm – small firm	6.6	7.0	7.4	7.0	3.4	4.0	7.8
Large firm – medium firm	9.0	8.9	12.7	8.9	5.8	5.8	10.5
Large firm – large firm	84.4	84.2	80.0	84.2	90.8	90.2	81.7
With social security – with social security	84.4	85.7	82.7	84.2	89.0	87.2	84.5
With social security – without social security	15.6	14.3	17.3	15.8	11.0	12.8	15.5
Without social security – with social security	16.0	15.4	21.7	15.4	14.8	20.5	12.2
Without social security – without social security	84.0	84.6	78.3	84.6	85.2	79.5	87.8

[a] Values are the percentage of workers who were employed.

[b] Values are the percentage of workers in each category who moved from the first state to the second. For example, for owner – self-employed, the value is the percentage of workers who were firm owners who became self-employed.

Source: IDB calculations based on EPH-INDEC for Argentina and ENEU-INEGI for Mexico.

Chapter

3

Changing Patterns in the Supply of Labor

In a typical workday, more than 210 million Latin Americans between the ages of 15 and 64 offer their skills to the labor market as wage earners, self-employed workers, employers, or job seekers. The labor force has increased at a remarkable pace during the past few years: about five million additional workers join the labor supply every year. Between 1990 and 2000, the labor force grew 2.5 percent a year, and in the previous decades the pace was even higher: more than 3 percent a year in the 1980s and 1970s.[1]

Although the rate of growth of the labor force is predicted to decline to 2 percent in the current decade and to 1.4 percent in the 2010s, its pace of increase will still be high compared with that of other regions. For example, although the labor force in Latin America was about the same size as the labor force in North America between 1950 and 1980, they are rapidly diverging. In 1980, the labor force in the two regions comprised about 120 million workers. Currently, the labor force in Latin America is 26 percent larger than that in North America, and by 2010 this gap is projected to swell to 87 million workers (Figure 3.1).[2]

This comparison shows the magnitude of the challenge the region faces in the years ahead to absorb the increasing number of workers in productive activities and offer them satisfying working conditions. It also reveals a great opportunity because the region is in the midst of a unique demographic phase in which the number of people of working age is growing substantially faster than the number of those more likely to be economically dependent on account of their age. Thus, if the region capitalizes on this phase, it will be able to raise per capita income levels and improve social and working conditions.

Labor supply trends are determined to a large extent by demographic trends that can be taken as given in the medium term. However, labor supply is also affected by the labor force participation decisions of those of working age and by the possibility that the supply of workers in each country is expanded by immigration or reduced by emigration flows. These factors also depend on demographic forces, but other economic, social, and cultural factors influence them as well. Demography, labor force participation, and migration decisions alter not only the size of the labor force, but also its composition in age, gender, and other dimensions. These changes in turn affect the behavior of the

[1] Based on calculations from the ILO LABORSTA database.

[2] The supply of labor in Latin America and the Caribbean in 2010 and 2020 is predicted by multiplying the estimated regional labor force participation rate by population projections from the United Nations. The participation rate for the region is estimated from a weighted fixed-effects regression of participation rates from a panel of 93 household surveys for 18 countries in 1990-2000 (sample size 93). The regression controls for a year trend as well as age structure, specifically, the share of population in the 15-24, 25-49, and 50-64 year age groups.

Figure 3.1 The Labor Force in Latin America and North America, 1950-2010
(Millions of people)

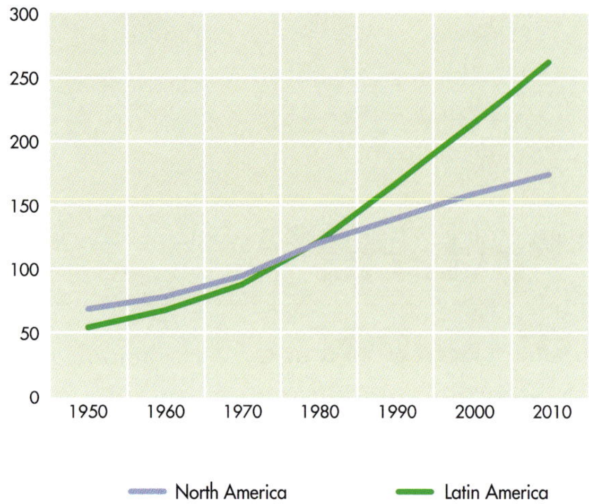

Note: North America includes Canada, the United States, Bermuda, Greenland, and Saint Pierre and Miquelon.
Source: ILO LABORSTA Labour Statistics Database copyright 1998-2003 for Latin America and the Caribbean and North America from 1950 to 2000. ILO projections for North America in 2010, and IDB projections for Latin America and the Caribbean in 2010.

labor market. This is because the propensity to become unemployed, change jobs, or be self-employed differs by age and gender. The purpose of this chapter is to illustrate these changing labor supply trends, their main driving forces, and their implications for the functioning of the labor market in Latin America and the Caribbean.

A Labor Supply Panorama

Demographic trends, changes in labor force participation, and migration flows determine the size and trends of the supply of labor. For Latin America and the Caribbean as a whole, the increase of 47 million workers in the labor supply during the 1990s, representing an annual rate of growth of 2.5 percent, was due mostly to the steady growth of the population of working age. More precisely, demographic trends accounted for 92 percent of the increase, changes in labor force participation accounted for 13 percent, and net migration outflows accounted for -5 percent (a decline in the size of the labor force).[3]

In many respects, countries in Latin America and the Caribbean are heterogeneous, and this is also the case with respect to labor supply trends. In most of the poorest countries, growth in the supply of labor exceeded 3 percent a year during the 1990s. However, Mexico, Costa Rica, and Venezuela, three relatively high-income countries, experienced similar rates. In Bolivia, Guyana, and Haiti, which are among the poorest countries, the labor supply grew by less than 3 percent a year. Only five countries had labor supply growth rates below 2 percent (Barbados, Guyana, Jamaica, Suriname, and Uruguay). These countries are small, but otherwise vary in terms of income level and other aspects of economic and social development.

Without exception, demography is the main driving force in the increase in labor supply in the countries of the region (Figure 3.2a). However, while in Uruguay it is responsible for an annual increase of just 0.8 percent (three-quarters of total growth in the labor supply), in Nicaragua demographic trends cause an annual increase of 3.6 percent (97 percent of total growth).

Although less important than demography, labor force participation changes are a major source of expansion of the labor supply (Figure 3.2b). This is especially so when excluding Brazil, which represents about a third of the total Latin American labor force, but was one of only three countries (along with Haiti and Jamaica) where participation rates declined in the 1990s.[4] Excluding Brazil, changes in labor force participation con-

[3] A simple equation was used to decompose the increase in the labor supply into (1) the change in the size of the working age population times the regional participation rate in 2000 plus (2) the change in the regional participation rate times the population size in 1990. The first component can be broken up into the part contributed by natural population increase as well as the part contributed by net migration if the participation rate of migrants is assumed to be the same as for nonmigrants. The source of data for labor supply and participation rates is the International Labour Organization LABORSTA Labour Statistics Database. Migration data were available only for 1995-2000 from United Nations (2002) and net migration rates were assumed to be the same for 1990-95. In addition, 76 percent of migrants were assumed to be in the working age population according to Clark, Hatton, and Williamson (2003, Table 3).

[4] Although participation rates for 15-64 year olds declined in Brazil during the 1990s according to ILO data, national household survey data for Brazil do not exhibit a decline in participation rates for the same age group.

Figure 3.2 Factors Driving Growth in the Supply of Labor in Latin America and the Caribbean, 1990-2000
(Percent)

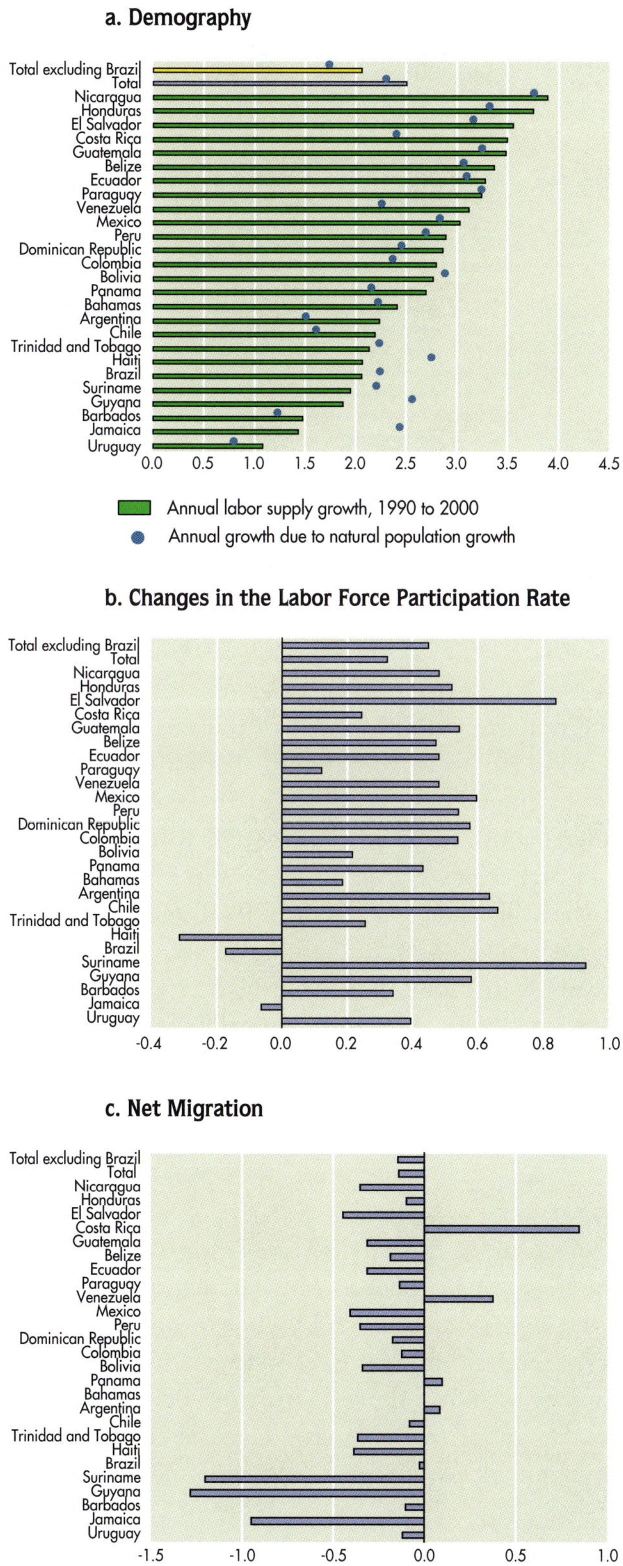

Source: IDB calculations based on ILO LABORSTA database for 1990 and 2000, and United Nations Popuation Division (2002) for net migration rates for 1995-2000.

tributed 22 percent of the expansion of the labor supply. This contribution was more than 30 percent in Chile, Guyana, Suriname, and Uruguay, and less than 10 percent in only a handful of countries.

For the region as a whole, net migration flows are not a major factor behind the changing patterns in the labor supply. Thus, they account for a decline of the labor force of just 0.14 percent a year, which represents about 5 percent of the total growth rate. However, Latin America has the highest net emigration rates in the world. Especially among the English-speaking Caribbean countries, emigration rates are astonishingly high. Figure 3.2c shows that the flow of migrants to other countries reduces Jamaica's labor force growth rate by 1 percentage point. Other sources of data, which cover migration flows only to the United States, show that large migration flows also affect labor supply trends and composition in other Caribbean and Central American countries.

Subsequent sections of this chapter discuss in greater detail the influence of demographic trends, changes in labor force participation, and migration flows on the composition of the labor force and the functioning of Latin American labor markets. However, it is useful to look at how some of the main features of the supply of labor have changed in the past decade.

The labor force in Latin America is aging and becoming more gender balanced, urban, and educated. The typical worker was 35.2 years old in 2000 and 34.4 in 1990. Considering the diversity of demographic conditions among the Latin American countries, the average age of the labor force is remarkably similar across countries. Of the 12 countries in Figure 3.3, Argentina has the oldest labor force, with an average age of 37.4 years, while Nicaragua has the youngest one, with an average age of 32.8 years. It is important to notice that the average age of the total population of working age is somewhat lower (35.7 in Argentina and 31.5 in Nicaragua). This reflects the fact that labor force participation rates are lowest for the younger groups. Labor force participation rates tend to decline after age 50, but the relative size of the older age groups is relatively too small to shift the calculation in that direction.[5]

[5] Unless otherwise noted, the household surveys and years used are those outlined in Appendix Table 3.1.

Figure 3.3 **Average Age of the Labor Force**

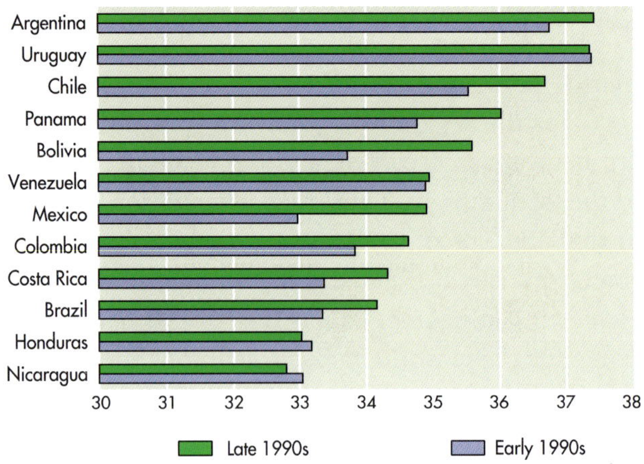

Source: IDB calculations based on household surveys.

Figure 3.4 **Women in the Labor Force**

(Women per 10 men)

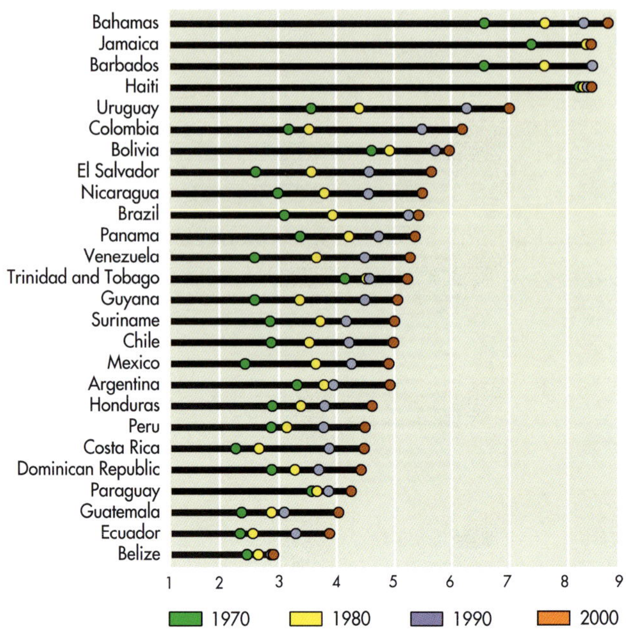

Source: World Bank (various years).

The labor force is aging in almost all the countries. The most extreme cases are Bolivia and Mexico, where the typical worker is nearly two years older than at the beginning of the 1990s. In Bolivia, a larger proportion of those between 50 and 64 years old are participating in the labor market, while in Mexico, labor force participation among the young has declined. However, the typical worker in Honduras, Nicaragua, and Uruguay is now slightly younger than a decade ago, in the first two cases due to the large numbers of young entering the labor market, in the latter due to greater participation of young people, especially women. Although both the male and female components of the labor force are aging in most countries, the average age of women is increasing faster than that of men. The reason is that larger proportions of women in their forties and fifties are participating at higher rates in the labor market. Although the age profile of participation is becoming more similar between women and men, large differences remain in average job seniority because labor force attachment is less interrupted for men than women.

The gender gap in labor force participation has been declining for several decades in Latin America. In the 1960s, for every 10 men in the workforce, there were only three women. This ratio increased to four in 1980s and to more than 5.5 in 2000 (Figure 3.4).[6] The highest shares of working women are found in some of the English-speaking Caribbean countries: in the Bahamas, Barbados, and Jamaica, there are nine women for every 10 men in the workforce. Although women in these countries have greater labor force participation than they had several decades ago, they have always had much higher participation rates than women in most Latin American countries, which suggests that cultural patterns may be behind these differences. Surprisingly, however, the country with the lowest share of women in the workforce is another English-speaking country: Belize, where there are three times more men than women in the labor force.

Among the Spanish-speaking countries, the highest female labor force participation rates are in Uruguay, Colombia, and Bolivia, a remarkable fact given the differences in economic and social development among these countries. Ecuador, Guatemala, and Paraguay have large shares of native indigenous populations, and are among the coun-

[6] In order to provide a long-term perspective, World Bank data are used in Figure 3.4, which is not strictly comparable with other estimates used in this Report, which are based on recent household surveys.

tries with the lowest female labor force participation rates. However, Costa Rica and the Dominican Republic also have relatively low female labor force participation rates.

Overall, the labor force in Latin America is becoming more gender balanced. This has been the trend in every country, with the exception of Haiti, which had the highest share of women in the labor market among all the countries in the region in the 1960s and 1970s.

The labor force in Latin America is becoming increasingly urban, partly as a direct result of the process of urbanization, and partly due to the increasing rates of labor force participation among urban women and, to a lesser extent, the declining labor force participation rates of children in rural areas. Available data provide a complete picture of these trends only since the early 1990s (Figure 3.5).[7] The share of the labor force residing in urban areas is highest in the countries that have traditionally enjoyed the highest income levels in the region, such as Uruguay, Argentina, and Venezuela. It is lowest in poor countries, such as Haiti and Guatemala. However, the pace of urbanization of the labor force does not seem to be a mechanistic result of economic growth: Costa Rica is among the least urban countries in Latin America in spite of its high level of development. Meanwhile, urbanization is advancing most rapidly in three of the poorest countries of the region (Haiti, Honduras, and Bolivia), none of which has experienced stellar rates of growth.

The typical Latin American worker has about eight years of education. Although education levels have been increasing, the pace has been notoriously slow, as is discussed in greater detail in the section on education in this chapter. During the 1990s, the average gain in education by the typical worker was a mere 0.6 years. According to estimates based on household surveys, Mexico was one of the few countries where progress was substantial: the average years of education of the workforce went from 7.3 in the early 1990s to 8.5 in 2000.

A large proportion of the labor force in most Latin American countries consists of workers with no more than primary education: about 40 percent of today's Latin American workers never went to

Figure 3.5 Share of the Labor Force Residing in Urban Areas
(Percent)

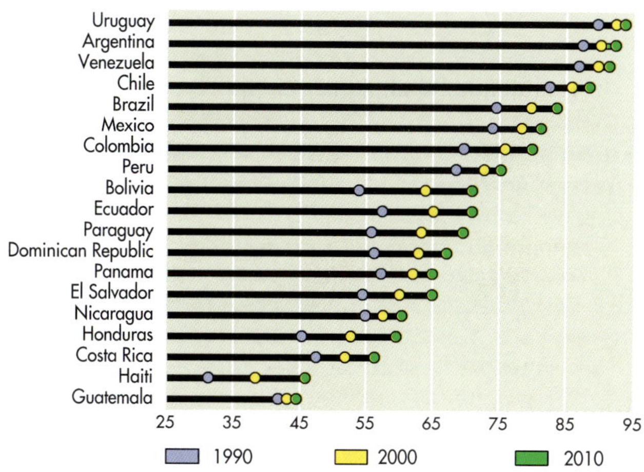

Source: ECLAC (1999).

secondary school. Although this proportion has declined from 45 percent a decade ago and more than 50 percent in earlier decades, in Honduras, Nicaragua, and other low-income countries, more than half the workers have at most primary education (Figure 3.6).

By international standards, the share of workers with (at least some) tertiary education is not low in most Latin American countries. About one of every four workers in Argentina, Chile, and Panama has some college education. In Costa Rica, Uruguay, Venezuela, and even low-income Bolivia, more than 15 percent of the workforce has some university education. As has long been recognized, the main weakness of education systems in Latin America does not lie in their ability to attract students who have completed secondary education to the numerous universities and other post-secondary education institutions, but to retain children at school until they complete secondary education.

In summary, the supply of labor is still growing rapidly in Latin America due to the combined forces of demography, labor force participation, and migration. Along with changing education patterns, these forces are also reshaping the composition of the labor force, which is becoming older,

[7] The trends in urbanization were estimated and predicted by Centro Latinoamericano de Demografía (CELADE) and published by ECLAC (1999).

Figure 3.6 Share of the Labor Force by Education Level
(Percent)

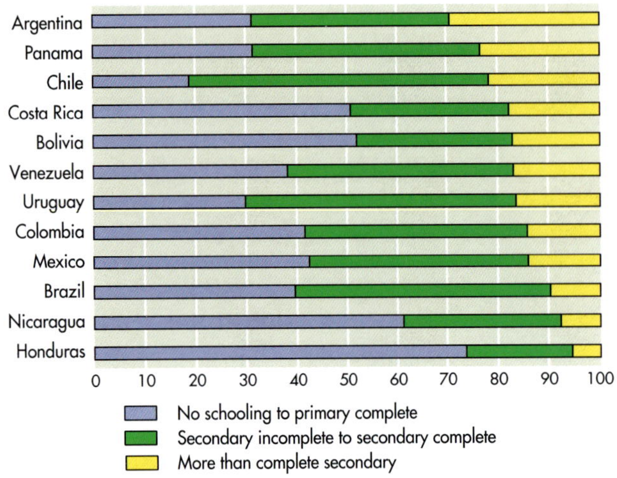

Source: IDB household surveys.

Figure 3.7 Population Growth in Latin America and the Caribbean, 1950-2010
(Average annual percent)

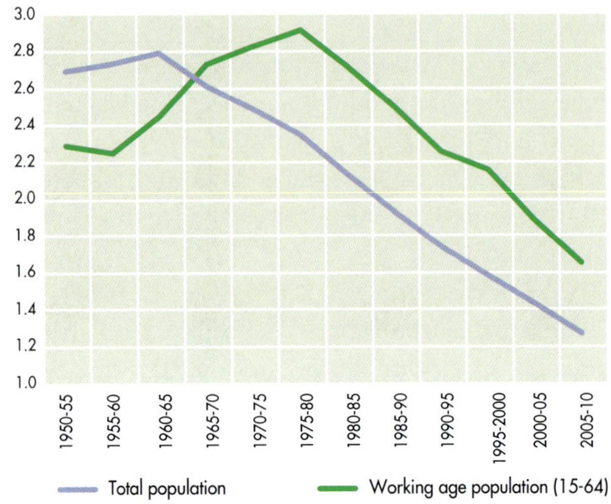

Source: United Nations Population Division (2002).

more gender balanced, more urban, and more educated. As the rest of this chapter discusses, each of these forces influences labor market behavior.

The Demographic Transition

The main force behind the changing patterns in the supply of labor is the demographic transition, that is, the process of change in the population from an equilibrium of high birth and mortality rates to one with low birth and mortality rates. During the several decades that this process takes, the rate of growth, age, and gender composition of the labor force experience important changes.

The typical demographic transition begins with a sharp decline in the mortality rate, usually as a result of improved health conditions that reduce infant and child mortality rates. After a lag, this has an effect on fertility as parents gradually become aware that their children are more likely to survive and expectations about family size adjust. The lag between falling mortality rates and declining birth rates means that countries first see a rapid growth in population, which then gradually subsides as the demographic transition matures. The speed of this process determines the relative size of each generation and the population share of each age group.

Population growth in Latin America peaked around 1965, at a rate of about 2.8 percent a year. Total population in the region is growing 1.4 percent a year (United Nations 2002). With a lag, these trends are reflected in the rate of growth of the working age population, which peaked around 1980 and has been declining since then (Figure 3.7). These trends are also observed in the labor force, although not in a mechanistic way because the labor force participation of adult women tends to increase when fertility declines, but that of young men and women is likely to decline as families become more able to give their children more years of education.[8]

The rapid growth of the working age population toward the middle of the demographic transition creates a window of opportunity, whereas dependency rates decline. Since fertility rates are declining, the share of those below the official working age tends to fall, while the share of those beyond the typical retirement age is still small. After several decades, the process reverses as a large segment of the population becomes older and dependency rates increase.

[8] An adult worker is defined as age 25 or older.

Possibilities for economic and social progress are extraordinary during this intermediate stage of the demographic transition. There is in effect a window of opportunity to increase the incomes of families (and thus the economy as a whole), boost savings and investment, and offer a better education to what will be a smaller share of children in the new generation. But it can also be a time of great challenge, especially from the point of view of labor, because sources of employment must be created quickly and employment conditions must be adapted to a labor force that is changing fast in age, gender, and education composition. The final section of this chapter discusses important implications for labor and social security policies.

A Closer Look

Countries can be classified according to their current stage in the demographic transition. Bolivia and Haiti are the only two Latin American countries still in the early stage in this process, with crude birth rates substantially higher than in all other countries and death rates in the uppermost range. The moderate population growth rates in these two countries are lower than predicted by the classic demographic model, but this is likely explained by the high rates of net emigration (Table 3.1). Belize, Guatemala, Honduras, Nicaragua, and Paraguay are in the second stage of the demographic transition, in which mortality rates have already declined substantially but birth rates are still high (around 30 per thousand). Population growth rates in these countries are the highest in the region, all above 2 percent.

Most Latin American countries have already passed the first two stages of the demographic transition. Most of the middle-income countries are already experiencing low mortality rates and moderate, although still declining, birth rates. Population growth rates in these countries range between 1.2 percent in the case of Brazil and slightly below 2 percent in the cases of Costa Rica, Panama, and Venezuela.

The English-speaking Caribbean countries and Argentina, Chile, and Uruguay are the only countries in the region already in the last stage of the demographic transition. Birth rates in these countries are typically below 20 per thousand, and death rates are between low and intermediate (possibly reflecting the growing share of the older groups). Population growth rates in this group of countries are below 1.2 percent a year (partly due to high emigration rates among the Caribbean countries).

Latin America as a whole is already in the midst of the period of demographic opportunity. The (adjusted) dependency rate has been declining since the early 1960s and is already approaching its lowest point, before starting to increase rapidly. This means that the share of those of working age is now approaching its peak. By 2020, about 70 percent of the Latin American population will be of working age.[9] However, countries in the first two stages of the demographic transition are just beginning to enter this period of opportunity. In Bolivia, the dependency rate is just starting to decline, and in Nicaragua—a typical country in the second stage—is yet to decline markedly for at least two decades. At the other extreme of the regional demographic spectrum, Chile is already experiencing a mild increase in the dependency ratio, due to the increasing share of older groups, a trend that will intensify in the next three decades (Figure 3.8).

Labor force trends clearly reflect these patterns of the demographic transition. Bolivia, still in the first stage of the demographic transition, is one of the few countries where the rate of growth of the economically active population is predicted to be higher over the current decade (2000-2010) than in the previous decade. However, the highest rates of growth of the labor force are found for countries in the second stage of the transition. The number of workers in Guatemala, Honduras, Nicaragua, and Paraguay grew at about 3.6 percent a year in the previous decade and will grow at only a slightly lower rate over 2000-2010. The large group of countries in the third stage of the demographic transition has

[9] The adjusted dependency rate reaches its lowest level around a decade earlier than the share of those of working age reaches its peak because of the adjustment factor, whereas each person 65 years or older weighs as much as four children in the calculation of that rate (reflecting the relative costs of their social security needs).

Table 3.1 Demographic Transition in Latin America and the Caribbean

Country	Projected crude death rate[a] 2000-2005	Projected crude birth rate[a] 2000-2005	Projected net migration rate[b] 2000-2005	Projected population growth 2000-2005	Projected labor supply growth[c] 2000-2010
Stage I: High mortality, high fertility, population growth typically about 2.5 percent with 0 net migration					
Bolivia	8.1	29.3	-2.3	1.9	2.9
Haiti	14.6	30.3	-2.5	1.3	1.8
Stage II: Drop in mortality, high fertility, higher population growth (typically about 3 percent with 0 net migration)					
Belize	5.3	27.0	-1.2	2.1	3.7
Guatemala	6.7	34.2	-2.0	2.6	3.5
Honduras	5.7	30.0	-0.9	2.3	3.0
Nicaragua	5.1	31.6	-2.2	2.4	3.5
Paraguay	5.1	29.6	-0.9	2.4	3.0
Stage III: Low mortality, falling fertility, lower population growth (typically about 2 percent with 0 net migration)					
El Salvador	5.9	25.1	-3.7	1.6	2.9
Venezuela	4.6	22.8	0.3	1.9	2.6
Ecuador	5.8	23.0	-2.3	1.5	2.4
Peru	6.1	23.3	-2.2	1.5	2.0
Mexico	5.0	22.4	-2.9	1.5	2.0
Dominican Republic	7.0	23.3	-1.4	1.5	1.9
Costa Rica	3.9	19.1	4.1	1.9	2.5
Colombia	5.4	22.2	-0.9	1.6	1.9
Panama	5.0	22.7	0.7	1.8	2..7
Brazil	7.1	19.7	-0.1	1.2	1.8
Stage IV: Low mortality, low fertility, low population growth (typically about 1 percent with 0 net migration)					
Bahamas	8.2	19.4	0.0	1.10	1.3
Jamaica	5.7	20.5	-5.6	0.92	2.0
Trinidad and Tobago	7.3	13.7	-2.9	0.34	1.4
Chile	5.6	18.2	-0.3	1.23	1.2
Argentina	7.6	19.0	0.3	1.17	1.9
Uruguay	9.1	16.8	-0.6	0.72	1.1
Barbados	7.8	12.2	-0.9	0.35	0.3

[a] Number of deaths (or live births) during the year per 1,000 mid-year population.

[b] The number of immigrants minus the number of emigrants over that period per 1,000 population.

[c] Labor supply projections for 2010 are predicted from a weighted fixed effects regression of participation rates from household survey data for 18 countries over 1990 to 2000 (n=93). The regression controls for a year trend as well as the age structure.

Note: The crude death rate can increase in stage IV as the population of elderly persons grows. For example, the share of persons over age 60 was greater than 10 percent in 1995 in Argentina, Uruguay, and Barbados, and these countries also have the highest crude death rates among the stage IV countries.

Source: United Nations Population Division (2002).

experienced slower rates of growth of the labor force, a trend that will become stronger in the current decade. Typically, in this group of countries, the rate of growth of the labor force will decline from 2.3 to 1.5 percent from the current to the next decade. Finally, in the group most advanced in the transition, the labor force will grow at a moderate rate over the next two decades, below 1.5 percent (Figure 3.9).

It is important to mention that the calculations of these projections assumed that participation rates of the working age population would increase 2 percentage points per decade, which reflects past trends. The projections also take into account the changing age composition of the population because there is a strong relationship between age and labor force participation profiles. Of course, the projections are a gross simplification. As the next section shows, labor force partici-

Figure 3.8 **Demographic Opportunity: The Dependency Ratio**

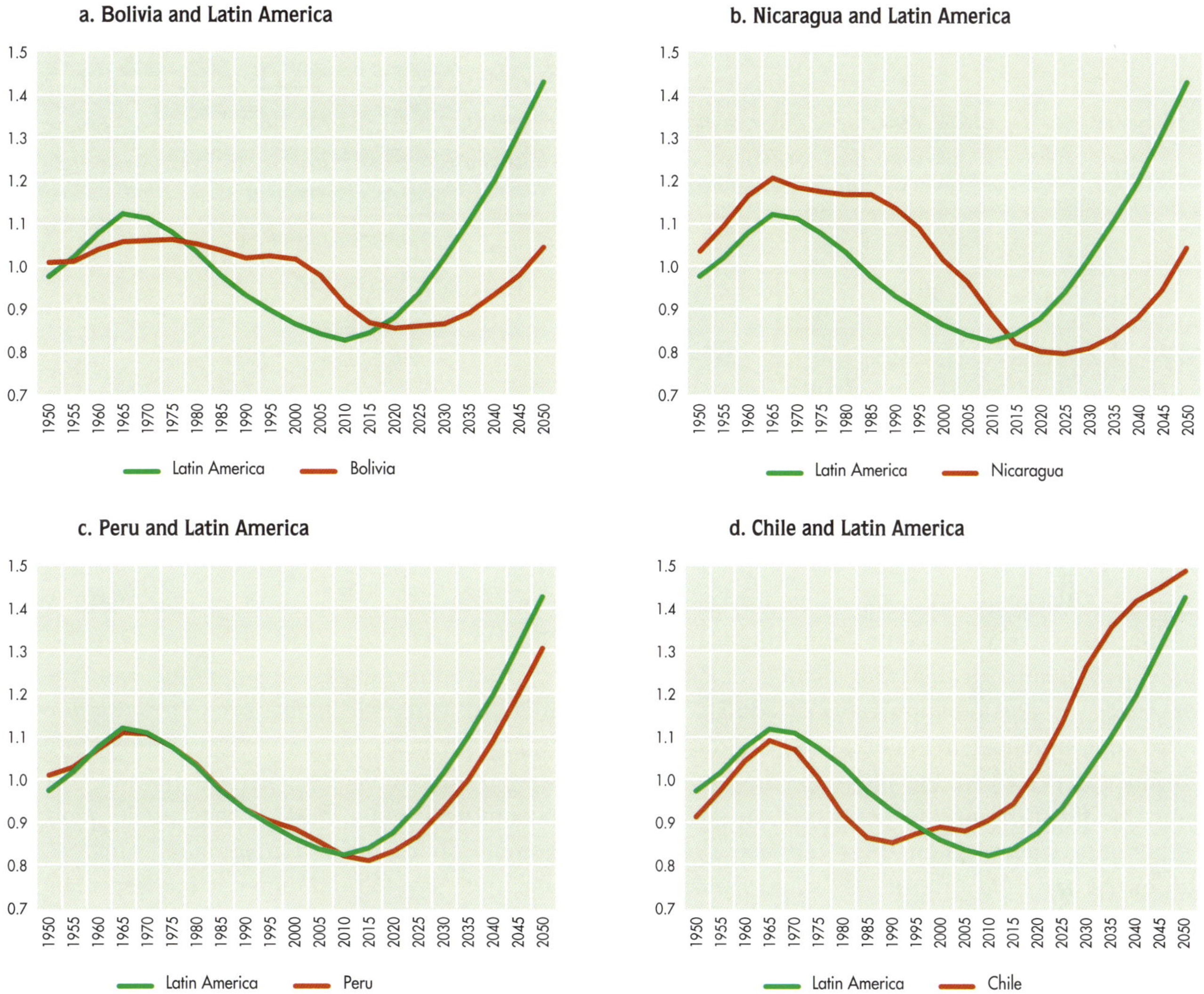

Note: Dependency ratio = (population age 0 to 14 + 4 * population age 65 and older) / population age 15 to 64.
Source: United Nations Population Division (2002).

pation is governed by a host of factors, some of which are difficult to forecast years, let alone decades, ahead.

Labor Force Participation

More than 90 percent of the increase in the labor supply in the past decade was due to the sheer increase in the size of the Latin American population. Only about 13 percent was the result of changes in labor force participation patterns (migration flows accounted for a small decrease). However, changes in labor force participation are far more important for understanding the changing patterns of the labor supply than this decomposition suggests because changes in labor force participation affect the composition of the labor supply much more than the purely demographic factors.

Since prime-age (25-55 years old) adult men have high labor force participation rates in almost any circumstances, changes in labor force participation mostly come from movements in or out of the labor force by adult women (and to a lesser

Figure 3.9 Labor Force Growth Rates for Countries at Different Stages in the Demographic Transition
(Percent)

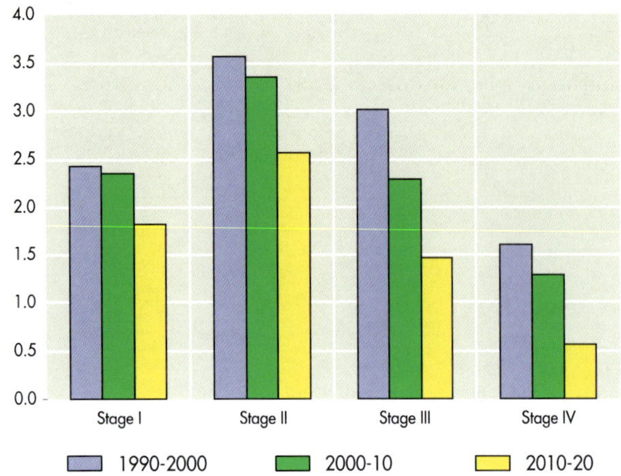

Source: Table 3.1.

Figure 3.10 Female Labor Force Participation Rates

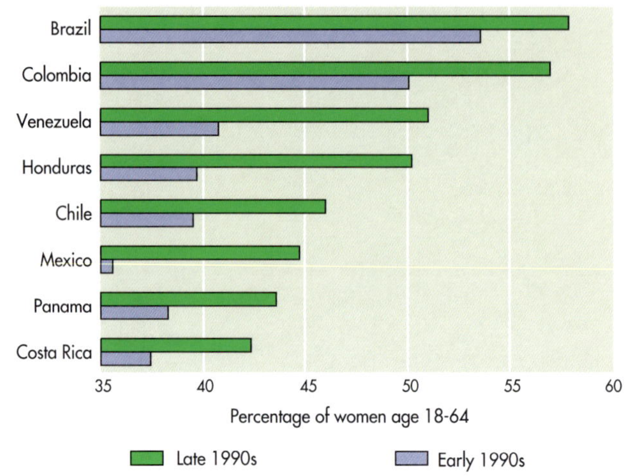

Note: Includes urban and rural areas.
Source: Updated from Duryea, Cox Edwards, and Ureta (2001).

extent by those beyond these age limits). Between 80 and 90 of every 100 adult Latin American men have participated in the labor market in the past decades; the participation rates of adult women have gone from 24 percent on average in the 1950s to about 33 percent in the 1980s and nearly 50 percent by the turn of the century.[10] As a result, although women accounted for only about a quarter of the labor force in the 1960s and 1970s, their share increased to 36 percent three decades later.

Child labor is a small fraction of the total labor supply, and has declined in most—although not all—countries in the region. However, child labor is a major social problem that requires specific policy attention (see Box 3.1).

The trend toward increased participation of women in the labor force was as least as pronounced in the 1990s as in previous decades and common to all countries. In Mexico, Venezuela, and Honduras, female labor force participation rates increased as much as 10 percentage points during the 1990s, while the average increase for the eight countries in Figure 3.10 was 7 percentage points.[11] The obvious implication is that women now contribute a larger share to the incomes of their households and, by extension, the economy as a whole. The most extreme case is Uruguay, where women contribute nearly half of household income. In most countries in the region, women contribute around a third of household income (Figure 3.11).[12]

Several factors are behind the trend of increasing female labor force participation. One important factor is a rather mechanistic one: the age groups with higher participation rates are becoming a larger share of the female population. Female labor force participation rates increase with age up to age 45 (and then decline, especially after age 55, see Figure 3.12). As age composition has gradually shifted toward this peak in most countries, female labor force participation has increased. Up to a third of the increase in female labor force participation in the 1980s and as much

[10] Data for the 1950s and the 1980s are from Psacharopoulos and Tzannatos (1992).

[11] The change in female labor force participation may differ from the trends shown in Figure 3.10 for the following reasons: (1) only two points are taken in this case and the differences are not annualized; that is, there is no control for the number of years between the early and late points; (2) the national household survey is used for Mexico rather than the urban labor force survey; and (3) the sample is for 18-64 year olds rather than 15-64 year olds.

[12] The share of household income earned by females has been calculated as a simple average across all households regardless of household composition or income level. Note that the increase in women's earning power does not appear to be driven by economic necessity, but as an increase in the share of female-headed households. If the samples are restricted to households in which at least one adult male and one adult female are present, the results are qualitatively the same.

Box 3.1 Trends in Child Labor

The supply of labor is not necessarily limited to adults, but also includes millions of children and adolescents in the region. The International Labour Organization estimates that 21.5 million children in Latin America and the Caribbean are involved in economically productive activities that directly or indirectly raise family income (ILO/IPEC 2002b). It can be difficult to accurately capture children's work in household surveys, given its intermittent nature and sensitive status, so that comparisons across countries are problematic (Duryea and others 2003).

Surprisingly, although social indicators including school attendance rates and child survival rates have generally improved in the region, rates of child labor have increased over the past decade in countries such as Honduras, Mexico, and Venezuela (see figure). Hurricane Mitch, which occurred in October 1998, is behind the increase in child labor observed in Honduras during the first months of 1999. The Progresa program, which began after 1998 (and is now called Oportunidades), may have contributed to turning around a similar trend toward higher child labor in Mexico. Trends have been favorable in Brazil, Colombia, Costa Rica, and Uruguay (see figure).

Child labor is strongly associated with poverty. However, although the propensity of poor families to send their children to work does respond to income, it does so in a weak manner. Parental levels of education seems to matter much more, as regression results reveal, but this is a route that would take even longer than economic growth to make a dent in the problem.

The region has seen a proliferation of conditional transfer programs in which families receive a subsidy for agreeing that their children will regularly attend school. Bolsa Escola in Brazil, Superémonos in Costa Rica, and Progresa in Mexico are examples of these programs. Rigorous evaluations of these programs have consistently found that beneficiary children are more likely to attend school; but the impact on child and adolescent labor seems to be mixed. Bolsa Escola in urban Brazil is widely regarded for its impact on school attendance, but is described as having a negligible impact on child labor (Yap, Sedlacek, and Orazem 2002). Similarly, the Superémonos program in Costa Rica has been found to have positive effects on school attendance, but no effect on adolescent labor (Duryea and Morrison 2003). However, reductions in child labor were found in the case of Oportunidades (formerly Progresa) in Mexico, and in Brazil's PETI.

The success cases suggest that the effects on child or adolescent labor may be larger when economic subsidies are combined with additional interventions. For example, PETI required that children attend after-school sessions, which effectively limited the time available for working. Hours of work were estimated to be reduced by half and the probability of working was reduced by at least 5 percentage points (Yap, Sedlacek, and Orazem 2002). In the case of Oportunidades, additional interventions came primarily in the form of home visits by community promoters, nutritional interventions, and health seminars. The probability of working fell by approximately 10-15 percent for 8-17 year old beneficiaries, with larger effects for 12-15 year old children (Skoufias 2001).

This comparison of results across countries suggests that programmatic interventions in addition to economic subsidies are needed to enhance the effects of programs to reduce child labor. Evaluations find larger effects in the programs that were limited to rural areas, and it is in those areas where the problem is more acute in several countries.

Trends in Child Labor, Employment Rates for 10-14 Year Olds

a. Rising in Venezuela, Mexico, and Honduras

(Percent)

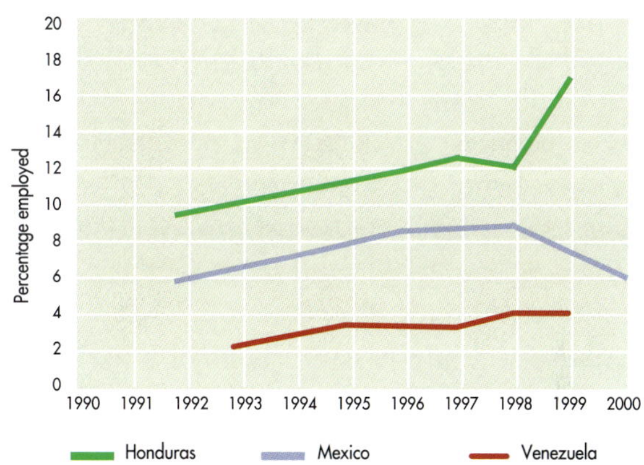

b. Falling in Brazil, Colombia, Costa Rica, and Uruguay

(Percent)

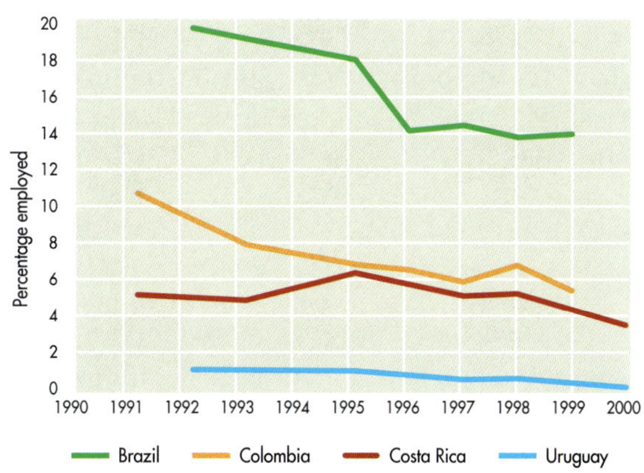

Note: For Costa Rica the age group is 12-14.
Source: IDB calculations based on household surveys.

Figure 3.11 Share of Household Income Earned by Females
(Percent)

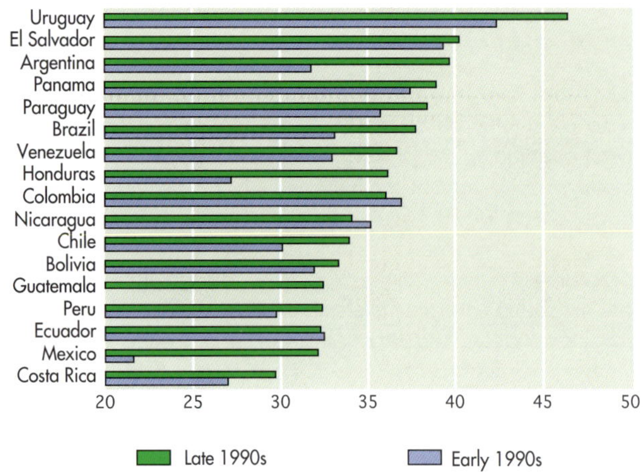

Source: Updated from Duryea, Cox Edwards, and Ureta (2001).

Figure 3.12 Labor Force Participation by Age and Gender
(Percent)

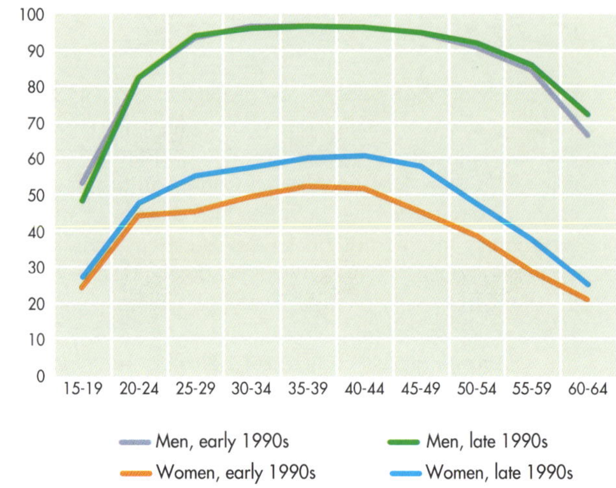

Source: IDB household surveys.

as a fifth of the increase in the 1990s could be explained by this recomposition (Duryea and Székely 2000). This process will intensify in the future, as women age 15-29 are expected to represent 35 percent of the labor force by 2020. Women in this age group have the lowest participation rates of all working age women and represented about 44 percent of all working age women in 2000.

Apart from purely compositional forces, education has been a main factor behind increased female labor force participation. A well-established fact is that the higher is the level of education of women, the higher is the probability that they join the labor market. Figure 3.13 confirms this pattern for the 12 countries in the region with comparable data from household surveys. One reason for this relationship is that education increases the value of women's time in the labor market relative to the value they place on their time spent at home. Usually this is also reinforced by the fact that more educated women tend to have fewer children, which may make labor force insertion more feasible.

But education (even if combined with fertility decisions) is far from the whole story. There are large differences in participation rates for similar education levels across countries (Figure 3.14).[13] For instance, seven in 10 Nicaraguan women age 30-45 in urban areas who have completed primary school are in the labor market, compared with only four in 10 in Mexico (although Nicaraguan women have more children on average). In Uruguay, eight in 10 women who have completed secondary school participate in the labor market, which is similar to the number in Guatemala, which has much lower incomes, and nearly twice as high as the figure for Chilean women, who have a similar level of education as women in Uruguay.

That education is only part of the story can also be seen in the shifting patterns in female labor force participation by education level in the 1990s. Women at all levels of education are participating more than they did a decade ago, but the biggest increases have taken place among the least educated women (Figure 3.13).[14]

To put in perspective the relative importance of education, it is useful to calculate the impact

[13] Notice that these estimates differ from those presented in chapter 1 and Figure 3.10, which cover both urban and rural areas and refer to women age 15-64 in chapter 1 and age 18-64 in Figure 3.10.

[14] Figure 3.13 is based on urban data for Bolivia, Brazil, Chile, Colombia, Costa Rica, Honduras, Mexico, Nicaragua, Panama, Peru, and Uruguay, and national data for Venezuela. Only six countries were used to calculate the average labor force participation rate for women with no schooling, since these countries had more than 4.5 percent of the schooling distribution at this level. The following countries were not used in the zero schooling calculation because of concerns about precision and whether the sample was representative: Chile, Colombia, Costa Rica, Panama, Peru, and Uruguay.

Figure 3.13 Female Urban Labor Force Participation by Education Level in Latin America
(Percent)

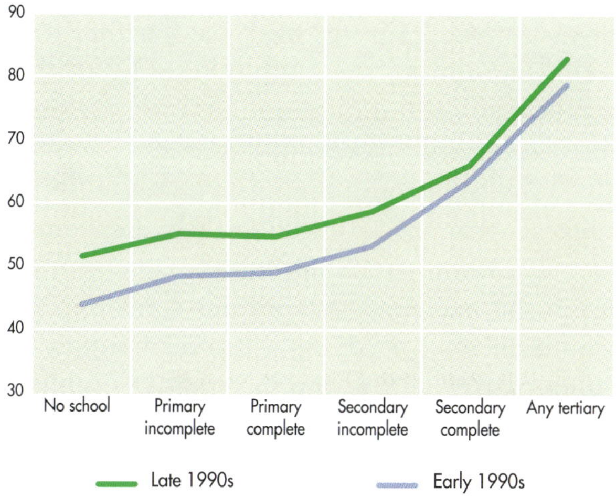

Note: Values are for women age 30-45, averages for 12 countries. No school is the average for 6 countries.
Source: Updated from Duryea, Cox Edwards, and Ureta (2001).

Figure 3.14 Female Labor Force Participation by Education Level and Country
(Percent)

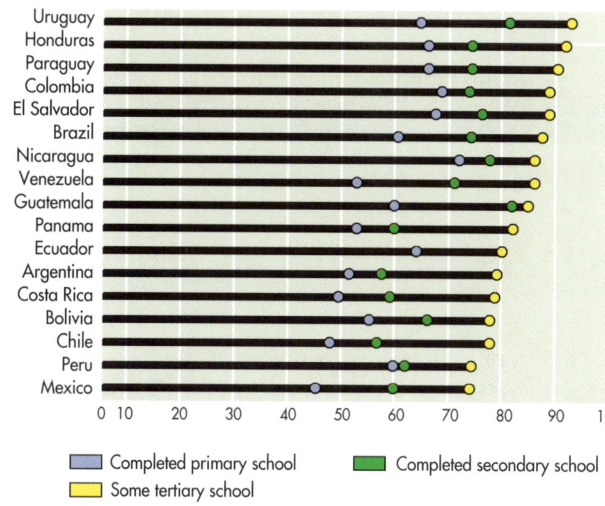

Note: Values are for women age 30-45 in urban areas.
Source: Updated from Duryea, Cox Edwards, and Ureta (2001).

that education improvements could have had on the rate of labor force participation if nothing else had changed. The result is that increased education levels during the 1990s account for only about a quarter of the increase in female labor force participation rates (1.6 percentage points of the 6.2 points of increase observed in the seven countries considered).[15]

Since education is only one of the factors influencing women's decision to join the labor force, it is tempting to think that the economic hardships of their families and countries are a more important factor. Some evidence could lend support to this idea. In several countries, men's earnings by the end of the 1990s were lower than at the beginning of the decade, while female labor force participation increased. Furthermore, in some countries, female labor force participation increased the most among the socioeconomic groups in which men's wages declined more sharply, suggesting that wives were pushed into the labor market by the decline in their husbands' earnings.

Figure 3.15 presents the changes in husbands' earnings and wives' labor force participation by socioeconomic decile.[16] Figure 3.15b shows the case of Mexico, in which larger increases in female labor force participation took place among lower socioeconomic groups, which also experienced larger declines in husbands' earnings (due either to wage declines, reduced working hours, or even unemployment). In other countries where husbands' earnings declined, wives' labor force participation also increased, but it is less clear that the two events were connected. For instance, in Argentina, declines in husbands' earnings were substantial among all but the richest socioeconomic groups, but wives' labor force participation increased significantly only for the three lowest deciles (Figure 3.15a). In Venezuela, labor force participation also increased strongly among

[15] Values are calculated for Brazil, Chile, Colombia, Costa Rica, Honduras, Panama, and Uruguay in Duryea, Cox Edwards, and Ureta (2001).

[16] This empirical examination follows the approach used by Juhn and Murphy (1997). Socioeconomic groups are constructed on the basis of predicted, rather than observed, per capita income as derived by regressing actual per capita household income on the age and education level of the husband and wife, the number of children in the household, and the number of retired or older persons. The classification of households into deciles was performed by first sorting couples into three experience groups based on the potential work experience of the male in the couple and then constructing income deciles within each experience group. In this manner, each decile of predicted per capita income contains individuals with different experience levels. Urban labor force surveys were used for Brazil (Pesquisa Mensal de Emprego) and Mexico (Encuesta Nacional de Empleo Urbano) rather than national household surveys.

Figure 3.15 **Changes in Husbands' Real Earnings and Wives' Labor Force Participation by Income Decile, 1992-2000**

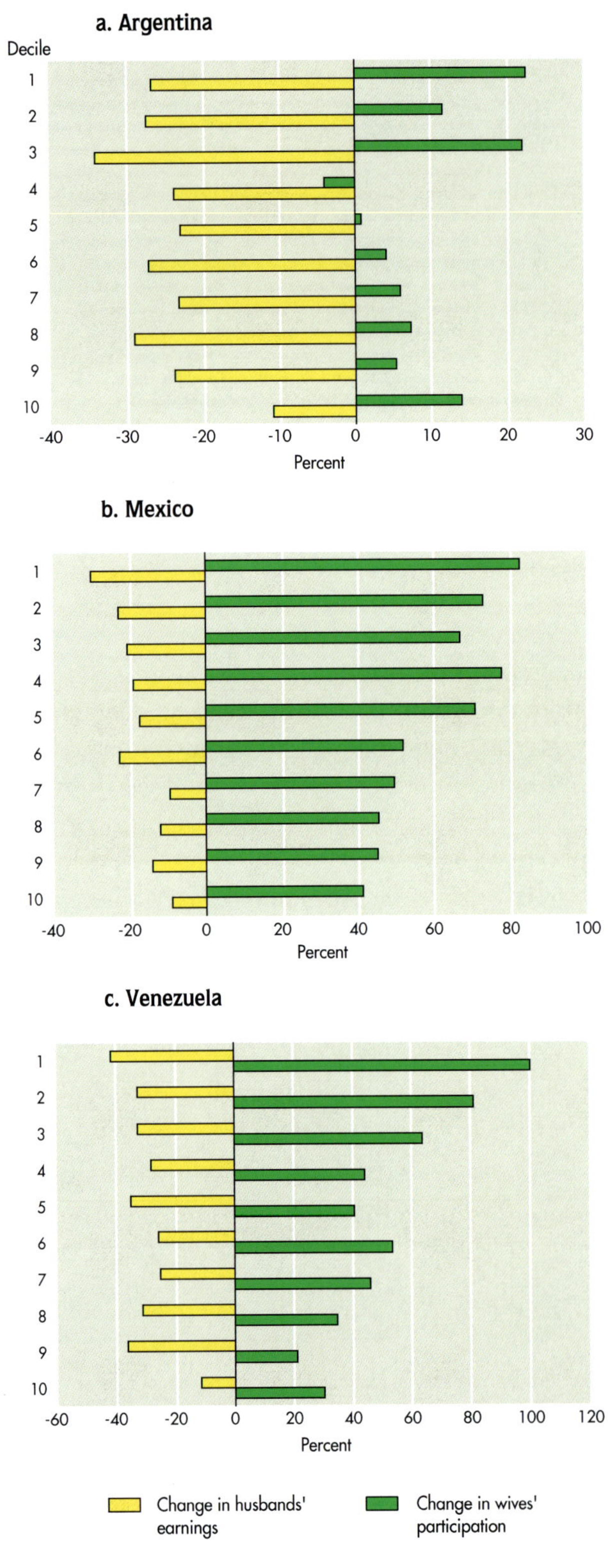

Note: 10 is the highest income decile.
Source: IDB household surveys.

women in the lower deciles, while husbands' earnings declined throughout the socioeconomic scale. Since other factors may have been at play, it is difficult to infer from this evidence whether women were pushed into the labor market by their husbands' economic difficulties, or were attracted by increased labor market opportunities.

The behavior of the relative wages of women suggests that the latter could have happened. In fact, if women were pushed into the market, it would be expected that women's relative wages would decline, partly as a result of supply pressures, partly due to the fact that the additional entrants probably would have less motivation and skills than their competitors. However, relative wages moved in favor of women during the 1990s. Of course, relative wages may be rising over time due to compositional changes, such as faster increases in the schooling of female workers. However, after correcting for compositional changes, the female wage penalty closed at a rate of about 1 percentage point a year (such that over the decade women's wages increased from lagging men's by 25 percent to lagging by 17 percent). These results suggest that women's earning opportunities in the labor force relative to men's have been steadily improving over time and may have played a role in attracting women to the labor force (Duryea, Edwards, and Ureta 2001).

Whether women are pushed or pulled into the labor market has been the subject of a long debate by economists and social scientists. The discussion has usually been framed within a short-term perspective. A well-known hypothesis about the labor market behavior of women (and other "secondary workers," such as teenagers) states that women join the labor market when economic conditions deteriorate and pull out of the market when conditions improve. In contrast to this added worker hypothesis, an alternative possibility—known as the discouraged worker hypothesis—is that women join the labor market in response to better labor opportunities (and withdraw when conditions deteriorate).

Both hypotheses are reasonable, according to economic theory. The added worker effect may occur for two reasons. First, the leisure of wives and husbands may be substitutable in home production. Second, families may be liquidity constrained and unable to smooth consumption during the husband's unemployment spell. Such individuals may leave the labor force when economic conditions improve and the primary earner is again employed on a regular basis. The extent to which such movements in and out of the labor force take place depends on whether women are becoming more firmly attached to the labor force.

The discouraged worker effect suggests that during times of high unemployment, when individuals become unemployed, they may become discouraged and drop out of the labor force after a fruitless period of job search. Others who are outside the labor market may postpone labor force entry until economic conditions improve. Discouragement is due to the decline in the perceived reward to market work because of the difficulty of locating an acceptable job. As economic conditions improve, previously discouraged workers may become encouraged and enter the labor force.

Both of these effects could operate at the same time for different households. The net effect of economic conditions on labor force participation depends on whether discouraged workers or added workers predominate in the aggregate. Since this is an empirical question, it is not surprising that the results differ across types of workers and across countries. Figure 3.16 compares (detrended) labor force participation rates of unskilled men and women[17] with the (also detrended) level of real gross domestic product (GDP) in Mexico, Brazil, and Argentina.[18]

In all three countries, the labor force participation of male workers is procyclical, meaning that it increases with increases in the level of real GDP and decreases with declines in real GDP. This applies both for unskilled and skilled workers (not shown in the figure). It thus appears that for adult males, independent of skill level, the discouraged worker effect dominates the decision to participate in the labor market.

Whether the labor force participation rate of adult women is countercyclical or procyclical seems to vary from country to country. In Mexico, for example, the labor force participation of unskilled female workers is countercyclical, meaning that it increases with declines in the level of real GDP. This was particularly clear during the 1995 Tequila crisis, when it reached a peak.[19] In Brazil, female labor force participation is procyclical, but in Argentina there seems be a change in the cyclical pattern between the early 1990s and the later part of the decade. For example, in 1992-95, female participation appears to have been countercyclical, but the pattern seems to have broken down in 1996-98.

In sum, the cyclical behavior of female labor supply does not reveal a common pattern across countries. In Mexico and Argentina up to the mid-1990s, the added worker hypothesis seems to hold; Brazil behaves more in tune with the discouraged worker hypothesis, with the pattern of women's labor force participation appearing similar to that of men.

Are Women to Blame?

Since women are joining the labor force in large numbers, they are partly responsible for the fast rate of growth of the supply of labor and its changing composition. Are they also to blame for increased unemployment and the decline of good quality jobs? It is plausible that, since women tend to experience higher rates of unemployment and be employed in jobs that are more flexible and less stable, the increasing share of women in the labor market has brought about these undesirable aggregate outcomes.

[17] Unskilled workers are those with up to nine years (junior high school) of education in Mexico and Brazil, and 12 years (high school) in Argentina.

[18] The detrended labor force participation rate was obtained from the residual of a first-stage regression of cohort-specific mean labor force participation rates on a constant term and dummy variables for birth year of cohort and cohort age. Thus, the labor force participation presented in the figures is net of a linear time trend, but also net of cohort/generation effects and age effects affecting labor force participation over the life cycle. Along similar lines, detrended real GDP was obtained from the residual of a regression of annual real GDP against a linear trend variable and a constant term. Urban labor force surveys were used for Mexico and Brazil because they are available at higher periodicity than the national surveys, which are interrupted during census years.

[19] The cyclical pattern of unemployment rates and self-employment rates of skilled and unskilled females in Mexico reveals that periods of increased labor force participation are accompanied by increases in the rate of unemployment and in the rate of self-employment during the same periods.

Figure 3.16 **Detrended Gross Domestic Product and Labor Force Participation Rates of Unskilled Workers by Gender in Mexico, Argentina, and Brazil**

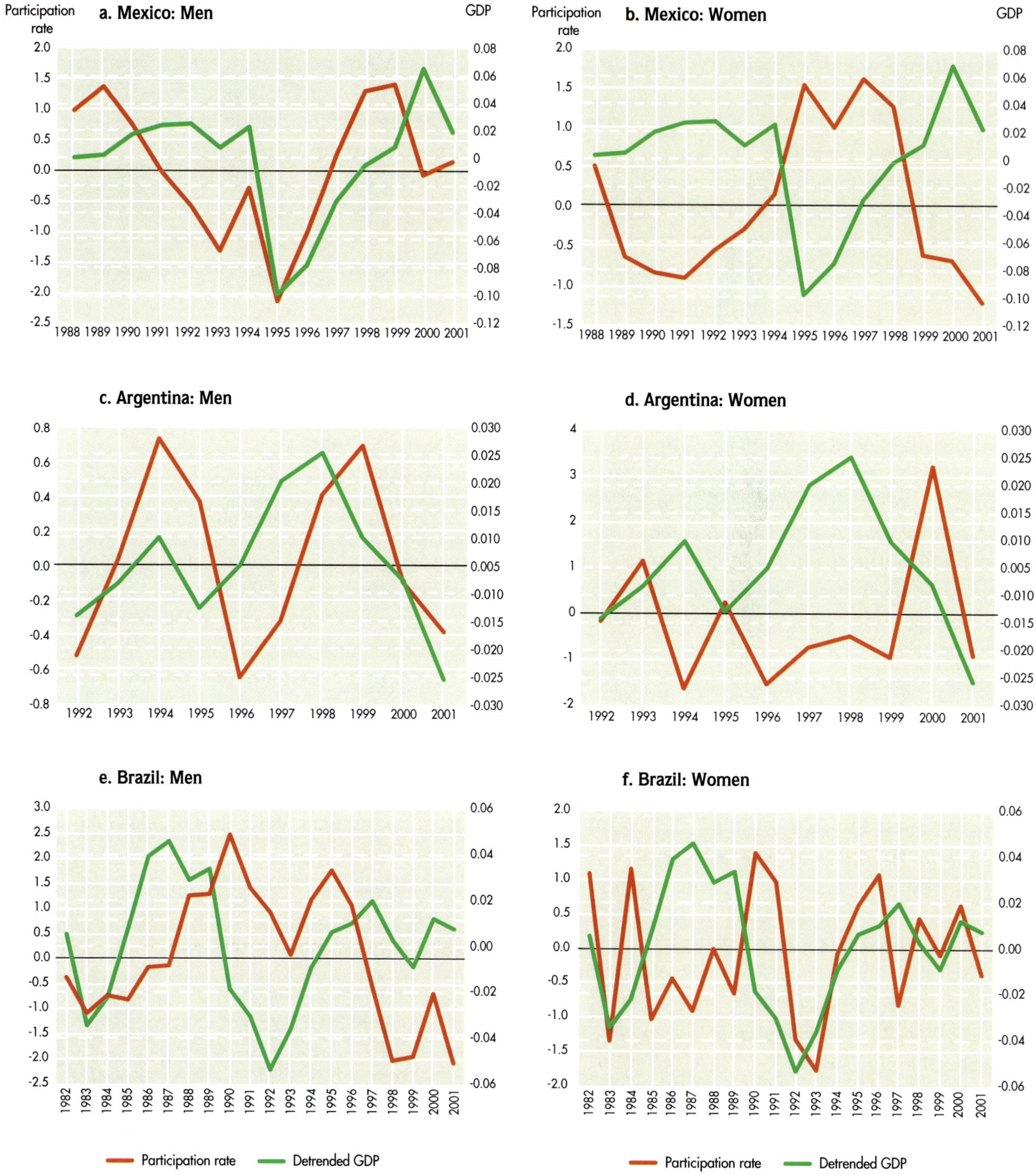

Note: GDP detrended using a linear trend. The participation rate is the number of employed and unemployed in each category divided by the working age population of that category, (expressed in percent).
Source: IDB household surveys and World Bank data for GDP.

Table 3.2 Changes in Unemployment and Labor Force Composition
(Percentage points)

Country	Period	Total change in unemployment rate	Cause of change in unemployment rate: Feminization of the labor force	Change in age composition of the labor force	Urbanization
Argentina[a]	1992–2000	7.42	0.00	–0.16	
Bolivia[a]	1993–99	–1.51	–0.01	–0.08	
Brazil	1993–99	3.73	0.06	–0.14	0.10
Chile	1992–98	4.45	0.11	–0.37	0.12
Colombia	1993–99	9.57	0.21	–0.10	0.11
Costa Rica	1993–98	1.56	0.04	–0.09	0.00
Honduras	1992–99	0.74	–0.01	0.01	0.08
Mexico	1992–2000	–1.49	–0.01	–0.44	0.02
Nicaragua	1993–2001	–8.43	–0.05	0.15	0.22
Panama	1991–2000	–2.33	0.05	–0.30	0.62
Uruguay[a]	1992–2000	4.81	0.08	–0.07	
Venezuela[a]	1993–99	5.53	–0.08	0.06	
Average		2.00	0.03	–0.13	0.16

[a] Urban only or rural and urban areas are not distinguished.
Source: IDB calculations based on household surveys.

Table 3.2 provides an answer to this question. The increased share of women in the labor market in the 1990s could have caused only a minute increase in the unemployment rate. In the 12 countries considered, the average contribution of the additional women in the labor market to the unemployment rate was just 0.03 percentage points, or less than 1 percent of the increase observed in the unemployment rate. In no country did the change in the gender structure of the labor force contribute more than 3 percent of the increase in the unemployment rate.

The table shows that the same conclusion applies to other compositional changes in the labor force. Young workers tend to experience higher unemployment rates than adult workers, either because they are entrants searching for their first jobs or because they are still in the process of exploring opportunities before committing themselves to a particular job or career. Since the share of young workers in the labor force declined in most countries, this compositional change does not help explain increasing unemployment rates. On the contrary, this would have caused a decline of 0.13 percentage points in the average unemployment rate in the 12 countries included in Table 3.2. In Chile, Mexico, and Panama, where youth participation rates decreased significantly, unemployment rates should have declined between 0.3 and 0.5 points on account of this factor.

Since unemployment rates are higher in urban areas than in rural areas, the process of urbanization did contribute to an increase in the overall rate of unemployment in most countries. However, this contribution was minimal: just 0.16 percentage points or about 1.5 percent of the actual increase in the unemployment rates of the eight countries considered for this computation. Only in Panama did the process of urbanization directly cause a noticeable increase in the unemployment rate in the 1990s, of about 0.6 percentage points.

The feminization of the labor force could also be behind the declining rates of social security coverage and the increasing trends of part-time work observed among the total labor force. However, as in the case for unemployment, feminization explains only a minor part of these patterns, and the same is valid for the other changes in the composition of the labor supply. Unemployment, lack of social security, and other undesirable labor out-

Table 3.3 Effects of Female Labor Force Participation on Male Wages and Unemployment

	Unskilled workers		Skilled workers	
Country	Male wages	Male unemployment	Male wages	Male unemployment
Mexico, 1988-2001	0.136	0.001	0.009	–0.002
	(1.48)	(0.04)	(0.10)	(0.23)
Brazil, 1982-2001	0.428	–0.045	0.21	–0.008
	(4.02)***	(2.16)**	(1.91)	(0.63)
Argentina, 1992-2001	–0.183	–0.097	0.024	0.061
	(1.69)	(2.13)**	(0.17)	(1.72)

** Significant at 5 percent.
*** Significant at 1 percent.
Note: Each coefficient comes from a separate regression (the dependent variable is the column heading). The female labor force participation rate and the following additional variables were included in the regressions but not reported: dummy variable identifying birth year cohort, dummy variable identifying aggregate time effects, cohort age, and age squared. Absolute values of t-statistics are in parentheses.
Source: IDB calculations.

comes affect all major groups of workers and cannot be explained, at least directly, by the changing structure of the labor force.

Could those changes indirectly cause undesirable labor market outcomes? It may be argued that the increasing number of women in the labor market could be weakening men's market power, forcing them to accept lower salaries and less desirable working conditions. In the longer run, women could displace men from the labor market since, from the point of view of employing firms, women could be considered less expensive substitutes. If these concerns were valid, higher female labor force participation would imply lower male wages and more serious unemployment for men.

Since competition between men and women would likely occur between men and women of similar ages, the labor force participation of female cohorts should be negatively correlated with the mean wage of men of the same age and positively correlated with their unemployment rates (after controlling for other factors that may affect the behavior of labor markets). But the data do not lend support to these hypotheses (Table 3.3). Among unskilled workers in the three countries in the table, Brazil is the only one where female labor force participation appears to be significantly correlated with male wages, but the correlation is positive, rather than negative. In Mexico, the correlation is also positive, but not significant, and in Argentina, it is negative, but insignificant. Among skilled workers, the higher is the participation of women in the labor market, the higher are the earnings of their male peers. The data also suggest that, if anything, higher female labor force participation tends to be associated with a lower probability that men become unemployed.

In summary, there are no grounds to blame women for the deteriorating performance of the labor market. The direct impact of their increasing labor force participation on the rate of unemployment and other undesirable labor outcomes turns out to be negligible. The indirect impact, if anything, goes in the opposite direction from what a hypothesis of competition for jobs would suggest.

Migration[20]

Latin America has the highest emigration rate in the world (Figure 3.17). For several centuries, the region was a net recipient of immigrants from Europe, Africa, and Asia. But the past 30 or 40 years

20 This section draws heavily on Clark, Hatton, and Williamson (2003).

Figure 3.17 Net Migration Rate by Region, 2000

(Per 1,000 population)

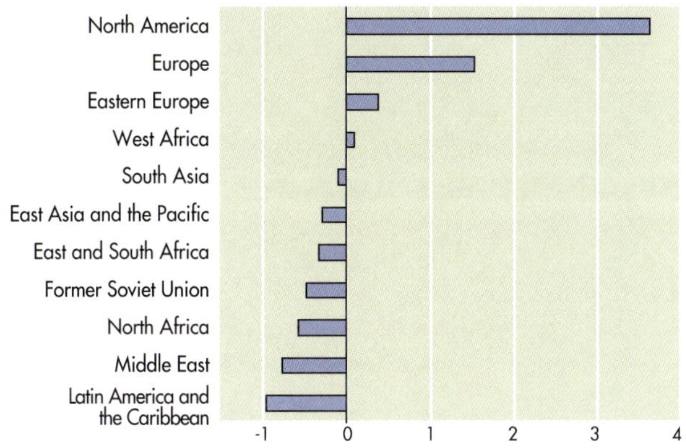

Source: Clark, Hatton, and Williamson (2003).

Figure 3.18 Net Migration Rate by Country, 1990s

(Per1,000 population)

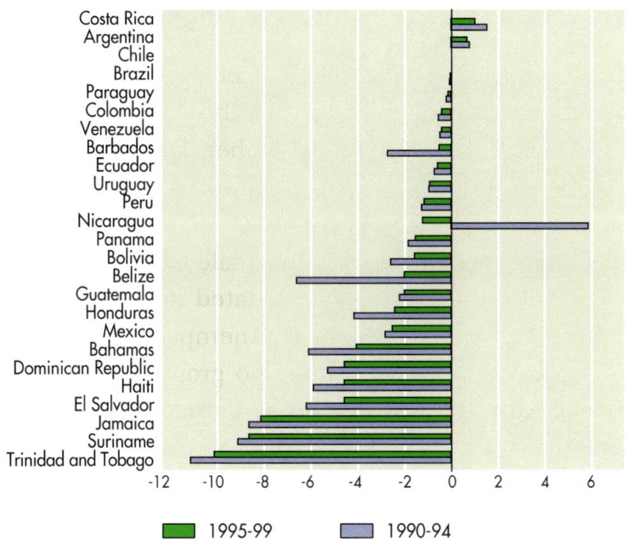

Source: Clark, Hatton and Williamson (2003).

Figure 3.19 Foreign Population by Origin

(Percent)

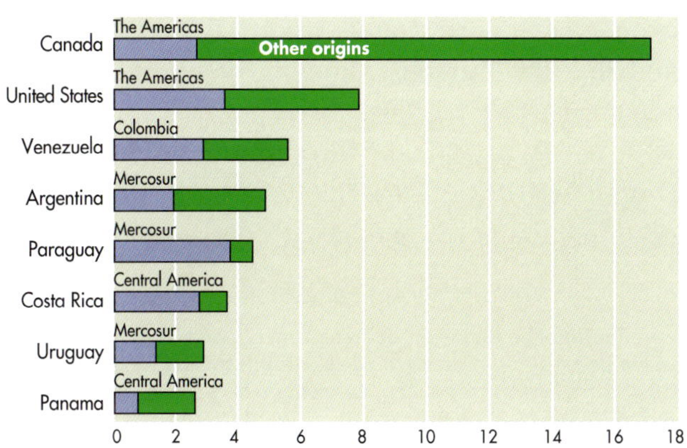

Source: Clark, Hatton, and Williamson (2003).

have been ones of net emigration, not net immigration. The largest net emigration rates in the 1990s were in English-speaking countries in the region: Trinidad and Tobago, Suriname, and Jamaica experienced emigration rates of approximately 10 per 1,000 population (Figure 3.18). Mexico and several Central American countries also had high net emigration rates (between two and six per thousand), although much lower than those of the English-speaking countries.

Latin American emigrants have increasingly favored the United States as their prime destination. By 2000, more than 55 percent of all immigrants in the United States were from Latin America, and about half of these were from Mexico. Although intraregional migration within Latin America has never been extensive, some important movements of workers have taken place in some periods, especially between neighboring countries. At the beginning of the 1990s, about 5 percent of the population of Venezuela was foreigners, many of them low-skilled workers from Colombia, who had come in the 1960s and 1970s, attracted by the oil boom (Figure 3.19).

Argentina has also attracted many Latin American immigrants, mainly from the other Southern Cone countries. During periods of good economic performance, Argentina has become a magnet for Paraguayans, Bolivians, and other workers from the Southern Cone. In Central America, Costa Rica is a magnet for low-skilled workers, mainly from Nicaragua. But apart from these magnets, Latin America has small foreign-born population shares compared with Canada and the United States. The share of foreigners in all of Latin America is only 1.4 percent (0.6 percent excluding Argentina and Venezuela); that of Canada and the United States combined is 8.9 percent.

Although the United States has never lost its importance as the principal destination for Latin American emigrants, they have started to explore new options, such as Australia, Canada, Japan, and some European countries (especially Spain, Italy, and the United Kingdom). In addition, adverse economic conditions in Latin America and improved conditions in Europe have contributed to some return migration on the part of descendants of pre-

Table 3.4 Latin American Immigrants in the United States, 1971-2000
(Thousands)

Country of origin	1971-80	1981-90	1991-2000	1997	1998	1999	2000
Latin America	1,813.8	3,460.6	4,319.2	348.9	288.2	304.1	384.6
Mexico	637.2	1,653.3	2,251.4	146.9	131.6	147.6	173.9
Caribbean	759.8	892.7	996.1	105.3	75.5	71.7	88.2
Cuba	276.8	159.2	180.8	33.6	17.4	14.1	20.8
Dominican Republic	148.0	251.8	340.9	27.1	20.4	17.9	17.5
Haiti	58.7	140.2	181.8	15.1	13.4	16.5	22.4
Jamaica	142.0	213.8	173.5	17.8	15.1	14.7	16.0
Trinidad and Tobago	61.8	39.5	63.3	6.4	4.9	4.3	6.7
Central America	132.4	458.7	531.8	43.8	35.7	43.2	66.4
Costa Rica	12.1	15.5					
El Salvador	34.4	214.6	217.4	18.0	14.6	14.6	22.6
Guatemala	25.6	87.9	103.1	7.8	7.8	7.3	10.0
Honduras	17.2	49.5	66.7	7.6	6.5	4.8	5.9
Nicaragua	13.0	44.1	97.7	6.3	3.5	13.4	24.0
Panama	22.7	29.0	23.9	2.0	1.6	1.6	1.8
South America	284.4	455.9	539.9	52.9	45.4	41.6	56.1
Argentina	25.1	25.7	24.3	2.0	1.5	1.4	2.3
Brazil	13.7	23.7	52.3	4.6	4.4	3.9	7.0
Chile	17.6	23.4	16.9	1.4	1.2	1.1	1.7
Colombia	77.6	124.4	131.0	13.0	11.8	10.0	14.5
Ecuador	50.2	56.0	76.4	7.8	6.9	8.9	7.7
Guyana	47.5	95.4	73.8			3.3	5.7
Peru	29.1	64.4	105.7	10.9	10.2	8.4	9.6
Venezuela	7.1	17.9	29.9	3.3	3.1	2.5	4.7
Europe	801.3	705.6	1,311.4	119.9	90.8	92.7	132.5
Asia	1,633.8	2,817.4	2,892.2	265.8	219.7	199.4	265.4
Canada	114.8	119.2	137.6	11.6	10.2	8.9	16.2
Africa	91.5	192.3	383.0	47.8	40.7	36.7	44.7
Oceania			48.0			3.7	5.1
All countries	4,493.3	7,338.1	9,095.4	798.4	660.5	646.6	849.8

Source: U.S. Census Bureau (various years).

vious European immigrants.[21] A similar pattern has emerged for Asian descendants.

Although significant numbers live in Europe, the overwhelming majority of Latin Americans outside the region (88 percent) live in the United States. Thus, explaining emigration from Latin America is largely a matter of explaining emigration to the United States. Table 3.4 reports flows of legal immigrants into the United States since 1971. The Latin American total rose two and a half times between 1971-80 and 1991-2000, from 1.8 to 4.3 million. Although U.S. immigration from all regions increased markedly over the three decades, the numbers arriving from Latin America far exceeded those arriving from Europe and Africa. And while the numbers arriving from Latin America in the 1970s exceeded those for Asia by only a small margin, by the 1990s they were about 70 percent larger. Legal immigration is, of course, only part of the story. Estimates for the stock of illegal immigrants in the United States (Table 3.5) show that these are even more concentrated among Latin Americans and that the numbers doubled between 1990 and 2000.

Latin American immigrants entering the United States are more likely to be labor-market-oriented adults compared with their home popula-

[21] In Europe, the definition of immigrant depends on the nationality of the parents (for instance, a person with two French parents would be granted French citizenship, no matter where he or she was born); in the United States and Canada, citizenship depends on the individual's country of birth.

Table 3.5 Estimates of Undocumented Immigrants in the United States, 1990–2000

Country of origin	1990	2000	Increase (percent)
Latin America	2,746	5,833	112
Mexico	2,040	4,808	136
El Salvador	298	189	-37
Guatemala	118	144	22
Colombia	51	141	176
Honduras	42	138	229
Ecuador	37	108	192
Dominican Republic	46	91	98
Brazil	20	77	285
Haiti	67	76	13
Peru	27	61	126
Other countries	754	1,167	55
China	70	115	64
Philippines	70	85	21
India	28	70	150
Korea	24	55	129
Canada	25	47	88
Total	3,500	7,000	100

Note: Previous estimates for 1996 indicated that there were 50,000 illegal immigrants from Jamaica, 50,000 from Trinidad and Tobago, and 70,000 from Nicaragua.
Source: U.S. Immigration and Naturalization Service, 2000.

tions: 76 percent of immigrants are of working age, compared with only 61 percent of the home population. This self-selection of labor-force-oriented adults has been true of international migrations since the early nineteenth century, and migrations have always self-selected young adults (Williamson 2001). Within this pattern, there is considerable variation by sending country. The Dominican Republic, El Salvador, Colombia, Nicaragua, and Peru are among the Latin American countries that have sent immigrants with the highest adult shares. Perhaps more relevant, however, is the difference between the adult share of emigrants and that of the sending country. There are large differences for Nicaragua (35.4 percent difference), El Salvador (23.1 percent), Guatemala (20.8 percent), Honduras (20.5 percent), and Haiti (18 percent). One of the countries with the weakest adult self-selection is Mexico, which seems to be due to the combination of two events. First, Mexico has one of the oldest U.S. immigration experiences, stretching back to the 1950s and 1960s. Second, the "family reunification effect," which became a part of U.S. immigration policy with the 1965 Act, has affected the age of Mexican immigrants.

Self-selection by skill is even more dramatic than by age. Latin Americans with legal immigration status in the United States have, on average, considerably higher levels of education than is true for their home country population.[22] For instance, the percentage of Latin Americans living in the United States who have completed at most secondary education is more than double (sometimes triple) the percentage in the country of origin. Although Latin American immigrants in the United States are more educated and more likely to be economically active than their compatriots at home, they are less educated, on average, than the Americans they join.

[22] Note that these numbers do not take into account that more than 50 percent of illegal immigrants in the United States come from Latin America (mostly from Mexico) and that this fact could influence some of these patterns.

Factors That Affect Migration

Examination of the determinants of U.S. immigration rates from a variety of countries sheds light on what drives emigration from Latin America compared with other source regions. This topic has been studied in recent years by a team of researchers headed by Jeffrey Williamson at Harvard University (see Clark, Hatton, and Williamson 2003). Their database includes 81 source countries (for which explanatory variables can also be documented), 22 of which are in Latin America, covering 1971-98. These source countries accounted for 82.5 percent of all U.S. immigration during this period. The dependent variable is the number of (legal) immigrants accepted into the United States who were born in another country as a proportion of that country's population.[23] The explanatory variables are those suggested by theories of migration, which are explained at greater length elsewhere (Clark, Hatton, and Williamson 2003; Hatton and Williamson 2002). Table 3.6 presents a regression equation that is estimated including all 81 source countries, and another that is estimated only for the 22 Latin American countries in the sample.

Relative income between the sending country and the United States is, of course, central to the migration decision. The regressions in Table 3.6 include the ratio of the source country purchasing-power-parity-adjusted GDP per capita to that of the United States. The coefficient is negative, as expected, and highly significant. Furthermore, the coefficient implies that a 10 percent increase in U.S. income (the leader surging ahead) or a 10 percent decrease in source country income (the follower falling behind) leads to a 15 percent rise in immigration from that country. However, the migration decision also depends on the relative returns to skills, not just income differentials, and hence the income effect must be deflated by relative skill levels. This is done using the ratio of the number of years of education of those age 15 and older in the source country relative to the United States, and, as expected, this variable has a negative impact on immigration. Holding income constant, a rise in the source country's average education level by 10 percent (equivalent to 0.55 years of schooling averaged across all sending countries) reduces the immigration rate by 7 percent.[24]

Migration theory also suggests that differences across countries in the returns to skills will select migrants from different parts of the skill distribution (Borjas 1987, 1991), which has come to be called the Roy model (Roy 1951). Roy model effects are captured here by the ratio of the Gini coefficient, a statistic describing the distribution of household income, in the source country relative to that in the United States. If a sending country has more inequality than the United States (which is the case for Latin America), then those at the top of the income distribution will have less incentive to emigrate, while those at the bottom will have more and vice versa. If inequality is similar in the source and destination, then, provided the destination has higher average income, there is an incentive to emigrate throughout the income distribution. Thus, unless poverty constrains poor potential immigrants from leaving the sending country, the immigration rate to the United States should follow an inverted U-shaped function of relative inequality. The results in Table 3.6 strongly support this hypothesis, with the peak immigration rate occurring at a ratio of 1.12, which is close to the point where inequality is about the same in the destination and source countries. In the Latin American case, this finding may need to be reinterpreted in terms of the qualification about poverty, namely, that poverty is likely to constrain the emigration of the very poor residing at the bottom of the income distribution in the sending country.

Unless return migration is very inexpensive, the discounted present value attached to any long-distance move should be higher at younger ages because the returns would be spread over a longer future working life.[25] Thus, source countries with

[23] Since this rate is bounded at zero, the variable actually used in the regressions is the log of that rate. The estimation technique is random effects, which exploits both the cross-section and time-series variation in the data.

[24] This does not imply that more education diminishes emigration rates, but rather only that GDP per capita differentials are explained in part by schooling differentials, and that the analysis must take this factor into consideration. If income differentials were instead documented by earnings differentials for individuals with the same level of schooling, it might affect the results on the schooling variable.

[25] If return migration is very inexpensive, migration is less likely to be permanent and more likely to be repeated.

Table 3.6 Immigration in the United States, 1971–98: Random Effects Regression Results

Variable	All source regions (81 countries)	Latin America (22 countries)
Constant	-8.72 (15.6)***	-10.64 (10.1)***
GDP per capita ratio (source/United States)	-1.49 (7.6)***	-2.55 (5.7)***
Schooling years ratio (source/United States)	0.69 (3.0)***	1.11 (3.1)***
Gini coefficient ratio (source/United States)	2.54 (5.8)***	5.83 (5.3)***
Gini coefficient ratio (source/United States) squared	-1.16 (6.3)***	-2.31 (5.6)***
Share age 15–29 in source population	0.52 (0.7)	4.09 (2.8)***
Immigration stock/source population (t-1)	7.18 (3.4)***	8.43 (4.2)***
Immigration stock/source population (t-1) squared	-39.7 (4.1)***	-34.69 (4.1)***
Distance	-0.21 (3.5)***	-0.24 (2.5)***
Landlocked	-0.46 (1.7)*	-0.52 (1.1)
English speaking	1.63 (6.4)***	2.01 (4.1)***
Civil war	0.22 (4.7)***	0.11 (1.7)
Eastern Hemisphere, 1971–78	-0.32 (9.3)***	
Western Hemisphere, 1971–78	-0.19 (3.6)***	-0.19 (3.8)***
Immigration Reform and Control Act, 1989-91	0.07 (7.5)***	0.06 (7.2)***
Dummy 1992–98	0.13 (4.1)***	-0.1 (1.8)*
Eastern Europe	-0.12 (0.3)	
Africa	-2.00 (5.0)***	
Oceania	0.51 (0.8)	
Middle East	1.31 (3.0)***	
Asia	-0.12 (0.3)	
Canada	-1.27 (1.4)	
Mexico	1.15 (1.4)	
Central America	0.72 (1.6)	-0.51 (0.8)
South America	0.06 (0.2)	-0.98 (1.3)
Caribbean	1.33 (2.6)***	-0.14 (0.2)
R^2 time series	0.20	0.44
R^2 between countries	0.76	0.88
R^2 overall	0.71	0.84
Number of observations	2,268	616

* Significant at 10 percent.

*** Significant at 1 percent.

Note: The dependent variable is the percentage of the source country population that are immigrants in the United States. Absolute values of t-statistics are in parentheses.

Source: Clark, Hatton, and Williamson (2003).

larger cohorts of young people should generate more migrants and higher emigration rates. In Table 3.6, the coefficient on the share of population age 15-29 is positive as expected, but it is not significant for the full sample of 81 countries (the opposite is true for Latin America alone).

Most observers also stress what has come to be called the "friends and relatives effect." An established stock of previous migrants from the same source country generates network effects that lower the costs and reduce the risks of migration and, through remittances by previous migrants, may even supply the initial investment necessary to finance the move by new migrants. Table 3.6 documents this friends and relatives effect, and, since this effect is sometimes thought to be nonlinear, the squared term is also included.[26] The values of the coefficients imply that the stock effect is most powerful at low levels and that it diminishes as the stock increases. At the average stock/population ratio, raising the expatriate stock by 1,000 generates an additional annual inflow from the source country of about 10 immigrants a year. This is a powerful influence indeed, with strong historical persistence.

Other country characteristics also matter. For example, distance from the destination, the gravity effect, is measured in Table 3.6 by the distance from Chicago in thousands of miles. The coefficient indicates that an additional 1,000 miles between the sending country and the United States reduces the immigration rate by 21 percent.[27] Whether the country is landlocked also has a large negative effect, although it is not quite significant at conventional levels. Even more important is whether the source country is English speaking, a factor that increases the number of immigrants from the sending country almost threefold. Political upheavals and violence, the most important source of which is civil wars, also have a significant effect, increasing the number of immigrants to the United States by about 22 percent.

U.S. immigration policy also matters in determining immigrant source, and Table 3.6 accommodates this with a series of dummies. Prior to 1978 there were separate quotas for the Western Hemisphere (chiefly Latin America) and the Eastern Hemisphere (the rest). The dummy for 1971-78 reflects the merging of these two quotas into a worldwide quota in 1979. The effect from 1979 onward seems to have been positive, especially for countries in the Eastern Hemisphere, despite some decrease in the overall quota.

The legalization of illegal immigrants (which is recorded as part of total immigration) under the Immigration Reform and Control Act of 1986 (effective 1988) is captured by a variable that represents the estimated stock of illegal immigrants by source country in 1980. This influence is applied only to 1989-91, when the program was in effect.[28] This effect varies across countries, with the largest impact on Mexico, where it doubled the immigration rate. The dummy for 1992-98 (for all source countries) is intended to reflect the expansion in the immigration quota that took effect following the Immigration Act of 1990 (effective 1992). This increased the number of immigrants by 13 percent (compared with the expansion of about 20 percent in the quota).

The analysis also includes regional dummies. Here the excluded region is Western Europe, so the coefficients on the other regions reflect differences from that benchmark. For the most part, the coefficients on regional dummies are small, suggesting that the fundamentals can by themselves explain regional differences in U.S. immigration rates. Notable exceptions are the large negative intercept for Africa and the fairly large positive intercept for the Middle East. Within the Americas, there are large coefficients for the border states—Canada and Mexico—and for the Caribbean. These results reflect the effects of contiguity as well as the place

[26] A lag is introduced on the premise that the friends and relatives effect has to be in place before the migrant makes the move.

[27] The gravity effect can be seen in Figure 3.18; countries in the Southern Cone (Argentina, Brazil, Chile, and Paraguay), which are farthest from the United States, have the lowest emigration (or highest immigration) rates. Of course, some of these countries have had relatively high wages, which also helps explain their high foreign-born population shares (Figure 3.19).

[28] The reason for using the estimated number of illegal immigrants in 1980 and not a later date is that legal immigration status was offered to those who had been living in the country since 1982 or longer.

in the United States (Chicago) from which distance is measured.[29]

Migration rates to the United States vary enormously in Latin America. What accounts for this variance? Are the same fundamentals at work as for the world at large? The second column in Table 3.6 reports estimates for the 22 Latin American countries. These are remarkably similar to those in the first column for all 81 countries. Hence, it appears that in general, Latin American emigration to the United States is driven by the same forces as for U.S. immigration as a whole, although the forces themselves may, of course, be larger or smaller.

However, there are some differences in the magnitudes of the estimated coefficients that are worth stressing. The most notable difference between Latin America and the rest is the large and significant effect of the share of population age 15-29. This regional difference may be explained by the fact that long-distance moves from Asia and Africa may more typically be family affairs, an issue that future research needs to explore. In any case, this result implies that an increase in the proportion of the population age 15-29 from, say, 25 to 30 percent would increase the typical Latin American country's U.S. immigration rate by 20 percent. Furthermore, the coefficients on income and schooling differences are larger for Latin America. Thus, a 10 percent increase in U.S. relative income increases immigration from the typical Latin American country by 25 percent. A 10 percent increase in U.S. relative education reduces immigration from the typical Latin American country by 11 percent. These effects are much larger than the effects for all sending regions combined.

The other coefficients are similar to those estimated for the full set of countries with the exception of the dummy for 1992-98, which is negative. This may reflect the effect of the increased favorable weight given to skills in the 1990 Immigration Act or it may simply reflect an increasing number of Latin Americans choosing illegal entry into the United States.

Inequality effects are also more powerful for Latin America, but the maximum immigration rate, where the Gini coefficient ratio is 1.26, is still fairly close to one. This inverse U shape implies that immigration to the United States is lower from those Latin American countries that are very equal or very unequal compared with the United States, and higher for those in between (that is, most like the United States). Note, however, that this is not quite the same as saying that Latin American immigrants into the United States came from middle-income groups.

Because Latin American income distributions are more unequal than that in the United States, migration should select from the bottom of the sending country's distribution, that is, mostly the very poor should move. However, there is also the "poverty trap" to consider. First, the very poor are unlikely to have the resources necessary to invest in the long-distance move to the United States. Second, the roughly constant absolute cost of migration across prospective migrants implies that the cost would be proportionately greater for poorer potential migrants. If either or both of these trap effects dominate, then higher poverty rates in the source country should serve to diminish U.S. immigration from that country.

Thus, although the migration incentives may be great for those at the bottom of the income distribution, poverty makes it impossible. At the top of the income distribution, there may be no financial constraint on emigration, but there is also far less incentive to move. Thus, it may be those in the middle of the sending country's distribution that actually emigrate. This is exactly what Chiquiar and Hanson (2002) find for Mexico in the 1990s, when U.S. immigrants came from the middle and top of the Mexican wage distribution. This issue is important and deserves further research on whether more liberal U.S. immigration policy would help to diminish poverty in Latin America.

Emigration: Blessing or Curse?

Since Latin America has the highest emigration rates in the world, it is important to discuss the

[29] Measuring distance from Los Angeles rather than from Chicago, for example, the intercept for Canada would be less negative and the intercept for Mexico would be less positive, but that for the Caribbean would be more positive.

effects of this phenomenon on the labor market. Can emigration help explain some of the ills of the labor market that were described in chapter 1?

The most notable effect of emigration in the source countries is the flow of remittances from migrants to their families. Remittances to Latin America and the Caribbean from abroad surpassed 32 billion dollars in 2002. The largest recipients were Mexico (10.5 billion dollars), Colombia, El Salvador, and the Dominican Republic (each with between 2 and 2.4 billion dollars).

Until recently, researchers and development agencies tended to underplay the importance of remittances or emphasize their potentially negative aspects. They feared that those receiving remittances would have no incentive to participate in the labor market or invest in income-generating activities. Furthermore, they thought that over time emigrants would lose contact with their home communities, leaving wives and children behind. Although some of these problems may exist, recent work on remittances reveals a far more complex picture. In the absence of adequate social insurance systems to protect families from the hardships of labor markets, remittances are an important source of income (see Box 3.2). Even if remittances are devoted to consumption only, their multiplier impact can be substantial, which has an effect on employment generation (Ouaked 2002; Samuel and Torres 2001).

The effects of emigration on the labor supply are less obvious than would appear at first sight. The direct effect is negative, but indirect effects may go in either direction depending on the participation response of family members remaining in the source country. Since family income may increase due to remittances, the labor force participation of the remaining members may decline, reinforcing the direct effect. But the family may substitute for the migrant in the local labor market if working opportunities improve and if the reduction in family size frees up time previously devoted to household activities. For example, in El Salvador during the civil war, the income effect dominated other effects, with the result that the reduction in labor supply exceeded the direct decline due to migration. Because of economic dislocation resulting from the war, these effects eased the unemployment problem rather than creating a labor shortage problem. In Puerto Rico, massive migration of low-skilled workers to the United States accounts for a minimum of one-fourth and probably much more of the long-term upward trend in real earnings. Migration has also contributed to reduce the rate of unemployment and the wage gap (Borjas and Freeman 1992).

However, not all the effects of emigration are positive. Since workers are attracted by the higher education returns in the destination country, emigration often takes the form of a "brain drain." The political and economic conditions of some countries have provided additional impetus to this process. In Latin America, a massive exodus of professionals took place in the 1960s and 1970s when military regimes in several countries targeted universities and other academic centers.

A continuous exodus of professionals affects many Caribbean countries, and probably contributes to widen the wage gap: there are 3.7 times more Jamaicans with some tertiary education living in the United States than in Jamaica. Although not as extreme, the cases of the Dominican Republic, El Salvador, Guatemala, and Mexico are also worrying. In these four countries, the number of immigrants in the United States who have some tertiary education represent between 16 and 40 percent of the pool of those with similar education levels residing in their own countries. These ratios are the highest of the 24 labor-exporting countries recently studied by Adams (2003).

Along with Mexico, the Philippines and India are the largest suppliers of workers with tertiary education to the U.S. labor market. However, in the Philippines and India, those in the United States represent just 11.7 and 2.8 percent, respectively, of the local population with similar skills.[30] Therefore, it is clear that migration is severely reducing the supply of skills in some Latin American countries. But international experience shows that when professional migrants return, or when they set up net-

[30] Coefficients for the Philippines and India would increase to 15.3 and 4.3 percent, respectively, if immigration to other developed countries were considered. These cases pale by comparison with Jamaica; there is roughly the same number of workers with tertiary education in Jamaica as in OECD countries (excluding the United States).

Box 3.2 Money Sent Home: Latin America's Largest Aid Program

Although Latin America's economic hardships in 2002 have been widely recognized, less obvious is the fact that millions of the region's emigrants, particularly in the United States, have mitigated the blow by sending home billions of dollars in direct assistance to their families.

According to the Multilateral Investment Fund (MIF), an affiliate of the Inter-American Development Bank (IDB), Latin American and Caribbean migrants living in industrial nations sent an unprecedented $32 billion to their home countries in 2002, a dramatic increase compared with $23 billion in 2001. These resources alleviated a great deal of suffering in the region during a recession year.

To put these amounts in perspective, in 2002 they roughly equaled direct foreign investment and outstripped overseas development aid to Latin America from all sources. In some countries, remittances make up more than 10 percent of the gross domestic product. Mexico received $10.5 billion in 2002, reflecting the large number of immigrants from that country throughout the United States, particularly in California and other border states. Three-quarters of remittances to Latin America and the Caribbean come from the United States. Important sums are also sent from Canada, Japan, Spain, and other European nations.

It is not the rich, but the poor who send the most money home. The typical remittance is around $250 to $300 a month, which represents a significant percentage of an immigrant's salary. Multiplied by millions, these sums add up to a major economic force. They help put roofs over heads, food on tables, and children through school. Some immigrants even manage to invest in real estate in their homelands or small businesses run by relatives. Experts believe that if demographic and economic trends persist, remittances will continue to mount. For this decade alone, Latin America and the Caribbean could receive more than $300 billion.

All this is happening at no cost to taxpayers, so why not leave well enough alone? The answer is simple: because the existing system is far from perfect. Last year, immigrants who sent money to Latin America and the Caribbean paid about $4 billion in transaction fees, mostly to money transfer companies that dominate this business. For every $100 an immigrant sent home, $12 went to financial intermediaries.

This level of service fee for Latin American emigrants sending home money from abroad is the highest in the world, and clearly unacceptable. It is 50 percent higher than fees charged for sending remittances to other areas of the world, such as India and the Philippines. If the costs of remittances dropped by two-thirds, billions of dollars more could reach some of the most needy people in the Western Hemisphere. The IDB believes that this is a reasonable and achievable goal.

Part of the solution is more competition. In recent years, the entry of new players in the market for remittance services has helped drive down costs, especially in major urban markets. Commercial banks and credit unions have started to engage Latin American immigrants with services that are increasingly tailored to their needs.

Another part of the solution will stem from expanding access to modern banking services to Latin Americans on both sides of the U.S. border. A recent report on remittances and Latin American immigrants conducted by the MIF and the Pew Hispanic Center shows that people who send money to Latin America tend to have little information on the alternatives to wire transfers. Many of them have no experience whatsoever with banks and are wary of formal financial institutions.

Fortunately, several U.S. federal agencies are pooling their resources to improve financial literacy among Latin American immigrants and help them open bank accounts. In some cases, these agencies are partnering with Mexican consulates to provide service to hundreds of people at public events. In one morning, a Mexican immigrant can obtain an ID card, known as the *matricula consular*, a taxpayer number from the U.S. Internal Revenue Service, and financial literacy materials in Spanish from the U.S. Federal Deposit Insurance Corporation, and open an account through a local bank representative.

Certainly more needs to be done in Latin America, where banks have traditionally focused on wealthy individuals and are just starting to court people who receive remittances. The IDB and MIF are giving priority to financial institutions that work with people of modest means, for example, assisting Mexican and Salvadoran credit unions in putting in place the regulations and technology that will allow them to take part in the remittance distribution business. It is hoped that these capital flows will grant many millions of Latin Americans access to the sort of financial services—automatic teller machines, savings accounts, credit cards, and loans—that most people in the United States take for granted.

Source: Adapted from the article by Enrique V. Iglesias originally published in *San Francisco Chronicle*, May 1, 2003.

works between their home and destination countries, they are likely to foster the transfer of technology, which could result in increased labor productivity. The mobility of skilled labor also bolsters the ability of the source country to attract global investment and trade linkages, with similar effects (Ouaked 2002).

Education

Education is the basis of workers' ability to generate income and have a satisfactory career and is therefore the most important quality dimension of the supply of labor. The positive relationship between schooling and earnings is well documented in the microeconomics literature for developed as well as developing countries. There has been intense discussion on whether the earnings of educated workers reflect their inherent abilities or instead reflect the increases in productivity associated with education. If the most able workers are those who can complete higher levels of education, education may be a way to signal higher ability. If this were an important part of the story, expansion in education would not necessarily lead to more productivity. However, recent research suggests that higher earnings do indeed demonstrate that education imparts knowledge and skills that increase workers' productivity (Krueger and Lindahl 2001). Given this relationship, low educational attainment of the labor force could be a leading cause of low labor earnings and a high level of poverty (IDB 1998, 2000).

Education Outcomes

Low levels of education, poor quality, and deep inequalities characterize education outcomes in Latin America. Educational attainment in Latin America lags behind attainment in other regions. Using estimates from the Barro and Lee (2000) data set on education, Figure 3.20 shows that the population age 25 and older in Latin America on average attained approximately 6 years of schooling in 2000. With averages of more than 11 years in Canada, Sweden, and the United States, attainment in

Figure 3.20 Educational Attainment for Population Age 25 or Older

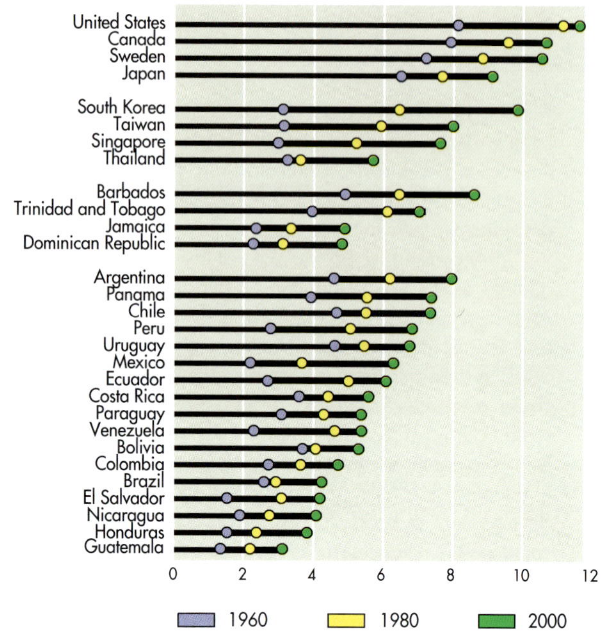

Source: Barro and Lee (2000).

these countries is twice the Latin American average. There is, of course, dispersion in average schooling levels within Latin American and the Caribbean; Guatemala (3.1 years) has the lowest average attainment and Barbados (8.5 years) has the highest.

The share of population with at least complete secondary schooling is a simple indicator of the availability of skills. Canada, Japan, South Korea, Sweden, Taiwan, and the United States have at least double the skill availability compared with most Latin American and Caribbean countries. For example, 42 percent of adults age 25 or older in Taiwan have completed at least secondary school, whereas the average for Latin America is 22 percent. Among the countries with the lowest share of workers with completed secondary schooling, in Brazil, El Salvador, Guatemala, Honduras, and Nicaragua, less than 15 percent of the adult population has completed secondary school.

Of particular concern, not only are attainment levels low, but progress has also been slow, especially in recent decades. The average years of schooling for the population older than age 25 in Latin America increased from about 3 years in 1960 to 4.5 years in 1980 and 6 years in 2000. Thus, the average years of schooling increased less than 1 year per decade in the region in 1960-80 and in 1980-2000.

Some countries have been more successful than others; Argentina, Chile, Mexico, Panama, and Peru increased their schooling by one year per decade between 1980 and 2000. In others, such as Colombia, Guatemala, Paraguay, and Venezuela, average years of schooling grew at a dismal rate. This is particularly troubling because some of these countries were already among the worst performers in 1980.

Although measures of the quality of schooling in Latin America are scarce, they all point to the same conclusion: the quality of schooling in the region is very low. Only a few countries participate regularly in internationally comparable achievement tests, making comparisons across countries and regions difficult. However, on the few occasions when a Latin American country has participated, students have performed below other countries, particularly relative to those in East Asia.[31] Colombia and Mexico participated in the International Mathematics and Science Study in 1996. Colombia ranked 40th out of 41 countries and Mexico refused to release the results. Similarly, Chile participated in the same test in 1999 and finished 35th out of 38 countries, below any participating Asian, Eastern European, or Middle Eastern country.

Moreover, the only test that allows for comparison across countries within Latin America—although it is not comparable with countries outside the region—indicates that most countries would achieve even lower levels on internationally comparable tests. In 1998, UNESCO's Latin office developed the first regionally comparable test in the subjects of language and mathematics (UNESCO/OREALC 1998). The results indicated that Chile was among the best performers in the region (after Argentina and Cuba in math scores and after Argentina, Brazil, and Cuba in language). The Dominican Republic, Honduras, Peru, and Venezuela were the lowest performers in both math and language tests.

Opinion surveys applied to firms in 75 countries confirm that the quality of public schools in Latin America is very low. Out of 20 Latin American countries considered by the *Global Competitiveness Report* of 2001, only the public schools in Costa Rica, Jamaica, Trinidad and Tobago, and Uruguay were performing at quality levels comparable with those of countries in Eastern Europe or East Asia and the Pacific. These opinion surveys also point to another serious problem in the Latin American education systems: profound inequality. According to the firms surveyed, differences in the quality of schools available to rich and poor children are greater in Latin America than in any other region (see Figures 3.21 and 3.22).

This is not the place to discuss the causes of the failures of the education system in Latin America. Suffice it to mention that several studies have identified as potential culprits the low level of education expenditure per student, lack of mechanisms of control and accountability in most education systems, inadequate pay for teachers, and credit constraints and other barriers that drive parents to take their children out of school (IDB 1996, 1998).

Lack of Education

Unemployment, low wages, and the increasing wage gap are often attributed to the failures of the education system. The deficiencies are so acute and palpable that there is little doubt that such is the case. But is it? Unemployment is easily dismissed: unemployment rates are usually lower among less educated than educated people, and increases in unemployment, where they have occurred, have affected both low-skilled and high-skilled workers, as discussed in chapter 1 and a previous section of this chapter. The other two arguments—namely, that lack of education is the main reason behind low productivity and the increasing wage gap—deserve further discussion.

Lack of education is often at the root of the problem of low labor productivity and poverty. However, it may not be the main reason for these

31 For more information on the quality of education in Latin America, see PREAL (2001).

Figure 3.21 Quality of Public Schools
(Index, 1-7)

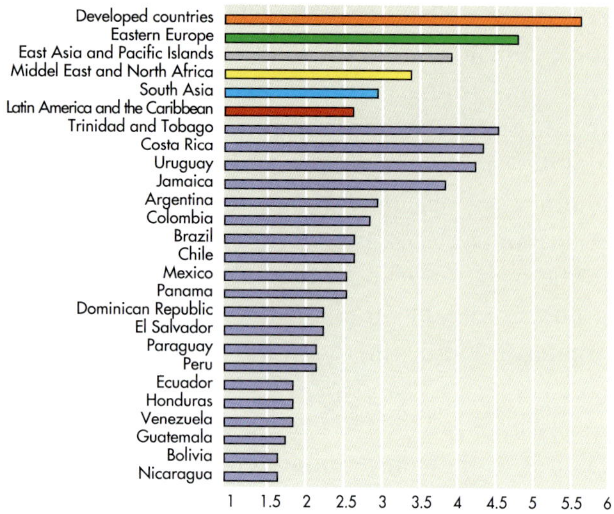

Note: The survey asked respondents to rank schools as follows: Public (free) schools in your country are (1=of poor quality, 7=equal to the best in the world).
Source: World Economic Forum (2001).

Figure 3.22 Equality in the Quality of Schools
(Index 1-7)

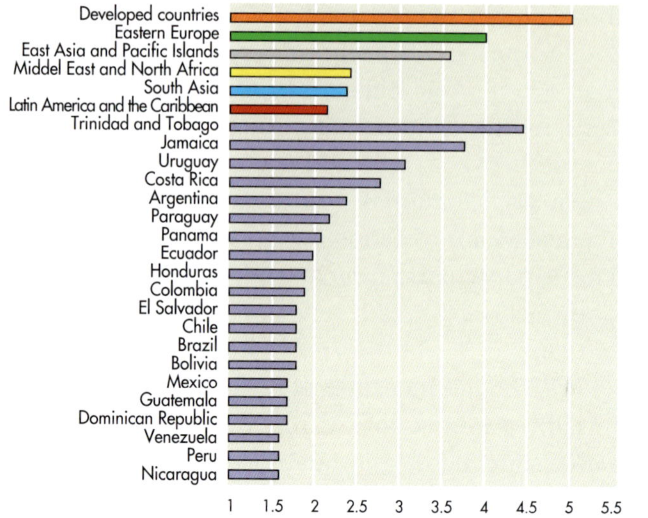

Note: The survey asked respondents to rank schools as follows: The difference in the quality of schools available to rich and poor children in your country is (1=large, 7=small).
Source: World Economic Forum (2001).

problems because workers' productivity depends, to a large extent, on factors outside the control of workers. If the economic and institutional environment discourages investment and innovation, or if finance and basic infrastructure are absent, labor productivity will be impaired and efforts to increase the level of education will not be an effective way to improve labor outcomes.

To grasp the relative importance of education vis-à-vis these other factors as alternative causes of low labor productivity, define a worker to have "low productivity" if he or she earns less than $1 an hour in the primary job.[32] The $1 threshold must be adjusted in each country to reflect differences in the cost of living. This definition of low productivity is both simple and meaningful because it connects neatly with standard poverty measures.[33] Table 3.7 shows the share of low-paid workers among urban males age 30-50 for 12 countries in the region at the end of the 1990s. In this sample, more than 45 percent earn less than the $1 threshold in Bolivia, El Salvador, Nicaragua, and Peru, while fewer than 25 percent have hourly earnings below $1 in Argentina, Chile, Costa Rica, Mexico, and Panama.

These figures suggest that wages and productivity levels are very low for a large share of workers in most countries. This is only partly the result of lack of education, because in some countries a large proportion of workers with relatively high levels of education have very low levels of productivity. In Bolivia, 41 percent of workers with secondary education and 18 percent with four years of university education earn less than $1 an hour. These percentages are similarly high in Nicaragua and Peru. By contrast, in Mexico only 5 percent of workers with secondary education and 1 percent with university schooling are poor according to this measure.

To examine whether increases in education can solve the problem of low wages in the short

[32] Results are computed based on income from the primary job. However, except when otherwise mentioned, the results do not differ much when they are based on a more comprehensive measure of income that includes all jobs.

[33] Thus, considering that the average worker in the region works an average of 44 hours a week and shares his or her income with two dependents, earnings of less than $1 an hour (adjusted for purchasing power parity, PPP) result in per capita household income of less than PPP$2 a day, a standard measure of moderate poverty. Duryea and Pagés (forthcoming) show that the proportion of workers earning less than PPP$1 an hour is correlated with the share of moderate poverty at the country level (the correlation coefficient is 0.84).

Table 3.7 Male Workers Age 30–50 Earning Less than a Dollar an Hour
(Percent)

		Education level			
Country	Year	All education levels	Primary	Secondary complete	Four or more years of higher education
Argentina	1999	17.00	15.32	7.54	5.66
Bolivia	1999	45.62	65.70	41.30	17.60
Brazil	1999	34.80	47.40	15.70	2.70
Chile	1998	21.38	38.90	16.80	2.40
Costa Rica	1998	18.55	30.60	14.70	2.20
El Salvador	1998	49.63	69.20	35.90	6.30
Guatemala	1998	39.92	29.81	8.56	0.33
Mexico	1998	15.89	27.70	5.10	1.00
Nicaragua	1998	53.96	71.00	43.50	14.00
Panama	1999	17.64	33.20	15.10	2.70
Peru	2000	45.83	72.80	48.10	19.00
Uruguay	1998	30.35	28.37	18.16	8.09

Source: Duryea and Pagés (forthcoming), based on household surveys.

run, it is useful to simulate the results of making secondary school universal. This can be done by computing the effect on incomes and the share of poor workers if all workers who had completed less than secondary school in the late 1990s had actually completed secondary school. It should be noted that this simulation ignores the possible reduction in the returns to secondary school caused by an increase in the supply of skilled workers. Therefore, it must be interpreted as an upper limit on the scope for the change in education to directly affect hourly wages in the short run. The results appear in Figure 3.23.

While the share of poorly remunerated workers would fall by more than half in Brazil, Guatemala, and Mexico, in four countries (Bolivia, El Salvador, Nicaragua, and Peru), 30 percent or more would still earn below the threshold. Even in Uruguay, almost 20 percent of the workers would still qualify as having low productivity. Taking the average across countries, the percentage of low-paid workers would fall by about one-third, that is, from 33 to 23 percent of all workers. Although such a reduction is impressive, it would take an extraordinary effort to achieve. In some countries, such as Argentina, Chile, Costa Rica, Panama, and Peru, this increase could be achieved in two decades if current progress were maintained in the future, or in one decade if progress in education attained the levels achieved in East Asia. However, in other countries, the required progress in education is huge. In Brazil, it would be necessary to increase average years of education by at least four years, which at historical rates of progress would require another 40 or 50 years.

These results highlight the fact that lack of education can only partly be blamed for the low productivity and wages that affect many workers in Latin America. Expansion in education alone will not lift everyone's productivity and earnings above the poverty level in a short time span. In order for expansions in education to have a large effect on individual incomes, the effect of every additional year of education on wages (the so-called returns to education) would have to be large. But this is not where the problem lies.

Despite widespread failure in the quality of education and the poor results obtained on internationally comparable exams, in Latin America the percentage increase in earnings associated with

Figure 3.23 Scenarios for Reducing Low-productivity Jobs
(Percentage of workers earning less than $1 an hour)

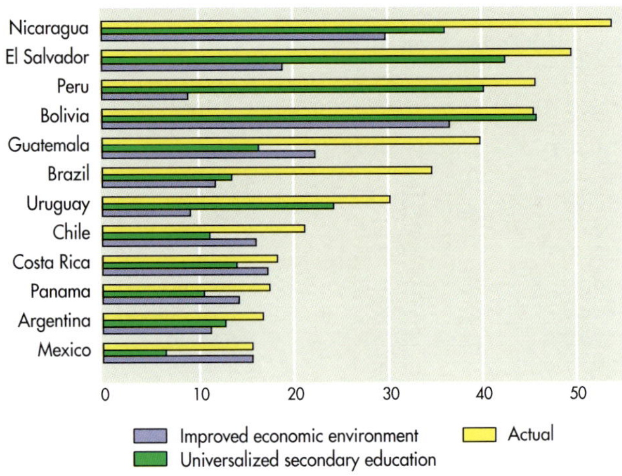

Source: Duryea and Pagés (forthcoming).

one extra year of primary, secondary, or tertiary education is quite high. Table 3.8 presents the estimated returns to one year of education across countries.[34] In the 12 countries in the sample, the median return to one additional year of primary schooling is 7 percent, while the median return to secondary and tertiary schooling is even higher (9 and 16 percent, respectively).[35] By comparison, Krueger and Lindahl (2001) report average returns to schooling across all schooling levels from 3 percent in Sweden, to 6-7 percent in Canada, 9 percent in the United States, and 13 percent in Austria.

Large returns to schooling are only a necessary but not sufficient condition for education to have a large effect on poverty level wages. After all, returns to schooling are measured in percentage rates. This implies that the final impact on absolute wages depends on the base to which that percentage applies. Since in Latin America a worker without education or skills may earn little in absolute terms, a relatively large increase in the wage (in percentage terms) as a result of education may still leave the worker with low wages.

The hourly wages of a worker without education or experience is a reflection of the productivity that an unskilled worker is able to obtain with other factors of production, such as physical capital, or public goods, such as institutions or infrastructure. Therefore, wages reflect the quality of the institutional and economic setting in which workers live and produce. To gauge the importance of the environment, consider the effect of a hypothetical simulation in which countries could instantaneously achieve the economic and institutional conditions of Mexico—the country with the best underlying conditions in the sample—as measured by the earnings of a person without education or labor market experience. The share of poor workers would decline substantially: Peru's share of low-paid jobs would drop dramatically, from 46 to 9 percent, while El Salvador's share would decline from 49 to 20 percent.

These results demonstrate that lack of education cannot be considered the sole explanation for the problems of low productivity and wages that affect a large proportion of workers in several Latin American countries. This does not imply that efforts to expand education are worthless in the short run, but rather that they need to be supported by an improvement in the underlying economic and institutional conditions. In the long run, a better-educated workforce should attract investments in capital and technology leading to higher growth and productivity.

But could lack of education be singled out as the main reason behind the problem of the increasing wage gap described in chapter 1? The wage gap between workers with complete tertiary education and those with complete secondary education has been growing 1.4 percent a year according to the estimates in Table 3.9.[36] In two decades, that would represent an increase of 32 percent, but some countries have had much larger increases. According to estimates by de Ferranti and others (2003, p.

[34] See Duryea and Pagés (forthcoming) for a description of the methodology used to estimate returns to schooling in Latin America.

[35] The coefficients do not measure returns, but wage effects, since in order to capture returns to education, it would be necessary to subtract foregone earnings and other costs of education. The results do not change qualitatively when improvement in the quality of education is included in the analysis.

[36] The estimates presented here differ somewhat from those in chapter 1 because the data coverage and estimation methods are not identical. However, both sets of estimates as well as those by de Ferranti and others (2003, p. 50) reach the same conclusion: returns to tertiary education (relative to secondary) have increased. (See Box 1.4 in chapter 1 for a further explanation of alternative methods of estimation.)

Table 3.8 Returns to Education and Experience, Urban Male Workers Age 30–50
(Percentage change in hourly wage)

Country	Year	Returns to: Primary education	Secondary education	Tertiary education	Five years of experience	Hourly earnings of a worker without schooling or experience[a]
Argentina	1999	5	8	17	22	0.48
Bolivia	1999	5	3	13	18	0.44
Brazil	1999	12	15	22	18	0.28
Chile	1998	7	12	24	9	0.50
Costa Rica	1998	6	6	19	14	0.54
El Salvador	1998	5	8	20	20	0.29
Guatemala	1998	8	13	14	17	0.37
Mexico	1998	7	10	15	18	0.55
Nicaragua	1998	9	13	15	10	0.30
Panama	1999	6	8	16	10	0.51
Peru	2000	10	9	15	9	0.24
Uruguay	1998	9	9	15	22	0.31

[a] Earnings are in purchasing-power-parity adjusted dollars.
Source: Duryea and Pagés (forthcoming), based on household surveys.

50), during the 1990s, "the relative wages of workers with tertiary education increased by an incredible 72.9 percent in Colombia, by 48.3 percent and 45.4 percent in Mexico and Bolivia, and 'only' by 19.7 percent and 11.7 percent in Argentina and Brazil." By contrast, the relative wages of workers with complete secondary education with respect to workers with complete primary education have not shown a clear trend; the share with secondary education has increased in Bolivia and Mexico (until the mid-1990s), but declined in Argentina, Brazil, Chile, and Colombia.

The relative supply of educated workers is, to some extent, the reason for this contrasting pattern between the relative wages of workers with tertiary education vis-à-vis those with secondary education on the one hand, and the relative wages of the latter with respect to those with primary education on the other. Thus, although the relative supply of workers with tertiary education (vis-à-vis that of secondary) has been falling at a rate of 0.1 percent annually, the relative supply of workers with secondary education (vis-à-vis that of primary) has been expanding at the astonishing rate of 4.3 percent. Therefore, there is some weight to the argument that slow progress in education is behind the increasing wage gap. Notice, however, that the argument holds true only if slow progress in tertiary education is the problem. But progress in tertiary education has been slow only in relative terms, not because it has remained stagnant in absolute terms. Therefore, the widening gap could also be seen as the result of progress in secondary education. Compared with international patterns, most Latin American countries lag behind in secondary education, not in tertiary education (IDB 1998). Therefore, the increasing gap is a natural result of the region's efforts to catch up with those patterns.

Furthermore, the increasing gap may be a byproduct of the higher (although still mediocre) rates of economic growth in the region, especially up to the mid-1990s. Although relative wages and the relative supply of labor are related in the expected way, the relationship is surprisingly weak. In Figure 3.24, the relative wage of workers with tertiary education tends to fall as the relative size of this group of workers increases. However, the relationship is barely significant at the 10 percent level and the elasticity is very low: the relative supply of workers with tertiary education would have to double to reduce the wage gap by 15 percent. The reason is that relative wages are not only

Table 3.9 The Wage Gap in Latin America

Gap	Wage gap trend	Relative supply trend	Relative demand trend: Elasticity = -2	Relative demand trend: Elasticity = -1.33
Tertiary education vs. secondary education	0.014 (3.99)***	–0.009 (1.80)*	0.019 (2.32)**	0.024 (1.72)*
Number of observations	70	70	70	70
Secondary education vs. primary education	–0.001 (0.22)	0.043 (10.24)***	0.042 (6.38)***	0.085 (7.41)***
Number of observations	70	70	70	70

* Significant at 10 percent.
** Significant at 5 percent.
*** Significant at 1 percent.
Note: Each coefficient comes from a separate regression with country fixed effects. Absolute values of t-statistics are in parentheses.
Source: IDB calculations based on data from a panel of household surveys for 12 countries between 1986 and 1999.

Figure 3.24 Relative Supply and Relative Wages of Workers with Tertiary Education in Latin America

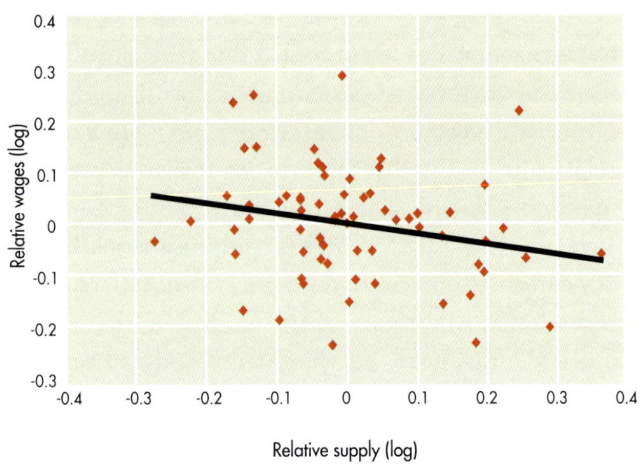

Note: Each dot represents an observation for a country, after controlling for fixed effects by country. Coefficient = -0.15; standard error = 0.85.
Source: IDB calculations based on household surveys.

a matter of relative supply, but also of relative demand, which is probably influenced by economic growth and other factors that affect the demand for skills.

To gauge the importance of relative demand, Table 3.10 shows how the relative wages of workers with tertiary education have increased as relative supply has declined. However, the decline in supply was too small to explain the price increase, which could happen only if, for some reason, demand was tilting toward more use of skilled than unskilled workers. The last two columns in the table measure the importance of changes in relative demand using a standard production function and a range of elasticities common in the literature on this subject (for a technical explanation, see the appendixes in chapter 6). While the relative supply of workers with tertiary education has been falling 0.1 percent a year, the relative demand for those workers has grown between 1.9 and 2.4 percent. Clearly, changes in demand are behind the widening wage gap. The same reasoning explains why the wages of workers with secondary education have not fallen relative to those of workers with less education: although the relative supply of workers with secondary education has increased at an annual rate of 4.3 percent, relative demand has been at least as dynamic.

The reasons behind the fast increase in the relative demand for skills are not clearly understood. It is likely that economic growth induces a higher demand for skills. When an economy grows vigorously, new firms are created, investment rises, and the variety and quality of all types and goods and services expand. In this process, the demand for labor could grow faster for skilled than unskilled workers. Empirical evidence lends some support to this hypothesis. According to the estimates in Table 3.10, the relative wages of workers

Table 3.10 Relative Wages and the Relative Supply of Workers with Tertiary Education in Latin America, 1986–99

Variable	(1)	(2)	(3)	(4)
Relative supply (tertiary/secondary)	–0.163	–0.149	–0.114	–0.121
	(1.83)*	(1.69)*	(1.25)	(1.26)
GDP per capita PPP (log)	0.326		0.079	
	(3.09)***		(0.45)	
GDP per capita trend		0.386		0.089
		(2.95)***		(0.21)
GDP per capita detrended		0.291		0.267
		(0.94)		(0.86)
Trend			0.011	0.009
			(1.78)*	(0.73)
Number of observations	70	70	70	70
R^2	0.79	0.80	0.80	0.80

* Significant at 10 percent.
*** Significant at 1 percent.
Note: The dependent variable is relative wages. All variables are in logarithms. All regressions include country fixed effects. Absolute values of t-statistics are in parentheses.
Source: IDB calculations.

with tertiary education (with respect to those with secondary education) tend to increase 3.3 percent for every 10 percent increase in GDP per capita (after controlling for changes in relative supply). More precisely, the estimates suggest that permanent (rather than cyclical) changes in GDP per capita may have an effect on wage gaps.

Since the relative supply of workers with tertiary education has been almost stagnant (the share of workers with secondary education has increased faster than that of college graduates), the results in Table 3.10 would suggest that the widening wage gap observed in the past decade was mainly due to economic growth. However, the estimates also suggest that other factors, apart from economic growth, could explain the increasing demand for skills. In fact, the estimates are unable to distinguish between the influence of permanent increases in GDP per capita and a common time trend for all countries, which could reflect trends in technological change or other factors.

Furthermore, the estimates implicitly assume that the supply and demand for skills are independent forces, but it is not unlikely that the demand for skills is influenced by supply. A possible reason is that the productivity of skilled workers is enhanced when there are more workers with similar abilities and education around them. If that were the case, the increasing wage gap could at least partly be a result of the changing educational composition of the labor supply. Chapter 6 discusses this and other hypotheses to explain the widening wage gap.

To summarize, although increasing the level and quality of education is desirable for good reasons, it is not a silver bullet against unemployment, low productivity, and the widening wage gap. If nothing else changed in the functioning of labor markets, more education probably would lead to more rather than less unemployment, and would not solve the problem of low productivity that affects millions of workers in countries with inadequate economic or institutional environments. It is not even clear that greater efforts to increase the supply of skills at the tertiary level would reduce the wage gap in a substantial way. This chapter offers a word of caution against the expectation that education will suffice to alleviate the ills of Latin America's labor markets. However, education should not be discarded as a source of productivity and economic growth or as a means of improving social development.

Conclusion: Channeling Labor Supply Trends

The supply of labor is rising fast in Latin America and the Caribbean due to the combination of demographic trends and higher female labor force participation. Although in some English-speaking countries and a few Central American countries large emigration flows are mitigating growth in the supply of labor, most countries in the region are going through a period of fast expansion in the number of workers, most of whom are relatively young. The process of deceleration of the labor supply has started already in a few countries, but it will take several decades before most of the region moves to a phase of low labor supply growth. In the meantime, the labor force will gradually become older, more gender balanced, more urban, and more educated, trends that are already apparent almost everywhere.

Fast labor supply growth should not be seen with anxiety, but as a potential source of economic and social benefit. The region is currently enjoying a window of demographic opportunity in which the share of those of working age in the total population is increasing. This implies lower costs of education and social security per family and as a share of total public expenditures, which should lead to better opportunities for increasing savings and incomes. As young dependency rates decline, a larger share of women will join the labor market, further helping increase income per capita levels. Meanwhile, as already observed in some countries, the labor force participation rates of the young will tend to decline, as families will be able to afford more years of education for their children.

However, these gains will not be automatic. Whether they are reaped depends to a large extent on the institutions and policies in place. Of special importance will be the set of labor regulations and institutions that can influence labor force participation decisions and improve the ability of the new entrants to find productive jobs. Reaping the benefits of the demographic bonus will also depend on the support that the macroeconomic and institutional environment provide to families, companies, and governments to increase their saving rates and create a financial cushion for the foreseeable increase in the share of retirees.

Traditional mechanisms for protecting labor in Latin America were designed to provide stability to formal employment rather than to encourage the involvement of women in economic activities or stabilize income from labor and other social protection for all workers. While policies that lead companies to discriminate against women should be avoided in principle, the economic costs of these policies increase with the size of the female labor force. Examples are restrictions on part-time hiring, rigid work schedules, high severance payments, and high maternity costs to be paid by firms (rather than the social security system). Women may seek more flexible working arrangements or may have higher rates of job separation if they also have primary responsibility for child or elder care. Well-intended but ultimately misguided protection efforts reduce their employment possibilities and should be replaced when possible by collective protection mechanisms against unemployment, illness, and old age. The high minimum wages in effect in some countries also cause discrimination against women and against workers with less education. (These policies and institutions are further discussed in chapters 7 and 8.)

In order for women to be incorporated into more productive economic activities, they must be freed up from household tasks. The lack or unreliability of water, electricity, and sewage services limits women's participation and lowers their productivity potential. The incorporation of women into regular employment is also limited by lack of help with childcare and health services for children.[37] As this chapter has shown, there is no basis for arguing that higher female labor force participation takes place at the expense of men's labor possibilities. Reducing women's household chores would benefit everyone.

Labor creation in many Latin American countries is constrained by high entry costs to new firms. As chapter 2 shows, a fluid process of creation and destruction of jobs is part and parcel of

[37] For a discussion of these policies, see IDB (1998).

any dynamic economy and should not be restrained for fear of causing job instability. In order to assimilate large numbers of entrants into the labor market, hiring must be eased by facilitating the creation of new firms. A worldwide study of 75 countries finds that some Latin American nations are among those that require the most procedures to start a business (Djankov and others 2000). Typically, prospective firms need to complete more than 10 separate procedures to start operations in Latin America, while developed countries require only three procedures. Theoretically, these requirements guarantee that labor and tax rules are enforced, and that worker and consumer rights are protected. However, in practice, cumbersome procedures have the opposite effects, and by granting implicit protection to incumbent firms, too many procedures distort the process of destruction and creation of jobs. This worsens the working possibilities of new entrants and all those who require greater job mobility and flexibility.

By restricting job creation and mobility, many Latin American countries may be squandering the opportunities of the current phase of fast growth of the supply of labor. This phase should also be an opportunity to increase savings to cover future pension costs. Traditional pension systems in Latin America operate on a pay-as-you-go basis in which today's workers cover the pensions of workers from previous generations who are now retired, with the implicit commitment that when today's workers reach retirement, the workers of the future will pay for them. But this mechanism does not impose the same costs on all generations. Today's working generations are large in comparison with the number of those retired, and are therefore contributing too little. But they will also be large in comparison with the size of future generations, which means that, with the current pay-as-you-go system still in place in many countries, they will become a heavy burden for future generations of workers. The countries that are still enjoying the demographic bonus ought to take advantage of it to pay for pensions by generating the savings that will make it possible to cover such expenses in the future.

Good use of the savings potential during the period of demographic opportunity is essential not only to avoid imposing a heavy burden on future workers, but also to increase the basis of productive capital with which they will work. Chapter 6 shows that capital-labor ratios are low and stagnant in Latin America, limiting labor productivity. Exploiting the savings potential of the demographic opportunity requires a sound macroeconomic environment and efficient and secure mechanisms for channeling those resources toward productive investments.

Part of the increased savings potential of families during the period of demographic opportunity will be devoted to improving their children's education. From a macroeconomic point of view, this will also be facilitated by the decline in the ratio of children to taxpayers. In order to take advantage of this opportunity, there must be better organization of education systems on the supply side, enabling them to respond to the changing needs of families, and support mechanisms to help pay the costs incurred by low-income families in sending their children to school on the demand side. Programs of this type, such as Mexico's Progresa (recently renamed Oportunidades) have proved to be an effective way of improving school attendance, while facilitating parents' work activities (see IDB 2002b). Although only part of the solution, better education systems will be essential to remedy the current ills of Latin America's labor markets.

Appendix Table 3.1 Household Surveys

Country	Early 1990s	Late 1990s	Survey
Argentina[a]	1992	2001	Encuesta Permanente de Hogares
Bolivia		1999	Encuesta de Condiciones de Hogares de Vida
Brazil	1993	1999	Pesquisa Nacional por Amostra de Domicílios
Chile	1992	1998	CASEN
Colombia	1993	1999	Encuesta Nacional de Hogares
Costa Rica	1993	1998	Encuesta de Hogares de Propósitos Múltiples
Ecuador		1998	Encuesta de Condiciones de Vida
El Salvador		1998	Encuesta de Hogares de Propósitos Múltiples
Guatemala		1998	Encuesta Nacional de Ingresos y Gastos Familiares
Honduras	1992	1999	Encuesta Permanente de Hogares de Propósitos Múltiples
Mexico	1992	2000	Encuesta Nacional de Ingresos y Gastos
Nicaragua	1993	2001	Encuesta Nacional de Hogares de Medición de Calidad de Vida
Panama	1991	2000	Encuesta de Hogares
Paraguay		1998	Encuesta Integrada de Hogares
Peru		2000	Encuesta Nacional de Hogares sobre Mediciones de Niveles de Vida
Uruguay[a]	1992	2000	Encuesta Continua de Hogares
Venezuela	1993	1999	Encuesta de Hogares por Muestreo

[a] The sample covers only urban areas.

Chapter 4

Working in a Volatile World: Macroeconomic Shocks and the Labor Market

Labor markets in Latin America operate in a volatile macroeconomic environment. This chapter documents the sources of this volatility and discusses its impact on the labor market. Although shocks affect both labor demand and labor supply, the chapter focuses on the former (movements in labor supply are discussed in chapter 3).

After documenting the high degree of macroeconomic volatility that characterizes Latin America, the chapter shows that shifts in labor demand translate into changes in employment or changes in wages (or both). The analysis explores why, compared with developed countries, Latin American countries tend to adjust more through wages and less through employment. It also discusses characteristics of emerging market countries that may amplify the impact of external shocks.

Disappointing Performance

Latin America's macroeconomic performance has been disappointing. The growth rate of the region's income can be described in two words: low and volatile. Over the past 30 years, average annual growth of income per capita in the region has been just above 1 percent, well below that of East Asia and the rest of Asia (which ranged between 3.5 and 6 percent) and developed countries (see Figure 4.1). Only Sub-Saharan Africa and the Middle East did worse than Latin America. In the long run, the difference between 1 and 4 percent is dramatic. At the end of 2000, Latin America's gross domestic product (GDP) per capita was 40 percent higher than it was in 1970. The corresponding figures for East Asia and developed countries were 320 percent and 80 percent, respectively.

Not only has Latin America's growth been slow, but it could also be described as "unsafe at any speed." Table 4.1 shows that Latin America is characterized by a high degree of economic volatility. Again, only Sub-Saharan Africa and the Middle East have been more volatile than Latin America. Studies suggest that this high degree of economic volatility contributes to the poor growth performance of the region.[1]

There are two main reasons why Latin America is so volatile. First, the region is subject to large shocks, and second, countries in the region are poorly equipped to cope with these shocks.

Latin America is subject to large terms of trade and capital flow volatility (again, only Sub-Saharan Africa and the Middle East are subject to larger shocks (Table 4.1). It is well-known that nega-

[1] Ramey and Ramey (1995) show that volatility leads to lower growth. Inter-American Development Bank (1995) discusses in greater detail the links between volatility and growth performance, and the determinants of macroeconomic volatility in Latin America.

Table 4.1 Growth and Volatility by Region, 1970–2000

Region	Average GDP growth	Volatility		
		Output gap	Terms of trade	Capital flows
Developed countries	2.10	0.04	6.65	6.47
Latin America	1.20	0.09	13.09	9.25
Africa	0.03	0.10	20.11	10.77
Middle East	0.70	0.14	28.42	22.64
East Asia	3.92	0.07	7.68	7.95
Rest of Asia	5.94	0.09	15.76	7.59

Note: Volatility is the standard deviation for the whole period.
Source: IDB calculations based on data from World Bank (various years).

Figure 4.1 Per Capita GDP Growth
(Percent)

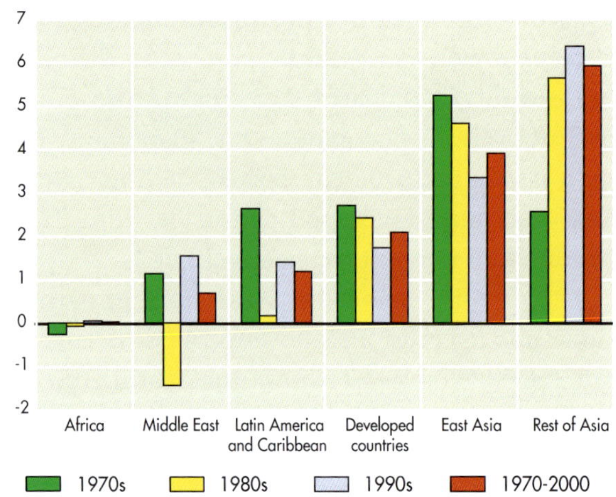

Note: Averages are weighted by GDP.
Source: IDB calculations based on data from World Bank (various years).

tive terms of trade shocks have a large impact on net exports and hence on aggregate demand; volatile capital flows are, if anything, even more destructive. When access to capital markets is closed, which happens with distressing frequency in Latin America, the collapse of real activity is dramatic. A sudden swing in the level of the capital account, or "sudden stop," sets in motion a destructive process as credit dries up throughout the economy and production is strangled.[2] The drastic growth slowdowns and recessions that follow sudden stops in net capital flows are striking. The difference in average growth between years with open access to financial markets and those with closed access to them is more than 2 percentage points. The magnitude of these external shocks is amplified by inability to conduct countercyclical policies (see Box 4.1).

Although macroeconomic volatility and low growth play an important role in explaining unemployment in the region, they cannot fully explain the behavior of unemployment. A simple way to show this is to look at the share of the variance of unemployment that is explained by the cyclical component of GDP. In a sample of 15 Latin American countries for which data are available, the business cycle explains more than 50 percent of the variance of unemployment in seven countries (Figure 4.2), but plays a limited role in explaining unemployment in the other eight countries. Figure 4.3 makes the same point by showing that the business cycle plays a modest role in explaining the difference in unemployment between the 1980s and the 1990s. In particular, the green bars in Figure 4.3 plot the difference between average unemployment in the 1990s and the 1980s and indicate that unemployment increased in nine of the 15 countries for which data are available. The red bars measure the difference in unemployment between the two periods that is not due to the cyclical component of GDP.[3] The figure shows that the output

[2] See Calvo, Izquierdo, and Talvi (2002).

[3] Technically, the red bars are the coefficients on a decade dummy (taking the value 1 for the 1990s and 0 for the 1980s) obtained by running a regression in which the dependent variable is the level of unemployment and the explanatory variables are the output gap and the decade dummy.

Box 4.1. How to Reduce Volatility

Greater openness, trade diversification, and ability to implement countercyclical policies are necessary conditions for reducing the impact of external shocks. Openness is important because, other things equal, the costs of the macroeconomic adjustment required by a sudden stop in capital flows is lower in countries that have a larger share of international trade (Calvo, Izquierdo, and Talvi 2002).[1] Trade diversification can play a role in reducing terms of trade volatility.[2] Stabilization funds can also reduce the negative impact of terms of trade volatility.

Macroeconomic policies could limit the impact of external demand shocks, but, contrary to most developed countries, Latin American countries have been unable to respond to shocks by implementing countercyclical monetary and fiscal policies. If anything, the region has been characterized by procyclical macroeconomic policies that magnify the effect of external shocks.

The inability to implement countercyclical policies is due to several factors. The most important are: (i) weak fiscal structure, (ii) procyclical international financing (that is, international financing often disappears during economic downturns when it is most needed to finance countercyclical policies), (iii) underdeveloped financial markets, and (iv) limited willingness (or ability) to let the exchange rate float freely. Political factors may also be significant. Rodrik (2001) suggests that there is a correlation between economic volatility and political systems that are under the control of a small elite. Some of these problems have a domestic solution, others require an international solution, and still others may have no clear solution, at least in the short run.

Developed countries can finance countercyclical fiscal policies by increasing public debt during recessions. There is a large literature (for a recent survey, see Braun [2003]) that shows that this may not be the case in developing countries. Talvi and Végh (2000) argue that procyclical policies arise from government's inability to accumulate surpluses during economic expansions. Gavin and Perotti (1997) and Gavin and others (1996) emphasize the role of limited creditworthiness and subinvestment-grade status in leading to a situation in which developing countries face higher borrowing costs and lack of access to capital markets during recessions. Although there is no easy solution for this problem, better budget institutions and cyclically adjusted hard budget constraints could help in reducing the effects of procyclical fiscal policies. In particular, policies that lead to accumulation of surpluses during periods of economic expansion would allow for limited countercyclical policies during recessions.

Better fiscal positions could also help in reducing the procyclical effects of international capital flows and international contagion. It should be pointed out, however, that it is unlikely that these problems will be fully solved by domestic measures. In this sense, international contagion can only be addressed by reforming the international financial architecture.

Underdeveloped financial markets are also part of the story. There is some evidence that financial intermediation dampens the macroeconomic effects of terms of trade volatility (Beck, Lundberg, and Majnoni 2001) and capital flow volatility (Caballero and Krishnamurthy 2001). Low inflation, better regulation and supervision, investor protection, and pension reforms are key conditions for deepening Latin American financial markets.

A floating exchange rate regime is important for conducting independent monetary policy. However, there is a lack of agreement on whether Latin American countries can afford such a regime. On the one hand, some analysts claim that, because of liability dollarization, countries in the region cannot respond to shocks with expansionary monetary policy.[3] On the other hand, others point out that, even in the presence of liability dollarization, emerging market countries can maintain a limited degree of monetary autonomy, and that dollarization and currency boards cannot solve the fundamental problems of emerging markets.[4]

Calvo and Mishkin (2003) argue that the debate on the exchange rate regime does not capture the main point that emerging market countries are fundamentally different from developed countries. In emerging markets, the institutional framework is often weak and the key to macroeconomic success is not the exchange rate regime, but the fundamental institutions underlying it—those associated with fiscal, financial, and price stability. Therefore, the debate should focus less on whether a float or an exchange rate peg is a better arrangement, and more on the deeper institutional arrangements that support the exchange rate regime of choice.

[1] Another option would be to impose restrictions on capital flows, but this may have costs in terms of growth. However, the evidence is not clear-cut; see Eichengreen (2001).

[2] If international trade is not diversified, greater openness could increase the macroeconomic effects of terms of trade volatility.

[3] See Calvo and Reinhart (2002) and Hausmann, Panizza, and Stein (2001).

[4] For the two sides of the debate, see Calvo (2000) and Sachs and Larraín (1999). Alternative proposals aim at dealing with liability dollarization head-on by developing mechanisms through which emerging market countries can increase their ability to borrow in their own currency. See Eichengreen, Hausmann, and Panizza (2002).

Figure 4.2 Variance of Unemployment Explained by the Output Gap

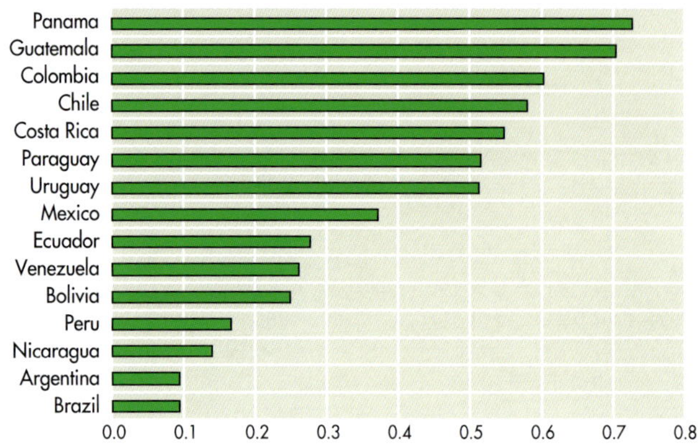

Note: The figure plots the R^2 of regressions of the level of unemployment over the output gap and lagged output gap. The output gap is measured as as the deviation between the log of actual GDP and the log of trend GDP (trend GDP is computed using a Hodrick-Prescott filter with λ=1000).
Source: IDB calculations.

Figure 4.3 The Difference between Average Unemployment in the 1980s and 1990s
(Percent)

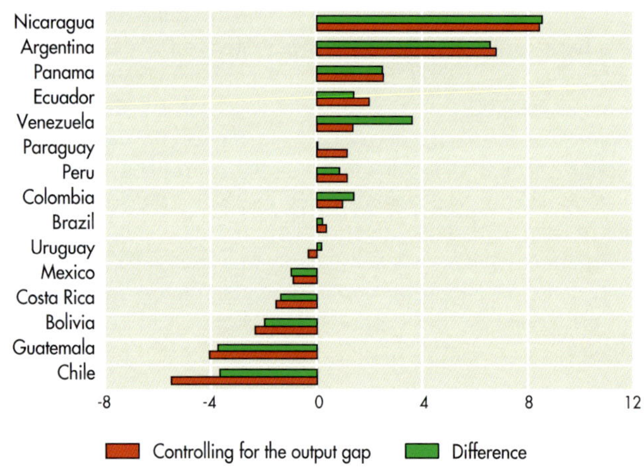

Note: Coefficients on a decade dummy (taking the value 1 for the 1990s and 0 for the 1980s) obtained by running a regression in which the dependent variable is the level of unemployment and the explanatory variables are the output gap and the decade dummy (trend GDP is computed using a Hodrick-Prescott filter with λ =1000).
Source: IDB calculations.

gap cannot explain the difference between average unemployment in the two decades (except in Chile and Venezuela).

The cases of Argentina and Nicaragua are particularly puzzling. Both countries exhibited a large increase in unemployment in the 1990s that could not be explained by GDP growth. The increase in unemployment in Nicaragua could be explained by the post-civil war adjustment in the early 1990s (there was a downward trend in unemployment in Nicaragua after 1993). But there is no explanation for the behavior of unemployment in Argentina, which, until the late 1990s, had excellent economic performance and increasing unemployment.

Employment

Most people find it intuitive that when economic conditions are good, employment increases (and unemployment decreases) and that when economic conditions are bad, employment decreases (and unemployment increases). But why is this? Is the relationship between economic activity and employment the same across countries and periods?

The economy could be in a situation in which all factors of production are fully employed, or in a situation with unemployed factors. In the first case, output growth could be due to either technological progress or an increase in the amount of available factors of production (more capital or more labor). Interestingly, growth could increase employment even in a situation of full employment. An increase in capital accumulation (or a positive technological shock) might increase the productivity of labor and, by increasing wages, attract new workers into the labor market. In this sense, long-run growth is key for employment growth.[4] Rather than determining employment, however, long-run growth is much more important in determining wages. Chapter 6 discusses the relationship between technological progress and wages.

The link between macroeconomic conditions and employment is stronger in the presence of unemployed resources or, in the jargon of econo-

[4] However, lack of aggregate demand can generate a situation in which a positive technological shock (that increases labor productivity) leads to higher unemployment. Increases in labor productivity and contractionary economic policies have been used to explain the increase in European unemployment (see Blanchard and Wolfers 2000).

Box 4.2. Wage or Employment Adjustment?

What determines cross-country differences in employment responses to changes in aggregate demand? In principle, the share of income that is captured by each factor of production is more or less constant over time.[1] Most studies show that in developed countries, labor captures two-thirds of production. (It is not clear whether labor shares are lower in developing countries; see Gollin [2002].) Thus, in a country with a GDP of $10 billion, workers would earn (including taxes and nonwage benefits) a total of $6.6 billion and the owners of capital would capture the remaining $3.4 billion. With constant factor shares, a negative shock that reduces total GDP by 10 percent would reduce the income captured by labor to $6 billion. Assuming that before the negative shock the economy employed one million workers (with average earnings of $6,600), employment after the shock could be maintained at one million only if average earnings dropped to $6,000. If average earnings remained constant at $6,600, employment would drop by about 91,000 units. This example shows that a negative macroeconomic shock does not necessarily lead to a proportional drop in employment. Part of the shock could be absorbed through an adjustment in wages. However, if wages did not adjust, the effect of the shock would fully translate into lower employment.

The Figure illustrates this idea. The vertical axis plots the change in employment and the horizontal axis plots the change in real wages brought about by a 1 percent change in income. The negative slope shows that there is a trade-off between employment and wage adjustment.

Employment and Wage Adjustment in Latin America

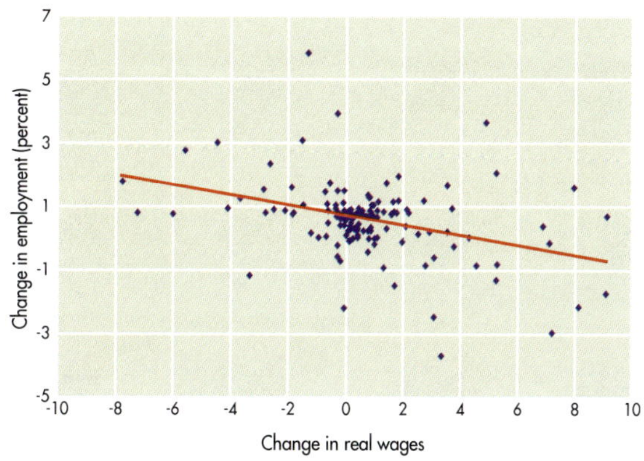

Note: Each point in the scatter is one year for one country in Latin American and shows changes in response to a 1 percent change in income.
Source: IDB calculations.

Countries that have a large adjustment in terms of wages have a smaller adjustment in terms of employment.

[1] This is true only in principle. Labor shares do change over time, but the changes tend to be small. In general, it is always true that the burden of a decrease in total production will be absorbed by both factors of production.

mists, when output is demand determined. In this situation, changes in aggregate demand determine how much is produced and, in turn, this determines the demand for factors of production. However, the employment response to changes in macroeconomic conditions is not constant across countries or across time within countries. In fact, there is a trade-off between adjustment in terms of real wages and adjustment in terms of employment or unemployment (see Box 4.2). For instance, Brazil, Costa Rica, Mexico, and Peru tend to adjust more through wages, and Chile, Jamaica, Panama, and Colombia through employment (Table 4.2).

But why do some countries adjust more in terms of wages and others more in terms of employment? One explanation has to do with differences in the willingness of workers to supply

Table 4.2 Employment and Wage Elasticity, Selected Countries, 1980–2000

Employment elasticity	Wage elasticity: Low	High	Very high
Very low			Argentina (1980s) Brazil Costa Rica Mexico Peru
Low	Argentina (1990s) Chile Jamaica Panama	Uruguay Venezuela	
High	Colombia		

Source: IDB calculations.

Figure 4.4 **Employment and Wage Adjustment**

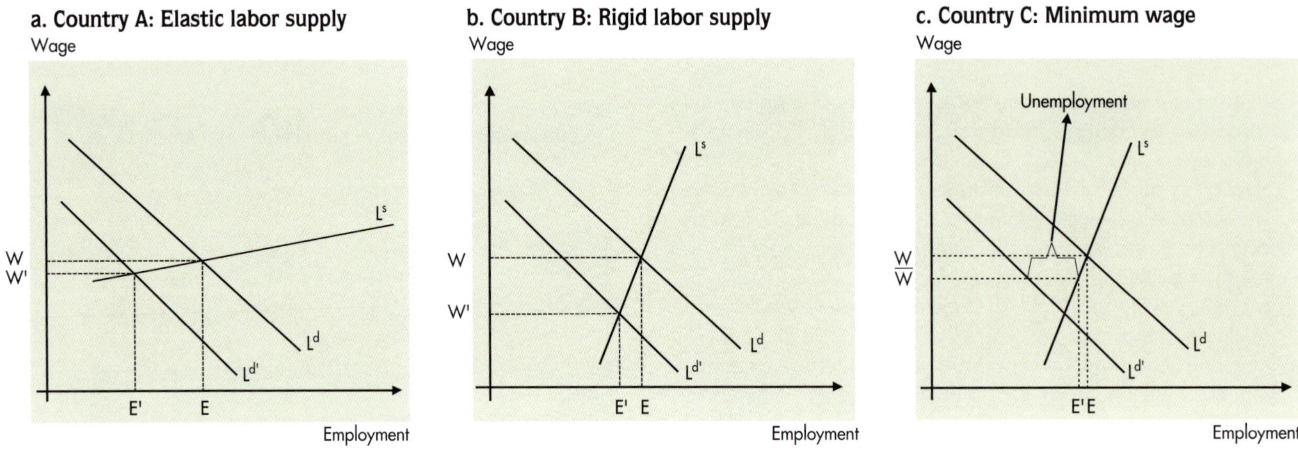

labor. In Figure 4.4, panels a and b represent two countries, A and B, that are subject to the same negative shock, resulting in a shift of labor demand (line L^d) to the left. This implies that, at any given wage, firms want to hire fewer workers. In country A, labor supply (line L^s) is relatively flat (or, in economic jargon, elastic). This means that small drops in wages will lead workers to drastically reduce the amount of labor they are willing to supply. In country B, labor supply is much steeper (inelastic). The figure shows that the same negative shock will lead to a larger drop in employment in country A and a larger drop in wages in country B. However, labor markets in both countries are in equilibrium, the decrease in employment is voluntary, and there are no unemployed workers in either country.[5] Workers in country A decide to exit the labor market rather than work at a lower wage. They may decide to stay home or go to school when wages are low, and go back to work when economic conditions improve. Their decision not to work is fully voluntary and the two situations cannot be ranked from a welfare point of view.

If the drop in employment brought about by a negative income shock were fully explained by high labor supply elasticity, there would be no need to worry. Economic activity would decrease, but workers would not be worse off because they would be happy to substitute working activity for leisure or to invest in education.[6] By contrast, if labor supply were inelastic, the observed decrease in employment would be involuntary and would lead to an increase in unemployment.

Research on developed countries finds that the hypothesis of high labor supply elasticity has limited empirical backing (Hall and Lilien 1986). Results of a set of simple regressions suggest that this is also the case for Latin America. A 1 percent increase in the growth rate of GDP per capita is associated with a 0.1 percent increase in the labor force participation rate (defined as labor force divided by population aged 15-64). In turn, this increase in participation can be decomposed into a 0.2 percent increase in the employment rate and a 0.1 percent decrease in the unemployment rate. However, estimation of these elasticities does not take into account the fact that female participation has increased over the past 20 years (see chapter 3). Including a time trend in the regressions helps control for this factor, and shows that a 1 percent

[5] The discussion in the text pushes the argument to the extreme by concluding that in the absence of rigidity, there are no unemployed workers. In the real world, all countries, even those with perfectly flexible labor markets, have positive voluntary unemployment. This is referred to as "frictional" unemployment and is determined by the time taken by workers to switch from one job to another. Frictional unemployment is the main determinant of what economists call the "natural" rate of unemployment (that is, the long-run equilibrium rate of unemployment).

[6] There is some evidence that in the case of Brazil school attendance increases during periods of economic downturn (but not during deep crises). See Duryea and Arends-Kuenning (2003).

Table 4.3 Volatility of Growth in Employment, Unemployment and Wages in Latin America and Developed Countries, 1980–2000

	Volatility					
	Employment growth		Unemployment growth		Wage growth	
Period	Latin America	Developed countries	Latin America	Developed countries	Latin America	Developed countries
1980–2000	0.024	0.019	0.243	0.185	0.100	0.024
1980–90	0.022	0.015	0.293	0.171	0.127	0.026
1990–2000	0.021	0.018	0.194	0.170	0.066	0.019

Note: Volatility is the standard deviation for the whole period. Values are calculated only for countries for which data are available for the 1980s. The sample includes 18 countries in Latin America and the Caribbean and 23 developed countries.
Source: IDB calculations.

acceleration in the growth rate of GDP per capita is associated with a 0.02 percent increase in the labor force participation rate, which can be decomposed into a 0.15 percent increase in employment and a 0.13 percent drop in unemployment.[7] Thus, the elasticity of labor force participation is rather low, and output shocks do have an effect on unemployment.

Several factors might lead to involuntary unemployment. In Figure 4.4, panel c illustrates the role of wage rigidity. In this case, labor supply is inelastic and hence workers would react to a negative shock by taking a wage cut rather than stopping working. However, rigidities in the labor market (in this case, the presence of a minimum wage at $\overline{W}$) do not allow the wage to move to the new equilibrium. This creates a situation in which some workers are involuntarily unemployed.[8]

This kind of rigidity is clearly inefficient because it leads to a waste of resources. Furthermore, it creates winners and losers. Workers who keep their jobs at a wage that is above that which would prevail in the absence of rigidities are clearly better off, but workers that are involuntarily unemployed are worse off.[9] In theory, losers could be compensated with transfers (unemployment benefits are a standard compensation method), but while this practice is rather common in developed countries, it is much less common in Latin America. Furthermore, the increase in unemployment is not homogenous across social classes. Those with low skills and low incomes are often the first to move to either unemployment or low-quality jobs. In this sense, recessions have negative distributional consequences and play an important role in increasing poverty. Therefore, mechanisms that guarantee wage flexibility might help in spreading the cost of recessions more evenly with respect to a situation characterized by wage rigidity.

VOLATILITY

So far, the chapter has discussed the volatility of GDP in Latin America, and that this volatility can be transmitted into wage and/or employment volatility. Table 4.3 compares average wage, employment, and unemployment volatility in Latin America with averages in developed countries. The differences between the two groups of countries are striking. Although Latin America's GDP is much more volatile than that of developed countries, the volatility in Latin American employment and unemployment is not very different from

[7] These estimations are averages for a group of heterogeneous countries. A detailed study of Chile (Cowan and others 2003) finds that workers exit the labor market during bad times and return during good times. This high elasticity of labor supply is in contrast with the results for Mexico, which indicate that the income effect dominates the substitution effect, leading to an increase in labor market participation during bad times (see chapter 3).

[8] There are other reasons, besides minimum wages, why nominal wages can be downward rigid. See Akerlof, Dickens, and Perry (2000).

[9] It should be pointed out that by giving extra bargaining power to low-income workers, a moderately binding minimum wage can also play a role in redistributing income from capital to labor.

Figure 4.5 Real Wage Volatility

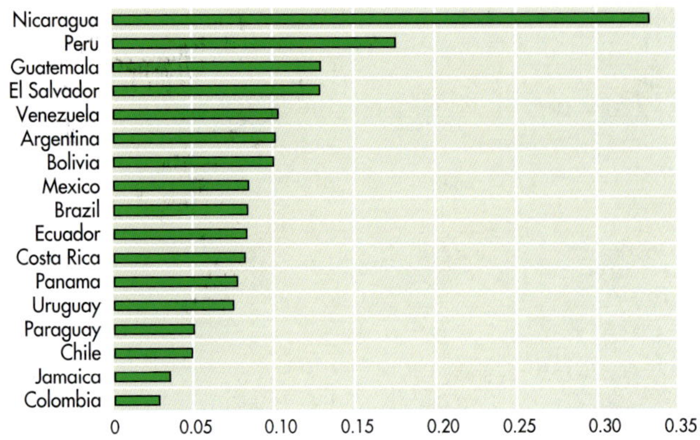

Note: Volatility is the standard deviation.
Source: IDB calculations.

Figure 4.6 Employment Volatility

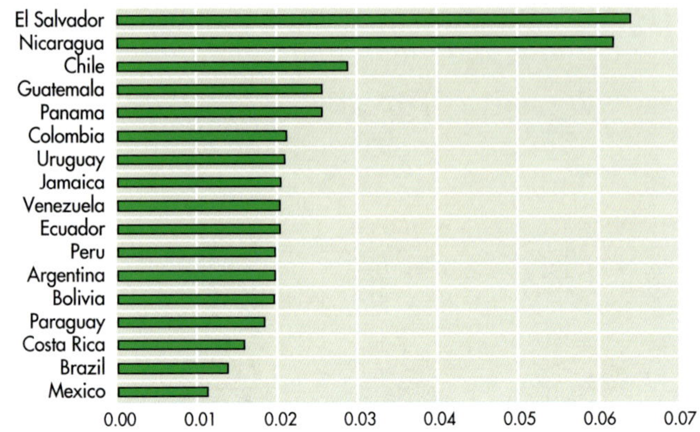

Note: Volatility is the standard deviation.
Source: IDB calculations.

those of developed countries. The relative stability in terms of employment is more than balanced by highly volatile real wages; Latin American real wages are five times more volatile than real wages in the sample of developed countries.

Average values mask large cross-country differences within Latin America. Real wages tend to be especially volatile in Nicaragua, Peru, Guatemala, and El Salvador, and relatively stable in Paraguay, Chile, Jamaica, and Colombia (Figure 4.5). Employment is highly volatile in El Salvador, Nicaragua, Chile, and Guatemala, and relatively stable in Costa Rica, Brazil, and Mexico (Figure 4.6).

Although looking at the volatility of wages and employment can give an idea of the most important channels through which the labor market adjusts to macroeconomic shocks, it should be recognized that these volatilities depend on the magnitude of the shocks. Thus, countries with a relatively stable macroeconomic environment would have lower wage and employment volatility than countries that are hit by larger shocks. (This is why some Central American countries appear to be very volatile in terms of both wages and employment.) A way to address this issue is to look at the response of wages and employment to a given income shock. For example, Figure 4.7 illustrates a message that is similar to that of Table 4.3. In developed countries, the effect of a 1 percent decrease in GDP is a 0.6 percentage point increase in unemployment, a 0.5 percentage point decrease in employment, and a 0.3 percentage point decrease in wages. In Latin America, the response is smaller for employment and unemployment (0.24 and 0.028 percentage points, respectively), and much larger for wages (1.00 percentage point).

Therefore, on average, Latin America seems to behave by the book. Compared with developed countries (which can provide better safety nets for unemployed workers), Latin America adjusts more

Figure 4.7 Effect of a 1 Percent Decrease in Output on Wages, Employment, and Unemployment
(Percent)

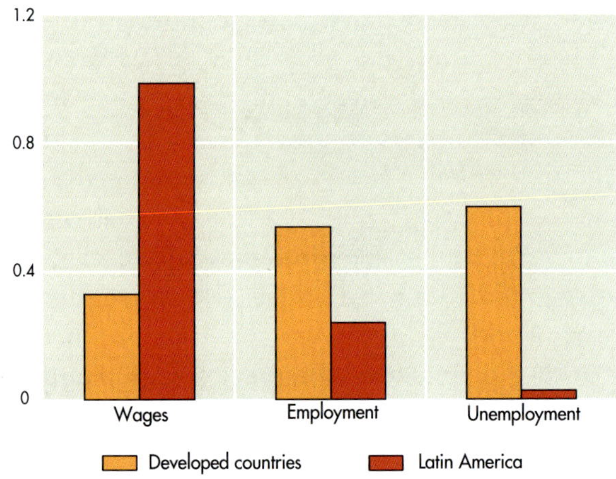

Note: The coefficients were obtained by running a set of fixed-effects regressions in which the dependent variable is real wage growth (or real employment or unemployment growth) and the explanatory variable is real GDP growth. The unemployment coefficient is the negative of the actual coefficient.
Source: IDB calculations.

Figure 4.8 Wage, Employment, and Unemployment Elasticity

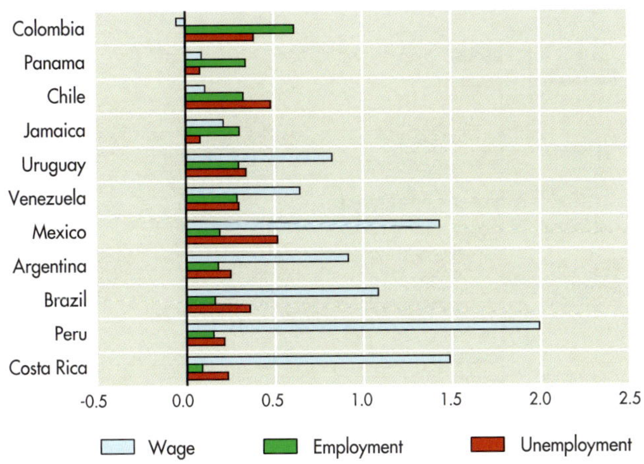

Source: IDB calculations.

through wages than through employment.[10] This helps in spreading the cost of an economic crisis more evenly. The problem lies in the fact that, in Latin America, crises are particularly painful for workers. Rough estimations indicate that the share of income that goes to labor tends to change over the business cycle. In developed countries, workers tend to receive a larger share of income during downturns (a 1 percent drop in GDP is associated with a 0.8 percent drop in income accrued to labor); in Latin America, the share of income that goes to labor tends to decrease during downturns (a 1 percent drop in GDP is associated with a 1.2 percent drop in income accrued to labor).

However, there are large cross-country differences within Latin America (Figure 4.8). On the one hand, Colombia, Panama, Chile, and Jamaica are characterized by low wage elasticity and relatively high employment and unemployment elasticity. On the other hand, Mexico, Argentina, Brazil, Peru, and Costa Rica have high wage elasticity and low employment and unemployment elasticity. Furthermore, these elasticities are not constant within countries. In the case of Argentina, for instance, wage elasticity in the 1980s was about 10 times higher than wage elasticity in the 1990s, and employment elasticity in the 1990s was twice as large as employment elasticity in the 1980s. This provides prima facie evidence for an argument developed later in the chapter, that is, that inflation stabilization may have reduced wage flexibility and increased employment volatility.

Adjustment Costs

High wage flexibility is not the only possible explanation for the relatively low employment volatility that characterizes Latin American countries. An alternative explanation focuses on the response of labor demand to changes in the demand for final goods. A series of country and industry-specific characteristics—including adjustment costs and product market competitive structure—influences the level and timing of the demand for labor in response to the demand for final goods. Oligopolistic industries are likely to have less responsive labor demand than industries that are more competitive.[11] In turn, industries with low adjustment costs are likely to have more responsive labor demand.

In particular, there is a concern that labor market regulation—high hiring and firing costs, for example—may have a negative effect on labor flexibility in Latin America, leading to a low response of labor demand to aggregate or idiosyncratic shocks. If true, this has important welfare consequences: after a demand or productivity shock, the faster the economy reallocates resources to their new best use, the sooner it will reach an efficient allocation of inputs.

To explore the degree to which labor market institutions (or other variables, like the presence of credit constraints) might affect labor adjustment costs in Latin America, it is useful to analyze

[10] Clearly, the availability of unemployment insurance and other safety nets plays a role in determining the higher employment elasticity observed in developed countries. These factors increase workers' reservation wage and their willingness to remain unemployed during periods of economic downturn. In this sense, unemployment insurance reduces the cost of layoffs. Therefore, there should be a positive correlation between the generosity of unemployment insurance and employment volatility.

[11] Campa and Goldberg (2001) find that demand for labor in industries with lower markups is more responsive to changes in demand for final goods.

employment flows across subsectors in manufacturing after reallocation shocks for a large set of countries. The purpose of this exercise is to determine whether labor adjustment costs in the region are abnormally high or low. With high labor adjustment costs, firms would move slowly to their new desired level of employment. Lower costs would induce firms to reach their desired level of employment in a short time.[12]

One way to measure adjustment costs is by computing the speed of employment adjustment. Caballero, Engel, and Micco (2003) provide a method for calculating the desired level of employment. Based on that method, the estimated speed of employment adjustment can be calculated for different regions during the 1980s and 1990s. Normalizing the English-speaking developed countries (this group excludes the United States) to 1, East Asia shows the fastest speed of adjustment, about 1.8 (statistically different from both English-speaking developed countries and Latin America). At the other extreme, Continental Europe has significantly higher adjustment costs, with a speed of adjustment of 0.8. For Latin America, the speed of adjustment is about 1.6. Thus, Latin American countries adjust more slowly than East Asian countries, but significantly faster than the English-speaking developed countries and Continental Europe. This suggests that differences in adjustment speed are not the key to explaining the relatively low employment elasticity of Latin American countries.

Inflation Stabilization

There are two problems with the estimations of wage and employment elasticity discussed so far. First, they are based on a small sample. Second, they assume no structural change over the period of estimation (1980–2000). This is a problematic assumption because this was a period when most countries in the region went through a process of structural reforms and macroeconomic stabilization that may have affected the degree of rigidity of the labor market. (It was already pointed out that, in the case of Argentina, wage flexibility decreased substantially during the 1990s.)

Figure 4.9 Wage and Unemployment Elasticity during Deep Recessions, 1980s and 1990s

Note: The figure considers the 1985 and 1995 recessions for Argentina, the 1982 and 1999 recessions for Chile and Uruguay, the 1992 and 1995 recessions for Mexico, and the 1983 and 1999 recessions for Venezuela.
Source: IDB calculations.

Interestingly, although labor market reforms may have increased the degree of flexibility of the Latin American labor market (see chapter 7), the disinflation process may have had the opposite effect. González (2002) studies labor market flexibility in 13 Latin American countries since the 1960s. He computes employment, unemployment, and real wage Okun coefficients and argues that structural reforms and the disinflation process may have affected how all three variables responded to output shocks.[13] González shows that in countries that went through a disinflation process, employment elasticity increased and wage elasticity decreased. He concludes that price stabilization reduces wage flexibility and hence increases the cost of labor market regulations.

Figure 4.9 compares wage and (the negative of) unemployment elasticity during the deep recessions of the 1980s and 1990s (the sample is restricted to countries for which there are data for both periods)

[12] Because of data limitations, the exercise focuses on the manufacturing sector. Adjustment speeds are estimated using a measure of the desired level of employment based on the method suggested by Caballero, Engel, and Micco (2003). For more on this methodology, see Hamermesh (1993).

[13] The Okun coefficient measures the unemployment (or employment or wage) response to a 1 percent change in GDP.

and confirms that, in most countries, wage flexibility was higher in the 1980s. In the case of Argentina and Chile, the drop in wage elasticity was associated with a large increase in unemployment elasticity. The opposite is true in the case of Mexico. In the case of Uruguay and Venezuela, there were no substantial changes in unemployment elasticity.

The behavior of Mexico and Argentina during the "Tequila" crisis—which originated in Mexico and spread contagion waves throughout Latin America—illustrates the costs and benefits of wage rigidity. Although the effect of the crisis on output was much stronger in Mexico than in Argentina (per capita GDP dropped by nearly 8 percent in Mexico and by 4 percent in Argentina), the effect on unemployment was much stronger in the latter. The Mexican unemployment rate went from approximately 3.5 percent to a peak of 7.5 percent and then quickly dropped back to its original level (Figure 4.10). In Argentina, the unemployment rate moved from an already high level of 11 percent to a peak of 18.5 percent and then stabilized at a level well above 13 percent (Figure 4.11).

Differences in wage rigidity are key in explaining the difference in the behavior of Mexican and Argentinean unemployment. Mexican real wages fell immediately after the crisis (and the effect on wages was uniform across income groups, with workers in the top and bottom quintiles of the earnings distribution observing similar drops in earnings). In the case of Argentina, the crisis had no effect on the earnings of workers in the top income quintile and a limited effect on workers in the bottom quintile (the cumulative drop in real wages over a two-year period was 12 percent compared with more than 35 percent in Mexico).

The Tequila crisis affected Mexican workers mostly through lower wages, and Argentinean workers mostly through higher unemployment. Although it is difficult to make value judgments on which adjustment mechanism is better, it should be recognized that wage adjustment helps spread the cost of the crisis, while unemployment has a more unequal effect. This can be seen by looking at the effect of the crisis on poverty, which increased by 20 percent in Mexico (7 percentage points) and by more than 50 percent in Argentina (9 percentage points), notwithstanding the fact that the drop in total output was much larger in Mexico.[14]

Figure 4.11 shows that although Argentinean real wages did not drop during the 1995 crisis, they

Figure 4.10 Unemployment and Wages in Mexico

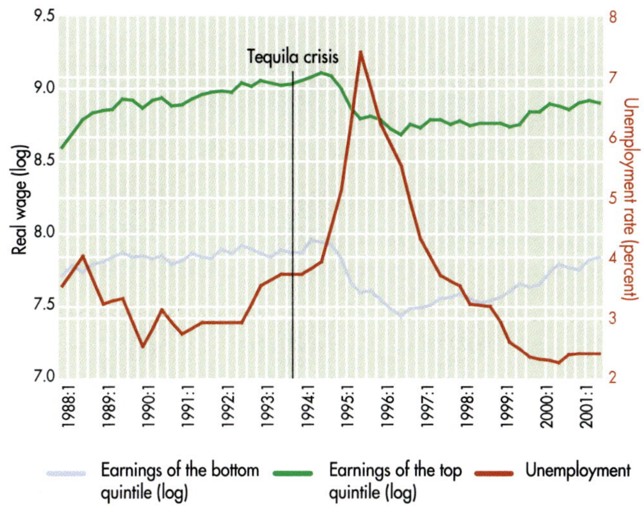

Source: IDB calculations based on household surveys.

Figure 4.11 Unemployment and Wages in Argentina

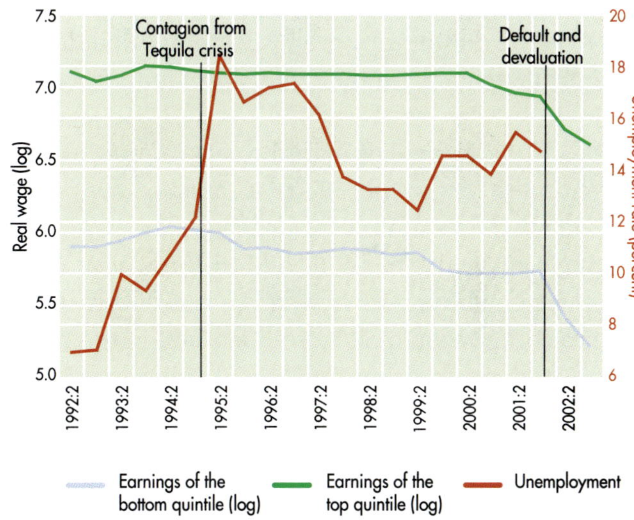

Source: IDB calculations based on household surveys.

[14] Data on poverty are from World Bank (2001, Table 9.1, p. 163).

dropped substantially after the default and devaluation that occurred at the end of 2001. This suggests the presence of nominal rigidities and indicates that inflation may play an important role in increasing wage flexibility in times of crisis.

The idea that increases in prices, by allowing real wages to drop by more than nominal wages, may reduce the employment cost of a recession is one of the central tenets of Keynesian economics. In this sense, inflation can offset nominal wage rigidities and play a beneficial role by "adding grease" to the wheels of the labor market. However, there is also a "sand" view of inflation, championed by Milton Friedman. According to this view, high and volatile inflation leads to errors in the wage-setting process. These errors, together with the costs associated with firms' attempts to avoid them, lead to inefficiencies and resource misallocation and increase the natural level of unemployment.[15]

Empirical evidence has not been kind to the grease hypothesis.[16] However, the relationship between inflation and wage flexibility should be highly dependent on the rigidity of nominal wages, which, in turn, may depend on the strictness of labor market regulations. The lack of success in identifying the grease effect of inflation may thus be due to the focus on the U.S. labor market, which, being among the most flexible in the world, does not need much grease. It would be expected that the grease effect should be more important in the highly regulated European and Latin American labor markets than in the fairly flexible U.S. market.

Figure 4.12 looks at whether the interaction between inflation and labor market regulations affects how employment responds to changes in output (the employment Okun coefficient). It shows that in developed countries with highly regulated labor markets, inflation reduces the sensitivity of employment to changes in output (labor market regulations are measured with the Heckman and Pagés [2000] index of job security).[17]

The figure shows that in unregulated labor markets, inflation increases the elasticity of employment to output shocks. When the index of labor market regulations is 0.25 (the mean value in the sample), inflation becomes neutral, and when labor market regulations are high (the index is

Figure 4.12 Employment Elasticity, Labor Market Regulations, and Inflation in Developed Countries

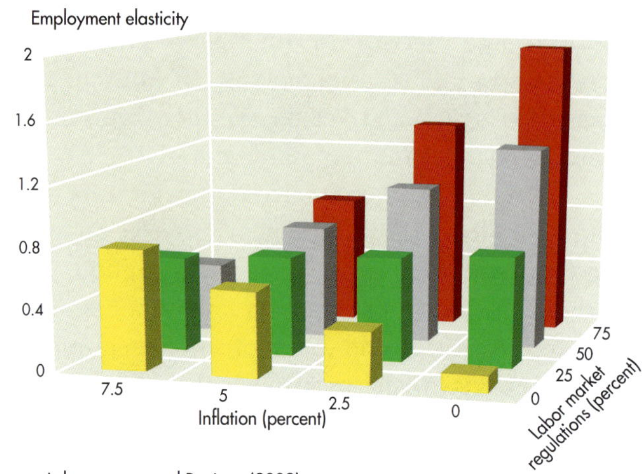

Source: Loboguerrero and Panizza (2003).

above 0.4), inflation starts greasing the wheels of the labor markets by substantially reducing employment elasticity. In particular, when the index of labor market regulations is 0.5, moving from 0 to 5 percent inflation reduces the employment Okun coefficient by 50 percent. Therefore, in developed countries with highly regulated labor markets, the grease effect of inflation dominates the sand effect. The opposite is true for developed countries that are characterized by more flexible

[15] For details on the "grease" view of inflation, see Tobin's (1972) presidential address to the American Economic Association. The grease hypothesis suggests that inflation can speed the adjustment to long-run equilibrium but is consistent with the idea of a vertical long-run Phillips curve. A second class of models rejects the idea of a vertical long-run Phillips curve and, by using near-rational wage-setting behavior, shows that at low levels of inflation, there is a long-run trade-off between inflation and unemployment (Akerlof, Dickens, and Perry 2000). For details on the "sand" view of inflation, see Friedman's (1977) Nobel Lecture.

[16] See Card and Hyslop (1996) and Groshen and Schweitzer (1996).

[17] It is important to note that the empirical strategy assumes that the index of labor market regulations affects both firing costs and wage flexibility. Bertola and Rogerson (1997) provide a rationale for that assumption. They point out that without wage rigidities, job protection makes little sense because entrepreneurs would have the option to drive real wages close to zero and thus make job protection irrelevant. The same would apply to a situation in which entrepreneurs cannot touch real wages but can fire at will. It is therefore natural that the political and economic institutions that lead to a high level of job protection will also lead to wage rigidity. The results are robust to using alternative measures of labor market regulations (for details, see Loboguerrero and Panizza [2003]).

labor markets. In this set of countries (including the United States), inflation increases the elasticity of employment and, thus, the sand effect of inflation dominates the grease effect. This suggests that inflation greases the wheels of the labor market, but only for those that squeak the most (Loboguerrero and Panizza 2003).

In Latin America, it is more difficult to find a statistically significant correlation between employment elasticity, inflation, and labor market regulations. There are four possible reasons why it is hard to find such a correlation. First, the lack of results may be due to the fact that the explanatory variables are measured with less precision in developing countries (see the section on data quality in chapter 1). In this case, the lack of a statistically significant result could be purely due to what econometricians call attenuation bias. Second, it may be due to the presence of widespread indexation mechanisms that offset the grease effect of inflation (Argentina and Brazil had wage indexation mechanisms until the early 1990s and Chile still has one). Third, because of lack of enforcement, labor market regulations may not be binding. In this case, de jure regulations would be very different from de facto regulations, which would explain the lack of a statistically significant relationship among inflation, de jure labor market regulations, and employment elasticity. A fourth and related explanation has to do with the presence of many firms that do not abide by labor laws. As a result, developing countries may end up having high levels of labor market flexibility even in the presence of strict regulations (see, for instance, the discussion in Calvo and Mishkin [2003]).[18]

In fact, Latin American economies are likely to have maintained a high degree of flexibility, with workers moving from the manufacturing sector to other sectors characterized by lower wage rigidity. Box 4.3 provides some evidence in this direction. To control for the fact that de jure labor market regulations may differ from de facto labor market regulations,[19] it is possible to divide the sample of Latin American countries into two groups. The first group contains all the observations where an index that measures the quality of the rule of law takes a value that is higher than the minimum value observed in the sample of developed countries. This is the group where de jure regulations are likely to coincide with de facto regulations. The second group includes countries with low rule of law. In this group, labor market regulations are likely to be less stringent (either because they are not enforced or because there is a large informal sector) than what would be predicted by their de jure value. Figure 4.13 suggests that inflation does grease the wheels of the labor market in developing countries with large and effective labor market regulations.

This finding has important implications for Latin America because it indicates that the disinflation process of the 1990s may have increased labor market rigidities and hence increased the negative effect of output shocks on employment. The policy implication is not to return to high inflation or a system that, by having low respect for the rule of law, makes labor market regulations ineffective. Inflation and poor institutional quality are likely to have costs that more than outweigh the increase in labor market flexibility they may bring. The clear policy prescription is that the disinflation process should have been accompanied by labor market reforms that, by reducing wage rigidity, reduce the employment costs of recessions, especially when no widespread social insurance mechanisms are provided for the unemployed (see chapter 8).

External Shocks

This section discusses the importance of external shocks for employment outcomes in Latin America, emphasizing how these shocks interact with each other and domestic variables.

Capital Flows Volatility

Table 4.1 shows that Latin America is subject to high capital flows volatility. Box 4.4 discusses the sudden stop in capital flows that followed the Russ-

[18] It is also possible that the Latin American result is driven by the fact that the assumption of a strong correlation between employment protection and wage rigidity does not hold for this region.

[19] Chapter 1 presents data on social security coverage (lack of it is a proxy for informality).

Box 4.3. Employment Reallocation across Sectors

Compared with developed countries, Latin American countries have low employment and unemployment elasticity. This may be because, in the absence of social protection programs and unemployment benefits, during recessions workers move from well-paid jobs in large firms to poorly paid jobs in small firms or become self-employed. It is therefore interesting to look at which sectors of the economy bear the largest burden of a given output shock. The table below uses data on employment shares from the International Labour Organization to look at the correlation between the business cycle and employment across sectors.

It is important to note that the estimations suffer from two fallacies of composition. First, the data are expressed as shares of total employment. The shares need to add to one so that if the employment share drops in one sector, by construction it has to increase in at least one other sector. This does not necessarily mean that employment has increased in the latter sector. It only means that employment decreased less than in other sectors. Second, firms tend to shrink during recessions and hence an increase in the employment share of small firms may just capture firms that used to be large and now are small.

With these caveats in mind, the table below shows that there is always a positive correlation between the output gap and the share of workers employed in large firms (indicating that the share of workers employed in large firms contracts during recessions). This correlation is particularly strong for Chile, Costa Rica, Mexico, and Venezuela. There are large cross-country differences in the correlation between the output gap and the share of workers employed in small firms. Peru, Colombia, and Brazil have positive values, and Chile, Paraguay, and Venezuela have negative values. However, the correlation between output gap and employment share in small firms is never statistically significant. Public employment appears to be countercyclical (or less procyclical than other types of employment), except in Brazil and Colombia, but, again, the correlation is never statistically significant. The same holds for self-employment (the exception is Argentina) and domestic services. In fact, domestic services is the only sector that is significantly countercyclical in at least five countries (Argentina, Chile, Colombia, Costa Rica, and Venezuela).

How the Share of Employment Responds to an Output Shock, Selected Countries,1980-97

Country	Large firms	Small firms	Public sector	Self-employed	Domestic services	Wage employment
Argentina	0.313	0.162	–0.392	0.09	–0.518**	0.077
Brazil	0.319	0.199	0.30	–0.542**	–0.233	0.48**
Chile	0.628**	–0.208	–0.354	–0.362	–0.676**	0.58**
Colombia	0.156	0.209	0.043	–0.296	–0.422**	0.351
Costa Rica	0.571**	0.002	–0.409	–0.11	–0.537**	0.30
Mexico	0.572**	–0.004	–0.261	–0.197	–0.004	0.22
Paraguay	0.096	–0.18	–0.32	0.374	–0.286	–0.28
Peru	0.466	0.378	–0.343	–0.459	–0.002	0.53
Venezuela	0.496**	–0.127	–0.646	–0.466	–0.417**	0.55**

** Significant at 5 percent.

Note: The figures were obtained by regressing the output gap (calculated as the deviation from a Hodrick-Prescott trend) on the deviation of employment shares over their long-run trends.

Source: IDB calculations.

Figure 4.13 **Employment Elasticity in Latin America: The Role of Effective Labor Market Regulations, 1990s**

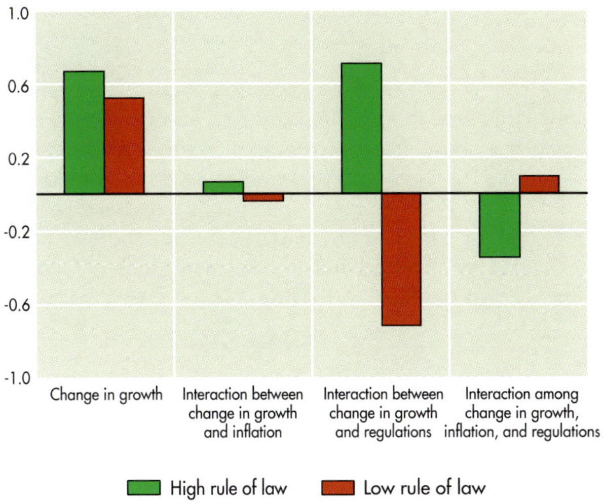

Source: Loboguerrero and Panizza (2003).

Figure 4.14 **Capital Flows and the Unemployment Rate**

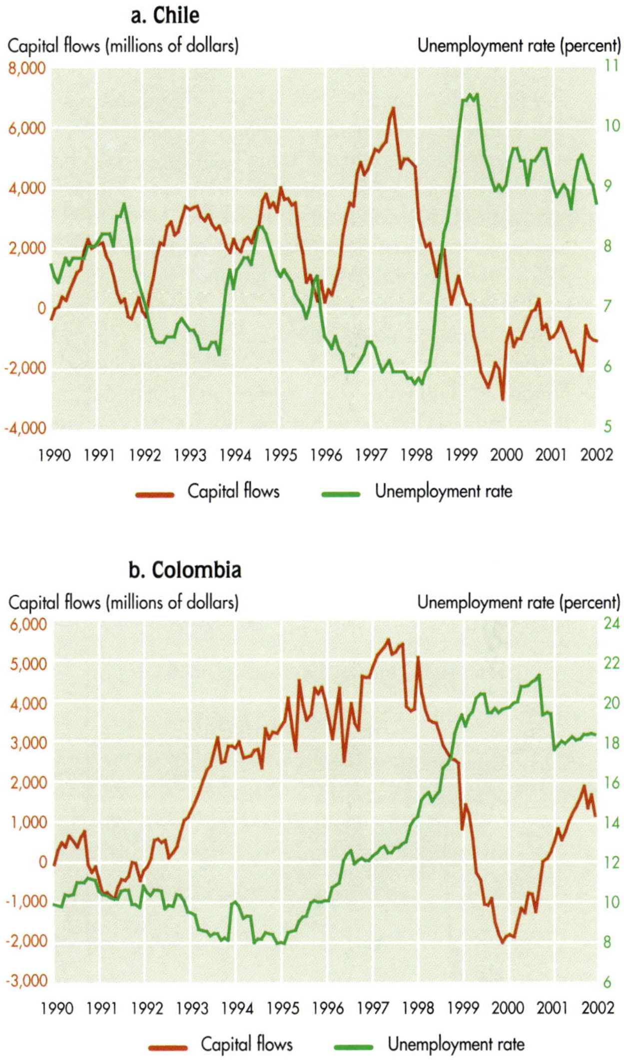

Source: Galindo and Izquierdo (2003).

ian crisis of 1998.[20] But why is capital flows volatility so important? The direct link between access to finance and unemployment is fairly obvious. Without funding, capital goods cannot be purchased, production cannot be undertaken, and, hence, other factors of production (such as labor) are not hired. Even if a particular industry does not use capital intensively, lack of access to credit may restrict working capital and impact employment decisions. This strong link between capital flows and unemployment is particularly clear in Chile and Colombia (Figure 4.14). The link has been especially strong following the 1998 sudden stop.

Capital Flows and Terms of Trade

Financing restrictions can affect output and employment indirectly in the presence of other external shocks, such as terms of trade shocks, contributing to the magnification of negative shocks and preventing countries from exploiting positive ones. Recent empirical work has shown that developing countries respond differently to terms of trade shocks under different conditions in international capital markets. Under "normal" conditions, positive and negative terms of trade shocks tend to have a similar impact. Galindo and Izquierdo (2003) estimate that for the average emerging country, a 12 percent fluctuation in the terms of trade[21] increases (or decreases, depending on the sign of the shock) the rate of employment growth by nearly 0.84 percentage points. This is a sizable impact, given that the average growth rate of employment in the sample is nearly 2 percent a year. However, in periods of sudden stops in capital flows, the same shocks have very different effects.

[20] For a discussion of capital flows volatility in Latin America, see Moguillansky (2002).

[21] This corresponds with the standard deviation of terms of trade fluctuations in the 1990s for their sample of emerging countries.

Box 4.4. Sudden Stops and the Russian Crisis

The Russian crisis of 1998 is a striking example of the destructive power of sudden swings in capital flows. Massive capital inflows that set sail to Latin America in the early 1990s, financing high growth rates and large current account deficits, came all of a sudden to a standstill following Russia's partial foreign debt repudiation in August 1998. It was a real challenge for analysts to imagine how a crisis in a country with little if any financial or trade ties to Latin America could have such profound effects on the region. This puzzle brought into question traditional explanations for financial crises (based on current account and fiscal deficits) and led to studies that focused on the intrinsic behavior of capital markets.[1]

In Figure 1 below, bond spreads for emerging markets display a dramatic increase following the Russian crisis.[2] For most emerging markets, higher interest rates were accompanied by a large reduction in capital inflows. Latin American markets were no exception. Figure 2 shows that the decline was sharp, particularly for portfolio flows, mimicking the sharp interest rate hike. As this phenomenon originated in Russia's crisis, the slowdown of capital inflows contained a large unexpected and exogenous component. "Large" and "unexpected" are the two defining characteristics of what the literature calls a "sudden stop" (Calvo and Reinhart 2000).

[1] In this respect, it was argued that prevailing rules for transactions at the heart of capital markets, such as margin credit, might have been responsible for the spread of shocks from one country to other regions (see, for example, Calvo [1999]).

[2] Emerging market spreads measure the difference between the interest paid by emerging market bonds and the interest rate paid by risk-free U.S. Treasury bonds.

1. Emerging Market Spreads, 1997-2003

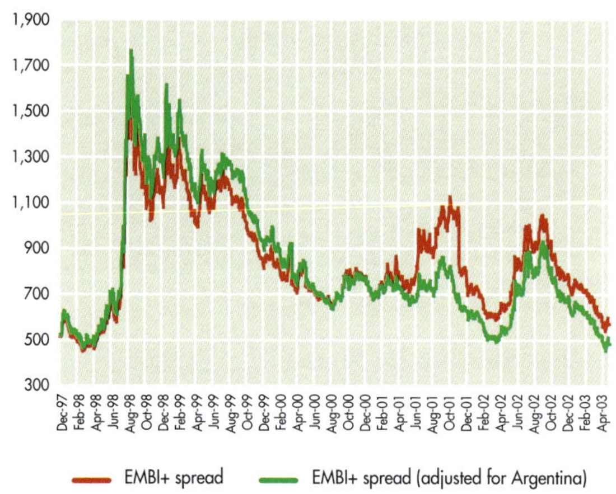

Source: Bloomberg.

2. Capital Flows and the Current Account in Latin America, 1996-2002
(Percentage of GDP)

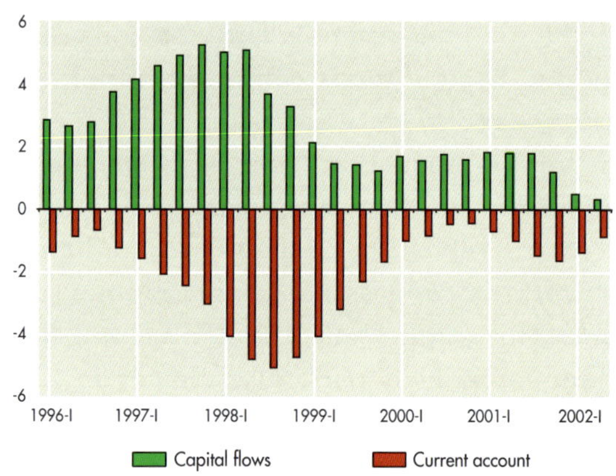

Note: The countries included are Argentina, Brazil, Chile, Colombia, Mexico, Peru, and Venezuela.
Source: Latin Macro Watch.

A 12 percent fall in the terms of trade reduces employment growth by nearly 1.4 percentage points, while a positive shock of similar size has almost no impact on employment. In this sense, capital flows help countries smooth out negative shocks, whereas when capital is not available, firms cannot expand to take advantage of favorable demand conditions.

The cases of Chile and Colombia are illustrated in Figure 4.15, which shows the response of employment to positive and negative terms of trade shocks in an environment such as the sudden stop in capital flows that followed the Russian crisis of 1998. Lack of access to financing magnifies the effects of a negative shock and neutralizes the effects of a positive one, once again confirming the

Figure 4.15 Effects of Terms of Trade Shocks on Employment under Sudden Stops in Capital Flows, Chile and Colombia

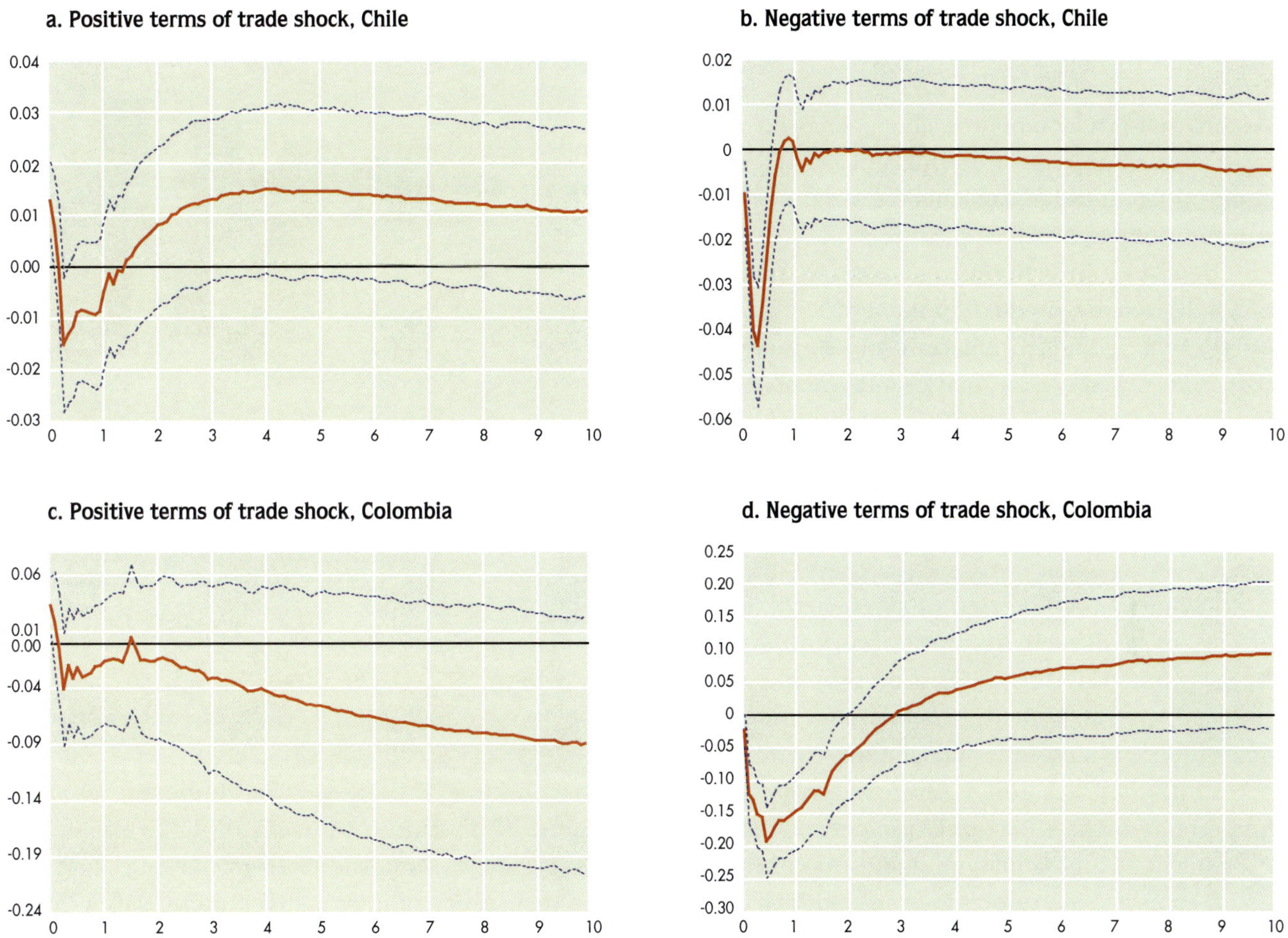

Note: Values are impulse responses to terms of trade shocks in a VAR system that includes employment, industrial output, capital flows, the real exchange rate, and wages. Data are in logs.
Source: Galindo and Izquierdo (2003).

relevance of the credit channel in determining responses to shocks, which are thus asymmetric under credit constraints.

These findings are particularly relevant for understanding the situation of many Latin American countries during the late 1990s. Not only were they exposed to a standstill in capital flows, which generated a contraction in output and employment, but they also experienced a sharp deterioration in their terms of trade, much of which may have been unexpected.

Real Exchange Rate Volatility

Sudden stops are typically accompanied by large contractions in international reserves and declines in the relative price of nontradables with respect to tradables (that is, a depreciation of the real exchange rate).[22] Fluctuations of the real exchange

[22] Calvo, Izquierdo, and Talvi (2002) show that economies with currency mismatches, as well as relatively closed and highly indebted economies, are more vulnerable to sharp relative price swings following a sudden stop.

rate can impact real activity and employment through different channels. Tradable sectors, especially firms that export, can benefit from the relative price adjustment, increasing their production and employing more labor. The opposite is true for sectors that produce nontradable goods and import most of their inputs. If output and factor markets have no friction and are characterized by perfect competition, real exchange rate fluctuations will only lead to employment reallocation: some sectors will increase production and employment and others will reduce production and employment, with zero net effect on total employment. However, the presence of imperfect competition, labor market frictions, and uncertainty about the duration of the shock can slow down the reallocation process and lead to changes in aggregate employment.

What is the international evidence on the effects of real exchange rates on employment? Burgess and Knetter (1998) find that in Canada, Italy, Japan, the United Kingdom, and the United States, there is a positive and significant correlation between a depreciation of the real exchange rate and employment; the correlation between the real exchange rate and employment is weaker in France and Germany. Márquez and Pagés (1998b) study the correlation between real depreciation and employment in a sample of 18 Latin American countries and find that depreciations are positively correlated with employment growth. Klein, Schuh, and Treist (2000) and Campa and Goldberg (2001) show that the impact of real exchange rate fluctuations on sector employment depends on both firm and country characteristics. Firms that export or that face competition from imported products tend to benefit from real exchange rate depreciation, while firms that have a high component of imported inputs are hurt by it.[23]

Most of the existing studies focus on developed countries and do not consider some of the peculiar characteristics of emerging market countries. One transmission channel that may be irrelevant in developed countries but important in developing countries is the impact of depreciation on firms' balance sheets. The main idea is that, in the presence of foreign currency debt, a real devaluation increases the domestic currency value of debt and, by weakening firms' balance sheets, prevents them from having access to finance, thus reducing investment, labor hiring, and output.[24]

The empirical evidence on balance sheet effects is not clear-cut. Although Bleakley and Cowan (2002) find no significant effect of liability dollarization, other studies find that the impact of real exchange rate fluctuations on employment

Figure 4.16 Employment Growth, Real Exchange Rate Depreciation, and Liability Dollarization in Five Latin American Countries

(Percent)

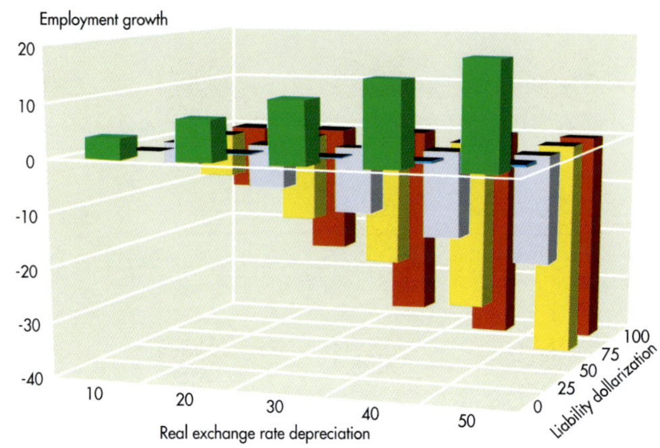

Note: Results control for lagged value added growth, the level of liability dollarization, country, industry, and year fixed effects. Countries included are: Argentina, Brazil, Chile, Colombia, and Peru.
Source: Appendix Table 4.1.

[23] Klein, Schuh, and Treist (2000) analyze job flows in U.S. manufacturing industries and find that the degree of openness to international trade explains the differences in responses across firms. In addition, they find evidence of asymmetries in the response to negative and positive shocks. Appreciations play a significant role in job destruction, but job flows do not respond to real exchange rate depreciations. Campa and Goldberg (2001) find that in the United States, responses of employment to real exchange rate changes are small but significant and vary depending on the competitive structure of industries and net exposure to trade. Firms in lower markup industries are more sensitive to exchange rate fluctuations. Gourinchas (1999) finds that employment in the tradable sector is highly sensitive to real exchange rate fluctuations in France. Reif (2001) discusses the channel through which devaluations may have contractionary effects via the cost of imported inputs.

[24] See Aguiar (2002), Bleakley and Cowan (2002), Forbes (2002), and Nucci and Pozzolo (2001).

varies substantially depending on the degree of liability dollarization. In particular, Figure 4.16 shows that the net effect of devaluation on employment growth can turn from positive to negative for liability dollarization exceeding 25 percent.[25] This finding may be quite relevant, given that the average degree of liability dollarization in the sample is around 40 percent.

Conclusion

Latin America suffers from an extremely volatile macroeconomic environment. Although output volatility explains a share of the variance in unemployment in the region, thanks to high levels of real wage flexibility, the responses of employment to output shocks are smaller in Latin America than in developed countries. This is likely to be a good thing because, while real wage volatility distributes the cost of a recession over a large share of the population (the effect is not completely uniform because less-skilled workers are likely to suffer larger wage cuts during recessions), employment and unemployment volatility have unequal effects. They leave unscathed those who do not lose their jobs, but cause large losses for those who become unemployed.[26]

However, there are indications that things may be changing. The chapter suggests that the high level of wage flexibility that characterized Latin America during 1980-2000 was due to high levels of inflation and poor enforcement of labor regulations. The disinflation process that characterized the region during the 1990s, together with a process of institutional reforms aimed at increasing institutional quality and improving respect for the rule of law, are likely to remove the margins of flexibility described above and, hence, may increase the unemployment cost of recessions.

This points to the need for Latin American countries to pursue two lines of action in order to reduce workers' vulnerability to adverse macroeconomic conditions. First, they should reduce macroeconomic volatility (see Box 4.1). Second, they should recognize that, even in the best-case scenario, they would not be able to fully isolate themselves from shocks. As macroeconomic volatility tends to have a strong impact on poverty and disproportionately affects individuals with low levels of wealth and skills (see Braun 2003), it is important to develop policies that protect the most vulnerable segments of the population. Clearly, social programs and unemployment insurance are important, but, given the weak fiscal situation of most countries in the region, they are unlikely to fully isolate the poor from the negative consequences of economic crises.[27] In this sense, labor reforms that maintain the high degree of wage flexibility that has characterized the region in the past are necessary to spread the burden of adjustment.

[25] See Appendix 4.1 for details on the estimation of the effect of real exchange rate fluctuations on employment. These results contrast with the findings of Bleakley and Cowan (2002), who find no significant effect of liability dollarization.

[26] Although social protection programs could make the two effects equivalent by compensating those who lose their jobs during recessions, the highly procyclical government budgets in Latin America are unlikely to allow the creation of widespread social protection programs.

[27] Unemployment insurance could be viable if it were privately financed from an accumulated fund.

Appendix 4.1 Employment and Real Exchange Rate Fluctuations

Fluctuations in the real exchange rate can impact real activity and employment through different channels. On the one hand, sectors that export can benefit from the relative price adjustment, increasing their production and employing more labor. In economics jargon, this is known as a competitiveness effect and is derived from standard Mundell-Fleming types of models. However, there is a large and growing literature on how currency and maturity mismatches affect firms' balance sheets and the overall level of economic activity.[28] The main point in the literature is that a real devaluation increases the domestic currency value of dollar debt and, by weakening firms' balance sheets, prevents firms from having access to finance, thus reducing investment, labor hiring, and output.

Empirical results suggest that the impact of real exchange rate fluctuations on employment varies substantially depending on the degree of liability dollarization. Using various econometric techniques and measures of liability dollarization, Appendix Table 4.1 shows the net effect of devaluation on employment growth for a sample of five Latin American countries for which data are available (Argentina, Brazil, Chile, Colombia, and Peru).[29] The effect can turn from positive to negative once liability dollarization exceeds 25 percent. This finding may be quite relevant, given that the average degree of liability dollarization in the sample is around 40 percent.

Appendix Table 4.1 The Effects of Real Exchange Rate Fluctuations on Employment Growth

	Fixed effects		GMM-difference		GMM-system	
Variable	**(1)**	**(2)**	**(3)**	**(4)**	**(5)**	**(6)**
Change in employment lagged			0.317	0.319	0.327	0.350
			(0.135)**	(0.132)**	(0.112)***	(0.111)***
Change in real exchange rate *(RER^{jt})*	0.400	0.447	0.467	0.413	0.428	0.444
	(0.227)*	(0.251)*	(0.288)*	(0.278)	(0.243)*	(0.276)*
Change in real exchange rate *(RER^{jt})* $DEBT\text{-}US^{ijt}$*	−1.680	−1.888	−1.334	−1.303	−1.041	−1.137
	(0.584)***	(0.687)***	(0.637)**	(0.714)*	(0.486)**	(0.627)*
$DEBT\text{-}US^{ijt}$	0.104	0.065	0.077	0.089	0.003	−0.020
	(0.039)***	(0.049)	(0.061)	(0.063)	(0.036)	(0.035)
log VA^{ijt}-1	−0.035	−0.029	−0.094	−0.089	−0.016	−0.013
	(0.049)	(0.049)	(0.057)*	(0.075)	(0.004)***	(0.005)**
Observations	571	571	447	447	447	447
R^2	0.44	0.45				
Sargan test (P-value)			0.996	0.990	0.591	0.516
First-order autocorrelation (P-value)			0.052	0.044	0.042	0.036
Second-order autocorrelation (P-value)			0.235	0.217	0.245	0.369
Year effects	Yes	Yes	Yes	Yes	Yes	Yes
Country-industry effects	Yes	Yes	Yes	Yes	Yes	Yes

* Significant at 10 percent.
** Significant at 5 percent.
*** Significant at 1 percent.

Note: Columns 1, 3, and 5 use the industry's average value of debt dollarization for a sample of firms. Columns 2, 4, and 6 use the industry's median value. The dependent variable is the change in the log of employment in industry *i* in country *j*. *RER* is the bilateral real exchange rate of each country with the United States. DEBT-US is the mean or average of the ratio of foreign to total debt of industry *i* in country *j*. *VA* is the value added of industry *i* in country *j*. Robust standard errors are in parentheses.

Source: IDB calculations.

[28] See, for example, Aguiar (2002), Bleakley and Cowan (2002), Forbes (2002), and Nucci and Pozzolo (2001).

[29] Additional specifications included the interaction between a measure of openness and the real exchange fluctuation as a regressor. This interaction is not significant and results regarding the dollar debt interaction hold when it is included.

Chapter 5

The Effects of Structural Reforms on Employment and Wages

The 1990s witnessed major changes in economic policies. In the macroeconomic realm, primarily in order to reduce inflation, monetary authorities were given more independence and steps were taken to reduce fiscal deficits. Structural economic policies were aimed at facilitating the operation of markets, thereby improving efficiency and economic growth. To that end, governments reduced restrictions on international trade, lifted controls on financial systems, simplified tax systems, and privatized companies, primarily in infrastructure services, which traditionally had been managed by the state. Some countries extended privatization to pension systems, and a few introduced reforms to make labor markets more flexible.

These combined steps are usually associated with what came to be called the "Washington Consensus," which from the early 1990s onward summarized the prevailing approach to economic policies in Latin America.[1] This chapter examines the effects on labor of the pro-market reforms that were adopted as part of the Washington Consensus.[2] The chapter describes structural reforms, their scope and impact, and the labor effects of the main reforms. It examines the extent to which the reforms have achieved the favorable effects sought by the reformers, or the unfavorable effects attributed to them by the critics.

The analysis is largely prompted by the contrast between what the advocates of the reforms hoped for, based on what was predicted by economic theory, and the criticisms leveled at the structural reforms from various angles. In essence, the reformers expected that in the medium run these steps would lead to increased productivity and investment, which would translate into better work opportunities and higher wages. Two reasons were given for that expectation. First, the reforms would eliminate distortions and interference, which were obscuring price signals, lessening efficiency, and hindering the use of productive resources, including labor. Second, the reforms as a whole, and liberalization of international trade in particular, would stimulate the demand for labor as a factor of production that is abundant in the coun-

[1] In 1990, a group of Latin American ministers of finance and economy met in Washington, D.C. with development experts and academics in a conference organized by the Institute for International Economics. In an influential article published after the conference, Williamson (1990) noted that the participants had substantially agreed on the need for a certain package of economic reforms. This package, which Williamson named the "Washington Consensus," included greater fiscal discipline, more government spending on education and health, interest rates set by the market, competitive exchange rates, free trade policies, openness to foreign direct investment, privatization, deregulation, and respect for property rights. The Latin American economic officials enthusiastically adopted the Washington Consensus and the region witnessed an unprecedented wave of reforms.

[2] Although macroeconomic stabilization policies were also a part of the Washington Consensus, this chapter does not study them (see chapter 4).

tries of Latin America and the Caribbean, and hence they would increase remuneration to labor. Even so, the reformers were aware that in the short run these steps could increase unemployment and reduce wages in the sectors most directly affected.

The optimistic prospects for the medium-run effects of the reforms stand in contrast to the adverse judgments they have received, especially in terms of their impact on the labor market. One of the best efforts to gather opinions on the labor and social impact of the reforms was recently undertaken by the Structural Adjustment Participatory Review International Network (SAPRIN), which used participatory methods to examine the experiences of nine countries, three of them in Latin America.[3] According to this study, the effects of the structural reforms on labor have been predominantly negative:

"Domestic manufacturing sectors and employment have been hit hard by indiscriminate import liberalization [while] increased exports have failed to generate significant domestic economic activity and employment." (pp. 174-76)

"Coupled with trade liberalization measures, financial-sector reforms have had a particularly devastating impact on small and medium-sized firms and the large number of jobs they provide." (p. 175)

"Unemployment and job insecurity have increased and working conditions have often deteriorated with the increase in privatizations and the introduction of flexibilization measures." (p. 180)

Likewise, an ambitious participatory project recently carried out by the World Bank in 23 countries (four of them in Latin America) gathered the opinions of poor people, who clearly stated their concern about the effects of the reforms on labor. According to Narayan and Petesch (2002):

"Depending on the country, poor people mentioned privatization, factory closures, the opening of domestic markets [...] and other related changes as having depleted their assets and increased their insecurity." (pp. 471-72)

"In all four countries of Latin America and the Caribbean, people described the economic and social devastation of their communities in the wake of macroeconomic crises and policy reforms. They felt directly harmed by numerous plant closures, the shift to a service economy, and the rise of the informal economy." (p. 474)

"A common theme underlies the sentiments expressed by men and women [...] in Argentina: the quality of their lives has deteriorated. In urban areas, they attribute the decline mostly to unemployment and crime. In their words, a dramatic picture emerges of the personal and social consequences of market reforms and factory closures." (p. 335)

And in Ecuador, "many urban study participants say the 1990s brought deep declines in their well-being, and they express little support for the economic reforms made by the government." (p. 400)

In general, Latin American public opinion on the reforms has not been favorable, and in recent years it has turned even more critical. In 2001, 63 percent of those surveyed by Latinobarometer in 17 countries did not believe that privatization had been beneficial for their countries; three years earlier, 43 percent had opposed privatization. Similarly, in 2001, 45 percent of Latin Americans stated that they disagreed with the basic principle of the reforms that "the state should leave productive activity to the private sector," whereas one year previously that percentage had been only 28 percent. Although it cannot be determined directly from this survey system whether the opposition to the reforms is due to their possible effects on labor, it is revealing that according to the surveys, unemployment is the main concern of Latin Americans (Figure 5.1).

Both the forecasts of the reformers and the criticisms leveled at the reforms are somewhat exaggerated, although both sides contain significant pieces of truth. The reforms really did increase productivity and economic growth, but modestly and perhaps temporarily, conceivably because they did not reallocate productive resources, including labor, as may have been predicted on the basis of

[3] See SAPRIN (2002). The countries included are Bangladesh, Ecuador, El Salvador, Ghana, Hungary, Mexico, the Philippines, Uganda, and Zimbabwe.

Figure 5.1 Survey Responses: The Main Concern of Latin Americans
(Percentage of respondents)

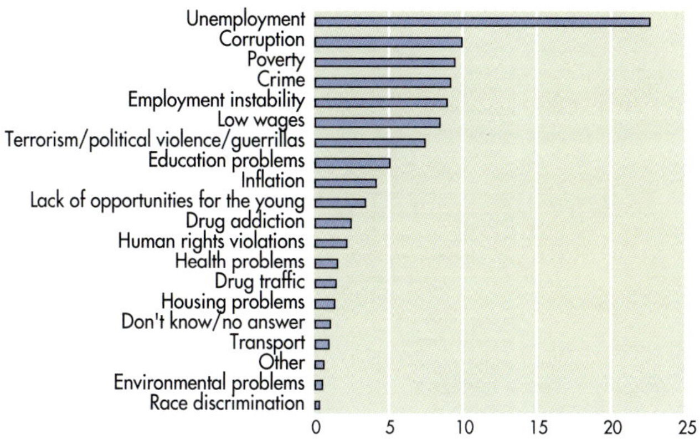

Source: Latinobarometer (2001).

theory. For the same reason, except in some of the privatized industries, such as railways and ports, the reforms did not lead to massive job losses or great shifts of workers from some areas to others. The changes in the sector composition of employment, which were quite significant in some countries, do not seem to have been due to structural reforms.

While the reforms did increase productivity, they did not have the expected effect on wages, which fell in the sectors most subject to competition, especially those of lower-skilled workers. Thus, the reforms contributed to widening wage gaps, although to a lesser extent than is generally believed. Furthermore, the reforms have had a mixed impact on labor conditions. Contrary to popular fears, the new jobs that have emerged in the export sector offer better conditions than other alternative occupations. The financial reforms, far from discriminating against small businesses, are in fact helping them by driving a strong market in lending that helps such businesses and thus improves their working conditions. Previously existing jobs in the tradable goods sector have not become more unstable and have not worsened. The same cannot be said, however, of labor conditions in the privatized sectors, which are generally more demanding and offer fewer benefits than in the past, and where there are indications that the countries that opened their economies to international competition with very rigid labor markets are registering increased employment in very small production units, presumably with inferior labor conditions. In short, the picture of the effect of the reforms on labor is full of nuances and lessons for the reformers and critics alike.

Structural Reforms

The structural reforms of the past two decades reoriented policies in international trade, finance, taxation, and private sector participation in areas previously reserved to the state. Although the reforms largely shared the objective of facilitating the operation of the market, this section shows that they varied substantially from country to country in their composition, depth, and application.[4]

Sector or microeconomic reforms complemented macroeconomic policy measures aimed at correcting fiscal imbalances and stabilizing the economy. In some countries, social policies and institutions and other areas of public administration also underwent deep reforms, but this chapter does not deal with these issues.[5]

Trade Liberalization

The core of trade liberalization was the lowering of barriers to imports that formerly sought to protect domestic production, especially in manufacturing. Between the mid-1980s and the beginning of the 1990s, countries in Latin America began trade liberalization programs, with reductions of at least 15 percentage points in the average tariff rate, which fell from an average of 48.9 percent in the prereform years to 10.7 percent in 1999. The dispersion of tariffs was also significantly reduced, although in most countries tariffs remain higher for consumer goods than for intermediate and capital goods, and are higher for agricultural goods than for industrial goods.

[4] For a more detailed description, see Lora (2001).

[5] Chapter 8 examines social policies directly related to the operation of labor markets.

By the end of the 1990s, only two countries (out of 24 for which information is available) had an average tariff of more than 15 percent. Nontariff trade restrictions, which were applied to 37.6 percent of imports in the pre-reform period, affected only 6.3 percent of imports by the mid-1990s (IDB 1996). Lower tariff and nontariff restrictions enabled imports to rise as a percentage of gross domestic product (GDP) in most countries (Figure 5.2a). For the Latin American and Caribbean region as a whole, imports increased from 22.6 percent in 1983-85 to 36.2 percent in 1998-2000. It should be noted that during this period, export-to-GDP ratios also increased, albeit by much less, from 23.3 to 29.6 percent (Figure 5.2b).[6]

Figure 5.2 **Imports and Exports, 1983-85 and 1998-2000**
(Percent of GDP)

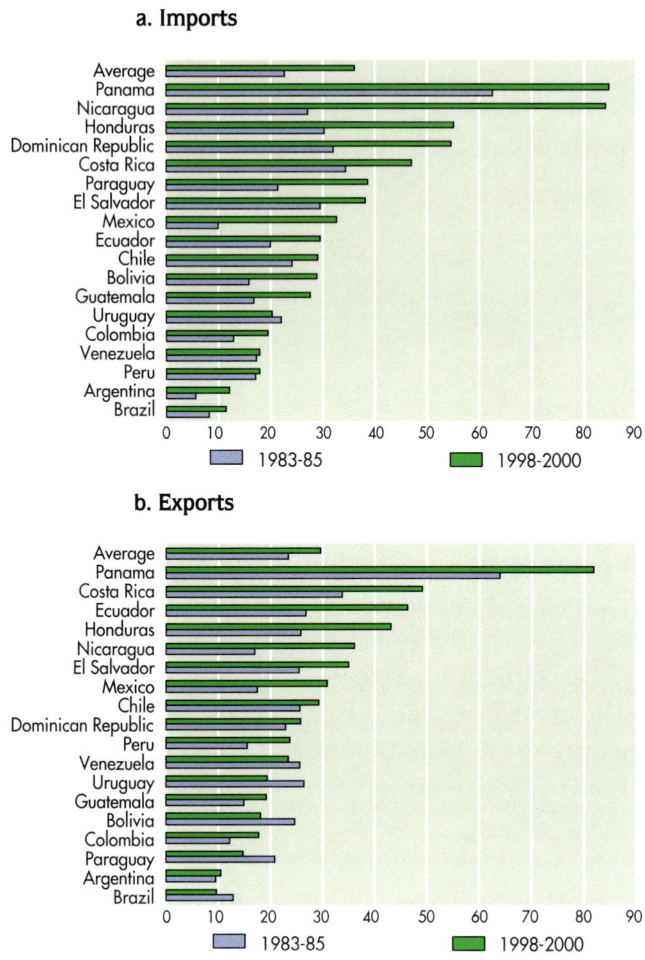

Source: IMF (various years).

Financial Liberalization

The main objectives of the financial reforms were to grant financial intermediaries greater freedom to operate and to strengthen mechanisms for prudential regulation and oversight. Liberalization consisted of lowering reserve ratios, eliminating controls on interest rates, and dismantling mechanisms of forced investment and directed lending. Between 1990 and 2000, effective reserve requirements were reduced in 15 countries in Latin America and the Caribbean (out of 22 for which data are available), and in five of them the reductions were 20 points or more. As a result, by the end of the 1990s, in 13 countries reserve requirements were no higher than 20 percent of demand deposits. Comprehensive controls on interest rates were dismantled in all the countries before 1995. With a few exceptions, however, various forms of government interference in loan agreements were retained.[7] Systems of obligatory investments and directed lending that sought to favor certain productive sectors, particularly agriculture and construction, were also eliminated or substantially reduced in all the countries. However, there are still obligatory investments (other than reserve requirements) in seven countries as well as credit requirements for specific sectors in five countries (out of the 21 for which there is information).

A central component of the wave of financial reforms in the region was the implementation of a modern system of prudential regulation. All countries adopted the minimum capital requirements weighted by risk established by the Basel Agreement on prudential regulation. However, the application of other prudential regulations to assure adequate capital coverage was uneven, as were other aspects that determine the effectiveness of regulation and oversight. This was largely a reflection of differences in the quality of public administration and the rule of law.

[6] For a more detailed description of export performance in the past two decades, see IDB (2001).

[7] The most common forms of interference have to do with systems for calculating and paying interest, the highest levels that certain lending modalities may have, and the periods of some types of loans.

Other noteworthy components of the financial reform process were the privatization of government banks, the opening of the sector to foreign investment, and the shift toward universal banking systems, with fewer restrictions on the services and activities of banks and other financial intermediaries. In all these aspects, the process is still quite uneven across countries (IDB 2001).

Tax Reforms

Far-reaching reforms were also made in the area of taxation, although they were much more uneven across countries. Their most common features were the search for neutrality, legal and administrative simplification, and increased collection. Taxes on foreign trade, which represented on average 18 percent of the tax revenues of countries in the region in 1980, were partially replaced by greater domestic collection. By the mid-1990s, they generated only 13.7 percent of total collection.[8] In order to moderate the distorting effects of taxation on production and savings decisions, 23 countries have adopted value-added tax (VAT) systems in order to tax consumption. Basic VAT rates range from levels of less than 10 percent in Panama and the Dominican Republic to more than 20 percent in Argentina and Uruguay. However, the effective rates of VAT collection are much less than the statutory rates, due to the exclusion of many final goods and services from the tax bases and to difficulties of administration and oversight, all of which further limit the neutrality of this tax.

Marginal tax rates on personal incomes, which in many countries were more than 50 percent, were cut drastically. Only Chile, Belize, and Barbados have maximum rates of 40 percent or more. The most common rates are 30 and 25 percent, which are in effect in seven and five countries, respectively. For reasons of fairness, these maximum rates begin to apply only for income levels that in some countries are quite high in comparison with average income levels. Tax rates on company earnings were also lowered and, with only two exceptions (Honduras and Barbados), they are less than 40 percent. The most common are also rates of 30 and 25 percent, which are in effect in seven and four countries, respectively. Although the reforms may have improved tax neutrality, most countries still maintain tax incentives by activity, sector, or region. The most common incentives are aimed at the primary sectors and tourism.

Privatization

For the region as a whole, the scope of privatization has been remarkable, but also uneven across countries. The 396 sales and transfers to the private sector carried out in Latin America between 1986 and 1999 represented more than half the value of privatization operations in all developing countries.[9] The largest amounts of privatization took place in Brazil and Argentina: US$61,000 million and US$25,000 million, respectively. Three countries carried out privatizations that cumulatively represented more than 10 percent of the GDP of their economies in 1999, and a total of 17 countries privatized more than 1 percent of GDP in a single year.

Fifty-seven percent of the amount of privatizations in the region during the 1990s took place in infrastructure sectors, which traditionally have been closed to private participation, and in which the potential for obtaining productivity and efficiency gains was great. Another 11 percent came from the sale of banking and similar entities, thus reinforcing financial reform trends. However, the composition of privatizations by sector has differed considerably across countries.

Labor Reforms

As Rodrik (1996) notes, various countries in Latin America adopted more trade and financial liberalization policies and more privatizations in a short time period than the countries of East Asia did in the course of three decades. Even in the tax area, where policy changes were very uneven, the depth of the reforms was striking. By contrast with the

[8] Calculations are based on data from World Bank (2001).

[9] This leaves out privatizations carried out through massive distribution of coupons in Eastern European countries.

four previous areas of reform, changes in the labor area were fewer and lesser in scope. Only six countries implemented significant labor reforms between the mid-1980s and 1999: Argentina (1991), Colombia (1991), Guatemala (1990), Panama (1995), Peru (1991), and Venezuela (1998). These reforms were focused on lowering worker dismissal costs and facilitating temporary hiring, thereby introducing a certain mobility around the edges of formal employment.

An Index of Reforms

A system of indicators originally presented in IDB (1997) may be used to describe in summary fashion the magnitude of the reforms. The system uses a set of indices that capture the main features of the reforms just described. These indices make it possible to compare the state of the different areas of policy within a country or between countries. The total index is an average of all the reform areas and makes it possible to measure the magnitude of the reforms on a scale of 0 to 1.

The total index, calculated for 17 Latin American countries, increased from 0.34 in 1985 to 0.58 by the end of the 1990s. This change implies a significant degree of reform, although it also suggests there is still considerable and unexplored room for further reforms in many countries (up to the maximum value of 1). The most dynamic reform period was between 1989 and 1994, when 0.12 points of the total 0.24 improvement for the whole period were gained. However, reforms took place in all years and countries, although at varying paces.

Figure 5.3 compares the state of the reforms in 1985 and 1999 for the countries with the highest and lowest indices in 1999. The five countries with the highest indices are Bolivia, Jamaica, Peru, Trinidad and Tobago, and Argentina, all of which have final index values above 0.6 and increases of at least 0.2 points over their starting situation. The five countries with the fewest reforms are (starting with the lowest) Uruguay, Mexico, Venezuela, Ecuador, and Costa Rica, with indices located between 0.48 and 0.55. However, even in this group of countries, there were noteworthy changes in comparison with the starting point; by the end of the 1990s, all of them were above what had been the regional average at the outset of the period.

Figure 5.3 Index of Structural Reforms, 1995 and 1999
(Index, 0-1)

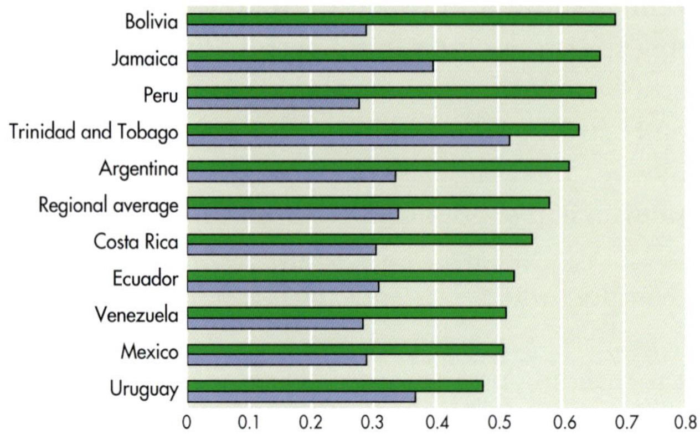

Source: Lora and Panizza (2002).

Figure 5.4 The Extent of Reform in Latin America (Margin of reform used)
(Percent)

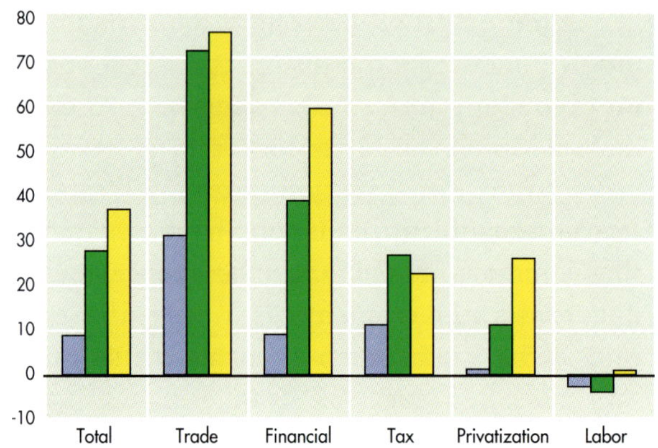

Source: Lora and Panizza (2002).

The scope of the reforms was more unequal by area of reform than between countries. Figure 5.4 shows the magnitude of the reforms for the total and by type of reform (measured relative to the average of each index in 1985). The potential for liberalization in 1985 was attained quite profoundly in the areas of trade and finance, substantially less in the areas of tax policy and privatization, and very little in labor reform.

The reforms in trade and finance in the first half of the 1990s were deep and encompassed all countries. Hence, it is not surprising that since then the pace of change in these areas has been moderate. Tax and privatization reforms, by contrast, have been much more uneven because, although there were reforms throughout the region, they varied significantly across time and countries. All of the countries have made changes in the area of taxes in recent years—not because of lack of reforms, but because of the need for greater revenue collection, even at the expense of tax neutrality. Privatization has been most dynamic since the mid-1990s. Labor reforms have been the most limited and focused on specific issues in a few countries.

Have the Reforms Achieved Their Objectives?

Although economic growth in Latin America improved over the previous decade, in the 1990s it was disappointing, and less than the averages for the 1960s and 1970s (Table 5.1). Indeed, whereas during the so-called "lost decade" of the 1980s annual growth in the region was only 1.2 percent and per capita income fell 0.7 percent, in the 1990s those rates rose to 3.8 and 2.1 percent, respectively. However, in the 1960s and 1970s, average annual growth was more than 5 percent and per capita income increased by around 3 percent. Something similar may be observed with regard to trends in total factor productivity, which are the best available measurement of efficiency in the use of the combined productive resources of the economy. In the 1990s, total factor productivity contributed practically nothing to the average growth of countries in the region, after having fallen sharply in the 1980s (when it took away around 2 percentage points of growth). Productivity improvements typical of the 1990s were not substantially different from those typical (also very low) of the 1960s and 1970s.

These results could be taken as an indicator that the reforms failed to achieve their central objective of speeding up economic growth through more efficient use of productive resources. It should not be surprising that under such conditions the performance of employment and wages was weak. Yet it would not be right to leap directly to that conclusion. First, it should not be forgotten that these averages conceal notable differences between some countries and others in the region. In terms of per capita income, for example, 10 of the 26 countries in question performed better in the 1990s than in the 1960s and 1970s. Some countries, such as Argentina, Chile, Guyana, and El Salvador, had significant increases in the rate of growth. An equal number of countries also registered improvements in overall factor productivity, which outpaced that of the 1960s and 1970s. Second, structural reforms significantly differed from one another in depth, pace, and manner of implementation from one country to another.

Finally, it should be kept in mind that the structural reforms were not the only factor influencing productivity and growth in recent decades. In this regard, it should be emphasized that growth trends in developed countries and in the world economy as a whole, which had been encouraging in the 1950s and 1960s, fell in the following decades. In the 1990s, per capita income growth in the developed countries was the same as that of Latin American countries (1.5 percent a year for Latin America, 1.7 percent for the entire world), whereas in the 1970s it had been 4.3 percent (4.1 percent for all countries). The international context has also limited Latin American countries because of instability in the international prices of the region's typical exports and because of the major changes in the amounts and costs of capital resources for the region. Growth was also affected by the quality of macroeconomic policies and other circumstances specific to each country.

Given the multiplicity of factors that can influence growth and productivity, it is not surprising that experts have different opinions about the effects of the reforms. Empirical studies try to isolate the effects of the reforms from the possible effects of outside circumstances, such as world economic growth, the availability of financing, or international prices, or internal factors, such as macroeconomic stabilization policies or the institutional or political environment. However, some of

Table 5.1 Growth and Productivity in Latin America and the Caribbean, 1961–2002
(Average annual percent)

Period	Growth rate: GDP	Per capita GDP	Total factor productivity
1961–70	5.3	2.7	1.01
1971–80	5.5	3.4	–0.34
1981–90	1.2	–0.7	–1.95
1991–99	3.8	2.1	0.13
2000–02	0.6	–1.1	

Source: Loayza, Fajnzylber, and Calderón (2002); World Bank (2001).

these factors are difficult to measure and isolate, and in some cases they interact with the reforms themselves, thereby modifying the effect of the latter on growth. In any case, until a few years ago, the prevailing opinion on the effectiveness of the reforms was quite optimistic.

Table 5.2 presents the results of five studies that evaluate the effects of the reforms. The first three studies analyze the reforms up to the mid-1990s and have consistent results (Easterly, Loayza, and Montiel 1997; Fernández-Arias and Montiel 1997; Lora and Barrera 1997). According to these studies, the effects were positive and substantial. For example, using the previously mentioned indices of reform, Lora and Barrera find that the reforms had a significant and ongoing impact on growth, productivity, and investment. According to their estimates, until the mid-1990s, the economic reforms raised Latin America's growth rate by 1.9 percentage points (that is, to 2.2 percentage points including the impact of macroeconomic stabilization).

More recent studies point to less encouraging effects. Escaith and Morley (2001), who use a modified version of the same indices for 1970-95, also find a positive effect, although smaller in magnitude and less robust than those reported in previous articles. By using the same indices for 1985-99, Lora and Panizza (2002) make new estimates of the effects of the reforms on growth. They find that the effects were more modest and of a transitory nature because they seemed to be diluted after the reforms were in place for some time. For example, during their high point (1991-93), the reforms increased annual growth by 1.3 percentage points. When the reform period began to slow down, the growth effect declined considerably, and in 1997-99 it entailed only 0.6 percentage points of additional growth (compared with a hypothetical situation with no further reforms; Figure 5.5). The study also finds that the effectiveness of the reforms depended crucially on the institutional environment in which they took place. In particular, the reforms seem to have had a greater effect in countries with good rule of law, possibly because it lessened uncertainty about the new rules and limited the undue interference of interest groups in the design and implementation of regulations. Loayza, Fajnzylber, and Calderón (2002) also find more modest effects of the reforms in their update of the estimates of Easterly, Loayza, and Montiel (1997).

Opening up to international trade is an area of structural reform whose effects on growth have been the subject of much debate. According to most studies that make comparisons between countries, there is a clear and positive correlation between opening to international trade and economic growth (Dollar 1992; Sachs and Warner 1995; Frankel and Romer 1999; Ben-David 1993; Edwards 1998; Dollar and Kraay 2001). Studies of domestic experiences reach the same conclusion (see a summary in Srinivasan and Bhagwati [1999]). Although criticisms have been raised about the validity of

Table 5.2 Effects of Reforms on Growth in Selected Countries

(Percentage points)

Source	Simple average	Weighted average
Easterly, Loayza, and Montiel (1997), 1991–93 vs. 1986–90	2.2	1.7
Lora and Barrera (1997), 1993–95 vs. 1987–89	2.2	2.2
Fernández-Arias and Montiel (1997), 1991–95 vs. 1986–90	1.6	1.7
Lora and Panizza (2002), average for 1988–99	1.0	
Loayza, Fajnzylber, and Calderón (2002), 1990s vs. 1980s	1.3	

Figure 5.5 Average Effect of Reforms on Growth in Latin America, 1988-99

(Percentage points)

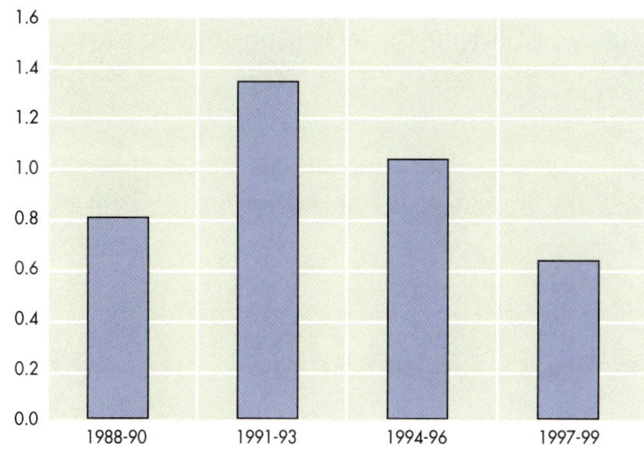

Source: Lora and Panizza (2002).

some of these studies,[10] no study has suggested that opening up to trade has adverse effects on growth. Studies more specifically focused on Latin America also find a positive relationship between liberalization and growth (Lora and Barrera 1997; Stallings and Peres 2000; Loayza, Fajnzylber, and Calderón 2002).

Likewise, reforms in the financial and infrastructure sectors have had positive effects when the reforms have generated a climate favorable to competition and an adequate regulatory system. According to a recent study based on the experience of 37 developing countries in the 1990s, when these conditions were met, the effect on growth of financial reform and the privatization of telecommunications was more than 2 percentage points (Mattoo, Rathindran, and Subramanian 2001). Although this estimate may exaggerate the permanent effects of these measures, it brings out the importance of having comprehensive reforms in these two areas.

In short, despite the differences between the various studies, the conclusion that can be drawn is that the reforms have had a positive but modest effect on growth. Even considering the more optimistic calculations, which place the effect at close to 2 points of additional growth, the reforms by themselves could not have raised per capita growth from -0.7 percent in the 1980s to rates around 3 percent, like those seen in the 1960s and 1970s. One of the reasons for the modest impact of the reforms may have been that they were incomplete, did not have enough internal institutional support, and took place in an unstable international environment, especially in the realm of financing, which in turn may have compromised national macroeconomic policies. This debate, which remains unresolved and is not the main subject of this chapter, nevertheless suggests that the reforms changed the operation of the economy less than is generally assumed and hence their impact on labor must likewise have been modest.

[10] According to Harrison and Hanson (1999) and Rodríguez and Rodrik (2001), the literature that finds a positive relationship between liberalization and growth is plagued by problems of methodology and data errors, and the results are not particularly solid in comparison with alternative specifications and data series. Rodrik (2000) likewise asserts that contrary to what is suggested by Srinivasan and Bhagwati (1999), the evidence for liberalization derived from country studies is far from overwhelming. Nevertheless, Jones (2001), commenting on the article by Rodríguez and Rodrik, shows that the standard results of a positive relationship between market opening and growth are quite solid, and that few of the results commonly accepted in the economic literature would pass the strict evidence of robustness of Rodríguez and Rodrik. Wacziarg and Welch (2002) take up the discussion begun by Rodríguez and Rodrik and find that their criticisms are valid for cross-section analyses, from which it cannot be concluded that opening helps growth. Nevertheless, time-series panel results do show high and robust effects of liberalization on growth.

The remainder of this chapter discusses the effects that the reforms had on employment, wages, and quality of work, starting from the assumption that the effect on growth was positive although modest. The discussion concentrates especially, but not exclusively, on trade liberalization and privatization, the two areas most criticized and the ones that have received the most attention from analysts.

Effects of Liberalization

Many critics believe that policies adopted since the late 1980s of lifting controls on imports have had various adverse effects on labor. The first and most worrisome effect seems to have been loss of employment. For example, according to SAPRIN (2002, p. 55): "The decline in domestic manufacturing has followed the flooding of local markets with cheap imports that have displaced local production and goods." As a result, "many local manufacturing firms, particularly innovative, small and medium-size ones that generate a great deal of employment, have been forced out of business."

In Argentina, "many poor people also blame mechanization and competition from foreign producers for the unemployment crisis." (Narayan and Petesch 2002, p. 338) In Jamaica, "unemployment is widely viewed as the leading cause of poverty [...] People point to problems of increased foreign competition. In urban areas, people speak repeatedly of factory closings and layoffs, and in rural areas they indicate that large plantations and processing plants used to offer many more jobs." (Narayan and Petesch 2002, p. 433)

The aim of liberalization was to reallocate resources from previously protected sectors toward more efficient sectors, especially export sectors. In almost all countries in the region, exports actually did perform much better in the 1990s than during the previous decade (see Figure 5.2). Nevertheless, the prevailing opinion is that the export sector did not manage to make up for the destruction of employment in the previously protected sectors and that the jobs created have been inferior in terms of pay, stability, and other labor conditions.

According to SAPRIN (2002, pp. 55-56): "Export growth has been concentrated in a few activities that do not create links to the local economy and has typically been very narrowly based on a few resources and items produced with low-skilled labor.[...] Employment growth occurring subsequent to trade liberalization has been no match for the volumes of new entrants to the labor market. The limited employment that has been generated is highly concentrated in export enclaves or in similar low-wage services [while] employment losses have occurred mostly in the domestic market-oriented sector."

According to Stallings and Peres (2000, pp. 200-201): "The reforms did not deliver the expected employment growth in the tradables sector [...] Only the maquila assembly plants, operating under conditions that differ from those of the rest of the economy, provided the strong growth in highly labor-intensive activities that the reforms were expected to produce."

The second issue of concern is the effect that trade liberalization had on pay for labor. The reformers expected that at least in the medium run liberalization would raise wages because of its expected effect on investment and productivity and by leading to the reallocation of employment toward the more efficient sectors. But this does not seem to have happened. On the contrary, it is widely held that liberalization lowered wages, especially for lower-skilled workers, thereby helping to widen pay inequality. According to SAPRIN (2002, pp. 55-56), after trade liberalization, "real wage rates have tended to decline, income inequality has increased, and job insecurity and 'informalization' have become more pervasive."

Goldín (1997, p. 112) notes: "Market inequality has increased in many countries of Latin America in terms of gender, age, and social class as a result of liberalization policies. Unequal terms are more profound in the countryside, however, deepening the already existing unequal relations of production." And Díaz (1997, p. 45) observes: "Economic crisis and neoliberal economic adjustment have increased social inequality throughout

Latin America, primarily by lowering median and minimum wages."

A third criticism, closely connected to the foregoing, has to do with the low pay and quality of the new employment created out of the liberalization processes. Poor people in São Paulo, Brazil said that, "in the past, everybody worked in the factories and the wages were good. [. . .] but today the men often work at jobs with less security as car washers, janitors, night watchmen, construction workers, or tradesmen. Most women clean houses or offices or wash laundry in addition to their responsibilities as housewives." (Narayan and Petesch 2002, p. 363)

Although the poor in Brazil recognize that there are new formal sector jobs, "many new jobs created in the formal sector are unskilled and low paid. While workers laid off from the manufacturing and financial sectors find these jobs preferable to those in the informal sector, these new positions do not provide an income level that allows workers to adequately support their families." (Narayan and Petesch 2002, p. 368) Similarly, the authors make the following observation on informal employment in Jamaica: "When Jamaican farms and industries faced increased competition in global markets during the 1990s, many formal work opportunities for poor men and women disappeared. Although jobs are tighter, poor Jamaicans engage in trades, run small shops, higgle (sell) on the streets, work as domestics, drive taxis, take factory and daily farm wage jobs, fish, and migrate in large numbers to other areas of the island and overseas in search of more opportunity." (Narayan and Petesch 2002, p. 455)

Some observers note that job creation is not only concentrated in a few activities such as the maquiladoras, but also that these new jobs have been of poor quality. According to the International Labour Organization (ILO), which has analyzed the opinions of many people and institutions related to export processing zones (EPZs), "wages, working conditions (including safety and health) and labour relations are the three areas in which there has been the most criticism about the situation of workers in EPZs."[11]

The following opinion reflects concerns about the quality of work in such zones: "Millions of textile, clothing and leather workers around the world are employed in free trade zones, special economic zones designed to attract foreign investment and promote export-led industrialisation. The ITGLWF [International Textile, Garment and Leather Workers' Federation] deplores the exploitation of workers in many of these zones, where trade union rights are often ignored."[12]

Many opinions on the effects of the reforms on labor are based on comparisons between the situation before and after the reforms, and often point to specific sectors, regions, or groups of workers or companies. These comparisons are a good starting point for identifying problems, but do not provide sufficiently general proof of the effects of the reforms because they do not allow for isolating the influence of other factors that may affect the impact on labor. And they do not make it possible to know whether these observations are representative of what may have happened to a larger number of workers or companies. This type of analysis would require econometric methods available only to specialists, and extensive databases that exist only in some countries. Hence the debate is inevitably inconclusive because in many cases it is impossible to verify (or reject) whether the problems identified by observers are the result of liberalization (or other factors) and whether they are a common phenomenon. Even when data exist, the results of econometric studies may be inconclusive for technical or interpretation reasons. Despite these limitations, some conclusions on the labor effects of liberalization may be advanced on the basis of available evidence.

Unemployment

It is possible that the impact of liberalization on employment was initially—and still is—the main reason for political and public opposition to this reform. There may be many reasons for such a rejection. Perhaps it is thought that imports dis-

[11] See ILO, www.transnationale.org/pays/epz.htm.

[12] The International Textile, Garment and Leather Workers Federation, 2003, www.itglwf.org/focus.asp?Issue=EPZ&Language=ENS.

place domestic production, prompting companies to lay off workers, or that, although liberalization promotes exports, there may not be enough jobs created to offset the losses in the sectors that compete with imports (for example, because in some countries exports are natural resource intensive and not labor intensive). Another possible reason for expecting greater unemployment after opening the economy is that during the process of reallocating resources from sectors that are no longer viable toward those that may be so, more workers will be looking for jobs.

Figure 5.6 suggests that there is no relationship between the degree of liberalization and the recent high unemployment rates in Latin American countries. From Table 5.3, this kind of cross-section comparison does not show statistically significant correlations with other liberalization measures, such as (changes in) trade deepening rates (exports plus imports as a percentage of GDP)[13] or the trade balance (exports minus imports as a percentage of GDP). This should not be surprising because unemployment rates are affected by factors specific to each country, such as per capita income and the institutions that regulate the labor market. Hence, it is more appropriate to ask whether variations in unemployment rates have had a relationship with trade liberalization over time, isolating the influence of the factors that are specific to each country. Márquez and Pagés (1998b) take such an approach in their analysis of the relationship between unemployment and liberalization in 18 Latin American countries since the 1970s. They conclude that trade liberalization has no effect on unemployment.

These long-range analyses may be limited by the quality of information because in many countries, definitions of unemployment and measurement methods have changed over the years. Hence, in order to calculate unemployment rates with uniform methods, this chapter uses a battery of 85 household surveys in 10 countries in the region. Although coverage by country is irregular and discontinuous over time, the results are illustrative. The central conclusion is once more that there is no statistically solid relationship between unemployment and any of the indicators of liberalization used (average tariff rate, trade-to-GDP ratio, trade balance, or exports or imports-to-GDP ratio). The only significant correlation found is that between unemployment and the trade balance, which suggests that both variables tend to move in the same direction (more unemployment when there is a higher trade surplus), possibly because both depend on common causes, such as the business cycle. Indeed, when the influence of the business cycle is isolated, this correlation is no longer significant (Table 5.3). Inasmuch as the results are similar when workers with different education levels are considered, there are no grounds for saying that liberalization is one of the factors helping to explain trends in unemployment rates.

This finding does not rule out that in specific cases changes in trade policy may have produced unemployment, but thus far there is no econometric evidence supporting that possibility. Liberalization may also have had transitory effects on employment levels and unemployment rates because liberalization processes have led to some reallocations of employment between sectors. In a few countries around the world, unemployment

Figure 5.6 Unemployment and Openness

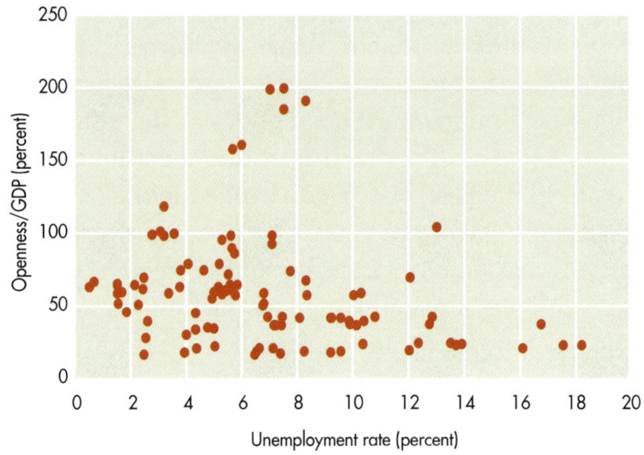

Note: Openness is the sum of exports plus imports over GDP. Each point in the scatter is a year for one Latin American country.
Source: IMF (various years); IDB household surveys.

[13] de Ferranti and others (2001) reach similar conclusions.

Table 5.3 Trade Reform and Unemployment

Variable	Number of observations	Type 1 regressions	Type 2 regressions
Tariffs (average)	83	0.038	0.050
		(1.05)	(1.17)
Trade penetration (exports plus imports/GDP)	85	–0.002	0.035
		(–0.07)	(1.32)
Trade balance (exports minus imports/GDP)	85	0.146	0.087
		(2.09)**	(1.16)
Exports/GDP	85	0.045	0.072
		(1.05)	(1.48)
Imports/GDP	85	–0.081	0.039
		(–1.14)*	(0.68)

* Significant at 10 percent.
** Significant at 5 percent.
Note: The dependent variable is the unemployment rate. The estimations are based on unbalanced panel data from the mid-1980s to 2001. Each coefficient comes from a separate regression in which country fixed effects are also included but not reported. Type 1 regressions also control for country trend. In addition, type 2 regressions control for GDP cycles and real exchange rate indices by country. t-statistics are in parentheses.
Source: IDB household surveys for the unemployment rate; IMF (various years) for exports, imports, and GDP; and Lora (2001) for tariffs.

rates have increased by about 10 points starting from the time when the economy opened up and lasting for a period of more than a decade before falling back to levels similar to and lower than initial unemployment (Rama 2001). This pattern does not seem to have occurred in the wave of reforms during the past decade in Latin America, however, because unemployment rates generally have not been higher since the time when the economy was opened up (Figure 5.7).[14] Nor does this pattern seem to have been common in the past, as shown by a set of studies on episodes of trade liberalization in the post-war period up to the mid-1980s. Based on the experiences of 19 countries, including six in Latin America (Argentina, Brazil, Chile, Colombia, Peru, and Uruguay), the authors note that, "based on the data and analysis of country studies it can be concluded that on the whole attempts at liberalization have not had significant transition costs in terms of unemployment." (Michaely, Papageorgiou, and Choksi 1991, p. 80)

Figure 5.7 Unemployment before and after Trade Reform

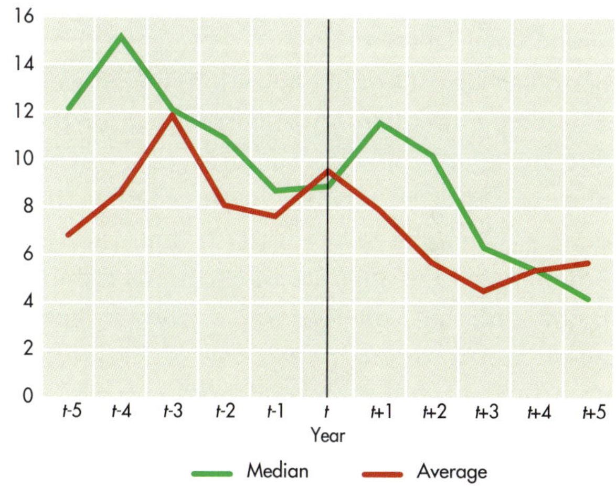

Source: Unemployment rates are from ECLAC (2001). t is the year of major reduction in tarriffs between 1985 and 1999 according to Lora (2001).

Aggregate Employment

Evidently, there are no empirical grounds for attributing unemployment to liberalization. Nevertheless, there may have been adverse effects on aggregate employment, which would not be reflected in unemployment if the workers affected opted to leave the labor market.

[14] Figure 5.7 shows the trend of unemployment rates before and after the year of greatest tariff reductions, without isolating the influence of any other variable that may have affected unemployment.

A few studies have established that *controlling for product level* (and other macro variables) the lowering of tariffs reduced aggregate employment levels (Stallings and Peres 2000; IDB 1997). However, strictly speaking, these studies do not provide a basis for claiming that liberalization has reduced employment. The only thing that can be said based on them is that liberalization increased labor productivity because it reduced employment *for each product unit.* Márquez and Pagés (1998b) is the only study that analyzes this issue, and the results are quite illustrative. When controlling for the product level, the finding is the same as in the other studies, namely that liberalization had negative effects on total employment. It is estimated that an increase of 1 percent of GDP in trade flows with the rest of the world leads to a reduction of 0.06 percent in aggregate employment, a modest effect, albeit statistically significant. Inasmuch as trade deepening increased 20 percent in the average Latin American country between the mid-1980s and the end of the 1990s, employment would have fallen a total of 1.2 percent during this period as a result of liberalization, which would be a modest effect. However, controlling for the production level, this effect is reduced even further and ceases to be significant, suggesting that the effects of increased productivity and the level of production have opposite implications for employment and that, on the whole, they cancel one another out.

In the battery of household surveys assembled by the IDB for 10 countries, there is a negative relationship between tariffs and employment rates (controlling for the fixed factors specific to each country). This relationship, which stands even controlling for product level, suggests that reducing tariffs had favorable effects on employment. The other measurements of liberalization have a statistically insignificant relationship with employment rates, regardless of controlling for product level or the business cycle (Table 5.4). Consequently, no basis has been found for saying that reducing tariffs or increasing trade has lessened overall employment (although there is evidence that it caused a decline in employment in the manufacturing sector in some countries).

The scarce impact of the trade reforms on employment levels is surprising when it is assumed that imports (total imports or net of exports) displace domestic production. Although this assumption may make some sense at the micro level, it tends to lose relevance in the aggregate (see Box 5.1).

The conclusion that liberalization has scant effects on employment is consistent with the conclusion of the studies on episodes of trade liberalization in the post-war period: "The overwhelming impression [...] is that import ratios and employment were correlated either very weakly or not at all." (Michaely, Papageorgiou, and Choksi 1991, p. 76)

In short, statistical evidence does not provide a basis for saying that liberalization processes have lowered total levels of employment or raised unemployment rates. The explanation for recent high unemployment rates in Argentina, Colombia, Uruguay, and Venezuela should be sought in macroeconomic factors and labor legislation that are analyzed in other chapters in this Report. However, this conclusion does not eliminate the possibility that liberalization may have had other effects on labor. Rather, if liberalization did not cause changes in employment or unemployment, it may have been because adjustment to changes in the level and composition of demand for labor took place through the sector composition of employment, wage levels, or quality of jobs.

Sector Composition of Employment

The bulk of (net) additional employment in the 1990s was created in services and commerce. The modern service sectors (electric power, water, transportation, telecommunications, and financial services) generated net employment at a faster pace than the traditional service sectors, but because of their small size, their contribution to total employment was modest. Industry and construction generated little additional employment, and employment levels declined in agriculture (Table 5.5). Within this overall pattern, the differences between countries and sectors are important. In Argentina, jobs in industries in the automotive

Table 5.4 Trade Reform and Employment

Variable	Number of observations	Type 1 regressions	Type 2 regressions
Tariffs (average)	83	–0.074	–0.067
		(–2.28)**	(–1.69)*
Trade penetration (exports plus imports/GDP)	85	0.010	0.002
		(0.43)	(0.07)
Trade balance (exports minus imports/GDP)	85	–0.067	–0.024
		(–1.20)	(–0.32)
Exports/GDP	85	–0.009	–0.004
		(–0.24)	(–0.10)
Imports/GDP	85	0.056	0.014
		(1.24)	(0.28)

* Significant at 10 percent.

** Significant at 5 percent.

Note: The dependent variable is employment. The estimations are based on unbalanced panel data from the mid-1980s to 2001. Each coefficient comes from a separate regression in which country fixed effects are also included but not reported. Type 1 regressions also control for country trend. In addition, type 2 regressions control for GDP cycles and real exchange rate indexes by country. t-statistics are in parentheses.

Source: IDB household surveys for employment; IMF for exports, imports, and GDP; and Lora (2001) for tariffs.

Box 5.1. Imports and Job Destruction

Opposition to trade liberalization measures is usually based on the fear that imports (total or net of exports) displace domestic production and thereby destroy jobs. In its extreme form, this approach implies that there is a one-to-one relationship between imports and domestic production. A 1 percent (in terms of GDP) increase in the rate of imports should lead to a similar percentage drop in total employment (or even worse, if it is thought that industries that compete with imports use labor more intensively than other sectors). Because imports affect the manufacturing sector more intensely, there would presumably be many of job losses in this sector. Sectors that do not compete directly with imports could also be affected insofar as they produce inputs for those sectors that do compete with imports.

The fundamental mistake of this approach is to assume that any increase in imports (total or net of exports) displaces domestic production, at least partially. In practice that is not what happens, for several reasons. Many imports do not compete with, but complement domestic production (machinery or inputs not produced domestically), and therefore help increase production. But even those that compete do not do so perfectly, nor do they encounter rigid domestic demand. Greater imports partly generate changes in quality and other attributes of domestic goods, and partly lower costs, helping to partially or completely offset the direct effect of displacement that would occur if the domestic and imported goods were identical and demand were rigid.

A further and perhaps more important reason is that imports can raise productivity both in the sectors with which they compete and in others where benefits include greater variety, quality, or technology associated with imports. Productivity increases mean a reduction in the need for labor per product unit and hence they can be seen as another factor in employment loss. However, productivity increases make it possible to reach broader markets, both domestic and foreign, thereby partially or completely offsetting possible employment reductions and allowing for higher pay for labor. Finally, an increase in imports may extend possibilities for production and consumption of goods that previously did not exist, opening employment opportunities.

Table 5.5 Employment Growth by Sector in Selected Countries, 1990s

(Average annual percent)

Sector	Argentina	Brazil	Chile	Colombia	Costa Rica	Honduras	Mexico	Panama	Uruguay	Venezuela
Agriculture, hunting, forestry, and fishing		0.2	–0.8	0.7	0.5	2.9		–2.3		1.3
Mining and quarrying	–5.4	–6.3	–1.9	–6.1	4.1	–6.3	0.0	1.6	4.7	–0.6
Manufacturing	4.8	–0.7	–0.4	–0.1	0.4	6.1	5.3	2.7	–4.3	1.7
Electricity, gas, and water	1.2	–2.2	3.5	–0.5	–0.3	–0.1	5.2	–3.6	–2.2	0.0
Construction	12.6	2.1	3.9	2.0	3.7	7.2		12.1	1.4	4.1
Wholesale and retail trade, restaurants, and hotels	9.5	3.3	3.7	3.3	5.3	7.6	7.2	4.9	1.1	6.0
Transport, storage, and communications	8.3	1.5	4.4	3.8	7.7	1.1	7.3	4.3	–1.5	4.5
Finance, insurance, real estate, and business services	13.2	–3.5	1.4	6.0	6.1	7.4	1.1	9.0	4.3	2.6
Community, social, and personal services, government services	11.1	2.7	4.6	4.1	3.4	1.9	6.4	3.4	–4.4	3.6
Total	9.2	1.5	2.4	2.4	2.9	4.3	6.8	3.2	–1.7	3.6

Note: Data for Argentina, Mexico, and Uruguay are for urban areas only.
Source: IDB household surveys.

sector were massively destroyed; in Brazil, employment in grains dropped by one-fourth; and in Mexico, there was a significant decline in employment in livestock and grains. In other sectors, the declines were less significant or employment increased (in chemicals and grains in Argentina and intermediate industry in Mexico).[15] Were these changes in the composition of employment the result of liberalization or other factors? For example, the abundant supply of foreign capital during a part of the decade ought to have reduced the prices of tradable goods vis-à-vis services, promoting increased employment in the latter. Similarly, technological change could have led to changes in the composition of employment.

Liberalization does seem to have affected industrial employment, albeit by a surprisingly small amount in view of the extent of reductions in tariffs and other mechanisms for protecting industry. Consider the case of Mexico, where, as in most countries in the region, tariffs and import controls were cut sharply. The average tariff fell from 23.5 percent in 1985 to 12.5 percent in 1990, and the maximum tariff dropped from 100 to 20 percent during the same period, while import licenses, which were formerly applied to 92 percent of imports, covered only 20 percent in 1990 and have covered even less since then. These major changes in protection had little effect on sector employment: based on data from industrial establishments, for every percentage point decline in tariffs, employment throughout manufacturing fell by an estimated 0.02 to 0.03 percent, and hence declines in employment were minimal (Revenga 1997). Other studies have found equally modest effects, which were concentrated among factory workers because employment in administrative activities showed practically no change (Feliciano 1994; Hanson and Harrison 1999). The explanation lies partly in the fact that the adjustment took place through wages and partly because tariff reductions had little impact on production in the affected sectors.

In Colombia, the liberalization of the 1990s also seems to have had little effect on industrial employment. It dropped markedly during the 1980s, despite tariff and nontariff protection, and deepened only marginally after the tariff reduction

[15] For a more detailed description of these changes, see de Ferranti and others (2001).

in the early 1990s. This phenomenon was partly the result of the trade opening that helped lower the price of capital in relation to labor. Other factors operating in the same direction were the appreciation in the exchange rate and increased payroll taxes (Cárdenas and Gutiérrez 1997).

By contrast, in Uruguay, tariff reductions seem to have had a strong effect on industrial employment, which is reasonable considering the small size of the economy. It has been estimated that in Uruguay, for every percentage point that protection was reduced, industrial employment fell between 0.4 and 0.5 percent in the same year (Rama 1994). With a reduction of some 20 points in tariffs from the mid-1980s until the end of the 1990s, liberalization may have caused a 10 percent drop in industrial employment.

Although each case may have been different, the effects of liberalization on industrial employment seem to have been small for the average of the 18 countries analyzed in the Márquez and Pagés (1998b) study. According to their calculations, for every percentage point decline in the average tariff, industrial employment fell between 0.2 and 0.3 percent. With a 30 point decline, as was typical in Latin America, industrial employment fell between 6 and 9 percent. Alternatively, for every 1 point increase in trade flows, employment in industry declined between 0.1 and 0.14 percent. These calculations do not take into account the indirect effect of trade or tariffs on the level of industrial production. If this effect were also adverse, the result would be a greater decline in employment. However, when this effect is incorporated, declines in industrial production are found to be less, again suggesting that liberalization did not have the destructive effects on industrial production (and thereby on employment) that are often attributed to it.[16]

Liberalization may have had greater effects on agricultural employment. However, as noted in a study by the Economic Commission for Latin America and the Caribbean (ECLAC) based on the experience of nine countries, "the most important transformations in the agricultural sector resulted not only from the reforms, but also from processes that began at least a decade earlier. The most significant were the incorporation of new technologies, reduction of cultivated land, increased land dedicated to livestock and forest plantations, and employment decline." (Stallings and Peres 2000, p. 179) Consequently, although liberalization may have caused significant labor displacement in some agricultural operations that were exposed to competition, it would be a mistake to think that this was the main cause of the decline in employment in agriculture. Unfortunately, few econometric studies have attempted to calculate the effects of liberalization on the agricultural sector because for this sector, unlike manufacturing, the information on production and employment needed for such measurements is not available.

What is known for certain, however, is that the catastrophic predictions of displacement of employment, which were based on calculating the labor requirements for agricultural goods that could not compete internationally, have not come true. It was feared that the North American Free Trade Agreement (NAFTA), which forced Mexico to sharply reduce protection for corn and other farm products, would cause the displacement of up to 15 million workers (de Janvry, Sadoulet, and Davis 1997). Actually, what happened was unexpected: the areas devoted to corn, the product most affected, expanded and although productivity declined, there was only moderate displacement of labor. However, income from production fell and environmental sustainability may have deteriorated in some areas (Nadal 2000).[17]

In short, although some sectors suffered loss of employment as a result of a reduction in tariffs and other import protection, the general changes in employment levels were minor, both in the

[16] See also Tybout (1996) on Chile in 1979-86. This case, like that of the other developing countries, shows that the sector composition of industrial production is insensitive to changes in policies to protect against imports. Likewise, Michaely, Papageorgiou, and Choksi (1991), on the basis of 19 episodes of liberalization in developing countries, show that trade liberalization has little effect on reallocation or loss of employment. Indeed, employment increased in practically all the cases examined, including Brazil between 1965 and 1973 and Peru after the 1978-79 liberalization.

[17] However, other factors counteracted this decline, notably the support of the Procampo program and an appreciation in the real exchange rate (de Janvry, Sadoulet, and Davis 1997).

aggregate and in the sectors in which protection was reduced. However, these conclusions refer to net changes in employment, behind which are concealed large flows of employment creation and destruction. Although it has not had a major impact on levels of aggregate or sector employment, liberalization may have affected the flows of employment creation and destruction, and hence employment stability. This point is important given the perception of labor insecurity among many Latin Americans. According to Latinobarómetro surveys of 17 countries in 2001, 63 of every 100 people thought that they were very likely to lose their jobs.

Employment Stability

Liberalization seems to have had a modest effect on the extent of reallocation of employment between sectors of production. In their analysis of the experiences of 25 countries at different stages of development (13 of them in Latin America), Seddon and Wacziarg (2001) find that the extent of changes in the composition of employment between the major sectors declined after trade liberalization.[18] In their examination of subsectors of manufacturing industry, they do find that the recomposition of employment increased after liberalization, but the estimated effects were small and statistically weak.[19]

Similar results are found in an analysis of the industrial sector in 11 Latin American countries based on data from surveys of manufacturing establishments between 1985 and 1998. There is no relationship between trade reform and the extent of reallocation of employment between industrial subsectors.[20] And there is no relationship with the other areas of reform studied in this chapter (the indicators of reform in all cases are the indices described in the previous section; see Table 5.6). However, there are differences across countries. For example, in Colombia, an increase in the rate of reallocation of employment between industrial sectors is indeed found, starting from the year when the major reforms for opening the economy were introduced. Before liberalization, 19.7 percent of industrial employment was reallocated each year, but the rate increased to 23.5 percent after liberalization,[21] primarily because companies were more sensitive to their own circumstances, as opposed to changes that they shared with other companies in the same subsector.

The fear that liberalization and globalization in general are making employment permanently more unstable finds support in the positions of noted academics, like Rodrik (1997), who argues that globalization has made the demand for labor more unstable because of increased competition between domestic and foreign markets and because companies can turn to imported inputs as a way of lowering production costs. Because companies now find it easier to substitute imported for domestic inputs and can even go outside the firm to contract a major portion of the production process, production tends to be more unstable and this greater instability tends to fall on workers, especially those with lower skills who are easily replaceable.

The empirical evidence does not sustain the claim that liberalization will permanently have such a destabilizing effect on Latin America.[22] In Brazil, no evidence has been found that employment or wages have become more sensitive to variations in export and import trade (Paes de Barros, Corseuil, and Gonzaga 1999). In Chile, Colombia, and Mexico, where Rodrik's hypothesis has been studied more explicitly, no coherent evidence has been found that trade liberalization policies or various measures of trade deepening are behind the changes observed in the elasticity of employment demand. According to the authors of the study, "if

[18] This is based on the one-digit classification in UNIDO's ISIC system. The changes in employment composition (or rate of reallocation of employment) are the sum of increases minus declines in employment in each sector, divided by total employment in all sectors.

[19] UNIDO three-digit ISIC classification.

[20] ISIC three-digit classification for manufacturing industry sectors, according to UNIDO data.

[21] These values are the average rates of reallocation of employment in 1978-91 and 1992-2000, respectively, based on statistics reported by Medina, Meléndez, and Seim (2003). The difference between the two rates is statistically significant at 1 percent.

[22] However, this claim may be valid for the United States, where the elasticity of demand for factory labor doubled between 1979 and 1991. For a short overview, see Brown (2000).

Table 5.6 Structural Reforms and Employment Reallocation between Manufacturing Sectors

Variable	(1)	(2)	(3)
Structural reform index	–0.018 (–0.039)		
Trade index		–0.011 (0.018)	
Privatization index			0.006 (0.034)

Note: The dependent variable, change in sector of employment, is measured as the sum of employment changes (in absolute values) between manufacturing sectors (according to the three-digit ISIC classification), relative to total employment in the manufacturing sector. The estimations are based on unbalanced panel data from the mid-1980s to 2001. The regressions use data for 11 countries in Latin America. Standard errors are in parentheses.
Source: UNIDO for change in sector of employment and Lora (2001) for the indexes.

globalization is making the lives of workers more unstable, it is probably through other mechanisms." (Fajnzylber and Maloney 2001)

Wage Levels

There is no empirical basis for claiming that greater openness to trade permanently worsens the wages of all workers in a country. However, international evidence suggests that wages may drop initially with liberalization and that some groups suffer significant losses of income.

Because increased openness to trade tends to increase the productivity and income levels of countries, wages should be expected to rise more rapidly in countries that are more integrated internationally. The growth pattern of wages in a sample of 70 countries from all regions of the world backs that presumption: in those developing countries that were more open to world trade, average real wages in the 1990s were 30 percent higher than in the 1980s; in those that were less open, the increase was only 13 percent; and the percentage for developed countries was around 20 percent (Figure 5.8).[23]

However, although openness to trade may help increase wages, the effect is not instantaneous. According to the calculations in Figure 5.9, a trade increase of 1 percent of GDP tends to be associated with an initial 0.3 percent decline in wages. It is only after the third year that, on average for the 70 countries considered, wages increase.[24] According to these estimates, an increase of 20 percentage points of GDP in trade penetration, which was the average in Latin America, could explain an initial 6 percent drop in real wages if it happened all at once. It is important to note that these calculations have to do with changes in the degree of penetration of imports and exports, and hence they do not necessarily reflect the effects of tariff reductions. Moreover, these results should be received with caution because they may be skewed by the presence of reverse causality, as an initial drop in wages may facilitate greater trade.

Using a battery of 78 household surveys for 10 countries, an effort has been made to verify the negative influence of trade on real wages. This effect also occurs in Latin America, but only in tradable sectors (agriculture and industry), not in services. When the effect of the business cycle on wages is isolated, the elasticity obtained is similar to that estimated for the world (-0.3). It also stands taking into account the (negative and significant)

[23] Nevertheless, these statistics do not demonstrate that increased trade caused higher wages; both could be the result of other factors.

[24] Although these estimates seem to be of the "before and after" type, they do not suffer from the methodological problems mentioned at the outset of this section because they are based on numerous observations, thereby making it possible to isolate the fixed effects associated with each country, occupation, and year. See Rama (2001).

Figure 5.8 Growth in Wages by Type of Country, 1980s to 1990s
(Percent)

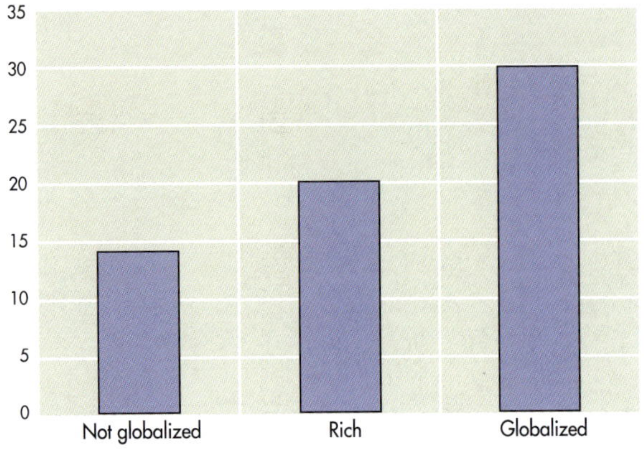

Note: Sample includes 70 countries around the world.
Source: Rama (2001).

Figure 5.9 Increased Trade and Wages over Time
(Percent change in wage level)

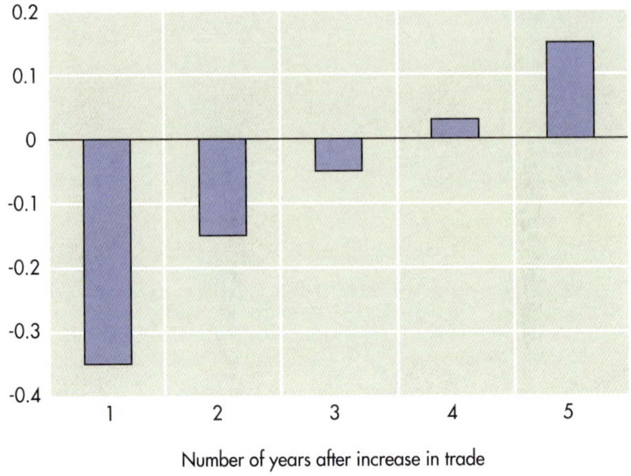

Note: Sample includes 70 countries around the world. Values show the change in wages after a 1 percent of GDP increase in trade.
Source: Rama (2001).

Table 5.7 Real Wages and Trade Penetration

Variable	(1)	(2)	(3)
Trade penetration effect on tradables[a]	−0.204	−0.321	−0.299
	(−2.09)**	(−3.05)***	(−2.78)***
Trade penetration effect on nontradables[a]	−0.001	−0.002	−0.002
	(−1.42)	(−2.08)**	(−1.97)**
GDP trend[b]		0.062	0.068
		(0.95)	(0.40)
GDP cycle[b]		0.606	0.424
		(2.55)**	(1.67)*
Real exchange rate index			−0.142
			(−2.03)**

** Significant at 5 percent.
*** Significant at 1 percent.
[a] Trade penetration is measured as imports plus exports over GDP.
[b] GDP trend and cycle are calculated applying Hodrick and Prescott filters to the GDP time series.
Note: The dependent variable is (log) real wages. The estimations are based on unbalanced panel data from the the mid-1980s to 2001. Values are estimated using fixed effects for country and sector. The sample is 85 surveys for 10 countries with nine sectors in each country. t-statistics are in parentheses.
Source: Household surveys for the dependent variable; IMF (International Financial Statistics) for independent variables.

influence exercised by devalued exchange rates on wages (Table 5.7). On the basis of available information, it cannot be determined whether these effects on wages tend to be corrected over time.

Some studies of individual countries have focused on analyzing the effects of lower tariffs on wages in industry (rather than the entire economy). In the case of Mexico, it has been estimated that in the companies that were affected by a 40 point drop in tariffs, real wages fell between 8 and 10 percent. For the manufacturing sector as a whole, it is calculated that the tariff reductions in the late 1980s caused a 3-4 percent drop in wages. The elimination of quantitative controls on imports may have had an even greater effect, but it is difficult to quantify with precision (Revenga 1997). In

Colombia, where the average tariff fell from 50 percent in 1984 to 13 percent in 1998, the effect on the average wage in manufacturing was also 3-4 percent;[25] in the industrial sectors that were initially protected, the effect may have been as much as 7 percent. In addition, increases in import penetration may have had some additional effect on industrial wages (Goldberg and Pavcnik 2001). Due to their short time horizon, the studies do not provide a basis for saying whether these wage drops were permanent or whether they would tend to be diluted over time and with the changes in productivity prompted by liberalization.

It is perhaps surprising that the effects of liberalization on wages have been relatively pronounced in comparison with the modest changes in employment and its composition. There is no definitive explanation for this phenomenon, but one possible hypothesis is that workers were sharing in the rents (and inefficiencies) that protection afforded companies. The lowering of tariffs could be accommodated without major changes in employment by improved productivity and elimination of those rents.

Wage Gaps

The impact of liberalization measures on wage gaps has been one of the most studied aspects of the structural reforms of the past decade. The issue arouses interest because the increase in wage gaps between skilled and unskilled workers has been striking in some countries and was unexpected by many economists, who had predicted that lowering tariffs would increase the demand for unskilled labor, and hence would help narrow wage gaps (see Box 5.2).

The widening of wage gaps caused by education has been significant, although less pronounced than is sometimes claimed. Comparing the wage incomes of workers with a university degree with those with a high school diploma, the gap increased by 10 percent in the 1990s (average for 12 countries in the region), which is a modest increase. However, if workers with a university degree are compared with those who have completed elementary school, the increase was 7 percent. By contrast, if the calculation is between workers with a high

Figure 5.10 Wage Gap between Workers with Complete Tertiary vs Complete Secondary Education
(Percent)

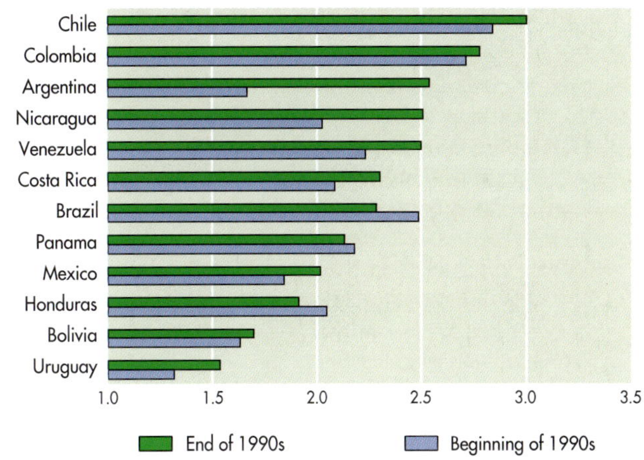

Source: IDB household surveys.

school diploma and those who have completed elementary school, a slight reduction in the gap over the entire decade may be noted. For example, in the case of the gap between university and high school, Argentina and Nicaragua display significant increases (53 and 24 percent, respectively), whereas Brazil, Honduras, and Panama had modest reductions (Figure 5.10). In several countries, the trend toward wider gaps that were observed at the beginning of liberalization has halted or reversed in recent years. In Mexico, the trend stopped after 1994, when NAFTA went into effect, and in Colombia, the sharp increase early in the 1990s was completely reversed in subsequent years.

Many studies have examined the relationship between the wage gap and the process of opening up to international trade in the past few decades. Although various studies establish a significant relationship between the two variables, there is consensus that the influence of liberalization on the wage gap has been modest and indirect, possibly reflecting the influence of technological change. (However, as is discussed in greater detail in chapter 6, this conclusion is far from overwhelming.)

[25] Goldberg and Pavcnik (2001) report a value of 4 percent, but it is based on the assumption that the tariff is entirely eliminated.

Box 5.2. Trade Liberalization and Relative Wages

The theory of international trade is based on the classic principle of comparative advantage articulated by David Ricardo. According to that principle, a country tends to export those goods that more intensively use the resources in which it is more abundant (and hence that are relatively cheaper) than in the countries with which it trades, and to import goods that use more intensively those resources that are scarcer (and hence more expensive). Both countries come out ahead in this exchange because they both receive a relative price for the goods exported (in terms of the other good) that is greater than what the exchange ratio of these goods would be when traded within the confines of each country.

If the only two factors of production were unskilled and skilled labor, developing countries would be expected to export goods that are intensive in unskilled labor and import those that are intensive in skilled labor. As a result of trade, the wages of unskilled workers in developing countries would be higher and closer to those of their peers in developed countries than they would be without trade, and the wages of skilled workers would be less (and also closer to those of their peers in developed countries).

In this conceptual framework, when a developing country restricts international trade (through tariffs or other devices), it necessarily lowers the relative wage of unskilled workers (and raises that of skilled workers). Hence, liberalization should be expected to reduce the wage gap in that country.

This conclusion does not necessarily hold, however, if there are more than two factors of production, or if the world does not divide neatly into two groups of countries. If natural resources are considered an additional factor, the relative abundance of factors in a developing economy may not be in unskilled labor, but in these resources. Liberalization would increase income from these sources, but not necessarily the relative wages of unskilled workers. Indeed, if natural resources require skilled rather than unskilled labor for their production, liberalization would widen the wage gap.

Other assumptions may likewise change the outcomes. What would happen if a country's capital endowment were not fixed but changed thanks to liberalization (for example, because liberalization attracted foreign investment or increased domestic investment rates) is relevant for Latin America. If capital complements skilled labor but replaces unskilled labor, greater investment would widen the wage gap.

The results would also vary depending on whether pre-liberalization tariffs sought to provide greater protection for those industries that make intensive use of unskilled labor, as was the case in various Latin American countries. Under such conditions, lowering tariffs would tend to lower rather than raise the relative pay of unskilled workers.

Hence, based on the classic theory of international trade, the conclusion that liberalization reduces the wage gap is assured only under rather restrictive assumptions.

The case of Argentina is especially interesting because it had the largest increase in the wage gap between university-educated workers and those with a high school education or less during the 1990s. Because the relative supply of university-educated workers has been increasing, the increase in the gap means that there is considerable demand pressure for workers with this level of education. Economic studies are in agreement that greater import penetration influenced this trend, although in a rather limited way. Greater import penetration of industrial goods explains only 10 percent of the increase in the wage gap favoring workers with a university education between 1992 and 1999 (see Galiani and Sanguinetti [2000] and Sanguinetti, Arim, and Pantano [2001]).[26] Although these studies have established that in sectors where import penetration was greater, the wage gap increased more, they do not clearly show why. The most common explanation is that greater competition from imports induced companies to adopt more sophisticated technologies that require relatively more skilled labor.[27]

In the cases of Colombia and Costa Rica, there is also evidence that liberalization helped widen the wage gap in industry by increasing relative demand for more skilled workers, apparently due to increased investment and the adoption of technologies skewed toward such workers (Cárdenas

[26] See also Robbins, González, and Menéndez (1997).

[27] This explanation is consistent with the fact that the wage gap has increased more in those sectors that have imported more machinery (Acosta and Montes Rojas 2002).

and Gutiérrez 1997; Robbins and Gindling 1999; Robbins 1996). However, there could be other mechanisms behind such processes, as will be seen in the analysis of other countries.

In the case of Uruguay, import penetration has not been found to directly impact the wage gap in industry (Sanguinetti, Arim, and Pantano 2001). There is evidence, however, that import penetration weakened the negotiating capacity of labor unions and eroded the wage advantages that used to benefit workers in the more highly unionized sectors (Cassoni, Allen, and Labadie forthcoming). Because the wage gap tends to be narrower when union power is greater, increased international trade may widen the wage gap not for technological reasons, but because it alters the negotiating power of less educated workers.

The cases of Brazil and Mexico offer evidence that greater openness to international trade does not necessary lead to a wider wage gap. Brazil is an interesting case because with the trade liberalization that occurred between the late 1980s and the mid-1990s, the wage gap between workers with a high school education or more fell vis-à-vis workers with less education, and the concentration of all wages was reduced. Lower tariffs seem to have been the main cause of this behavior by decreasing the prices of goods that were more intensive in skilled labor and reorienting employment toward sectors that were more intensive in the use of low-skilled labor (Gonzaga, Menezes Filho, and Terra 2002).[28] There is evidence that the subsectors that were under increased competition from imported goods became more intensive in the use of skilled labor, but that did not bring about an appreciable increase in wage inequality (Pavcnik and others 2002; Green, Dickerson, and Arbache 2001; Carneiro and Arbache 2002).

Finally, the case of Mexico is illustrative because it combines two well-defined phases of trade liberalization since 1985: first, the unilateral decision to implement a sharp reduction in tariffs and more uniform tariffs, and second, integration with the United States and Canada, starting with NAFTA in January 1994. During the first phase, the wage gap increased, but in the second phase, it tended to decrease slightly (Robertson 2002). A portion of the initial increase in the wage gap may have been due to tariff reduction because the most protected sectors tended to use low-skilled and highly unionized workers (Revenga 1997; Hanson and Harrison 1999).[29] However, there are few indications that this was the predominant effect. There is little relationship between the extent of the changes in tariffs and the changes in product prices or in the wage gap between high and low-skilled workers in companies in the affected sectors. However, there is a relationship between the wage gap in different companies and the weight of exports in their sales or indicators of the adoption of new technologies (Hanson and Harrison 1999).[30]

In the second phase, the relative price increased for goods that were intensive in low-skilled labor, which is consistent with the narrowing of wage inequality. This could be explained by the fact that in this phase, tariffs on such goods were lowered further, and because Mexico exports to the United States and Canada goods requiring more low-skilled labor than those it imports from those countries (Robertson 2002). Integration with the United States affected the wage structure, not only through changes in tariffs, but also through greater direct investment in Mexico, especially in the maquila sectors and through the geographical relocation of industrial employment (see Box 5.3).

Nevertheless, another possible explanation for the slight reduction in wage inequality in Mexico is that liberalization has different short and long-term effects. The increased inequality that may occur in the initial phases is not necessarily a per-

[28] Although Blom and Vélez (2001) find a strong trend toward a wider wage gap between workers with advanced education and those who have completed secondary school, they attribute 60 percent of this increase to asymmetrical expansion of the education system and only 40 percent to a displacement of demand toward more highly-skilled work. But, as de Ferranti and others (2001, p. 146) note, "even this 40 percent seems not to be related to trade liberalization per se."

[29] In Brazil and Colombia, greater tariff reductions also occurred in sectors that were intensive in unskilled labor and were more protected (Pavcnik and others 2002).

[30] In Brazil, there is also a positive relationship between export performance and the behavior of wages by sector (Pavcnik and others 2002). Chapter 6 provides a more detailed discussion of the solidity and interpretation of these results, which may not be sufficient proof of the influence of technology on the wage gap.

Box 5.3 Mexico: Effects of Integration with the United States on Employment

Integration between Mexico and the United States did not begin with the signing of NAFTA in 1994. It has in fact been an ongoing process that has influenced the labor market in both countries. The most important transmission channels of the process—at least for Mexico—include the *maquiladoras* and migration to the United States and various regions in Mexico.

The expansion of the *maquila* plants accounted for more than 50 percent of the widening of the wage gap between skilled and unskilled workers at the end of the 1980s, and it has continued to exert substantial pressure because the foreign-owned *maquila* plants—like other enterprises with investment from the same source—demand higher-skilled workers and pay better than domestic companies in the same sectors. In fact, foreign-owned companies pay skilled workers 21.5 percent more and unskilled workers 3.3 percent more than domestically-owned companies pay. This may be because the foreign-owned companies use better technologies, which raise the productivity of their workers, or because they attract more productive workers or benefit from rents that they share with the workers.

Integration with the United States has influenced the geographic distribution of labor opportunities in Mexico. In 1980, five years before the first phase of trade liberalization, 46 percent of employment in manufacturing was located in Mexico City and 21 percent in the states bordering the United States. By 1993, Mexico City's share had fallen to 29 percent and the border states had reached 30 percent. By 1998, four years after the signing of NAFTA, Mexico City held only 23 percent of manufacturing employment and the border states had 34 percent. Moreover, in the past decade, manufacturing employment throughout the country has clustered along the transportation routes toward the United States (including highways, railways, and ports) and has declined in the less connected areas.

The relocation of industrial employment has reflected trends in relative wages between regions: wages in the border areas have increased in comparison with the interior, and those in the better connected regions have increased more than those in more remote regions. With greater integration with the United States after NAFTA, the importance of these factors has grown and, along with it, inequality in wages between regions.

Labor migration toward the United States has had significant effects on the Mexican labor market (and, of course, on the U.S. labor market). At least since 1990, the historic rates of emigration from Mexican states have been strongly correlated with rates of growth of wages, thereby suggesting that emigration exerts an upward pressure on wages in states where the labor force is decreasing through this behavior. Likewise, the incomes of those who stay behind in those states increase as a result of remittances from relatives in the United States; it is estimated that each Mexican emigrant transfers approximately US$2,500 in remittances per year to his or her country.

Source: IDB (2002); Hanson (2003); Meardon (2003).

manent effect, as suggested by Chile's somewhat longer experience. Chile's liberalization began in 1973 and deepened during the 1980s. Wage inequality—measured by the ratio of pay between the highest-wage 10 percent and the lowest-wage 10 percent—increased from around three-to-one in the early 1970s to almost five-to-one in 1988, but from that point it began to decline until it returned to close to the starting point (de Ferranti and others 2001, p 143). This suggests that changes in labor remuneration are an economic signal to which producers respond by introducing technologies that allow for more efficient use of costly human resources, and to which individuals respond by investing in those types of education that are best rewarded by the market.

Regardless of whether the effects of liberalization on wage gaps are permanent (about which there is still little evidence), the most important conclusion of all these studies is that liberalization and inequality do not necessarily go hand in hand. This is the conclusion also reached by the few examinations of common patterns in the influence of liberalization in various countries. An econometric study based on a panel of household surveys for 18 countries in the past two decades finds no evidence that liberalization processes have had a discernible effect on the wage gap between education levels (Behrman, Birdsall, and Székely 2000). The authors observe the effects of both tariffs and trade penetration on the wage gap, without distinguishing between industries. By contrast, a study that includes Argentina (1986-99), Brazil (1982-99), Chile (1966-99), Colombia (1982-99), and Mexico (1987-99) finds that the wage gap by subsector of the manufacturing industry has common patterns of behavior that are associated with changes in the demand for labor, possibly for technological reasons. First, increases in the wage gap occurred within sectors and in the same sectors in all countries. Second, the intensity of this phenomenon was related to the import penetration of inputs and capital goods of those industries. Third, the increase in the wage gap proved to be more sensitive to the technological content of those imports than to their penetration (Sánchez-Páramo and Schady 2003).[31] This evidence notwithstanding, the extent of these effects is modest and it could even be consistent with phenomena other than technological change.[32]

These conclusions about Latin America are not surprising in light of world experience. Indeed, although wage inequality has increased in many countries over the past two decades, this phenomenon has not been shown to be explicable by changes in trade liberalization policies or by the volume of trade flows.[33] Although evidence available for previous periods is limited, an analysis of import liberalization experiences up to the mid-1980s concluded the following: "No clear patterns emerge. The presumption that liberalization is bound to worsen income distribution, making the poor poorer, is not borne out." (Michaely, Papageorgiou, and Choksi 1991, p. 103)

Quality of Employment

Although the effects of liberalization on total employment or on the relative pay of major groups of workers seem to have been modest, liberalization may have affected the quality of work. Has liberalization replaced employment under good conditions of social protection in traditional industry with jobs where social security is weak and there is little compliance with labor standards? Are the new jobs being created in the export sector of poor quality?

It is true that the traditional ways of hiring labor have been partially replaced by new arrangements, such as subcontracting services and temporary employment.[34] However, trade has played no more than a marginal role in this process, whose real driving forces have been technological and organizational changes on the labor demand side and pursuit of greater flexibility, especially for female labor, on the supply side.[35] The assumption that nontraditional ways of hiring harm workers or are associated with "precarious" jobs is not necessarily correct. First, new forms of hiring may be better suited for some workers, and second, nontraditional practices do not necessarily take away social security services or other benefits.

It is likely that greater exposure to international trade will induce firms to make greater use of more flexible methods of hiring labor. If international trade means that firms are exposed to more unstable and unpredictable demand, it is reasonable for them to seek to depend less on a stable workforce whose hiring and dismissal costs are higher than having temporary workers (or workers connected indirectly through providers who operate informally). Based on a theoretical model justifying such a decision, Goldberg and Pavcnik (2003) analyze its validity for Brazil and Colombia from the mid-1980s to the end of the 1990s. These two countries are interesting because their liberalization coincided with the loss of legally protected employment in the manufacturing industry (defined by the proportion of workers with a labor

[31] The last two points could only be established for Chile, Colombia, and Mexico. The technological content of imports was measured by research and development spending in the countries of origin of these imports.

[32] For example, as discussed in chapter 6, the change in the structure of employment within sectors may be due to a recomposition of firms and not necessarily to the adoption of technologies skewed toward skilled work in existing firms.

[33] Freeman and Oostendorp (2000) analyze wage inequality by occupation on the basis of information for 150 countries between 1983 and 1998 and find no relationship to trade policies or to the volume of trade flows. For a summary of the evidence on the effects of international trade on wage gaps in developed countries, see Brown (2000).

[34] For the case of Mexico, see Maloney (1998).

[35] Trends toward temporary and seasonal employment in agriculture have been common throughout Latin America and date back at least to the 1980s, associated with the expansion of agroindustry and seasonal export crops, such as fruits and vegetables (Kay 1995).

contract in Brazil, and those enrolled in social security in Colombia). Moreover, in both countries, the rise of unprotected employment in industry was due almost completely to changes *within* industrial subsectors (and not to changes in the composition of employment *between* sectors). Therefore, it could have been due to common patterns in the behavior of companies in some sectors, possibly in response to liberalization. However, in Brazil unprotected employment did not increase more in those sectors that were more exposed to competition. In Colombia it did so, but only until a labor reform was introduced to make the hiring and dismissing of new workers considerably more flexible. Therefore, the fear that liberalization worsens the quality of employment might be valid only in countries with more rigid labor systems.

Partial evidence from a broader group of countries provides support for such a conclusion. On the basis of 69 household surveys in 11 countries in the region, Table 5.8 shows how changes in tariff rates affected the employment rate in companies with more than five workers. Ignoring differences in labor legislation, there is a negative, albeit insignificant, relationship between tariffs and the employment rate (controlling for other factors that may affect the composition of employment). This suggests that for the average of the countries considered, lower tariffs seem to have increased the share of employment in companies with more than five workers. In considering the interaction between tariffs and labor legislation (measured by the labor reform index described in this chapter), the relationship between liberalization and employment composition seems to depend strongly on such legislation. For the countries with the most rigid labor markets in the region, such as Venezuela and pre-reform Colombia, the share of employment in companies with more than five workers tends to rise with tariffs (in the hypothetical case of a country with the greatest rigidity observed in the various aspects of labor legislation, this elasticity could rise to 0.7). Hence, in these cases there seem to be grounds for the fear that liberalization lessens the weight of companies with more than five workers, although that is not the case for countries with more flexible labor markets.

The econometric results set forth in Table 5.8 also indicate that these effects are not limited to the manufacturing sector because they can also occur in the service (nontradables) sector. This fact may be consistent with the conceptual framework of Goldberg and Pavcnik (2003) because liberalization may prompt manufacturing companies to subcontract with small companies to perform services that they used to handle internally. However, there may be other ways to explain this relationship. For example, greater ease in purchasing imported equipment may help service companies to become organized in small units in those countries where labor legislation is more rigid. However, as suggestive as this evidence might be, it should be taken with caution because it comes from databases that are uneven over time and between countries, and whose level of detail is insufficient for specifying the extent, solidity, and sources of these effects.

Employment in the Export Sector

According to ECLAC, the new export patterns in the region follow essentially two models: one based on agricultural and natural resource exports, characteristic of a number of South American and Central American countries, and the other based on manufacturing exports that are intensive in low-skilled labor, characterized especially by *maquiladoras* in Mexico and some Central American and Caribbean countries (Stallings and Peres 2000). Hence, it is enlightening to focus on evidence on the quality of work in these two sectors.

Liberalization processes have encouraged the expansion of nontraditional agricultural export goods. In Costa Rica, nontraditional agriculture increased from 8.7 percent of agricultural production in 1984 to 16.3 percent in 1998, thereby contributing to the rapid growth of the agricultural sector in that period (6.2 percent annually). The new goods use capital and skilled labor more intensively than traditional agricultural products (but not more so than the industrial sector). The effect on the quality of employment has been twofold. Salaried employment has risen more rapidly than other forms of employment (4.2 percent compared

Table 5.8 Tariffs and Employment

Variable	(1)	(2)	(3)	(4)
Tariffs	–0.107		0.733	
	(–1.38)		(2.54)**	
Tariffs * labor reform index			–1.412	
			(–3.14)***	
Tariff effects on tradables sector		–0.219		1.093
		(–1.06)		(2.29)**
Tariff effects on nontradables sector		–0.220		0.489
		(–2.17)**		(1.24)
Tariffs * labor reform index effect on tradables sector				–2.251
				(–3.00)***
Tariffs * labor reform index effect on nontradables sector				1.171
				(–1.80)*

* Significant at 10 percent.
** Significant at 5 percent.
*** Significant at 1 percent.
Note: The dependent variable is the employment rate in firms with more than five workers. The estimations are based on unbalanced panel data from the mid-1980s to 2001. Values are estimated using fixed effects for country and sector. The sample is 69 surveys for 11 countries with nine sectors in each country. t-statistics are in parentheses.
Source: IDB household surveys for the employment rate; Lora (2001) for tariffs and the labor reform index.

with 2.7 percent) and full-time jobs in these activities have offered pay and security conditions that are relatively favorable compared with other options. Even so, unskilled labor has been concentrated in temporary work in which workers are paid less and have less stability than those who work full time (Sánchez Cantillo 2001).[36]

The relatively intensive use of skilled labor in full-time work in nontraditional agriculture does not seem to be unique to Costa Rica, where it might be due to high average education levels. The same pattern is observed in Ecuador, for example, where around 70,000 permanent workers are employed in the production of flowers, broccoli, and various tropical fruits, which contribute more than 20 percent to the country's total exports. In Guatemala, exports of fruits, vegetables, ornamental plants, and organic crops represent approximately 9 percent of total exports. And in the Petrolina-Juazeiro region in northeast Brazil, 30 percent of the labor force is employed in growing tropical fruits and other nontraditional farm products. In some of these areas, these new operations have replaced extensive cattle ranching, which generated little employment, and created a demand for female labor that previously did not exist.

The low educational level of the workforce in these areas has forced producers to train workers and pay them higher wages than they would receive in alternative work in order to avoid higher costs for training new workers. For example, in the flower sector in Ecuador, women earn wages that are 40 percent higher than those of other rural women, and men earn a third more than they would in alternative employment in the countryside (Newman, Larreamendy, and Maldonado 2000). In Chile, wages in fruit export industries are 50 percent higher than in other jobs (Jarvis and Vera-Toscano 2001). Although health problems have arisen in various countries among those working with some kinds of nontraditional crops, a clear trend toward improved working conditions has nevertheless been noted, especially driven by the fear companies have of creating a bad image among their customers in the importing countries. That is why these companies tend to be more willing to negotiate better working conditions than higher wages (Damiani 2000).

36 These trends go back at least to the 1980s and can be explained by technology.

The flower export industry in Colombia provides an example of improved working conditions partly prompted by accusations (whether well founded or not) common in the 1980s that the sector violated workers' human rights, used child labor, and caused health problems due to improper use of agrochemical inputs. To forestall such criticisms, which would be harmful to the reputation of Colombian flowers on the international market, in the 1990s, the producers' association set up environmental and social programs that have become a model for other sectors. Companies participating in these programs say that their labor turnover rate is only 1 or 2 percent. An informal survey shows that workers in this sector, mostly women, felt satisfied with their working conditions.[37]

Small producers of nontraditional crops in Guatemala in the area of Sacatepéquez export vegetables through cooperatives that provide the producers technical assistance and training. For the community as a whole, producing nontraditional crops for export has been associated with considerable improvement in living conditions and the economic situation. Nontraditional crops have generated many jobs for the community, and most workers interviewed said that if they had more money or more land, they would use it to produce more crops (Hamilton, Sullivan, and Asturias 2001).

Nevertheless, the effects of the good labor conditions and poverty reduction produced by vegetable exports in Guatemala have not occurred in other cases of agricultural export development. In Paraguay, exports of cotton and soybeans from large plantations have contributed to the displacement of peasant crops, and little employment has been generated for poor workers. In Chile, fruit exports have resulted in a hybrid pattern in which the generation of employment has favored poor workers, but changes in land tenure structure have harmed them (Carter, Barham, and Mesbah 1996). This variety of experiences offers important lessons on the labor and social implications of agroexport development (see Box 5.4).

The *maquilas* (also known as export processing zones or free trade zones) have been a dynamic source of job creation in many countries (Table 5.9). In Mexico, *maquila* employment increased from 118,000 people in 1980 to 446,000 in 1990, and to more than one million after 1998 (1.2 million people in 2001). In 1998, *maquila* employment represented 14.6 percent of employment in the manufacturing sector and 2.6 percent of all employment in the economy. In the four border cities where this activity is concentrated (Ciudad Juárez, Matamoros, Nuevo Laredo, and Tijuana), the *maquila* plants generate 43 percent of total employment and 53 percent of female employment. In the Dominican Republic, free trade zones employed 500 workers in 1970. In 1988, this number had risen to more than 85,000 people, and hence 4 percent of total employment in the country, and by 1996 it was more than 164,000 people. Similarly, in the English-speaking Caribbean countries, assembly plants are a significant source of (primarily female) employment.

The *maquila* plants did not arise from the structural reforms considered in this chapter or from the free trade agreements, which basically have not changed the competitive dynamic of the *maquila* plants (Sargent and Matthews 2001). They were started in Mexico in 1965 to replace the opportunities lost with the end of the farm labor program with the United States. In most countries, the *maquila* plants are a legacy of the former import control mechanisms and other policies that, by isolating domestic industry from international trade, impeded the development of exports. The dynamism of assembly plants after liberalization may therefore seem paradoxical. However, the assembly plants are still being favored with special treatment, not only in the area of international trade (particularly the reduction or complete elimination of levies on the use of imported raw materials and simplified import and export procedures), but also in the area of tax incentives and a variety of other policies, from financing to labor legislation, depending on the country.[38] In some Central American and Caribbean countries, the expansion

[37] See *Los Angeles Times*, February 14, 2003, "Everything's Coming Up Roses for Colombia's Flower Industry."

[38] Madani (1999) presents a summary of incentives in nine Central American and Caribbean countries.

Box 5.4 Lessons on the Relationship between Agricultural Exports and the Rural Poor

Evidence from the latest push for agroexport growth in Latin America reveals variations in the impact on the rural poor. Farm-level data gathered in booming regions in Chile, Guatemala, and Paraguay demonstrate that in all three cases, the amount of labor absorbed per unit of land in the boom crop decreases as the size of the operation grows. The social welfare impact of export booms thus depends in the short run on which classes adopt the crops; in the longer run, the impact depends on the patterns of structural change that shift land between classes (and alter levels of employment). If the adoption of export crops favors smallholders, as it has in the Guatemalan highlands, then positive impacts on the rural poor will tend to be magnified, and more and more so over time if the boom renders smallholders more competitive in the land market.

In the frontier region of Paraguay, the boom in wheat and soy production has given rise to precisely the opposite interaction. The boom, which directly favors large-scale farmers who absorb relatively little labor per hectare, has occasioned a pattern of structural change over time in which the shift of land to large farms has accentuated the negative impact of the boom on the rural poor, creating a highly exclusionary growth trajectory that leaves peasants out as both producers and workers.

The Chilean experience falls somewhere in between these two cases. The fruit export boom has bypassed the traditional smallholder sector and the small-scale farm sector created from the remnants of the agrarian reform. Over time, land ownership has shifted from smallholders to larger holdings. At the same time, export crops on large farms seem to absorb more labor than the traditional crops (and farms) that they displace. Restructuring of the workforce toward more seasonal labor has probably aggravated the effects on social welfare of the partly exclusionary fruit export boom.

On the whole, competitive biases seem to be working against small-scale producers. The human capital intensity of many export crops, price-quality measurement concerns, product perishability and the resulting need for vertical integration, extended gestation periods for investments, and absence of insurance markets tend to favor medium and large-scale producers. Labor interactivity, highly fragmented holdings that make land consolidation costly, and (where they exist) contractual relations and cooperative institutions that reduce some of the other biases seem to favor small-scale producers.

Source: Reproduced with permission from Carter, Barham, and Mesbah (1996).

Table 5.9 Employment Creation in Export Processing Zones

Country	Year	Employment	Percentage of economically active population
Costa Rica	1992	15,000	1.24
	1996	47,972	3.59
Dominican Republic	1992	142,000	4.71
	1996	164,639	4.92
El Salvador	1991	6,500	0.33
	1996	50,000	2.10
Honduras	1991	19,000	1.00
	2000	106,000	5.01
Jamaica	1996	16,804	1.11
Mexico	1990	446,000	1.69
	2001	1,187,525	3.00
Nicaragua	2000	40,760	3.00

Source: Madani (1999); ECLAC (1999); INTAL.

of *maquila* plants may have been spurred by trade liberalization agreements, like the United States-Caribbean Basin Trade Partnership Act, which have favored producers that use inputs from the United States.[39] The future of export assembly plants is currently in question because of the commitment made by World Trade Organization member countries (except for those considered poor) to dismantle the differential systems that favor them.

However, although the export assembly plants are not a result of the recent liberalization processes, for many observers, they symbolize the dangers of the globalization toward which countries that have opted for trade liberalization policies are heading. The plants are accused of paying low wages, exploiting workers, discriminating against women, providing inadequate safety conditions, and hindering labor organizing rights.

Many of these criticisms may be valid in various instances, and it is the duty of the ILO and other bodies to be on guard to detect and correct irregularities. However, such accusations have not been proven on a broad scale. With regard to wages and working conditions, periodic ILO reviews show that "on the whole, wages and working conditions in EPZs (free trade export zones) compare favourably with those outside the zones." (Romero 1995, p. 252) For various reasons, *maquila* wages tend to be higher than those received on average by the same kind of workers elsewhere: the companies are larger and are better monitored for compliance with minimum wage and overtime requirements. In some countries, such as Guatemala, Honduras, and El Salvador, minimum wages in this type of work have sometimes been better than in other activities. However, in other instances, *maquila* zones have been exempted from complying with minimum wage regulations (such as in the Dominican Republic until 1993) or have had low minimum wages (such as in Panama in the mid-1990s).[40]

Foreign-owned companies, which are governed by the practices of their head offices and the requirements of their customers, tend to offer productivity bonuses and other incentives aimed at attracting and keeping trained workers so as to meet production and quality targets. Anecdotal evidence also suggests that pay conditions tend to improve rapidly with the experience of workers and gradually as plants become more sophisticated. Analyses of apparel plants in the Dominican Republic show that the learning curve and pay increases rise sharply during the first three years, but then tend to level off, suggesting that on-the-job training and learning are effective for improving basic levels of qualification, but not for reaching highly sophisticated skill levels (Madani 1999).

With regard to discrimination against women, the studies show that on average, pay for women workers is significantly lower than that for men. However, "ILO research and surveys provide no evidence that these disparities are due to the deliberate setting of different gender-based wage rates and emoluments [...]. Rather, they appear to be more the result of gender-based biases with respect to the recruitment and promotion of staff, which result in a severe under-representation of women in the better-paid, skilled, technical and managerial jobs." (Romero 1995, p. 255) It may be that the characteristics of the jobs and the concentration in activities requiring little training help explain the overrepresentation of women in *maquila* plants. In fact, as the average wages in such work have been rising and approaching the national average, overrepresentation has been declining (Fleck 2001).

With regard to labor organizing rights, it is true that *maquila* plants have low rates of unionization. Although all countries in the region have legal rights for labor organizing, low membership could be due to high turnover, ineffective protection of rights of association, and workers' fear of losing their jobs, among other reasons (Romero 1995; Maskus 1997). However, there are no empirical studies supporting (or rejecting) these hypotheses.

The debate about working conditions in *maquila* plants is unlikely to be resolved by the few studies thus far available for countries in the

---

[39] According to Sargent and Matthews (2001), this has not been the case for *maquila* plants in Mexico, which are still using the same sources of inputs.

[40] According to Madani (1999), based on other sources; these minimum wage comparisons are for 1995.

Box 5.5 The Relative Attractiveness of Employment in the Maquiladoras

The *maquilas* are often accused of exploiting workers. But is that criticism well founded? Sargent and Matthews (1999) thought that the workers themselves would be a valuable source of information about this debate, and so they interviewed 59 production-level workers in the Mexican cities of Ciudad Juárez and Chihuahua. The authors conclude the following:

"The majority of *maquila* workers interviewed for this study indicated that they worked in a *maquila* due to the availability of *maquila* employment. Also, the majority of people that had worked in jobs outside the *maquila* industry considered their *maquila* jobs more attractive even though they might be receiving less in direct compensation. The majority of *maquila* workers also planned to continue working in the *maquilas*. A minority of workers indicated that they felt they had the opportunity, if they wanted, to find employment outside the *maquila* industry. This group frequently indicated that they worked in a *maquila* for such reason as the work was easier, they liked working indoors, there were more advanced opportunities, and that there was more time off. [...] The statements made by the *maquila* workers suggest that the charges of widespread worker exploitation in the *maquilas* appear somewhat exaggerated." (Sargent and Matthews 1999, pp. 224-25)

region. However, the discussion should not ignore the opinions of those who work in the export assembly plants (see Box 5.5).

Summary: Labor after Liberalization

Liberalization was one of the major reforms of the 1990s in Latin America. It had a positive impact on efficiency and economic growth, although much less than what its advocates had expected. The same can be said about the fears of its effects on labor. Some of these effects were negative, at least in the short run, but apocalyptic predictions of job destruction and deteriorating working conditions were not fulfilled.

First, the biggest surprise that emerges from a review of empirical research on the effects of liberalization on labor is that it has not had much effect on employment allocation. This is a surprise to those economic analysts who, on the basis of the theory of comparative advantage, expected resources to move massively toward activities that were potentially more efficient and more intensive in the use of the most abundant resources. It is also a surprise for people who imagined that increased exports would displace employment in the sectors producing tradable goods.

Second, because the changes in employment composition were modest, the fact that liberalization did not have very pronounced effects on unemployment may likewise be explained. This is also a surprise for many economists, who expected the unemployment associated with the transition of workers from some sectors to others would increase, at least initially. The fact that little employment was reallocated between sectors does not mean that companies or workers did not suffer traumas due to liberalization, or that the labor market lacked the vitality to respond to such an important policy change. On the contrary, the continual gross creation and destruction of jobs in each company and the appearance and disappearance of companies in each industry were mechanisms that helped adjust production methods and organization, change the composition of production, and reorient production toward particular markets in response to liberalization.

A third surprise is that liberalization seems to have lowered real wages, especially in industry, at least in the short run. This is a surprise for economists trained in neoclassical analysis who usually assume that wages correspond to workers' marginal productivity, and that liberalization should lead to more productive use of all resources, including labor, elimination of rents that favor capitalists, and lower prices for agricultural and industrial goods consumed by workers. What seems to have happened (although there is no direct evidence supporting it) is that workers were sharing in these rents and were forced to give them up in order to hold onto their jobs. The fact that in many countries tariffs (and import controls) were higher for those sectors that were more labor intensive (especially in unskilled labor) also helps explain this paradox. Another possible explanation is that liberalization may have lowered wages in industry by allowing entry into domestic markets of goods from countries with lower production costs.

A fourth surprise, possibly the one most debated in public and academic circles, is that liberalization helped widen the wage gap between skilled and unskilled workers. Economists have paid so much attention to this phenomenon that many of them may now find it surprising that this effect was actually less pronounced than is currently believed, and that the explanation may be found more in the area of technology and other little understood mechanisms than in the mechanics of relative prices directly associated with international trade. Whatever the mechanisms may have been, however, trade liberalization does not go very far toward explaining the wider wage gap in some countries.

Liberalization produced two more surprises, both related to the quality of work. On the one hand, it is striking that the new jobs generated in the export sector are comparable in quality and pay to alternative jobs, or even better. The increase in labor-intensive exports in many countries (even before liberalization) has helped to raise workers' wages and improve their living conditions, contrary to what is often claimed. On the other hand, there is some evidence (far from definitive) that lower tariffs or greater penetration of imports has widened informal labor in some countries (understanding informal labor to mean employment without social security and other benefits, or employment in a company of up to five workers). However, this phenomenon does not seem to be occurring in all countries, but only where labor legislation is more restrictive.

The lesson from this series of surprises is one of modesty for economists and moderation for critics. At the same time, evidence is limited by lack of information, the shortness of the time period for observing some of the effects of liberalization, and conceptual and technical barriers to interpreting the results. Moreover, the evidence is restricted by the inclinations of academic research, which do not necessarily coincide with the concerns and fears of the public. Finally, none of the foregoing surprises constitutes a rule because there are many variations among country experiences.

Impact of Privatization on Labor

Privatization may entail job loss, deterioration in labor conditions, and other changes in the organization of labor for those who remain in their jobs in privatized companies. Table 5.10 summarizes the most common concerns of workers, some of which are also reflected in the following opinions on the effects of privatization:

"Unemployment and job insecurity have increased overall. Layoffs accompanied privatization across the board, and new employment generation did not always compensate for jobs lost. Privatization has fostered discontent among those workers who did not lose their jobs, because workloads have increased, employment has become less secure, and the power to organize and negotiate with employers has been weakened." (SAPRIN 2002, p.108)

"Privatization has contributed to increasing inequality. Income distribution has worsened as large numbers of low-skilled, low-wage workers have been the first to be laid off. This has been particularly detrimental to minority groups and women, who tend to lack specialized skills. Job training or other similar programs, where they have existed, have been either ineffective or insufficient to address the problems of the newly unemployed. Although new employment generated in privatized firms has tended to be better paid, these jobs have required higher skill levels." (SAPRIN 2002, p. 108)

The reforming governments were aware of the social and political risks of the job loss and increased unemployment that privatization could bring (Williamson 1990). However, they believed

Table 5.10 Possible Effects of Privatization on Employment

Employment effects	Employment conditions	Management-labor relations
• Reclassification of posts • New job patterns • Labor retrenchment and direct job losses • Gender-biased employment policies • Discrimination against labor representatives • Medium and long-term employment gains due to increased investment, growth of privatized firms, and diversification of services	• Greater job mobility • Diminished guarantee of tenure and job security • Need for retraining and skill upgrading • Longer working hours and/or increased workload • Payment by results schemes and pay freezes • Loss of seniority and service grades • Wider wage differentials with greater incentive components • Loss of pension rights • Loss of social benefits (housing, transport, childcare, and health insurance schemes) • Abolition of the prohibition on strikes and industrial actions	• Greater emphasis on professionalism • More discretionary power in making management decisions and formulating enterprise policies • More emphasis on strict implementation of these decisions and policies • Marginalization of unions' influence and bargaining power • More tedious wage bargaining with preferences for individual rather than collective agreements • Tougher stance of management on workers' performance and work discipline • Efficiency arguments and profit making gain importance over social objectives

Source: World Bank (2003), based on UNCTAD.

that privatization was necessary in order to solve the problems of inefficiency and high cost of some government enterprises, especially in the public service sector.

Employment

Employment loss has been one of the main reasons for popular rejection of privatization. Because state-run companies have often been used to create employment for political reasons, it is not surprising that cutting jobs is necessary to keep these companies viable in the private sector. Anecdotal evidence indicates the magnitude of the problem:

• Before privatization, the railway payroll in Argentina totaled 60 percent of total company revenues. In 1990, although railways were moving less than 10 percent of traffic, they were incurring losses equal to 2 percent of GDP (Birdsall and Nellis 2002; Kikeri 1998).

• In the late 1980s, 50,000 people were employed in Mexico's telecommunications company, and labor productivity was half the international standard of 10.5 workers for every 1,000 lines (Kikeri 1998).

• In 1990, AeroPeru had 2,300 employees for only six planes, almost four times the maximum industry standard (World Bank 2003).

International experience has shown that personnel reductions are common but not universal in privatized companies. In a set of 27 cases of privatization studied by various authors, 14 show declining employment after privatization (27 percent of employees on average), two show substantial reductions (amount not specified), and the rest had increases or changed very little. In a second set of 17 cases, employment was lost in seven (equivalent to 45 percent of personnel), increased in four (by 23 percent on average), and there was little change in the rest (Birdsall and Nellis 2002, based on various ILO studies). In a third set of recently privatized companies in 21 developing countries (including the most active privatizers), employment increased in 60 percent of the cases (with increases of 10 percent on average), and the companies recently exposed to competition were the ones most likely to lose employment (Boubakri and Cosset [1996] cited by Kikeri 1998).

The intensity of the personnel reductions has differed across sectors in developing countries. The most draconian cuts have been in railways and ports, more modest cuts have been made in water and electric power, and employment has actually often increased in telecommunications (World Bank 2003).

The experience of Latin American countries illustrates the extent of employment changes in privatized companies. In seven companies privatized in Argentina in the early 1990s, approximately 113,000 jobs were lost, or 50 percent of the personnel of these companies before they were sold. The reductions ranged from 3 percent in the telecommunications company to 81 percent in railways (Kikeri 1998). For privatized companies as a whole, employment fell from 223,000 people in 1987-90 to 73,000 in 1997. This drop in employment was equivalent to 2 percent of the urban workforce (or 3.5 percent of the workforce in Buenos Aires, where most of the layoffs were concentrated). If all the workers laid off had remained unemployed (which was not the case), privatization would have been responsible for 13 percent of the increase in the unemployment rate during this period (Table 5.11). Under this assumption, privatization would have meant an 8 percent increase in the number of poor people and would have raised the Gini coefficient of income concentration by 3 percent (McKenzie and Mookherjee 2002).

Although Bolivia carried out more privatization (as a percentage of GDP) than Argentina, layoffs seem to have been substantially fewer. There are no statistics encompassing all the privatizations, but those that took place in the electric power and telecommunications industries, which were the most important ones in the 1990s, led to employee reductions of only 1,700 persons, around 0.1 percent of the urban labor force. Again, under the assumption that these people did not find jobs, these layoffs would explain only 3 percent of the rise in unemployment between 1995 and 2000.

The case of Mexico seems to lie halfway between that of Argentina and Bolivia. At the start of privatization in 1983, state companies employed 4 percent of the urban workforce; a decade later, they employed slightly less than 2 percent (McKenzie and Mookherjee 2002). In a pattern that is not exclusive to Mexico, a large proportion of the job losses took place before privatization. A study of 218 firms privatized in a variety of industries shows that approximately 50 percent of employees were laid off during the four years before privatization (La Porta and López-de-Silanes 1999). In four steel production plants employment dropped from 35.6 thousand people in 1985 to 17.5 thousand, with the largest cuts just before privatization in 1991. In the case of Mexicana Airlines, employment was cut 40 percent before privatization at the request of potential buyers (previous privatization efforts had failed because the conditions of sale prohibited laying off workers). At Ferrocarriles Nacionales de Mexico (National Railways of Mexico), employment was cut from a high of 83,000 employees in 1990 to approximately 44,000 when the privatization process began in January 1997, and between that time and June 1999 cutbacks affected another 3,000 people (La Porta and López-de-Silanes 1999).

The case of railways in Brazil was similar: employment had fallen from 110,000 people in 1975 to 42,000 in May 1995, before the pre-privatization restructuring of the company began. From that time on, approximately 18,000 more people were cut from the payroll until the company was transferred to the concessionaires, who cut an additional 14,000 workers from the payroll (Estache, Schmitt de Azevedo, and Sydenstricker 2000; Andalón and López-Calva 2001).

Labor unions, governments, and potential buyers tend to prefer that cutbacks in staffing take place before privatization. Indeed, although they are opposed to cutbacks, labor unions have more power to obtain better compensation before layoffs take place. Governments are attracted by the incentive of improving the sale price if they lower labor costs, and potential buyers prefer to avoid the conflicts and economic uncertainty that may be entailed in the layoff process. Given the many incentives, it is not surprising that cutbacks are often made before privatization. Based on a sample of 308 companies privatized in developing coun-

Table 5.11 Employment Contraction in the Private Sector in Argentina, Bolivia, and Mexico
(Percent)

	Argentina	Bolivia	Mexico
Urban workforce in privatized sector prior to privatization	7	Less than 0.5	4
Employment cutbacks in urban workforce	2	0.13	1
Employment cutbacks before privatization in the privatized firms	75	30	50
Increased unemployment caused by employment cutbacks[a]	13	3	-100
Re-employment rate within the same sector[b]	80–90		45–50

[a] Values are for 1987/90–1997 for Argentina, 1995–2000 for Bolivia, and 1983–94 for Mexico.
[b] Within four years for Argentina and within one year for Mexico.
Source: McKenzie and Mookherjee (2002).

tries between 1982 and 2000 (101 in Latin America), Chong and López-de-Silanes (2003a) calculate that in 78 percent of the cases, job positions were cut before privatization (82 percent in Latin America). The dismissals did not affect the various groups of workers in the companies equally because in many cases the criteria for making layoffs were seniority, workers' age, or lack of training; only 32 percent of the companies (worldwide and in Latin America) used voluntary retirement programs.[41]

Although this section has focused on privatization, it should be noted that significant cutbacks were made in public sector employment in the 1990s in a number of countries in the region. Approximately 406,000 federal government jobs were cut in Argentina between 1990 and 1992; more than 263,000 were dismissed from the Peruvian civil service between 1991 and 1993, although 112,000 were rehired; 40,000 people were dismissed from the civil service in Ecuador between 1992 and 1994; and 12,000 were dropped from the Ministry of Transport and Tourism in Colombia between 1990 and 1992 (Haltiwanger and Singh 1999). The decline in public sector employment has been a noteworthy phenomenon in most countries in the region (Box 5.6).

New Jobs

Comparing employment before and after privatization can be deceptive because successful restructurings that boost productivity and enable services to be expanded may completely or partially make up for jobs lost in privatization. For example, in Argentina, the YPF oil company took a contracting approach with 210 companies formed by 5,300 former workers at the firm. Likewise, the railway company subcontracted repair work to labor-intensive cooperative enterprises. And the new telecommunications sector companies, which had laid off approximately 10 percent of the employees, rehired most of them through service contracts (Kikeri 1998; Petrazzini 1996). In Peru, around 20 percent of employees dismissed by privatization became subcontractors for the same companies, which created many small companies in transportation, water, mining, ports, and electricity (Kik-

[41] However, there is conflicting evidence on the effects of pre-privatization layoffs on the sale price. Chong and López-de-Silanes (2003a) observe that labor restructurings as a rule do not help raise prices (and when retirement programs are voluntary, they clearly lower the price). But for the case of Mexico, López-de-Silanes (1996) finds that previous layoffs had the effect of raising prices by 6 percent. He also finds that transferring labor contingencies to the buyers lowered the price by 3 percent, and the prior occurrence of strikes lowered the price by 18 percent.

Box 5.6 Public Employment in Latin America

The public sector in Latin America has been considered a privileged one for a long time for at least three reasons. First, although the pay is, other things equal, lower than in the private sector, the benefits, related amenities, and workload more than compensate for this. Second, job security has been unprecedented even in a region that has historically been characterized by dramatic labor rigidities. Third, access, power, and political clientelism have provided intangible benefits that are difficult to match in the private sector. As a consequence, in recent decades overemployment in the public sector ran rampant in the region. The structural reforms and related market-friendly policies that several Latin American countries pursued during the 1990s, along with severe cutbacks in government spending due to fiscal crises, were intended to put an end to this. As economies liberalized trade and deregulated markets, the public sector with its soft budget constraint was also touched.

As a consequence, employment in the public sector as a whole fell in most Latin American countries, not only as a consequence of privatization but also because of public administration downsizing. As is shown in the figure, the share of public sector employment in total urban employment fell for all Latin American countries except Brazil and Chile. However, although the average public sector share of total urban employment fell only during the 1990s, this drop hides large differences in the evolution of public sector employment within countries.

In part, these changes in employment patterns and the employment shocks suffered by specific segments of the population are behind the weak support for reform in Latin American countries. Reductions in public sector employment meant that fewer of the jobs that have traditionally been shielded from economic fluctuations were protected. The number of jobs created in high-productivity sectors was not enough to replace the jobs lost in low-productivity but formerly high-rent sectors. This fact, coupled with a modest evolution of overall productivity and the need to reduce costs was not compatible with the high cost associated with the legal requirements of entering the formal sector that resulted in dramatic relative growth in the informal sector in recent years. Hence, informal contractual relations also became more frequent. Under these adverse circumstances, many of those workers displaced from the public sector were not able to find another job with the same level of protection, earnings, and social benefits or were not able to find a job at all.

Share of Public Sector Employment in Total Employment
(Percent)

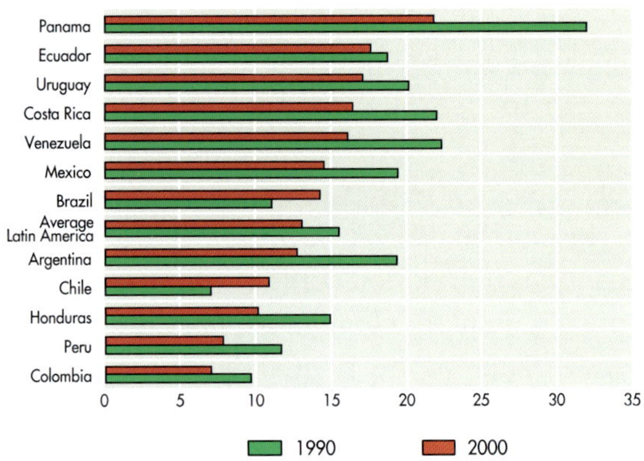

Source: ILO (2001).

Source: Chong and Saavedra (2003); Saavedra (2003).

eri 1998). When ports were reformed in Mexico, public employment declined, but greater port activity meant that employment grew rapidly in the private companies that received concessions to provide services. Thus, the port of Manzanillo, which had 2,100 workers in 1993, had twice that number four years later, and in Veracruz, employment increased from about 6,000 workers to more than 8,000 (Estache, González, and Trujillo 2001). In the railway industry in Mexico, where cutbacks were quite large, 54 percent (23,300 workers) of those laid off during the privatization process were rehired by the new companies in the industry (Andalón and López-Calva 2001).

Thus, a good portion of the jobs initially lost in privatized companies may be offset by new hiring in the same companies or in others linked to them as suppliers or contractors of the original companies. For Argentina, it has been calculated that between 80 and 90 percent of the staff reductions in the privatized companies were offset by reemployment procedures within the same sectors in the four years after privatization (which does not mean that the same people who were laid off were rehired). For Mexico, the rate of reemployment in the same sectors has been calculated to be between 45 and 50 percent in the first year after privatization (McKenzie and Mookherjee 2002). In their sample of 308 companies privatized throughout the world, Chong and López-de-Silanes (2003a; 2003b) find that 44 percent expanded their payrolls after privatization (54 percent in Latin America), and 11 percent rehired employees who had been laid off (21 percent among companies privatized in Latin America). The likelihood of rehiring employees who had been laid off before privatization increased substantially when the criterion for dismissal was the age of the employees; the likelihood of rehiring decreased when the criterion was workers' abilities.

Pay and Working Conditions

Improved productivity resulting from privatization processes often makes it possible to raise wages and other forms of pay for the workers who keep their jobs. In Chile, the new owners of the electric power companies privatized in the 1980s (Chilgener and Enersis) raised wages and introduced profit-sharing systems. In Argentina, the real wages of the employees of Entel and the water concession in Buenos Aires rose 45 percent in the three years after privatization. In Mexico, according to a broad sample of privatized companies up to 1993, wages rose 76 percent on average, which was far more than in the rest of the economy (Kikeri 1998). Even more surprising, wages rose substantially more for workers than for office staff (122 percent compared with 77 percent in 1983-94, as calculated by La Porta and López-de-Silanes [1999]).

In many privatized companies, workers also benefited from shared ownership programs that were introduced to increase their interest in privatization. In an electric power company in Chile, 85 percent of the workers acquired shares, the price of which quintupled over the next three years. In Mexico, the Telmex union bought shares at a price close to half the basic offer price for privatization. The workers then benefited from a considerable rise in the market price. When Entel was privatized in Argentina, workers bought shares at one-sixth of the purchase price from the new owners, and by 1994 the average worker's share had risen in value by US$25,000. These mechanisms for participation in ownership represented not only a net wealth benefit, but an incentive for workers to cooperate in improving the company (Kikeri 1998).

Even so, some labor conditions worsened during the privatization process or afterward. In preparation for privatizing Argentina's Entel, the government lengthened the workday, eliminated job security guarantees, and severely restricted the possibility of worker organization (Petrazzini 1996). In the case of Telmex in Mexico, in exchange for wage increases, workers agreed that contracts could be made uniform, employees could be shifted within the company, and service contracts could be extended to nonunionized companies (Kikeri 1998).

These organizational changes inside the companies have usually been accompanied by significant changes in labor practices, which may entail a lessening of worker well-being as a result of longer workdays and more frequent accidents and health problems, attributable in some cases to greater use of temporary contracts (World Bank 2003; McKenzie and Mookherjee 2002). There is also evidence that privatization has weakened the ability of unions to exert influence. However, in some instances, new mechanisms for worker representation have been developed, and have enhanced workers' influence on working conditions. For example, the International Federation of Chemical, Energy, Mine, and General Workers' Unions (ICEM) has reached a global agreement with Endesa in Spain to improve working conditions in all its companies, while the worldwide union of telecommunications workers has done something similar with Telefónica (both companies own stock in many privatized companies in Latin America; see World Bank [2003]).

What Happens to Laid-off Workers?

Little is known about the fate suffered by workers who are laid off by privatized companies (those who are not rehired directly or indirectly by the same industry). In compensation for the losses that they might suffer, they generally receive severance pay and other monetary benefits. According to some estimates, these compensations more than surpass the average cost of hunting for a new job (Galal and others 1994).[42] Fragmentary information on some companies also suggests that retirement packages have usually been generous and were voluntarily accepted by most of the workers in the companies where they have been offered. In railway, telecommunications, and steel companies in Argentina, the average compensation was equivalent to two years of wages, and in the Brazilian railways, it was three years. Although severance packages have generally represented large outlays, the evidence suggests that this practice has been the only politically acceptable alternative for correcting excess employment, and has turned out to be beneficial from a fiscal standpoint, given the savings in labor costs, transfers, and subsidies (Kikeri 1998).

A case study based on surveys of former workers in the federal railways of Brazil offers a sense of how they returned to work. Around half of those dismissed between January 1995 and October 1997 who replied to the survey were self-employed in early 1998; only 18 percent had formal jobs, 4 percent were government employees, and 13 percent were working without a legal contract. In September 1998, only 10 percent were unemployed (especially those who were older and/or less educated), but 53 percent were earning less than when they worked for the railways (Estache, Schmitt de Azevedo, and Sydenstricker 2000).

The experience of employees of the Central Bank of Ecuador who were dismissed in the 1994 reform is illustrative, although it was not a privatization and may not be representative of the employment patterns of privatized companies. Fifteen months after their dismissal, 30 percent of the 363 affected employees had jobs, 51 percent were self-employed, and 6 percent were unemployed. Of all those dismissed, after three months 43 percent were earning lower incomes than before and after 15 months, that figure had risen to 46 percent. This evidence suggests that job possibilities and pay declined for a significant proportion of those who lost their jobs (Rama and MacIsaac 1999).

It may well be that workers dismissed have difficulty finding new jobs, especially if their abilities are specific to the work that they did in the now-privatized company, or if their training or work discipline has been neglected due to their working conditions. These difficulties may be partly remedied by training and support programs for them to return to work. In Latin America, there are examples of such programs in Argentina, Brazil, Mexico, and Peru, as well as elsewhere. Evaluations of these experiences show that their effectiveness has varied a great deal. Focused programs have generally been more effective than those with broad coverage, and programs that offer guidance for job hunting have had better results than retraining programs, which are often plagued by problems in terms of the competence of the management, the relevance of the programs, and the low learning ability of the participants.

Summary: Effects of Privatization

Although substantial in relation to the permanent payroll of companies before they were privatized, the effects of privatization on the labor force or unemployment were actually modest and tended to be rapidly compensated, to a great extent by the rehiring of personnel at the same companies or their suppliers. In some cases, the labor conditions of those who kept their jobs deteriorated over the course of the process (but not their incomes). There is also evidence that health and safety conditions worsened, as did workers' ability to organize, and the influence of labor organizations. Through its impact on company productivity or family living conditions, privatization may have had other indirect effects on labor that have not been considered in this analysis. Naturally, the appropriateness of privatization cannot be judged solely on the basis of its effects on labor, and the adverse opinion of Latin Americans toward this area of reform may be only partly due to its effects on labor.

42 This study considers six cases of privatization in Chile and Mexico and other countries.

Other Structural Reforms

The chapter thus far has discussed evidence of the effects on labor of liberalization and privatization, which are no doubt the two most visible and controversial areas of reform. Although they are less important from a labor standpoint, other reforms may also have contributed to the problems of employment and low incomes for some groups of workers. SAPRIN (2002) makes the following observations:

"*Reforms have allowed financial assets to become more concentrated.* [...] Instead of helping producers that need capital to maintain or expand their operations, financial intermediaries have directed financing toward large (usually urban) firms and extended the largest share of loans to a few, powerful economic agents. *This has hindered the development of small and medium-size enterprises, an important source of employment generation.*" (p. 68)

"*Important sectors of the economy and population groups have been unable to access affordable credit. Small and medium-size firms, rural and indigenous producers and women have very limited access to the formal financial system, as high interest rates resulting from liberalization and obstacles to qualifying for financing have prevented them from borrowing.*" (p. 68)

Financial Reforms

Evidence of the effects of the financial reforms on labor is scarce and concentrated in a few countries. Although the central conclusion from the few existing studies is that small businesses and microenterprises are not suffering major limitations on credit because of the reforms, it is not clear whether this conclusion can be generalized.

The closing of many state banks is one of the factors that may have reduced credit for small and medium enterprises (SMEs). However, the evidence for Argentina, Chile, and Colombia shows that state banking devotes a substantially smaller proportion of its resources to SMEs than private banks do. In Chile and Colombia, this trend seems to be compounded by the fact that government banks are pursuing this market less vigorously than private banks. Between 1997 and 2000, growth in real lending by state banks to SMEs in Chile was 19 percentage points less than that of private banking, and in Colombia it was 15 percentage points less (Clarke and others 2002). Consequently, insofar as the financial reforms have allowed for greater expansion of lending by private banks, the SMEs are being better served.

Another cause of reduced lending to small businesses could be the greater importance attained by foreign banking in Latin America. Foreign banks may have pushed domestic banks out of the market and focused on larger businesses, which could be served with less information and lower monitoring costs. Evidence provides sufficient basis for this fear. In Argentina, Colombia, and Peru, foreign banks devote an average of 21 percent of their portfolio to small businesses, whereas this rate rises to 26 percent in domestic banks. In Argentina and Chile, moreover, foreign banks grew more slowly in this market segment than domestic banks. Curiously, these differences between domestic and foreign banks are due to the smaller size of the foreign banks, because the large banks, whether domestic or foreign, tend to lend to SMEs in similar proportions (Clarke and others 2002). However, inasmuch as foreign banks have not displaced domestic banks, but have contributed to the growth of the entire financial system, their effects on SMEs would be favorable. Opinion surveys carried out with more than 4,000 companies in 38 developing countries indicate that greater penetration by foreign banks improves both the amount of credit and loan conditions for companies of all sizes. The benefits seem to be greater for larger firms, but the smaller ones also benefit (Clarke, Cull, and Martínez Pería 2001).

The evidence mentioned thus far has to do with lending to SMEs, which may be irrelevant for the poor, who can receive credit only in very small amounts. Is there any evidence that financial reform policies have hindered the development of microlending? The answer is a resounding "No." Microlending has not only developed rapidly in the past decade in Latin America, but a good proportion of this development has taken place in the traditional financial sector. According to statistics based on an inventory of microcredit in 17 countries for 1999, commercial banks granted 29 percent of total lending received by microenterprises. Nongovernmental organizations (NGOs) that became regulated financial entities provided another 45 percent, along with other specialized financial intermediaries. Hence, the regulated financial institutions that were almost uninvolved in microlending five years ago are now channeling 74 percent of loans to microenterprises and serving 53 percent of their customers. Although the microlending of regulated entities is made in amounts two-and-a-half times higher than those of unregulated entities, the average amount of each operation is just US$800, which represents approximately six months of the per capita income of the countries where they operate. Consequently, the institutionalization of microlending does not seem to be leading to a diversion of the product toward wealthy sectors. Some observers believe that these trends indicate that lending to the poor is finally becoming a significant component of the menu of services of the financial system (Christen 2000).

These advances cannot be attributed completely to the financial reforms of the past decade. However, it can be said that they have undoubtedly been favored by the growth of the credit system, greater competition, an improved regulatory environment, and greater flexibility granted to financial intermediaries to develop new products and operate in diverse markets. That is what is suggested by the results of a study performed in 78 developing countries, which shows that 44 percent of the banks providing services to SMEs are motivated primarily by greater competition in the credit market for medium and large companies (Jenkins 2000). Nevertheless, the development of microlending has been uneven across countries for reasons that are not well understood. The number of microlending operations in Bolivia reaches 80 percent of the estimated population of microenterprises, suggesting that the microlending market is saturated. Indicators of coverage are also high in Nicaragua (36 percent) and El Salvador (35 percent), and a little lower but also significant in Paraguay, Peru, and Chile (between 18 and 13 percent). By contrast, in Argentina, Brazil, Mexico, Uruguay, and Venezuela, microlending is virtually nonexistent. With the noteworthy exception of the Banco do Nordeste in Brazil, microlending has not captured the attention of the large financial entities in those countries (Christen 2000).

Tax Reforms and Other Reforms

The labor implications of the tax reforms have received much less attention than the other reforms discussed in this chapter. The general orientation of the tax reforms involved simplifying tax systems, reducing tax rates on capital and higher labor incomes, and broadly extending the use of the value-added tax. However, the scope and continuity of these reforms has varied depending on the country.

Four fundamental questions ought to be asked about the effects of these measures on labor. The first is whether the reforms affected the demand for labor by making it cheaper to use capital. Some studies on Colombia suggest that in manufacturing, the tax reforms, along with other measures, made capital cheaper and reduced the demand for unskilled labor, while raising the demand for skilled labor, which complements capital (Cárdenas and Gutiérrez 1997).

The second question is whether the reforms affected labor demand by changing the incentives to work. Discussion of this issue, which has been intense in Europe and the United States, is less relevant in Latin America, where taxes are levied only on relatively highly paid workers (IDB 1998) and where few people have incomes sufficiently high so that the tax level would influence the decision of whether to work. Even so, two important aspects must be considered. First, income taxes may influence the composition and quality of employment by affecting people's decision to work as employees or as self-employed workers, and companies' decision to be organized in a transparent and consolidated way or opaquely and through small production units. Second, the level of taxes may influence high-income workers' decision to migrate and accordingly affect relative wages between skilled and unskilled workers.

The third question has to do with the effects

of tax reforms on the incidence of taxation, that is, those on whom tax burdens ultimately fall. Given the greater importance of the VAT, it might seem that workers have been harmed by the tax reforms. Indeed, it is often claimed that the VAT is a regressive tax, contrary to the income tax, which is regarded as progressive. That conclusion is not necessarily correct, however, for several reasons:

- In most Latin American countries, many basic consumption items, such as food, which weigh more heavily in workers' basic market basket, especially for low-income workers, are excluded from the VAT (IDB 1998).
- If a tax reform is not neutral in terms of total collection, tax incidence analysis must take into account the use of extra revenues collected, which tend to have greater benefits for those who receive social services. Further revenues collected may benefit workers through health and pension social security programs.
- Conventional analyses of the impact of taxes tend to assume that the cost of the VAT is passed on entirely in the price of final goods, but it does not happen that way in practice (Shah and Whalley 1991). This means that a portion of the tax may fall on the producers, or on the workers in sectors producing the goods to which the VAT is applied.

The fourth question is related to the issue of incidence and has to do with interaction between tax reforms and other reforms. The issue emerges because the incidence of any tax depends on how factor and goods markets operate. Because the other reforms changed the operation of these markets, they may be expected a priori to have modified the incidence of previously existing taxes. For example, changes in tariffs affect only the beneficiaries of import quotas and have no incidence on producers or consumers. But when quotas disappear, tariff changes tend to be shifted to both producers and consumers and thus they may affect workers. Another example is the possible effect of rationing of credit on the incidence of taxation on companies. In this case, the burden of income tax falls on those who receive rationed credit. But if a financial reform eliminates rationing, the tax will tend to fall partly on consumers. Except for some simulation runs made with general equilibrium models, little is known about the relevance and size of these labor effects (Shah and Whalley 1991; Lora 1995).

In short, tax reforms (and the interaction of other reforms with the tax system) may have had effects on employment and the real wages of workers, but these issues have not received much attention in the heated debate on the effects of the reforms.

Conclusions and Policy Implications

Unemployment, low wages, and labor instability are problems that concern most Latin Americans. Liberalization, privatization, and other structural reforms aimed at smoothing the operation of the market have not been sufficient to solve these problems, and it is widely believed that those very reforms may even have aggravated them.

This chapter has shown that there is no basis for some of these criticisms. The effects of liberalization and privatization on unemployment (or on total employment) were limited in scope and duration, so much so that there is no evidence (in this study or others) that these reforms help explain the differences in unemployment (or employment) rates between some countries and others, or the changes in those rates over time. Nor can it be maintained that liberalization made employment unstable or worsened working conditions in the sectors exposed to competition from imports or the new export sectors. Nor are there grounds for claiming that financial liberalization has reduced lending to small companies or microenterprises, thereby helping to aggravate labor problems.

Nevertheless, some criticisms are valid. Liberalization led to wage decreases in sectors affected by lower tariffs and increased imports. It may also have helped increase informal labor in countries where labor legislation was more rigid. Privatization caused sharp declines in earnings and instability for employees laid off from the privatized companies. Both liberalization and privatization weakened the negotiating power of workers, contributing to lower wages and labor benefits.

These conclusions are relevant for future reforms. An important implication is that it may be impossible to determine the labor effects of a structural reform in advance. This is especially true for the lifting of restrictions on imports and other reforms in the international trade system (such as international integration agreements).

The situation described above is due not only to a lack of knowledge about the possible impact of these reforms on various sectors, but also to the nature of how the labor market works. The great fear of governments when they began liberalization processes was that unemployment would rise because it would be difficult for workers who lost their jobs in the previously protected sectors to find new jobs due to lack of job retraining or information about employment opportunities. This fear reflected a failure to see that labor markets are fluid due to high rates of job creation and destruction in all sectors, and that their fluidity would help facilitate the reforms without causing major changes in unemployment. Governments and analysts also failed to foresee that a large portion of the adjustment of the labor market to the reforms would take place through falling wages, especially those of unskilled workers in the sectors that were receiving rents due to lack of competition.

Given this lack of knowledge, efforts to compensate the losers or to ease social costs would have been inadequate. They might have focused on establishing or enhancing worker training courses or temporary minimum employment programs, as in fact happened in some countries. Had governments anticipated the true adjustment mechanisms of labor markets, they would have noticed that it is difficult to identify precisely who is losing from the reforms, and hence the effectiveness of these active policies of intervening in the labor market would have been called into question. Hence, it would have been more appropriate to bolster labor policies of a passive nature (such as unemployment insurance and other general protective measures) and to foster the creation of new jobs through reforms in labor legislation and a policy environment favorable to economic growth.[43]

Nevertheless, in some reforms it is possible to identify those groups of workers that may be among the losers and take steps to help them. That is the case with privatizations or programs to restructure public administration, where those affected by job loss can be helped by programs that may include a variety of active policies, from counseling and help in job hunting, to community job creation plans. The effectiveness of most of these policies depends on whether they can target specific groups of workers, although that is not the only condition for success.[44]

The conclusions of this chapter are also relevant for analysts and researchers. Many of the effects of the structural reforms were unexpected by economists. Liberalization may have produced favorable (although modest) effects on productivity and growth, but it did not have the favorable effects that were expected in the composition of production or employment or in labor remuneration. For reasons that have not been sufficiently studied, the sector composition of production and employment changed far less than what was expected after the modifications in the relative prices of products or the penetration of net imports. The adjustment seems to have occurred partly through falling wages, especially those of unskilled workers, who may have been sharing in the rents resulting from import protection. However, this hypothesis has not been sufficiently proven, and it is still not clear whether its validity depends on the presence of labor unions, wage negotiation mechanisms, or other factors. Researchers have paid a great deal of attention to the relationship between liberalization and widening wage gaps. The most common hypothesis for explaining it regards competition from imports (or increased exports) as having facilitated and encouraged the adoption of technologies skewed toward the use of more highly qualified labor. Nonetheless, as is discussed in the next chap-

[43] See chapters 7 and 8 for a discussion of the pros and cons of various labor policies and institutions.

[44] See chapter 8, particularly Box 8.2.

ter, the statistical and analytical support for this hypothesis is far from overwhelming.

Economic research has devoted little attention to the labor effects of financial and tax reforms. Fragmentary evidence on financial reform indicates that its labor effects have been positive because apparently it has helped widen access to credit for small businesses and microenterprises. However, the issue has been studied too little for a definitive conclusion. There is no proof of a direct correlation between these two phenomena, and it is not known why micro lending systems have developed in only some countries. Nor is it known whether it can correctly be assumed, as is implicit in these analyses, that lending that is aimed at more labor-intensive companies has a greater effect on aggregate employment. The gaps in research on tax reform are even more striking. Its effects on labor supply and demand are not known, little is known about its influence on the pay actually received by workers, and it is not known whether the interaction between tax reform and other reforms has changed tax incidence.

In short, the structural reform process has brought many labor surprises to reform governments and their critics and economists, teaching all concerned a lesson in caution and humility.

Chapter 6

Employment Outcomes and the Role of Technology

Previous chapters have described and analyzed the disappointing labor market outcomes in Latin America during the 1990s. With some exceptions, Latin American countries generally suffered from stagnant wages, rising unemployment, and increasing wage inequality associated with rising returns to education. As mentioned in chapter 1, there are several (not mutually exclusive) hypotheses for these labor market phenomena. This chapter focuses on explanations associated with technological change.

The main conclusion that emerges from the analysis is that technology provides a good explanation for stagnant wages but not for rising unemployment. Wage growth has been low because productivity has barely increased in the region. Since over long periods of time productivity growth is associated mainly with technological change, it follows that wages have failed to increase as expected because of slow technological progress in the region. In other words, the problem is not that labor markets have allocated rents in a way that has hurt workers; it is that the economic system has failed to generate rents that can be allocated to workers.

This conclusion casts doubt on explanations that blame other labor market pathologies, such as rising unemployment, on technological change. Moreover, cross-country analysis clearly shows that high or rapidly growing productivity is not correlated with high or rapidly growing unemployment rates.

An additional conclusion is that the claim that rising returns to education are due to skill-biased technological change, perhaps caused by trade liberalization and other structural reforms, turns out to be surprisingly weak. This is not to dispute the validity of the more general notion that technological change must be skill biased in the long run; technological change must be skill biased to reconcile the long-term increase in the supply of skilled workers with the absence of a secular decline in the returns to education. The point is rather that it is difficult to find convincing evidence that technological change is the cause of the recent increase in the returns to education. The chapter does not reach a strong conclusion on this point, but instead warns the reader that more research is needed in order to understand the causes of the rising skill premium in the region. Moreover, even if skill-biased technological change were indeed the cause of this phenomenon, there is still much to be learned about the specific technologies (such as information technology and automated equipment) behind skill-biased technological change and the specific skills for which demand is rising.

Technology and Stagnant Wages

One point on which economists generally agree is that, in the long run, the main determinant of the wage level is labor productivity. This is clearly the case if the share of labor in GDP (that is, total wages paid as a proportion of total income) is constant over time; in this case, the rate of growth of the wage is equal to the rate of growth of productivity.[1] Moreover, if labor's share does not vary with income levels across countries, this would imply that richer countries pay higher wages because they have higher levels of labor productivity.

The constancy of labor's share has been one of the "stylized facts" of growth accepted by economists for many decades (Kaldor 1961). This is partly because of the remarkable stability of labor's share in the United States, where total wages and salaries paid as a fraction of total income remained at 60 percent from 1950 to 2002. Considering a more inclusive measure of labor compensation, which includes employers' contributions to social insurance and other labor income in addition to wages and salaries, leads to the conclusion that labor's share has increased slightly over this period, implying that wages have actually grown faster than labor productivity in the United States.

The constancy of labor's share has also been observed in East Asian countries, which have experienced fast rates of growth (Young 1995). Consistent with this finding, Gollin (2002) shows that labor's share does not vary systematically with income level across countries. Putting together all the available data across countries and time, he finds that labor's share clusters in a range from 0.6 to 0.85, with no tendency over time or across countries.

Unfortunately, the evidence is not as conclusive as these papers and findings suggest. For example, Blanchard (1997) shows that labor's share of national income declined during the 1980s and 1990s in several countries in Continental Europe. More generally, Harrison (2002) shows that, whereas labor's share appears to have no trend when all countries are taken together, this masks differences in experience among countries at different income levels. Her detailed analysis suggests that poor and middle-income countries have exhibited a negative trend in labor's share over 1960-97.

Labor saving technological progress might be a reason why labor's share could fall over time. Technological progress is said to be labor saving if it raises the demand for capital by more than it raises the demand for labor.[2] With flexible wages and a constant stock of capital, this would imply that wages do not rise as fast as output, and hence the share of income accruing to labor falls. Of course, it also implies that the returns to capital increase and hence in the long run the supply of capital would respond positively. This would lower the returns to capital and increase wages, allowing labor's share to remain constant. This is a good description of what happens in the long run in developed countries and perhaps even in less developed countries, but it may fail to capture relevant dynamics in the medium run, when the capital stock does not adjust fully. For example, Blanchard (1997) argues that the decrease in labor's share in Europe in the 1980s and 1990s was caused by labor saving technological change (itself the result of labor market rigidities and high labor taxes), which was not accompanied by an expanded supply of capital. Could this be happening in Latin America? Are stagnant wages a result of the decrease in labor's share in the region?

Before looking in detail at the data for Latin America, it is useful to look again at Harrison's findings. The negative trend in labor's share for countries in the middle and lower portions of the income distribution turns out to be small: labor's share falls by 1 percentage point each decade. This would contribute little to the explanation of stagnant wages in Latin America.

To look into this matter more directly, this chapter investigates the statistical relationship between wages and labor productivity across countries in Latin America using data on wages from the Inter-American Development Bank (IDB), Econom-

[1] To see this, note that if the wage (w) is a constant fraction of labor productivity (Y/L, where Y is total output and L is total workers), that is, $w = \alpha\ (Y/L)$, then total wages paid will be a constant fraction of total output or GDP: $\alpha = (wL)/Y$.

[2] Barro and Sala-i-Martin show that for there to exist a steady state in a neoclassical growth model, technological change has to be labor saving. Given that developed countries (such as the United States and the United Kingdom) have exhibited roughly constant growth rates for more than a century, steady-state growth is an attractive feature of growth models. This is a strong argument that technological progress must ultimately be labor saving.

Figure 6.1 Wages and Labor Productivity in Latin America

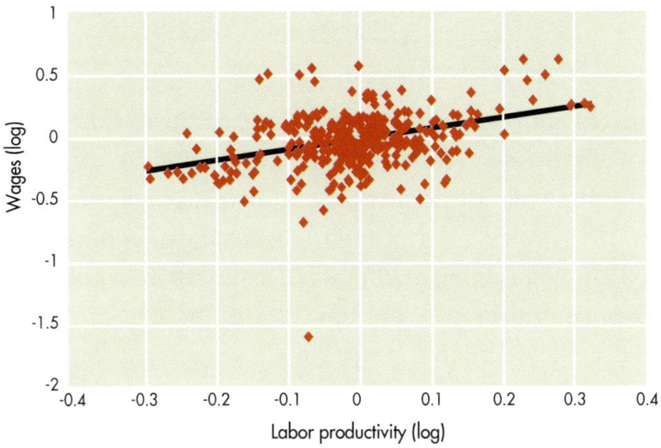

Note: Each point in the scatter corresponds to one Latin American country and one year.
Source: IDB calculations based on ILO data.

Figure 6.2 Labor Productivity Growth: Contributions from Technology and Capital Deepening, 1985-2000
(Percent)

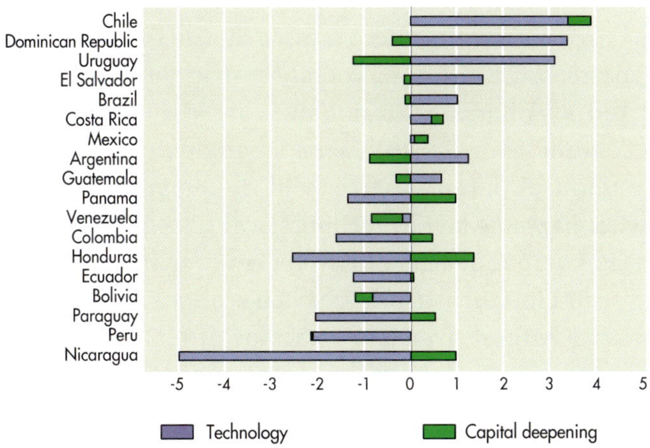

Source: IDB calculations.

ic Commission for Latin America and the Caribbean (ECLAC), and International Labour Organization (ILO).[3] For the IDB and ECLAC data sets, the statistical analysis suggests that wages move more than proportionally with labor productivity. For the ILO data set, the estimated coefficient is 0.86, implying that when labor productivity increases by 1 percent, wages increase by 0.86 percent. But even in this case, the standard error of the regression is such that the analysis cannot reject the hypothesis that the true coefficient is equal to one. Figure 6.1 shows the corresponding partial correlation of labor productivity and wages (in logs) for the ILO data set. In general, the statistical analysis suggests that wages move one for one with labor productivity.

This analysis suggests that the failure of wages to grow rapidly is due to slow growth in labor productivity. As Figure 6.2 shows, the average annual growth rate of labor productivity in 1985-2000 was low in the region.[4] Out of 18 countries in the sample, nine exhibited negative growth rates. The simple average of the growth rate in the 18 countries was –0.03 percent, far below the U.S. growth rate of 1.95 percent in the same period. Thus, the general tendency has been one of stagnation in labor productivity in the region in the post-crisis period. Only four countries (Chile, Dominican Republic, El Salvador, and Uruguay) have shown rates of growth in labor productivity above 1 percent a year.

It falls outside of the scope of this Report to conduct a full analysis of the sources of low growth in labor productivity in the region.[5] Here the analysis is limited to an exploration of the role of technological change in this phenomenon. Since technological change cannot be measured directly, the conventional approach entails looking at the growth of output that cannot be explained by increases in inputs (this is commonly referred to as total factor productivity, TFP) as an indirect measure of technological change.[6] In this way, growth in

[3] Formally, a regression was run of the log of the wage level on the log of labor productivity, using year and country dummies. The regression used PPP labor productivity numbers from the Heston, Summers, and Betina (2002) database. Three sources of wages were used to perform three exercises. The first used average wages from the household surveys (IDB database). The second used data from ECLAC (PADI database) on average real wages in the manufacturing sector in the countries of the region. The third used data for manufacturing real wages from the ILO.

[4] The data come from the Heston, Summers, and Betina (2002) database.

[5] See Loayza, Fajnzylber, and Calderón (2002), for a thorough analysis.

[6] This is a good approach for the long run; for example, it is not disputed that the source of growth for developed countries over the long run has been technological change. Over shorter periods, however, TFP growth may be induced by factors other than technological change, for instance, a better allocation of resources across sectors, or a reallocation of resources away from rent seeking and into productive activities. Moreover, TFP growth is affected by the business cycle: in a downturn, capital utilization decreases, and this is usually not captured in capital input measures, so that it would lead to an underestimation of TFP growth.

labor productivity can be broken down into two components: a contribution from technological change and a contribution from capital deepening (see Figure 6.2).[7]

During 1985-2000, technological progress contributed nothing to growth in labor productivity in the region.[8] Whereas in the United States technology contributed 1.57 percent to growth in labor productivity, the average for the region was -0.1 percent. Technology contributed more than 1 percent to growth in labor productivity in only six of 18 countries in the study sample (Argentina, Brazil, Chile, Dominican Republic, El Salvador, and Uruguay).[9]

It is worth investigating whether the stagnation during 1985 to 2000 was due to negative results in the second half of the 1980s. To explore this possibility, the statistical analysis subdivides the whole period into three five-year subperiods: 1985-90, 1990-95, and 1995-2000. Appendix 6.2 describes the details of this analysis. The main result is that there is no statistically significant difference in the rate of growth of labor productivity across the three subperiods. Analysis of the contribution of technology to the growth in labor productivity across the three subperiods yields the same result. The only statistically significant difference arises in the contribution of capital deepening to growth in labor productivity, which shows an improvement from a -1 percent in 1990-95 to 1.2 percent in 1995-2000.

The result that growth in labor productivity is not statistically greater in the first half of the 1990s with respect to the second half of the 1980s is surprising in light of the fact that growth in income per capita increased markedly across the two five-year periods. Indeed, a similar statistical analysis reveals that the growth rate of income per capita increased from -1.1 percent a year in 1985-90 to 1 percent in 1990-95. This improvement was not due to a higher growth rate in labor productivity, but rather to a significant increase in labor force participation: the contribution of this component went from a -0.7 percent in the second half of the 1980s to 0.9 percent in the first half of the 1990s. In the words of Paul Krugman, the growth spur in 1990-95 was more "perspiration" than "inspiration" (Krugman 1994).

Technological Progress and Employment

In the 1990s, growth in employment failed to match growth in the number of people looking for work. As chapter 1 showed, this led to rising rates of unemployment in several countries, particularly in South America. In popular discussions, a hypothesis that has been implicitly formulated to explain this phenomenon is that technological progress reduced the need for workers.

The idea that technological progress has a detrimental effect on employment growth is not new. But a casual look at economic history clearly rejects the idea. For example, there was fast technological progress and a high rate of growth in employment in Great Britain following the Industrial Revolution. This was also the case in the United States during the whole twentieth century, with an important intensification of both technological change and employment growth during the 1990s.[10] The reason for this, of course, is that output is not fixed and hence it is not the case that when an economy can use less labor to produce the same amount of output, then it will do so. Simply put, what happens is that technological change leads to rising output instead of rising unemployment.

Still, it is instructive to take a look at recent data. The best available indicator of technological change is TFP growth. Using TFP growth rates calculated by Klenow and Rodríguez-Clare (2003), it is possible to check the relationship between changes

[7] See Appendix 6.1 for an explanation of the decomposition of growth in Figure 6.2.

[8] This growth decomposition does not adjust for capacity utilization or human capital, but the results would only be strengthened if these adjustments were made (see Loayza, Fajnzylber, and Calderón 2002).

[9] Interestingly, of the four countries where labor productivity grew by more than 1 percent a year, only one experienced a positive contribution from capital deepening (Chile), and even there the contribution was barely more than 10 percent of the total growth in labor productivity. This result should not be surprising: it is well known in the literature that high growth of labor productivity is usually the result of high TFP growth rather than capital deepening (Klenow and Rodríguez-Clare 1997; Easterly and Levine 2001; Loayza and others 2002).

[10] Europe was an exception during the 1970s, 1980s, and 1990s, with slow employment growth, but it is not clear that this was due to rapid technological change.

in employment rates and TFP growth rates for a pool of countries for 1990-95 and 1995-2000. There is no statistically significant relation between the variables: it is not the case that countries with higher TFP growth rates suffer from declining employment rates.[11] A similar analysis, but with the increase in the number of personal computers per person instead of TFP growth as a measure of technological progress, yields similar results.[12]

A slightly different hypothesis holds that periods of high technological change go together with low employment rates (or high unemployment rates), although not necessarily decreasing employment rates. This alternative was explored by checking the statistical relationship between the employment rate at the end of the subperiod and the change in TFP over the subperiod for the two subperiods mentioned above. Again, the results show no statistically significant relationship between these variables. The same results arise when the change in computers per person rather than TFP growth is used as an indicator of technological progress.

A more sophisticated and subtle version of the "technological change is bad for jobs" hypothesis is framed in a cross-industry setting. The idea is that the industries that have been growing fast in the region are ones that have also experienced fast technological progress, and hence have generated low employment growth. More formally, the hypothesis is that fast technological change goes together with slow employment growth at the industry level. In theory, this would happen if the industry faced a steep (inelastic) demand curve: in that case, an improvement in technology (a rightward shift in the supply curve) would lead to a large decline in price and a small increase in output in the new equilibrium. Given the higher productivity associated with the improvement in technology, the small increase in output could actually be produced with a lower employment level. This could have aggregate implications—at least in the short run—if industries that experienced fast technological progress fired workers that were not rapidly absorbed by the rest of the economy. This would lead to higher unemployment during a transition period.

To check this "industry version" of the hypothesis, it is necessary to turn to cross-industry data. Although the focus is Latin America, it is helpful to start the analysis with the United States, which has high-quality data for the manufacturing sector at a disaggregate level. It turns out that, in contrast with the proposition above, there is a positive and statistically significant relation between TFP growth and employment growth at the industry level.[13] In other words, high technological progress goes together with higher rates of employment growth at the industry level.

Is this also the case in Latin America? Unfortunately, the data for Latin America are incomplete and available only at a higher level of aggregation. Thus, the exercise is less reliable than for the United States. However, the analysis yields a positive and statistically significant relation between TFP growth and employment growth at the industry level for a pool of seven Latin American countries for which the necessary data are available.[14] Thus,

[11] The regression was of the change in the log of the employment rate (employment over labor force) on the changes in the log of TFP in 1990-95 (48 countries) and 1995-2000 (32 countries). The estimated coefficient is positive but statistically insignificant.

[12] Data on personal computers per person are from World Development Indicators, World Bank.

[13] Formally, this result comes from running a regression of change in the log of industry employment on change in the log of industry TFP. The data come from the NBER-CES Manufacturing Industry Database maintained by Bartelsman, Becker, and Gray (http://www.nber.org/nberces/nbprod96.htm). This database provides information for each of the 459 1987 SIC four-digit industries. The period for which changes in the main variables are calculated is 1960-96. TFP is calculated using the five-factor TFP index developed by the National Bureau of Economic Research. The estimated coefficient is 0.36 with a standard error of 0.07. It can be shown that if there is unrestricted labor mobility across industries, then this estimated coefficient plus 1 is an unbiased estimate of the elasticity of substitution in demand between industry outputs (Klenow 1998). If there are restrictions on cross-industry labor flows, then this would establish a lower bound for the elasticity of substitution. Thus, this finding is consistent with an elasticity of substitution among goods greater than 1.

[14] The seven countries are Bolivia, Chile, Colombia, Ecuador, Mexico, Panama, and Venezuela. The data come from the UNIDO database for three-digit industries according to the ISIC classification. Thus, instead of 459 sectors, the data are for 32 sectors per country. $\ln TFP = \ln(Y_i/L_i) - \alpha_i \ln(K_i/L_i)$ is computed for each country, where i is a sector index, and α_i is the capital share in sector i. The industry capital stock was constructed using data on industry investment deflated by the country's investment deflator from the Penn World Tables. For α_i the capital share for each industry in the United States is used. The period of analysis is 1983-91. The regression uses country dummies and yields a coefficient on change in log of TFP equal to 0.1, with a standard error of 0.039 (t-statistic of 2.6).

similar to the United States, industries enjoying faster TFP growth exhibit faster employment growth, rejecting the subtle version of the hypothesis that technological change is bad for jobs.

In sum, the evidence presented in this section shows that it is difficult to make the argument that technological progress at the aggregate or industry level leads to an increase in unemployment. The next section turns to a more interesting possibility, namely that technological change may have different effects on different types of workers and, in particular, that it could lead to an increase in wages for skilled workers in relation to those of unskilled workers.

Technology and the Rising Skill Premium in Latin America

Chapters 1 and 3 presented evidence of a rising skill premium in Latin America. This, of course, is only a general trend; there are countries where the skill premium did not increase, but they are the exception.

The phenomenon of the rising skill premium has received a lot of attention in the region because of its effect on income inequality, which is already the highest in the world. Moreover, the expectation was that trade liberalization would lead to a reduction in wage inequality, so the fact that it has increased certainly calls for an explanation.

A simple explanation for the rising skill premium is that it is due to the large increase in the supply of workers with secondary education in most countries. In other words, this explanation posits that workers with tertiary education have become scarcer relative to workers with only secondary education, thereby allowing the former to command a higher relative wage. As discussed in chapter 3, this "supply-side" explanation is not sufficient because the supply of workers with tertiary education has declined only slightly relative to the supply of workers with only secondary education. Thus, it is necessary to explore an additional "demand-side" explanation for the rising skill premium. Indeed, chapter 3 showed the existence of a regional positive trend in the relative demand for workers with tertiary education of between 1.9 and 2.4 percent a year. What explains this rising relative demand for skilled workers?

At a general level, the increasing relative demand for skills could come from a between-sectors phenomenon or a within-sector phenomenon, or from a combination of both. Some sectors are more skill intensive relative to others. For example, the financial services sector is skill intensive in relation to the agricultural sector. If the financial services sector expands and the agricultural sector contracts, then the overall skill intensity increases, implying an increase in the relative demand for skills at the aggregate level. This is a between-sectors phenomenon because it arises as resources are reallocated between sectors. Alternatively, the increase in demand for skills at the aggregate level could come from a tendency for sectors to become more skill intensive, which would be a within-sector phenomenon.

The distinction between the within and between effects is important because it points to different sources of the increase in the relative demand for skilled labor. For example, the effect of trade liberalization on the skill premium should show up as an increase in the relative demand for skilled workers associated with a between-sectors effect. The effect of technological change on the relative demand for skills, by contrast, would be expected to arise through a within effect.

The most important between-sectors effect in the past decades has been associated with reallocation of workers from agriculture and manufacturing toward services. This reallocation has contributed to the increasing demand for skills because the services sector is more skill intensive than either the manufacturing or the agricultural sector. Indeed, if the skill intensity of a sector is defined by its share of college educated workers, the skill intensity of the services sector was 14.8 percent in Brazil in 1999, whereas the skill intensity of the agricultural and manufacturing sectors was only 7.4 and 8.1 percent, respectively. Similarly, in Chile in 1998, the skill intensity of the services sector was 28.5 percent, whereas it was only 5.1 and 17.6 percent in the agricultural and manufacturing sectors, respectively. This relation holds true for all

Figure 6.3 Decomposition of Change in Relative Demand for Skilled Labor, 1990s

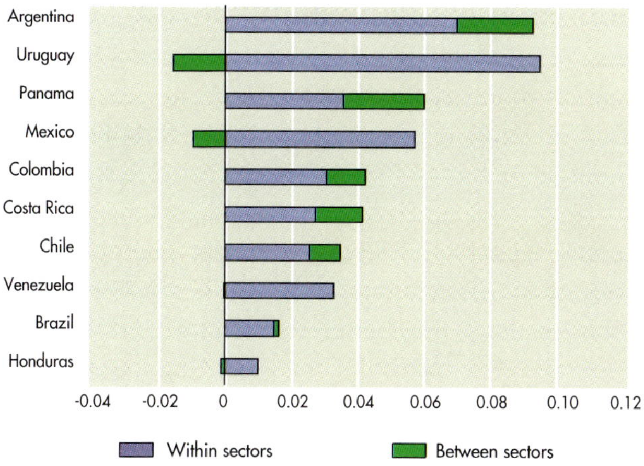

Source: IDB calculations.

Figure 6.4 Increases in Skill Intensity Across Sectors in Latin America

(Percent)

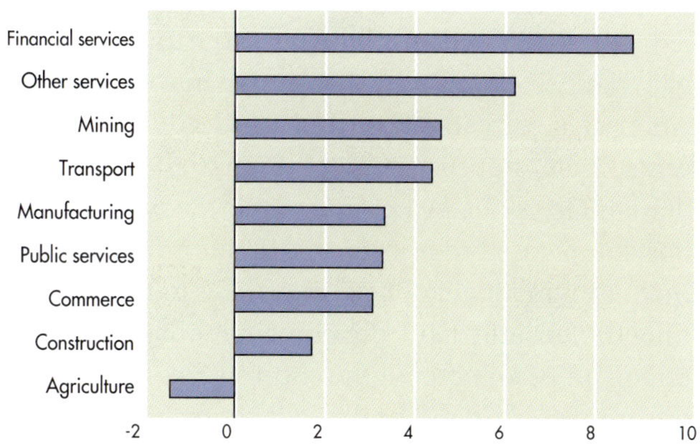

Note: Financial services includes finance, insurance, real estate and business services. Other services includes community, social, and personal services. Mining is mining and quarrying. Transport includes transport and storage. Public services includes electricity, gas, and water. Commerce includes wholesale and retail trade, and hotels and restaurants. Agriculture includes agriculture, hunting, forestry, and fishing.
Source: IDB calculations.

countries and years for which the relevant data are available.

According to this analysis, the within effect explains most of the increase in the demand for skills in Latin America. For instance, Argentina's skill intensity increased by 9.2 percent because the share of workers with tertiary education increased from 22.9 to 32.1 percent in 1992-2000. Of the total increase, the within effect accounted for 7 percent, whereas the between effect accounted for 2.3 percent.[15] Figure 6.3 shows the decomposition of the total increase in the skill intensity at the aggregate level (all sectors combined) for the 10 countries for which data are available.[16] In three of the countries, the between effect goes in the wrong direction and therefore the within effect overexplains the increased skill intensity. In the other countries, the within effect accounts for most of the total increase in skill intensity.

This sector analysis leads to the additional conclusion that rising skill intensity is a phenomenon that is not concentrated in manufacturing, as has sometimes been presumed. On the contrary, the phenomenon is present in many sectors. To see this, it is useful to calculate the average increase in skill intensity in each sector for the 10 Latin American countries in the sample. According to this measure, the sector that experienced the strongest increase in skill intensity was finance, insurance, real estate, and business services. The sector with the second-highest average increase was community, social, and personal services. In general, all sectors experienced an increase in skill intensity, except for agriculture. Moreover, as shown in Figure 6.4, manufacturing experienced only a moderate increase in skill intensity.

A caveat of this analysis is that it is done at a high level of aggregation, in which the economy is grouped in nine large sectors, such as manufactur-

15 This exercise uses data from household surveys, which provide the education level and sector of occupation for workers. Workers are classified in nine sectors: (1) agriculture, hunting, forestry, and fishing; (2) mining and quarrying; (3) manufacturing; (4) electricity, gas, and water supply; (5) construction; (6) wholesale and retail trade and hotels and restaurants; (7) transport and storage; (8) finance, insurance, real estate, and business services; and (9) community, social, and personal services. The economywide skill intensity is a weighted average of the skill intensity across sectors, with the weights given by the share of employment of each sector. For the decomposition, note that the change in this weighted average is equal to the sum of two components: the within effect, which is the weighted average of the change in skill intensity across sectors with weights given by the employment shares in the initial year, and the between effect, which is the sum across all sectors of the skill intensity in the final year multiplied by the change in the employment share for each sector.

16 The periods of analysis vary across countries due to data availability: Argentina, 1992-2000; Brazil, 1988-99; Chile, 1990-98; Colombia, 1991-99; Costa Rica, 1989-2000; Honduras, 1992-99; Mexico, 1989-2000; Panama, 1991-2000; Uruguay, 1989-2000; and Venezuela, 1989-99.

ing and agriculture. Perhaps the increase in skill intensity for some of these broad sectors is itself caused by a between phenomenon across subsectors. For example, the increase in skill intensity in manufacturing could be caused by a reallocation of resources from apparel to machinery, which is more skill intensive. This issue has been explored in several recent papers for the manufacturing sector, which is the only sector for which the required data are available. The consistent finding in these studies is that the between effect is small (Berman and Machin 2000; Sánchez-Páramo and Schady 2003). Thus, most of the increase in skill intensity at the sector level is also caused by a within effect at the subsector level.

One explanation for this phenomenon at the subsector level that has been discussed in the literature starts with the accepted proposition that capital is complementary to skilled labor, and a substitute for unskilled labor. Thus, if a higher investment rate leads to capital deepening (as reflected in an increasing capital-output ratio), then it would be expected that the relative demand for skilled labor would increase. However, a problem with this hypothesis is that, for plausible elasticity parameters, capital deepening explains only a small part of the increase in the relative demand for skills (see Berman and Machin 2000). But more importantly, data from Heston, Summers, and Bettina (2002) for 1985-2000 show that there is a negative trend in the capital-output ratio in Latin American countries, so there is no capital deepening whatsoever.[17]

The discussion so far can be summarized in three statements. First, an increase in the relative demand for skills, and not a fall in the relative supply of skills, has caused the increase in the skill premium. Second, a within-sector effect rather than a between-sectors phenomenon has caused the increase in the relative demand for skills at the aggregate level. And third, the capital deepening explanation for the within effect is not consistent with the data.

An understanding of the causes of the rising skill premium requires an understanding of the causes of the rising relative demand for skills within sectors. A widely accepted explanation for this phenomenon is technological change that is biased in favor of skilled workers. This is commonly referred to as skill-biased technological change. The rest of this section is devoted to exploring this explanation of the rising skill premium in the region.

Exploring the validity of the skill-biased technological change (SBTC) hypothesis for the case of Latin America turns out to be important because a better understanding of the causes and characteristics of the rising demand for skills may prove valuable in designing better technology and education policies. For example, the ambitious study by de Ferranti and others (2003) puts forward an interesting argument, which begins with recent research arguing that trade liberalization, foreign direct investment flows, and other reforms have increased technology adoption in Latin America and the Caribbean. Coming from the rich, skilled-labor abundant countries, the argument goes, these adopted technologies are skill biased, so they have led to a rising demand for skills. In contrast to what has happened in other regions, however, Latin America's unresponsive and rigid education systems have not been able to match this rising demand for skills. According to this study, the result has been an increase in the skill premium and increased inequality. The bright side to this story is that the greater skill premium presents a golden opportunity to increase the supply of skills to match the greater demand and produce fast growth and prosperity with falling inequality.

This chapter explores the SBTC hypothesis as it applies to the Latin American and Caribbean region to understand whether these conclusions are warranted. In particular, what specific technologies has the region adopted recently? Are they specific to manufacturing or do they have broader relevance, like information technology? What has been the role of international trade in inducing and

[17] This statement comes from running a regression of the capital-output ratio on a time trend, using country dummies. The coefficient of the time trend in this regression is -0.0103, with standard error 0.002 (t-statistic -4.31). The decline in the capital-output ratio is due to lower investment rates in the 1980s and 1990s compared with the ones that prevailed in the 1960s and 1970s. The good news is that there was a trend to recuperate those high investment rates in the 1990s. The bad news is that this trend broke down in the late 1990s.

allowing technology adoption in the region? What are the skills whose demand has increased the most (engineers, information technology professionals, business administrators, accountants, or others)? These are, of course, difficult questions, but they provide the proper motivation to guide the investigation.

Although there has been some research conducted recently addressing these questions in the context of Latin America, most of the related research has been focused on the United States. The next section looks at this literature, which provides several useful clues for the analysis of Latin America and the Caribbean.

Skill-biased Technological Change in the United States

During the past two decades, and especially in the early 1980s, there was a marked increase in the skill premium in the United States (Card and DiNardo 2002). This led to a large literature exploring the causes of this phenomenon. Given that the rising skill premium coincided with a rising relative supply of skilled workers, the necessary conclusion was that the demand for skills was increasing.

Initially, increasing international trade with less developed countries received a lot of attention as a plausible explanation for the rising demand for skills because standard trade theory would predict this for a developed country like the United States. According to this view, opening up trade channels with less developed countries would lead a country abundant in skilled labor to specialize in goods intensive in skilled labor. This would increase the relative size of sectors producing these goods and thereby increase the aggregate demand for skilled workers. Soon, however, people realized that the reallocation of resources toward sectors intensive in skilled labor explained only a small fraction of the rising aggregate demand for skills. The new consensus became that the source of the increasing demand for skilled workers was at the industry or sector level, that is, the consensus was that it was a within-sector phenomenon, such as the one observed in Latin America.

The SBTC hypothesis has become the most widely accepted explanation of the rising skill premium in the United States because it provides a plausible explanation for the observed increasing intensity in skilled labor across a large set of industries or sectors. Exemplifying the way good science is done, the SBTC hypothesis soon began to be contrasted with the data in different ways. This section briefly reviews this literature in an effort to better understand the SBTC hypothesis and its plausibility for the Latin American case. The next section turns to the literature that specifically analyzes the hypothesis for Latin America.

Skill-biased technological change generally brings to mind two things: computers and equipment that displaces manual labor on the factory floor. Doms, Dunne, and Troske (1997) use plant-level data to examine the relationship between adoption of advanced production machinery and skill intensity. The data come from plant-level responses to a survey of manufacturing technology conducted by the U.S. Census Bureau. The survey asked firms whether they used any of 17 particular technologies that included computer aided design/computer aided manufacturing, networks, and robots. According to the study's authors, these technologies increase the level of automation in a factory:

> The primary way workers control these technologies is through keyboards, pointing devices, and video display terminals. At a minimum, workers using these technologies must be able to use such devices and thus have reasonable language skills, reading skills, and, in some cases, basic math skills. Thus, we expect that plants that are more automated will employ relatively more educated and skilled workers than plants that rely on more traditional technologies with mechanical interfaces (i.e., levers and switches). (Doms, Dunne, and Troske 1997, p. 260)

The Doms, Dunne, and Troske study finds that, indeed, firms that use more of these technologies also have a higher share of skilled workers, as measured by the share of workers that have at least a college degree. This applies both to production and nonproduction workers. But, surprisingly, when the study turns from cross-section to time-series analysis, firms do not become more skill intensive when they adopt more technology.[18] From these seemingly contradictory results, the study concludes that the relationship between factory floor automation technologies and skills does not match that which the SBTC hypothesis postulates (adoption of these technologies increases the relative demand for skills), but rather skill intensity leads to technology adoption: firms with more skilled workers are more likely to adopt advanced technology.[19]

Doms, Dunne, and Troske turn to computers as an alternative driver of skill-biased technological change. They perform a similar analysis and find that firms that invest more in computers and computer peripherals in relation to total investment do become more skill intensive, as measured by the share of nonproduction workers.

This last result corresponds to the notion that firms that increase their use of computers become more skill intensive. Moreover, it seems that there has been an increase in demand for people with knowledge about computers and software. However, wages for electrical engineers and people with computer science degrees relative to those with degrees in humanities and social sciences stagnated or decreased during the 1980s and early 1990s (Card and DiNardo 2002). Has a supply effect prevented prices from reflecting a change in demand? That is, was there a large increase in the supply of people with engineering and computer science degrees? According to data presented in Romer (2000), the fraction of engineers in the total U.S. labor force has remained constant since the early 1970s.

Perhaps this interpretation of the SBTC hypothesis is too narrow. As Bresnahan, Brynjolfsson, and Hitt (2002) argue, investments in computers and information technology go together with changes in organizational form and product mix that lead firms to increase their demand for a wide range of skills, not only computer-related skills. In their words:

> Firms do not simply plug in computers or telecommunications equipment and achieve service quality or efficiency gains. Instead they go through a process of organizational redesign and make substantial changes to their product and service mix. This raises the possibility that computers affect labor demand not only directly, as has been previously studied, but indirectly through other firm-level changes. That is, IT is embedded in a cluster of related innovations, notably organizational changes and product innovation. These three complementary innovations—a) increased use of IT, b) changes in organization practices, and c) changes in products and services—*taken together* are the SBTC that calls for a higher-skilled labor mix. (Bresnahan, Brynjolfsson, and Hitt 2002, p. 341)

The study confirms that the three elements of this particular version of the SBTC hypothesis vary together at the firm level, so that the data do not reject the proposition that falling prices of information technology equipment have led to organizational changes that in turn have led to greater relative demand for skills.

This could well be the most interesting and plausible version of the SBTC hypothesis. However, most of the increase in the skill premium in the United States occurred in the 1980s, whereas the effect of technological change led by information technology should have been felt during the 1990s. A possible explanation could be that the skill premium increased rapidly in the 1980s not because of

[18] It might be possible that firms *first* hire more skilled workers and then adopt the new technology. In this case, an empirical study looking for skill upgrading *after* technology adoption would find none. It is difficult to claim that the Doms, Dunne, and Troske (1997) study suffers from this problem, however, because it covers 1977-92 and most of the technologies considered became available after 1977. It seems unlikely that by 1977 firms had already adjusted their workforce in response to those skill-biased technologies.

[19] Doms, Dunne, and Troske (1997) alert the reader that this finding should be interpreted with care because it is only about the dynamics of individual firms. Technology adoption could still have aggregate implications if firms that adopted technologies grew faster or had a higher probability of survival: in that case, it would be expected that there would be an increase in the share of resources managed by firms that are more intensive in skilled labor. If this were the case, then there would be a process of increasing relative demand for skills caused by technology adoption that would not be captured in the exercise performed by Doms, Dunne, and Troske.

a faster rate of increase in the relative demand for skills, but because of a slower rate of increase in their relative supply (Katz and Murphy 1992). But this explanation requires the rate of increase in the relative supply of skills to have risen during the 1990s, as this would be required to explain the considerable slowdown in the rate of increase in the skill premium. However, as Beaudry and Green (2002) show, this did not happen.

Beaudry and Green propose a different framework for thinking about this matter. The idea is that during the 1980s and 1990s, the U.S. economy was (and perhaps still is) in transition toward a new skill-intensive technology associated with information technology.[20] In this transition process, the old technology coexists with the new technology, and factor prices are affected by both the evolution of the stock of factors of production (skilled labor, unskilled labor, and capital) and the rate at which the economy adopts the new technology. Given some plausible assumptions about the intensity with which the old and new technologies use the factors of production, Beaudry and Green show that—contrary to what has been emphasized in the literature—an increase in the relative supply of skills *increases* the skill premium. Moreover, an increase in the capital stock *decreases* the skill premium, in spite of the fact that skills are complementary to capital in the new technology.

The explanation for these surprising results rests on the notion that changes in factor supplies are accompanied by changes in the adoption of the new technology. Thus, an increase in the relative supply of skills leads to faster adoption of the new skill-biased technology; in turn, this increases the relative demand for skills and thereby prevents the skill premium from falling. Were it not for the introduction of capital into the model, this would imply that changes in the relative supply of skills do not affect the skill premium.[21]

Beaudry and Green introduce capital into the model and make two reasonable assumptions. First, the new technology exhibits capital-skill complementarity in the sense that the capital-labor ratio in the new (skill-intensive) technology is higher than in the old technology. Second, the new technology is capital efficient relative to the old technology in the sense that fewer units of capital are required to produce one unit of output with the new technology than with the old technology.[22] Under the first assumption, adoption of the new technology leads to a higher demand for capital. In turn, with constant capital stock, this leads to a higher rental rate for capital, and—under the second assumption—this increases the skill premium.

Beaudry and Green show that this framework is consistent with the U.S. data and provides an explanation for the evolution of the skill premium in the United States during the 1980s and 1990s. According to this explanation, rather than ongoing skill-biased technological change, the behavior of the skill premium has been determined by imbalances in the accumulation of skills and capital. During the 1980s, the skill premium increased because the supply of capital failed to match the increase in educational attainment; the skill premium stopped increasing toward the end of the 1980s and in the 1990s thanks to faster capital accumulation in relation to the rate of increase in educational attainment.

What are the implications for Latin America? In broad terms, it is clear that technological progress must have been skill biased during the twentieth century in the United States. There is no other way to explain the stability of the skill premium in spite of the significant increase in the relative supply of skilled labor during this period.[23] When it comes to explaining the recent increase in the skill premium in the United States, the simple SBTC hypothesis is not sufficiently informative and is even inconsistent with recent experience because it fails to explain the slowdown in the rising skill premium in the 1990s. Thus, perhaps a more appealing explanation is the one provided by Beaudry and

[20] Caselli (1999) explains this idea in depth. Beaudry and Green (2002) introduce capital and propose a coherent explanation for the U.S. experience since the mid-1970s.

[21] The intuition behind this result is the same as the intuition for factor price equalization in trade models.

[22] These two assumptions are consistent only when the share of skilled labor in the new technology is much higher than in the old technology, which is what Beaudry and Green (2002) implicitly assume.

[23] See Goldin and Margo (1992) and Acemoglu (2002).

Green, in which the evolution of the skill premium is determined by imbalances in the accumulation of skills and capital during the transition from the old to the new, general-purpose, skill-intensive technology, such as information technology.

Skill-Biased Technological Change in Latin America

The discussion about the determinants of the skill premium in the United States points to two related frameworks for thinking about this matter in Latin America. In both frameworks, the new technologies are associated with information technology and affect all sectors of the economy. The difference is that in the first framework (the exogenous SBTC hypothesis), the relative demand for skills is determined solely by exogenous skill-biased technological change, whereas in the second framework (the technology revolution hypothesis), the relative demand for skills is determined by a more complex process in which both the adoption of the new technology and the supply of skills and capital interact.[24]

According to the exogenous SBTC hypothesis, the skill premium increases when the relative supply of skills does not match the increase in the relative demand for skills caused by exogenous skill-biased technological change. In turn, skill-biased technological change in less developed countries can be seen as the result of the diffusion of skill-biased technologies developed for rich countries that are abundant in skilled labor (Acemoglu and Zilibotti 2001). By contrast, the technology revolution hypothesis posits that the skill premium increases when educational attainment increases faster than the supply of capital (Beaudry and Green 2002).

This section begins with an exploration of these ideas using the available household survey data for Latin America. It then moves on to analyze several specific questions. First, which technologies are behind the increasing relative demand for skills? Second, has trade liberalization caused the adoption of skill-biased technologies? And third, which skills are most in demand?

The Aggregate Data

The exogenous SBTC hypothesis suggests that the skill premium is determined by the relative supply of skilled labor and a time trend that captures rising relative demand for skills caused (presumably) by ongoing skill-biased technological change. It is instructive to follow Katz and Murphy (1992) in running a regression of the relative wage of skilled workers on the relative supply of skilled workers and a time trend for the region for the 1990s.[25] The estimated coefficient on the time trend is positive and statistically significant, but—contrary to the results in Katz and Murphy—the estimated coefficient on the relative supply of skilled workers is not statistically different from zero.[26] This should not be surprising in light of Beaudry and Green's (2002) results, which show that the Katz and Murphy results no longer hold in the United States when implemented for a period that includes the 1990s.

To deal with some econometric problems with this exercise, an alternative approach, also proposed by Katz and Murphy, involves using standard estimates of the relevant elasticities to derive the implied relative demand for skills from data on relative supply and relative wages, as explained in

[24] This discussion does not explicitly address a third framework, proposed by Acemoglu and others (see Acemoglu 2002), in which skill-biased technological change is itself caused by the increased relative supply of skills in developed countries. This endogenous SBTC hypothesis is interesting and relevant for the discussion in developed countries, but does not help much beyond the exogenous SBTC hypothesis from the point of view of understanding the recent experience in Latin America.

[25] This exercise follows the literature in thinking of skilled workers as workers with complete tertiary education and unskilled workers as those with complete secondary education. This is appropriate because, as mentioned in chapters 1 and 3, it is the wage of workers with tertiary education relative to workers with only secondary education that has been increasing in the region. All the data come from the IDB's collection of household surveys for Latin American countries. The supply numbers come from the surveys restricted to workers between 25 and 49 years of age, and who work at least five hours a day. The relative wages relate only to males, to avoid compositional effects. The regression is done for an unbalanced panel for Latin America with country dummies.

[26] The coefficient of the log of the relative supply is –0.106 with a t-statistic of 1.19. Not only is this coefficient not statistically different from zero, but it also implies an elasticity of substitution between skilled and unskilled labor of around 10, which is implausibly large. The coefficient of the time trend is 0.013 with a t-statistic of 3.62. These results are similar to the results of Sánchez-Páramo and Schady (2003).

Table 6.1 Evolution of the Relative Demand for Skills in Latin America

Variable	(1)	(2)	(3)
Trend	0.017	0.018	0.102
	(2.05)**	(2.22)**	(2.65)**
GDP per worker (log)	0.359		
	(0.74)		
Total factor productivity (log)		0.227	
		(0.37)	
Computers per capita (log)			–0.359
			(2.08)**
Number of observations	70	70	52
R^2	0.87	0.87	0.90

** Significant at 5 percent.
Note: The dependent variable is relative demand for skilled labor, with elasticity –2. All regressions use country dummies (not reported). Absolute values of t-statistics are in parentheses.
Source: IDB calculations.

Appendix 6.3. The intuition is that the evolution of the skill premium and the relative supply of skills must imply an increase in the relative demand for skills. But by how much does demand increase? This is determined by the relevant elasticities, which are obtained from standard estimates in the empirical literature.

This approach yields the implied relative demand for skills for all the countries and years for which relevant data are available from the household surveys. A simple statistical analysis of the derived relative demand for skills shows the existence of a positive trend in the region from the mid-1980s to the end of the 1990s. This is suggestive of skill-biased technological change, but requires further analysis. In particular, if the rising relative demand for skills is caused by skill-biased technological change, it is natural to expect that countries whose labor productivity or TFP has grown faster should have experienced a larger increase in the relative demand for skills.[27]

The statistical analysis reveals that this is not true: a regression of the relative demand for skills on productivity variables (labor productivity or TFP) and a time trend yields an estimated coefficient for the productivity variable that is not statistically different from zero (Table 6.1). Instead, using the number of computers per capita as a way to capture the diffusion of information technology, the coefficient becomes statistically significant, but of the wrong sign: the regression implies that countries where the diffusion of personal computers has been faster have experienced a lower rate of increase in the relative demand for skills (Table 6.1).

The next step should be to explore the empirical relevance of the technology revolution hypothesis, in which, instead of exogenous skill-biased technological change, there is a transition from old to new skill-biased technology. Unfortunately, lack of data prevents a thorough exploration of such an alternative framework. At most, the data would allow for exploring a crude approximation of Beaudry and Green's framework, by running a regression of the skill premium on the ratio of the supply of skilled workers to the capital stock (the Beaudry and Green ratio) plus a time trend. According to this framework, the coefficient on the time trend should be close to zero, whereas the coefficient on the Beaudry and Green ratio should be positive. The results generated by a simple regression

[27] This assumes that the degree to which technological change is biased toward skilled labor is exogenous to less developed countries, as in Acemoglu and Zilibotti (2001). Thus, if a country adopts technology at a faster pace than another, it is natural to expect both faster TFP growth and a higher rate of increase in the relative demand for skills.

do not match these predictions: the estimated coefficient on the time trend is positive and statistically significant, whereas the estimated coefficient on the Beaudry and Green ratio is negative, although statistically not different from zero.

These results show that there is no simple model that fits the available data for Latin America. Perhaps this should not be surprising: it would be quite remarkable if a simple framework such as any of the ones mentioned here could consistently explain the Latin American experience of the past two decades. The rest of this section adopts a more eclectic approach, in which the two major technological explanations for the rising skill premium (exogenous skill-biased technological change and the technological revolution) have some relevance for recent experience in Latin America.

Rising Relative Demand for Skills

Doms, Dunne, and Troske (1997) analyze plant-level data to explore the relationship between adoption of production automation technologies and skills upgrading. The authors conclude that although increased skills lead to technology adoption, it is not the case that technology adoption leads to increased demand for skills. Is there some evidence on this matter for Latin America?

Pavcnik (2002) follows a similar strategy to the one implemented by Doms, Dunne, and Troske using Chilean plant-level data.[28] As proxies for technology adoption, Pavcnik uses indicator variables for whether a plant receives foreign technical assistance, pays for patent use, or imports a portion of its materials. She finds basically the same result as Doms, Dunne, and Troske derive for the United States. Unfortunately, Pavcnik did not have data on information technology investment to check whether this kind of investment led to increases in skill intensity.

The results of this study are certainly not definitive, but do call into question the conclusion that technologies adopted recently in the manufacturing sector have led to an increase in the relative demand for skills. More importantly, given the small size of the manufacturing sector, it is unlikely that this, by itself, could have had a large aggregate effect. Perhaps a more appropriate interpretation is that investment in information technology has, as in Bresnahan, Brynjolfsson, and Hitt (2002), led to increased relative demand for skills (college graduates) of a wide variety, not only engineers and information technology professionals, and that this has happened not only in manufacturing but also in services and other sectors.

Trade Liberalization

In some studies, including de Ferranti and others (2003), the SBTC hypothesis is accompanied by a second hypothesis that states that the adoption of technologies intensive in skilled labor has been fueled in part by trade liberalization. What is the evidence for this claim?

A large literature discusses the role of trade in the diffusion of technology. In the extreme, trade is essential because new technologies almost always require imported equipment and other inputs. Thus, closing off trade completely surely would have a significant effect on reducing technology diffusion. But the relevant question is whether trade liberalization, *of the magnitude experienced in Latin America*, has led to faster technology diffusion.

To investigate this matter, it is instructive to start by examining the evolution of tariffs on capital goods in Latin America during the 1990s. As shown in Figure 6.5, there is no significant trend toward a reduction in these tariffs. In fact, in many countries, tariffs on capital goods increased during this period.

Given the well-known problems with tariff data, it is instructive to look directly at price data on capital goods and output to find out whether the relative price of capital goods has fallen in the region. Data on the price of capital goods relative to output for most of the countries in Latin America are from Heston, Summers, and Bettina (2002). In a regression of this relative price on a time trend, using country dummies, the estimated coefficient turned out negative and significantly different from zero.[29]

[28] This is the only study that uses appropriate data with appropriate econometric techniques. What is crucial is that the econometric identification comes from the time-series dimension of a panel, as opposed to the cross section, where endogeneity problems may be severe.

[29] The coefficient is –0.0059 and the standard error is 0.0017, with t-statistic –3.4.

Figure 6.5 Import Tariffs on Capital Goods
(Percent)

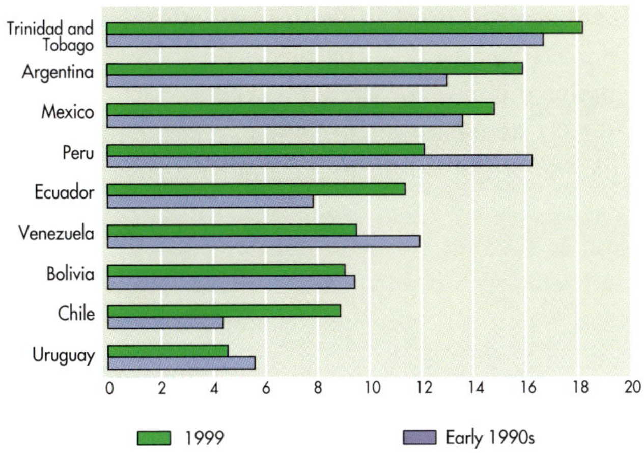

Source: UNCTAD database.

Thus, the hypothesis that there is a negative time trend in the relative price of capital goods in Latin America cannot be rejected.

Is the declining relative price of capital a consequence of trade liberalization? To explore this, note that there is a long-run trend in the United States of decline in the relative price of investment (Greenwood, Hercowitz, and Krusell 1997). It is natural to expect that this trend, which is surely due to faster technological change at the level of investment goods than general output, would also benefit Latin America because technology diffuses from developed to less developed countries. Thus, even without trade liberalization, a decline in the relative price of capital in the region would be expected. In a regression of the relative price of capital in Latin American countries against the same price in the United States, the hypothesis that the coefficient is 1 cannot be rejected.[30] Thus, the entire decline observed in the relative price of capital in the region could be due to the general trend in developed countries that has existed for many decades.

Since it is commonly understood that investment goods are more tradable than consumption goods, it is important to examine how the real exchange rate (RER) has affected the relative price of investment goods. Given that the RER is a good indicator of the relative price of tradable goods in terms of nontradable goods, it would be expected that a lower (appreciated) RER would lead to a lower relative price of investment. In a regression of the price of investment relative to output on the corresponding price in the United States and the RER in each country, together with country dummies, the coefficients for both independent variables turn out significantly different from zero and of the expected sign: the coefficient on the relative price of investment in the United States is positive and statistically not different from 1, and the coefficient on the RER is positive.[31] The regression was also run including the index of trade reform developed by Lora and Barrera (1997) and updated by Lora and Panizza (2002). This index goes from 0 to 1, with 1 being the most liberal trade regime in the region in the period under consideration (mid-1980s to 2000). If trade reform led to cheaper prices for investment goods, then trade reform would have a negative coefficient. In fact, the coefficient is positive, although it is not significantly different from 0 at the 10 percent level of confidence.

The analysis so far casts doubt on the idea that trade liberalization has led to a decrease in the relative price of investment and, hence, an increase in imports of capital goods, which in turn has led to an increase in the relative demand for skilled labor. As a final check on this idea, the analysis evaluates whether there has been an increasing share of imported capital goods in the total capital stock in Latin American countries. A series was constructed on the total capital stock and the part of that stock that is composed of imported capital goods.[32] A regression of the imported capital component on a

[30] The regression used country dummies and was conducted for 1985-2000 (or until the last year for which data were available). The resulting coefficient is 0.82, with standard error 0.38 (t-statistic 2.15).

[31] The coefficient for the relative price of investment in the United States is 1.39 and the standard error is 0.54 (t-statistic 2.59); the coefficient for the RER is 0.0025 and the standard error is 0.00066 (t-statistic 3.79).

[32] To do this, both series were computed using the permanent inventory method with a depreciation rate of 6 percent. For the initial year, 0 was used as the value of the capital stock for both series. For total capital stock, the initial year was 1950, and the investment data are from Heston, Summers, and Bettina (2002). For the imported capital goods, the data are from the ECLAC Yearbook (table 295) and the initial year was 1960. Since the analysis is on the period from the mid-1980s onward, the value of the capital stock in the initial year is irrelevant. The ratio of stock of capital imported over total capital is obtained by dividing these two series.

time trend shows that there is a positive time trend.[33] A new regression of the imported capital component on Lora and Panizza's (2002) index of trade reforms (with country and year dummies) is run to examine whether this positive time trend is a result of trade liberalization. The coefficient on trade reform is basically 0. The same exercise, but using tariffs on capital goods instead of the index of trade reform, yields a similar result.

Thus, the analysis so far does not provide evidence for the hypothesis that trade reform has led to imports of capital goods, which in turn have increased the relative demand for skilled labor. But perhaps trade reform has led to skill-biased technological change that is not associated with more imports of capital goods. This idea hinges on the notion that trade liberalization leads to technological change. On this matter, there is strong disagreement among economists, and it is not the place here to review this literature (see Rodrik 1995). Suffice it to say that there is no consensus that trade liberalization has led to faster technological progress in the region. It is safe to say that trade liberalization, together with a set of "right conditions," would indeed lead to faster technological progress, but that unfortunately those right conditions have not prevailed in many countries in Latin America in the 1990s.[34]

Two recent papers that study the direct link between trade liberalization and skill-biased technological change are relevant here. Sánchez-Páramo and Schady (2003) obtained data on imports and the relative demand for skilled workers for a group of manufacturing industries in Chile, Colombia, and Mexico. They regress the relative demand for skilled workers on import penetration, using country-sector specific dummies, and find a positive and statistically significant coefficient. This is consistent with the results in Pavcnik and others (2002) for Brazil; they show that the sectors where import penetration increased more rapidly were also the ones where the share of skilled workers increased the most. These results must be interpreted with caution, however, because they use industry data to get at what is in essence a plant-level phenomenon. Thus, the results admit different interpretations. It could well be, for instance, that increasing import penetration goes together with contraction of the domestic sector. If contraction occurs through the exit of low-productivity firms or through reduced plant size, then this by itself could cause the observed increase in the relative demand for skilled workers.

To avoid these problems, instead of import penetration it is better to use more exogenous measures of trade liberalization, like tariffs. Pavcnik and others (2002) do this and find no statistically significant relationship between tariff reduction and rising relative demand for skilled workers. Examination of data for Mexico leads to similar results.[35]

Which Skills Are Most in Demand?

The appropriate policy response to increases in demand for skilled workers caused by technological change is to facilitate the appropriate supply response, which requires knowledge about the skills whose demand is increasing the most. Some commentators have implicitly or explicitly assumed that technological change has increased the demand for engineers and scientists. Is this true?

Data availability limits the study of this issue, but some knowledge can be gained from household surveys. In particular, for the case of Mexico, these surveys contain information about the supply and wages of college educated workers by educational attainment for two broad categories: scientists and engineers, and other professionals.[36] Figure 6.6

[33] This regression included country dummies. The coefficient on the time trend is 0.001, with standard error 0.00009 and t-statistic 10.3.

[34] Beyond the right macroeconomic conditions and appropriate education levels, there is debate about the "right conditions." For some, they are an effective national innovation system (de Ferranti and others 2003). For others, they are the right institutions (Rodrik, Subramanian, and Trebbi 2002). Others would argue that what is required is a cluster-based policy toward certain sectors.

[35] Using the data described in López-Córdoba (2003), a regression of plant-level skill intensity (measured as production to total workers in each plant) on industry-level import penetration and year dummies was run for 1994-2000. The estimated coefficient on import penetration turned out negative (increasing import penetration implies *less* skill intensity), but statistically indistinguishable from 0.

[36] Scientists and engineers include four subcategories: (1) physicists, chemists, and related professionals; (2) mathematicians, statisticians, and related professionals; (3) computing professionals; and (4) architects, engineers, and related professionals. Other professionals include five subcategories: (1) business professionals; (2) legal professionals; (3) archivists, librarians, and related professionals; (4) social and related science professionals; and (5) writers and creative and performing artists.

Figure 6.6 Evolution of Relative Wages of Scientists and Engineers in Mexico
(Percent)

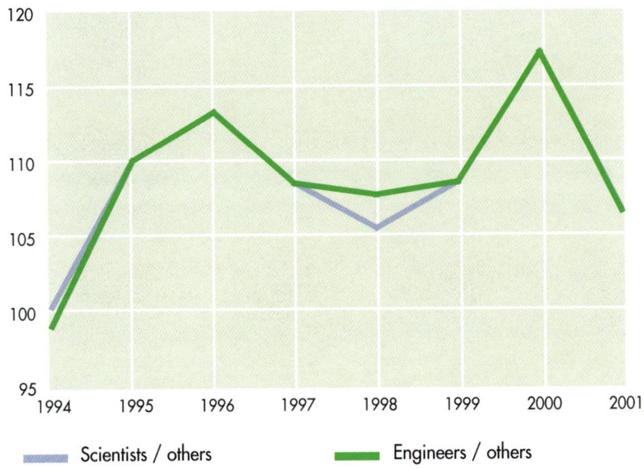

Source: IDB calculations based on household surveys.

Figure 6.7 Evolution of Relative Supply of Scientists and Engineers in Mexico
(Percent)

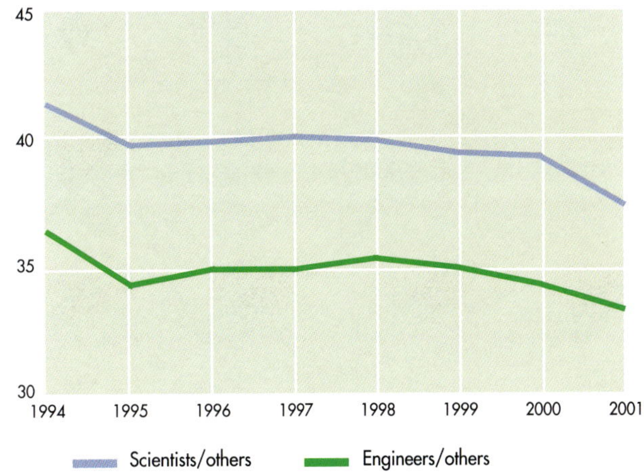

Source: IDB calculations based on data from Encuesta Nacional de Empleo Urbano Mexico.

shows the evolution of wages for scientists and engineers relative to those for other professionals for 1994–2001.[37] The figure reveals significant swings from one year to the next, so it is difficult to infer a clear trend. Figure 6.7 shows that the relative supply of workers with technical degrees has been falling, which is contrary to what would be expected in the presence of increasing relative demand for workers with technical degrees. From these figures, it is difficult to infer an increasing relative demand for workers with technical degrees.

For the rest of the countries, there are no available data on wages and labor supply according to educational degree, but there are data classified according to occupation.[38] Figures 6.8 and 6.9 show the evolution of the wages and share of workers in technical jobs relative to those in other jobs for the countries for which household and labor survey data are available. From Figure 6.8, it is difficult to draw the conclusion that the relative wages of workers in technical occupations have increased; the only countries for which this appears to be true are Mexico and Panama. Is this due to an increase in the relative supply of workers in technical areas, which has compensated for an increase in the relative demand for such workers? Experience has varied across countries for workers in technical occupations:

- In Argentina, Brazil, and Uruguay, the relative wage fell and the relative supply increased. Thus, there is no clear conclusion about the relative demand for technical workers.
- In Panama, the relative wage increased and the relative supply decreased. Thus, there is no clear conclusion about the relative demand for technical workers.
- In Colombia, there was a slight fall in the relative wage, while relative supply also dropped. This suggests a decrease in the relative demand for technical workers.
- In Mexico, the relative wage increased and relative supply was constant. This suggests an increase in the relative demand for technical workers.

In sum, there is no clear evidence of an increase in the relative demand for technical workers in the countries in Latin America for which data are available.

---

37 Unfortunately, there are no consistent data for a longer period (there was a change in codification in 1994).

38 The analysis focuses on data for hourly wages for males, although the implications are similar for other variables (monthly income and females).

Figure 6.8 Evolution of Relative Wages of Technical Workers
(Percent)

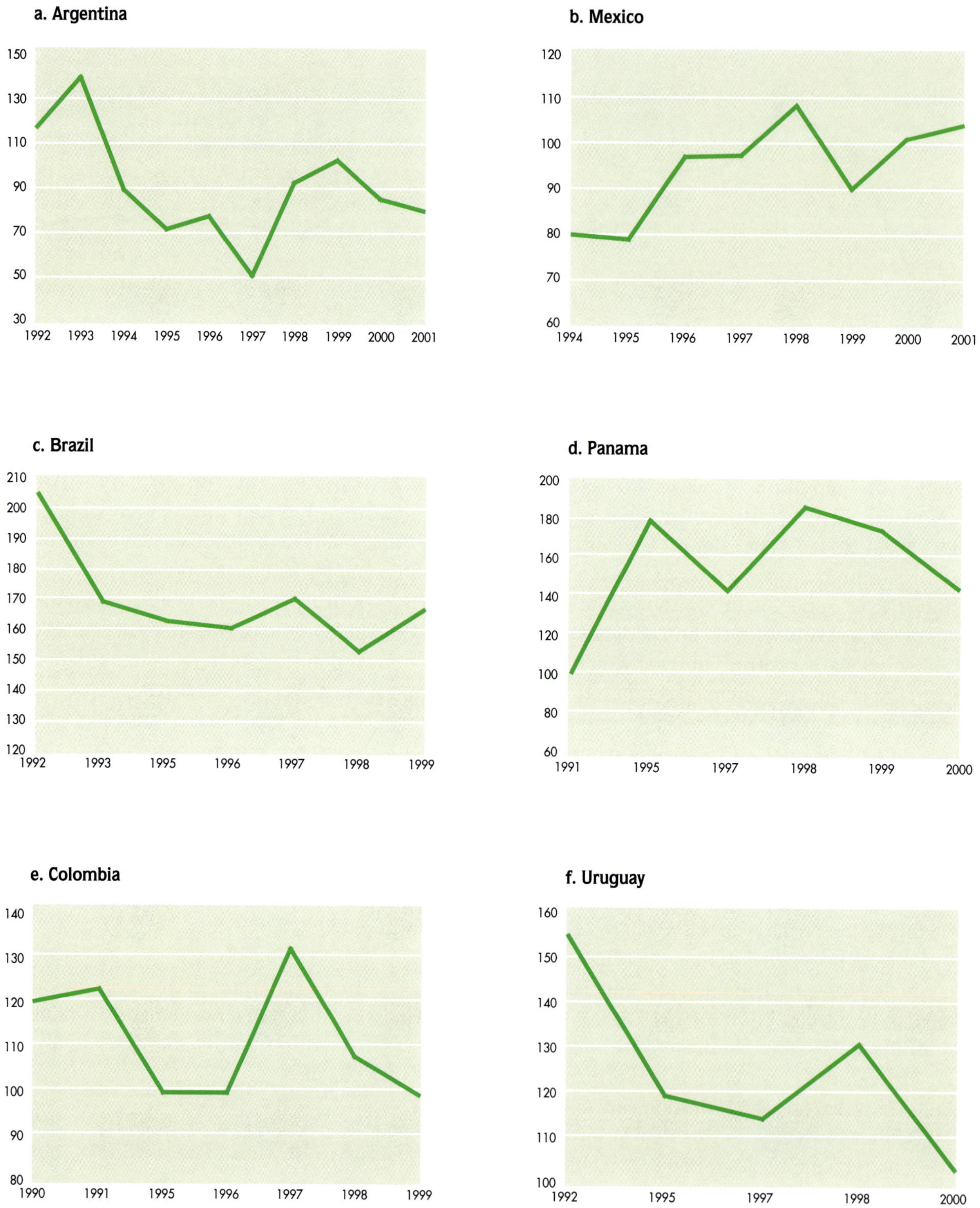

Note: Sample includes only salaried workers.
Source: IDB calculations based on household surveys.

Figure 6.9 Evolution of Relative Supply of Technical Workers
(Percent)

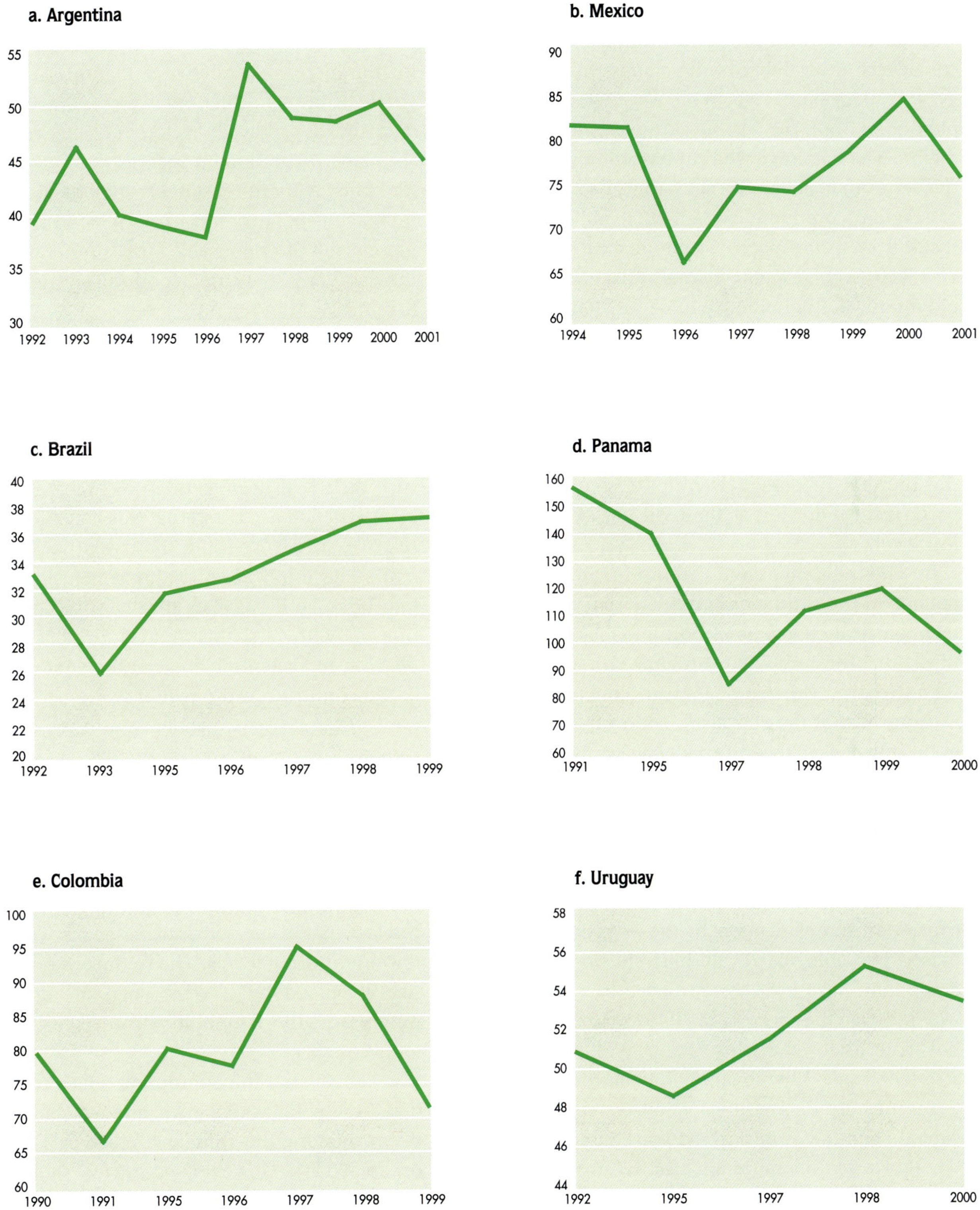

Note: Sample includes only salaried workers.
Source: IDB calculations based on household surveys.

Conclusion

This chapter has discussed the role of technology in labor markets in Latin America. In particular, it has considered the validity of the claims that technology is responsible for stagnant wages, rising unemployment, and the rising skill premium in the region. The data reviewed support the first claim in the sense that stagnant wages appear to be a result of stagnant productivity, which itself could well result from a slow pace of technological change.

The second claim, namely that rising unemployment is the consequence of technological progress, is clearly rejected by the data: it is not the case that countries with high TFP levels have lower employment rates, nor is it true that countries experiencing faster TFP growth have lower or declining employment rates. The same conclusion emerges if the number of personal computers per capita is used (instead of TFP) as the indicator of technological level.

The evidence and literature reviewed in regards to the third claim, namely that skill-biased technological change is responsible for the increasing skill premium in the region, are mixed and inconclusive. However, a clear conclusion that emerges is that the simplistic notion that trade liberalization has allowed firms to import production automation equipment that has replaced unskilled labor, and that this has led to the rising relative demand for skilled workers (especially in technical areas) is clearly wrong.

First, it is not clear that trade liberalization has caused an intensification in the adoption of skill-biased technologies. Trade barriers for importing equipment have not been removed in a significant way because they were already low. Moreover, it is not true that countries that have engaged in stronger trade liberalization have experienced a faster increase in imported capital as a share of total capital. And the empirical evidence is not clear on whether trade liberalization has led to faster technological adoption through other mechanisms (such as increased competition).

Second, the evidence rejects the notion that adoption of production automation technologies in manufacturing plants has led to an increase in skill intensity in those plants. More importantly, given the small and declining size of the manufacturing sector in the region, it is difficult to make the case that something specific to this sector is responsible for the increasing relative demand for skills in the whole economy. This conclusion is strengthened by data showing that all sectors, not just manufacturing, have experienced increased relative demand for skills. A more reasonable hypothesis is that the increasing penetration of information technology has caused the rising skill intensity in all sectors of the economy. But this hypothesis awaits clear confirmation in the region.

Third, the evidence does not support the claim that the relative demand for skilled workers is concentrated in workers with technical skills, as opposed to more general skills. Data from various countries show that the relative wages of workers with technical degrees or in technical occupations have not increased, and that this is not due to rising relative supply keeping their relative wages stagnant. The implication of this conclusion is important because it suggests that it would be wrong at this point to push for greater emphasis on engineering and scientific areas in the education efforts of the countries in the region.

Without a clear understanding of the specific causes of the rising skill premium, it is difficult to draw specific policy recommendations to deal with this phenomenon. But this should not be the main issue regarding technology and labor markets in the region. Of much greater importance than the rising relative wage of workers with tertiary education is the fact that wages have stagnated for workers with lower education levels. The finding that this is most likely caused by a slow pace of technological progress in the region should receive much more attention.

This is not the appropriate place to discuss in detail the policies that governments could follow to improve along this dimension (see de Ferranti and others 2003). However, countries should devote more energy to develop higher education systems that respond rapidly and effectively to the productive sector's demand for labor. Just as education policies by themselves are not the solution to the labor market problems affecting the region (as discussed in chapter 3), it is also true that without strong universities graduating high-quality professionals that respond to the needs of the private sector, it is doubtful that the region would improve its track record in terms of technology adoption and innovation. Moreover, a more responsive higher education system could prevent relative wages from deviating much in the medium term.

Given that the education sector is plagued by market imperfections, the role of the government is crucial. But public intervention in this area has not necessarily done much good: it is common to find governments transferring large sums of money to public universities that end up allocating these resources without placing adequate weight on private sector demand. As long as governments continue to transfer resources to public universities (and there are arguably good reasons for continuing to do so), it is important to make sure that these resources have a high social rate of return.

In this area, small changes could go a long way. For example, governments could slow the rate of growth of these transfers and allocate the freed-up resources toward projects in which universities collaborate with the private sector in terms of curriculum design, teacher training, investment in equipment, and research. This would help in promoting closer cooperation between universities and private sector associations at the sector level, so that the training provided by the universities would closely match the needs of firms. This collaboration should extend to national training institutes and technical schools.

Beyond public universities, governments should pay attention to improving the functioning of the higher education market. It is crucial to establish a system to improve information flows and decisionmaking regarding education choices. Prospective students should have better information about the labor market conditions (wages and the probability of employment) for various careers and universities. They should have better information regarding the quality of public and private universities, through a system of voluntary certification of universities and educational programs. And they should have access to loans in order to act on this information. These are all areas where government intervention could foster high returns.

Appendix 6.1 Decomposition of Growth in Labor Productivity

This appendix explains the analysis behind columns (2) and (3) in Appendix Table 6.1. As is customary in the literature, the analysis assumes a Cobb-Douglas production function in which labor's share is two-thirds: $Y = K^{1/3} (AL)^{2/3}$, Y is output, K is the capital stock, L is the quantity of workers, and A is a variable that captures the level of technology. This production function can be rearranged so that: $Y/L = TFP(K/L)^{1/3}$, where $TFP = A^{2/3}$. Taking logs and differentiating with respect to time yields the usual growth decomposition equation:

$$g = g(TFP) + (1/3)g(K/L)$$

where g is the growth rate of labor productivity, $g(TFP)$ is the growth rate of TFP, and $g(K/L)$ is the growth rate of the capital-labor ratio.

The problem with this approach is that part of the growth of the capital-labor ratio could be due to technological change. To see this, note that the rate of return to capital is $(1/3)A^{2/3}(K/L)^{-2/3}$, which is the marginal product of K in the production function above. As A increases, the rate of return to capital increases, and the natural consequence is more capital accumulation. It is natural to assume that in equilibrium the rate of return to capital is constant; for this to be the case, an increase in A requires a proportional increase in the capital-labor ratio. Thus, the decomposition above attributes to capital deepening what is really a contribution of technology.

There is another way to see this same point. Consider a model in which A and L grow at constant and exogenous rates g_A and g_L, respectively. Given the usual equation for the accumulation of capital ($\dot{K} = I - \delta K$, where $\dot{K}$ is the time derivative of K and δ is the rate of depreciation of capital), it can be shown that the capital-output ratio is given by:

$$\frac{K}{Y} = \frac{s}{g_A + g_L + \delta}$$

where s is the investment rate, assumed constant here. If the savings rate does not increase, the capital-output ratio does not increase. But the capital-labor ratio depends on both A and the capital-output ratio: $K/L = A(K/Y)^{3/2}$. Thus, even with a constant investment rate, an increase in A would lead to an increase in the capital-labor ratio.

This argument suggests a different decomposition, which comes from noting that $Y/L = A(K/Y)^{1/2}$. This leads to the following growth decomposition:

$$g = g(A) + (1/2)g(K/Y).$$

The benefit of this second approach is that, in contrast to the capital-labor ratio, the capital-output ratio does not depend on A. For instance, if all that happens is that A increases by 10 percent, then it would be expected that the capital-labor ratio would also increase by 10 percent. In the traditional decomposition, the increase in labor productivity is explained by both growth in TFP and growth in the capital-labor ratio. In this alternative decomposition, all the growth would be accounted for by growth in A.

This decomposition is shown in columns (2) and (3) in Appendix Table 6.1, where $g(A)$ is labeled technology and $g(K/Y)$ is labeled capital deepening.

Appendix 6.2 Growth in Labor Productivity across Countries and Time

This appendix explains the statistical analysis to uncover differences across countries and subperiods in the growth rates of labor productivity and its two components (technology and capital deepening). The analysis assumes that the growth rate of labor productivity in each country in each subperiod is the result of three elements: a country-specific element that is common across the three subperiods, a subperiod-specific element that is common across all countries, and a country and subperiod-specific element.

In other words, the analysis assumes that:

$$g_{ct} = \alpha + \gamma_c + \gamma_t + \varepsilon_{ct}$$

where g_{ct} is the growth rate of the variable of interest (labor productivity, the level of technology, or the capital-output ratio divided by two), subscript c denotes the country and subscript t denotes time (subperiod), and γ_c and γ_t are country and subperiod dummies. The associated regression was run imposing the constraints that both the sum of the country dummy coefficients and the sum of the subperiod dummy coefficients equal 0. In this way, the coefficients of the country and subperiod dummies can be interpreted as deviations from the sample means.

The results of this exercise reveal that only Chile and the Dominican Republic have rates of growth of labor productivity that are statistically higher than the sample mean, whereas Nicaragua has a growth rate of labor productivity that is statistically lower than the sample mean. For Chile and the Dominican Republic, the higher-than-average growth rates are due to statistically higher-than-average contributions from technology, not capital deepening. The reverse is true for Nicaragua.

The results for the subperiod dummies are interesting. Appendix Table 6.1 shows that there are no statistically significant differences across subperiods in the growth rate of labor productivity or the contribution from technology. Capital deepening made a statistically negative contribution in 1990-95 and a statistically positive contribution in 1995-2000.

Appendix Table 6.1 Subperiod Effects on Growth in Labor Productivity, 1985–2000

Subperiod	Labor productivity	Technology	Capital deepening
1985–90	–0.005	–0.004	–0.001
	(0.004)	(0.006)	(0.005)
1990–95	0.001	0.007	–0.010
	(0.004)	(0.006)	(0.005)**
1995–2000	0.003	–0.002	0.012
	(0.004)	(0.006)	(0.005)**
F tests of differences across subperiods			
1985–90 vs. 1990–95	0.67	1.04	1.28
1985–90 vs. 1995–2000	1.19	0.03	2.54
1990–95 vs. 1995–2000	0.07	0.71	7.43**

** Significant at 5 percent.
Note: t-statistics are in parentheses.
Source: IDB calculations.

Appendix 6.3 The Implied Relative Demand for Skills

Is there a generalized trend in the demand for different skill groups? Consider N skill groups and M countries. Output is produced according to the following CES production function:

$$Y_{jt} = \left(\sum_{i=1}^{N} (A_{ijt} L_{ijt})^{\sigma} \right)^{1/\sigma}$$

where L_{jit} is the quantity used of labor type $i = 1, 2, \ldots N$ in country $j = 1, 2, \ldots M$ at time t, and where the elasticity of substitution among labor types is $\varepsilon = -1/(1 - \sigma)$ with $\sigma < 1$. Equality of supply and demand for labor type i at time t implies the following:

$$w_{ijt} = Y_{jt}^{1-\sigma} A_{ijt}^{\sigma} L_{ijt}^{\sigma-1}.$$

Dividing the wage of labor type i by the wage of labor type 1 and taking logs gives the following:

$$\ln\left(\frac{w_{ijt}}{w_{1jt}}\right) = \sigma \ln\left(\frac{A_{ijt}}{A_{1jt}}\right) - (1 - \sigma) \ln\left(\frac{L_{ijt}}{L_{1jt}}\right).$$

Assuming a particular value for σ, say 0.5 (so that $\varepsilon=-2$) or 1/3 (so that $\varepsilon=-1.5$), and using data for the left-hand side of the equation and the second term on the right-hand side, the implied $\ln(A_{ijt}/A_{1jt})$ for each skill group/country/year triplet can be calculated.

Chapter 7

Labor Market Regulations and Institutions

Labor laws regulate the conditions of wage employment by establishing the types of contracts that can be issued to workers, the length of the workweek, conditions for dismissal, conditions under which contracts can be negotiated collectively, wage floors, and other aspects of the relationship between employees and employers. In some instances, the stated objective of this wide body of rules is to increase the bargaining power of workers; in others, the aim is to balance social, economic, and political objectives. However, judging from the level of contention and disagreement that these laws generate in the region, the balance has seemingy not been achieved. Many employers, economists, and politicians claim that labor regulations impede the ability of labor markets to function well. They argue that, by setting conditions that are not market driven, regulations may force some workers out of work; cause inefficient allocations of employment across sectors, firms, and plants; and drive workers and firms to evade labor laws. Moreover, by impeding the normal functioning of labor markets, regulations may reduce productivity growth. Against this negative backdrop, others point to worrisome high levels of inequality, employment instability, and deplorable labor conditions; they argue that without regulations, work conditions, job stability, and social protection would be even worse.

This chapter documents the nature of regulations and labor market institutions in Latin America and the Caribbean relative to other regions. It also examines the effects of regulations and labor market institutions on the behavior of labor markets in the region. To what extent do regulations and institutions alter the functioning of labor markets? Could labor markets do without them? Are the high rates of unemployment observed in some countries a consequence of poorly designed regulations and institutions? Do regulations force workers and firms to evade labor laws? Is there a trade-off between flexibility and workers' welfare, and if so, in which areas, and what can be done about it?

The chapter borrows from a growing literature that examines the effects of regulations and institutions on multiple dimensions of the labor market. The main conclusions are the following. First, regulations are necessary in labor markets. The issue is not how or when to deregulate, but which set of rules and regulations will improve the functioning of labor markets and whether the rules and regulations already in place achieve such goals. Second, by international standards, Latin American countries have highly protective regulations in labor codes; however, their effect is diluted by the high rates of evasion and noncompliance. Third, although regulations and institutions have the potential to generate welfare gains and improve the functioning of the labor market, oftentimes they do not do so, but instead create winners and losers. Mandatory benefits and minimum wages, for example, can bring welfare gains if they are set at levels consistent with overall economic conditions, but may cause loss of employment when they are set above such levels. Severance payments might help unemployed workers, but at the same time reduce the employment rates of young and unskilled workers. Unions can benefit their members but also reduce investment and growth. The bottom line is that regulations and institutions do not always work in favor of those that they are meant to protect. Policymakers should carefully evaluate the costs and benefits of regulatory changes.

Two fundamental questions feed the debate on regulations. The first, a favorite of economists, asks whether the labor market needs regulations. From the point of view of economic analysis, with the right set of conditions in place, labor markets by themselves and without intervention would be expected to deliver efficient outcomes. The second question asks what determines labor market regulations. That is, do the rules that govern labor markets respond to market failures or to political, cultural, or legal pressures? Such pressures may have little to do with improving the functioning of labor markets but may still be important for achieving desirable social outcomes. For example, redistributing income from employers to workers or from one group of workers to another might be a desirable social outcome, but labor markets that do this might produce high unemployment or discriminate against certain types of workers. In the worst-case scenario, these outcomes could undo the benefits intended by the law.

Do regulations help or hinder labor markets? To assess whether they could be expected to work without regulations, it is useful to describe how a well-behaved labor market would work. In such an ideal market, many workers would compete for comparable jobs and many firms would compete for comparable workers. Informed workers would examine their options and accept offers of employment that provided the best labor conditions and the highest wages for the same expected effort. Firms that offered poor labor conditions might not be able to hire workers or might lose workers to other firms. Therefore, all firms would end up offering similar wages for similar work. This process would ensure that wages equaled the value of workers' marginal product (that is, the value of the goods and services that they produce). However, this unregulated labor market would not necessarily ensure adequate conditions and wages for all workers; those with less education or ability might produce little and therefore be paid little in the market.

Although this streamlined depiction of the labor market is useful for describing some aspects of labor market behavior, many other aspects, particularly in developing countries, do not square well with this textbook scenario. For instance, most workers do not have the resources to sustain long periods of job search, reducing their ability to look for the best jobs available. Workers may not have the resources to move to where the jobs are, reducing the competition for jobs and workers in the labor market. Moreover, barriers to the entry of firms in the market, either in the form of credit constraints or red tape, reduce the number of vacancies available to workers. Pervasive market failures mean that labor markets alone would not offer the conditions for workers (and firms) warranted under the perfect market scenario. Therefore, the fundamental question is not how or when to deregulate, but *which set of rules and regulations will improve the functioning of labor markets and whether the rules and regulations already in place achieve such goals.* Box 7.1 lists some guiding principles for labor market regulations.

This chapter relies on new original evidence on whether different types of regulations affect key labor market variables such as job creation and destruction, net employment growth, unemployment, employment rates, wages, the percentage of workers covered by employment laws, and the percentage of self-employed workers. The chapter looks at regulations and institutions in four areas: (1) working conditions, (2) job security, (3) the minimum wage, and (4) labor unions.

Box 7.1 Principles for Designing Labor Regulations

Be Clear about the Objectives

Regulations should ensure balance so that the fundamental rights of workers are protected and yet the labor market is allowed to function adequately. Likewise, the objectives pursued must be distinguished from the instruments for attaining them. Depending on the economic, social, and institutional situation of a country, some instruments are more appropriate for reaching the desired objectives.

Identify the Market Imperfection to Be Resolved

Policymakers should address the issue of how and why the market fails and how regulations would improve the situation.

Analyze Who Gains and Who Loses

Labor legislation must consider the possible beneficiaries as well as who might lose and by how much. Regulations can cause some groups of workers to gain in terms of employment or wages, but they can also make other workers lose. The difficult job for policymakers is to find a compromise between costs and benefits.

Ensure That Compliance Is Feasible

Protection cannot seek to grant benefits that cannot be sustained given productivity, overall economic conditions, and workers' preferences. Large disparities between workers' wages and preferences and the benefits that the law supposedly grants may lead workers and companies to ultimately evade such payments, thereby leading to informal employment.

Understand That Labor Costs Are Set by the Market

Legislation establishes who nominally pays social benefits, that is, whether it is the employer or the worker. Who really pays over the long run, however, depends on the conditions of the market.

Increase the Share of Workers with Benefits

Regulations should aim for the principle of universality. They will be easier to comply with the greater the correspondence between the benefits granted by the law and the possibility of granting them to workers.

Consider the Impact on Investment and Growth

Calculations of costs and benefits of legislation should include the net number of jobs gained or lost, the change in productivity, the effect of the regulations on the growth of the economy, and their effect on the well-being of workers.

Promote Increased Productivity

Increased productivity is the main mechanism for raising wages. Therefore, legislation should assure that incentives are established so that both companies and workers will invest in technology and training as a way to increase productivity.

Allow for Flexibility

Legislation should be sufficiently flexible so that it can be corrected should unforeseen, undesired effects be detected. Labor legislation will be more flexible the greater is the separation between objectives and instruments. Ideally the objectives should be formulated based on social consensus with a medium or long-range horizon, while it should be possible to vary the instruments in the short and medium run if their design hinders the attainment of the objectives sought or imposes great costs on particular groups.

Source: Pagés and Saavedra (2002).

Social Security Regulations

A large share of labor market regulations aims at setting minimum standards for the conditions of wage employment. Another important group of regulations establishes conditions for qualifying for social security benefits and the contributions to such programs. Although different in nature, both sets of regulations mandate some transfer from the employer to the worker, which might be in the form of a paid vacation, overtime premium, or contribution to a social security program. Employers often argue that providing these benefits makes hiring workers less attractive. For many others, regulations are essential for keeping the workplace humane.

How Does Latin America Compare with Other Regions?

Labor laws in Latin America are protective by international standards. Figure 7.1 provides a comparison of an index of conditions of employment in world regions and Latin American countries. Higher values of the index indicate a greater number of regulations and more protective regulations for workers. The index captures what is written in the laws and regulations of each country on the maximum number of hours in a workweek, overtime work, night shifts, holidays, hours of work, maternity leave, other types of leave, and vacation days.[1] It should be emphasized that this is a "de jure" indicator, that is, it does not reflect whether these regulations are enforced; it only measures conditions according to the letter of the law.

Surprisingly, less developed countries have more statutory working conditions than developed countries do. Latin America is only surpassed by Eastern Europe and Central Asia in its level of de jure protection of workers. Within Latin America, the labor codes of Bolivia, Venezuela, Brazil, and Panama provide the most protective working conditions to workers. Jamaica, Uruguay, and Chile have the least protective regulations. Both across world regions and within Latin America, regulation of employment conditions tends to be more protective in countries that are poorer and in those with a legal system based on French civil law (Djankov and others 2003).

Social security benefits (and contributions) are lower in Latin America and other developing countries than in developed countries. In Figure 7.2, the social security index is the sum of three indices summarizing benefits received from old age pensions, health, and maternity and unemployment insurance programs.[2] The index takes a greater value for programs with greater benefits and for those with greater benefits relative to contributions. According to this measure, social security regulations are less protective of workers in Latin America than in English-speaking developed countries and countries in Eastern Europe and Central Asia. However, the index for Latin America is higher than for other developing regions, including East Asia. Within Latin America, Jamaica, Bolivia, and Peru have the lowest social security benefits, whereas Colombia, Panama, and Argentina have the highest level of protection, with levels that are above the average in English-speaking developed countries.

Figure 7.1 Conditions of Employment
(Index, 0-1)

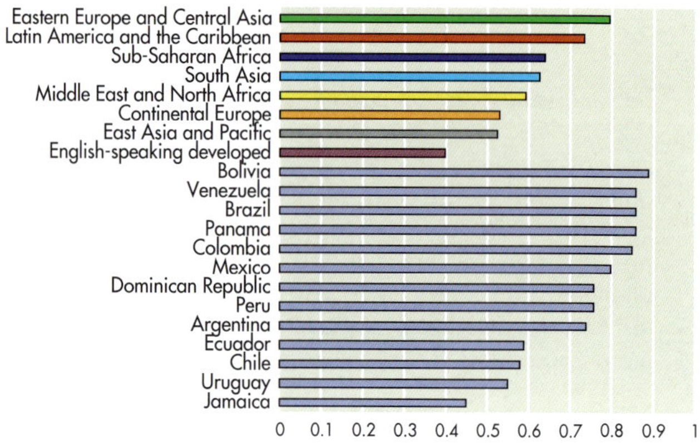

Source: Djankov and others (2003).

These indicators suggest that, at least on paper, Latin America is well endowed with laws and regulations aimed at improving the welfare of workers. The indicators also suggest that, in many aspects, lawmakers in Latin America have gone above and beyond the levels provided in other countries. Are Latin American labor markets overburdened by these regulations?

Cost of Regulations

If regulations that seek to improve working conditions and benefits did exactly that at no cost, the task of lawmakers would be rather simple. They would just have to agree on which benefits the laws

---

[1] See Djankov and others (2003) for more on calculating this measure.

[2] The source of this index is Djankov and others (2003). The index is the normalized sum of the following components: the difference between retirement age and life expectancy; months of contributions required for normal retirement; contributions to pensions, disability, health, and unemployment insurance programs; the replacement rate for pensions; the replacement rate for health insurance benefits; months of contributions to qualify for health insurance benefits; and the waiting period for health insurance benefits.

Figure 7.2 Social Security
(Index, 0-1)

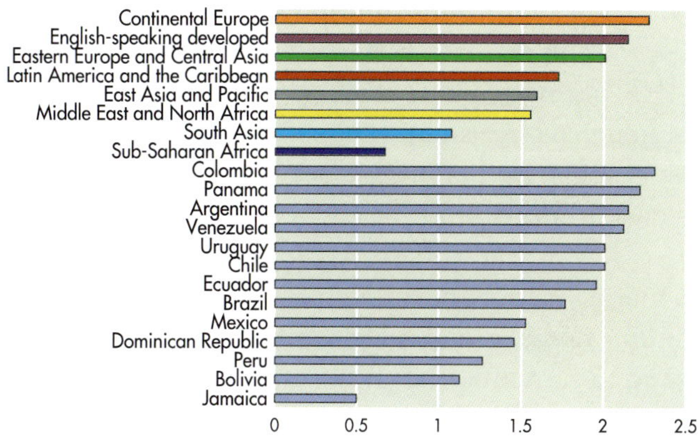

Source: Djankov and others (2003).

and regulations should address and provide resources for enforcement. Unfortunately, it is not that simple. Regulations are mandatory transfers from employers to employees and the effect of such regulations on labor market outcomes depends on who effectively bears the cost of such transfers. A transfer does not necessarily imply an extra cost for employers or a disincentive to hire labor; this would depend on whether employers are able to transfer the costs to workers in the form of lower pay.

Consider, for example, a new regulation that increases mandatory holiday time from two to four weeks. Would this provision be a gift for workers and an extra burden for employers? Employers would likely respond by offering lower wages to new hires to compensate for the increase in costs. Some workers would find the lower wages unacceptable and would withdraw from the labor market, while others would be willing to work for lower wages because they valued the extra vacation time. If workers were willing to take a pay cut exactly equivalent to two weeks of salary, total output would decline and leisure time would increase, but employers would not bear any extra cost. Alternatively, if workers were willing to take a pay cut equal to less than two weeks of pay, employment and wages would decline and the cost of the regulation would be borne partly by workers (via lower wages) and partly by firms (via higher costs). Thus, the incidence of a mandatory transfer is not determined by regulations but by the workings of the labor market.

One implication of this analysis is that regulations that mandate benefits for which workers have a high willingness to pay will increase the welfare of workers without affecting the labor market, while regulations or benefits for which workers have little desire will lead to loss of jobs. This is particularly relevant in the case of contributions to social security programs. In many countries in Latin America, demographic trends and actuarial imbalances imply that workers would get less out of such programs than they did in the past, while contributions rise (Lora and Pagés 1997). These effects might reduce the willingness of workers to pay for social security programs.

Another implication is that if minimum wages or other wage floors prevented the adjustment of wages, regulations that in principle could be neutral might reduce employment and increase unemployment. This suggests that similar regulations could have different effects across countries due to interactions with other regulations.

Empirical Evidence

What is the empirical evidence on these effects? Are workers willing to pay for benefits? Does employment decline substantially after regulations increase benefits? Drawing on the empirical evidence, it is important to assess the existence and magnitude of possible trade-offs between mandatory benefits and employment.

A simple and telling empirical exercise correlates measures of regulations with labor market and economic performance measures across a sample of Latin American and developed countries. The results give an indication of whether countries with more stringent regulations have better or worse performance. Since the level of development of a country is correlated with performance, the analysis controls for per capita gross domestic product (GDP). The results reported in Appendix Table 7.1 suggest that more protective working conditions and higher social security contributions (and benefits) are correlated with lower employment rates and lower employment growth across countries. The correlation with unemployment is positive but not statistically significant, suggesting that losses in aggregate employment result in people withdrawing from the labor force rather than remaining unemployed. However, higher social security benefits are correlated with a higher percentage of long-term unemployed workers (one year or more). This is consistent with a picture in which higher contributions and benefits lead to lower job creation and greater difficulty in finding jobs.

The evidence also suggests that more protective conditions of employment increase self-employment. Thus, there is some evidence that the higher are the transfers mandated from firms to workers, the lower is the creation of jobs in the wage employment sector. There is no evidence, however, that higher social security contributions lead to more self-employment.[3] Finally, there is some correlation at the cross-country level between higher social security benefits and lower total factor productivity growth.

Although these correlations are suggestive, they are based on a limited number of countries and observations. Some other studies provide results based on more disaggregated data or longer time horizons. For example, Heckman and Pagés (forthcoming) survey the existing literature on the effects of mandatory benefits and social security contributions on wages and employment. They conclude that, "All in all, the available evidence for Latin America suggests that at least part of the cost of non-wage benefits is passed on to workers in the form of lower wages." A few studies find evidence that workers pay for the entirety of benefits, but the majority find that employers bear a share of the cost.[4] According to Heckman and Pagés, based on a panel of cross-country and time-series information for Latin America and developed countries, in Latin America, workers absorb between 52 and 90 percent of the cost while employers pay the rest.

There are effects on employment as well. Heckman and Pagés estimate that an increase of 10 percentage points in social security contributions leads to a 1.7 percentage point decline in overall employment-to-population rates. Although these effects are much smaller than the ones that would be obtained if employers bore all the cost, they are still significant. These estimates are consistent with those obtained from individual country studies and the regressions reported in Appendix Table 7.1. Therefore, the evidence is fairly robust that although a large share of benefits is likely to be paid by employees, mandatory benefit regulations have a cost in terms of lower employment.

Given that workers pay for a large share of the benefits, it could be argued that labor market regulations do not really make workers better off. However, this argument does not take into account that regulations may help to achieve results that could not be attained by individuals in an uncoordinated manner. For instance, a worker might be willing to negotiate a pay cut in exchange for paid leave, but may not dare to do so for fear of being labeled as lazy or uncommitted by the employer. If all workers wanted more vacation time but individually could not attain such a goal, a labor market regulation that specified minimum vacation time would likely to be welfare enhancing even if workers fully paid for such a benefit.

However, a country would suffer from excessive regulation if lawmakers went beyond what workers were willing to pay or contribute in order to achieve those benefits. This issue is particularly relevant in the context of low and middle-income countries. If poorer people value the goods that can be afforded with cash income (such as food, clothing, and housing) more than richer people do, overly ambitious regulations might reduce wages below what poor workers would be willing (or able) to accept. In this case, workers might be willing to exchange lower protection for higher wages.

Excessive protection may be part of the explanation of why compliance with social security regulations is low. As mentioned in chapter 1, three out of five workers in Latin America are not cov-

[3] It would have been useful to correlate mandatory benefit measures with the percentage of workers in the social security system; however, these data are available for only a few countries.

[4] Gruber (1994) for the United States and Gruber (1997a) for Chile find that workers bear all the costs. Mondino and Montoya (forthcoming) and MacIsaac and Rama (1997) find that the cost is shared by employers and employees.

Figure 7.3 Percentage of Wage Employees without Social Security Benefits, 1990s

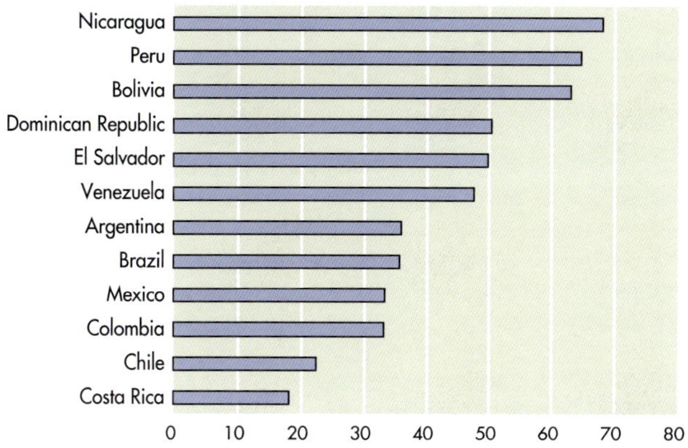

Source: IDB household surveys.

ered by mandatory social security programs. This is not just because a large share of workers is self-employed and therefore not required to contribute.[5] Fifty percent or more of employees are not covered in Nicaragua, Peru, Bolivia, the Dominican Republic, and El Salvador (see Figure 7.3). Excessive protection may also explain why in Latin America it is less likely that social insurance programs cover poorer workers than middle or higher-income workers. Of course, an alternative explanation is that low-income workers are more likely to be employed in firms that evade regulations, but then it would be necessary to explain why poorer workers are concentrated in these firms to begin with. Excessive protection may also explain why younger workers (who are likely to be covered by the contributions of other members of the household) are less likely to be covered than prime-age and older workers.

Table 7.1 and Figure 7.4 show some regularity in the coverage of social security programs in Latin America. Encouragingly, male and female wage workers have on average the same coverage rate. However, coverage increases with the level of education. On average, while only 45 percent of workers with incomplete primary education are protected, coverage increases to 85 percent for workers with at least some tertiary education (Figure 7.4, panel a).

Across industries, agriculture and construction are the least protected sectors (around 40 percent coverage), while the utility, community and social services, and financial services sectors have high coverage (around 70 percent on average). In addition, 67 percent of urban workers are protected, compared with 52 percent of rural workers (Figure 7.4, panel b).

The head of the family is more protected than the spouse, siblings, and other relatives living in the same house. Social security programs protect the prime-age worker more than the young: coverage increases from 52 percent for workers between 15 and 24 years old to 71 percent for workers between 24 and 49 (Figure 7.4, panel c).

Finally, only 20 percent of workers in very small firms (fewer than five employees) are protected; 82 percent of workers are protected in companies with more than 100 employees. Coverage is biased toward high-wage earners: while only 25 percent of workers who earn the minimum wage have coverage, 80 percent of workers with salaries greater than three times the minimum wage are protected (Figure 7.4, panel d).

Poor Performance in the 1990s

Is excessive regulation to fault for the poor performance of labor markets during the 1990s? Increased benefits have a cost in terms of total employment rates. They may also have a cost in terms of coverage of the system because many workers and firms may pull out of systems they cannot afford or to which they do not want to contribute. But what about the changes experienced during the 1990s? Do mandatory benefits explain the increase in unemployment and decline in covered employment?

Social security contributions increased in some countries (most noticeably in Colombia, El Salvador, Mexico, Uruguay, and Brazil) in the 1990s and this effect is likely to have increased unemployment rates. However, regressions of unemployment changes against changes in social security contributions and GDP growth confirm that social security contributions are positively associated with

[5] In some countries, contributions are also mandatory for self-employed workers.

Table 7.1 Social Security Coverage in Latin America

(Percentage of salaried employment)

Worker characteristic	Argentina 2001	Brazil 1999	Bolivia 1999	Costa Rica 2000	Chile 2000	Mexico 2001	Peru 2000
Gender							
Male	66.34	64.71	34.86	73.84	79.03	66.66	36.15
Female	60.69	63.57	40.80	68.18	72.82	68.22	33.17
Education							
No school		35.36		49.28	56.00	43.12	
Primary incomplete	37.36	46.13	15.11	55.49	59.21	45.94	14.38
Primary complete	50.31	59.21	5.46	64.63	67.07	56.71	17.71
Secondary incomplete	50.59	60.88	22.48	71.86	70.06	64.13	17.47
Secondary complete	71.69	81.80	40.48	84.99	82.29	79.71	30.53
At least some tertiary	79.61	88.64	61.51	90.07	88.84	79.83	55.80
Activity							
Agriculture, hunting, forestry, and fishing		31.91	5.98	62.69	61.36	40.81	6.27
Mining and quarrying	86.04	67.99		96.54	93.50	69.48	
Manufacturing	66.86	78.79	29.43	79.05	83.24	80.72	38.83
Electricity, gas, and water supply	86.03	94.25		94.62	89.34	91.04	
Construction	31.96	41.93	11.68	53.04	72.82	42.83	16.38
Wholesale and retail trade, hotels and restaurants	52.76	67.50	24.41	71.35	79.23	63.12	21.18
Transport and storage	57.17	78.18	17.08	74.53	73.39	53.67	20.63
Finance, insurance, real estate, and business	79.79	86.94			85.55	84.91	49.20
Community, social, and personal services	80.83	65.26	64.12	83.44	76.70	64.93	53.27
Age							
15–24	44.06	49.56	12.20	55.85	62.18	55.81	10.25
25–49	68.95	70.62	45.27	78.48	79.18	71.85	43.02
50–64	67.25	65.36	49.73	76.86	79.10	66.82	46.34
Location							
Urban	63.93	67.50	38.54	76.54	78.54	67.25	39.86
Rural		44.00	26.22	67.11	61.68		17.16
Family							
Head	71.44	70.09	43.46	81.58	81.96	71.56	43.27
Spouse	64.24	66.77	57.92	63.87	73.80	69.15	39.16
Children	54.67	56.51	19.00	63.60	70.69	61.49	26.01
Firm size[a] (number of workers)							
Very small	25.78	37.77	12.26	42.30	52.32	16.45	8.17
Small	57.80	62.07	14.22	61.60	70.34	46.03	27.46
Medium	81.57	85.43	42.24	76.09	79.55	74.90	49.81
Large	87.60		61.51	90.52	86.58	85.94	65.17
Very large	92.38		72.08		91.59	90.02	73.80
Wage (multiple of minimum wage)							
Less than 90 percent	50.41	11.65	10.58	62.46	53.53	18.68	11.63
90–120 percent	25.96	41.18	13.39	81.96	75.49	28.67	28.82
121–200 percent	45.39	60.03	16.68	87.55	84.64	42.50	43.68
200–300 percent	65.45	73.61	28.79	86.08	88.46	62.33	68.75
300 percent or more	77.26	83.66	55.67	77.85	82.39	76.66	67.54

[a] For Argentina and Mexico, very small firms have 1-5 workers; small firms, 6-15; medium firms, 16-50; large firms, 51-100; and very large firms, more than 100. For Brazil, very small firms have 1-5 workers; small firms, 6-10; and medium and other firms, 11 or more. For Bolivia, very small firms have 1-4 workers; small firms, 5-19; medium firms, 20-49; large firms, 50-99; and very large firms, more than 100. For Costa Rica, very small firms have 1-5 workers; small firms, 6-9; medium firms, 10-19; and large and very large firms, 20 or more. For Chile, very small firms have 1-5 workers; small firms, 6-9; medium firms, 10-49; large firms, 50-199; and very large firms, 200 or more. For Peru, very small firms have 1-5 workers; small firms, 6-10; medium firms, 11-50; large firms, 51-100; and very large firms, more than 100.

Source: IDB household surveys.

Figure 7.4 Percentage of Employed Wage Workers with Social Security by Category Median for Latin America

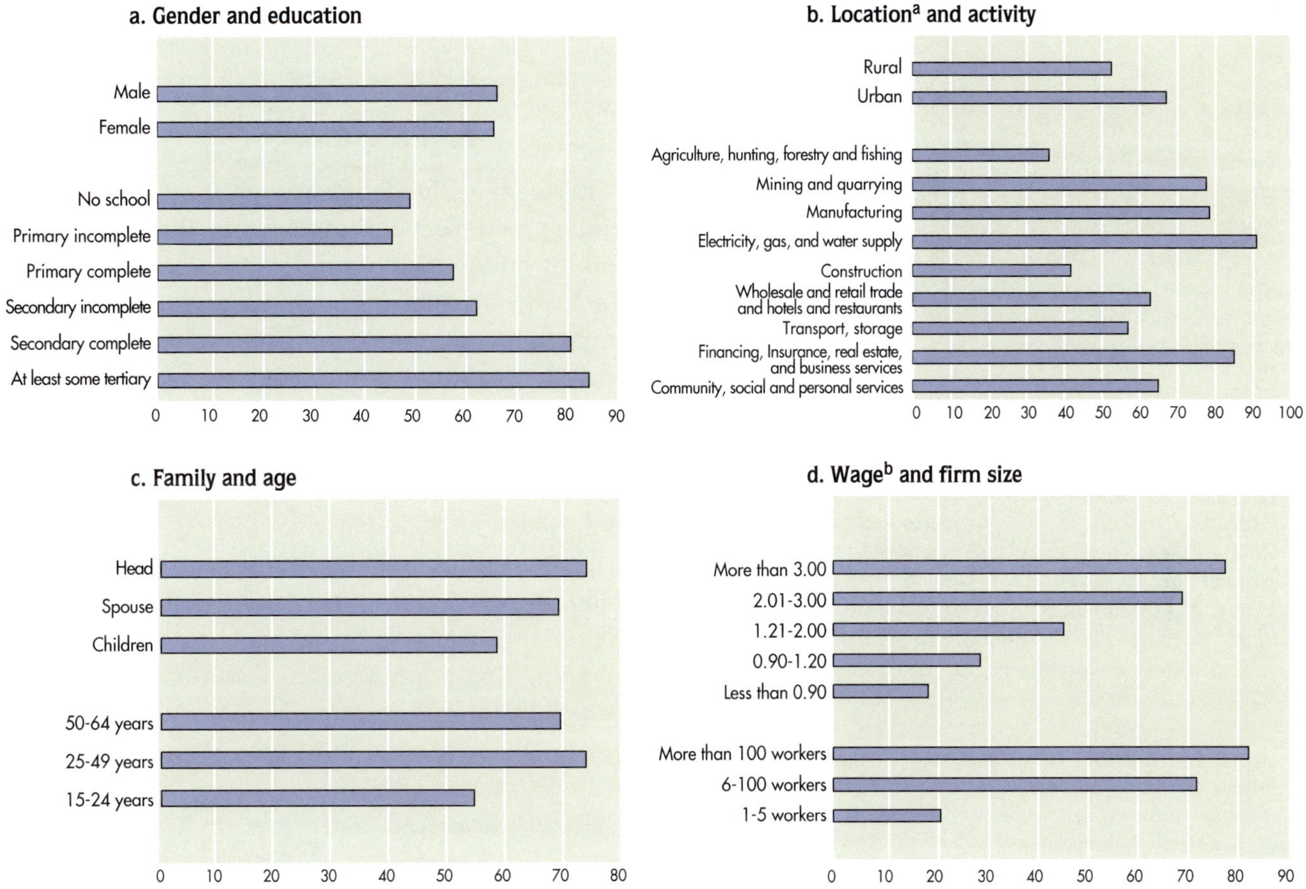

[a] Includes only countries for which national data are available.
[b] Multiple of minimum wage.
Note: The figure includes the countries and years in Table 7.1.
Source: IDB household surveys.

unemployment rates, but that the variance in unemployment explained by social security contributions is very low. This suggests that although social security regulations are relevant, other factors, such as low and volatile economic growth, have been more important in explaining the increase in unemployment rates. (See chapter 4 for an analysis of the relation between economic performance and unemployment.)

During the 1990s, many countries in the region implemented reforms transforming pay-as-you-go systems into full or partial capitalization systems. One of the advantages of such schemes is that they tend to increase the link between contributions and benefits; therefore, these schemes are likely to increase the willingness of workers to accept lower wages to participate in such programs. However, at the same time, in many countries, contributions had to increase in order to reduce actuarial imbalances. The effect of reforms on employment is therefore ambiguous: higher links between contributions and benefits may reduce employment costs while higher contributions can raise them.

There is no evidence that pension reforms have increased the willingness of workers or firms to pay for benefits. Heckman and Pagés (forthcoming) show that, if anything, the negative effect of social security contributions on employment increases after reforms. The explanation may lie in the fact that as workers move from pay-as-you-go to the capitalization system, their contributions not only finance individual accounts but also the pen-

Box 7.2 Effects of Mandatory Benefit Regulations

Indications

Mandatory benefit regulations provide valuable benefits for workers such as paid vacation, maternity leave, health benefits, pensions, work injury insurance, and unemployment insurance. The benefits are especially appropriate when private negotiation between workers and employers cannot achieve the same objective as mandatory regulation.

Side Effects

Benefits should be legislated with care because they can have undesired side effects. Benefits need to be valued by workers, that is, workers should be willing to pay for them in terms of lower wages. If mandated benefits are too high for workers and firms to afford, they are likely to seek to evade the law. Regulating mandatory benefits that are not compatible with workers' or firms' willingness to pay could cause the following side effects:

- In countries with good rule of law and enforcement, reduced employment, especially for young, female, and unskilled workers.

- In countries with poor enforcement, movement of workers, particularly young, female, and unskilled workers, into uncovered sectors without any protection. This is the case in many Latin American countries where ambitious mandatory benefit regulations result in good benefit packages for a few and no protection at all for the majority of workers.

Caution

After an increase in benefits, the following indicators should be monitored: employment and unemployment rates (particularly for female, young, and unskilled workers), wages, and coverage of benefits. This last indicator is especially important because a decline in the percentage of workers that have access to these benefits might be a signal that they are set too high.

sions of those left in the old system. That is, workers may have little willingness to pay for contributions that clearly fund someone else without offering anything in return.

Improving Mandatory Benefit Regulations

Mandatory benefit regulations improve the welfare of workers in the formal sector (see Box 7.2 for a summary of the benefits and costs of mandatory benefit regulations). However, in addition to the employment cost of these policies, the current system of protection *ends up excluding the majority of the workforce*. This is obviously a worrisome and inequitable situation, more so because there are few alternative ways to obtain protection against unemployment, sickness, or old age risk outside the national social security system. How can countries establish an appropriate level of protection for the widest possible majority of workers?

Countries should examine whether the level (and bundling) of benefits prescribed by their national labor code is optimal, with the understanding that more is not necessarily better. Thus, benefits that are too ambitious in relation to workers' level of productivity and wages may force many workers and firms to opt out and remain or become uncovered. Therefore, it is important to assess how benefits (and contributions) relate to wages and the size and nature of risk, and whether workers can buy or subscribe to different bundles depending on worker or industry characteristics. For instance, self-employed workers might be more likely to contribute to the social security system if they could buy disability insurance without contributing to the pension program. Unbundling the contributions to these programs could be a way to extend protection to uncovered workers. Similarly, separating health insurance from pension contributions could reduce the number of workers with no protection because health insurance tends to be in higher demand than old age insurance.

Another possible way to expand coverage would be to increase the resources devoted to enforcement. Adequate enforcement of laws and regulations is a pending subject in most Latin American countries. It should be made into a rule that any regulation or law has to be assigned the necessary resources to enforce it. However, it should also be made a rule that all regulations or laws should only be approved after an extensive analysis of their benefits and costs. The empirical evidence discussed above suggests that greater enforcement could bring greater compliance but at the cost of lower employment rates.

Finally, it is important to mention that, contrary to what is often argued, shifting the financing of social security systems from payroll contributions to income or consumption taxes is not likely to reduce the employment costs of such programs. First, workers might be more willing to pay for programs whose benefits they know and value than for general taxes whose uses are less well known. Second, if contributions are not valued (and therefore are considered taxes), then taxes on labor operate through the wedge between labor costs for employers and the net wage that a worker receives. In general, shifting from wage and payroll contributions to income or consumption taxes (by an equivalent amount) does not alter this difference. To see this, assume a country where workers and firms pay a contribution of 10 and gross wages are 95. In this economy, firms' cost of labor is 105, while net wages are 85. Assume now that a reform eliminates social security contributions and increases income taxes to 20. Since the workers are only willing to work for 85 or more and firms are only willing to employ at 105 or less, firms will pay wages of 105 and net wages will be 85. This implies that the reform would not alter the disemployment effects of the original policy; it only shifts the nominal burden of the tax.[6]

Job Security Regulations

One of the objectives of labor laws in Latin America, as well as in other parts of the world, is to promote job stability. Labor codes mandate a minimum advance notice period prior to termination, specify which causes justify dismissal, and establish the compensation to be awarded to workers (and paid by the firm) depending on the cause of termination. Labor codes also limit or forbid the use of contracts that can be terminated at no cost (such as temporary contracts). In some cases, labor codes require firms to be involved in lengthy consultations with the authorities prior to undertaking collective dismissals; in other cases, workers can be reinstated in their post if a labor court judges the cause of separation to be unfair.

Regulators seek to limit the dismissal of workers by making it costly for employers, especially when insurance, such as unemployment insurance, is not available. However, although some aspects of job security (such as advance notice and severance pay) can be considered an insurance mechanism, attempting to stabilize employment may have costs. Indeed, it is argued that excessive rigidity increases the cost of hiring labor, and that restrictions on hiring and firing are incompatible with a highly volatile economic environment. This section looks at whether Latin American countries have more or less job security provisions than other countries in the world. It also examines the extent to which claims of excessive rigidity are supported by the empirical evidence.

The analysis uses information gathered by Djankov and others (2003) to compare job security provisions across world regions. The job security index constructed by these authors is a normalized sum of the following four dimensions of protection: (1) whether employment at will is allowed and whether termination for economic reasons is considered a fair cause for dismissal, (2) procedures that an employer must follow and approvals it must seek prior to individual or collective dismissals, (3) advance notice and severance payments, and (4) whether job security is enshrined in a country's constitution. In Figure 7.5, Latin America and the Caribbean is the region with the most protected job security. English-speaking developed countries have the lowest levels of statutory protection. Within Latin America, Mexico, Peru, and Brazil exhibit high job security according to this measure, and Uruguay, Jamaica, and Chile have low job security.

[6] Shifting taxes from labor to total income will increase the price of capital relative to labor. However, if both the elasticity of substitution between capital and labor and the capital share of earnings are low, then a shift in the relative price of capital will not affect the employment costs of social security programs.

Figure 7.5 Job Security
(Index, 0-1)

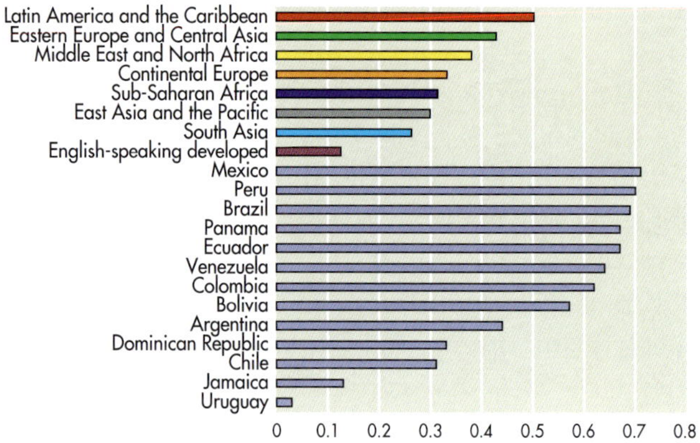

Source: Djankov and others (2003).

Figure 7.6 The Cost of Job Security, 1988 and 1999
(Multiple of monthly wage)

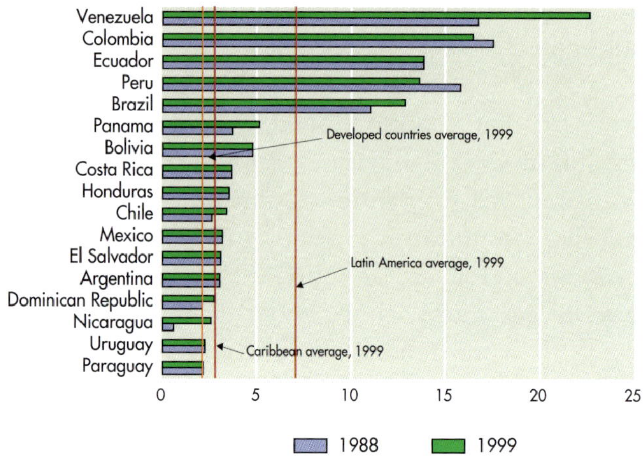

Source: Heckman and Pagés (forthcoming).

Heckman and Pagés (forthcoming) provide an alternative measure of job security that takes into account the monetary transfer that by law a firm has to pay to a worker on dismissal. The measure includes advance notice, severance pay, and mandatory contributions to individual savings accounts.[7] Other costs, such as those associated with consultations with the authorities prior to collective dismissals, are not considered. Although this is a less complete measure of employment security, it has the advantage that it records variations in time associated with recent labor reforms. In addition, it provides a measure of the level of benefits awarded to workers in case of separation.

Figure 7.6 summarizes the ranking of countries and the changes in regulation recorded by the Heckman and Pagés measure for Latin American countries. It shows that dismissing a worker in Latin America involves a larger mandatory transfer to the worker than it would in developed countries. However, the ranking of countries is somewhat different when job security is compared according to this measure. At the end of the 1990s, firms in Venezuela, Colombia, and Ecuador had the highest mandatory transfers to workers, and dismissed workers in Nicaragua, Paraguay, and Uruguay received the lowest benefits. Mexico, which ranks as highly protective according to Djankov and others (2003), appears relatively flexible in the Heckman and Pagés measure. This is because a large part of employment protection in Mexico comes in the form of lengthy procedural requirements rather than a high mandatory transfer.

Contrary to the common belief, employment protection for permanent workers did not weaken in most countries in the 1990s. At the end of the 1980s, labor reforms in Colombia and Peru reduced the total amount of the transfer to be paid to workers. In Brazil, Venezuela, Chile, the Dominican Republic, Nicaragua, and Panama, labor reforms increased this amount. However, in many cases, reforms increased one component of the transfer and reduced another one. Thus, for instance, Venezuela and Panama reduced severance pay considerably, but increased mandatory contributions (or payments) to individual savings accounts. In Colombia, reforms reduced the amount that firms paid to such savings accounts and increased severance payments for workers with more than 10 years of seniority.[8]

---

[7] In a number of countries in Latin America, labor codes mandate firms' periodic contributions to workers' individual accounts. The funds deposited in these accounts plus interest income can be withdrawn only in the event that a worker separates from a job either voluntarily or involuntarily.

[8] Reforms also eliminated these workers' right to sue for back pay and reinstatement; however, this is not captured in the index.

Patterns of job security across countries are inversely correlated with income levels (Heckman and Pagés forthcoming; Djankov and others 2003). This correlation suggests that poor countries make up for the lack of well-developed insurance markets or state-run unemployment insurance systems with mandatory job security provisions. For countries with weak institutions and states, it is easier to mandate firms to pay benefits to workers or to impose constraints on layoffs than to set up a system in which firms and workers contribute to an insurance pool from which workers draw when unemployed. The legal tradition of a given country is also an important determinant of its level of job security regulation. Countries that have adopted the French legal system, as most Latin American countries have, tend to have higher regulations than other countries have. The English-speaking Caribbean countries, which belong to the common-law legal system, tend to be less regulated.

Given the high levels of employment protection prevalent in Latin America (judging by the labor codes), it is important to assess its effects on the labor market. If such policies bring unwanted costs, then these effects are going to be more pervasive in Latin America than in other regions of the world.

In general, cross-country regressions of the two job security measures discussed above on a set of indicators of performance, controlling for income per capita, do not provide much evidence that job security regulations are significantly correlated with measures of performance. However, given the limited number of countries and periods, it is important to rely as well on other studies using more disaggregated data and longer time horizons. The following subsections summarize the literature on the effects of job security.

Turnover in the Labor Market

How do the high levels of de jure job security found in Latin America compare with actual turnover rates? Does higher employment protection increase job stability for Latin American workers? Since the main objective of job security laws is to make dismissals costly, it would be expected that countries with higher levels of employment protection would

Figure 7.7 Job Security and Annual Gross Job Flows

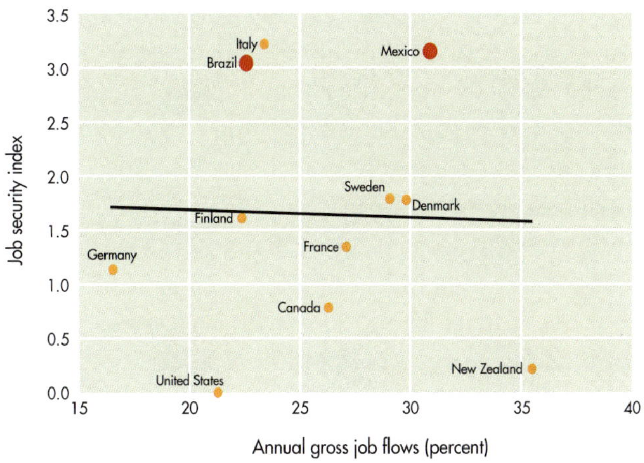

Source: Djankov and others (2003) for the job security index, and Figure 2.1 for annual gross job flows.

have lower turnover rates. Surprisingly, the comparison of turnover rates across countries does not show this effect. Figure 7.7 plots average turnover rates and the Djankov and others (2003) job security measure across a sample of OECD countries and two Latin American countries.

Job turnover is the sum of the job creation and job destruction figures for a given year. Job creation is computed as the percent increase in employment at the plant or establishment level for all plants whose employment increased over the course of the year, weighted by each plant or establishment's employment rate. Job destruction is computed in a similar manner. A job turnover rate of 25 percent indicates that one in four jobs is created or destroyed each year.[9]

One of the most remarkable stylized facts of labor markets across the world is that rates of job creation and job destruction are large regardless of the level of job security. For instance, countries with low employment protection, such as the United States and Canada, have similar turnover rates as Italy and France, which have higher job security. Moreover, Mexico and Brazil, which have higher employment protection than the United States,

[9] Chapter 2 offers a more extended discussion of job creation and destruction in Latin America.

both have higher turnover rates. This is particularly surprising considering that turnover rates for Mexico and Brazil are computed using data from social security registries that capture turnover in the formal sector. Does this imply that more protective job security measures do not reduce turnover in the labor market? The economic literature offers at least three explanations for this puzzling stylized fact.

First, Bertola and Rogerson (1997) explain the similar rates of job creation and destruction found in Continental Europe (rigid) and the United States and Canada (flexible). They argue that countries with high job security are also likely to have institutions that promote wage rigidity.

Second, job security provisions may not prevent firms from closing or downsizing their labor force in the face of permanent negative shocks. For instance, Albaek, Audenrode, and Browning (1999) compare the nature of mass layoffs in Belgium (high employment protection) with those in Denmark (low employment protection) and find that most of the layoffs in Denmark were attributed to firms adjusting their labor force, while in Belgium, a large share was attributed to firm closures. Blanchard and Portugal (2001) find evidence for OECD countries indicating that job security reduces short-term employment flows (that is, those computed between one quarter and the quarter before), while it may not affect yearly flows (computed between one year and the year before). This suggests that the main effect of job security on turnover may be to reduce short-term seasonal fluctuations and not the necessary reallocation induced by permanent shocks.

Third, crude measures such as gross job flows do not control for the size of macroeconomic shocks or other relevant differences across economies that may be important in determining turnover. Some recent studies suggest that, controlling for these differences, job security affects turnover in the expected way. For instance, Kugler (forthcoming) examines the effect of job security on the duration of employment in Colombia. She compares the average duration of a job before and after 1990, when a labor reform reduced certain components of job security. She finds that job instability increased after the reforms and that this change occurred across all sectors and not only in the tradable sectors (as would be expected if these changes were mostly caused by contemporaneous trade reforms). Gonzaga (2003) explores the effect of a constitutional reform in Brazil that substantially increased job security in 1988 on the ability of firms to adjust employment to economic shocks. Higher adjustment implies less job stability as firms swiftly modify their labor forces in response to economic shocks. Gonzaga finds that employment responded less to changes in economic activity after 1988. However, the change in the adjustment seems to be quite small.

Appendix 7.1 presents a measure of the speed of adjustment of employment levels following the methodology of Caballero and Engel (1993). This measure captures how swiftly employment in a given sector adjusts to changes in economic activity; it is an average across sectors for each country. The estimates suggest that higher dismissal costs are associated with lower speed of adjustment. Thus, although international comparisons of gross job flows suggest that all countries tend to have high rates of job turnover, the evidence suggests that job security regulations reduce turnover in the labor market.

Costs of Job Security

What about costs? Are labor markets incurring large efficiency losses as a result of job security policies? This section examines the evidence on three fronts: employment and unemployment, the duration and composition of employment, and productivity growth.

Employment and Unemployment

In some respects, job security regulations can be interpreted as mandatory benefits, so the analysis of the latter also applies to these regulations. Thus, the impact of job security provisions on employment depends on whether the cost associated with such provisions can be transferred to workers in the form of lower pay. If workers were willing to accept lower average wages in exchange for higher employment security plus compensation in case of dismissal, then the policy could make workers better off without affecting the behavior of the labor market.

However, job security regulations differ from regular mandatory benefits in that the regulations specifically seek to alter firms' decisions regarding hiring and firing workers. The result is fewer layoffs in bad times, but also less hiring in good times. In the face of positive shocks, firms become more conservative in their hiring decisions in order to avoid costly adjustments in case economic conditions do not turn out as expected. This effect implies that even if the cost of severance pay and other job security provisions could not be fully shifted to workers, employment rates may not decline because the negative effect of fewer hires could be outweighed by the effect of reduced layoffs. In fact, the empirical evidence on the effect of job security on employment and unemployment rates is far from conclusive. Addison and Teixeira (2001) survey the literature for developed countries and report that while a large group of studies find a negative effect of job security on employment, others do not. The evidence on the effects of job security on unemployment is equally ambiguous.

Heckman and Pagés (forthcoming) review the literature for Latin America and find that while some individual country studies suggest that regulations promoting job security reduce employment, cross-country time-series estimates for Latin American and OECD countries do not show those results. The strongest results are found by Saavedra and Torero (forthcoming) for Peru and Mondino and Montoya (forthcoming) for Argentina. In both studies, the authors find that greater job security is associated with lower employment rates in manufacturing. However, studies examining labor reforms in Chile and Brazil find no evidence of statistically significant effects.[10]

Thus, although some studies suggest that reducing job security in Latin America holds the promise of higher employment and lower unemployment rates, others do not. These results may imply that the effects of labor market deregulation differ across countries, depending on the circumstances accompanying such reforms.

Duration of Unemployment and Composition of Employment

Two areas in which job security regulations are found to have important and undesirable effects are: the duration of unemployment and the composition of employment by age, gender, and skill. The evidence suggests that more stringent job security provisions tend to increase the duration of unemployment. This is explained by a decline in hiring rates. As firms become more reluctant to hire workers (for fear of expensive dismissal costs in the future), unemployed workers have greater difficulty finding new jobs.[11] For Colombia, Kugler (forthcoming) finds that after a reform in 1990 that reduced job security, the average duration of unemployment declined from its prereform levels. Her analysis suggests that job security provisions simultaneously increase the duration of employment and the duration of unemployment. Thus, it is possible that job security provisions create higher perceptions of insecurity among workers as the welfare losses associated with unemployment increase.

The evidence also suggests that job security provisions create winners and losers. In a study of OECD countries, Nickell (1997) reports that while job security does not seem to have an effect on prime-age male employment rates, it is associated with lower employment rates for women and youth. Two studies on Chile find that job security provisions are not neutral across age and skill groups. More stringent job security regulations are found to bias employment toward prime-age and older workers while reducing the employment share of younger workers. Moreover, higher employment protection is associated with a decline in the demand for unskilled workers relative to skilled workers (Pagés and Montenegro 1999; Montenegro and Pagés forthcoming). The effects are quite sizable. For instance, a 10 percent increase in job security reduces the employment rate of

[10] See Pagés and Montenegro (1999) for Chile and P. de Barros and Corseuil (forthcoming) for Brazil.

[11] See Nickell and Layard (1999) and the references therein.

young, unskilled workers by almost 0.5 percentage points (see Figure 7.8). For skilled youth, the effect is smaller but still significant. For older workers, these effects are reversed and employment rates increase with job protection. To give an idea of the magnitudes, the 1990 Chilean reform increased job security by about one-third. The estimates suggest that this reform could have reduced the employment rate of unskilled youth by 1.5 percentage points.

Figure 7.8 Effect of an Increase in Employment Protection on the Probability of Employment in Chile, 1960-98

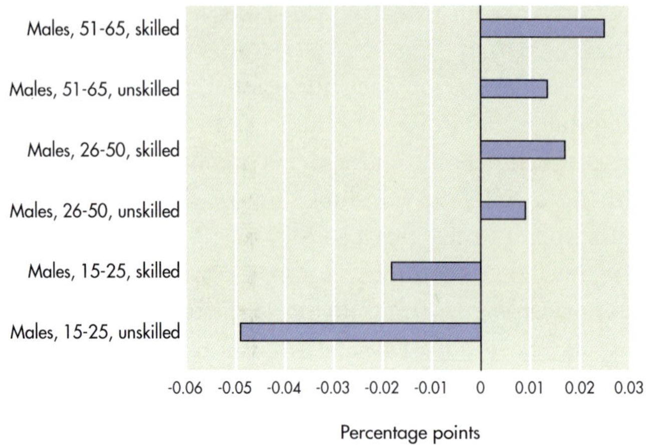

Source: Montenegro and Pagés (forthcoming).

Productivity Growth

Do job security regulations have an effect on productivity growth? A traditional argument is that job security reduces productivity growth because it reduces the reallocation of workers from less productive to more productive activities (Hopenhayn and Rogerson 1993; Blanchard and Portugal 2001). The evidence suggests that job security slows down reallocation, but the relationship between labor market institutions and growth is far from conclusive. Although job security provisions may reduce reallocation, they may increase within-firm productivity growth. This is likely to be especially true in industries that rely on within-firm knowledge and specific skills. In these sectors, loss of workers may be detrimental to the firm's know-how and new workers may take a long time to learn and be productive. In these types of industries, job security may increase the incentives of workers to invest in specific skills because they expect to stay longer at a given firm. It may also motivate firms to provide training. In other types of industries, the skills and abilities required by firms might change often; in these industries, job security regulations might restrict productivity growth.

There is scant empirical evidence on whether job security decreases (or increases) productivity growth. Nickell and Layard (1999) examine the effect of job security provisions on productivity growth in a panel of OECD countries and conclude that there is no evidence in their sample that countries with more stringent job security have lower labor (or total) productivity growth. This result is driven by the fact that in the period considered in their study (1976-92), countries such as the United States, Canada, and New Zealand, which are characterized by low job security, had lower average productivity growth than countries such as Spain, Italy, and Belgium, which had high job protection.

Scarpetta and Tressell (2002) analyze a panel of countries, sectors (manufacturing and services), and years. They find that although on average countries with higher job security tend to experience lower productivity growth, this effect is statistically significant only in countries with intermediate levels of coordination/decentralization in collective bargaining. They interpret these findings as suggestive that job security provisions do not have negative effects in countries where incentives for firms to train existing workers are high (as is the case in countries with coordinated/centralized collective bargaining) or in countries that have few restrictions on hiring the required mix of skills in the market (decentralized bargaining). These results might be good news for Latin America, where, with few exceptions, collective bargaining is decentralized.

Other Effects

High job security also interacts with other variables leading to undesired effects in the labor market. Two effects that are discussed in other chapters of this Report worth mentioning here are the possible interactions between high job security and trade liberalization (chapter 5) and between high job security and low inflation (chapter 4).

High job security and stringent labor market regulations may lead to adverse effects of trade reforms on the coverage of labor laws and social protection. Goldberg, Koujianou, and Pavcnik (2001) and the results presented in chapter 5 suggest that in highly regulated labor markets, trade reforms lead to an employment reallocation from jobs covered by labor laws to jobs that are not covered.

Stringent job security provisions also appear to reduce the ability of wages to adjust to adverse economic conditions. This in turn magnifies the response of unemployment to adverse shocks. Such an effect was not an issue in the past when inflation rates were high and rigid real wages were quickly eroded by inflation. However, as inflation reaches single digits, the adverse effects of negative shocks on unemployment become more pronounced. This might explain why unemployment reacted so virulently to the economic crisis at the end of the 1990s.

Box 7. 3 Job Security Regulations

Indications

Job security regulations provide a form of insurance against unemployment when better forms of insurance cannot be provided.

Side Effects

Regulations reduce the ability of firms to react to changes in economic conditions, possibly slowing down a powerful engine of growth: the reallocation of workers from less to more productive ends. Job security regulations also have important redistribution consequences because they tend to favor the employment of male adults and skilled workers, relative to female, young, and unskilled workers. Finally, research indicates that these regulations increase the duration of unemployment, reducing workers' chances of finding new jobs when displaced.

Labor Market Reforms

Although the high level of de jure job security in Latin America provides some insurance for some workers, the available evidence suggests that job security provisions are not cost-free. (See Box 7.3 for a summary of benefits and costs of job security provisions.) Reforms have not been possible in many countries, and the reason is quite simple. Although unskilled or young workers would be likely to benefit from reforms, prime-age and skilled workers fear the loss of security and benefits associated with labor reforms. Since the latter tend to be better organized and have greater voice than the former, it is difficult to implement reforms. In many cases, reformers have not attempted to provide alternative means of insurance. In others, interest groups have resisted giving up job security even when alternative insurance mechanisms were considered. Given these circumstances, some countries have worked out alternatives to labor market reforms, such as temporary contracts and various forms of unemployment insurance.

Temporary Contracts and Other Schemes

Many countries have introduced or are considering partial reforms, creating special contracts with limited duration and no severance payment obligations. To prevent firms from exclusively hiring workers under this modality, the use of these contracts is restricted. In some instances, they cannot be renewed. In others, after a given number of renewals, workers have to be hired under permanent, regular contracts.

These types of new modalities were introduced in Argentina in 1991 and extended in 1995. Employment promotion contracts could be awarded to unemployed workers, allowing a 50 percent reduction in severance pay (Saavedra 2003). For some types of contracts, severance pay was removed entirely. However, these contracts were eliminated in 1998, after the share of workers under these modalities had increased substantially. Peru and Colombia also lifted restrictions on the use of these types of programs in the early 1990s.

In both cases, the number of workers hired under these modalities increased enormously—for Peru, from 20 percent of salaried employees in 1990 to 55 percent in 2000, and in Colombia, a similarly high increase. In Brazil, the use of such contracts was deregulated in 1988.

Does the introduction of employment promotion contracts improve the situation of the labor market? Is partial reform better than no reform at all? Temporary contracts may have perverse effects by increasing firms' incentives to hire more workers at the entry level, employ them for a short while, and then dismiss them without giving them permanent jobs. This increases rotation, particularly among the young, but does not necessarily increase employment rates or reduce unemployment because the effect of more workers hired is outweighed by the effect of increased layoffs. Moreover, the use of fixed-term contracts for some workers might strengthen the bargaining position of permanent workers because they know that there is a buffer of temporary workers that will be laid off first in the face of adverse economic conditions. This stronger bargaining position might result in higher wages for permanent workers relative to a situation without temporary contracts, and lower overall employment rates. The evidence from both developing and developed countries suggests that these alternative contracts tend to account for a large share of employment creation, and that they are concentrated among the young. The evidence also suggests that turnover increases, but there is no evidence that unemployment declines as a result of this measure.[12]

Temporary contracts also seem to have negative effects on the accumulation of human capital. As the probability that workers are converted to permanent status declines, so does the incentive to accumulate human capital or provide training. Since the contracts are concentrated among young and female workers, incentives for productivity growth are reduced for those workers with lower wages. These effects become larger the greater is the difference in dismissal costs between permanent and temporary workers. The lesson is that the more effective is the legislation of employment protection, the larger are the distortions and negative consequences of partial reforms. Therefore, despite the difficulties in passing comprehensive reforms, partial reforms are not a good substitute.

Other Forms of Insurance

Although job security may bring unintended costs, this policy, as a means of providing unemployment insurance in low and medium-income countries, has an advantage: the transfer to the unemployed is paid directly by the employer. This is not a small thing. In poorer countries, one of the most difficult challenges to overcome is to find out who needs the transfer. The lack of registries implies that an insurance system run by a third party would be difficult and costly to administer.

However, improvement in the current system requires an understanding of the secondary effects of job security. Two particularly relevant aspects are the relation between job security and tenure, and the unemployment insurance properties of job security.

Job security tends to increase with tenure. This implies that it is less costly to dismiss workers who have been at a firm for less time. Thus, when firms need to adjust, they tend to concentrate layoffs among women, youth, and unskilled workers because they tend to have lower tenure. Weakening the link between severance pay and tenure, for instance, by imposing a maximum amount a worker can obtain, would reduce the bias that job security imposes against workers with less tenure.

Job security can have negative effects on economic performance by reducing the adaptability of firms to changes in the economic environment. There are three types of reforms that preserve the unemployment insurance properties of job security without imposing a tax on layoffs.

The first one is to convert severance pay into an *individual* savings account. This is the strategy followed in Peru, Colombia, Ecuador, and to some extent Brazil. In these countries, employers regularly deposit a given fraction of each worker's wage

[12] See Saint-Paul (2000) for Spain, Blanchard and Landier (2001) for France, and Hopenhayn (forthcoming) for Argentina.

in an individual account. If for any reason the relationship between the worker and the firm is terminated, the worker can withdraw the funds plus the interest income accumulated in the account. An important limitation of this system (and of systems based on severance pay) is that workers with short tenures prior to termination may not receive enough funds in their accounts to survive an unemployment spell. In this respect, individual savings accounts are self-insurance mechanisms because there is no pooling of risk across workers.

The second alternative is to convert severance pay into a *collective* savings account. In this format, regular contributions are pooled in a collective account from which dismissed workers can obtain a predetermined amount. Under this modality, there is an insurance mechanism if workers that have contributed for a long time subsidize workers with shorter tenures. The possibilities of insurance increase the larger and more diversified is the pool of workers that contribute to the collective account. One risk that cannot be diversified away is aggregate or systemic risk. If a large percentage of workers is laid off at once, the collective account may be quickly depleted.

The third option to reduce the welfare cost of unemployment is found in the traditional unemployment insurance mechanisms established in developed countries. These systems look a lot like the collective savings account mechanisms described above, with the difference that payments to the unemployed are not performed in a lump-sum fashion. Instead, there is a predetermined schedule of payments that lasts for a given number of periods while the worker is unemployed. This system provides two layers of insurance: payments are less dependent on contributions and workers that suffer longer unemployment spells receive payments for a longer period (up to a maximum). Most developed countries provide a third layer of insurance against systemic risk, as the state adds resources to the collective account in case of financial imbalances.

The road to insurance is paved with difficulties. The higher the level of cross-subsidy among workers, the higher are the employment costs because workers with low risk are less willing to pay. In addition, for developing countries, the cost of administration of collective programs may be very high because it requires identifying who becomes and who remains unemployed. The presence of a large informal sector in which workers can be employed without being registered means that many workers could be receiving an unemployment subsidy while employed at an informal job.

All these difficulties imply that each country should choose modalities that are compatible with its institutional capabilities and income level. In some cases, a mix of schemes may be the appropriate solution. For example, the new unemployment insurance scheme in Chile is a mix of individual savings accounts supplemented with a solidarity scheme that provides partial insurance to workers that become unemployed and have less than a given amount in their accounts. This system may be appropriate for a country like Chile, which has a relatively small informal sector, but may not work in poorer countries, such as Peru or Bolivia, where the size of the informal sector would make it too costly to administer.

The Minimum Wage

Public discussion of the minimum wage is often heated, for good reasons. The minimum wage is a key distribution variable because, at least at the microeconomic level, it has opposite effects on the earnings of workers (especially unskilled workers) and firms. The minimum wage is also controversial within governments because it can be used as a policy tool for very different purposes. From the standpoint of the economic authorities, the minimum wage tends to be seen as an anti-inflation policy tool that affects production costs, expectations of price increases, and public spending. From the standpoint of social policy, however, the minimum wage is viewed as a tool for reducing poverty and inequality. The minimum wage also generates intense disputes among economists. The prevailing opinion in the profession is that the minimum wage is a market distortion that, if effective, generates unemployment or informal labor and leads to

Box 7.4 Reasons for the Minimum Wage

If the labor market were like the potato market, there would be no reason for a minimum wage. A multitude of sellers and buyers operating competitively would spontaneously find the price that would make supply and demand meet at all times, and that price would change continually in order to adjust to the fluctuations of supply and demand. But the labor market is different. To begin with, some companies may have sufficient market power to depress wages below where they would be if there were perfect competition with other buyers. Even when many companies exist, there may be market power because information on work opportunities and conditions is imperfect and difficult for jobseekers to acquire. Moreover, in the labor market, wages represent the price of a transaction that does not take place instantaneously but over the time of the labor contract, or until one of the two parties decides to interrupt it. The product sold in the labor market is not homogeneous because workers differ in their skills and abilities. Nor is it a product that is fully known beforehand, because it depends not only on the skills of individuals but on the effort that they put into their work.

These characteristics of the labor market may justify the existence of the minimum wage. The minimum wage may help to counteract the monopsonistic power of firms, whether because there are few companies or as a result of information problems. The minimum wage may help reduce labor turnover and facilitate the hiring of low-skilled workers and hence may help reduce the costs entailed in the recruiting, hiring, and ongoing training of new workers. When the minimum wage is moderate, it may even help raise employment levels. The minimum wage may lead workers to put greater effort into their work out of fear of losing their jobs or being left with lower-paying jobs. None of these potentially good effects of the minimum wage is guaranteed, however, because they depend on many factors. But the claim that minimum wages are distorting or inefficient cannot be accepted without qualification.

Source: Card and Krueger (1995).

loss of efficiency and social welfare. However, others justify the minimum wage for reasons of efficiency or as an intervention aimed at correcting market failures (Box 7.4).

Before taking a side in this heated debate, it is useful to review the data and results of available studies.

Changes in the Minimum Wage

In most countries in Latin America, the average level of the minimum wage (in constant prices) between 1991 and 2000 was lower than in the previous decade (Figure 7.9). The largest drops, of 40 percent or more, took place in Peru, Mexico, Uruguay, El Salvador, and Argentina; there were major declines in Venezuela and Brazil as well. Only in Chile and Costa Rica did the purchasing power of the minimum wage rise appreciably from one decade to the next.

The real minimum wage on average displayed the same instability in both periods. In both decades, minimum wages were most unstable in real terms in Argentina. Venezuela and Peru displayed greater instability in the 1990s than in the previous decade. In these three countries, real wages typically varied by more than 25 percent from one year to the next, and in Nicaragua it was close to 20 percent. In the other countries, the real minimum wage has been less volatile, with typical annual variations of around 5 percent (Figure 7.10).

Inflation is one of the factors that influences the stability of the purchasing power of the minimum wage. In economies with low inflation, the minimum wage is more likely to be more stable in real terms. However, the opposite is not necessarily true. For example, in the past two decades, Brazil has gone through periods of high inflation, but has managed to keep the minimum wage relatively stable. For much of the 1990s, Colombia had a rate of inflation higher than most countries in the region, but adjustments in the minimum wage have closely followed price increases.

Although the minimum wage as a proportion of per capita income has fallen in practically all countries, in some cases it is still high (Figure 7.11).

Figure 7.9 Changes in Real Minimum Wage between 1981-90 and 1991-2000
(Percent)

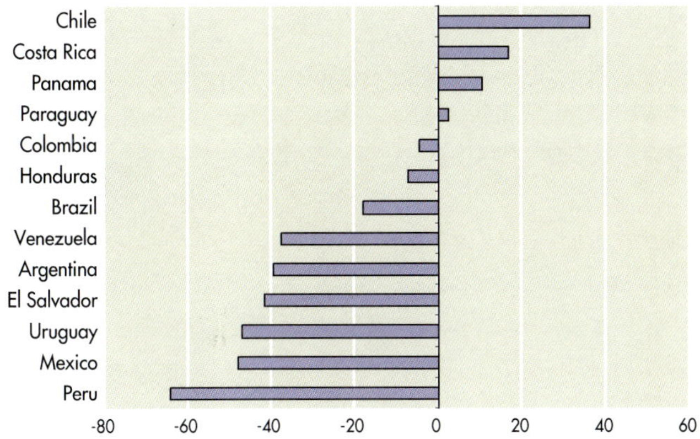

Source: IDB based on official country data.

Figure 7.10 Real Minimum Wage Volatility
(Percent)

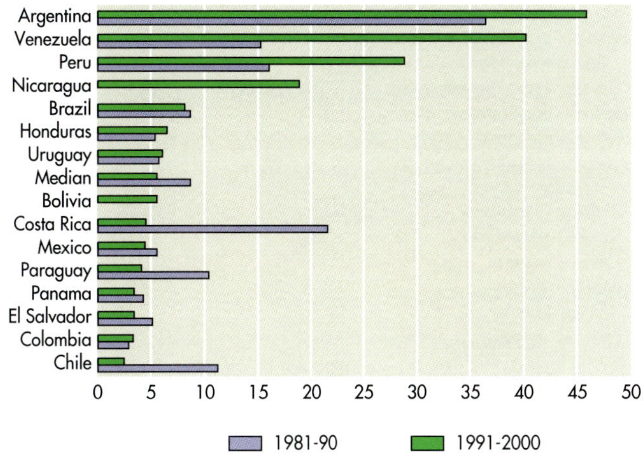

Source: IDB based on official country data.

For example, in Honduras, Nicaragua, and Paraguay, the minimum wage in the 1990s was higher than per capita income when calculated using official statistics. However, it may be that in these three countries, official statistics underestimate per capita income. Less susceptible to these problems is the comparison between the minimum wage and the median wage (that is, the pay received by the median worker). According to this measurement, differences between countries are less substantial. The highest minimum wages since the mid-1990s are found in Nicaragua, Colombia, and Venezuela, where they represent around 80 percent of the pay of the average worker. In most countries for which there are data, this relationship is between 30 and 60 percent. The lowest minimum wage in relation to the pay of the typical worker is found in Uruguay, where it is less than 20 percent (Figure 7.12).

Coverage and Effectiveness

Compliance with the minimum wage differs notably from country to country. On average in the 1990s, rates of noncompliance with the minimum wage were more than 20 percent in Colombia and Nicaragua, and less than 5 percent in Argentina, Bolivia, Mexico, El Salvador, and Uruguay. These rates are the percentage of employees between ages 26 and 40, working more than 30 hours a week, who say that they receive net incomes that are below what would be required by the minimum wage and the regulation of contributions to social security.[13]

Compliance with the minimum wage is partly related to where it stands in relation to the wages of the typical worker. The largest percentages of workers who earn less than the minimum wage are found in Nicaragua and Colombia, countries where the minimum wage is relatively high (Figure 7.13). This relationship clearly suggests that efforts to raise the minimum wage are largely undermined by evasion of the regulations and, as would be expected, evasion increases as the minimum wage rises. However, this relationship is not mechanical. For example, Chile has a relatively low level of noncompliance for the level of its minimum wage. Respect for the law and more generally the institutional climate may influence compliance. The stability of the real minimum wage might also have a

[13] These calculations are based on IDB household surveys starting in 1990. To calculate the net minimum wage, the payroll deductions from workers for Social Security, Medicare, and retirement plans were taken into account according to the data compiled by the U.S. Department of Health and Human Services (1998).

Figure 7.11 Minimum Wage as a Percent of Per Capita Income

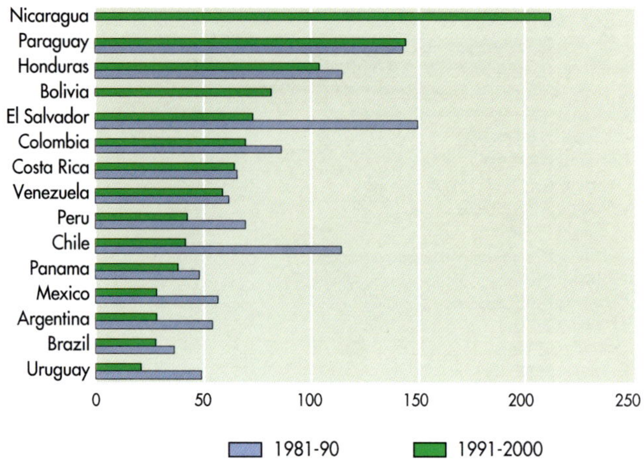

Source: IDB based on official country data.

Figure 7.13 Minimum Wage Level and Enforcement

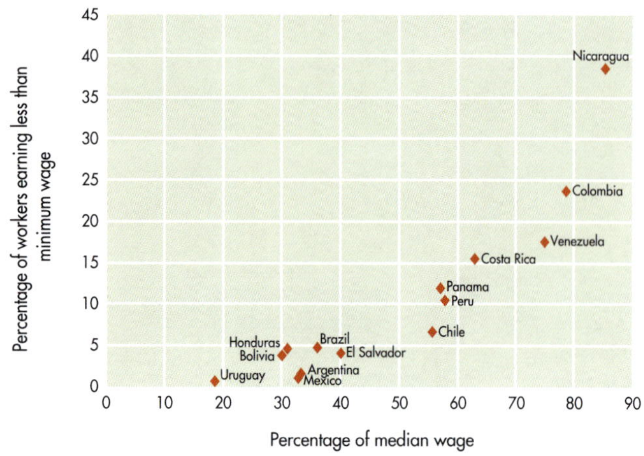

Note: The wage used for comparison is the median wage for workers beween 26 and 40 years old that work for more than 30 hours a week in the survey reference period.
Source: IDB based on official country data.

Figure 7.12 Minimum Wage as a Percentage of the Median Wage, 1996-2001

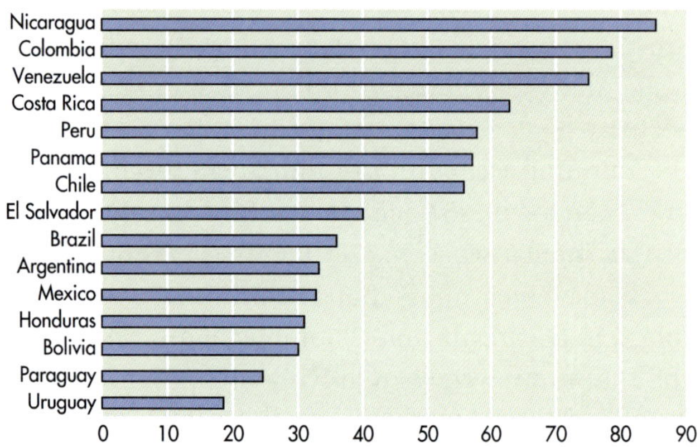

Note: The wage used for comparison is the median wage for workers beween 26 and 40 years old that work for more than 30 hours a week in the survey reference period.
Source: IDB based on official country data.

bearing, but these issues have not been studied in Latin America.

As would be expected, rates of noncompliance are highest among less educated workers. In the typical country in the region, around 21 percent of workers who have completed elementary school earn less than the minimum wage (Table 7.2). In Colombia, Nicaragua, and Peru, approximately two out of three less educated workers are paid less than the minimum wage. The rate of noncompliance for workers with a secondary education drops to 5 percent for the typical country, but in Colombia, Nicaragua, and Peru, it is more than 20 percent. For workers with a university education, it is typically less than 1 percent, although in Peru approximately one out of every 10 workers with that level of education is paid less than the minimum.

Failure to comply with minimum wage laws is a much more serious problem in rural areas than in cities. Typically, whereas only one worker out of 22 earns less than the minimum in urban areas, the ratio in rural areas is one in four. The differences are also notable according to the type of company involved. Typically, one out of every six workers in companies with up to five employees is paid less than the minimum, but that is the case for only one out of 37 in larger companies. However, as the next section explains, that does not mean that the minimum wage has no impact on those segments of the labor market that are usually called "informal."

Effects of the Minimum Wage

Differences between countries and over time in the level and coverage of the minimum wage are so

Table 7.2 Minimum Wage Noncompliance Rates by Education, Location, and Firm Size

(Percent)

		Education			Location		Firm size (number of workers)		
Country	Year	Primary	Secondary	Tertiary	Rural	Urban	Less than five	More than five	Total
Argentina	2001	8.90	2.64	0.54		3.07	8.51	7.67	3.07
Bolivia	1999	5.01	0.43	0.00	0.36	1.21	4.53	0.06	1.10
Brazil[a]	1999	16.16	2.21	0.08	20.38	3.84	21.69	0.37	5.83
Chile	1998	26.72	7.36	0.77	22.96	5.41	17.54	4.38	7.25
Colombia	1999	59.37	23.62	40.6	54.37	17.38			26.90
Costa Rica	2000	29.02	9.72	2.48	23.25	9.21	42.45	7.98	15.66
El Salvador	1999	7.98	2.00	0.23	8.34	2.00	7.87	2.72	3.58
Honduras	1999	10.31	1.42	0.69	11.07	3.19	16.01	2.70	5.88
Mexico	2001	1.48	0.35	0.16		0.52	2.18	0.19	0.52
Nicaragua	2001	59.83	22.88	6.23	56.82	27.58	61.49	26.95	35.58
Panama	2000	32.79	17.60	2.08	19.22	13.19	53.09	6.95	14.78
Peru	2000	66.21	27.26	9.20	52.31	16.38	46.11	14.69	23.46
Uruguay	2000	1.23	0.34	0.13		0.46	2.18	0.15	0.46
Venezuela	1999	35.83	14.31	6.09			41.37	12.20	17.91
Median		21.44	5.00	0.73	21.65	3.84	17.54	2.72	6.57

[a] Firm size refers to employees with and without a contract, not to the number of workers.

Note: Rates are calculated based on the number of employees between 25 and 40 years old working more than 30 hours a week.

Source: IDB household surveys.

vast that it would be rash to make statements of a general nature on its effects. When the minimum wage has been unstable in a country and its coverage low, its influence on other wages and on the level and structure of employment may be less than in another country where the minimum wage is characterized by its stability and acceptance. The examples in this section show that, in general, when the minimum wage is highly effective, it helps raise the wages of those who earn around the minimum wage (including slightly below it) but at the cost of reducing employment possibilities for those workers. This also applies to "informal" workers, that is, those who work in small companies or who do not have a labor contract. The balance between the benefits of higher wages and the cost of decreased possibilities of employment tends to be positive and, at least in the short run, increases in the minimum wage improve the distribution of labor income.

In Colombia, the minimum wage is effective because a high percentage of workers earn around the minimum. Figure 7.14 illustrates the high percentage of workers whose wages are around the minimum wage.

The minimum wage seems to have an impact not only on less skilled workers employed in formal companies, but also on the wages of relatively highly educated workers and those who work for small companies of up to five workers.

The rise in unemployment in Colombia since the mid-1990s is explained primarily by slow economic growth and a drop in private investment, made worse by problems in the financial sector and economic insecurity. Nonetheless, the question has to be asked whether the adjustments in the minimum wage helped aggravate the problem, because in the most critical period of low growth (1997-99), those adjustments were higher than the rate of inflation, which fell rapidly, partly due to the recession. Maloney and Núñez (forthcoming) focus precisely on this period and find that for every percentage point rise in the minimum wage, employment falls by 0.15 percent. This means that the 9

Figure 7.14 Distribution of Workers by Wage Level in Colombia

a. Skilled workers

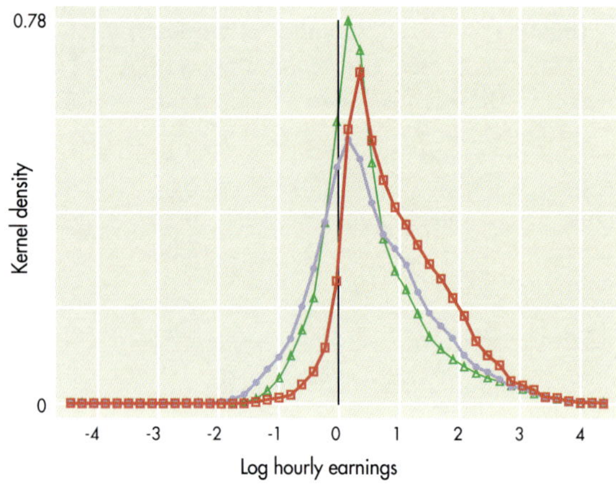

b. Unskilled workers

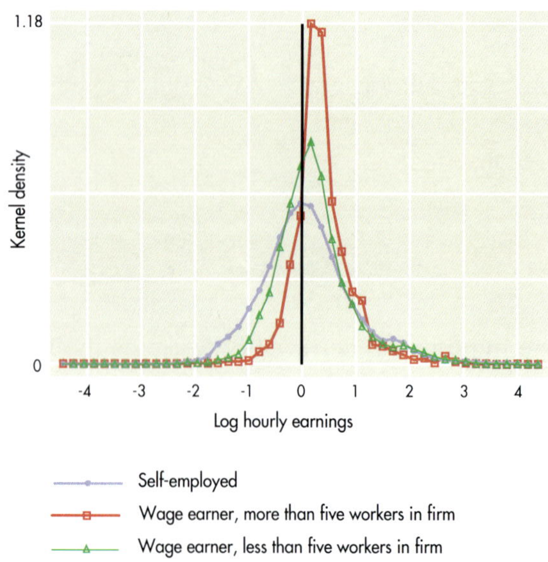

Note: On the horizontal axis, 0 is equivalent to the minimum wage.
Source: IDB based on official country data.

Figure 7.15 Effect of the Minimum Wage on Wages and Employment in Colombia

Source: Maloney and Núñez (forthcoming).

percent increase in the real minimum wage in 1999 reduced employment by 1.4 percent.[14]

The likelihood of losing a job due to an increase in the minimum wage does not affect all workers alike. It is greater for those who earn low wages, and may be as much as double for those who earn less than the minimum wage. The reason for this effect is that increases in the minimum wage are reflected disproportionately in the short run in pay to workers whose wages are slightly below the minimum. (The effect is less than proportional for higher paid workers; see Figure 7.15.) The strong contemporaneous effect of the minimum wage on lower wages—which has also been found in the United States (see Neumark, Schweitzer, and Wascher 2000)—challenges the belief that the formal and informal segments of the labor market are neatly separated, and that those who fall into the latter category are outside the direct influence of labor laws. This result suggests that the minimum wage may operate as a strong pay-setting signal when, as is the case in Colombia, the amount is widely known and socially respected. This also means that the minimum wage exercises a positive influence on income distribution, and possibly on poverty levels in the short run, which is consistent with cross-section studies. It must be kept in mind that these effects refer to the short term (a quarter) and may dissipate over time.

As the experience of Colombia shows, the short-term effectiveness of the minimum wage is a double-edged sword that cuts both ways because, although it helps protect the lowest wages, it does

[14] This elasticity is somewhat lower than that obtained by previous studies for Colombia. Bell (1997) estimates that the 10 percent rise in the real minimum wage between 1981 and 1987 was responsible for a reduction in employment in the range of 2 to 12 percent.

so at the cost of job creation. In a recession, the minimum wage should be allowed to drop to avoid higher unemployment, but that policy option is hard to apply, especially when, as happened in Colombia, the recession was combined with a steep decline in inflation.

The effectiveness of the minimum wage in Brazil is also quite high and is not limited to workers employed in accordance with labor regulations. Indeed, in Brazil the percentage of workers who receive exactly the minimum wage is higher among those who do not have a labor contract (informal workers) than among those who do. However, among the latter, it often happens that wages are set in multiples of the minimum wage, which thus operates as a calculation unit for defining labor remuneration (Neri, Gonzaga, and Camargo 2001). Fajnzylber (2001) studies the influence of the minimum wage on pay and employment in Brazil using a set of 22 quarterly panels between 1982 and 1997, making it possible to follow the work life of more than half a million individuals.

As in the case of Colombia, when the minimum wage rises in Brazil, workers with wages slightly below the minimum wage benefit the most in the short run (in this instance, a year). The elasticity is 1.4 for workers under a contract who earn less than 0.9 times the minimum wage, 1.08 for those who earn around the minimum, and 0.4 for those earning high wages (around 40 times the minimum wage). The other side of the coin is that low-income workers are more affected by job losses when the minimum wage rises: 1.6 percent of those who have a contract and earn less than 0.9 times the minimum wage lose their jobs when the minimum wage increases by 10 percent (and 0.9 percent of those who earn around the minimum suffer the same fate). These short-term effects dissipate over time: after a year, around half of the wage gains disappear for those earning less than two times the minimum wage, and around half of the job losses are corrected.

These results are similar for workers who have no contract, suggesting, as in the case of Colombia, that the boundaries between formal and informal work are quite porous. The effects on the wages of workers without a contract are slightly lower, and tend to be diluted more quickly than for workers with a contract, but the implications for job loss are greater. When the minimum wage increases by 10 percent, in the first year, 3.5 percent of wage earners without a contract who are earning less than 0.9 times the minimum wage lose their jobs (as do 2.5 percent of those who earn around the minimum). The loss in informal employment is greater, although it is partially corrected in the next year. A portion of unemployed informal workers decides to seek jobs with a contract, attracted by higher wages, and a portion withdraws from the workforce, discouraged by higher unemployment.

The studies of Colombia and Brazil show that the informal sector does not operate as a residual segment with flexible wages where those who have no other options end up. If that were the case, when the minimum wage rose, informal employment would increase and earnings from it would drop, but this is the opposite of what happens. Because the minimum wage in these two countries operates effectively as a signal, setting wages in both segments, it has favorable effects on the incomes of low-wage workers, but it also lessens possibilities for job creation, albeit less than proportionally. This entails costs and benefits that should be considered, bearing in mind the macroeconomic context.

It should also be emphasized that the balance of the effects may be different in countries where conditions are different. An analysis using the same methodology for the United States shows that increases in the minimum wage have an adverse net effect on the pay of low-wage workers because the unemployment effects and fewer hours of work are stronger than the effects of the wage increase (Neumark, Schweitzer, and Wascher 2000). Unfortunately, there are no strictly comparable studies to establish whether this is also the case in other relatively more developed countries in the region, such as Argentina, Uruguay, or some countries in the English-speaking Caribbean. There is only some evidence for the case of Chile, suggesting effects more similar to those in the United States than to those in Brazil or Colombia.

In Chile, the rate of compliance with the minimum wage, defined as the percentage of wage workers who earn at least the minimum, is higher than in Colombia (Figure 7.13). Until 1998, the minimum wage was comparatively lower in Chile than in Brazil or Colombia, at around 45 percent of the median wage of unskilled workers. However, since 1998 it has increased by around 10 percent a year, and in 2002 it reached 60 percent of the median wage of unskilled workers. The impact of these increases was highly concentrated on workers within the range in which the minimum wage changed, contrary to what happened in Brazil and Colombia, where the strongest impact was felt by workers below the minimum wage, and where there were also significant impacts (albeit gradually less) at higher pay levels.

Calculations made by Cowan and others (2003) suggest that wage employment declined by 6 percent in Chile due to increases in the minimum wage. Those most affected were unskilled workers (up to 11 years of schooling) with little experience (up to 8 years). Thirteen percent of this group lost their jobs as full-time salaried workers. Surprisingly, the real wages of those who kept their jobs seem to have changed very little, even at levels close to the minimum. Hence, in the case of Chile, the dominant effect of the increase in the minimum wage seems to have been the loss of full-time salaried jobs, especially among unskilled workers. These results are consistent with a study on Chile by Montenegro and Pagés (forthcoming) that likewise shows that increases in the minimum wage reduce chances for employment of youth in comparison with other age groups and improve the likelihood of employment of women as compared with men. The latter might be the case because the minimum wage strengthens the bargaining position of women or because it brings more women into the job market (Montenegro and Pagés forthcoming).

In contrast with the previous three cases, in Mexico the minimum wage is set low in comparison with average wages and there is little concentration of wages around the minimum, suggesting that it is not very effective. As would be expected under such conditions, changes in the minimum wage are unlikely to produce major consequences. Bell's (1997) analysis of Mexico in 1981-87, when the real minimum wage fell by 45 percent, concludes that there was no effect on employment in the manufacturing sector. This does not rule out the possibility that the decrease in the minimum wage might have had the effect of creating employment in other sectors. And it does not necessarily mean that it is desirable for the minimum wage to be extremely low or ineffective.

The minimum wage does not seem to have a great impact on pay rates in Ecuador because of its low level and the complexity of laws on pay for work in effect until 2000. In Ecuador, minimum wages are set by occupation within each industry by each of the Industry Wage Commissions, which include representatives of government, business, and workers. There are 118 minimum wages, a number that has remained practically unchanged for the past decade. Until 2000, obligatory wages were also affected by a variety of supplementary payments that had to be paid in different proportions and at different times in the year. With this legal complexity and few tools for enforcing the regulations, the minimum wage does not seem to be effective. According to MacIsaac and Rama (1997), a significant proportion of supplementary payments was handled by lowering the basic wage paid to workers, which could happen because the minimum wage was low and ineffective.

Costa Rica has traditionally had a complex system of minimum wages differentiated by industry sector and occupation. In the 1970s and 1980s, there were approximately 350 different levels; in the early 1990s, this number was reduced to around 80. Costa Rica is interesting because it was one of the few countries where the average minimum wage rose in the 1990s, both in real terms and as a percentage of the wage of the average worker. Because Costa Rica is also one of the few countries where inequality of pay for work has not tended to increase since the mid-1980s, it is important to ask whether these results are related. That is in fact the case according to econometric studies by El-Hamidi and Terrell (2001). They estimate that for every percentage rise in the minimum wage by sector relative to the average wage in that sector, inequality drops typically by between 0.9 and 1.7 percent. The effects are greater in those sectors where the relative minimum wage is lower, and lesser (or even negative) in those sectors where the relative minimum wage is higher.

The impact of the minimum wage on poverty has been studied for a set of developing countries (in contrast to the case studies of other effects of the minimum wage surveyed in this section). Lustig and McLeod (1997) use time-series data from 22 countries (13 in Latin America) to determine whether changes in the real minimum wage influence poverty levels. They conclude that increases (or decreases) in the real minimum wage are associated with reductions (or increases, respectively) in short-term poverty levels. This relationship obtains for different measures of poverty whether the economies are expanding or contracting, for both rural and urban populations, and in Latin America and elsewhere. This conclusion is consistent with case studies of Colombia, Brazil, Chile, and Costa Rica. It is also consistent with other analyses that show that increases in the minimum wage have a favorable influence, albeit modest in size, on income distribution (IDB 1998).[15] Moreover, Lustig and McLeod (1997) observe the following:

> These results, however, are not an outright endorsement of minimum wage increases as a cost effective policy to reduce poverty. Higher minimum wages do seem to increase unemployment. Minimum wage increases may also reduce efficiency and competitiveness. If minimum wage laws have a negative effect on growth, they could hurt the poor over the long term. Even if raising the minimum wages can be shown to reduce poverty in the short run, in the long run it could reduce employment opportunities.

Why the Minimum Wage Is Needed

The minimum wage may have some favorable effects on poverty and income distribution, but it is not the most appropriate tool for those aims. The main justification for the existence of the minimum wage is the need to control the market power that companies may have over individual workers who lack the information, influence, or means to find better-paying jobs (Blanchard 2002). The extreme case is that of agricultural or mining enclaves where, in practice, a single company constitutes the sole demand for labor in that location. But there does not have to be this extreme case in order for the minimum wage to be justified. (See Box 7.5 for a summary of the benefits and costs of minimum wage laws.) In order to fulfill its function, the minimum wage must meet various requirements. The most important is that it be widely known and that the companies and workers as a whole regard it as unacceptable that any worker be paid less. This means that the level at which the minimum wage is set constitutes a social convention that must be dictated by the economic and social realities of the country. No government is in a position to impose a minimum wage that companies and workers by mutual agreement are willing to violate because they regard it as excessive or arbitrary or because it produces unemployment levels that are too high. Because the minimum

Box 7.5 **The Minimum Wage**

Indications

The minimum wage provides support to low-wage earners in their individual negotiating with their employers, and facilitates the hiring of workers by small and medium firms. Increases in the minimum wage benefit low-wage workers and have beneficial, although mild, effects on inequality, at least in the short run.

Side Effects

The minimum wage increases unemployment rates among low-wage and young workers.

Caution

If the increase of the minimum wage is too large, its effectiveness will be severely reduced or even lost. The medium and long-term effects of minimum wage increases are largely unknown.

[15] On the other hand, it is not consistent with studies for the United States, which show that the minimum wage does not help reduce poverty (Neumark and Wascher 2002).

wage must facilitate the hiring of labor under conditions that are acceptable to companies and workers, it ought to meet the following requirements:

- *Simplicity.* In almost all countries in the region, the previously common practice of setting different minimum wages by industry sector, region, or type of company has been abandoned because such differences are difficult to enforce and have the major disadvantage of obscuring the tool. Setting different minimums did not help strengthen workers in their individual dealings with companies.
- *Reasonableness.* A minimum wage that is too high in relation to average pay levels would not constitute a floor and hence would tend to be ignored. A minimum wage that is too low does not grant any power to the individuals who are seeking employment, and hence does not prevent them from taking excessively low-quality and low-productivity jobs.
- *Stability but not rigidity.* A highly fluctuating real minimum wage would produce abrupt redistributions of income that would tend to be perceived as unjust and undermine the credibility of the tool. The same thing would happen with a completely rigid real minimum wage that failed to take into account the state of the economy, the unemployment level, or changes in worker productivity.
- *Broad discussion and agreement.* Since the minimum wage is ultimately a social convention, it should be based on a broad debate with participation not only by organized workers and large companies, as happens in some countries, but by society as a whole and government officials formulating economic and social policies. Any minimum wage level chosen will have costs and benefits, and society as a whole should be aware of them.

Labor Unions

Labor unions represent a crucial achievement by workers, and have made possible spectacular gains in working conditions and pay for significant groups of workers. Unions facilitate relations between companies and workers by reducing uncertainty and improving information flows between both parties. Collective bargaining helps reconcile the interests of workers and companies in the aggregate and prevents the adverse consequences that may result from uncoordinated bargaining activities and their ensuing conflicts.

At the same time, labor unions have imposed work rules that impede improvements in productivity and are a device for seeking to extract rents from companies. Labor union activity may have the effect of reducing investment and making businesses less competitive. Unions may also be harmful at the macroeconomic level if they become an obstacle to adopting adjustment policies or to allowing for greater economic flexibility.

The real impact of union action depends on the balance between these costs and benefits, which are in turn influenced by the economic, political, and organizational environment in which labor organizing and collective bargaining take place. Hence, rather than trying to identify an impact that will vary from country to country or between sectors within each country, this section presents an overview of trends in unionization and the laws governing it, and the results of research that has analyzed the impact of unions on the well-being of workers and society as a whole.

The levels of unionization in Latin America are modest and have declined in most countries over the past decade. The legal framework within which labor unions operate in the region is relatively favorable to union organizing and protective of workers, with significant differences among countries. Contrary to the rest of the world, in Latin America, workers who are less educated are less likely to belong to a labor union than those who are more educated. This partly explains the view of unions as defenders of a labor elite (and as increasing pay inequality). As in the rest of the world, labor unions in Latin America seek to achieve their primary objective: raising the income level of their members. However, this ability has been weakened by the processes of economic liberalization, privatization, decline in government jobs, and other factors that have eroded the market power of companies and hence of unions as well.

Labor unions can produce significant macroeconomic effects, depending on the degree of coordination among unions and among companies in the collective bargaining process. Experience in developed countries indicates that the risks of higher unemployment or inflation resulting from uncoordinated actions by labor unions can be moderated when there are mechanisms for high-level coordination and companies are more exposed to international competition.

Unionization in Latin America

By international standards, unionization rates in Latin America are moderate. Average union membership in the past three decades was 18.3 percent of the workforce, which was less than the world average (23.8 percent) and substantially less than in developed countries and Eastern Europe (Figure 7.16). Nonetheless, in Latin America, labor unions represent a greater percentage of the workforce than elsewhere in the developing world.

Household surveys can be used to analyze the factors that explain the differences between unionization rates in the region in comparison with Canada and the United States. Most of the personal and employment characteristics explained by unionization in developed countries have the same effect in Latin America. Workers in manufacturing, public services, transportation, large firms, and the public sector tend to have higher levels of unionization (see Box 7.6). The exception to this uniformity is education: in Latin America, workers who have not completed high school tend to be less unionized than their peers who have a high school diploma or more. This membership pattern suggests that by defending the interests of a relatively more educated labor elite, labor unions may actually increase wage inequality.

Thus, the relatively low rates of unionization in the region are not necessarily the result of political factors (such as repression of labor organizing), but may result from differences in the composition of workforces in the region. The youth of the region's labor force in itself hinders unionization. At the same time, differences in unionization levels between countries that are similar in terms of their income level and labor force composition suggest the importance of the regulatory framework as crucial for levels of union density.

Figure 7.16 Unionization Rate, 1970-99
(Percentage of the labor force)

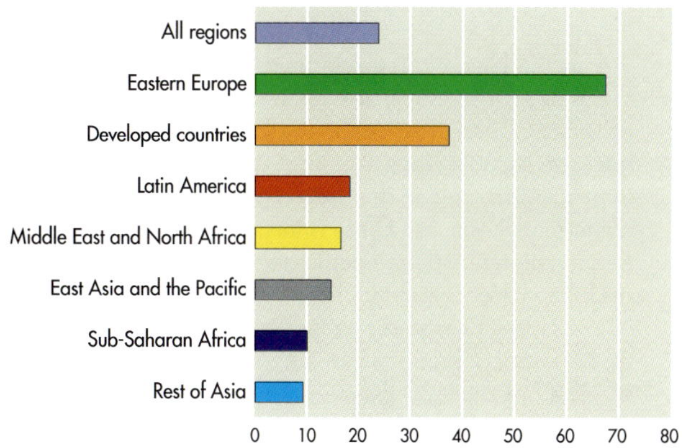

Source: Forteza and Rama (2002).

In the 1990s, unionization rates fell in most countries in the region. In Brazil and Mexico, where unionization had increased between the late 1970s and the late 1980s to more than 35 percent, it fell to 24.8 and 22.4 percent, respectively, in the first half of the 1990s. Only in Chile, Costa Rica, and El Salvador did union coverage increase in the 1990s, although it did not reach more than a modest 15 percent of the workforce (Table 7.3).

The declining importance of unions is related to changes in economies in recent decades. In particular, declining government employment, expanding temporary employment, and increasing competition in industry have contributed to the drop in unionization. Changes in legislation governing how unions operate have also had a great influence.

According to Saavedra and Torero (forthcoming), reduced government employment and the expansion of temporary work are the two primary factors explaining the drop in the rate of unionization in Peru from 40 percent in 1986 to 30 percent in 1991. But after 1992, the diminished protection granted to labor unions in Peru was the main reason for the even sharper decline in unionization (to 10 percent in 1998). In Uruguay, where unions were prohibited until 1985, unionization among factory workers reached 60 percent three years later. Since 1991 it has dropped sharply, partly

Box 7.6 Unions and the Public Sector

The public sector in the region is highly unionized relative to the overall economy. It is often argued that this high level of unionization has detrimental effects on performance because arcane work rules and wage increases unrelated to productivity growth hinder the development of better production methods. Nowhere is this debate more crucial than in education, where the public sector dominates production and the workforce of teachers is highly unionized.

Two recent studies shed some light on the question of the impact of unions in the mostly public education sector. The first difficulty these studies had to overcome was to choose one method to measure product and productivity. Both chose variants of the education production function approach (Hoxby 1996) to analyze the influence of unions on student achievement (measured by some form of standardized test). The production function approach allows the analyst to control for other factors, such as physical inputs and socio-demographic characteristics of the population, to better isolate the impact of unions, which is measured as the difference in students' standardized test scores.

Zegarra and Ravina's (2003) study of schools in Peru finds that most of the decline in union density is associated with changes in work rules that allowed the hiring of temporary teachers, who were less likely to belong to a union, given the temporary nature of their contracts. This decline in union density curtailed the ability of unions to influence budgets at the school or district level. However, unions could still influence the effort that teachers put into the process and the physical inputs. This analysis weakly supports the hypothesis that unionized workers have access to more complementary inputs, at least at the intermediate *multigrado* schools. More interestingly, the authors find that unions do not have a statistically significant influence, either on teacher effort or student test scores.

Murillo and others (2002) analyze Argentina's public education system, which has been decentralized since the early 1990s. The peculiar trait of this system is that the role of provincial authorities is larger than usual and schools have limited autonomy. The authors find that in provinces where there is a higher frequency of strikes, there is also more competition between unions, and unions have more adversarial relations with the government. This suggests that neither competition between unions nor adversarial managerial relations (both supposedly disciplining forces for public sector unions) work well in this case. In contrast with Zegarra and Ravina's study of Peru, Murillo and others show that unions in Argentina (weakly) influence class size and teacher satisfaction in ways favorable to higher student achievement in test scores. They also report that the education budget is determined by the overall fiscal situation; the only impact unions have is on the distribution of the budget toward more personnel.

Both studies suggest that unions have a weak effect on the performance of the education system, and the effect is dwarfed by the impact of availability of complementary inputs and the socio-demographic characteristics of the students.

More importantly, both studies show how the framework in which unions operate to improve the lot of their members is important in shaping outcomes. In Peru, the lack of influence of unions in determining either district or school budgets explains to a large extent why the authors find no impact of unions on student performance. The study on Argentina shows that the "discipline the unions" approach does not work, confirming what a multitude of private sector studies have found: hostile management-union relationships are bad for productivity. If public sector reforms are to be successful, they require the development of a cooperative framework of operations for unions and management in the education sector.

because of changes in regulations and competition introduced into industry by economic liberalization (Cassoni, Allen, and Labadie forthcoming).

Laws Governing Industrial Relations

Legislation on industrial (or collective) relations provides the legal framework within which labor unions operate. The laws govern the balance of power between unions and labor organizations on one side and individual companies or sets of companies on the other. In keeping with the typology recently developed by Djankov and others (2003), the topics regulating this legislation may be organized under three headings: (i) collective bargaining, (ii) participation of workers in managing companies, and (iii) group conflicts. These researchers have proposed a system of indicators of these three aspects of the legislation that seeks to measure the degree of protection granted to workers and labor organizations.

In the area of collective bargaining, it is thought that unions are more protected if employers have a legal obligation to bargain with unions, collective bargaining agreements extend to third parties, the law allows for hiring to be conditional

Table 7.3 Unionization Rates in Latin America, 1976–95
(Percent)

Country	1976–80	1981–85	1986–90	1991–95
Argentina		28.2	26.5	21.5
Bahamas	25	25	25	
Bolivia	32	28.8	25.2	16.4
Brazil	19.6	34.8	38.1	24.8
Chile		9.1	9.5	13.1
Colombia		17.7	12.1	
Costa Rica		14.3	14.9	15.0
Dominican Republic		12.2	15.3	13.4
Ecuador		15.0	14.3	13.5
El Salvador		8.0	14.1	15.0
Guatemala			8.1	4.4
Honduras			20.0	20.0
Jamaica	28.3	22.2	20.3	16.3
Mexico	19.1	27.3	35.3	22.4
Nicaragua	3.7	32.0	32.0	23.4
Panama	12.5	15.0	17.0	14.2
Paraguay	5.0	2.8		
Peru	25.0	40.0	13.0	12.9
Trinidad and Tobago	27.2	31.0	25.4	22.0
Uruguay			19.3	16.3
Venezuela		18.0		
Median	25.0	20.1	18.15	16.3

Source: Forteza and Rama (2002).

on union membership, and labor organization and collective bargaining rights are enshrined in the constitution. By international standards, the protection granted to unions in their collective bargaining processes is high in Latin America. On a scale of zero to one, the typical country in Latin America offers protection at 0.67, above the world standard (0.44) and that of developed countries in relative terms (0.39). Argentina, Mexico, Peru, and Venezuela have substantially higher protection (0.89), whereas Bolivia, Jamaica, and Panama offer the least protection in the region, which is at the world level (Figure 7.17).

In the area of participation by workers in company management, workers are believed to have greater collective protection when they or their unions have the right to appoint representatives to serve on the company board of directors, it is obligatory that there be worker councils or similar bodies in companies, and participation by workers in company management is enshrined in the constitution.

Figure 7.17 Protection of Collective Bargaining
(Index, 0-3)

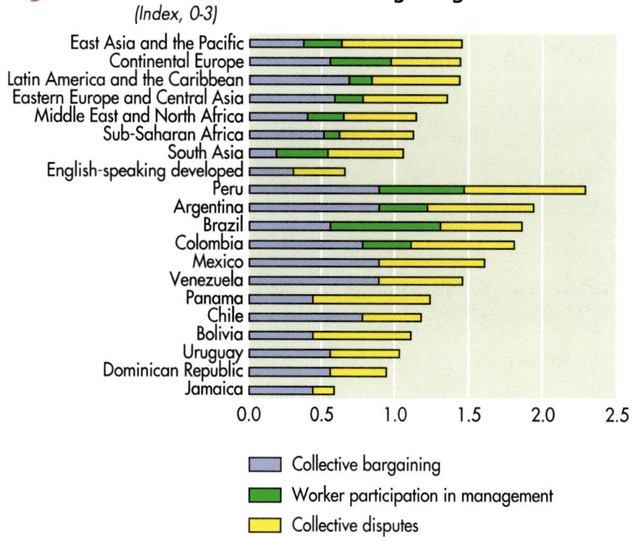

Source: Djankov and others (2003).

In Latin America, these participation mechanisms are not legally protected, nor are they commonly used in the rest of the world. However, there are great differences between countries; for example, among developed countries, Norway meets all the criteria, whereas English-speaking developed countries and Japan meet none of them. In Latin America, only Brazil, Peru, Argentina, and Colombia concede importance (in that order) to some of these mechanisms for participation by workers.

The field of collective bargaining conflicts is the area of legislation that is most difficult to typify, and where measurements are therefore most likely to be arbitrary. The system used by researchers from Harvard and Yale considers a set of 11 criteria that measure the level of protection of the right to a strike, the absence of procedural restrictions on exercising this right, the degree of restriction of actions of defense that may be taken by employees if arbitration is legally required by the government or third parties, and whether the constitution protects rights in a labor action. Typically in Latin America, in collective bargaining disputes, workers are more protected than elsewhere in the world or in countries with higher relative development. The index for this group of indicators is 0.6 for the typical country in the region, as compared with 0.53 worldwide or 0.48 among more developed countries. Peru, Panama, Argentina, Mexico, and Brazil (in that order) offer the most protection, whereas Jamaica, the Dominican Republic, Chile, and Uruguay offer the least protection.

Hence, in two of the three areas of industrial relations legislation—collective bargaining and labor disputes—greater protection tends to be offered to workers in Latin America than in the rest of the world or in more developed countries. The index that summarizes all aspects considered shows Latin America to have relatively high levels of protection, especially in Peru, Argentina, Brazil, Colombia, and Mexico.

Who Benefits from Labor Unions?

Who wins and who loses through union activity and collective bargaining disputes is an area of disagreement, not only between the parties directly involved, but also among analysts. Disputes are sharpest precisely when it is implicitly assumed that the labor relationship is a zero-sum game in which some can win only at the cost of others. The discussion on the effects of unions also becomes difficult when it is mistakenly believed that the consequences of labor union action are similar in different contexts, and when positive or negative experiences may be transplanted to different contexts. On this issue, the starting point must be the recognition that neither theory nor empirical evidence offers a final conclusion on the impact of labor union activity. Box 7.7 explains the theoretical reasons for this ambivalence. This section summarizes the results of empirical research on the benefits and costs of unions.

The primary objective of any labor union is to improve the well-being of its members. By this standard, unions tend to be successful. Labor union members generally receive higher pay than those who are nonunionized. In the United States, the differential has been estimated at 15 percent, and in most other countries it is between 5 and 10 percent. There is a great deal of variation in developing countries, possibly because of the diversity of market conditions in which firms operate. As a rule, the wages of unionized workers are better in companies that operate under less competitive conditions in the product market (Aidt and Tzannatos 2002). Hence, the wages of unionized workers are better in companies protected by tariffs or other restrictions on imports because the unions can share in the rents that the companies derive from such restrictions (Harrison and Hanson 1999). The wage differential favoring unionized workers may be cut back with the freeing of international trade, as has happened in Mexico, Uruguay, and other countries (see chapter 5).

Labor unions help reduce wage disparities, especially between skilled and unskilled workers (Aidt and Tzannatos 2002). However, in Latin America, the influence of unions on income distribution may be favorable in some countries and unfavorable in others, for reasons that are not well understood. Cross-section statistical analysis that compares several countries shows that the greater the union membership, the better the income dis-

Box 7.7 The Usefulness of Union Action

Unions generate both costs and benefits for society. In theory, they can produce monopoly costs insofar as they interfere with the free operation of the labor market, and rent-seeking costs insofar as they try to create other distortions and seek to extract rents from society. But they benefit society by acting as channels of information and coordination between companies and workers and as mechanisms for cooperation in work. The impact of labor union action therefore depends on the balance between the costs and benefits produced by their activities.

Monopoly Costs

The main objective of unions is to improve the working conditions of their members. In an elementary theoretical framework, this objective can be achieved if unions succeed in reducing the supply of labor to which companies have access and thereby obtain higher wages so as to seize some of the extra earnings that companies may achieve by operating in markets that are not fully competitive. Unions have to control the labor supply because otherwise companies would hire nonunion workers at lower wages. The markets for the companies' products must not be completely competitive because otherwise there would be no rents to share. In this theoretical framework, unions generate monopoly costs to society by discouraging investment in the sectors where they operate, causing employment in lower productivity sectors to expand, and generating unemployment among workers attracted to unionized sectors by the differential between their wages and those of the nonunionized sector.

The discussion of monopoly costs of unions implicitly assumes that the labor market would be perfectly competitive in the absence of unions. But if that is not the case, for example, because firms have monopsonistic power (that is, market power to hire workers at lower pay than would be the case with perfect competition in the labor market), unions could help resolve the inefficiencies produced by this original distortion. In addition, it is not clear that a multitude of negotiations between each company and its individual workers is a more efficient way to set wages and other labor conditions than an arrangement negotiated with a union, which sets general guidelines for individual contracts, thereby reducing negotiation costs and uncertainty.

Costs of Rent Seeking

Unions can generate other costs to society because it is in their interest to increase the rents received by companies so that they can receive a share. Therefore, unions may support distortionary policies that may be expensive for society but benefit companies and unions. Import controls are a good example. They have social costs because resources flow to sectors that are artificially more profitable to the detriment of others that may be more productive, and because resources are devoted to disputes over claiming the rents, rather than to productive activities. Rent seeking by unions may also be harmful to innovation. Companies that fear that unions may seize the earnings from their inventions may opt to reduce their investment in research and development. Hence, through various routes, unions can generate rent-seeking costs.

Benefits from Participation and Resolution of Disputes

Unions play a role in the organization of companies by acting as channels of information between management and workers and as mechanisms for facilitating cooperation in the workplace. Unions are the collective voice of workers; they allow the exchange of information on concerns that workers individually would not be able or want to express. Thus, unions can help companies improve the work environment, offer more training that is more adequate to workers' needs, and facilitate on-the-job learning. Unions can also help maintain procedures for dialogue between companies and workers, thereby lowering the risk of costly disputes and strikes. And unions can help assure that agreements between companies and workers are observed, reducing uncertainty, which can be harmful to investment and to workers adopting abilities specific to the company. Finally, when a cooperative environment between a company and a union is developed, the latter can help adopt better techniques and work methods to improve productivity for the benefit of both sides. These are all benefits of participation and dispute resolution that may be provided by unions to the companies or sectors in which they operate.

In sum, theory is ambiguous on whether unions are beneficial to society. It depends on the balance between costs and benefits.

Source: Based on Aidt and Tzannatos (2002, chapter 3).

tribution, even controlling for the impact of other factors that may influence income distribution (such as taxes, government spending, or social security payments to families). According to Pagés and Shinkai (2002), a 10 percent increase in union membership is associated with a 6 to 10 percent reduction in wage inequality. Therefore, the decline in union membership between the 1980s and the 1990s could account for a 6.6 percent increase in wage inequality, which is greater than what actually took place (3.1 percent).

However, a more detailed country-by-country analysis indicates that this conclusion must be accepted with caution because it does not apply equally to all cases. For example, in Mexico and Venezuela, union membership helps lessen wage inequality among unionized workers, although unions benefit skilled more than unskilled workers. This effect is so strong that unions reduce total wage inequality. According to Pagés and Shinkai, in Venezuela the wage variance of all workers would be 20 percent greater without unions, and in Mexico it would be 13 percent greater.[16] In Brazil, by contrast, unionization has the opposite effect on inequality because unions contribute to increased inequality among unionized workers and between them and other workers.[17]

Unions also seem to contribute to reduced wage gaps between men and women among unionized workers. In Mexico, unionization produces a similar effect for indigenous people (Aidt and Tzannatos 2002).

Unions achieve other benefits for their workers. Voluntary turnover is less and job permanence is greater in unionized companies (although at the cost, at least partly, of more involuntary dismissals).[18] Work hours are less for unionized compared with nonunionized workers, and other benefits, such as severance pay, vacations, and pensions, are greater. Furthermore, unionized workers receive more training than their nonunionized peers, especially training directly related to company activities, although the evidence comes primarily from developed countries (Aidt and Tzannatos 2002). Whether this can be generalized to Latin American countries is not known.

Effects of Unions on Companies

Unions do benefit their members, but does this benefit occur at the expense of companies or other sectors of society? In relation to the effects on companies, the evidence is mixed. It has been found quite consistently that unionized companies are less profitable, especially when such companies enjoy market power. However, unions seem to be sufficiently restrained to avoid bringing companies to bankruptcy. Indeed, there is no evidence that unionized companies go bankrupt more often than nonunionized ones do (Aidt and Tzannatos 2002; Kuhn 1998). The presence of unions in companies seems to have negative effects on investment, as indicated by evidence for the United States and the United Kingdom. However, no uniform pattern has been found in the effect of unionization on productivity. Differences are great from one industry to another, but they tend to be positive where companies operate in competitive markets and in an atmosphere where industrial relations are not very conflictive.

Although most studies of the effects of unions on company performance have to do with developed countries, the main conclusions seem to bear out for Latin American countries as well. Utilizing a set of companies in the manufacturing sector in Peru, Saavedra and Torero (forthcoming) find that the presence of unions reduces company profitability, and that this effect increases with higher unionization. In Guatemala, a study of coffee farms finds negative effects of unionization on productivity (Urizar and Lee 2003). Menezes Filho and others (2002) establish that in Brazil, the presence of unions lowers the profitability of manufacturing companies.[19] However, Brazil is one of the few countries where worker participation in certain aspects of company management is mandatory. Menezes Filho and others find that the introduction of these mechanisms (particularly profit sharing) contributed to company performance in terms of productivity and profitability, and that this effect

[16] In the United States, unions reduce inequality by 8 percent, according to the same study.

[17] These conclusions of Pagés and Shinkai (2002) for Brazil are consistent with the findings of Arbache (1999).

[18] Yet this is not true in Uruguay, one of the few countries in the region where this phenomenon has been studied. In Uruguay, those working in the more unionized industries are less likely to be fired (Cassoni, Allen, and Labadie forthcoming).

[19] According to this study, union density has a nonlinear effect on productivity—it is positive and growing to intermediate levels and then gradually declining until it reaches the negative point.

was greater in the more unionized companies, possibly because unions facilitate communication between company management and workers.

Effects of Unions on the Economy

An issue that requires caution before leaping to any conclusion is the effects of unions on the economy as a whole. This is due not only to limitations of empirical research, but also to the fact that the influence of labor union action depends crucially on contextual aspects and especially on coordination between unions and/or companies.

Aidt and Tzannatos (2002) review comparative studies among countries (most of them in the OECD) and make the following observations:

> • Union density (the proportion of all workers who are union members) per se has a weak association, or perhaps no association, with economic performance indicators such as the unemployment rate, inflation, the employment rate, real compensation growth, labor supply, adjustment speed to wage shocks, real wage flexibility, and labor and total factor productivity. There is, however, one significant exception: union density correlates negatively with labor earnings inequality and wage dispersion. However, even this conclusion must be taken with caution for Latin American countries.
>
> • Bargaining coverage (the proportion of the workforce that is covered by a collective agreement) tends to be associated with higher real wage growth (with no impact on productivity growth), lower employment rates, higher unemployment rates, and higher inflation. As with union density, bargaining coverage correlates negatively with larger earnings inequality and age dispersion. (Aidt and Tzannatos 2002, p.11)

The foregoing conclusions mean that union action can have important effects for society as a whole. However, those effects depend critically on circumstances that differ between countries, particularly the degree of coordination between unions and/or between companies in wage negotiations. For example, in Uruguay between 1985 and 1991, unions operated under an arrangement of three-way industry negotiations with government involvement, thereby entailing a high degree of coordination. Since 1992, unions have been free to bargain at the firm level with no government involvement. In this new system, chances of coordination are minimal.

It is important to distinguish coordination from centralization, which refers strictly to the level at which the negotiation takes place (in the plan, the company, the industry, or the economy as a whole). This means that there may be coordination between unions or companies even when the bargaining system is decentralized. The existence of labor and business organizations facilitates coordination between unions and companies, even when wage decisions are decentralized.

The evidence for developed countries suggests that countries where collective bargaining processes are coordinated at the national level tend to experience lower and less persistent unemployment rates, less wage inequality, and fewer disruptions because of strikes than those where coordination takes place at the industry level or where there is no coordination. There is also support for the claim that coordination at the intermediate or industry level produces the worst effects in terms of productivity and wage rigidity. Although these conclusions stand up better for the 1970s and 1980s than subsequently, the following statement remains generally valid for developed countries: "High union density and bargaining coverage do not contribute to poor unemployment performance so long as they are complemented by high bargaining coordination (particularly among employers)." (Aidt and Tzannatos 2002, p.13)

Hence, coordination of collective bargaining processes may avoid some of the negative effects that union action may have on the economy as a whole when unions or companies act without coordination. But coordination also brings its own risks, especially when it is based on centralized bargaining processes. It may reduce competitive pressure on companies, which, by acting together, can raise wages not supported by productivity improvements and thus translate into inflation, unemployment, or low growth. This risk is significant in economies that are not very integrated with the rest of the world. Centralized coordination can reduce incentives for collaboration between companies and their unions to share information and improve productivity, and raise the risks of national strikes that can have high costs for society as a whole.

Labor unions may influence the ability of economies to adjust and their willingness to adopt reforms, an issue that is quite relevant for Latin America. Of all the labor institutions discussed in this chapter, only labor unions seem to have an influence on the depth and effectiveness of macroeconomic and structural reforms, according to an analysis of the experience of more than 100 countries between 1980 and 1996 (Forteza and Rama 2002). The countries with the highest unionization rates tend to experience greater recessions before adopting adjustment measurements, and subsequently they are slower to recover. These results suggest that in most cases labor organizations help delay and dilute reform processes. However, it is not clear whether this applies to countries with different levels of coordination, collective bargaining, and other institutions that may influence interaction among governments, business sectors, and workers in macroeconomic decisionmaking.

In closing, as summarized in Box 7.8, labor unions can bring important gains to society, but also induce substantial costs, depending on institutional, economic, and cultural factors.

Box 7.8 Effects of Labor Unions

Indications

Labor unions provide a voice to workers and facilitate dialogue between workers and firms. Labor unions prevent conflict between firms and workers by finding win-win solutions to problems and helping to increase productivity. They raise wages, working conditions, and employment levels for those covered in the negotiations.

Side Effects

Labor unions often reduce profits and investment and may promote inefficient policies and rent-seeking that will benefit their members but not society at large. Side effects are much less of a concern in firms/sectors subject to internal and external competition.

Caution

Benefits and side effects are difficult to foresee in advance because they are sensitive to the legal framework governing industrial relations, the level of coordination among unions, and coordination among unions, government, and business organizations.

Appendix Table 7.1 Economic Effects of Labor Laws and Regulations, Latin American and Developed Countries, 1995–2001

Dependent variable	Employment rate	Unemployment rate	Growth in employment[a]	Percent self-employed	Total factor productivity growth rate[b]	Real GDP per worker growth rate[b]	Percent unemployed more than a year
Conditions of employment	-7.24	3.12	-2.53	12.67	0.38	1.35	31.83
t-statistic	(1.27)	(0.67)	(1.21)	(2.40)**	(0.27)	(0.89)	(1.64)
Number of observations	54	39	40	33	64	83	38
R^2	0.11	0.13	0.13	0.75	0.05	0.03	0.11
Social security	-3.61	1.02	-1.77	-0.87	-0.71	-0.30	
t-statistic	(1.62)	(0.71)	(2.31)**	(0.29)	(1.66)	(0.71)	
Number of observations	54	39	40	33	64	83	
R^2	0.12	0.13	0.21	0.7	0.09	0.02	
Social security contributions (percentage of wages)	-12.48	3.86	-3.16	-0.08	0.61	1.64	73.04
t-statistic	(1.97)	(0.93)	(2.14)**	(0.01)	(0.33)	(0.79)	(4.51)***
Number of observations	42	36	32	38	40	42	40
R^2	0.18	0.12	0.29	0.7	0.23	0.17	0.39
Job security (Djankov measure)	0.60	-0.64	1.67	0.77	-0.30	0.49	-3.45
t-statistic	(0.10)	(0.18)	(0.80)	(0.16)	(0.23)	(0.35)	(0.20)
Number of observations	54	39	40	33	64	83	38
R^2	0.08	0.12	0.11	0.7	0.05	0.02	0.05
Job security (Heckman and Pagés measure)	-1.38	-0.97	0.32	-0.36	0.05	0.17	-0.15
t-statistic	(1.37)	(1.52)	(1.08)	(0.36)	(0.16)	(0.67)	(0.47)
Number of observations	42	37	32	38	40	41	42
R^2	0.21	0.17	0.24	0.71	0.19	0.34	0.12

** Significant at 5 percent.

*** Significant at 1 percent.

[a] Number of employees, 1990–2001.

[b] 1995–99.

Note: Per capita GDP in U.S. dollars is used as a control in all regressions, and a constant is also estimated but not reported.

Source: Self-employment data are from Blanchard (2002) and IDB household surveys. Social security data are from Djankov and others (2003). Data on social security contributions as a percentage of wages are from Heckman and Pagés (forthcoming). Job security measures are from Djankov and others (2003) and Heckman and Pagés (forthcoming).

Appendix 7.1 The Speed of Adjustment and Labor Market Institutions

This appendix summarizes recent work by Caballero and Engel (2003), which analyzes the relationship between the speed at which firms adjust employment to changes in the economic environment and labor market institutions.

The first step is to compute a measure of the speed of adjustment, λ. The following setup is used:

$$(1)\quad \Delta l_{jit} = \lambda(l^*_{jit} - l_{jit-1}) = \lambda(l^*_{jit} - l_{jit} - \Delta l_{jit})$$

where l and l^* represent the observed and desired levels of employment (in logs) for sector i in country j and period t. To estimate the gap between the current and desired levels of employment, gap = $(l^*_{jit} - l_{jit-1})$, it is assumed that wages equal the nominal marginal productivity of labor in the absence of adjustment costs. After some algebra, the following expression is obtained:

$$(2)\quad l^*_{jit} - l_{jit} = \Omega \frac{nmpl_{jit} - w_{j,t} - \phi_{jit}}{1 - \alpha\gamma_i}$$

where *nmpl* is the nominal marginal productivity of labor (in logs) and w represents wages (also in logs).

To avoid the use of wages, they are proxied by the simple average of *nmpl* by country and year. The denominator is one minus labor's share in income and ϕ is a variable that accounts for the composition of workers across industries and countries.[1] This parameter is estimated as the simple average in t-2 and t-1 of the difference between *nmpl* and w. The parameter Ω is related to the substitutability between hours and employment, and is estimated by rewriting expression (2) as follows:

$$(3)\quad \Delta l_{jit} = -\Omega \frac{\Delta nmpl_{jit} - \Delta w_{j,t}}{1 - \alpha\gamma_i} + \Delta l^*_{jit}$$

and making use of the fact that the obtained coefficient is 0.3.

To compute equation (1), nominal output and employment data from the 2002 three-digit UNIDO Industrial Statistics Database are used. The UNIDO database contains data for 1963-2000 for the 28 manufacturing sectors that correspond to the three-digit ISIC code (revision 2). The analysis is based on data for 51 OECD and Latin American countries from 1980-2000 for which there is information on job security from Djankov and others (2003) and Heckman and Pagés (forthcoming).

Appendix Table 7.1 presents the results of estimation of equation (1). The first column reports the results without including the interaction term (gap * job security). As expected, the estimated coefficient on gap is positive and significantly different from zero at conventional confidence levels: changes in employment are proportional to the gap between wages and the marginal product of labor. The point estimates of the λ coefficient suggest that firms on average close 75 percent of the gap between the desired and current levels of labor.

The second column includes an interaction between the computed gap and the Djankov and others index of job security (a higher value implies more job security). The estimated coefficient on the gap * job security interaction is positive and (marginally) significant, contrary to the expected effect of job security on adjustment costs. A possible explanation for this finding is variation across countries in the degree of enforcement of labor market regulations.

To test this hypothesis, the third column includes an additional interaction term, gap * job security * rule of law. The estimated coefficient on this triple interaction should be (and is) negative and significant. Countries with higher job security and rule of law have a lower speed of adjustment. The effect of the estimated coefficients on the speed of adjustment is large. Moving from the low-

[1] Labor's share in income equals the labor-output elasticity divided by the markup. The coefficient is assumed to be equal across countries but varies across sectors.

Appendix 7.1 Table 1 Speed of Adjustment and Labor Market Regulation

	(1)	(2)	(3)	(4)	(5)	(6)	(7)	(8)	(9)
Gap	0.754	0.752	0.771	0.841	0.697				
	(0.011)***	(0.019)***	(0.018)***	(0.048)***	(0.019)***				
Gap* job security (Djankov)		0.007	–0.086	–0.090	–0.142	–0.152	0.197		
		(0.045)	(0.050)*	(0.050)*	(0.051)***	(0.051)***	(0.055)***		
Gap* rule of law			0.040	0.041			0.052		–0.001
			(0.016)**	(0.015)***			(0.017)***		(0.021)
Gap* job security (Djankov) * rule of law			–0.129	–0.130			–0.112		
			(0.041)***	(0.040)***			(0.041)***		
Gap* job security (Heckman)							–0.032	–0.032	
								(0.009)***	(0.009)***
Gap* job security (Heckman) * rule of law									0.001
									(0.008)
Gap* medium-high income					0.085	0.080	0.095	0.096	0.096
					(0.016)***	(0.017)***	(0.025)***	(0.025)***	(0.033)***
Gap* medium income					–0.001	0.007	0.007	0.013	0.013
					(0.001)	(0.004)*	(0.004)*	(0.005)***	(0.005)***
Gap* low income					0.179	0.179	0.203	0.152	0.155
					(0.024)***	(0.024)***	(0.032)***	(0.041)***	(0.060)***
Number of observations	20,332	20,332	20,332	20,332	20,332	20,332	20,332	10,676	10,676
R^2	0.71	0.71	0.72	0.72	0.72	0.72	0.72	0.73	0.73
Gap * ISIC dummies	No	No	No	Yes	No	Yes	Yes	Yes	Yes

* Significant at 10 percent.
** Significant at 5 percent.
*** Significant at 1 percent.
Note: The dependent variable is change in employment. Higher values represent lower contract flexibility. Each regression has a country-year fixed effect. Robust standard errors are in parentheses. Omega=0.3 The Djankov job security measure is from Djankov and others (2003); the Heckman measure is from Heckman and Pagés (forthcoming).
Source: IDB calculations.

est 20 percent of job security to the highest 20 percent reduces the speed of adjustment from around 0.6 to less that 0.1 with high rule of law. The same change has a lower effect for countries with weak rule of law: from 0.6 to 0.4.

These results are robust to the addition of sector-gap interactions to control for differences in the speed of adjustment of sectors (the fourth column), dummy variables for the level of income interacted with the gap interactions (the fifth through seventh columns), and an alternative measure of job security (the eighth column).

Chapter 8

A New Labor Policy Agenda

The labor market fulfills two parallel functions—allocation of resources and allocation of incomes—at the center of everyday market exchanges. All kinds of policies affect the labor market and, in turn, labor market performance affects outcomes in other policy areas. Growth is a fundamental force affecting the performance of the labor market; after all, the demand for labor is derived from the demand for the goods and services labor produces.

The mix and orientation of the policy instruments that have been used to affect labor market outcomes in Latin America and the Caribbean have not been static. In the 1970s and early 1980s, fiscal policy, particularly investment in large public projects, was the favorite tool for fighting unemployment. In the high-inflation 1980s, wage indexation policies and modest targeted employment programs were used to dampen the impact of low growth on the labor market. During the 1990s, when financial constraints forbade the use of fiscal policies, attention turned to the reform of labor regulations that increased labor costs for firms.

In spite of this variety of policy efforts, labor market outcomes in the region have been unsatisfactory. These outcomes are the product of more than labor policies. The preceding chapters of this volume have discussed in depth how labor market performance is affected by demographic trends (chapter 3), macroeconomic policies (chapter 4), the structural reforms of the 1990s (chapter 5), and technological change or lack thereof (chapter 6). Chapter 7 discussed the impact that labor regulation and institutions have on the performance of the labor market. This chapter returns to the discussion in chapter 2 on the reallocation of jobs and workers. It focuses on the set of policies needed to facilitate the labor market task of allocating resources and earnings across workers and firms.

These facilitating policies will operate in a volatile macroeconomic environment. Although monetary and fiscal policies are not as much of a source of instability as they used to be—during the 1990s they exhibited substantially lower volatility than in previous decades—other sources of volatility persist. The first section of the chapter briefly discusses some of the suggested policies for lowering volatility by reducing exposure to external shocks and improving the set of domestic policies that countries can use to deal with these shocks. The main point is that many of these macro policies involve structural changes—and as such are unlikely to have immediate effects on instability. Furthermore, falling inflation rates in many economies of the region may lead to higher real wage rigidity (as discussed in chapter 4) and therefore may deepen the unemployment effects of adjustment to external shocks. Thus, this section also explores some innovations in labor market policies that may help to minimize the negative effects of this unstable macroeconomic setting on labor market outcomes.

As the discussion about job and worker dynamics in chapter 2 explained, most of the action in the labor market happens around the flows of job creation and destruction, and it is at this level that labor policies need to operate. These flows involve a vastly larger number of workers than those who are unemployed; typically, relocation involves one-fourth of the total number of jobs in each period, a much larger number than the average 10 percent unemployment rate that is usually observed in the region. Even more compelling, normal job churning dwarfs the effects of macro and financial crises on worker and job relocation (see chapter 2).

The main normative message of this chapter is that labor policies should evolve away from the philosophy of "protecting the worker from the power of employers" that has often inspired the institutional design of labor policies in the region. Policies should instead facilitate the labor market's task of allocating resources and earnings across workers and firms.

This does not imply that workers' rights (both individual and collective, as established in conventions on core labor standards and in national labor codes) are not important. In fact, if anything, the status quo of implementation and enforcement in the region de facto ignores core labor standards, using a "better not to enforce bad regulations" justification. Rule of law is a social asset that is depreciated through noncompliance with regulations and should be taken more seriously. Reversing the past decade's degradation of the regulatory and enforcement function is a necessary condition for effective labor policy. Regulations can and should change, as discussed in chapter 7.

Switching labor policies toward a facilitating role implies far-reaching institutional changes. Countries in the region spend 0.5 percent of gross domestic product (GDP) on income support policies that operate through the labor market; OECD countries spend at least double that (Verdera 1998; OECD 1998). Given the modest amount of resources available in Latin America, the development of new public-private partnerships in the design and implementation of labor policies is crucial.

What would this new approach encompass? The vision that emerges from the discussion in this volume is a complex network of public and private institutions that fill four specific functions: (1) increasing the efficiency of matching, (2) adequately insuring workers against the risks of job churning, (3) enhancing the opportunities of workers by increasing their skills, and (4) enforcing regulations. With the exception of the insurance function, these are structural functions. That is, they entail expenditures and offer services that are permanent and independent of business cycles. The insurance function is highly countercyclical by design and therefore should adjust through the cycle. However, because services include cross-referral between income support, training, and intermediation subsystems, the whole system should exhibit countercyclical behavior.

However, the behavior of current fiscal and social policies hinders the task of insurance that, by definition, implies transferring income between good and bad times. The last section of this chapter discusses possible mechanisms to overcome the macroeconomic and political constraints that generate this procyclical behavior. In the long run, Latin American countries would likely benefit from a more developed welfare state, both through more macroeconomic stability and less risk for the population from unexpected shocks. However, in this process it is essential to bring in the lessons and avoid the mistakes made by those countries that began this process earlier.

Dealing with Macro Volatility

One of the main findings of chapter 4 is that when faced with a negative aggregate demand shock, Latin American countries have tended to adjust more through real wages and less through employment compared with developed countries. At the same time, falling inflation may have reduced this real wage flexibility, increasing the unemployment cost of recessions. The first line of defense against this vulnerability is to reduce the exposure to external

Box 8.1 Administratively Determined Wages and Wage Rigidity in Chile

A recent study by Cowan and others (2003) evaluates the impact of public sector and minimum wages on private sector wages in Chile in the past two decades. The figure below plots the behavior of an index of nominal wages in the private sector, an index of wages in the social and community services sector (a proxy for public wages), average output per worker in the economy, and an index of the minimum wage. The first fact that stands out is the high rate of growth in minimum wages, in particular during 1997-2000, when growth slowed down and unemployment picked up. Public sector wages also grew significantly in this period, more than private sector wages in fact. Real wages outran average productivity in the initial quarters of the slow-down (the third quarter in 1998). Neither minimum wages nor public wages fell after the economic slowdown.

Nominal Wages in Chile, 1996-2002
(Index, 1996=1)

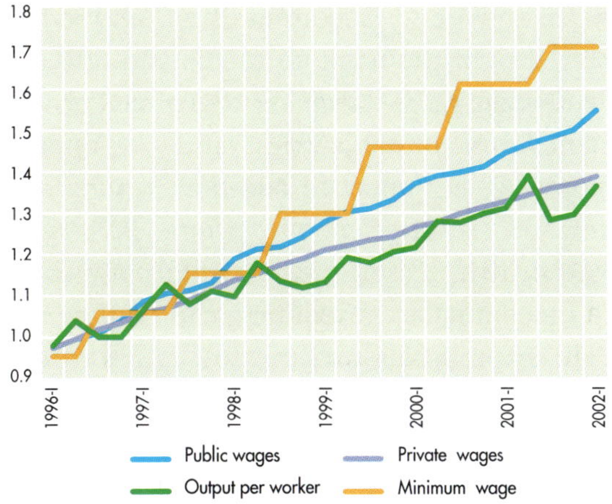

Note: Based on Cowan and others (2003, figure 5.3).
Source: Chilean National Institute of Statistics and Central Bank of Chile.

Did the high growth rate in minimum and public wages influence the downward rigidity of private sector wages in Chile? To answer this question, the authors carried out two exercises. First, they used data from household surveys to evaluate the impact of the minimum wage on the distribution of wages, finding that a substantial number of workers (6 percent) were directly affected by the rising minimum wage during 1997-2002. Second, they estimated the impact of public and minimum wages on private sector wages using monthly data for 1986-2002. They find a positive and significant correlation between the minimum wage and private sector wages. However, the parameter estimates and the timing of the effects suggest that the minimum wage in Chile only has a direct effect, and does not have a significant effect on workers earning more than the minimum wage. Moreover, if the effect of minimum wages is allowed to vary across periods (1986-97 and 1998-2000), only the estimated coefficient for the second period is significant—suggesting that the minimum wage becomes a binding restriction only in the period of low growth. The authors also obtain a positive correlation between private and public wages, although this coefficient is not significantly larger than zero at conventional confidence levels.

shocks and the impact of those shocks on the domestic economy. Because these policies are structural and therefore unlikely to have an effect in the short run, another set of policies needs to be adopted to deal with other sources of rigidities that arise from the cost of wage renegotiations and the consideration of labor contracts as an insurance device.

In addition to nominal rigidities that arise from the structure of wage contracts, wages set by governments—minimum wages or public sector wages—may also have an effect on wage rigidity. Both of these have a direct effect on those workers who receive the set wages, and may also have an indirect effect on the rest of the economy by affecting the opportunity cost of private sector workers. The effect of the minimum wage on wage rigidity will depend on the level of enforcement and on whether it constitutes a binding restriction. The effects of public sector wages will depend on the relative size of the public sector and the degree of worker mobility between the public and private sectors. Box 8.1 discusses the effects of these policies in Chile.

Reducing Exposure to External Shocks

Although terms of trade volatility in Latin America has fallen over the past two decades, it is still con-

Figure 8.1 Volatility of Prices of Main Export Products

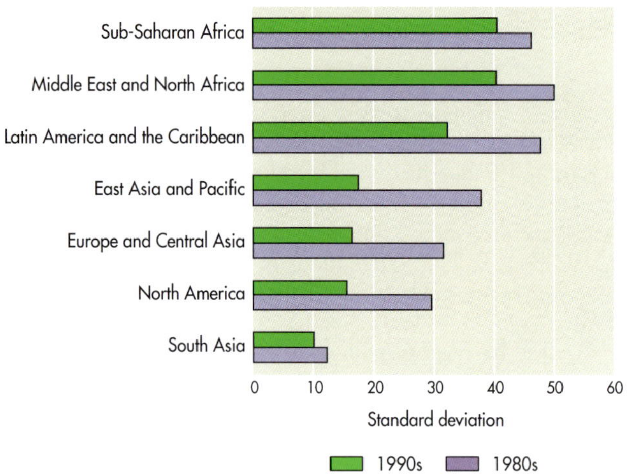

Note: Volatility is defined as the standard deviation of the annual price index of exports per decade. The main export products are the five SITC categories (3-digit, rev. 2) that make up the largest shares in each region's exports.
Source: IDB calculations based on World Integrated Trade Solution data from the World Bank.

Figure 8.2 Concentration of Exports
(Hirsch-Herfindal index, 0-1)

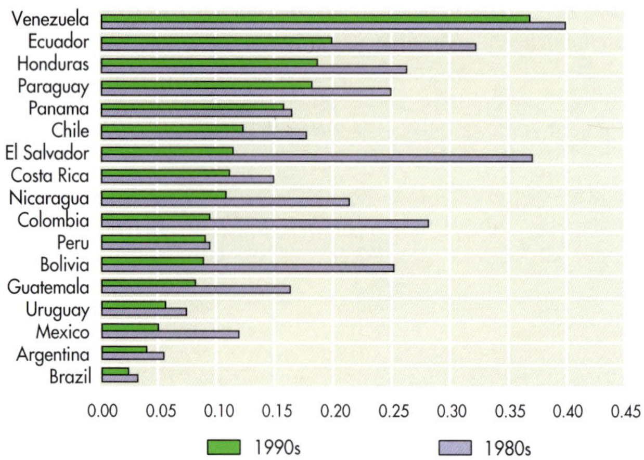

Note: The Hirsch-Herfindal index is calculated over 3-digit (rev. 2) SITC exports. Sample size is determined by data availability.
Source: IDB calculations based on World Integrated Trade Solution data from the World Bank.

siderably higher than that of East Asia and the developed countries (see chapter 4).[1] This high volatility of terms of trade is at least in part the result of low export diversification and a high share in total exports of goods with above average price volatility (see Figure 8.1). Although export diversification has been increasing in the region in the past decade (see Figure 8.2), further progress in this area is a necessary condition to reduce exposure to large fluctuations in external demand.

In addition to exposure to large fluctuations in external demand, weak international links limit the capacity of countries in the region to accommodate these temporary demand shocks. These weak links are reflected in the high volatility of capital inflows to the region.[2] Indeed, capital flows are often a shock in and of themselves. Sudden reversals of capital inflows, or "sudden stops," have large costs in terms of output and employment. There is widespread consensus on a series of medium-run structural policies aimed at improving external financial links. These include norms of transparency and accountability, and adequate supervision of the banking sector and other financial intermediaries—all measures aimed at improving the contractual setting and the quality of corporate governance. In addition to the domestic policies mentioned above, there is a growing debate on the importance of "international insurance mechanisms" in reducing capital flow volatility. These proposals run the full range from state contingent debt (see Borensztein and Mauro 2002), to contingent credit lines (see Caballero and Panageas 2003), to the privatization of state-owned companies (see IDB 1995).

Reducing the Impact of Shocks

As argued by Calvo, Izquierdo, and Talvi (2002), greater trade openness will reduce the costs of a reversal of capital inflows by limiting the size of the real exchange rate adjustment required to accommodate a given shock. Trade openness has increased in the region (from close to 22 percent of GDP in the early 1970s to more than 30 percent of GDP in the late 1990s). Nevertheless, this expansion has been smaller than the growth of capital inflows. Indeed, the ratio of the current account

[1] Based on terms of trade data from World Bank (various years), the variance of the terms of trade in the 1990s was significantly lower than that of the 1970s at conventional confidence levels.

[2] Table 4.1 documents the volatility of capital flows in different regions in the past three decades.

deficit to exports grew from 15 to 20 percent during the 1990s.[3] Additional efforts to increase trade openness are therefore needed to reduce the effects of capital flows volatility on output and employment.

Domestic financial markets play a key role in intermediating funds for investment, and hence play an important role in enhancing long-term growth and productivity. They also play an important role in intermediating liquidity, a role that is particularly important if a country's access to international capital markets is temporarily limited. Therefore, developing the domestic financial market may help to reduce the impact of temporary shocks to external demand on output.[4] In addition, by correctly pricing access to international capital markets, domestic financial development may also reduce exposure to capital flows volatility (Caballero and Krishnamurthy 2001). Finally, key conditions identified for the development of domestic financial markets (including adequate regulation and supervision and investor protection) are also likely to have a direct effect on international linkages.

The role of nominal exchange rates in the adjustment of relative prices (the real exchange rate) to an external shock is directly related to wage flexibility and hence to labor market policies. In a pegged regime, real exchange rate adjustments have to occur through changes in the domestic price and wage level. Shocks requiring a real depreciation—such as those experienced by Argentina after the Brazil devaluation—require a decline in the domestic price level in relation to trading partners to restore real exchange rate equilibrium. If wages and prices are rigid, the adjustment will be slow and costly in terms of output and employment. In a floating regime, by contrast, a misalignment of the real exchange rate can be quickly corrected through a change in the nominal exchange rate.[5]

A series of recent studies—inspired by the emerging market crises of the late 1990s—calls into question the central assumption that a depreciation of the exchange rate has an expansionary effect on the macroeconomy.[6] These studies indicate that a depreciation not only has the usual positive effects on aggregate demand, but also deteriorates net worth by inflating the domestic currency value of debt. Larger debt leads to an increase in the cost of external finance and (other things equal) to a reduction in investment.

Discussion of the optimal exchange rate policy for emerging markets must take into consideration both the degree of wage and price rigidity and the balance sheet effects brought about by liability dollarization. On the one hand, exchange rate flexibility reduces real wage rigidity in the presence of rigid nominal wage and price contracts. On the other hand, if financial contracts are indexed to the nominal exchange rate, then the stabilizing effects of real wage flexibility must be weighed against the (potentially) destabilizing effects the exchange rate may have on balance sheets.

Contracts and Renegotiations

As discussed in chapter 4, the response of the labor market to aggregate shocks depends to a large extent on the degree of real wage flexibility. This flexibility will in turn depend on the length of contracts and the indexation mechanisms included in them. With this in mind, the discussion turns to some possible determinants of contract structure and the implications of labor market policies for this structure.

Gray (1978) provides a useful framework for analyzing the determinants of labor contract length

[3] Data on trade and capital flows are from IDB (2002).

[4] Beck, Lundberg, and Majnoni (2001) provide some evidence that the development of financial intermediaries reduces the macroeconomic impact of terms of trade volatility.

[5] Perry and Servén (2003) find that the impact of a terms of trade shock on output is significantly lower in countries with floating exchange rate regimes, suggesting that nominal price rigidities are pervasive and therefore that nominal exchange rate flexibility can reduce the output cost of external shocks by increasing the flexibility of real exchange rates. This result extends previous research by Broda (2001).

[6] A first strand of the literature explores the macroeconomic implications of currency mismatches. In Krugman (1999a, 1999b) and Aghion, Bacchetta, and Banerjee (2001), the balance sheet effect is assumed to be large enough to dominate the expansionary effects. This strongly negative relationship between investment and depreciation can give rise to multiple equilibria, and hence the potential for an expectations-driven exchange rate crisis. The potentially destabilizing effects of a devaluation in the presence of dollar debt are also discussed in Céspedes, Chang, and Velasco (2000), although the authors emphasize that dollar debt does not necessarily lead to "macroeconomic damnation." For a recent survey of this literature, see Cowan and Do (2003).

in the context of real and monetary shocks. She argues that firms choose the optimal contract length taking into consideration the costs of renegotiating each contract and the expected costs of having a wage that may no longer be optimal if demand or cost conditions change during the life of the contract. Therefore, if uncertainty about future demand conditions increases, firms will negotiate shorter contracts. Increasing the costs of renegotiation will have the opposite effect—lengthening contracts and introducing greater nominal rigidity. A first implication is that countries with higher costs of renegotiating contracts will tend to have longer contracts. Another implication is that a reduction in the volatility of demand or productivity will lead to longer contracts and a reduction in nominal wage flexibility.[7] This being the case, it should be expected that contracts would become increasingly longer in Latin America if volatility were reduced.

Indexation to inflation increases the expected costs of a long wage contract if shocks are real, but reduces the costs if shocks are monetary (Fischer 1977; Gray 1978). This makes intuitive sense: if the money supply expands unexpectedly, pushing prices up, then indexed wages will adjust accordingly, leaving output and employment unchanged. For a real shock, on the other hand, indexation will limit the speed of adjustment of the real wage, and increase the effect in terms of unemployment. In the absence of legal restrictions, the degree of contract indexation will therefore depend on the perceived volatility of real and monetary shocks. Indexation will increase if the volatility of monetary shocks increases relative to the volatility of real shocks.[8]

It can be argued that wage indexation increases the cost of disinflation by increasing inflation persistence. This does not imply, however, that indexation should be restricted or removed. The benefits in terms of inflation inertia of restricting indexation must be weighed against the costs of pushing contracts away from the private optimum. Limiting indexation is likely to (1) shorten labor contracts, which will lead to higher negotiation costs, and (2) increase the effects of monetary shocks on output and employment.

Wage contracts will also be shorter, and nominal rigidity lower, if labor market regulations reduce the probability or duration of strikes—one of the main components of negotiation costs. Although a series of explanations has been put forward for strike activity, all of them appeal to some form of imperfect information.[9] If the profitability of the firm is unknown to union members, strikes may be viewed as screening devices, which allow workers to extract higher wages from more profitable employers. A firm with higher profits prefers to settle at a high wage without a strike; a firm with low profitability would be willing to endure a strike. Policies that affect information disclosure would therefore affect the probability of labor conflicts. In more general terms, legislation that increases the quantity and reliability of corporate accounting information would have a series of benefits, in addition to reducing labor conflicts. This is not always a feasible policy, however, as many firms are not required to keep, let alone publish, accounting information. For such firms, the rules of negotiation are likely to be more important than provisions affecting information disclosure.[10]

Information availability is also a key component of proposals that seek to increase wage flexi-

[7] Gray and Kandil (1991) and Kandil (2000) find evidence of this using aggregate wage data for a group of developed economies. In particular, they find that the response of nominal wages to aggregate shocks is lower in economies with lower uncertainty, which they argue is consistent with longer nominal wage contracts.

[8] Strictly speaking, indexation is often imperfect because it is based on lagged values of growth of the consumer price index. Jadresic (1997, 1998) discusses the implications of this lagged indexation for output volatility in the context of a small open economy.

[9] Alternative explanations for strikes are faulty negotiations (Hicks 1932) or incentives of union leaders (Ashenfelter and Johnson 1969).

[10] Because of lack of data, there is scarce careful empirical evidence for emerging markets on the impact of bargaining legislation on strike outcomes. Recent empirical data for a developed economy are presented in Crampton, Gunderson, and Tracy (1999). Using data on strike activity that exploit variations in labor codes across Canadian provinces, they find that negotiation policies have had a substantial effect on strike incidence, duration, and wage outcomes. Conciliation policies have been largely ineffective in reducing strike costs, but in general contract re-opener provisions make both unions and employers better off by reducing negotiation costs without systematically affecting wage settlements. Legislation banning the use of replacement workers leads to higher negotiation costs by increasing both the frequency and duration of strikes. In addition, replacement bans also result in significantly higher real wage settlements.

bility by incorporating some form of profit sharing into the wage structure. Share wages can take the form of profit sharing, a fraction of shares, or production bonuses—indeed, any form that ties wages to firm outcomes according to a previously defined rule. This type of contract potentially has the added advantage of increasing worker productivity. (See Bravo, Larrañaga, and Ramos [2001] for a discussion of share wages and their impact on volatility and productivity.)

Why are these share contracts not used extensively in Latin America, in particular considering the highly volatile macroeconomic environment in which labor markets in the region operate? As discussed above, information requirements are one explanation. Tying wages to profits or sales requires firms to produce timely and credible accounting. The other explanation relates to risk aversion and the role of long-term labor market contracts in providing insurance to workers.

Labor Contracts as Insurance

Either because firms have better access to capital markets or firm owners have a broadly diversified portfolio of assets, it seems reasonable to consider that firms are less risk averse than workers. This being the case, both employers and employees will benefit from a long-term contract that insulates workers from fluctuations in firm profits in exchange for lower average wages (Baily 1974; Azariadis 1975). Indeed, Baily (1974) shows that the optimal contract in this setting will guarantee a steady wage to workers, giving rise to long-term fixed wage contracts.

Finally, it should be noted that all the arguments and policies discussed in this section are based on the existence of long-term work contracts and hence are closely related to the existence of regulated and registered employment contracts. Any long-term promise is meaningless if workers (or employers) cannot enforce it in later periods when conditions change. As countries move toward higher levels of enforcement, they should therefore be aware of the possible effects of increased formality on wage flexibility.

Job-Worker Matching

The labor market has persistent gaps and lags between the demand for workers by employers and the supply of jobseekers.[11] In a world where one in four jobs is destroyed or created in any given year, these gaps and lags have significant economic costs. Many factors explain this failure to fully clear the labor market: limited dissemination of information about job openings, mismatches between the skills workers have and the skills employers need, jobseekers with poor skills for finding appropriate employment, and discrimination, just to mention a few.

Labor policies can help to increase the efficiency of the job-worker matching process. Policies that increase the effectiveness of job searches and reduce the cost of filling vacancies help to increase employment, while their direct effect on wages is ambiguous. However, the most important effect of these policies is to increase the productivity of job-worker matches in the labor market. Labor intermediation services are intended to improve the speed and quality of the match between available jobs and jobseekers. In this way, such services intermediate between labor supply and demand. The principal clients of such services are unemployed or underemployed workers and firms seeking new employees.

There are many advantages in making the match between jobseekers and jobs faster, less costly, and of better quality. A better quality match would mean the employee would more closely fit the job, be more productive, and likely stay in the job longer. A faster and less costly match would reduce the firm's output losses, increase productivity, and reduce staff time in personnel functions. It would also increase the worker's income and reduce the social and family costs of unemployment or underemployment. Lower costs would also result for the wider community in terms of reduced need for social services and reduced unemployment insurance or social service pay-

[11] This section is based on Mazza (1999).

ments, if applicable. As these services increase the transparency of labor market exchange mechanisms, they also help to reduce discrimination.

Intermediation services can fulfill a number of useful functions, but they cannot create jobs. If a country is facing a true employment crisis with conditions of high structural unemployment, it is generally more productive to look for, and hopefully solve, wage rigidities that impede employment generation. The principal economic purpose of labor intermediation is to create information useful for linking demand and supply, thus increasing productivity and social welfare, not to create jobs. However, labor intermediation services may also coordinate with income support or other safety net programs, thus fulfilling a function within the safety net.

Labor intermediation services are an important tool of labor policies. A number of evaluation results for OECD countries point to the fact that job search assistance is highly cost effective in helping to put workers in new jobs.[12] New evaluations of programs in Mexico also show that some low-cost interventions (such as subsidizing transportation costs for job interviews) help shorten the duration of unemployment. However, the challenges that labor intermediation services face in the region differ from those faced by their counterparts in more developed OECD countries. On the one hand, the prevalence of unregulated forms of employment contracts (including self-employment) dictates that labor intermediation services should include services adapted to the variety of labor market insertion of their clients (such as referral to microenterprise programs). On the other hand, given the limited size and scope of existing labor intermediation services in the region, reforms should start by fostering an adequate regulatory environment for private and nonprofit providers that facilitates the development of new public-private partnerships.

Labor Intermediation Services

Around the globe, there are new efforts to innovate and reform ways to better match jobs to jobseekers. National public employment services were first created in the developed economies around 1900. Today, many of these public employment services are being reformulated and reformed, private services are being expanded, and new partnerships are being sparked between the two. In these new policy reformulations of employment services, it is more accurate to call the emerging systems labor intermediation services because the range of services has become broader in intermediating between workers and jobs and between jobs and education and training, self-employment, and other needed social services.

Broader Range of Services

The core labor market intermediation services are job search assistance and job placement or brokering. The first encompasses actions to help the jobseeker in finding new employment through resume preparation, development of a job search strategy, occupational information, and contacts with employers. Job brokering, in turn, relies on the maintenance of a registry and information on current job openings; it seeks to match specific openings with specific applicants. This task is not as simple as it sounds because employers' job needs change rapidly. To be effective, the service must maintain a wide number of listings, keep them current, and be skilled at placing the right people in the right jobs in order to ensure that employers continue to use the service.

Research has continued to indicate that job search assistance is highly cost effective and productive as a method of assisting workers into new jobs. Positive impacts as well have been noted in job counseling, particularly with two or more sessions.[13] Job clubs have also been shown to assist the long-term unemployed in developed countries.[14]

[12] See OECD (1996) for OECD countries; Fretwell, Benus, and O'Leary (1999) for transition economies in Eastern Europe; Samaniego (2002) for Latin American countries; and Dar and Tzannatos (1999) for an overall review.

[13] A Canadian study finds that two or more sessions increased the level of job satisfaction (Government of Canada 1989).

[14] A European Commission report cites the range of participants receiving work after participation in a job club from 8 percent in Ireland to 73 percent in a small pilot project in the Netherlands (Commission of the European Communities 1991).

Table 8.1 Principal Functions of Labor Intermediation Services

Service category	Target clients	Types of services
Job search and employment profiling	• Jobseekers	• Skills testing or referrals to testing • Profiling of clients to determine services needed • Resume preparation • Job counseling • Phone banks for job search • Job search assistance • Job clubs • Case management
Job placement brokerage	• Employers • Jobseekers	• National database of job vacancies • Job placement • Vacancy intake (firms) • Candidate screening (for firms) • Outplacement • Recruitment for select positions (firms)
Training	• Jobseekers • Training providers • Employers	• Assessments of training needs and requirements • Referral to private and public training providers • Training directly by labor intermediation service (limited)
Specialized services for employers	• Employers	• Human resource assessments • Legal advice on employment • Screening and testing of job applicants • Sector promoters and liaisons • Staff training guidance
Labor market information	• Government (local and national) • Firms • Jobseekers	• Data and analysis on labor market trends
Unemployment insurance and social services; gateway to social services provision	• Jobseekers	• Administration of unemployment insurance benefits or referrals • Referral or coordination with social services • Referral to self-employment programs

Labor intermediation services include a range of secondary services designed to improve the quality and efficiency of intermediation. These services are secondary only in that not all systems of labor intermediation offer such services. In many cases, these services can be central to the efficient functioning of the match between workers and jobs. They include employment profiling and skill assessments (that evaluate the skills required by jobs and offered by searchers to develop a better search strategy), referral to training services, development of labor market information systems, and serving as a social and business service "gateway" (intermediating between searchers and other service providers, such as self-employment or credit programs). Additional labor intermediation services regulate private intermediation services and provide specialized services (mostly substitutes for human resource functions in firms). Table 8.1 summarizes the types of services that labor intermediation services offer.

Variety of Clients and Service Packages

The great variety of labor intermediation services reflects the fact that no one package of services fits the needs of every worker seeking employment through an intermediation service. Some workers need little assistance and others need a lot. For those job-ready clients who already have the skills and recent work history to find a new job relatively easily, low-cost resume preparation and job search orientation might be enough to get the individual into a new position.[15] Older workers with outmoded skills, workers with social difficulties that impede employment (such as alcoholism, poor work record, or poor skills), single parents who require integrated services (including child care), or indigenous or disadvantaged workers with cultural or linguistic barriers are best handled on a case management basis. Counselors could look at the complexity of their employment situation and help tailor the right combination of services and follow up closely with the many elements of a job and social services strategy. In the most likely intermediate case, a worker might be new to a field but have skills that are transferable or that could be developed through on-the-job training. In this case, services would need to include the intervention of a job counselor, referral to short-term training programs, development of a job search plan that includes identification of a range of positions in the vacancy database, direct solicitation of firms, and case follow-up.

Categories of employer clients have not been as easily classified. Typically, a labor intermediation service would distinguish between a set of basic services provided to all employers, including the critical service of registering job vacancies, and a set of enhanced services that would be provided on a fee-for-service basis to firms on request.

In assessing how to structure the services to be offered to each client, national intermediation services reflect different national philosophies about the nature of public service. As a matter of policy, in a number of European countries (for example, Austria and France), all services are offered to all clients, that is, services are universally offered. In other nations, services are not offered universally, but selectively, based on a personal or formula-based determination of which beneficiaries need the services the most (for example, Great Britain and the United States).[16]

Institutional Structure and National Public Service

Labor intermediation services have historically been seen as a monopoly public service. During the early post-World War II period, labor intermediation services in many OECD countries were a single, national public service run by the ministry of labor. The basic operational philosophy was reflected in the relevant International Labour Organization (ILO) conventions, which created a public monopoly of intermediation services.[17] Private employment agencies were seen as potentially exploiting workers by charging for placement, delivering poor quality service, and "creaming" the best candidates, relegating public services to the most difficult cases. Recently, however, the ILO has enacted new conventions that reverse the ban on private employment agencies and call for enhanced oversight and regulation.[18]

This regulatory development arises from experimentation by OECD countries to test new methods of making labor intermediation systems more effective, looking at how to reach a greater number of workers and firms in a more client-driven fashion. The new conventions take advantage of new technologies and demand more explicit and definable outcomes. These efforts are not just oriented to reform old public employment services, but modernize and design the larger system of public and private services. First, the reforms make public employment services more efficient, effective, and client-driven, introducing a number of pri-

[15] In a number of countries, such clients would be candidates for self-service services, that is, they could be left on their own to navigate the system's job database and resource library, asking for assistance only when needed.

[16] The United States has moved the farthest to an automated, formula-based assessment of which clients are most at risk for long-term unemployment and thus eligible for a wider range of services earlier. Those defined most at risk are eligible for social services and training. The profiling system utilizes a number of characteristics of the client—including age, length of time in previous employment, and occupation—to assess the potential for long-term unemployment. The system does not use characteristics such as race and ethnicity. This computer-based profiling system is relatively recent and there is widespread agreement that it is still "getting rid of teething problems" (OECD 1999, p. 195).

[17] The basic ILO Employment Service Convention (1948) establishes that placement services should be guaranteed free of charge to workers. The accompanying 1949 Fee-Charging Employment Agencies Convention bans private agencies that charge fees for placement of workers, effectively creating a public monopoly.

[18] In particular, the 1997 C181 Private Employment Agencies Convention and R188 Private Employment Agencies Recommendation, 1997.

vate sector practices.[19] Second, the services expand the use of private labor intermediation services, either as contractors to public systems, competitors, or partners in a national labor intermediation system.

Labor Intermediation in the Region

Recent reform and modernization of labor intermediation systems in Latin America and the Caribbean have had a distinctly different point of departure than reforms in OECD countries. In particular, the following characteristics of Latin American and Caribbean systems contrast with those of the OECD:

- Typically, Latin American national employment services are less extensive and have a lower investment level than their OECD counterparts.
- Private sector placement and employment services are generally less prevalent in Latin America and the few existing firms are newer. Some national employment services have a reputation of being politicized by local and regional authorities, thus discouraging the private sector from working more directly with these offices.
- The majority of Latin American countries do not have unemployment insurance, and so reform of labor intermediation services does not address the integration of such systems. As a consequence, potential cost savings in unemployment insurance is not a motivation for reform of the national labor intermediation service. Those countries in the region that do have unemployment insurance do not typically use a national employment service to administer unemployment insurance (for example, Argentina and Brazil).
- Discriminatory markets—lack of transparency, misinformation, and discrimination—are particular motivations for strengthening labor intermediation service systems in Latin America and the Caribbean. The region has a high reliance on informal networks and family/personal contacts, and this is typically viewed as reinforcing and perpetuating discrimination based on race, ethnic origin, gender, and economic class.
- Unregulated, precarious employment can exceed 50 percent of the national economy, with a concentration of poor and disadvantaged workers in these contracts. By definition, this shapes a different approach to labor intermediation designed to serve the regulated sector of the labor market.
- Latin American countries have less of a chronic problem of long-term unemployment in the workforce than a problem of low education and work skills.
- There is substantial internal and external migration in a number of countries, particularly within Central America and Mexico.

Currently in Latin America there are a number of public national employment services and a limited but growing private sector market in labor intermediation and placement. However, in the majority of countries in the region, there is a small public sector service that, with limited resources, typically serves the lower strata of the workforce.[20] National employment services in the region are typically administered by either the ministry of labor or the state-based national training institute (for example, SENA in Colombia). Latin American and Caribbean systems typically concentrate on the core functions of job brokering and job search.

The traditional target of labor intermediation services in the region has always been formal sector jobs, which have employers that more openly advertise and solicit employees. In countries that have an extensive unregulated sector and a high proportion of self-employed workers, there are clear benefits to improving the match of workers to jobs; however, special consideration needs to be given to the labor market placement of some types of workers. Labor intermediation services should include matching and referrals to programs in microenterprise, self-employment, and small busi-

[19] Key reforms pursued within the OECD countries include (1) integrating core functions, (2) expanding policy interventions for the long-term unemployed, (3) introducing and strengthening performance indicators, and (4) introducing market signals in the operation of public employment services.

[20] The directors of the public employment services of Central America, for example, stated that, historically, intermediation services in the region have been occupied with the strata with "low technical qualifications at the lowest levels of the occupational pyramid" (ILO 1998).

ness development, which are frequent (and sometimes the only) sources of employment for portions of the labor force, particularly older workers.[21] In most countries in the region, self-employment programs are provided by a range of providers, such as governments and nongovernmental organizations (NGOs), but rarely on a walk-in demand basis. Few clearinghouses provide information on a range of alternative programs and help candidates assess the best fit for their needs. Labor intermediation systems in the region should also consider whether intermediation centers can provide advice, information, and referrals on the formalization of businesses.

A word of caution is needed here. As in developed countries, countries in the region should clearly avoid putting labor intermediation services in a regulatory role that discourages participation in the service. It is useful to provide information on a voluntary basis in some cases, particularly if the government is offering expedited procedures to register businesses.

Many Latin American and Caribbean countries face major labor market challenges in the concentration of low skills, poor education, poverty, and labor market discrimination (employment and wage discrimination) among specific populations, especially women, ethnic/racial minorities, youth, and the handicapped. Among the greatest concerns in the evolution of labor market intermediation systems is how to more effectively reach these target populations. To provide for the social inclusion of these groups in the marketplace, labor intermediation services must be careful that the public/private market does not become so segmented that the national public service receives only the most disadvantaged clients. This would lead to increasing disuse by private employers. The challenge is in increasing the coverage of disadvantaged groups while simultaneously expanding the overall client and employer base in order to provide more opportunities to refer disadvantaged groups to better quality jobs.

For many of the poorer countries in the region, out-migration of labor—both legal and illegal—to higher-income countries has continued for several decades. Migration trends are increasing even within the region; for example, Nicaraguans work in Costa Rica and Peruvians work in Chile and Argentina. This migration can be seasonal, temporary, or permanent. For countries such as the Dominican Republic and El Salvador, worker remittances from abroad are a major source of national income and substantially affect the operation of the local labor market. For higher-income Caribbean countries, there is a reduction in job opportunities in the low season. A key question and controversy is whether a national labor intermediation service should play a role in regularizing temporary or seasonal migration or protecting or overseeing workers migrating within the region. Some countries in the region follow ILO conventions and guidelines in prohibiting private employment agencies from facilitating and charging for overseas placements. Other countries allow private agencies to play a role with the justification that this provides workers a legal and safe path for migration and safe return to their home country.[22]

Reforming Labor Intermediation Services

Reforming existing intermediation services requires fostering an appropriate regulatory environment for private nonprofit providers, a condition for creating new public-private partnerships. Staff of the labor intermediation services should be trained and information and performance-based systems introduced to measure the efficiency and effectiveness

[21] Ivan Gonçalves Ribeiro Guimarães, who runs the state employment service in Brasilia, Brazil, for example, says that workers over age 33 who have lost their formal sector jobs are particularly difficult to place. Statistics show that only about 2-3 percent of the unemployed in this age group find employment in the formal sector (interview with Ivan Gonçalves Ribeiro Guimarães, Brasília, 14 May 1998).

[22] Mexico, for example, has a specific arrangement between its public employment service and the Canadian government in which the service screens a set of agricultural workers who are provided legal visas and travel costs to work seasonally in Canada. The National Employment Bureau of Barbados lists seasonal overseas job opportunities under special programs largely in Canada and on U.S. cruise ships. The directors of the Central American employment services, for example, maintain the importance of continuing to meet on a regional basis to share national experience, propose adequate national policies, and seek ways to guarantee better conditions for migrating workers, actions which have implications for employment services (ILO 1999).

of the services. After these initial steps, there should be a more ambitious overhaul of the institutional framework and the roles of the private and public sectors. However, investment in information systems and development of a training registry and referral systems are critical investments at this stage to enhance the attractiveness of the services to employers and jobseekers.

Recent experimentation in the region has shown that three areas are promising for increasing the efficiency and cost effectiveness of labor intermediation services: (1) introducing and expanding information systems, (2) fostering partnerships with the private and nonprofit sectors, and (3) improving performance and expanding the client base.

Information and Internet Systems

Throughout the region, there is a clear trend toward putting new technologies to work in improving the performance of labor intermediation systems. Large investments in new information system technologies for intermediation systems have been more limited in Latin America and the Caribbean than in the OECD, but countries and local municipalities are beginning to invest in new computer-based systems.

Chile's Servicio Nacional de Capacitación y Empleo has developed the country's first electronic labor exchange. InfoEmpleo currently contains more than 29,000 resumes of jobseekers and receives more than 300 job vacancies a month.[23] Mexico has also made important advances and investments in information systems for its network of employment services, and has developed ChambaNet and ChambaTel, two innovative labor exchange programs that connect jobseekers directly to existing vacancies. Costa Rica, under financing and support from the National Apprenticeship Institute (INA) is developing a two-phase information system to revitalize its public employment service, expand to a network of private and nonprofit providers, and provide a national job registry with INA providing the central server.

Another important development in the region is the use of electronic *bolsas de trabajo*, not just on a single country basis, but also as part of a regional network. Under its program to modernize the labor ministries of Central America, Belize, Panama, and the Dominican Republic, the ILO is examining electronic job exchanges on a regional basis.[24] Under a regional project of the IDB Multilateral Investment Fund, eight countries—Central America, the Dominican Republic, and Panama—have developed a labor market information system in which labor market data can be jointly shared and analyzed on a regional basis, including data on employment, economic, and occupational trends.

Private and Nonprofit Services

Another emerging trend in the region is the expansion of the role of private employment agencies and initiatives to create partnerships between public, private, and nonprofit providers. Argentina is seeking to better link its public employment offices with the nonprofit and private employment agencies operating in the country. Peru created a network of public, private, and nonprofit providers, significantly increasing the reach of the system (Ministry of Labor and Social Security 2001). Guatemala is developing plans to create a network of employment services (Red de Servicios de Empleo) in which the local public office of the national employment service in each region or province would serve as a center for a local network that would include private and nonprofit providers. The pilot program of the network would begin in the metropolitan area of Guatemala City. As a first stage in opening up and regularizing a private sector market, a number of countries in the region are working to provide appropriate legal frameworks and institute regulations or oversight of private providers. For example, Panama passed a law in August 1995 permitting for-profit employment agencies and providing for the ministry of labor to have oversight over such agencies.

[23] http://www.sence.cl/.

[24] http://ns.oit.or.cr/matac.

Performance, Output, and Client Base

Countries in Latin America and the Caribbean are undertaking a series of actions to improve the performance, output, and client base of their systems. First, they are using job fairs as temporary one-stop centers. These *ferias de empleo* do more than just bring employers and jobseekers together face-to-face for one day. Job fairs, like those in Panama, are expanding to offer a range of services more akin to the type of one-day, one-stop shop that operates in OECD countries. Services available at the Panamanian job fairs include technical assistance for microenterprise, career information, resume workshops, information on training programs and needs, and assessments of jobseekers' work skills in addition to interviews with employers. In the Panamanian case, these fairs are self-financing, that is, they are fully paid for from the fees charged to employers establishing booths at the fairs. Mexico also has a comprehensive approach to job fairs, which serve as a hub for the national and local employment services to interact with private sector employer organizations.

Second, there is a more limited trend in the region toward decentralization of labor intermediation services to local municipalities and offices. The role and feasibility of decentralization in any country depends on a larger national strategy and trend toward decentralization and on the capacity of local institutions, particularly in relation to the variety in quality of service that can result without sufficient local capacity. For example, Chile has decentralized local employment offices to a network of more than 150 municipal employment agencies. These offices provide mediation services free of charge to workers. The Chilean National Training and Employment Service provides technical support to the network, plans and supervises training programs and institutions, and monitors the performance of the tax rebate plan for enterprise-based training (Martínez Espinoza 1998).

Third, systems in the region are working to improve the services that intermediation centers provide, for example, job search methodologies and assessments. Improvements include sharing information and tools across the region and providing information at international forums.

The Risks of Job Churning

The high level of macroeconomic volatility of Latin American economies, which is documented in chapter 4, has generated a strong social demand for mechanisms to protect the working population from the resulting risk of income loss. Traditionally, this demand has been met by the enactment of employment security regulations that penalize terminations either through high severance payments when terminations are allowed, or through direct prohibition of terminations. The region had high levels of employment protection until the mid-1990s, even relative to the protection enjoyed by workers in more developed OECD countries (Márquez 1997; IDB 1997; and chapter 7, this volume). For workers with regulated contracts, severance payments are quite high and employment protection regulations are strictly enforced both in practice and in the courts.

In a sense, employment protection works as privately implemented unemployment insurance with coverage limited to those workers with a regulated employment contract. These workers are protected both because the firm has a positive cost associated with termination (ensuring that layoffs and firings will be used sparsely as adjustment mechanisms), and because unemployed workers receive an income transfer through severance payments.

However, in most countries in the region, unregulated, precarious employment relations and self-employment account for more than 50 percent of the workforce. In a sense, the absence of job security for these segments of the population has provided wage flexibility, which has characterized the region until recently. However, as discussed in chapter 4, things are changing and the reduction in inflation and increasing demands for improvements in institutional quality (including rule of law in the labor market) are eroding the margins of wage flexibility and increasing the unemployment costs of downturns.

For workers who are not protected by labor market regulations and do not benefit from the protection of severance payments, the increasing unemployment risk is a serious threat. If countries are to protect the majority of their populations in the context of a broad social compact, more forms of social insurance are required. Labor policies can help workers cope with the risks of job churning and reduce the associated income loss before it drags entire families into poverty. In a world where 25 percent of the existing jobs are created or destroyed in any given year, how to insure against the cost of job loss is not a minor question.

A caveat is in order. It could be argued that many workers in regulated labor contracts are overinsured through severance payments. If a worker receives six months of current wages on firing and the average unemployment duration is three months, this worker is indeed overinsured. This overinsurance raises labor costs and therefore reduces employment (see chapter 7). The policy remedy is to substitute insurance mechanisms for incumbents, not to pile up additional insurance. The point is to move away from forms of proto-insurance and making individual severance payments in two directions.[25] Regulatory change and enhancement of the social protection network are essential tools for this task.

Regulatory change should seek to move away from severance payments and toward unemployment insurance for workers who have regulated labor contracts. Of course, this is easier said than done because such a change would have to overcome the political opposition of the labor movement. And its effectiveness would be conditional on significant organizational and institutional changes (including creation of individual savings accounts in the pension system). (This is discussed more fully below in the section on unemployment insurance.)

Financial and human resources should be invested in the maintenance (and in some cases establishment) of an effective network of institutions and policies to protect workers who have precarious labor contracts or are self-employed. Given the concerns about economic insecurity reflected in surveys such as Latinobarometer, sustaining political support for the modernization process will require the development of a broader social contract explicitly designed to operate in the context of more competitive, open, and therefore more vulnerable economies (Birdsall 2002; Graham 2002). Social insurance policies are a crucial piece of this new social contract, and their failure in the past decade helps explain many of the political difficulties faced by governments that are willing to deepen the modernization process. At the same time, experience shows that when income support policies are implemented in a transparent way and with efficient coordination between local and national authorities, they are effective in countering the negative effects of adverse external shocks (Ademar, Tergeist, and Torres 2000).

There is no single recipe for the design of social insurance. The unhappy equilibrium in the labor markets of many countries in the region today is the accumulated response to aggregate sector and idiosyncratic shocks. Each country has faced particular shocks and, even when reacting to aggregate regional shocks such as the Tequila or the East Asian crisis, each country has adjusted differently, and groups of workers have faced varying consequences. Even if countries faced a set of common labor market problems, policies in each country must take into account the nature of the adjustment of each economy. There is no one-size-fits-all policy; countries need to use different sets of policy instruments to help workers cope with income losses associated with job relocation.[26]

A common trait that requires attention is the number of workers that do not have legal employment contracts with benefits, but that are self-employed or working in casual, unregulated situations. This creates particular problems for the design of policies above and beyond the obvious problem of noncompliance with regulation of benefits and working conditions. New and innovative methods of collaboration between the public and private sectors are needed to provide social insurance for workers in these activities. Experience

[25] Blanchard (2002) refers to severance payments in a world with perfect information and different risk preferences of workers and firms as "proto-insurance."

[26] The flip side of this affirmation is that countries will need to invest in the development of labor policy institutions that collect, analyze, and process information, and that implement policies and enforce regulations.

indicates that this will require mainstreaming the informal sector into the institutions that govern market transactions, commercial contracts, and industrial labor relations. Mechanisms should be developed to provide social insurance tailored to the particular characteristics of work in the informal sector (Chen, Jhabvala, and Lund 2002).

The Toolbox

Tools for building a social insurance system originated in the efforts of the region's governments to cope with the crises of the 1990s and the renewed volatility in international capital markets. These efforts have created an opportunity to test some new ideas and disseminate innovative approaches to old problems. Labor-intensive public works programs, youth training programs, and semi-universal unemployment insurance systems all have became acceptable ideas to help sustain the incomes of affected workers. These programs developed historically as a response to the urgency of coping with the effects of crises. As such, the quest for mechanisms that could be set up quickly to transfer income to the poor in the most targeted way possible dominated optimal design considerations. By design, the expenditure in these programs should have been countercyclical; in practice, it was not, given the size of fiscal adjustments that had to be undertaken (Braun and di Gresia 2003).

The region's experience with income support programs shows that they can at least to some extent help compensate for the effects of economy-wide shocks on workers. A varied array of programs has been used to help workers cope with one or another of the damaging effects of these shocks. This battery of programs will be the backbone of any social insurance system, given organizational, political, and resource constraints that limit the ability of the government to create new programs.

However, social insurance mechanisms have different content and clientele compared with the safety nets of the 1990s. Although the rationale of safety nets is to protect the human capital of the poor during economic downturns, the objective of social insurance mechanisms is to help all workers (not just the poor) cope with the consequences of the job creation and destruction that characterize modern economies. For this reason, social and labor market policies require a higher dose of social insurance vis-à-vis poverty alleviation programs than what governments adopted and international financial institutions recommended during the 1990s. Unfortunately, social insurance mechanisms, such as unemployment benefits and other programs that provide income support, are less developed in Latin America than in OECD countries (Bourguignon 2000).

The mechanisms of social insurance should aim at providing a minimum income guarantee to the largest number of workers possible. To be feasible in financial and economic terms, they need to fulfill at least three requirements:

- Their design should minimize labor market distortions and, in particular, should not create incentives that result in reduced employment or output.
- Their coverage should be as wide as possible, given that the risk of unemployment affects all workers, including those in unregulated and precarious forms of employment contracts.
- Their budget allocation should be adjusted countercyclically, expanding in economic downturns when unemployment increases, and contracting in expansions when it decreases.

Coverage of unemployment insurance will not be wide enough to protect all workers, particularly the poorer ones. Part of what differentiates the poor from the nonpoor is the nature of their labor market insertion and, therefore, the mechanisms that need to be devised to insure them against the risk of income loss. Poor, low-productivity workers must rely on alternative mechanisms for protection because they cannot afford the cost of unemployment insurance, or they are in employment situations (self-employment or casual work with unregulated contracts) that make it unsuitable as an insurance mechanism. For these workers, a menu of alternatives needs to be provided based on the existing mechanisms of income support.

Table 8.2 presents a general vision of a social insurance system. At the center of the scheme, a

Table 8.2 The Design of a Social Insurance System

Program	Targeting	Financing	Institutional requirements
Unemployment insurance	Nontargeted, covering all workers in regulated contracts (in lieu of severance payments)	Financed from workers' and firms' contributions	Independent financial institution(s) System connected to pension system
Scholarships for short-term classroom training, apprenticeships, and job search assistance	Unemployed youth	Financed from training system payroll tax	Opening of the market for training services; network of nongovernmental providers
Employment generation programs			
Labor-intensive public works	Self-targeting	Financed from general revenues, strongly countercyclical	A solid network of local institutions able to apply selection criteria and develop works
Wage subsidies	Administrative	Exemption of payroll taxes, financed from general revenues	Sophisticated enforcement and verification system from labor authority
Cash transfers	Very narrow, based on family income below the poverty line	Financed from general revenues	Sophisticated targeting system

well-designed unemployment insurance system covers the group of workers that, given their employment contracts and productivity, can buy the insurance. Workers who are not clients of the unemployment insurance system can be referred to either a short-term training program or an employment generation scheme. For workers who exhaust their benefits in the system, cash transfer programs can provide limited income support.

Unemployment Insurance

Table 8.3 presents a summary description of unemployment insurance systems in the region. Few of the countries have legally and/or administratively enacted unemployment insurance systems, and even fewer have working unemployment insurance schemes. This is a consequence of the weak incentives for the development of unemployment insurance and other more socialized forms of income protection, given the fact that severance payments work as privately provided income insurance for workers in full-benefit employment contracts.

In those countries that do have unemployment insurance systems, coverage is limited to workers that have contributed while employed to the financing of the system. In other words, only workers in full-benefit employment contracts and working in firms that pay payroll taxes enjoy the benefits of the unemployment insurance system. The level and duration of benefits provided are low relative to the unemployment insurance systems in more developed countries. Replacement rates are normally on the order of 50-60 percent of the most recent wage, with the maximum linked to the minimum wage for higher salaries. Typically, benefits are granted for no longer than four months.

The unemployment insurance system in Argentina, for example, has a limited number of beneficiaries in spite of strong increases in the number of unemployed workers. Mazza (1999) reports that the number of beneficiaries has remained stable at between 100,000 and 125,000 workers, of which more than 70 percent are prime-age males and more than 50 percent are not household heads. Mazza also reports that an analysis of beneficiaries' personal and previous job character-

Table 8.3 Unemployment Insurance in Latin America and the Caribbean

Country	Law	Funding	Replacement rates[a]	Benefit duration	Benefits min./max.	Coverage	Requirements[b]
Argentina	1991 (reform in 1995)	Worker: 1 percent of wages Employer: 1.5 percent of payroll	60 percent	4–12 months	Min: minimum wage Max: 4 times the minimum wage	Employees	1 (12), 2, 3
Barbados	1982	Worker: 1.5 percent of wages Employer: 1.5 percent of payroll	60 percent, 10 weeks 40 percent, 16 weeks	26 weeks in a 52-week period		Employees age 16–64	1 (6)
Brazil	1986 1990	FAT[c] (0.65 percent tax on total sales)	1–3 times the minimum wage	4 months	Min: minimum wage	Employees	4 (36, 4), 5, 6
Chile	2001	Worker: 0.6 percent Employer: 1.6 percent, plus employer (0.8 percent of payroll) and state fixed contribution to solidarity fund	Amount is a function of accumulation in individual account; maximum of five payments from solidarity fund	1 payment per year of contribution to the unemployment insurance fund	Minimum from solidarity fund 30 percent of the last wage or $41–89 Maximum 50 percent or $103–171	Employees starting new contract, voluntary affiliation on existing contracts	2, 9
Ecuador	1958, 1988	Worker: 2 percent of salary Employer: 1 percent of payroll	One-time subsidy, amount decided each year			Employees	1 (24), 7
Mexico		Social security	95 percent of pension	5 years maximum		Employees age 60–65	Age 60–65
Uruguay	1981	Contributions to social security	Up to 50 percent	6 months	Min: 50 percent of minimum wage Max: 4 times the minimum wage	Employees in commerce and industry	1 (6), 5, 3, 8
Venezuela	1989 (reform in 1999)	Worker: 0.7 percent of wages Employer: 1.5 percent of payroll	Up to 60 percent	13–26 weeks	Max: $44	Employees	1 (12), 2

[a] Percentage of last wage.
[b] Beneficiaries also receive family support and medical and maternity benefits.
[c] Fundo de Amparo ao Trabalhador.
Requirements are as follows:
1 (s) – Employed s months before receiving subsidy.
2 – Availability to work.
3 – Does not receive other social security benefits.
4 (s, j) – Not having received more than s months of benefits in the past j years.
5 – Unemployed for reasons outside the conduct and willingness of the worker.
6 – Subject to economic need.
7 – Waiting period.
8 – At least 12 months between periods of receiving subsidy.
9 – Subject to availability of funds in individual account.
Source: Lora and Pagés (1997); U.S. Department of Health and Human Services; Acevedo (2003).

istics shows that there is a definite trend toward serving younger and middle-class displaced workers. This suggests that unemployment insurance is not fulfilling a safety net role for the poor in the case of Argentina.

Until it was surpassed by Chile, Brazil had the largest unemployment insurance system in the region, with 300,000 to 400,000 beneficiaries. Mazza (1999) reports that unemployment insurance in Brazil also serves younger (more than 50 percent of beneficiaries are younger than 30 years old) and more educated (45 percent of beneficiaries have completed eighth grade or better) workers.

In 2001, Chile enacted a new law implementing an unemployment insurance system, which began operations in October 2002. The Chilean system is based on a defined contributions/variable benefits regime. Workers and employers contribute to nominative individual accounts, and contributing workers are entitled to one monthly payment for each 12 months of contributions to the unemployment insurance fund, the amount of the payment being a function of accumulated funds. A solidarity fund, funded by employers and the treasury, pays benefits to workers with insufficient funds in their individual accounts. Affiliation is mandatory for workers in new labor contracts and voluntary for workers already in jobs. By March 2003, voluntary affiliation was much larger than expected, and the system is already covering more than 900,000 workers, or around 30 percent of potential affiliates. Following the general pattern in the region, the share of workers affiliated with the unemployment insurance system grows with the education level.[27]

In Venezuela, the unemployment insurance system was enacted in 1989, but was never implemented. The system was reformed in 1999, but again never implemented. The new system would protect beneficiaries through a mix of individual and collective insurance operated by competitive insurance providers. Given that only workers with regulated, tax-paying contracts are entitled to benefits, it is likely that the distribution pattern of beneficiaries would be similar to that in Argentina and Brazil.

Mexico and Uruguay have unemployment insurance programs operated by the social security system. In both cases, coverage is limited. In Mexico, coverage is just an advance payment of the old-age pension for a maximum period of five years. In the case of Barbados, the unemployment insurance system is comparatively generous, although quite well adapted to the needs of an island economy with frequent but short episodes of unemployment concentrated among workers in the tourism industry (Mazza 1999).[28]

Differences in design, coverage, and benefits make it difficult to present an overall assessment of the importance of unemployment insurance systems as part of a comprehensive social insurance mechanism; however, there are some common traits. First, unemployment insurance is normally a benefit in addition to the severance payment. The worker has the right to unemployment insurance as a supplementary source of income during the search for a new job. Therefore, income protection by the unemployment insurance system is targeted to workers that have had full-benefit employment contracts. This excludes from protection a sizable fraction of the workforce in the unregulated segment of the labor market, presumably those who are the most needy in terms of income protection.

Second, unemployment insurance systems generally lack connection with other labor market intermediation and placement services. Even in cases where the unemployment insurance system is operated through the labor ministry (as in Brazil), workers are not required to register with the intermediation service, and payment of the benefit is not contingent on verification of search effort. On the one hand, this lack of connection generates an opportunity for fraud. Even if it is illegal to have a job and receive unemployment insurance payments simultaneously, most operators complain of their lack of capacity to control what is perceived to be widespread fraud and collusion

[27] Notas del Seguro de Cesantía, año 1, no. 1, March 2003.

[28] Mazza (1999) notes that Barbados is the only example where severance payments were capped and eligibility limited when unemployment insurance came into being in 1967.

between firms and workers.[29] On the other hand, this lack of connection with labor market intermediation services makes the system a pure income transfer that does not ease the transition of the unemployed into a new job.

Third, most unemployment insurance systems are financed through payroll taxes, which are already high in the region. This partly explains the limited coverage, low replacement rates, and short periods of coverage. Any expansion of the system to cover hitherto unprotected segments of the population would likely face substantial opposition by the present beneficiaries and by firms operating in the regulated sector of the economy. However, in the case of Brazil, some expansion to new groups has been made (to traditional fishermen and workers affected by the drought in the northeast), but the expansion has been temporary and financed through the use of excess funds. If unemployment insurance were to work as part of the safety net in a crisis, the expansion of coverage would have to be produced just when the flow of benefits to already protected workers was highest, creating financial strains on the system and the need for additional funding. The question is whether this effort should go through the unemployment insurance system or through an alternative mechanism for income transfer that would be better suited to the needs of various groups of workers.

The design and target population of unemployment insurance make it suitable for protecting workers who have full-benefit employment contracts and that acquire rights to it through their contributions while employed. In terms of labor market distortions, the low level of benefits and their short duration apparently do not create an incentive against job search. In fact, reports of fraud in Argentina and Brazil suggest that workers use unemployment insurance as a means to obtain additional income while in a new job. As Hopenhayn and Nicolini (2001) show, it is possible to design optimal unemployment insurance schedules that do not induce reduction in search efforts. Furthermore, schemes of unemployment insurance based on nominative contributions to individual accounts that can be rolled over into retirement funds can minimize the negative impacts on search effort.[30]

In order to expand and contract countercyclically, unemployment insurance needs to be protected by transparent and well-enforced regulations. Under constant eligibility and benefit conditions, outlays increase when unemployment is rising and contract with the recuperation of employment. However, eligibility and benefits are seldom constant and those changes are expected. In the United States, for instance, the length of benefits is routinely increased during downturns. The political and institutional capability to manage this kind of decision in a fair and transparent way is thus a necessary condition for this variability to work.

There are two problematic aspects of unemployment insurance. The first is related to its employment effect. If the unemployment insurance system were well implemented, it would increase both the duration and level of unemployment via the incentive to extend the job search. This employment effect would be amplified by the indirect effect of unemployment insurance on labor costs; the larger the costs, the less inclined workers would be to accept lower wages in exchange for the additional insurance. Therefore, every effort should be made to ensure that labor costs are not affected by simultaneously enacting offsetting reductions in other components of labor costs (such as severance payments).

The second problematic aspect is related to coverage. For high-productivity workers, wages are high enough to make the benefits of paying for unemployment insurance (the expected value of benefits when unemployed) higher than the current income foregone by paying the contribution. However, for low-productivity workers, the utility gain from an increase in current income could be large enough to generate incentives to negotiate

[29] Mazza (1999) reports that some efforts have been made in Argentina to detect whether workers receiving unemployment insurance were working by using a common taxpayer identification number. It was found that a sizable number of workers were not only working, but also contributing to social security in a new job while continuing to receive unemployment insurance payments.

[30] For a proposal of an unemployment insurance system along these lines, see Cortazar and others (1995).

Table 8.4 Employment Generation Programs in the Region

	Beneficiaries		Expenditure	
Country	Thousands of workers	Percentage of total labor force	Millions of U.S. dollars	Percentage of GDP
Argentina	892.2	9.31	249.2	0.09
Brazil	221.8	0.49	1,188.8	0.21
Chile	4.3	0.10	1.4	0.00
Costa Rica	8.1	0.71	3.3	0.04
Jamaica	6.0	0.61	21.2	0.50
Mexico	1,024.0	4.42	1,802.0	0.51
Peru	27.8	0.93	100.0	0.19

Source: Based on data in Verdera (1998).

with employers a contract without benefits in exchange for higher current income.

Employment Generation Programs

Employment generation programs are a natural government reaction to increasing unemployment. Politically they show the concern of the government with the workers' plight and, by providing jobs, they directly attack unemployment. For analytical purposes, it is convenient to separate labor-intensive public works from wage subsidies to the private sector.

Table 8.4 presents a summary description of employment generation programs in seven countries in the region at the end of 1995: Argentina, Brazil, Chile, Costa Rica, Jamaica, Mexico, and Peru. These countries represent a wide spectrum of variation in terms of policy development, operational capabilities, and exposure to international capital market volatility. Verdera (1998) summarizes the program descriptions and characteristics and provides a more thorough discussion.

Argentina had the most varied set of employment generation programs, comprising a combination of public works and subsidies to private employment. The federal government also financed labor-intensive public works as an employment generation device. Trabajar and similar programs were financed and supervised by the federal government using the Fondo Nacional de Empleo (a fund financed through payroll taxes). The resources were used to build small-scale and labor-intensive public works (in many cases social infrastructure, but also roads and small sanitation works) executed by a wide variety of agencies, including local and state governments and NGOs.

By contrast, the PROGER program in Brazil operates through the establishment of credit lines offered through the national development banking system to small enterprises, cooperatives, NGOs, and other civil society associations. This mechanism serves to circumvent subnational governments for works execution in order to avoid the creation of budgetary entitlements. However, evaluations of PROGER are not optimistic about the results in terms of employment generation (Government of Brazil 1998).

By 1995, Chile did not have an employment generation program as such, although it had a number of small and narrowly targeted programs to address living conditions that might hinder the labor market insertion of particular groups. However, at the end of the 1990s, a number of incentives and programs were introduced to reduce the cost of the rising unemployment rate.

Costa Rica uses public works, wage subsidies, and credit to small enterprises as mechanisms to promote employment generation. Credit to promote employment generation in small firms is also widely used in Jamaica in a battery of programs, some of which also include a form of short-term training. Jamaica has a training and temporary employment program for unemployed youth, which is aimed at easing their labor market insertion.

Mexico uses public works (rural roads and other social infrastructure) as employment generation devices. The programs are financed by allocations from general revenues (not from payroll taxes) in the federal government budget, and states and local governments execute the works.

Finally, Peru uses legal incentives, a social investment fund, and a micro and small enterprise credit program as tools for employment promotion. The labor law reform of 1991 introduced a number of more precarious forms of employment contracts, allowing firms to hire workers without generating rights to severance payments under fixed-term contracts. FONCODES, a social investment fund, is also used as an employment generation device that can be quickly adjusted to the situation of local labor markets. However, it is not clear how much capacity or interest the management of FONCODES has in employment generation as opposed to the physical execution of civil works (Verdera 1998).

Labor-intensive public works. Labor-intensive public works have been the tool of choice for dealing with economywide shocks. The number and variety of programs in place in the region show that governments choose to spend more resources on employment generation than on other mechanisms for providing income support to unemployed workers. One of the main advantages of these programs is that they are self-targeted and, therefore, can be implemented without the delays necessary for implementing a targeting mechanism (Grosh 1994; Ravallion 1998).

Three characteristics of labor-intensive public works are crucial in their success as income support mechanisms. First, these programs are financed by the central government and executed by local organizations (local governments or NGOs), which normally are in charge of selecting the works to be performed and the beneficiaries. Thus, labor-intensive public works require an extensive and solid network of institutions at the local level, with the technical and operational capacity to choose the works to be done, organize the production process, and channel resources to the needy poor. A large part of the success of these programs hinges on a well-structured relationship between the central government and the executing agencies. There is no single way to design this relationship. To mention just two examples, Argentina finances works that are approved by a central government agency and executed mostly by local governments; Brazil allocates resources semiautomatically based on regional needs and subnational governments select the works. In any case, what is important is that the design of the relationship between financing and work execution be adequate for the institutional and political structure of the country. More federalist countries should respect local autonomy in work selection and allocate budgets on objective criteria; more centralized countries will be more able to select works and distribute resources at the central level while keeping responsibility for execution at the local level.

Second, the wage level and criteria for selection of beneficiaries are set at the central level, while local organizations are in charge of the selection of beneficiaries. Thus, there is a certain degree of tension between the criteria set at the central level and the local political and social reality within which the selection of beneficiaries takes place. There are multiple ways to solve or at least mitigate the consequences of this tension. Community participation is useful for overseeing that resources are not diverted through political favoritism or other forms of corruption, but there is no guarantee that the needed level of community participation will exist. A useful complement to community participation is a system of random sampling of projects and beneficiaries by the central government agency in charge of overseeing the program to check whether resources are being diverted. This implies a nontrivial investment of resources in sampling and supervision, but these resources will pay for themselves in more transparency and better targeting of beneficiaries.

Third, the virtue of self-targeting has the vice of low wages. In order to target resources on needy groups and avoid inducing distortions in local labor markets, wages in labor-intensive public works are set below the market wage of the relevant labor market. The literature on workfare in developed countries suggests that this targeting mechanism is not without costs in terms of stigmatizing workers who participate in the program (Lightman 1995), and in terms of political and social discrimination among workers by program administrators (Rose 1994). Low-income workers, in particular, may suffer from the stigma of participating in a make-work program where no skills are imparted. Graham (2002) and Grosh (1994) report similar stigmatizing effects on beneficiaries of the Chilean Programa de Empleo Temporal during the 1980s. There is no easy way out of this problem, short of raising wages to market levels, which in most cases would be impossible, given resource constraints.

In summary, labor-intensive public works do not generate important labor market distortions to the extent that they offer wages below the relevant market and can provide a source of income for temporarily unemployed workers. Coverage depends on the amount of resources allocated to the program, but there is no intrinsic reason why coverage of low-skill workers could not be as ample as needed to reduce unemployment to the target level. This same property, however, raises the problem that labor-intensive public works are countercyclical. Because the amount of resources dedicated to the program is a political decision, there is no way of guaranteeing that the program will move in sync with the economic cycle, expanding in downturns and shrinking in upturns. In fact, experience in the region shows that once the programs are in place, it is very difficult to reduce their size.

Wage subsidies. Subsidized private sector jobs are much less widespread than labor-intensive public works programs. Argentina is the only case where wage subsidies were widely used, and even there the scope of these programs has shrunk recently due to criticisms from the union movement.

Wage subsidies work through reducing the payroll tax and/or severance payments in employment contracts for particular groups of workers (such as youth, women, or ex-combatants). This characteristic makes them suitable for the introduction of more flexible (or precarious) employment contracts in a process of reform of labor market regulation. In fact, this was the role these programs fulfilled in Argentina in 1995. But at the same time, this makes them the center of a political debate on labor market flexibility, which in large measure explains why these programs were phased out in 1998.

However, because they target particular groups, wage subsidies change the relative prices of different types of workers in favor of the target group and induce large labor market distortions, not the least of which is the substitution of subsidized by nonsubsidized workers.[31] In order to mitigate this problem, there is normally an additionality requirement, by which subsidies are granted only for new net hires that expand the payroll. In turn, this requires the determination of a baseline number of employees and control of new hires. Theoretically, this is a task that the ministry of labor fulfills in the normal course of business. In practice, the ministries have little enforcement capability. This weakness makes impossible the task of determining baselines and controlling the hiring of subsidized workers, therefore making worker substitution a widespread problem. As a consequence, it is not clear whether these programs really create more jobs than those that would have been created without the subsidy.

In summary, wage subsidy programs tend to generate large labor market distortions by attempting to change the relative salaries of different types of workers. Because the programs have to be explicitly targeted by design, they require a comprehensive and often nonexistent enforcement apparatus, making the problem of targeting the program an intractable one. However, even in OECD countries with sophisticated recording and enforcement sys-

[31] More formally, deadweight effects appear when the subsidized jobs would have been created anyway without the subsidy, while substitution effects appear when subsidized workers replace nonsubsidized workers (Calmfors 1994). The additionality requirement addresses the deadweight effect, while substitution effects are only prevented at the margin.

Table 8.5 Training Programs in the Region

Country	Beneficiaries: Thousands of workers	Beneficiaries: Percentage of total labor force	Expenditure: Millions of U.S. dollars	Expenditure: Percentage of GDP
Argentina	133.0	1.4	95.6	0.04
Brazil	740.5	1.6	310.2	0.06
Chile	36.6	0.8	18.3	0.03
Costa Rica	13.1	1.2	60.6	0.73
Jamaica	43.5	4.4	18.6	0.44
Mexico	410.3	1.8	135.0	0.04
Peru	1.5	0.1	5.0	0.01

Source: Based on data in Verdera (1998).

tems, these subsidies are being minimized, given negative evaluation results (Martin and Grubb 2001).

The programs tend to be countercyclical, expanding and shrinking, and therefore requiring an administrative decision. To the extent that they are often perceived as a mechanism for introducing more flexible (or more precarious) employment contracts, they can become the center of political debate, making decisions about program implementation politically costly. This has been the experience in Argentina, where these programs were phased out and more far-reaching labor regulation reforms were rejected in 1998.

Training as Income Transfer Programs

Table 8.5 presents some summary statistics on the training programs used as an income transfer device in seven countries in the region at the end of 1995 (Verdera 1998). Training programs were widely used as a mechanism for transferring income, particularly to unemployed youth, through scholarships during the classroom training period (normally three to six months) and in some cases through job search assistance and/or apprenticeship stages in private firms. In most cases, the government financed these programs and private and NGO training providers delivered the programs with little or no intervention by the traditional national training institutions.

A caveat is that a common trait of this group of programs is that they use training activities, often as the result of a referral from an intermediation service. The programs are a peripheral part of the training system, which should be able to adapt countercyclically by expanding the programs while maintaining their core functions of skill training, intermediation, and education, which help lead the country to higher skill and income levels. Given the high public profile of the programs listed under this heading, they probably represent the greatest opportunity to reform the training systems.

The basic operational technology of these programs was based on Chile Joven, a pioneering youth training program that combines a scholarship for classroom training with a three-month paid apprenticeship in a private firm. Instead of direct purchasing of training services, resources are used to create a fund managed by a central government agency. The managing agency requests proposals for training projects, and funds are granted through open bidding. The proposals must describe the content of the courses to be taught and include a commitment from private sector firms to accept the trainees as apprentices for a period of time (normally three months). The provision of scholarships serves as an income transfer to beneficiaries, takes them out of the unemployment queue, and gives them some labor market experience during the apprenticeship. These three beneficial effects of the Joven program are adequately suited to situations characterized by high youth unemployment rates.[32] However, other countries in the region have emulated the contracting methodology of the Joven program to cater to the needs of other population groups.

Among the countries in the study reported here, Argentina, Chile, and Peru have programs inspired by the Chile Joven design, targeting low-income unemployed youth. Argentina has also used the contracting mechanisms of the Joven program to develop training programs for other groups and granted subsidies to private employers that hire apprentices under promotional employment contracts.

Brazil uses competitive bidding for training provision, but the program operates in a highly decentralized way. The PLANFOR program is financed through the Fundo de Amparo ao Traballhador, a fund financed by the payroll tax, and funds are allocated to states and local governments, who in turn hire providers (both private and public) through competitive bidding. States must present annual training plans to the PLANFOR administration, and funds are allocated in proportion to the state's share of the total workforce. This method of allocation is presently being changed to reflect the state's level of poverty and education and past experience with the execution of annual training programs. It is interesting to note that the national training institutions (in the case of Brazil, the SENAI-SENAC system) participate in the bidding process as another provider of training services, thus creating an interesting financial and institutional dynamic in the overall training system.

Costa Rica uses a national training institution as a channel for delivery of training services to semi-skilled and skilled unemployed workers. The national training institution uses its own facilities and instructors to schedule and deliver training programs for low-income workers in marginal urban areas, displaced public sector workers, and handicapped workers. A special line of action was established to enable the national training institution to contract out other training institutions, but no special targeting mechanism has been used.

Jamaica uses a number of programs to provide training for unskilled and young unemployed workers, but the mechanism for income transfer is temporary jobs rather than scholarships during training.

Mexico has the largest training and income transfer program in the region, and effectively uses it as a protective device for unemployed and displaced workers. The PROBECAT program expands and contracts according to the economic cycle. It provides scholarships for the beneficiaries, and the state offices of the labor ministry organize a variety of training programs that are delivered locally. Program evaluations have found that the program has been somewhat successful as a training program, increasing income and likelihood of employment for beneficiaries, although positive effects tend to increase with higher levels of education of the beneficiary (STPS 1995). After 1999, the new Mexican administration engaged in a number of reforms of the PROBECAT program, with the basic aim of streamlining intermediation services for unemployed workers and, in some cases, reducing the training component. The available evaluations indicate that enhancing the link with intermediation services has produced positive results and reduced the costs of interventions (GEA and Associates 2003).

Short-term training programs work as an income support device through the provision of scholarships to trainees during the classroom training and apprenticeship periods, normally between four and six months. The scholarships are below the relevant market wage, and the apprenticeships take place in private firms with which the training providers sign an agreement. The short duration of the classroom training makes these programs more adequate for providing young new entrants to the labor market with job search skills than for meeting the needs of skill updating or upgrading of workers displaced from declining sectors.

[32] The contracting mechanism of Chile Joven was in fact a way to create incentives for training providers to deliver good quality and labor market-relevant content in their courses. This created pressure for an institutional and content revamping of the training system, as firms accepting apprentices acted as controllers and gatekeepers of the relevance and adequacy of the training provided. The program was therefore rightly perceived as a tool to modernize and connect the training system with real productive activities.

The main challenge in the design of these training programs arises from the existence of a national training institution, normally a monopolistic public provider of training financed through a payroll tax with no incentive whatsoever to adapt the nature of its activities and clientele to the challenges of high unemployment. In order to circumvent this obstacle, a separate pool of resources managed by a specialized agent at the central government level organizes the programs. This agent in turn bids out resources to private providers that execute the training programs in a decentralized fashion. These decentralized providers must enter into agreements with private sector firms to ensure that trainees will have an apprenticeship stage, making private firms the effective gatekeepers of the quality and relevance of the training programs. Another interesting byproduct of this process is the development of stronger connections between firms and training providers, which make the latter effectively providers of job search assistance services.

Training programs tend to be more expensive on a per beneficiary basis compared with labor-intensive public works, given that a larger part of the resources goes to pay the training provider. However, calculations of benefits should include the long-term change in the structure of the training system and the development of job search assistance services, which are large positive externalities of these programs.[33]

The organization of the programs makes it easy for the program organizer to administratively target groups of the population, and the programs have been quite successful in attracting unemployed youth. However, it should be noted that the programs could be too effective in attracting the target group. For example, in Mexico in 1996, youth participation rates increased so much that even if the employment rate of the group rose, so did its unemployment rate. Although there is no formal proof that this was the result of the expansion of training programs (particularly PROBECAT) that year, there is a suggestive association between expansion of the programs, decline in school enrollment rates, and increase in labor force participation and employment of the target groups.

Elías, Cossa, and Ruiz-Núñez (2001) analyze the impact of one of the rounds of the Joven program in Argentina on wages and likelihood of employment. The program offered a scholarship for participation in a training program (between six weeks and three months of classroom training and two months of practical training in a firm) to particularly disadvantaged segments of the labor force. The target population of the program was unemployed individuals between 16 and 30 years old, with less than complete secondary education and scarce labor market experience. One-third of the beneficiaries were female and two-thirds were younger than 24. Using a variety of matching estimators, the authors conclude that the main impact of the program was on wages, with only weak non-significant effects on the likelihood of finding a job. The wage effect is around a 10 percent increase over the previous wage, and the effect is stronger for females, implying that female trainees tend to benefit more from the training received through the program. In terms of cost-benefit analysis, the authors conclude that, depending on the assumptions about costs and assuming that the effects of the program last for five years, internal rates of return vary between 2.4 and 7 percent.

Aedo and Núñez (2000) use control groups and stringent estimation techniques to evaluate the same program's impact on wages and likelihood of employment. They report that females over age 25 are the only group that benefits in wage increases and likelihood of employment.

Bravo and Contreras (2000) use a change in the rules between two different waves of the Chilean Joven program to infer how changes in the incentive structure that training providers face can alter the placement of trainees. Until 1994, training providers received payment for delivering classroom training and placing the trainee in an internship in an enterprise, with no additional

33 These emergency training programs have created the opportunity to introduce institutional innovation into a training system characterized by the monopolistic power of institutions financed by the payroll tax. Disseminating these innovations to the mainstream vocational training system will make it much more successful in addressing the needs of skill upgrading of workers caught in the normal process of job churning.

compensation if instead of an internship the trainee got a job contract. In 1995, a new rule was introduced in the program, by which the training provider would receive monetary compensation from the government if the trainee obtained a job contract instead of just an internship in a firm at the end of the training period. This change allowed the authors to compare placement rates before and after the change.

Bravo and Contreras conclude that changing the structure of financial incentives that training providers faced reduced the program's dropout rates and had a positive impact on placement rates. The authors calculate that placement rates increased by 13 percent after controlling for possible differences in the composition of the beneficiary group between the two waves using matching methodologies.

In summary, these programs tend to generate positive labor market externalities beyond the training process itself by easing the insertion of young workers and creating experience in the operation of labor market intermediation mechanisms (job search assistance). In terms of coverage, the nature of the training provided makes the programs suitable for unemployed youth. As is true for any training program, it should not be expected to create new jobs, but rather to provide new entrants with some labor market experience. Because youth unemployment is a permanent problem in the labor market, these programs should not be considered countercyclical devices, but rather a permanent feature of a well-functioning labor market intermediation system, which could be expanded and contracted following demand in a countercyclical way.

Cash Transfers

The most immediate and direct way to protect the income of unemployed workers is through cash transfers to families that fall below a predetermined income level. Although the criterion for receiving benefits from the program is formulated in terms of per capita family income, low family income levels are associated with unemployment or low wages (Hausmann and Székely 1999).

Cash transfer programs are usually targeted to the poorest segments of the population, which cannot obtain a minimum survival income level in the labor market. In many cases, a cash transfer is part of a more comprehensive program that aims to protect and further the ability of low-income families to maintain and accumulate human capital and, therefore, to graduate from the program.[34] Because these families are poor to begin with, economy-wide or even idiosyncratic shocks can put into question their ability to sustain minimum consumption levels. Therefore, a cash transfer could help them smooth their consumption levels.

The crisis in Argentina in 2001 was the scenario for a new type of cash transfer program, the Jefes y Jefas de Hogar, a basically universal program that targets unemployed household heads. The program provides a cash transfer to registered household heads and is not means tested. To be registered, the beneficiary needs to be unemployed and able to provide some hours of work, normally in a social service institution in the neighborhood. It is not clear whether this rule is well enforced, since control is in the hands of local government. Attempts to build social controls through the Grupos Consultivos, a consultation group formed by local authorities and civil society organizations, although not yet evaluated, seem to give mixed results. It is interesting that local authorities organize the works to be performed, but transfers are organized through the banking system. As access to the program is basically universal, benefits need to be rationed by queue, making the program's criteria for admission not quite transparent.

Cash transfers induce labor market distortions by increasing reservation wages and creating incentives against work. Because in most cases they do not require any counterpart work effort (making participation in the program effectively a free good), these programs also require a sophisti-

[34] The rationale for programs such as Bolsa Escola in Brazil, Programa de Asignaciones Familiares (PRAF) in Honduras, Becas de Retención Escolar in Argentina, and Beca Alimentaria en Venezuela is to avoid perpetuating a vicious circle of poverty. Thus, these programs require children to stay in school or women to attend primary health care facilities during pregnancy as mechanisms to prevent the transmission of poverty to the next generation.

cated targeting system and a complex system of verification and enforcement to avoid fraud by inclusion of families that are not needy and to avoid exclusion of needy ones. Cash transfers also tend to create strong entitlements among the beneficiaries, making it difficult to adjust either the number of beneficiaries or the amount of benefits in a countercyclical fashion.

Evaluations of conditional cash transfers show that the programs are effective in protecting the human capital of the poor. However, little is known from experience about the effects of unconditional transfers, such as the Jefes de Hogar program in Argentina. Recently, Argentina has released a new data set with information that would allow for an evaluation of this program.

Building Up a System

Skepticism about unemployment insurance in the region encompasses both the possibility of abuse and the negative effects on employment and output that would arise from reduced search effort by the insured unemployed. The concerns about abuse and corruption are quite understandable, particularly in countries where a large fraction of the workforce works in unregulated jobs or is self-employed. A poor record of enforcement of labor regulations does not help, as the absence of adequate registries of labor contracts with the labor authority make it difficult to imagine how eligibility for unemployment insurance would be assessed. Countries that do not have viable labor market enforcement and registration systems should privilege the creation of these capabilities over and above any discussion of unemployment insurance.

The possibility of establishing individual accounts increases social control over the insurance fund. This is an advantage for countries that have reformed the pension system to a system based on individual accounts (for example, as in Chile, Argentina, and Uruguay). Clear and well-enforced rules on contributions to the solidarity account from employers and the treasury should create enough formal controls for transparent and efficient operation of the system.

The creation of unemployment insurance raises concerns about the output and employment costs associated with reduced search efforts; these need to be weighed against the benefits that occur when longer searches by funded unemployed workers result in better matches and, therefore, a job mix that results in higher productivity and output. Acemoglu and Shimer (1999a) calibrate a model of the labor market for high school graduates in the United States; their results indicate that the benefits arising from better job matches of workers that searched longer outweigh the cost of foregone output and unemployment for moderate levels of unemployment insurance.

However, it should be stressed that unemployment insurance may increase labor costs and, therefore, have a negative effect on labor demand.[35] In order to minimize likely negative employment effects, unemployment insurance should be thought of as an offset for a reduction in legally established severance payments. In addition, unemployment insurance is sustainable only as a protective device and only for workers who have regulated and registered labor contracts. The temptation to temporarily extend benefits to noncontributors may arise for a government besieged by a macro crisis if eligibility conditions and benefits are not stable and well defined at the outset (even if they vary along the cycle). By contrast, well-defined eligibility conditions and reasonable costs may induce workers and employers to register labor contracts that otherwise would have gone unreported.[36]

For workers who do not have access to unemployment insurance, a variety of mechanisms need to be put in place, depending on the reasons for their lack of access. These programs are a form of income insurance. An early example of this kind of program is the redeployment support programs that were used in the early 1990s to cater to the needs of workers affected by privatization of public

[35] For a discussion of the issue of labor taxes and their impact on labor demand, see chapter 7.

[36] This is one of the explanations that have been suggested to explain the surge in enrollment in the new Chilean system, which quadrupled the projections for affiliations after nine months in operation.

Box 8.2 Redeployment Support

Redeployment support aims to help displaced workers reenter the job market or become self-employed. Redeployment programs are politically and socially valuable, providing a tangible demonstration of government's commitment to help workers. Targeted programs can help assist workers in finding alternative employment.

There are limits to what can be achieved by redeployment alone. Economic policies that generate sustainable economic growth will offer the best prospects for displaced workers in the medium term. However, redeployment may provide important support for displaced workers. The main types of redeployment support are the following:

Counseling

In addition to advice on services on support open to the displaced worker, counseling might include elements of trauma, financial, and life counseling. Counseling is the first and minimum level of support that the implementing agency can put in place to help displaced workers. There are many types of counseling. Although it is cost-effective, counseling is often neglected, partly because of lack of clear guidance.

Job Search Assistance

Job search assistance can be valuable because it helps identify and match workers' skills to available job opportunities. Job search efforts show positive results and, when targeted, can be cost-effective. Job search assistance might include the following:

- Placement assistance (employment intermediation) to match workers with opportunities in the job market
- Time off for job search prior to termination of employment
- Assistance in building skills and confidence to find a new job (interview skills, personal skills assessment, writing job applications, and job clubs).

Training

Retraining is often the biggest element of a redeployment program, and often the most costly. Retraining can be provided for both formal employment and self-employment. The record such programs has been mixed. Retraining needs to be targeted and demand driven if it is to be cost-effective. Training might include the following:

- Retraining and development of new skills
- Training in small business, microenterprise, or other new areas.

Employee Enterprise

Facilities are provided by the government or privatized enterprises to enable employees to set up their own businesses. Some governments have helped employees set up their own enterprises to contract services that were previously provided by the state enterprise, or set up workspace and small business incubators. Employee enterprise may only help a small group of workers, but it offers the prospect of creating secondary employment. Employee enterprise might include the following:

- Contracting out services to newly separated workers
- Providing simple workspace facilities (sheds, garages, or small offices)
- Creating business incubators and supporting workspace facilities with business advice, shared facilities (fax and photocopier machines), and a degree of mentoring.

Community-based Approaches

Community-based approaches look to local government, NGOs, and community self-help groups, alone or in coalition, to develop employment opportunities at the local level. These can include public works programs that provide temporary employment opportunities through large-scale, labor-intensive projects. Involving the community in redeployment schemes is valuable in many redeployment circumstances, but particularly in regions or mono-industrial towns with large levels of local unemployment. Where there is chronic unemployment, both community approaches and public works can provide elements of active and passive labor market support.

enterprises (see Box 8.2). They use mechanisms of the training and intermediation system to deliver income support to workers excluded from the benefits of unemployment insurance. Financing constraints dictate that these programs be targeted.

In the first place, short-term training courses could provide low-skilled new entrants with the training, labor market experience, and job search assistance necessary to access a regular job. Scholarships should be set at a level low enough as to not discourage search in the local labor market,[37] and targeting should concentrate resources on out-of-school unemployed youth. Careful attention should be given to attract exclusively individuals out of the school system, and therefore to deter school dropout caused by the program. Financing of this program should be obtained from the existing payroll tax earmarked for training, maintaining the system of decentralized provision with apprenticeships that has proved successful. Complementary funding (from either general fiscal resources or built-in reserves) should be provided in sync with demand for these services, and should be higher during economic downturns and lower during expansions.

This kind of program has numerous virtues, not the least important among them that it takes people out of the unemployment queue. However, there is an issue about the value of the training provided. In some cases, attending a training course should be an eligibility requirement; in others, the intermediation role of providing experience in the firm is more valuable. In any case, and given this design flexibility, programs of this nature should be subject to strict evaluation of their effects on wages and likelihood of employment (see Box 8.3).

For displaced low-skill workers, labor-intensive public works are the tool of choice in order to provide them with jobs at the local level. The innovation of these programs is that they do on a small scale what large public works did during the 1970s and part of the 1980s: stimulate labor demand through channeling public funds into construction works. The costs of providing complementary inputs are not trivial in a situation of fiscal contraction and, therefore, one of the temptations has been to reduce or simply eliminate the work effort requirement so as to reduce unit costs and expand the number of beneficiaries with the same resources. The paradox is, however, that these programs then become simple and unconditional cash transfers, losing a large part of the attraction of their original design.[38]

The design of labor-intensive public works programs requires taking into account the level of development of local government and the nature of its financial and political relationship with the central government. Many initiatives to set up employment generation programs have failed for not taking into account the organizational and political dimensions of the separation between financing and execution. Again, wage levels in the programs should be low enough so as not to crowd out alternative employment opportunities. Funding should be provided from general revenues and not, as is normally done, from payroll tax revenues.[39] Funding should be provided in sync with demand, with expenditure adjusting according to the evolution of the general or, if available, local unemployment rates.

Evaluations of the Trabajar program implemented in Argentina since 1997 present a number of important lessons about the design and impact of workfare programs. For example, the average gain for program participants in the late 1990s was about half the gross wage, and the distribution of gains was decidedly pro-poor (Ravallion 1999a, 1999b). The program's filtrations to the nonpoor are an essential element in maintaining the political support needed to implement the program. Not surprisingly, when it was cut in the midst of a deep fiscal adjustment, the program was cut in poorer areas and not in nonpoor ones (Ravallion 2000), thus increasing the anti-poor bias of fiscal adjustment.

The other member of the family of employment generation programs, wage subsidies, should be used sparingly, if at all, in spite of the conceptual attractiveness of the idea of generating real private sector jobs (as opposed to the make-work jobs of labor-intensive public works). The distortions caused by meddling with the relative wages of different types of workers are important enough as to counsel caution in this area. In any case, the sophisticated enforcement and supervision system

[37] The main criterion here is that the scholarship should be below the market wage that equivalent workers obtain in the labor market, and not a function of the overall average wage.

[38] It could be argued, for instance, that the Jefas y Jefes de Hogar program in Argentina is just a detargetting of the Trabajar program.

[39] The use of payroll tax resources (which increase the cost of labor and therefore reduce employment generation) to generate jobs is somewhat contradictory.

Box 8.3 Evaluation as a Tool

The rationale for program evaluation is straightforward. Without it, there is no reliable means for determining whether a program is achieving its objectives, whether the situation of the intended beneficiaries has changed, and what that situation might have been without the program. Anecdotal evidence and casual impressions alone are insufficient to manage programs that operate on a large scale and in some cases nationwide. Evaluations of programs and their impacts represent an important tool for testing the design and effectiveness of programs and determining whether time and money are well spent.

Moreover, evaluation at an early stage of a project can improve program design and targeting. Evaluation at an intermediate stage can further modify program design and increase the effectiveness of service delivery. In any event, the costs of evaluation represent only a small share of program costs, often less than 1 percent. The returns in terms of increased effectiveness of social spending and greater accountability are high.

Two main methods of evaluation are used. Both compare a treatment group of beneficiaries with a comparison group of nonbeneficiaries. When testing is conducted on a small scale, evaluators assume that the program has no impact on the economy as a whole. Evaluation of large-scale programs, however, should take macroeconomic effects into account.

The first method—the statistically ideal method—is experimental design. In this approach, members of the treatment and comparison (control) groups are randomly selected from a pool of eligible beneficiaries. Random selection serves both practical and ethical purposes. Many programs, particularly in their initial phases, simply do not have the resources to serve everyone who might benefit. Choosing members of the treatment group by what is in effect a lottery gives every member of the target population an equal chance of receiving benefits. The two groups can be compared for any indicator of interest, such as income, consumption, school attendance, or labor force participation. Randomization can also serve as a model for program expansion and later phases of testing.

A second approach is quasi-experimental design. Using a variety of statistical and econometric methods, analysts take survey information that is already available to construct approximations of treatment and comparison groups. As with experimental design, the groups are then compared according to the indicators of interest. This approach has both drawbacks and advantages in relation to experimental design. The most notable disadvantage is that this method does not equalize the various sources of selection bias between the treatment and comparison groups in advance. Consequently, evaluations conducted through quasi-experimental design may yield less reliable results.

The quasi-experimental approach nonetheless enjoys several practical advantages. First, this approach is generally less costly to implement, as it typically involves pre-existing surveys and no baseline (or pre-program) surveys. Second, quasi-experimental design can prevent delays in service delivery that would result from planning, carrying out, and analyzing an experimental design. Finally, a quasi-experimental approach may be better suited to accommodate political constraints: politicians are often (understandably) more interested in distributing benefits than waiting for the most accurate findings. Along similar lines, members of the public are more interested in receiving benefits than not.

Whatever method is used, some kind of evaluation is far better than none at all. Planning, managing, and expanding social programs without the tools of evaluation is inconceivable. When rigorous and thorough evaluations take place, policymakers and administrators can make better use of limited government funds and personnel and are thus able to direct resources to programs that have the greatest positive impact on social welfare.

needed to mitigate the deadweight and substitution effects of these subsidies is not present in most countries.

Finally, cash transfers to poor families are the last resort mechanism to support those families that fall through the other support mechanisms. This is the point where labor and poverty policies intersect in a strong way. The complications of their design and implementation are well known, and extreme caution is recommended, given that the program can create dependency traps for beneficiaries. Although it is too soon for a thorough evaluation of a program like Jefes y Jefas de Hogar in Argentina, it has undoubtedly fulfilled a positive role in at least temporarily containing the social consequences of the increase in unemployment at the end of 2001. The fact that in practical terms the program is not targeted to poverty, just to unemployment, makes it even more important to carefully evaluate the program's impact.

Updating and Improving the Workers' Skill Base

The fact that skill-related wage differentials are increasing in the region, unwelcome as it may be from the distributive point of view, creates an opportunity to increase the skill level of the workforce. The wage incentives are set as a clear signal of increased earning opportunities arising from higher skill levels. For this to happen, the education and training systems need to improve their operations.

The principles of training policies are well understood and essentially refer to the question of how to link effectively the demand and supply of skills. There is a widespread perception in the region that globalization and economic integration are making training policies more important. A well-trained workforce is key for providing domestic firms with a competitive edge, and workers require a higher level of skills to adapt to accelerating technical and market changes. At the same time, however, the increase in precarious and casual forms of labor contracts reduces the incentives that both firms and workers face to invest in developing and acquiring new skills.

Much of the policy debate focuses on the reform of public training institutions, rather than on the wider set of private and public institutions and practices that determine how workers acquire and apply new skills. Training is a public policy problem, but it affects both public and private actors. Interaction between the government and social partners (the private sector and unions) is key to any feasible solution. Improving the performance of the training system requires more than reforming public training institutions; changes in tax, education, and labor market policies are crucial in this task.

Private firms do train their workers, and the shape and intensity of this training effort are similar to what is done by comparable private firms in the United States and Canada (IDB 2001). Training policies have to operate in an institutional structure that involves the actions of workers and unions, firms and business organizations, and government. The institutional and organizational capabilities of each of these actors contribute to give the training system a particular shape in each country.

Training systems in the region have evolved differently from a common original model, mostly as a consequence of the different sets of circumstances and institutional capabilities that governments, the private sector, and unions have had in each country. Training systems are in a fluid organizational and institutional state. In most countries, the training system performs poorly and shows little or no ability to innovate. In some countries, however, the training system that has evolved allows for experimentation and innovation in training provision.

In spite of the variety of organizational contexts, there is a general perception that the performance of training systems is poor, and that its products are not relevant or even opportune in terms of the needed skills. Recent evaluation efforts suggest that this pessimistic assessment is not off the mark. For example, Medina, Meléndez, and Seim (2003) study the impact of the training system in Colombia. It encompasses a number of public and private institutions that offer training programs and the Servicio Nacional de Aprendizaje (SENA), an important public institution that regulates the system and owns and operates training facilities. The study finds that youth training has no statistically significant impact on income, except for a long-term impact on the future wages of young females who train in private institutions. For adults who train at SENA or other public institutions, training has no short or long-term impact on income. Adult males who train at SENA show a negative impact in the short term, but no impact in the long run. For adult females who train at SENA, the impact is positive in both the short and long term. Adults who train at private institutions enjoy a significant long-term increase in income, although there is no impact in the short run.

Tinkering with the institutional structure of a country's national training institute cannot solve this poor performance, although much needs to be done there. It is clear that neither provision nor regulation of training needs to be public, or even that being public would make the system work better. However, strong regulation and effective enforcement of quality and relevance standards for training programs are needed for any policy to work. The regulator should be separate and independent of any other entity that operates training programs to avoid conflicts of interest that could arise from bureaucratic encroachment. As in any market, regulation operates best when it is separate from provision.

Universalizing basic education and easing the transition between school and the labor market are crucial to give workers the opportunity to acquire the basic skills that are a prerequisite of the more specialized skills that firms may want to offer. Tax policies could also fulfill an important role, both to subsidize the cost of training for individuals that choose to invest in learning new skills, and to subsidize the investment that firms make in training their workers. At the least, investment in human capital should receive the same tax treatment as capital investment. Labor market regulations also need to be attuned to this process because productivity is a function of contractual relations and working conditions within the firm. Contractual innovations (including apprenticeship contracts) would allow workers and firms to share in the cost of training.

Achieving sustainable growth requires, among other things, a sustained rhythm of increase in labor productivity, which can only be the result of improved educational attainment for the population at large and a higher level of skill supply and demand. Training policies should not be seen in isolation: their effectiveness and success depend on a number of policies that structure the incentives for firms and workers to demand and supply skills.

First and foremost is the education policy. Universalizing basic education up to ninth grade is a necessary condition, but far from sufficient to support a process of skill development. The school system needs to show flexibility and attractiveness to give students the incentive to stay in the school system beyond basic education. This is not necessarily an argument in favor of vocational education as a specialized, closed-end feature of the education system. Rather, easing the transition between school and the labor market and vice versa is crucial for giving undereducated workers the opportunity to acquire the basic skills that are a prerequisite of the more specialized skills that firms may need. In this sense, the Mexican initiative *Educación para la vida y el trabajo* shows conceptual promise because it opens new channels of communication between school, training, and the labor market.

Adult education needs to be expanded, given the low educational attainment of the population at large and active workers in particular. Alternative models of delivery that are suitable for adults who are either working or looking for a job will be a necessity, probably implying a more intensive use of existing educational facilities and the design of accelerated, examination-based accreditation programs. Subsidizing the financial and foregone earnings costs of acquiring more education is a legitimate means for increasing the demand for adult education. In particular, these efforts should be expanded in periods of high unemployment, when the cost of foregone earnings falls substantially. If subsidization included the provision of income support contingent on results to adults reentering the education system, these programs would also have the nontrivial benefit of keeping workers out of the unemployment lines. However, policymakers should resist the temptation to use adult education as an income support program. If the quality of the education delivered is deficient, program participants will be stigmatized and the program will lose its effect on the future earnings of trainees.

In Chile, a tax rebate (the *franquicia tributaria*) subsidizes a wide variety of training programs, including programs for disadvantaged groups. This kind of intervention produces little or no interference in the training decisions of firms and workers. However, in the absence of strong regulations based on objective criteria about the quality and relevance of the training programs, this policy might be a waste of resources if firms and workers acted opportunistically.

Labor market regulations also need to be attuned to this process because productivity is a function of contractual relations and working conditions within the firm. Contractual innovations (including apprenticeship contracts) that allow workers and firms to share in the cost of training through a reduction in wages, and that eliminate the legal presumption of existence of an indefinite labor contract for trainees, serve to increase the supply and demand for skills. However, it should be kept in mind that opportunistic behavior could result in the use of trainees as a cheap labor force in the absence of strong and effective enforcement of quality and relevance standards for the training programs. If these innovations reduced separation costs below normal levels, firms and workers would have fewer incentives to acquire skills, given the increase in the likelihood of termination.

Workers and firms would benefit from wider availability of information about jobs and educational opportunities. Labor market intermediation services, which support unemployed workers' search efforts, could help to ease the flow of information and help workers find training opportunities while searching for a job. The post-1995 experience of operation of income-support programs shows that their effectiveness could be enhanced immensely by offering a menu of options (including training and educational opportunities), as opposed to just cash transfers (Márquez 2000).

Training programs should also be included in collective bargaining, thus giving firms and unions the opportunity and the mechanisms to bargain on the level of investment aimed at skill development. Unions and employers operate training facilities in a number of countries in the region, some of them of quite high quality. Regulation and direct government intervention to foster the creation and orderly use of local or regional councils of workers and firms aimed at development and operation of training programs would ease the coordination problem and probably increase the quality and relevance of the training offered. These programs operate at the local or regional level, where unions and employer organizations have more control over their performance.

Mechanisms to protect the income of unemployed workers (including severance pay and unemployment insurance) should include subsidies for training, preferably in the form of voucher-like instruments that workers could negotiate as part of their job search strategy. The post-1995 experience in the region shows that short-term training programs for unemployed workers are not star performers in increasing the future earnings of beneficiaries, although they seem to enhance employability at least for adult women. No experimental evidence is available on the impact of programs that send the unemployed back to school to acquire basic skills, but experimentation in this area should be encouraged and could be used to support the expansion of adult education.

There is no clear "best" model for the institutional layout of training systems, but there are a numbers of do's and don'ts that should orient policies in this area. The poor record of the traditional national training institutions in most countries in the region shows that the corporativist model of organization isolated the system from workers and firms, and that these institutes need to be redesigned. A strong public regulator of the training system needs to be in place in order to set and enforce quality and relevance standards for training programs. Because of the central nature of this institution in labor market policies, it is natural to think that it should depend on the labor ministry, rather than the education authority. The regulator should be separate and independent of any other public entity that operates training programs to avoid conflicts of interest that could arise from bureaucratic encroachment.

As in any market, regulation operates best when it is separate from provision. This does not imply the endorsement of an enlightened but isolated public bureaucracy: the regulator needs to earn the trust of the private sector and, for that, needs to interact with the institutional representations of workers and firms (and not just with training providers) and be governed by their demands. The corporativist model works only if the institutional representations are strong and focused on competitiveness (as seems to be the case in Brazil), rather than on the defense of the status quo. When unions and chambers of industry and commerce are weak, the corporativist solution degenerates into a bureaucratic quagmire that consumes inordinate resources with little or no social return.

More flexible forms of coordination with the private sector and unions should be stimulated, including the creation of local/regional and sector-specialized councils that can inform and direct public training policies in a setting and scale that are more agreeable with the institutional capabilities of unions and the private sector. Skill certification is an important tool in this process, in the sense that it solves an information problem by making the quality and quantity of workers' skills observable by potential employers. However, certification requires the strong institutional participation of firms, workers, and unions in the design of content standards and the mechanisms for accreditation.

The existing training systems have been charged with remedial training and education, and it is likely that they will continue to be involved in this area, given the deficits in basic skills of the labor force. The problem is that these programs tend to have little impact on beneficiaries and therefore low social returns. These programs should not be financed without stringent and continuous evaluation that allows for flexible redesign of program content, method of delivery, and clientele. On the positive side, these programs have served to open up the spectrum of training providers and have been strong forces for change in the training system. In particular, the programs need to be integrated with placement and intermediation mechanisms, keeping in mind that the ultimate objective of remedial training is to place trainees in productive jobs where they can continue to develop their skills. This implies that actions to facilitate job search, including subsidies and counseling, should be an integral part of remedial training programs. The labor ministry should profit from this opportunity to enhance the structure and performance of the placement and labor market intermediation services it provides.

In the past decade, governments in the region have implemented new programs and set up new institutional structures in the training system. This is a welcome process whose momentum should be kept up. However, most of these new programs have been set up as transitional devices to counteract the adverse consequences of unemployment and low incomes. Authorities should not forget that the ultimate mission of the training system is to provide the population at large with the level and mix of skills needed for workers and firms to create the more productive jobs associated with a more competitive economy. This implies that every action in the training system, from basic remedial training to the more sophisticated skill certification process, should be evaluated in terms of its effectiveness and cost efficiency in the attainment of that objective, rather than on its effectiveness in containing the adverse social consequences of unemployment.

Enforcing the Social Contract

Labor policies and regulations need to be enforced. In order to effectively enforce the social contract, countries will need to invest in the development of the institutions of labor policies, both those that collect, analyze, and process information, and those that implement policies and enforce regulations. Scarcity of resources and institutional deterioration are two traits that characterize the institutions in charge of labor policies (mostly ministries of labor). The low level of enforcement of labor regulations that results is not beneficial to the effectiveness of labor policies; important investments are needed in just setting up the institutional abilities and capabilities to implement labor policies. On the one hand, significant investments need to be made in labor market data collection and analysis. On the other hand, and more importantly, significant investments are needed to rebuild the capacity of the labor administration authority (normally the ministry of labor) to enforce regulations and analyze and design labor policies and instruments.

Hard data on enforcement resources are difficult to obtain. The data in Table 8.6 present the limited information that the labor ministries could provide regarding both a measure of human resources (number of inspectors per 100,000 workers) and an imperfect indicator of enforcement results (number of fines imposed in connection with noncompliance with some aspect of labor regulations per 100,000 workers).

Table 8.6 Enforcement Capacities of Labor Ministries in the Region

	Inspectors per 100,000 workers			Number of fines per 100,000 workers			
Year	**Argentina**	**Brazil**	**Peru**	**Argentina**	**Brazil**	**Mexico**	**Peru**
1990		5.61			1.41	0.26	
1991		4.99			1.46	0.24	
1992		4.27			1.44	0.22	
1993		3.95			1.89	0.21	
1994		3.54	0.24		1.67	0.21	
1995		3.20	0.55		1.54	0.44	
1996	4.40	4.64	1.13	7.95	1.54	0.51	
1997	4.10	4.37	1.12	7.30	1.82	0.50	
1998	4.03	4.00	1.11	6.24	1.58	0.45	0.62
1999		4.07	1.11		1.46	0.33	1.81
2000		3.82	1.09		1.31	0.29	2.88
2001		3.70	2.23		1.25		0.75
2002		3.63	2.21		1.17		1.76
2003			2.19				

Source: Data on the number of inspections and fines are from the ministries of labor; data on the number of employees are from IIMF (various years).

It is worth noting that many workers do not have employment contracts with full benefits; they are self-employed or work in casual, unregulated jobs. Massive noncompliance with benefit and working conditions regulations adds complexity to the enforcement task and new approaches need to be sought to expand the coverage of inspections and other mechanisms to increase compliance.

Labor ministries have an enormous regulatory task, encompassing occupational safety and health regulations and issues of basic labor rights, such as freedom of association and bargaining. The ministries are expected to organize a wide range of services, from intermediation to training. Based on their wide charter of action and shallow pool of resources, it is not surprising that the ministries have often failed in fulfilling their mission. Labor ministries need support in the areas of inspection services, labor administration, and registry.

Renewed efforts need to be directed toward enhancing the regulatory and enforcement capabilities of the labor authority, and new forms of fulfilling old (and new) functions need to be created. The evolution of training systems is an interesting example of how the new institutions of labor policy are being created. Of the numerous developments in this area, two areas deserve special consideration. One is the work on competency certification programs, in which the government and the private sector are working together to create a self-sustained system of standard setting and certification to enhance the mobility of workers across jobs (see Box 8.4). Another area where innovative efforts are being made relates to occupational safety and health (see Box 8.5). A common trait of these efforts is that they involve private (often for-profit) providers of intermediation, placement, and training services. These innovative new models of collaboration between the public and private sectors should be expanded.

Financing Labor Policies

Countries in the region invest a smaller fraction of GDP in unemployment insurance, employment generation, and training-cum-income transfer programs than a wide sample of more developed OECD countries invest.[40] Table 8.7 presents evidence for the seven countries in the region for which comparable data are available. On average,

[40] This section is based on Braun and di Gresia (2003).

Box 8.4 Skills Standards and Certification Systems[1]

Better information about workers' abilities and capabilities should increase both the productivity of search and the productivity of job-worker matches. This is the basic premise behind the new wave of skills standards and certification systems that a number of countries in the region are developing with (and some without) financing and technical assistance from the Inter-American Development Bank.

Skills standards are the abilities, skills, knowledge, and operations that an individual should posses for a specific occupation. Certification systems are institutional mechanisms that provide testable evidence of a worker's competency to perform the specific functions described by the applicable skills standard. Accreditation systems are necessary complements to ensure the quality of training delivered by a multiplicity of public and private providers. Once operational, the skills standards and certification system makes more information available on the skills and qualifications of workers, which benefits companies, workers, and society as a whole. For companies, the system provides objective information on workers' skills, thus reducing hiring costs and enhancing the ability to manage human resource development internally. For workers, the system provides a validated means of proving their skills and abilities, thus increasing their marketability and job mobility. For society as a whole, the skills system makes for more fluid and effective linkages between employment and skills, and provides an objective measure to assess the impact of training.

Developing comprehensive skills standards is a complex process. Experience shows that projects must be demand-driven so as to engage the productive sector in the design and utilization of the standards in everyday practice. Financing for the standards certification system should be provided by the private sector, although some initial government support may be needed. The system itself should be led by the private sector and managed by a body with a broad representation of labor and the public sector. Although standards will most likely be simple at the beginning, their quality and level of detail will need to evolve substantially with broader use. However, the crucial test of a skills standards system is whether it is used by the private sector as a tool in human resource management functions.

In Mexico, the development of skills standards was part of a public sector led initiative that is notable for its sheer scale. Between 1996 and 2000, more than 530 standards were developed and more than 42,000 workers were certified through the actions of the Consejo de Normalización y Certificación de Competencias Laborales (CONOCER). The hotel chain Grupo Posadas and the food retailer Bimbo, both major private sector companies, are adapting those standards for their own use. The Comisión Federal de Electricidad, a public electricity distributor, is planning to certify its 80,000 workers. Efforts are presently underway to strengthen the link with the training system through the adoption of competency-based training.

In Brazil, the Instituto de Hospitalidade was the hub of a national certification council that included representatives of business, labor unions, and government and educational institutions. Fifty-two standards were developed and validated in consultation with employers, workers, and trainers. As a result, nearly 12,500 workers were certified and more than 400 trainers were trained. Super Club, an international hotel chain operating in Brazil, is using the standards to train its entire workforce at its resort near Salvador.

In Chile, the Fundación Chile, an independent, nonprofit organization, worked closely with the National Training and Employment Service (SENCE) to produce 271 standards and train more than 4,000 workers over a three-year period.

The experimentation with skills standards and certification systems is a long-term process that has just recently begun in the region. There is a growing network of institutions through the region and much is being learned. There is an understandable enthusiasm among practitioners because of the increased private sector involvement that the skills system implies. However, this enthusiasm needs to be tempered by hard data on the impact of the skills system in increasing productivity in the firms and sectors involved.

Work needs to be developed in assessing the market penetration of the certification system. Evaluation of the impact of the skills system requires answers to the questions of who gets certified, which companies are purchasing certifications, and what competencies are being tested. Evaluations should be based on the market adoption of standards and use of certification, rather than on outputs (such as the number of standards and the number of certified workers).

[1] Based on Kappaz and Siegel (2002).

Box 8.5. Occupational Safety and Health Policies in the Region

Concerns about occupational safety and health extend well beyond the obvious health consequences of work-related illnesses, accidents, and deaths.[1] Occupational safety and health issues are directly linked to labor productivity, household income and poverty, the social security system, international trade, and even the environment. However, occupational safety and health issues have received little attention in Latin America and the Caribbean due to the lack of awareness regarding the importance of a safe and healthy work environment, and to the weakness of the institutions responsible for the promotion and enforcement of better working conditions.

Analysis of the incidence and impact of workplace diseases and accidents in Latin America and the Caribbean must take into consideration the limits imposed by widespread underreporting of accidents and illnesses and the frequent exclusion of entire sectors from information systems. Although reliable and comparable data on occupational accidents, injuries, and deaths are difficult to obtain, estimates for the region indicate that the social and economic impact of the unsafe work environment is significant: conservative figures show that it costs the region at least 27,000 deaths, 20 million injuries, and 4 percent of GDP. Furthermore, conditions observed in the region are more dangerous than those found in developed economies and even other developing regions. As a consequence, a substantial proportion of the regional effort to promote and develop its human resources is unnecessarily being lost in a workplace that is generally unsafe and unhealthy.

Addressing occupational safety and health problems requires dealing with overlapping responsibilities between ministries of labor and health, and between private insurers and social security institutes. It requires the cooperation of business associations and worker unions, international trade negotiators, and environmentalists. And it entails making decisions with significant distributional and health consequences. The key determinants of workplace health and safety conditions in the region require policy interventions that go well beyond the boundaries of occupational safety and health and into the realm of labor sector reform and social and macroeconomic progress.

The most obvious of the economic policies are those related to the labor market itself. Fiscal policies can also be used to promote low-risk activities and safe work environments through the use of fiscal incentives to encourage the use of safety equipment and/or to stimulate the development of low-risk industries. Furthermore, preferential interest rates and financing mechanisms can be used to support firms, particularly small and medium enterprises, in acquiring safer equipment and tools.

Health and safety conditions at work will not improve in the region without better standards and improved regulatory and incentive structures. Occupational safety and health standards need to be mandatory, universal, and enforceable. However, regulatory systems should not be limited to the traditional enforcement approach: the regulatory and incentive-based approaches are not mutually exclusive alternatives, but rather form a continuum that reflects the emphasis placed on one scheme or another. In fact, the two approaches tend to reinforce each other.

Efforts to improve regulations and incentives depend on each country's institutional capacity. Systems that emphasize regulations require a well-organized and

the countries in the sample spend less than 0.5 percent of GDP on these programs, while the average for the OECD countries is 2.4 percent of GDP. Only the United States and Japan, both countries with particular labor market structures, spend a smaller fraction of GDP on these types of programs.

Within the region, Mexico spends the most resources on employment generation (0.5 percent of GDP) to benefit around 4 percent of the total workforce. Argentina reports expenditure below 0.1 percent of GDP to benefit around 9 percent of the total workforce. Resources invested in training programs are of the same order of magnitude as those dedicated to employment generation programs, although the number of beneficiaries seems to be somewhat greater.[41] Furthermore, the countries in the region that have unemployment insurance systems (Brazil and Argentina) spend less on unemployment compensation than the OECD countries that spend the least on unemployment.

These figures suggest that there is room for expansion of expenditure on income support programs. Even doubling the expenditure on these programs (an increase well beyond any reasonable short-term expectation) would not make countries

[41] These figures exclude the expenditure of the traditional national training institutions.

financed government structure capable of defining, implementing, and enforcing appropriate principles, rules, and standards. An emphasis on incentives, by contrast, requires an insurance industry that is large enough to allow competition and sophisticated enough to be able to address the specificities of the different markets and individual firms, and a public sector with adequate institutional and regulatory capacity.

It must be noted, however, that the implementation of a structure of incentives is a complex proposition that imposes an important set of demands on the overall occupational safety and health system. First, the risk assessment and insurance functions need to be separated in order to avoid conflicts of interest. Second, the number of insurers and risk assessment firms must be large enough to ensure that neither market is an oligopoly or an oligopsony. Third, the definition of whether the firm or the insurer contracts the risk appraiser is critical: in the first case, the appraiser may have an incentive to underestimate the risk level of the firm in order to obtain a lower premium for its client; the opposite incentive would apply if the insurer were the client of the risk assessment company.

Smaller countries and/or those with weaker institutional capacity should maximize the capacity of the system to induce changes in the behavior of economic agents through a system that places relatively more emphasis on a regulatory structure based on clear and well-defined standards on which a good enforcement strategy can be executed.

Workers need to be better informed and educated in the use of occupational safety procedures and equipment, particularly in those industries that present relatively high risks, since the positive impact of these measures in such industries can be significant. Simple measures, such as adequate ventilation, proper use of safety equipment, and unobstructed work areas, could go a long way toward reducing occupational risks in the region. Health professionals need to be trained to recognize occupational injuries and particularly occupational diseases. Occupational safety and health inspectors also need to be trained. Better-trained workers, managers, health professionals, and regulators tend to generate better reporting and information systems, which, in turn, would provide the inputs to further improve the quality of training and education.

A strategy that coordinates the efforts and actions of the technical and financial multilateral agencies that are working with occupational safety and health issues in the region is particularly desirable. The relative strengths of each institution could be used to tackle the complexity of issues that determine the occupational safety and health conditions in the region.

Countries in Latin America and the Caribbean have many opportunities to improve occupational health and safety in ways that are cost-effective. Simple measures can go a long way toward reducing occupational risk in the region. In fact, there might not be a trade-off between improved safety and health conditions and costs because reducing occupational hazards may indeed improve labor productivity.

[1] Much of the information presented here is based on Giuffrida, Iunes, and Savedoff (2003).

in the region big spenders in international terms. However, size is not the only problem that affects expenditure on income support programs; lack of opportunity also hinders effectiveness. Because labor market programs are procyclical, as is overall fiscal expenditure, these programs tend to expand in good times and contract in bad times. Income support programs and social policy as a whole tend to follow this pattern.

Countercyclical fiscal policy is a key element for dealing with crises. Many of the recent proposals for reducing aggregate macro volatility in Latin America mention the importance of the potentially stabilizing role of fiscal policy (de Ferranti and others 2000). Most importantly, social insurance requires countercyclical fiscal policy by construction because it requires transferring income from booms to recessions. An adequate unemployment insurance scheme would automatically increase government expenditure as unemployment increases during a recession, and automatically reduce expenditure when employment recovers.

Countercyclical fiscal policy is also a key element for integrating social insurance with a well-funded safety net.[42] Unfortunately, the evidence

[42] That is, the elasticity of total spending to GDP per capita should be negative (and as large as possible).

Table 8.7 Expenditure on Labor Market Programs in OECD and Latin American Countries
(Percentage of GDP)

Country (year)	Training for unemployed	Employment generation	Unemployment compensation	Total
OECD countries				
Australia (1994–95)	0.23	0.21	1.62	2.06
Austria (1995)	0.13	0.05	1.30	1.48
Belgium (1995)	0.24	0.68	2.11	3.03
Canada (1994–95)	0.29	0.07	1.50	1.86
Denmark (1995)	0.86	0.36	3.06	4.28
Finland (1995)	0.60	0.68	3.57	4.85
France (1995)	0.67	0.40	1.43	2.50
Germany (1995)	0.44	0.44	2.08	2.96
Greece (1995)	0.04	0.09	0.44	0.57
Italy (1995)	0.39	0.69	0.68	1.76
Japan (1994–95)	0.03	0.06	0.39	0.48
New Zealand (1994–95)	0.44	0.15	1.26	1.85
Spain (1995)	0.33	0.31	2.46	3.10
Sweden (1994–95)	0.98	0.90	2.51	4.39
United States (1994–95)	0.07	0.01	0.35	0.43
Latin American and Caribbean countries				
Argentina (1995)	0.04	0.09	0.14	0.27
Brazil (1995)	0.06	0.21	0.19	0.46
Chile (1995)	0.03	0.00	0.00	0.03
Costa Rica (1995)	0.73	0.04	0.00	0.77
Jamaica (1995)	0.44	0.50	0.00	0.94
Mexico (1995)	0.04	0.51		0.55
Peru (1995)	0.01	0.19	0.00	0.20

Note: Training for unemployed includes training for unemployed adults and those at risk, plus measures for unemployed and disadvantaged youth and support of apprenticeship programs. Employment generation includes all forms of subsidized employment, plus direct job creation by the public and nonprofit sectors. Unemployment compensation includes all expenditure on benefits, independent of source of financing.

Source: For OECD countries, OECD (1998); for Latin American and Caribbean countries, Verdera (1998).

shows that fiscal policy tends to be procyclical in Latin America, thus leading to higher economic volatility and acting as a constraint on the possibility of establishing an adequate safety net. The recent literature on crises and poverty discusses options for reducing the volatility of Latin American economies and the design of adequate safety nets.[43] However, not much emphasis has been placed on studying specific ways of reducing the procyclical behavior of fiscal policy.

Social spending is strongly procyclical in Latin America: governments tend to increase pro-poor spending during expansions and reduce it during recessions.[44] Volatility is a key determinant of procyclical fiscal policy: the more volatile is growth, the more volatile is fiscal policy.[45] Braun and di Gresia (2003) analyze the correlation between pro-cyclical fiscal policy and GDP volatility for a sample of 88 countries including OECD and Latin American countries. Their results confirm that blessings come in pairs: OECD countries tend to have both low volatility and low procyclical fiscal policy, whereas Latin American countries have both high volatility and high procyclical fiscal policy. Latin American

[43] Ferreira, Prennushi, and Ravallion (1999); Lustig (1999); Lustig and Walton (1999); de Ferranti and others (2000).

[44] Wodon and others (2002) find that social spending per poor person falls by 2 percent for each 1 percent reduction in GDP per capita.

[45] Gavin and others (1996); Talvi and Végh (2000); Gavin and Perotti (1997).

governments are as pro-poor as OECD governments, but the adjustments in fiscal policy are relatively too large for the smaller Latin American governments to absorb. The differences between Latin American and OECD countries in procyclical social spending can be explained by the differences in the behavior of overall fiscal policy.

Countries in Latin America have been somewhat able to protect social expenditure, but are limited in their efforts by the depth of the fiscal adjustment needed. In more practical terms, protecting specific items of social spending during crises is often the only feasible policy and it may be an important second-best policy. However, the impact of such a policy is limited in scope given the size of the fiscal adjustment that is being undertaken at the same time.

Fiscal policy is particularly procyclical in Latin America because both the automatic and discretionary responses of the budget to the cycle are more procyclical than in developed countries (IDB 1997). It is difficult to disentangle the causality and relative importance of the competing explanatory factors of procyclical fiscal policies. However, there are several differences between Latin American and OECD governments. Fiscal policy is probably more procyclical in Latin America because the automatic response of fiscal policy is less countercyclical than in the OECD[46] because Latin America has smaller governments and a smaller proportion of automatic stabilizers in public spending (for instance, limited unemployment insurance). The discretionary response of fiscal policy (especially spending) is more pro-cyclical than in the OECD because Latin America is characterized by volatility, discretionary policies, political constraints, weak fiscal institutions that make saving in good times difficult, and limited creditworthiness.

What can governments do to limit this problem? Country experience suggests a menu of policy choices for reducing the procyclical effects of fiscal policy. The menu includes the following:

- Fiscal stabilization funds that would collect surpluses during good times and that could be spent during recessions
- Numerical fiscal rules to limit the growth of spending and debt during expansions
- Reform of the structure of federal fiscal transfers to reduce the procyclical effects of subnational spending[47]
- Increases in the proportion of automatic stabilizers in total spending
- GDP-indexed bonds, which would limit the need for fiscal adjustment during recessions by automatically reducing interest payments.

Unfortunately, the evidence shows that, in many cases, isolated measures do not work. For instance, fiscal rules and stabilization funds in many countries have failed due to unexpected shocks and politically motivated noncompliance.[48] Given that many of the above proposals do not alter underlying political incentives to increase spending during good times, the mixed results are not surprising. However, new developments in some countries, such as Brazil's Fiscal Responsibility Law and the Chilean structural surplus rule, and recent research allow for some optimism.[49] An integrated country-specific approach (as opposed to a one-size-fits-all approach) that takes political constraints seriously seems to be key for success.

Recent experience suggests working in at least three directions, as summarized in Table 8.8. In the first, policies should be adopted to increase the role of automatic stabilizers in the budget, as long as this can be done along a sustainable fiscal path. This is not easy; Bourguignon (2000) shows that Latin America's "welfare state" is similar in size and scope to that of Europe in the 1920s/1930s.

[46] Martner (1999) estimates that the average elasticity of the cyclical surplus to growth is 0.2 percent of GDP in Latin America, compared with estimates closer to 0.5 percent of GDP in the European Union.

[47] For example, making transfers constant, as opposed to linking them to procyclical tax revenues.

[48] See Braun and Tommasi (2002) for a discussion of some failures of fiscal rules in Latin America.

[49] Spiller and Tommasi (2000), for instance, develop an in-depth analysis of the Argentine political system, and use the framework to propose incentive-compatible policy proposals. Von Hagen, Perotti, and Strauch (1997) propose a multi-step process to achieve fiscal sustainability in the European Union.

Table 8.8 Summary of Policy Options for Reducing Procyclical Effects of Fiscal Policy

Objective	Domestic policy	International financial institutions
Increase automatic stabilizers	Unemployment insurance and other policies; increased size of government	Insist on transparency and accountability
Improve savings during good times	Fiscal rules to reduce discretion and limit spending and debt during good times; fiscal stabilization funds; reform of fiscal institutions	Countercyclical lending
Improve creditworthiness during bad times	GDP-indexed bonds	Countercyclical lending and contingent credit lines

Excluding spending on education, Latin American countries spend on average 10 percent of GDP on social protection, compared with 15 to 33 percent in developed countries.[50] It took Europe several decades of post-war economic growth to develop its current welfare state institutions. Recent literature suggests that efforts to improve the efficiency of the public sector, improve transparency in the budget, and fight tax evasion should be promoted (Alesina 1999). The objective should be to help Latin American countries "switch" toward a better equilibrium with improved social protection and lower tax evasion. However, results will probably not be forthcoming immediately.

The second prong should aim at implementing fiscal institutions that limit discretionary spending and pressures to increase spending during good times. A combination of macroeconomic volatility and political-institutional constraints explains to a large extent the lack of fiscal savings during economic expansions. Powerful groups struggle for parts of the common pool of fiscal resources. This struggle generates pressure for increased spending during good times, and the pressure is greater the larger the fiscal surpluses. Therefore, volatility—which generates large surpluses in booms and large deficits in recessions—makes savings during good times even harder. Approaches proposed in this direction include fiscal rules (Kopits and Symansky 1998), stabilization funds (Braun and Tommasi 2002), and revamping fiscal and political institutions (Hausmann and Stein 1996; Perry 2002; Stein, Talvi, and Grisanti 1998).

The third approach involves the development of financial instruments to improve access to credit during recessions or, in other words, to provide better insurance against shocks. A specific proposal by Borensztein and Mauro (2002) is to convert a significant proportion of debt issued by Latin American countries to GDP-indexed bonds. The idea is that bonds would pay higher interest when GDP growth is high, and less during recessions. This would reduce the need for rolling over debt or adjusting spending during recessions. Furthermore, increases in (inflexible) primary spending would be limited during expansions, because part of the extra surplus would automatically be used to pay debt service. Therefore, it would limit the problem of lack of creditworthiness and reduce procyclicality of spending. The role of international financial institutions is key in this kind of proposal because the markets for this type of security are still underdeveloped (Caballero 2003). Another way for international financial institutions to con-

[50] The conclusion is unchanged if pensions are excluded. Latin American average social spending excluding education and pensions is 4.8 percent of GDP, compared with a range of 9.4 percent (United States) to 24 percent (Sweden) in OECD countries.

Box 8.6 The Chilean Structural Balance Rule

Chile introduced its Structural Balance Rule (SBR) in 2000, when, for the first time in 20 years, the government was running a budget deficit. The main stated objective of this rule was to ensure a fiscal surplus of 1 percent of GDP in the medium run.[1]

The objectives of the rule were to introduce automatic stabilizers to fiscal policy, reducing the degree of procyclical fiscal policy and therefore the impact of external shocks on output and employment. A second stated objective was to improve the credibility of fiscal policy, which should in turn reduce financing costs and assure stable access to international financial markets.

The Chilean SBR is based on the IMF and OECD methodologies for calculating structural balances in developing economies, and published in IMF (various years). There are two main differences. The first is that the accounting principle is changed from one of "public sector financing needs" to that of "net equity changes." Specifically, income from privatizations is subtracted and income accruing to the copper and oil stabilization funds is added. Second, the cyclical component is only removed from income and special consideration is given to the price of copper.

Structural income (that is, without the cyclical component) is the sum of two structural components: tax income adjusted for cyclical variations in output around potential GDP and copper income adjusted for the cyclical variations in the price of copper around a long-run trend. The two key variables for this calculation are therefore the estimates of potential GDP and the long-run reference price for copper. How well the SBR operates will depend crucially on the accuracy and credibility of these estimates. Systematic overestimation of any of these variables will generate a deficit bias and erode credibility. To ensure independence, the Chilean authorities have delegated estimation of potential GDP and the reference price of copper to a panel of economists from various public and private institutions.

Expenditure is set so as to generate a 1 percent surplus with respect to structural income (see the figure). In periods of low growth (below the potential growth rate) or low copper prices (below the reference price), the realized surplus will be less than 1 percent. The result is a countercyclical fiscal policy that should generate a 1 percent surplus in the medium run.

Structural Balance Rule

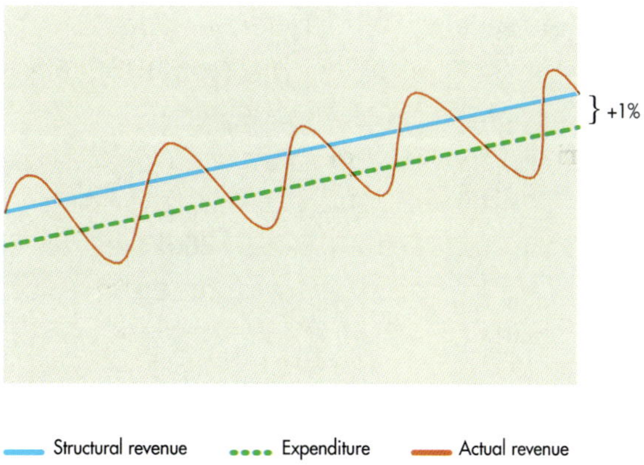

[1] See "Balance Central del Gobierno Estructural: Metodologia y Estimaciones para Chile: 1987-2000" at http://www.dipres.cl/publicaciones/Balance%20MH_1.html.

tribute to improve creditworthiness during recessions and limit higher spending during expansions is to make sure that disbursement of funds is more countercyclical, although this proposal is fraught with moral hazard problems.

Financing Countercyclical Fiscal Policies

Crises are common and recessions are deep in Latin America, and the poor and middle-income brackets are negatively affected. The procyclical behavior of fiscal policy—apart from increasing economic volatility—is a constraint on the ability of Latin American governments to protect the population from the risks of job churning. Efforts must be made to increase savings during expansions, access to credit during recessions, and the size of automatic stabilizers in the budget.

Simplistic applications of general principles, such as "make budget procedures more hierarchical" or "implement fiscal rules to limit spending and deficits" do not necessarily result in better fiscal outcomes. A more detailed, country-specific analysis is required to match detailed proposals to specific political contexts. This type of analysis is in its early stages, and international financial institutions should expand their efforts to enhance the knowledge about the particular mechanisms of operation in this area.

Voluntary approaches to fiscal rules and stabilization funds should be avoided; evidence shows that they do not work. More research is needed regarding what works in different political and economic environments. The same applies for reform of budget institutions. Probably hierarchical and transparent procedures would be good, but more country-specific analysis is needed on how to implement these broad ideas. It is clear that incentive problems with subnational spending are important. However, the cases studied by Dillinger, Perry, and Webb (2001) seem to indicate that easy solutions, such as stabilizing transfers, do not necessarily work. On the bright side, there are some encouraging experiences in the region, such as the Fiscal Responsibility Law in Brazil and the structural surplus rule in Chile (see Box 8.6).

In the long run, Latin American countries would likely benefit from a more developed welfare state, both through greater macroeconomic stability and less risk for the population from aggregate shocks. A step in the right direction would be for central banks and technical offices to actually start calculating the cyclical component of fiscal policy. However, the road in this direction is long. It will require "brilliant fiscal management" (Birdsall 2002), more trust of citizens in government, and more transparency and accountability. Automatic stabilizers, such as unemployment insurance, can be risky in a context of low transparency and state capacity, and it might be impossible to cut spending during booms if the government cannot control whether unemployment insurance beneficiaries are employed in the informal sector.

References

Acemoglu, D. 2002. Technical Change, Inequality, and the Labor Market. *Journal of Economic Literature* XL (March): 7–72.

Acemoglu, D., and F. Zilibotti. 2001. Productivity Differences. *Quarterly Journal of Economics* 116(2): 563–606.

Acemoglu, D., and R. Shimer. 1999a. Efficient Unemployment Insurance. *The Journal of Political Economy* 107: 893–928.

———. 1999b. *Productivity Gains from Unemployment Insurance*. NBER Working Paper no. 7352. National Bureau of Economic Research, Cambridge, MA.

Acevedo, G. 2003. Notas del seguro de cesantía, Year 1, No. 3, July, Santiago.

Acosta, Pablo, and Gabriel V. Montes Rojas. 2002. Trade Reform, Technological Change and Inequality: The Case of Mexico and Argentina in the 1990s. World Bank, Washington, D.C., and University of Illinois, Urbana-Champaign, IL.

Adams, Jr., Richard. 2003. International Migration, Remittances and the Brain Drain: A Study of 24 Labor-Exporting Countries. Unpublished.

Addison, J., and P. Teixeira. 2001. *The Economics of Employment Protection*. IZA Discussion Paper no. 381. Institute for the Study of Labor, Bonn.

Ademar, W., P. Tergeist, and R. Torres. 2000. Pushing Ahead with Reform in Korea: Labour Market and Social Safety-net Policies. OECD, Paris.

Aedo, C., and S. Núñez. 2000. The Impact of Training Programs in Latin America and the Caribbean: The Case of Programa Joven. Research Department, Inter-American Development Bank, Washington, D.C. Unpublished.

Aghion, P., P. Bacchetta, and A. Banerjee. 2001. Currency Crises and Monetary Policy in an Economy with Credit Constraints. *European Economic Review* 45(7).

Aguiar, M. 2002. Devaluation, Foreign Currency Exposure and Investment: The Case of Mexico. University of Chicago. Unpublished.

Aidt, Toke, and Zafiris Tzannatos. 2002. *Unions and Collective Bargaining: Economic Effects in a Global Environment*. Washington, D.C.: World Bank.

Akerlof, G., W. Dickens, and G. Perry. 2000. Near Rational Wage and Price Setting and the Long Run Phillips Curve. *Brookings Papers on Economic Activity* 1: 1–60.

Albaek, K., M. V. Audenrode, and M. Browning. 1999. Employment Protection and the Consequences for Displaced Workers: A Comparison of Belgium and Denmark. Article prepared for the CILN/Upjohn project, "Losing Work, Moving on: International Comparisons on Worker Displacement."

Alesina, A. 1999. Too Large and Too Small Governments. In V. Tanzi, K. Y. Chu, and S. Gupta, eds., *Economic Policy and Equity*. Washington, D.C.: IMF.

Andalón, Mabel A., and Luis F. López-Calva. 2001. What Happens to Workers When Governments Divest? Labor and the Privatization of Mexican Railroads. Universidad de las Américas-Puebla and Centro de Estudios Económicos, El Colegio de México.

Arbache, J. S. 1999. Do Unions Always Decrease Wage Dispersion? The Case of Brazilian Manufacturing. *Journal of Labor Research* 20(5).

Ashenfelter, O., and G. E. Johnson. 1969. Bargaining Theory, Trade Unions and Industrial Strike Activity. *American Economic Review* 59.

Azariadis, C. 1975. Implicit Contracts and Underemployment Equilibria. *Journal of Political Economy* 83(6).

Baily, M. N. 1974. Wages and Unemployment under Uncertain Demand. *Review of Economics and Statistics* 41(1).

Baldwin, John R. 1995. *The Dynamics of Industrial Competition*. Cambridge, UK: Cambridge University Press.

Barnes, M., and J. Haskel. 2002. *Job Creation, Job Destruction and the Contribution of Small Businesses: Evidence for UK Manufacturing*. Working Paper no. 461. Department of Economics, University of London.

Barnes, M., J. Haskel, and M. Maliranta. 2001. The Source of Productivity Growth: Micro-level Evidence for the OECD. Organisation for Economic Co-operation and Development, Paris. Unpublished.

Barro, R. J., and J. Lee. 2000. *International Data on Educational Attainment: Updates and Implications*. NBER Working Paper no. 7911. National Bureau of Economic Research, Cambridge, MA.

Beaudry, P., and D. A. Green. 2002. *Changes in U.S. Wages 1976–2000: Ongoing Skill Bias or Major Technological Change?* NBER Working Paper no. 8787. National Bureau of Economic Research, Cambridge, MA.

Beck, Thorsten, Mattias Lundberg, and Giovanni Majnoni. 2001. *Financial Development and Economic Volatility: Does Finance Dampen or Magnify Shocks?* Policy Research Working Paper no. 2707. World Bank, Washington, D.C.

Behrman, Jere R., Nancy Birdsall, and Miguel Székely. 2000. *Economic Reform and Wage Differentials in Latin America*. Working Paper no. 435. Inter-American Development Bank, Washington, D.C.

Bell, L. A. 1997. The Impact of Minimum Wages in Mexico and Colombia. *Journal of Labor Economics* 15(3).

Belussi, F. 1998. A Framework of Analysis for Self-Employment in Italy. Paper presented at the International Conference on Self-Employment, September 24–26, Burlington, Ontario.

Ben-David, D. 1993. Equalizing Exchange: Trade Liberalization and Income Convergence. *Quarterly Journal of Economics* 108: 653–79.

Bergoeing, Raphael, Andrés Hernando, and Andrea Repetto. 2003. The Effect of Policy Distortions on Aggregate Productivity Dynamics. Universidad de Chile and Harvard University. Unpublished.

Berman, E., and S. Machin. 2000. Evidence of Factor-biased Technological Change in Developing Countries. Boston University, Boston, MA. Unpublished.

Bernanke, B. S., and R. S. Gurkaynak. 2001. *Is Growth Exogenous? Taking Mankiw, Romer and Weil Seriously*. NBER Working Paper no. 8365. National Bureau of Economic Research, Cambridge, MA.

Bertola, G., and R. Rogerson. 1997. Institutions and Labor Reallocation. *European Economic Review* 41(6): 1147–71.

Bertola, Giuseppe, Tito Boeri, and Sandrine Cazes. 1999. Employment Protection and Labour Market Adjustment in Some OECD Countries: Evolving Institutions and Variable Enforcement. Employment and Training Department, International Labour Office, Geneva.

Birdsall, Nancy. 2002. *From Social Policy to an Open-economy Social Contract in Latin America*. Working Paper no. 21. Center for Global Development, Washington, D.C.

Birdsall, Nancy, and John Nellis. 2002. *Winners and Losers: Assessing the Distributional Impact of Privatization*. Working Paper no. 6. Center for Global Development, Washington, D.C.

Blanchard, O. J. 1997. The Medium Run. *Brookings Papers on Economic Activity* 1997(2): 89–158.

———. 2002. Designing Labor Market Institutions. Paper presented at the conference Beyond

Transition: Development Perspectives and Dilemmas, April 12–13, Warsaw.

Blanchard, O., and A. Landier. 2001. *The Perverse Effects of Partial Labor Market Reform: Fixed Duration Contracts in France*. NBER Working Paper no. 8219. National Bureau of Economic Research, Cambridge, MA.

Blanchard, O., and P. Portugal. 2001. What Hides behind an Unemployment Rate: Comparing Portuguese and U.S. Labor Markets. *American Economic Review* 91(1): 187–207.

Blanchard, Olivier, and Justin Wolfers. 2000. The Role of Shocks and Institutions in the Rise of European Unemployment: The Aggregate Evidence. *Economic Journal* 110: 1–33.

Blanchflower, D. 2000. *Self-Employment in OECD Countries*. NBER Working Paper no. 7486. National Bureau of Economic Research, Cambridge, MA.

Bleakley, H., and K. Cowan. 2002. Corporate Dollar Debt and Devaluations: Much Ado about Nothing? Massachusetts Institute of Technology, Cambridge, MA. Unpublished.

Blom, Andreas, and Carlos Eduardo Vélez. 2001. Brazil's Increasing Skill Premium: Growing Demand and Insufficient Supply? World Bank, Washington, D.C.

Boeri, Tito, and Katherine Terrell. 2001. *Institutional Determinants of Labor Reallocation in Transition*. William Davidson Institute Working Paper no. 384. University of Michigan, Ann Arbor, MI.

Borensztein, E., and P. Mauro. 2002. *Reviving the Case for GDP-indexed Bonds*. Policy Discussion Paper no. 02/10. International Monetary Fund, Washington, D.C.

Borjas, George. 1987. Self-Selection and the Earnings of Immigrants. *American Economic Review* 77(4): 531–53.

———. 1991. Immigration and Self-Selection. In J. Abowd and R. Freeman, eds., *Immigration, Trade, and the Labor Market*. Chicago, IL: University of Chicago Press.

Borjas, George, and Richard Freeman. 1992. *Immigration and the Work Force: Economic Consequences for the United States and Source Areas*. Chicago, IL: University of Chicago Press.

Boubakri, Narjess, and Jean-Claude Cosset. 1996. The Financial and Operating Performance of Newly Privatized Firms: Evidence from Developing Countries. Centre de recherche en économie et finance appliquées (CRÉFA), Faculté des sciences de l'administration. Université Laval, Québec.

Bourguignon, F. 2000. Social Protection in Industrial Countries: Which Lessons for LAC Countries? World Bank, Washington, D.C. Unpublished.

Braun, Miguel, and Luciano di Gresia. 2003. Towards Effective Social Insurance in Latin America: The Importance of Countercyclical Fiscal Policy. Paper presented at the Forty-fourth Annual Meeting of the Inter-American Development Bank, March 24–26, Milan.

Braun, Miguel, and Mariano Tommasi. 2002. Fiscal Rules for Subnational Governments: Some Organizing Principles and Latin American Experiences. Paper presented at the IMF/World Bank Conference on Rules-based Fiscal Policy in Emerging Market Economies, February 14–16, Oaxaca.

Bravo, D., and D. Contreras. 2000. The Impact of Financial Incentives to Training Providers: The Case of Chile Joven. Research Department, Inter-American Development Bank, Washington, D.C. Unpublished.

Bravo, D., O. Larrañaga, and J. Ramos. 2001. Una nueva agenda de políticas de empleo. *Revista Economía y Administración* 142.

Bresnahan, T. F., E. Brynjolfsson, and L. M. Hitt. 2002. Information Technology, Workplace Organization, and the Demand for Skilled Labor: Firm-Level Evidence. *Quarterly Journal of Economics* 117(1) February: 339–76.

Broda, C. 2001. Coping with Terms-of-Trade Shocks: Pegs versus Floats. *American Economic Review* 91(2).

Brown, Drusilla K. 2000. *International Trade and Core Labor Standards: A Survey of the Recent Literature*. Discussion Paper no. 2000-05. Department of Economics, Tufts University, Medford, MA.

Bulow, Jeremy I., and Lawrence H. Summers. 1986. A Theory of Dual Labor Markets with Application to Industrial Policy, Discrimination and

Keynesian Unemployment. *Journal of Labor Economics* 4(3) July: 376–414.

Burgess, Simon, and Michael M. Knetter. 1998. An International Comparison of Employment Adjustment to Exchange Rate Fluctuations. *Review of International Economics* 6(1): 151–63.

Butler, Inés, and Gabriel Sánchez. 2003. Market Institutions, Labor Market Dynamics, Growth and Productivity: Argentina. IERAL and Fundación Mediterránea. Unpublished.

Caballero, R. 2003. The Future of the IMF. Massachusetts Institute of Technology, Cambridge, MA. Unpublished.

Caballero, R., and E. Engel. 1993. Microeconomic Adjustment Hazards and Aggregate Dynamics. *Quarterly Journal of Economics* 108(2): 359–83.

Caballero, R., and M. Hammour. 2003. The Cost of Recessions Revisited: A Reverse-Liquidationist View. Massachusetts Institute of Technology, Cambridge, MA. Unpublished.

Caballero, R., and A. Krishnamurthy. 2001. *Dollarization of Liabilities: Underinsurance and Domestic Financial Underdevelopment.* NBER Working Paper no. 7792. National Bureau of Economic Research, Cambridge, MA.

Caballero, R., and S. Panageas. 2003. Hedging Sudden Stops and Precautionary Recessions: A Quantitative Framework. Massachusetts Institute of Technology, Cambridge, MA. Unpublished.

Caballero, Ricardo, Eduardo Engel, and Alejandro Micco. 2003. Microeconomic Flexibility in Latin America. Inter-American Development Bank, Washington, D.C. Unpublished.

Calmfors, Lars. 1994. *Active Labour Market Policy and Unemployment – A Framework for the Analysis of Crucial Design Features.* OECD Economic Studies no. 22. Organisation for Economic Co-operation and Development, Paris.

Calvo, Guillermo. 1999. Contagion in Emerging Markets: When Wall Street Is a Carrier. University of Maryland, College Park, MD. Unpublished.

———. 2000. The Case for Hard Pegs. University of Maryland. College Park, MD. Unpublished.

Calvo, Guillermo, Alejandro Izquierdo, and Ernesto Talvi. 2002. *Sudden Stops, the Real Exchange Rate and Fiscal Sustainability: Argentina's Lessons.* Working Paper no. 469. Inter-American Development Bank, Washington, D.C.

Calvo, Guillermo, and Frederic S. Mishkin. 2003. *The Mirage of Exchange Rate Regimes for Emerging Market Countries.* NBER Working Paper no. 9808. National Bureau of Economic Research, Cambridge, MA.

Calvo, Guillermo, and Carmen Reinhart. 2000. When Capital Flows Come to a Sudden Stop: Consequences and Policy Options. University of Maryland, College Park, MD. Unpublished.

———. 2002. Fear of Floating. *Quarterly Journal of Economics* 117: 379–408.

Campa, José Manuel, and Linda Goldberg. 2001. Employment versus Wage Adjustment and the U.S. Dollar. *The Review of Economics and Statistics* 83(3): 477–89.

Card, D. 1990. Strikes and Wages: A Test of an Asymmetric Information Model. *Quarterly Journal of Economics* 105(3): 625–59.

Card, D., and J. E. DiNardo. 2002. *Skill Biased Technological Change and Rising Wage Inequality: Some Problems and Puzzles.* NBER Working Paper no. 8769. National Bureau of Economic Research, Cambridge, MA.

Card, D., and D. Hyslop. 1996. *Does Inflation "Grease the Wheels of the Labor Market"?* NBER Working Paper no. 5538. National Bureau of Economic Research, Cambridge, MA.

Card, D., and A. B. Krueger. 1995. *Myth and Measurement: The New Economics of the Minimum Wage.* Princeton, N.J.: Princeton University Press.

Cárdenas S., Mauricio, and Catalina Gutiérrez. 1997. Impacto de las reformas estructurales sobre la eficiencia y la equidad. In Mauricio Cárdenas S., ed., *Empleo y distribución del ingreso en América Latina: ¿hemos avanzado?* Bogotá: Fedesarrollo-TM Editores.

Carneiro, F. G., and J. S. Arbache. 2002. The Impacts of Trade on the Brazilian Labor Market: A CGE Model Approach. Universidade de Brasília. Unpublished.

Carter, Michael, Bradford Barham, and Dina Mesbah. 1996. Agricultural Export Booms and the Rural Poor in Chile, Guatemala and Paraguay. *Latin American Research Review* 31(1): 33–64.

Casacuberta, Carlos, Gabriela Fachola, and Néstor Gandelman. 2003. Employment, Capital and Productivity Dynamics: Trade Liberalization and Unionization in the Uruguayan Manufacturing Sector. Universidad de la República and Universidad ORT, Uruguay. Unpublished.

Caselli, F. 1999. Technological Revolutions. *American Economic Review* (March): 78–102.

Cassoni, Adriana, Steven G. Allen, and Gaston J. Labadie. Forthcoming. Unions and Employment in Uruguay. In J. Heckman and C. Pagés, eds., *Law and Employment: Lessons from Latin America and the Caribbean*. Cambridge, MA: NBER; and Chicago, IL: University of Chicago.

Céspedes, L. F., R. Chang, and A. Velasco. 2000. *Balance Sheets and Exchange Rate Policy*. NBER Working Paper no. 7840. National Bureau of Economic Research, Cambridge, MA.

Chen, M. A., R. Jhabvala, and F. Lund. 2002. *Supporting Workers in the Informal Economy: A Policy Framework*. Employment Sector Paper no. 2002/2. International Labour Office, Geneva.

Chiquiar, D., and G. H. Hanson. 2002. *International Migration, Self-Selection, and the Distribution of Wages: Evidence from Mexico and the United States.* NBER Working Paper no. 9242. National Bureau of Economic Research, Cambridge, MA.

Chong, Alberto, and Florencio López-de-Silanes. 2003a. Privatization and Labor Restructuring around the World. Yale University, New Haven, CT. Unpublished.

———. 2003b. Privatization in Latin America: Myths and Stylized Facts. Paper presented at the Seventh Panel Meeting of *Economia*, Journal of the Latin American and Caribbean Economic Association (LACEA), April 24–25, Santiago.

Chong, Alberto, and Jaime Saavedra. 2003. Explaining Increases in Legal Informality during the Nineties in Latin America. Inter-American Development Bank, Washington, D.C. Unpublished.

Christen, Robert Peck. 2000. Commercialization and Mission Drift. The Transformation of Microfinance in Latin America. Consultative Group to Assist the Poorest, World Bank, Washington, D.C. Unpublished.

Clark, Ximena, Timothy J. Hatton, and Jeffrey G. Williamson. 2002. *Where Do U.S. Immigrants Come From and Why?* NBER Working Paper no. 8998. National Bureau of Economic Research, Cambridge, MA.

———. 2003. What Explains Cross-Border Migration in Latin America? Unpublished.

Clarke, George R. G., and others. 2002. *Bank Lending to Small Business in Latin America. Does Bank Origin Matter?* Policy Research Working Paper no. 2760. World Bank, Washington, D.C.

Clarke, George R. G., Robert Cull, and María Soledad Martínez Pería. 2001. *Does Foreign Bank Penetration Reduce Access to Credit in Developing Countries? Evidence from Asking Borrowers.* Policy Research Working Paper no. 2716. World Bank, Washington, D.C.

Commission of the European Community. 1991. Employment, Industrial Relations and Social Affairs Directorate, Employment in Europe, Office for the Official Publications of the European Commission, Luxembourg.

Cortázar, R., C. Echeverría, and P. González. 1995. Hacia un nuevo diseño de sistemas de protección a cesantes. *Colección Estudios CIEPLAN* 40 (March).

Cowan, K., and T. Do. 2003. *Financial Dollarization and Central Bank Credibility*. Policy Research Working Paper no. 3082. World Bank, Washington, D.C.

Cowan, K., A. Micco, A. Mizala, C. Pagés, and P. Romaguera. 2003. Un diagnóstico del desempleo en Chile. Inter-American Development Bank, Washington, D.C. Unpublished.

Crampton, P., M. Gunderson, and J. Tracy. 1999. The Effect of Collective Legislation on Strikes and Wages. *The Review of Economics and Statistics* 81(3).

Damiani, Octavio. 2000. *The State and Nontraditional Agricultural Exports in Latin America: Results and Lessons of Three Case Studies*. Working Paper no. RUR-103. Inter-American Development Bank, Washington, D.C.

Dar, A., and Z. Tzannatos. 1999. Active Labor Market Programs: A Review of the Evidence from Evaluations. World Bank, Washington, D.C. Unpublished.

Davis, S., and J. Haltiwanger. 1999. Gross Job Flows. In O. Ashenfelter and D. Card, eds., *Handbook of Labor Economics*, Volume 3. Amsterdam: North-Holland.

Davis, S., J. Haltiwanger, and S. Schuh. 1996. *Job Creation and Destruction*. Cambridge, MA: MIT Press.

de Ferranti, D., G. Perry, I. Gill, J. L. Guasch, C. Sánchez-Páramo, N. Schady, and W. Maloney. 2003. *Closing the Gap in Education and Technology*. Washington, D.C.: World Bank.

de Ferranti, D., G. Perry, I. Gill, and L. Servén. 2000. *Securing Our Future in a Global Economy*. Washington, D.C.: World Bank.

de Ferranti, D., G. Perry, D. Lederman, and W. Maloney. 2001. *From Natural Resources to the Knowledge Economy: Trade and Job Quality*. Washington, D.C.: World Bank.

de Janvry, Alain, Elisabeth Sadoulet, and Benjamin Davis. 1997. *NAFTA and Agriculture: An Early Assessment*. Working Paper no. 807. Department of Agriculture and Resource Economics, University of California, Berkeley, CA.

Díaz, Alvaro. 1997. New Developments in Economic and Social Restructuring in Latin America. In William C. Smith and Roberto Patricio Korzeniewicz, eds., *Politics, Social Change, and Economic Restructuring in Latin America*. Coral Gables, FL: North-South Center Press.

Dillinger, W., G. Perry, and S. Webb. 2001. Is Fiscal Stability Compatible with Decentralization?: The Case of Latin America. World Bank, Washington, D.C. Unpublished.

Djankov, S., R. La Porta, F. López-de-Silanes, and A. Shleifer. 2000. *The Regulation of Entry*. NBER Working Paper no. 7892. National Bureau of Economic Research, Cambridge, MA.

Djankov, S., R. La Porta, F. López-de-Silanes, A. Shleifer, and J. Botero. 2003. *The Regulation of Labor*. NBER Working Paper no. 9756. National Bureau of Economic Research, Cambridge, MA.

Dollar, D. 1992. Outward Oriented Developing Economies Really Do Grow More Rapidly: Evidence from 95 LDCs 1976–85. *Economic Development and Cultural Change* 40: 523–44.

Dollar, D., and A. Kraay. 2001. Trade, Growth, and Poverty. Development Research Group, World Bank, Washington, D.C.

Doms, M., T. Dunne, and K. R. Troske. 1997. Workers, Wages, and Technology. *Quarterly Journal of Economics* 112(1): 253–90.

Duryea, Suzanne, and Mary Arends-Kuenning. Forthcoming. School Attendance, Child Labor and Local Labor Market Fluctuations in Urban Brazil. *World Development*.

Duryea, Suzanne, Alejandra Cox Edwards, and Manuelita Ureta. 2001. *Women in the LAC Labor Market: The Remarkable 1990's*. William Davidson Institute Working Paper no. 500. University of Michigan, Ann Arbor, MI.

Duryea, Suzanne, Jasper Hoek, David Lam, and Deborah Levison. Forthcoming. Dynamics of Child Labor: Labor Force Entry and Exit in Urban Brazil. In Guilherme Sedlacek and Peter Orazem, eds., *Eradicating Child Labor in Latin America in the 90s: The Promise of Demand Side Interventions*. Washington, D.C.: World Bank and IDB.

Duryea, Suzanne, Olga Jaramillo, and Carmen Pagés. 2003. *Latin American Labor Markets in the 1990s: Deciphering the Decade*. Research Department Working Paper no. 486. Inter-American Development Bank, Washington, D.C.

Duryea, Suzanne, and Andrew Morrison. 2003. An Ex-Post Impact Evaluation of the Superémonos Program on Children's School and Work Outcomes in Urban Costa Rica. Unpublished.

Duryea, Suzanne, and Carmen Pagés. Forthcoming. Human Capital Policies: What They Can and Cannot Do for Productivity and Poverty Reduction in Latin America. In Ana Margheritis, ed., *Latin American Democracies in the New Global Economy*. Coral Gables, FL: North-South Center Press; and Boulder, CO: Lynne Rienner Publishers.

Duryea, Suzanne, and Miguel Székely. 2000. Labor Markets in Latin America: A Look at the Supply-Side. *Emerging Markets Review* 1(3): 199–228.

Easterly, W., and R. Levine. 2001. It's Not Factor Accumulation: Stylized Facts and Growth Models. *The World Bank Economic Review* 15(2): 177–219.

Easterly, W., N. Loayza, and P. Montiel. 1997. Has Latin America's Post Reform Growth Been Disappointing? *Journal of International Economics* 43: 287–311.

Economic Commission for Latin America and the Caribbean (ECLAC). 1999. *Latin America: Economically Active Population, 1980–2025.* Demographic Bulletin no. 64. Santiago: ECLAC.

Edwards, S. 1998. Openness, Productivity and Growth: What Do We Really Know? *Economic Journal* 108: 383–98.

Ehrenberg, R., and R. Oaxaca. 1976. Unemployment Insurance, Duration of Unemployment, and Subsequent Wage Gain. *American Economic Review* 66(5): 754–66.

Eichengreen, Barry. 2001. Capital Account Liberalization. What Do the Cross Country Studies Tell Us? University of California, Berkeley, CA. Unpublished.

Eichengreen, Barry, Ricardo Hausmann, and Ugo Panizza. 2002. Original Sin: The Pain, the Mystery and the Road to Redemption. Inter-American Development Bank, Harvard University and University of California at Berkeley. Unpublished.

El-Hamidi, F., and K. Terrell. 2001. The Impact of Minimum Wages on Wage Inequality and Employment in the Formal and Informal Sector in Costa Rica. University of Pittsburgh and University of Michigan Business School. Unpublished.

Elías, V., R. Cossa, and F. Ruiz-Núñez. 2001. An Econometric Cost-Benefit Analysis of the Young Training Program in Argentina. Research Department, Inter-American Development Bank, Washington, D.C. Unpublished.

Escaith, H., and S. Morley. 2001. El efecto de las reformas estructurales en el crecimiento económico de América Latina y el Caribe: una estimación empírica. *El Trimestre Económico* 68: 469–513.

Estache, Antonio, Marianela González, and Lourdes Trujillo. 2001. *Technical Efficiency Gains from Port Reform: The Potential for Yardstick Competition in Mexico.* Policy Research Working Paper no. 2637. World Bank, Washington, D.C.

Estache, Antonio, José Antonio Schmitt de Azevedo, and Evelyn Sydenstricker. 2000. *Labor Redundancy, Retraining, and Outplacement during Privatization: The Experience of Brazil's Federal Railway.* Policy Research Working Paper no. 2460. World Bank, Washington, D.C.

Eurobarometer. 1996–97. European Public Opinion Survey. Directorate-General Press and Communication, European Commission, Brussels.

Fajnzylber, P. 2001. *Minimum Wage Effects throughout the Wage Distribution: Evidence from Brazil´s Formal and Informal Sectors.* Texto para Discussão no. 151. Universidade Federal de Minas Gerais, Facultade de Ciências Econômicas, and Centro de Desenvolvimento e Planejamento Regional, Belo Horizonte.

Fajnzylber, Pablo, and William F. Maloney. 2001. Labor Demand and Trade Reform in Latin America. World Bank, Washington, D.C. Unpublished.

Fay, Robert G. 1996. *Enhancing the Effectiveness of Active Labour Market Policies: Evidence from Programme Evaluations in OECD Countries.* Labour Market and Social Policy Occasional Paper no. 18. Organisation for Economic Co-operation and Development, Paris.

Feliciano, Zadia. 1994. Workers and Trade Liberalization: The Impact of Trade Reforms in Mexico on Wages and Unemployment. Harvard University, Cambridge, MA. Unpublished.

Fernández-Arias, E., and P. Montiel. 1997. *Reform and Growth in Latin America: All Pain, No Gain?* Research Department Working Paper no. 351. Inter-American Development Bank, Washington, D.C.

Ferreira, F., G. Prennushi, and M. Ravallion. 1999. Protecting the Poor from Macroeconomic Shocks: An Agenda for Action in a Crisis and Beyond. World Bank, Washington, D.C. Unpublished.

Fischer, S. 1977. Wage Indexation and Macroeconomic Stability. In K. Brunner and A. Meltzer, eds., *Stabilization of the Domestic and International Economy.* Amsterdam: North-Holland.

Fleck, Susan. 2001. A Gender Perspective of *Maquila* Employment and Wages in Mexico. In Elizabeth G. Katz and María G. Correia, eds., *The Economics of Gender in Mexico: Work, Family, State, and Market.* Washington, D.C.: World Bank.

Forbes, Kristin. 2002. *How Do Large Depreciations Affect Firm Performance?* NBER Working Paper no. 9095. National Bureau of Economic Research, Cambridge, MA.

Forteza, A., and M. Rama. 2002. Labor Market "Rigidity" and the Success of Economic Reforms across More Than One Hundred Countries. Universidad de la República, Uruguay, and World Bank, Washington, D.C. Unpublished.

Frankel, J., and D. Romer. 1999. Does Trade Cause Growth? *American Economic Review* 89: 379–99.

Freeman, Richard B., and Remco H. Oostendorp. 2000. *Wages around the World: Pay Across Occupations and Countries.* NBER Working Paper no. 8058. National Bureau of Economic Research, Cambridge, MA.

Fretwell, D., J. Benus, and C. O'Leary. 1999. *Evaluating the Impact of Active Labor Programs: Results of Cross Country Studies in Europe and Central Asia.* SP Discussion Paper no. 9915. World Bank, Washington, D.C.

Friedman, M. 1977. Nobel Lecture: Inflation and Unemployment. *Journal of Political Economy* 85(3): 451–72.

Galal, Ahmed, Leroy Jones, Pankaj Tandonand, and Ingo Vogelsang. 1994. *Welfare Consequences of Selling Public Enterprises: An Empirical Analysis.* Washington, D.C.: World Bank; and New York: Oxford University Press.

Galiani, Sebastián, and Pablo Sanguinetti. 2000. Wage Inequality and Trade Liberalization: Evidence from Argentina. Universidad Torcuato Di Tella, Buenos Aires. Unpublished.

Galindo, Arturo, and Alejandro Izquierdo. 2003. Terms of Trade Shocks, Sudden Stops and Asymmetric Employment Responses: Evidence for Emerging Markets. Inter-American Development Bank, Washington, D.C. Unpublished.

Gallie, D. 1997. Employment, Unemployment and the Quality of Life: The Employment in Europe Survey 1996. *Eurobarometer* 44.3. Report prepared for the European Commission.

Gavin, M. 1997. *A Decade of Reform in Latin America: Has It Delivered Lower Volatility?* Working Paper no. 349. Inter-American Development Bank, Washington, D.C.

Gavin, M., R. Hausmann, R. Perotti, and E. Talvi. 1996. *Managing Fiscal Policy in Latin America and the Caribbean: Volatility, Procyclicality and Limited Creditworthiness.* Working Paper no. 326. Inter-American Development Bank, Washington, D.C.

Gavin, Michael, and Roberto Perotti. 1997. Fiscal Policy in Latin America. In Ben Bernanke and Julio Rotemberg, eds., *NBER Macroeconomic Annual.* Cambridge, MA: MIT Press.

GEA and Associates. 2003. Evaluación del programa de becas de capacitación para desempleados. Mexico City.

Giuffrida, A., R. F. Iunes, and W. D. Savedoff. 2003. Occupational Safety and Health in Latin America and the Caribbean: Overview, Issues and Policy Recommendations. Policy Brief. Inter-American Development Bank, Washington, D.C.

Goldberg, Pinelopi Koujianou, and Nina Pavcnik. 2001. *Trade Protection and Wages: Evidence from the Colombian Trade Reforms.* NBER Working Paper no. 8575. National Bureau of Economic Research, Cambridge, MA.

———. 2003. *The Response of the Informal Sector to Trade Liberalization.* NBER Working Paper no. 9443. National Bureau of Economic Research, Cambridge, MA.

Goldin, C., and R. A. Margo. 1992. The Great Compression: The Wage Structure in the United States at Mid-Century. *Quarterly Journal of Economics* 107(1) February: 1–34.

Goldín, Liliana R. 1997. Economic Restructuring and New Forms of Market Participation in Rural Latin America. In William C. Smith and Roberto Patricio Korzeniewicz, eds., *Politics, Social Change, and Economic Restructuring in Latin America.* Coral Gables, FL: North-South Center Press; and Boulder, CO: Lynne Rienner Publishers.

Gollin, Douglas. 2002. Getting Income Shares Right. *Journal of Political Economy* 110(2) April: 458–74.

Gonzaga, G. 2003. Labor Adjustment Dynamics in Brazilian Manufacturing. Unpublished.

Gonzaga, Gustavo, Naércio Aquino Menezes Filho, and Cristina Terra. 2002. *Trade Liberalization and the Evolution of Skill Earnings Differentials in*

Brazil. Texto para Discussão no. 463. PUC-Rio, USP, EPGE-FGV.

González, J. A. 2002. *Labor Market Flexibility in Thirteen Latin American Countries and the United States: Revisiting and Expanding Okun Coefficients.* Working Paper no. 136. Center for Research on Economic Development and Policy Reform, Stanford University, Palo Alto, CA.

Gourinchas, Pierre-Olivier. 1999. Exchange Rates Do Matter: French Job Reallocation and the Exchange Rate Turbulence, 1984–1992. *European Economic Review* 43: 1279–1316.

Government of Brazil. 1998. Relatório da Força-Tarefa sobre Políticas de Emprego: Diagnóstico e Recomendações. Ministério de Trabalho, Brasília.

Government of Canada. 1989. *Employment and Evaluation of the National Employment Service.* Ottawa: Employment and Immigration Service.

Government of the United States. 1998. *Social Security Programs throughout the World.* Washington, D.C.: U.S. Social Security Administration.

Government of the United States. Various years. *Statistical Abstract of the United States.* Washington, D.C.: U.S. Census Bureau.

Graham, Carol. 2002. *Crafting Sustainable Social Contracts in Latin America: Political Economy, Public Attitudes, and Social Policy.* Working Paper no. 29. The Brookings Institution, Washington, D.C.

Gray, J. A. 1978. On Indexation and Contract Length. *Journal of Political Economy* 86(1).

Gray, J. A., and M. Kandil. 1991. Is Price Flexibility Stabilizing? A Broader Perspective. *Journal of Money, Credit and Banking* 23(1).

Green, F., A. Dickerson, and J. S. Arbache. 2001. A Picture of Wage Inequality and the Allocation of Labor through the Period of Trade Liberalization: The Case of Brazil. *World Development* 29: 1923–39.

Greenwood, J., Z. Hercowitz, and P. Krusell. 1997. Long-run Implications of Investment-specific Technological Change. *American Economic Review* 87(3) June: 342–62.

Gronau, Reuben, and Haim Regev. 1997. *The Demand for Labor and Job Turnover: Israeli Manufacturing 1970–1994.* Working Paper no. 378. Industrial Relations Section, Princeton University, Princeton, NJ.

Grosh, Margaret E. 1994. *Administering Targeted Social Programs in Latin America: From Platitudes to Practice.* Washington, D.C.: World Bank.

Groshen, E., and M. Schweitzer. 1996. *The Effects of Inflation on Wage Adjustments in Firm-Level Data: Grease or Sand?* Staff Reports, no. 9. Federal Reserve Bank of New York, New York, N.Y.

Gruber, Jonathan. 1994. The Incidence of Mandated Maternity Benefits. *American Economic Review* 84(3): 622–41.

———. 1997a. The Consumption Smoothing Benefits of Unemployment Insurance. *American Economic Review* 87: 192–205.

———.1997b. The Incidence of Payroll Taxation: Evidence from Chile. *Journal of Labor Economics* 15(3): S72–S101.

Hall, Robert. 1995. Lost Jobs. *Brookings Papers on Economic Activity* 1: 221–56.

Hall, Robert, and David Lilien. 1986. Cyclical Fluctuations in the Labor Market. In O. Ashenfelter and R. Layard, eds., *Handbook of Labor Economics.* Volume 2. Amsterdam: North-Holland.

Haltiwanger, John, and Manisha Singh. 1999. Cross-Country Evidence on Public Sector Retrenchment. *The World Bank Economic Review* 13(1): 23–66.

Hamermesh, D. S. 1993. Labor Demand. Princeton, N.J.: Princeton University Press.

Hamilton, S., G. Sullivan, and L. Asturias. 2001. *Economic and Social Impacts of Non-traditional Export Crop Production in Highland Guatemala: Impact Perception Survey.* IPM CRSP Working Paper no. 01-3. Office of International Research and Development, Virginia Tech, VA.

Hanson, Gordon. 2003. *What Has Happened to Wages in Mexico since NAFTA? Implications for Hemispheric Free Trade.* NBER Working Paper no. 9563. National Bureau of Economic Research, Cambridge, MA.

Hanson, Gordon, and Ann Harrison. 1999. Trade and Wage Inequality in Mexico. *Industrial and Labor Relations Review* 52(2): 271–88.

Harrison, A. 2002. Has Globalization Eroded Labor's Share? Some Cross-Country Evidence. University of California, Berkeley, CA. Unpublished.

Harrison, Ann, and Gordon Hanson. 1999. Who Gains from Trade Reform? Some Remaining

Puzzles. *Journal of Development Economics* 59: 125–54.

Hatton, T. J., and J. G. Williamson. 2002. *What Fundamentals Drive World Migration?* NBER Working Paper no. 9159. National Bureau of Economic Research, Cambridge, MA.

Hausmann, Ricardo, Ugo Panizza, and Ernesto Stein. 2001. Why Do Countries Float the Way They Float? *Journal of Development Economics* 66: 387–414.

Hausmann, Ricardo, and Dani Rodrik. 2002. *Economic Development as Self-Discovery.* KSG Faculty Research Working Paper Series no. RWP02-023. Harvard University, Cambridge, MA.

Hausmann, Ricardo, and Ernesto Stein. 1996. Searching for the Right Budgetary Institutions for a Volatile Region. In R. Hausmann and H. Reisen, eds., *Securing Stability and Growth in Latin America.* Paris: OECD.

Hausmann, Ricardo, and Miguel Székely. 1999. *Inequality and the Family in Latin America.* Working Paper Series no. 393. Inter-American Development Bank, Washington, D.C.

Heckman, James, and Carmen Pagés. 2000. *The Cost of Job Security Regulation: Evidence from Latin American Labor Markets.* Research Department Working Paper no. 430. Inter-American Development Bank, Washington, D.C.

———. Forthcoming. Law and Employment: Lessons from Latin America and the Caribbean. An Introduction. In J. Heckman and C. Pagés, eds., *Law and Employment: Lessons from Latin America and the Caribbean.* Cambridge, MA: NBER; and Chicago, IL: University of Chicago.

Herrera, J., and D. Rosas Shady. 2003. Labor Market Transitions in Peru. Unpublished.

Heston, A., R. Summers, and A. Bettina. 2002. Penn World Table Version 6.1. Center for International Comparisons at the University of Pennsylvania (CICUP).

Hicks, J. 1932. *The Theory of Wages.* London: Macmillan Press.

Hopenhayn, Hugo. Forthcoming. Labor Market Policies and Employment Duration: The Effects of Labor Market Reform in Argentina. In J. Heckman and C. Pagés, eds., *Law and Employment: Lessons from Latin America and the Caribbean.* Cambridge, MA: NBER; and Chicago, IL: University of Chicago.

Hopenhayn, Hugo, and Juan Pablo Nicolini. 1997. Optimal Unemployment Insurance. *Journal of Political Economy* 105: 412–38.

———. 2001. Heterogeneity and Optimal Unemployment Insurance. In Nora Lustig, ed., *Shielding the Poor.* Washington, D.C.: Brookings Institution Press and IDB.

Hopenhayn, Hugo, and Richard Rogerson. 1993. Job Turnover and Policy Evaluation: A General Equilibrium Analysis. *Journal of Political Economy* 101(5): 915–38.

Hoxby, C. M. 1996. How Teachers' Unions Affect Education Production. *Quarterly Journal of Economics* 111(3): 671–718.

Inter-American Development Bank. 1995. *Overcoming Volatility.* Washington, D.C.: IDB.

———. 1996. *Making Social Services Work.* Washington, D.C.: IDB.

———. 1997. *Latin America after a Decade of Reforms.* Washington, D.C.: IDB.

———. 1998. *Latin American Economic Policies.* No. 5. Fourth Quarter. Office of the Chief Economist, Inter-American Development Bank, Washington, D.C.

———. 1998–99. *Facing Up to Inequality in Latin America.* Washington, D.C.: IDB.

———. 2000. *Latin American Economic Policies.* Fourth Quarter. Research Department, Inter-American Development Bank, Washington, D.C.

———. 2001. *Competitiveness: The Business of Growth.* Washington, D.C.: IDB.

———. 2002. *Beyond Borders: The New Regionalism in Latin America.* Washington, D.C.: IDB.

———. 2003. *Ideas for Development in the Americas.* Vol. 1. Second Quarter. Research Department, Inter-American Development Bank, Washington, D.C.

International Labour Organization (ILO). 1996. *Panorama laboral '96: América Latina y el Caribe.* Lima: ILO.

———. 1997. *World Labour Report 1997–98: Industrial Relations, Democracy and Social Stability.* Geneva: ILO.

———. 1998. Seminario-taller sobre la estructura y el funcionamiento de los departamentos de empleo y de los sistemas de intermediación en el mercado de trabajo. ILO, September 8–9, documento de conclusiones.

———. 1999. Segundo seminario-taller sobre la estructura y el funcionamiento de los departamentos de empleo y de los sistemas de intermediación en el mercado de trabajo. ILO, May 12–13, documento de conclusiones.

———. Various years. LABORSTA Labour Statistics Database, Copyright International Labour Organization 1998–2003. Geneva.

———. 2001. *Panorama laboral 2001: América Latina y el Caribe*. Geneva: ILO.

———. 2002a. *Panorama laboral 2002: América Latina y el Caribe*. Geneva: ILO.

———. 2002b. *IPEC Action against Child Labour: Highlights* 2002. Geneva: ILO.

Jacobson, Louis S., Robert J. LaLonde, and Daniel G. Sullivan. 1993. Earnings Losses of Displaced Workers. *American Economic Review* 83(4): 685–709.

Jadresic, Esteban. 1997. *What Type of Contracts Underlie Aggregate Wage Dynamics?* Working Paper no. 97/67. International Monetary Fund, Washington, D.C.

———. 1998. Wage Indexation and the Cost of Disinflation. *IMF Staff Papers* 43(4).

Jarvis, Lovell S., and Esperanza Vera-Toscano. 2001. Seasonal Adjustment in a Market for Temporary Agricultural Workers: Fruit Workers in Chile. World Bank, Washington, D.C. Unpublished.

Jenkins, Hatice. 2000. *Commercial Bank Behaviour in Micro and Small Enterprise Finance.* Development Discussion Paper no. 741. Harvard Institute for International Development, Harvard University, Cambridge, MA.

Jones, Charles I. 2001. Comment on "Trade Policy and Economic Growth: A Skeptic's Guide to the Cross-National Evidence." In B. S. Bernanke and K. Rogoff, eds., *NBER Macroeconomics Annual 2000*. Cambridge, MA: MIT Press.

Juhn, Chinhui, and Kevin Murphy. 1997. Wage Inequality and Family Labor Supply. *Journal of Labor Economics* 15(1) January: 72–97.

Kaldor, Nicholas. 1961. Capital Accumulation and Economic Growth. In Friedrich A. Lutz and Douglas C. Hague, eds., *The Theory of Capital*. New York: St. Martin's Press.

Kandil, M. 2000. *Wage Flexibility and Economic Performance: Evidence across Industrial Countries*. Working Paper no. WP/00/137. International Monetary Fund, Washington, D.C.

Kaplan, D., G. Martínez González, and R. Robertson. 2003. Worker- and Job-flows in Mexico. Instituto Tecnológico Autónomo de México (ITAM), Instituto Mexicano del Seguro Social (IMSS), and Macalester College. Unpublished.

Kappaz, C., and W. Siegel. 2002. The Role of the Multilateral Investment Fund in Skills Standards and Certification. Millennia Consulting l.l.c., Washington, D.C.

Katz, L., and K. Murphy. 1992. Changes in Relative Wages, 1963–1987: Supply and Demand Factors. *Quarterly Journal of Economics* 107(1): 35–78.

Kaufmann, D., A. Kraay, and P. Zoido-Lobatón. 1999. *Aggregating Governance Indicators*. Policy Research Working Paper no. 2195. World Bank, Washington, D.C.

Kay, Cristóbal. 1995. Rural Development and Agrarian Issues in Contemporary Latin America. In John Weeks, ed., *Structural Adjustment and the Agricultural Sector in Latin America and the Caribbean*. New York: St. Martin's Press.

Kikeri, Sunita. 1998. *Privatization and Labor: What Happens to Workers When Governments Divest*. Technical Paper no. 396. World Bank, Washington, D.C.

Klein, Michael, Scott Schuh, and Robert Treist. 2000. *Job Creation, Job Destruction, and the Real Exchange Rate*. NBER Working Paper no. 7466. National Bureau of Economic Research, Cambridge, MA.

Klenow, P. 1998. Ideas vs. Rival Human Capital: Industry Evidence on Growth Models. *Journal of Monetary Economics* 42(1) August: 3–24.

Klenow, P., and A. Rodríguez-Clare. 1997. The Neoclassical Revival in Growth Economics: Has It Gone Too Far? In B. S. Bernanke and J. Rotemberg, eds., *NBER Macroeconomics Annual 1997*. Cambridge, MA: MIT Press.

———. 2003. Externalities and Growth. Paper in progress for the *Handbook of Economic Growth*.

Kopits, G., and S. Symansky. 1998. *Fiscal Policy Rules*. Occasional Paper no. 162. International Monetary Fund, Washington, D.C.

Krueger, Alan, and Mikael Lindahl. 2001. Education for Growth: Why and for Whom? *Journal of Economic Literature* 39(4): 1101–36.

Krugman, Paul. 1994. The Myth of Asia's Miracle. *Foreign Affairs* 73(6) November-December: 62–78.

———. 1999a. Analytical Afterthoughts on the Asian Crisis. At *http://web.mit.edu/krugman/www.*

———. 1999b. Balance Sheets, the Transfer Problem, and Financial Crises. *International Tax and Public Finance* 6(4).

Kugler, Adriana. 2002. *From Severance Pay to Self-Insurance: Effects of Severance Payments Savings Accounts in Colombia*. CEPR Discussion Paper no. 3197. Centre for Economic Policy Research, London.

———. Forthcoming. The Effect of Job Security Regulations on Labor Market Flexibility: Evidence from the Colombian Labor Market Reform. In J. Heckman and C. Pagés, eds., *Law and Employment: Lessons from Latin America and the Caribbean*. Cambridge, MA: NBER; and Chicago, IL: University of Chicago.

Kuhn, P. 1998. Unions and the Economy: What We Know; What We Should Know. *Canadian Journal of Economics* 31(5): 1033–56.

La Porta, Rafael, and Florencio López-de-Silanes. 1999. The Benefits of Privatization: Evidence from Mexico. *Quarterly Journal of Economics* 114(4): 1193–1242.

Latinobarometer. Various years. Latin American Public Opinion Survey. Corporación Latinobarómetro, Santiago.

Lightman, E. S. 1995. You Can Lead a Horse to Water, but...: The Case against Workfare in Canada. In J. Richards and W. G. Watson, eds., *Helping the Poor: A Qualified Case for Workfare*. Toronto: C. D. Howe Institute.

Loayza, Norman, Pablo Fajnzylber, and César Calderón. 2002. Economic Growth in Latin America and the Caribbean: Stylized Facts, Explanations, and Forecasts. World Bank, Washington, D.C. Unpublished.

Loboguerrero, Ana María, and Ugo Panizza. 2003. *Inflation and Labor Market Flexibility: The Squeaky Wheel Gets the Grease*. Research Department Working Paper no. 495. Inter-American Development Bank, Washington, D.C.

López-Córdova, José Ernesto. 2003. NAFTA and Mexico's Manufacturing Productivity: An Empirical Investigation Using Micro-level Data. Paper presented at the Seventh Panel Meeting of *Economia*, Journal of the Latin American and Caribbean Economic Association (LACEA), April 24–25, Santiago, Chile.

López-de-Silanes, Florencio. 1996. *Determinants of Privatization Prices*. NBER Working Paper no. 5494. National Bureau of Economic Research, Cambridge, MA.

Lora, Eduardo. 1995. Los modelos de equilibrio general computable en análisis de incidencia fiscal. *El Trimestre Económico* LXII(1): 21–78.

———. 2001. *Structural Reforms in Latin America: What Has Been Reformed and How to Measure It*. Research Department Working Paper no. 466. Inter-American Development Bank, Washington, D.C.

Lora, Eduardo, and Felipe Barrera. 1997. *Una década de reformas estructurales en América Latina: el crecimiento, la productividad y la inversión, ya no son como antes*. Working Paper no. 350. Inter-American Development Bank, Washington, D.C.

Lora, Eduardo, and Carmen Pagés. 1997. La legislación laboral y el proceso de reformas estructurales de América Latina y el Caribe. In Mauricio Cárdenas S., ed., *Empleo y distribución del ingreso en América Latina: ¿hemos avanzado?* Bogotá: Fedesarrollo-TM Editores.

Lora, Eduardo, and Ugo Panizza. 2002. *Structural Reforms in Latin America under Scrutiny*. Research Department Working Paper no. 470. Inter-American Development Bank, Washington, D.C.

Lustig, N. 1999. Crises and the Poor: Socially Responsible Macroeconomics. Paper presented at the Fourth Annual Meeting of the Latin American and Caribbean Economic Association (LACEA), October 22, Santiago.

Lustig, N. C., and D. McLeod. 1997. Minimum Wages and Poverty in Developing Countries: Some

Empirical Evidence. In S. Edwards and N. C. Lustig, eds., *Labor Markets in Latin America: Combining Social Protection with Market Flexibility*. Washington, D.C.: Brookings Institution Press.

Lustig, N., and M. Walton. 1999. Crises and the Poor: A Template for Action. Paper presented at the conference, Social Protection and Poverty, February 4–5, Washington, D.C.

MacIsaac, D., and M. Rama. 1997. Determinants of Hourly Earnings in Ecuador: The Role of Labor Market Regulations. *Journal of Labor Economics* 15(3): S136–S165.

Madani, Dorsati. 1999. A Review of the Role and Impact of Export Processing Zones. World Bank, Washington, D.C. Unpublished.

Maddison, A. 1995. *Monitoring the World Economy, 1820–1992*. Paris: OECD.

Maloney, William F. 1998. *The Structure of Labor Markets in Developing Countries: Time Series Evidence on Competing Views*. Policy Research Working Paper no. 1940. World Bank, Washington, D.C.

———. 1999. Does Informality Imply Segmentation in Urban Labor Markets?: Evidence from Sectoral Transitions in Mexico. *The World Bank Economic Review* 13(2): 275–302.

Maloney, William F., and Jairo Núñez. Forthcoming. Measuring the Impact of Minimum Wages: Evidence from Latin America. In J. Heckman and C. Pagés, eds., *Law and Employment: Lessons from Latin America and the Caribbean*. Cambridge, MA: NBER; and Chicago, IL: University of Chicago.

Márquez, Gustavo. 1997. Protección al empleo y funcionamiento del mercado de trabajo: una aproximación comparativa. In Empleo, flexibilidad laboral y protección social, Proceedings of the II Technical Meeting, Círculo de Montevideo, Montevideo, Uruguay, UNDP.

———. 2000. *Labor Markets and Income Support: What Did We Learn from the Crises?* Research Department Working Paper no. 425. Inter-American Development Bank, Washington, D.C.

Márquez, Gustavo, and Carmen Pagés. 1998a. *Ties That Bind: Employment Protection and Labor Market Outcomes in Latin America*. Research Department Working Paper no. 373. Inter-American Development Bank, Washington, D.C.

———. 1998b. *Trade and Employment: Evidence from Latin America and the Caribbean*. Research Department Working Paper no. 366. Inter-American Development Bank, Washington, D.C.

Martin, J., and D. Grubb. 2001. *What Works and for Whom: A Review of OECD Countries' Experiences with Active Labour Market Policies*. IFAU Working Paper no. 2001:14. Institute for Labour Market Policy Evaluation, Uppsala.

Martínez Espinoza, Eduardo. 1998. Chile: Experiences in a Market-oriented Training System. International Labour Organization, Geneva.

Martner, Ricardo. 1999. El papel de los estabilizadores automáticos en la política fiscal en América Latina. Dirección de Programación del Sector Público, ECLAC, Santiago.

Maskus, Keith E. 1997. *Should Core Labor Standards Be Imposed through International Trade Policy?* Policy Research Working Paper no. 1817. World Bank, Washington, D.C.

Mattoo, Aaditya, Randeep Rathindran, and Arvind Subramanian. 2001. *Measuring Services Trade Liberalization and Its Impact on Economic Growth: An Illustration*. Policy Research Working Paper no. 2655. World Bank, Washington, D.C.

Mazza, Jacqueline. 1999. *Unemployment Insurance: Case Studies and Lessons for Latin America and the Caribbean*. Working Paper no. 411. Inter-American Development Bank, Washington, D.C.

———. 2001. Labor Intermediation Services: A Review for Latin American and Caribbean Countries. Paper prepared for the First Technical Meeting on Labor Market Issues, November 26–27, Panama City, Panama.

McKenzie, David, and Dilip Mookherjee. 2002. Distributive Impact of Privatization in Latin America: An Overview of Evidence from Four Countries. Research report presented to the IDB. Stanford University and Boston University.

Meardon, Stephen. 2003. Geography, Trade, and Regional Disparities: The Case of the Missing

Middle of Mexico. Inter-American Development Bank, Washington, D.C. Unpublished.

Medina, Pablo, Marcela Meléndez, and Katja Seim. 2003. Productivity Dynamics of the Colombian Manufacturing Sector. Inter-American Development Bank, Washington, D.C. Unpublished.

Menezes Filho, Naércio Aquino (coordinator). 2003. Labor Market Dynamics in Brazil. Final report. Fundação Instituto de Pesquisas Econômicas, Universidade de São Paulo and Fipe-USP.

Menezes Filho, N., H. Zylberstajn, J. P. Chahad, and E. Pazello. 2002. *Unions and the Economic Performance of Brazilian Establishments*. Research Network Working Paper no. R-464. Inter-American Development Bank, Washington, D.C.

Michaely, Michael, Demetris Papageorgiou, and Armeane M. Choksi, eds. 1991. *Liberalizing Foreign Trade: Lessons of Experience in the Developing World*. Volume 7. Cambridge, MA: Basil Blackwell, Inc.

Mincer, Jacob, and Boyan Jovanovic. 1981. Labor Mobility and Wages. In Sherwin Rosen, ed., *Studies in Labor Markets*. Chicago, IL: University of Chicago Press.

Ministerio de Trabajo y Promoción Social del Perú (MTPS), Dirección Nacional de Empleo y Formación Profesional (DNEFP) and Sistema de Información Laboral. 2001. La modernización del servicio nacional de empleo en el Perú: una propuesta aplicable a países en desarrollo. Paper presented at the conference, Fifth World Congress of the World Association of Public Employment Services, May 29–June 2, Bergen, Norway.

Moguillansky, Graciela. 2002. Inversión y volatilidad financiera en América Latina. *Revista de la CEPAL* 77: 47–66.

Mondino, Guillermo, and Silvia Montoya. Forthcoming. The Effects of Labor Market Regulations on Employment Decisions by Firms: Empirical Evidence for Argentina. In J. Heckman and C. Pagés, eds., *Law and Employment: Lessons from Latin America and the Caribbean*. Cambridge, MA: NBER; and Chicago, IL: University of Chicago.

Montenegro, Claudio E., and Carmen Pagés. Forthcoming. Who Benefits from Labor Market Regulations? Chile 1960–1998. In J. Heckman and C. Pagés, eds., *Law and Employment: Lessons from Latin America and the Caribbean*. Cambridge, MA: NBER; and Chicago, IL: University of Chicago.

Morandé, Felipe, and Klaus Schmidt-Hebbel. 2000. *Chile's Peso: Better Than (Just) Living with the Dollar?* Working Paper no. 68. Central Bank of Chile.

Mundell, R. 1961. A Theory of Optimal Currency Areas. *American Economic Review* 51(3): 657–65.

Murillo, M. V., and others. 2002. *The Economic Effects of Unions in Latin America: Teachers' Unions and Education in Argentina*. Research Network Working Paper no. R-463. Inter-American Development Bank, Washington, D.C.

Murphy, K., and R. Topel. 1997. Unemployment and Nonemployment. *American Economic Review* 87(2) May: 295–300.

Nadal, Alejandro. 2000. The Environmental and Social Impacts of Economic Liberalization on Corn Production in Mexico. Oxfam and WWF International, London. Unpublished.

Narayan, Deepa, and Patti Petesch, eds. 2002. *Voices of the Poor: From Many Lands*. Washington, D.C.: World Bank; and New York: Oxford University Press.

Neri, M., G. Gonzaga, and J. M. Camargo. 2001. Salário Mínimo, Efeito-Farol e Pobreza. *Revista de Economia Política* 21(2): 78–90.

Neumark, D., M. Schweitzer, and W. Wascher. 2000. *The Effects of Minimum Wages throughout the Wage Distribution*. NBER Working Paper no. 7519. National Bureau of Economic Research, Cambridge, MA.

Neumark, D., and W. Wascher. 2002. Do Minimum Wages Fight Poverty? *Economic Enquiry* 40(3): 315–33.

Newman, Constance, Pilar Larreamendy, and Ana María Maldonado. 2000. Women and Floriculture: Changes and Consequences in the Home. World Bank, Washington, D.C. Unpublished.

Nickell, S. 1997. Unemployment and Labor Market Rigidities: Europe versus North America. *Journal of Economic Perspectives* 11(3) Summer: 55–74.

Nickell, S., and R. Layard. 1999. Labor Market Institutions and Economic Performance. In O. Ashenfelter and D. Card, eds., *Handbook of Labor Economics*. Volume 3. Amsterdam: North-Holland.

Nucci, Francesco, and Alberto F. Pozzolo. 2001. Investment and the Exchange Rate: An Analysis with Firm-Level Panel Data. *European Economic Review* 45(2): 259–83.

Oi, W. 1999. Firm Size and Wages. In O. Ashenfelter and D. Card, eds., *Handbook of Labor Economics*. Volume 3. Amsterdam: North-Holland.

Organisation for Economic Co-operation and Development. 1987. *OECD Employment Outlook*. Paris: OECD.

———. 1996. *OECD Employment Outlook*. Paris: OECD.

———. 1997. Labour Market Policies: New Challenges. Enhancing the Effectiveness of Active Labour Market Policies: A Streamlined Public Employment Service. Paper presented at Meeting of the Employment, Labour and Social Affairs Committee at the Ministerial Level, October 14–15, Paris.

———. 1998. *OECD Employment Outlook*. Paris: OECD.

———. 1999. *The Public Employment Service in the United States*. Paris: OECD.

———. 2000. *OECD Employment Outlook*. Paris: OECD.

———. 2001. Labour Market Policies and the Public Employment Service: Proceedings of the Prague Conference, July 2000. Paris: OECD.

Ouaked, Said. 2002. Transatlantic Roundtable on High-skilled Migration and Sending Countries Issues. *International Migration* 40(4): 153–66.

Paes de Barros, Ricardo, and Carlos Henrique Corseuil. Forthcoming. The Impact of Regulations on Brazilian Labor Market Performance. In J. Heckman and C. Pagés, eds., *Law and Employment: Lessons from Latin America and the Caribbean*. Cambridge, MA: NBER; and Chicago, IL: University of Chicago.

Paes de Barros, Ricardo, Carlos Henrique Corseuil, and Gustavo Gonzaga. 1999. *Labor Market Regulations and the Demand for Labor in Brazil*. Texto para Discussão no. 398. Departamento de Economia, Pontifícia Universidade Católica, Rio de Janeiro.

Pagés, C., and C. Montenegro. 1999. *Job Security and the Age-Composition of Employment: Evidence from Chile*. Working Paper no. 398. Inter-American Development Bank, Washington, D.C.

Pagés, C., and N. Shinkai. 2002. Union Membership and Wage Distribution. Research Department, Inter-American Development Bank, Washington, D.C. Unpublished.

Pagés, Carmen, and Jaime Saavedra. 2002. Legislación laboral: algunos principios fundamentales, evidencia empírica y políticas en América Latina. Paper presented at the seminar, Desarrollando Consensos en Torno al Mercado de Trabajo y las Políticas de Empleo en el Área Andina, July 18–19, Lima.

Partnership for Educational Revitalization in the Americas (PREAL). 2001. Lagging Behind: A Report Card on Education in Latin America. Report of the Task Force on Education, Equity, and Economic Competitiveness in the Americas. Santiago.

Pavcnik, Nina. 2002. What Explains Skill Upgrading in Less Developed Countries? Dartmouth College, Hanover, N.H. Unpublished.

Pavcnik, Nina, Andreas Blom, P. Goldberg, and Norbert Schady. 2002. Trade Liberalization and Labor Market Adjustment in Brazil. Dartmouth College, Hanover, N.H. Unpublished.

Perry, G. 2002. Can Fiscal Rules Help Reduce Macroeconomic Volatility in LAC? Paper presented at the IMF/World Bank Conference on Rules-based Fiscal Policy in Emerging Market Economies, February 14–16, Oaxaca.

Perry, G., and L. Servén. 2003. *The Anatomy of a Multiple Crisis: Why Was Argentina Special and What Can We Learn from It?* Policy Research Working Paper no. 3081. World Bank, Washington, D.C.

Petrazzini, Ben. 1996. Telephone Privatization in a Hurry: Argentina. In Ravi Ramamurti, ed., *Privatizing Monopolies. Lessons from the Telecommunications and Transport Sectors in Latin America*. Baltimore and London: Johns Hopkins University Press.

Psacharopoulos, George, and Zafiris Tzannatos. 1992. Women's Employment and Pay in Latin America: Overview and Methodology. Regional and Sectoral Studies. World Bank, Washington, D.C.

Rama, Martín. 1994. In Michael Connolly and Jaime de Melo, eds., *The Effects of Protectionism on a Small Country: The Case of Uruguay*. Washington, D.C.: World Bank.

———. 2001. Globalization and Workers in Developing Countries. World Bank, Washington, D.C. Unpublished.

Rama, Martín, and Donna MacIsaac. 1999. Earnings and Welfare after Downsizing: Central Bank Employees in Ecuador. *The World Bank Economic Review* 13(1): 89–116.

Ramey, Valery, and Garey Ramey. 1995. Cross-Country Evidence on the Link between Volatility and Growth. *American Economic Review* 85(5): 1138–51.

Ravallion, M. 1998. *Appraising Workfare Programs*. SDS Working Paper no. POV-102. Inter-American Development Bank, Washington, D.C.

———. 1999a. Is More Targeting Consistent with Less Spending? *International Tax and Public Finance* 6(3): 411–19.

———. 1999b. Monitoring Targeting Performance When Decentralized Allocations to the Poor Are Observed. World Bank, Washington, D.C.

———. 2000. *Are the Poor Protected from Budget Cuts? Theory and Evidence for Argentina*. Policy Research Working Paper no. 2391. World Bank, Washington, D.C.

Ravallion, M., and J. Jalan. 1999. Income Gains from Workfare and Their Distribution. World Bank, Washington, D.C.

Reif, Tania. 2001. The Real Side of Currency Crises. Columbia University, New York, N.Y. Unpublished.

Revenga, Ana. 1997. Employment and Wage Effects of Trade Liberalization: The Case of Mexican Manufacturing. *Journal of Labor Economics* 107(1): 255–84.

Robbins, Donald J. 1996. *Stolper-Samuelson (Lost) in the Tropics? Trade Liberalization and Wages in Colombia: 1976–1994*. Development Discussion Paper no. 563. Harvard University, Cambridge, MA.

Robbins, Donald J., and T. H. Gindling. 1999. Trade Liberalization and the Relative Wages for More-Skilled Workers in Costa Rica. *Review of Development Economics* 3(2) June: 140–54.

Robbins, Donald J., Martín González Rozada, and Alicia Menéndez. 1997. Dispersión salarial y comercio en Argentina. In Mauricio Cárdenas S., ed., *Empleo y distribución del ingreso en América Latina: ¿hemos avanzado?* Bogotá: Fedesarrollo-TM Editores.

Roberts, M., and J. Tybout. 1996. *Industrial Evolution in Developing Countries: Micro Patterns of Turnover, Productivity, and Market Structure*. Oxford University Press.

Robertson, Raymond. 2002. Relative Prices and Wage Inequality: Evidence from Mexico. Department of Economics, Macalester College, St. Paul, MN. Unpublished.

Rodríguez, F., and D. Rodrik. 2001. Trade Policy and Economic Growth: A Skeptic's Guide to the Cross-National Evidence. In B. S. Bernanke and K. Rogoff, eds., *NBER Macroeconomics Annual 2000*. Cambridge, MA: MIT Press.

Rodrik, Dani. 1995. Trade and Industrial Policy Reform. In J. R. Behrman and T. N. Srinivasan, eds., *Handbook of Development Economics. Volume 3*. Amsterdam: North-Holland.

———. 1996. Understanding Economic Policy Reform. *Journal of Economic Literature* 34(1): 9–41.

———. 1997. *Has Globalization Gone Too Far?* Washington, D.C.: Institute for International Economics.

———. 2000. Comments on "Outward-Orientation and Development: Are Revisionists Right?" by T. N. Srinivasan and J. Bhagwati (September 1999 version). *http://ksghome.harvard.edu/~.drodrik.academic.ksg/Bhagwati-Srinivasan-percent20piecepercent_response_.pdf*.

———. 2001. ¿Por qué hay tanta inseguridad económica en América Latina? *Revista de la CEPAL* 73: 7–32.

Rodrik, Dani, Arvind Subramanian, and Francesco Trebbi. 2002. *Institutions Rule: The Primacy of Institutions over Geography and Integration in Economic Development*. NBER Working Paper no. 9305. National Bureau of Economic Research, Cambridge, MA.

Romer, P. 2000. *Should Governments Subsidize Supply or Demand in the Market for Scientists and Engineers?* NBER Working Paper no. 7723. National Bureau of Economic Research, Cambridge, MA.

Romero, Ana Teresa. 1995. Labour Standards and Export Processing Zones: Situation and Pressures for Change. *Development Policy Review* 13(3): 247–76.

Rose, Nancy E. 1994. *Put to Work: Relief Programs in the Great Depression.* New York: Monthly Review Press.

Roy, A. D. 1951. Some Thoughts on the Distribution of Earnings. *Oxford Economic Papers* 3 (June): 135–46.

Saavedra, Jaime. 2003. Labor Markets during the 1990s. In Pedro-Pablo Kuczynski and John Williamson, eds., *After the Washington Consensus: Restarting Growth and Reform in Latin America.* Washington, D.C.: Institute for International Economics.

Saavedra, Jaime, and Máximo Torero. Forthcoming. Labor Market Reforms and Their Impact on Formal Labor Demand and Job Market Turnover: The Case of Peru. In J. Heckman and C. Pagés, eds., *Law and Employment: Lessons from Latin America and the Caribbean.* Cambridge, MA: NBER; and Chicago, IL: University of Chicago.

———. 2002. *Union Density Changes and Union Effects on Firm Performance in Peru.* Research Network Working Paper no. R-465. Inter-American Development Bank, Washington, D.C.

Sachs, Jeffrey, and Felipe Larraín. 1999. Why Dollarization Is More Straightjacket Than Salvation. *Foreign Policy* 116 (Fall): 80–92.

Sachs, Jeffrey, and Andrew Warner. 1995. Economic Reforms and the Process of Global Integration. *Brookings Papers on Economic Activity* 1: 1–118.

Saint-Paul, G. 2000. *Flexibility vs. Rigidity: Does Spain Have the Worst of Both Worlds?* Discussion Paper no. 144. Universitat de Pompeu Fabra, Barcelona.

Samaniego, N. 2002. *Las políticas de mercado de trabajo y su evaluación en América Latina.* Serie Macroeconomía del Desarrollo no. 19. ECLAC, Santiago.

Samuel, Wendell, and Federico Torres. 2001. Remesas y redes migratorias. Paper prepared for the conference, Simposio sobre migración internacional en las Américas, December, Santiago.

Sánchez Cantillo, Marco V. 2001. *Trade Reform and Comparative Advantage: Expectations for Costa Rica's Agricultural Development.* Working Paper no. 346. ORPAS, Institute of Social Studies, The Hague.

Sánchez-Páramo, Carolina, and Norbert Schady. 2003. Off and Running? Technology, Trade and the Rising Demand for Skilled Workers in Latin America. World Bank, Washington, D.C. Unpublished.

Sanguinetti, Pablo, Rodrigo Arim, and Juan Pantano. 2001. Changes in Production and Employment Structure and Relative Wages in Argentina and Uruguay. Universidad Torcuato Di Tella, Buenos Aires. Unpublished.

Sargent, John, and Linda Matthews. 1999. Exploitation or Choice? Exploring the Relative Attractiveness of Employment in the Maquiladoras. *Journal of Business Ethics* 18(2): 213–27.

———. 2001. Combining Export Processing Zones and Regional Free Trade Agreements: Lessons from the Mexican Experience. *World Development* 29(10): 1739–52.

Scarpetta, Stefano, Philip Hemmings, Thierry Tressel, and Jaejoon Woo. 2002. *The Role of Policy and Institutions for Productivity and Firm Dynamics: Evidence from Micro and Industry Data.* Economics Department Working Paper no. 329. Organisation for Economic Co-operation and Development, Paris.

Scarpetta, Stefano, and Thierry Tressel. 2002. *Productivity and Convergence in a Panel of OECD Industries: Do Regulations and Institutions Matter?* Economics Department Working Paper no. 342. Organisation for Economic Co-operation and Development, Paris.

Secretaría de Trabajo y Previsión Social (STPS). 1995. Capacitación y empleo: evaluación del programa de becas de capacitación para desempleados. Mexico City.

Seddon, Jessica, and Romain Wacziarg. 2001. Trade Liberalization and Intersectoral Labor Movements. Stanford University, Palo Alto, CA. Unpublished.

Shah, Anwar, and John Whalley. 1991. The Redistributive Impact of Taxation in Developed

Countries. In Javad Khalilzadeh-Shirazi and Anwar Shah, eds., *Tax Policy in Developing Countries*. Washington, D.C.: World Bank.

Shavell, S., and L. Weiss. 1979. The Optimal Payment of Unemployment Insurance Benefits over Time. *Journal of Political Economy* 87(6): 1347–62.

Skoufias, Emmanuel. 2001. PROGRESA and Its Impacts on the Human Capital and Welfare of Households in Rural Mexico: A Synthesis of the Results of an Evaluation by IFPRI. International Food Policy Research Institute, Washington, D.C.

Spiller, P., and M. Tommasi. 2000. *Los determinantes institucionales del desarrollo argentino: una aproximación desde la nueva economía institucional.* Documento no. 33. Centro de Estudios para el Desarrollo Institucional, Buenos Aires.

Srinivasan, T. N., and J. Bhagwati. 1999. Outward-Orientation and Development: Are Revisionists Right? Yale University, New Haven, CT. Unpublished.

Stallings, Barbara, and Wilson Peres. 2000. *Growth, Employment, and Equity: The Impact of the Economic Reforms in Latin America and the Caribbean*. Washington, D.C.: Brookings Institution Press.

Stein, Ernesto, Ernesto Talvi, and Alejandro Grisanti. 1998. *Institutional Arrangements and Fiscal Performance: The Latin American Experience*. Working Paper no. 367. Inter-American Development Bank, Washington, D.C.

Structural Adjustment Participatory Review International Network (SAPRIN). 2002. *The Policy Roots of Economic Crisis and Poverty*. Washington, D.C.: SAPRIN.

Talvi, E., and C. Végh. 2000. *Tax Base Variability and Procyclical Fiscal Policy*. NBER Working Paper no. 7499. National Bureau of Economic Research, Cambridge, MA.

Tobin, J. 1972. Inflation and Unemployment. *American Economic Review* 62(1): 1–18.

Tybout, James R. 1996. Chile, 1979–86: Trade Liberalization and Its Aftermath. In Mark Roberts and James Tybout, eds., *Industrial Evolution in Developing Countries*. New York: Oxford University Press.

United Nations Population Division. 2002. *World Population Prospects: The 2002 Revision and World Urbanization Prospects: The 2001 Revision*. New York: United Nations.

UNESCO/OREALC. 1998. Laboratorio Latinoamericano de Evaluación de la Calidad de la Educación. Primer Estudio Internacional Comparativo.

Urizar, H., and S. Lee. 2003. *The Effects of Unions on Productivity: Evidence from Large Coffee Producers in Guatemala*. Research Department Working Paper no. 473. Inter-American Development Bank, Washington, D.C.

Verdera, Francisco. 1998. Análisis comparativo de los programas de empleo e ingresos en América Latina y el Caribe. In Inter-American Development Bank and International Labour Organization, eds., *Programas de empleo e ingresos en América Latina y el Caribe*. Washington, D.C.: IDB; and Lima: ILO.

von Hagen, J., R. Perotti, and R. Strauch. 1997. *Sustainability of Public Finances.* CEPR Discussion Paper no. 1781. Centre for Economic Policy Research, London.

Wacziarg, Romain, and Karen Horn Welch. 2002. Integration and Growth: An Update. Stanford University and National Bureau of Economic Research. Unpublished.

Williamson, Jeffrey G. 2001. Demographic Shocks and Global Factor Flows. In J. N. Little and R. K. Triest, eds., *Seismic Shifts: The Economic Impact of Demographic Change*. Boston, MA: Federal Reserve Bank of Boston.

Williamson, John. 1990. What Does Washington Mean by Policy Reform? In J. Williamson, ed., *Latin American Adjustment: How Much Has Happened*. Washington, D.C.: Institute for International Economics.

Wodon, Q., N. Hicks, B. Ryan, and G. González. 2002. Are Governments Pro-Poor but Short-Sighted? Targeted and Social Spending for the Poor during Booms and Busts. World Bank, Washington, D.C. Unpublished.

World Bank. Various years. *World Development Indicators*. Washington, D.C.: World Bank.

World Bank. 2000. *World Development Report 2000/2001: Attacking Poverty*. Oxford: Oxford University Press.

———. 2001. *World Development Indicators*. CD-ROM. Washington, D.C.: World Bank.

———. 2003. *Public-Private Infrastructure Advisory Facility (PPIAF) Toolkit*. Washington, D.C.: World Bank.

World Economic Forum. 2003. *The Global Competitiveness Report 2002–2003*. New York and Oxford: Oxford University Press.

World Economic Forum, with Center for International Development and Institute for Strategy and Competitiveness. 2001. *The Global Competitiveness Report 2001–2002*. New York and Oxford: Oxford University Press.

Yap, Y., G. Sedlacek, and P. Orazem. 2002. Limiting Child Labor through Behavior-Based Income Transfers: An Experimental Evaluation of the PETI Program in Rural Brazil. Unpublished.

Young, Alwyn. 1995. The Tyranny of Numbers: Confronting the Statistical Realities of the East Asian Growth Experience. *Quarterly Journal of Economics* 110(3) August: 641–80.

Zegarra, Eduardo, and Renato Ravina. 2003. *Teacher Unionization and the Quality of Education in Peru: An Empirical Evaluation Using Survey Data*. Research Network Working Paper no. R-474. Inter-American Development Bank, Washington, D.C.

Appendix
Labor Market Indicators (CD-ROM)

The appendix on the accompanying CD-ROM contains comparable labor market indicators for 18 countries in Latin America since 1990. The indicators are based on analysis of more than 100 household surveys that were conducted by national statistical agencies.

Information is available on labor force participation, employment rates, self-employment, involuntary part-time work, child labor, youth work, unemployment rates, unemployment duration, composition of employment, employment tenure, average work hours, and the educational achievement of the labor force. Most indicators are computed separately by gender, geographic location, education level, and age group. The data appendix also contains estimates of returns to education, Gini coefficients, and other measures of wage inequality. Some countries have longer series of data than others; all 18 countries have at least one observation for the late 1990s or later.

The data are not intended to serve as official figures for any particular country, but rather to provide a comparable set of labor market indicators for the region. Updates will be available at http://www.iadb.org/res/ipes.